The Petrograd Workers in the Russian Revolution

Historical Materialism Book Series

The Historical Materialism Book Series is a major publishing initiative of the radical left. The capitalist crisis of the twenty-first century has been met by a resurgence of interest in critical Marxist theory. At the same time, the publishing institutions committed to Marxism have contracted markedly since the high point of the 1970s. The Historical Materialism Book Series is dedicated to addressing this situation by making available important works of Marxist theory. The aim of the series is to publish important theoretical contributions as the basis for vigorous intellectual debate and exchange on the left.

The peer-reviewed series publishes original monographs, translated texts, and reprints of classics across the bounds of academic disciplinary agendas and across the divisions of the left. The series is particularly concerned to encourage the internationalization of Marxist debate and aims to translate significant studies from beyond the English-speaking world.

For a full list of titles in the Historical Materialism Book Series available in paperback from Haymarket Books, visit:
https://www.haymarketbooks.org/series_collections/1-historical-materialism

The Petrograd Workers in the Russian Revolution

February 1917–June 1918

David Mandel

Haymarket Books
Chicago, IL

First published in 2017 by Brill Academic Publishers, The Netherlands

Published in paperback in 2018 by
Haymarket Books
P.O. Box 180165
Chicago, IL 60618
773-583-7884
www.haymarketbooks.org

ISBN: 978-1-60846-006-9

Trade distribution:
In the US, Consortium Book Sales, www.cbsd.com
In Canada, Publishers Group Canada, www.pgcbooks.ca
In the UK, Turnaround Publisher Services, www.turnaround-uk.com
All other countries, Ingram Publisher Services International, ips_intlsales@ingramcontent.com

Cover design by Jamie Kerry and Ragina Johnson.

This book was published with the generous support of Lannan Foundation and the Wallace Action Fund.

Printed in the United States.

10 9 8 7 6 5 4 3 2 1

Library of Congress Cataloging-in-Publication data is available.

To the memories of

Leopold H. Haimson (1927–2010)
my teacher and defender

Ivan Kupriyanovich Naumov (1895–1938)
Vyborg district worker, Bolshevik, Left Oppositionist to Stalinism

∴

Contents

List of Tables and Maps

Tables

Map

Glossary

census society – the propertied classes (landed aristocracy and bourgeoisie)

defencists – socialists who argued that as a result of the February Revolution the war on Russia's part had ceased to be imperialist and that the people had a duty to support the military efforts of the Provisional Government against German imperialism

internationalists – socialists who argued that the war being waged by the Provisional Government remained imperialist and should be opposed; included Bolsheviks, Menshevik-Internationalists and Left SRs

Kadet party – Constitutional Democrats, liberal party

PSFMO – Petrograd Society of Factory and Mill Owners

revolutionary democracy (or democracy) – the workers, peasants and soldiers, as well as the members of the intelligentsia who identified with them; for all practical purposes, the constituency of the socialist parties

SRs – Social Revolutionaries – Russia's peasant party, successor to the nineteenth-century populists; in the autumn of 1917 the Left SRs (internationalists) officially broke off to form a separate party

Sovnarkhoz – regional Council of National Economy, established by a decree of 23 December 1917

Sovnarkom – Council of People's Commissars, the Soviet government elected by the Second Congress of Soviets in October, responsible to the TsIK and ultimately the Congress of Soviets

State Duma – Russia's parliament, established in 1906 as a result of the 1905 revolution with extremely limited powers and an unequal franchise strongly biased in favour of the propertied classes

TsIK – All-Russian Central Executive Committee of Soviets of Workers' and Soldiers' Deputies, elected by the All-Russian Congress of Soviets of Workers' and Soldiers' Deputies

VSNKh – Supreme Council of National Economy, established in December 1917

Introduction

Few historical events arouse stronger political passions than revolutions, and no statement about the events in Russia in 1917 provokes more controversy than the claim that it was a proletarian revolution, a view that some historians have summarily relegated to 'the realm of revolutionary mythology'.[1] Yet, the present study of the workers of Petrograd, the heart of the revolution, supports the view that the Russian Revolution was, in fact, a workers' revolution.

Of course, so complex and multi-faceted an event cannot be reduced to any simple formula. The revolutions of 1917 were also, among other things, a soldiers' mutiny, a peasant uprising, a movement of liberation of national minorities. Moreover, the overthrow of the monarchy in February was facilitated by the *krizis verkhov*, the disaffection of the propertied classes, which had ripened towards the end of 1916 and embraced even the most conservative members of the dominant classes, represented by the United Nobility,[2] as well as significant sectors of the state bureaucracy and the military élite. While these privileged elements certainly did not desire a popular revolution, once it broke out, they were not prepared to join battle to save the deeply discredited Tsarist regime.

Despite these other dimensions of the revolution, the workers constituted the main force in the political struggle that culminated in the soviets' seizure of power in October. They provided the revolutionary movement with leadership, organisation and a disproportionate proportion of its active participants.

The aim of this book is to present a coherent account and analysis of the evolution of the attitudes and collective actions of the industrial workers of Petrograd in 1917 and in the first half of 1918, as they related to the major issues of the revolution: the war, the organisation of the economy, and the one question that subsumed all others – political power.

Too often historians of the revolution have left the workers at the margins of their accounts. When workers entered the picture, they were frequently portrayed as an elemental, anarchistic force that the Bolsheviks, the true authors and victors of October, were able to harness and manipulate for their own purposes. That version was promoted in particular by the Mensheviks following their defeat: the conscious, urbanised workers, they argued, had been diluted by the wartime influx into industry of peasants, a *stikhiya*, an elemental force, disoriented and politically illiterate, that drowned out the voice of the discip-

---

1 Keep 1976, p. xiv.

2 An organisation of the big landed aristocracy formed in 1905.

lined, class-conscious workers. A similar view has sometimes been echoed in sociological literature on revolutions, presenting popular participation in them as irrational, little different, in fact, from the acts of lunatics and criminals.[3]

Soviet historians, understandably, did not share that view. But they were obliged to emphasise the 'leading role of the party'. As a result, their analyses in their own way also tended to reduce the workers to objects, not of elemental instincts or demagogic propaganda, but of the party's 'leading role'. Their radicalisation in the course of 1917 was often presented as a lineal process, in the course of which the masses, aided by the party, overcame their initial illusions and errors. For example, their strong support for dual power and for the moderate socialists in the first months of 1917 was explained as the product of a 'petty bourgeois wave' that swept over the working class during the war, a curious echo of the Mensheviks' argument adduced to explain the workers' radicalism in the latter months of 1917.[4] The possibility that support for dual power might have been a rational position from the workers' point of view in the early months of the revolution was not seriously entertained.

The evidence available to me when this study was originally undertaken convinced me that the workers' participation in the revolution is best understood in fundamentally rational terms, rather than as responses to alleged elemental drives or demagogic propaganda. Materials that have become available since that time have only reinforced that view. The present edition reproduces the original study with mostly minor changes, except for the final chapters that cover the post-October months and which have been expanded to include more considerable new materials. But the fundamental analysis and interpretation have not changed in any substantive way.

I argue in this book that the overwhelming support among workers for the Bolsheviks in October 1917 was based upon a reasonable understanding of their interests in the existing political and economic circumstances. In demanding that the soviets take power the workers were not moved by irresponsible Bolshevik promises of a socialist paradise just around the corner. (While the prospect of revolutions in the West did boost hope in the success of the October Revolution, it was not itself a primary motivating factor.) Nor did Bolshevik agitation make such extravagant promises. Instead, it presented Soviet power as the only alternative to counterrevolution. And if the workers agreed with that analysis, it was because it corresponded to reality that they experienced.

---

3 Johnson 1966, p. 152.

4 Sobolev 1973, p. 182.

The workers' radicalisation in the course of 1917 was largely a defensive reaction to the threat posed by the propertied classes to the 'bourgeois-democratic' revolution of February. In that revolution, the workers' main goals had been the establishment of a democratic republic, an active peace policy aimed at bringing the war to a rapid and democratic conclusion, the introduction of the eight-hour workday, and land reform for the peasantry. The radicalisation of the workers' aims over the following months to include workers' control of the factories, state regulation of the national economy, and the transfer of power to the soviets, was a response to concrete problems they faced. In the end, it all came down to their realisation that defence of the revolution, still conceived in largely 'bourgeois-democratic' terms, demanded the exclusion of the propertied classes from influence on government policy. Hence, their support for soviet power, which meant a government of workers and peasants with no representation of the bourgeoisie and landowners.

Even so, most workers in October were not rushing to join battle. Most adopted a cautious, wait-and-see attitude, preferring to leave the initiative to others. For they had a quite sober understanding of what the transfer of power to the soviets meant: people who had spent their lives carrying out orders issued by others, would be assuming responsibility for running the state and the economy; and moreover, they would be doing so against the active, and no doubt armed, opposition of the propertied classes, who had the support of the vast majority of the intelligentsia, people with higher and specialised education. For that reason, the initiative in the October Revolution fell to the most determined section of the working class, members of the Bolshevik party or workers close to it. This was a stratum of workers whose class consciousness, whose sense of personal and class dignity, and whose aspiration to independence from the propertied classes had been forged over years of intense struggle against the autocracy and the industrialists.

But the other workers almost unanimously welcomed their initiative. And most continued to support Soviet power in the spring of 1918, despite the serious deterioration of their material situation and coercive measures against opposition protest adopted by the Soviet government. The alternative to Soviet power that the Mensheviks and the Socialist Revolutionaries (SRs) were proposing – an all-class, 'all-national' (*vsenarodnoe*), i.e. all-class government to be created by the Constituent Assembly, a government, so they argued, that could avert civil war, was indeed tempting. And yet most workers did not consider that option realistic. They saw the alternatives in the same way as the Bolsheviks: Soviet power and civil war imposed by the propertied classes or a victory of the counterrevolution.

It follows from the preceding that the evolution of the workers' politics in the period covered by this study is best understood against the background of the changing relations among the principal classes of Russian society. These relations are the basis of this study's periodisation.

The weeks between the February Revolution to the April crisis were the so-called 'honeymoon period' of the revolution, when a certain sense of national unity prevailed. But even though 'census society' (the propertied classes) had in the end rallied to the revolution, the workers, at least those who were not new arrivals to industry, had not forgotten the recent history of bitter opposition of the bourgeoisie to their aspirations. Hence, the soviet's conditional support for the liberal government and the establishment of 'dual power', understood by workers as the exercise of 'control' over the government.

In the months between the April crisis and the July Days, the old class polarisation broke through the veneer of national unity. A majority of the capital's workers came to suspect the employers of conducting a 'hidden lockout', of sabotaging production with the aim of creating mass unemployment in order to weaken the workers' movement. The government's decision to pursue the imperialist war further angered the workers. Meanwhile, the bourgeois press and politicians were speaking out with increasing boldness against the pernicious influence of the soviets on Russia's political life. A majority of workers reached the conclusion that dual power had failed and that the soviets had to directly assume power. The demand for transfer of power to the soviets meant just that: establishment of a 'democratic dictatorship' of workers and peasants, of 'revolutionary democracy' to the exclusion of the propertied classes from influence on state policy.

But matters took a turn for the worse in the July Days, when the Mensheviks and SRs, the moderate socialists who controlled the Central Executive Committee of Soviets (the TsIK) and who were now participating in a coalition provisional government with the liberals, supported repressive measures against the workers. Suddenly, the workers were made acutely aware of their situation: they faced an alliance of the propertied classes with that large part of 'revolutionary democracy' that supported the TsIK. That included most of the peasantry and the intelligentsia, and a large part of the workers and soldiers outside of the capital. The political situation seemed to have entered a dead-end, since the workers who wanted soviet power could not move forward without provoking a civil war within the ranks of the popular classes, something they did not want and they knew they could not win. The soviets, which until that time had been viewed as vehicles for realising the workers' aspirations, suddenly appeared as obstacles. Nevertheless, the workers' attachment to the soviets remained strong and they did not support Lenin's position, who called (at that time) to abandon the soviets as the future organs of popular power.

By September 1917, the Bolsheviks had won majorities in the major urban soviets and garrisons, so that the fears of isolation subsided, though they remained very much in the workers' minds since the peasants' disillusionment with the SRs, their traditional party, was still far from complete. As for the intelligentsia, it was clear that it would be hostile to exclusion of the propertied classes from representation in the government. These political concerns, and the deepening economic crisis, made workers hesitate.

It was in this period, therefore, that the initiative shifted to the Bolshevik party, which included in its ranks the most determined elements of the working class. The working class of Petrograd was virtually unanimous in welcoming the October insurrection and the formation of a Soviet government. But most workers, including Bolsheviks, hoped that, now that the Rubicon had been crossed, it would be possible to restore the unity of revolutionary democracy. They overwhelmingly supported negotiations among all the socialist parties with a view to the formation of a coalition government. But when it became clear that the moderate socialists, the Mensheviks and SRs, would not participate in a government responsible solely to the soviets, that they continued to insist on inclusion, in one way or another, of representatives of the propertied classes, worker support for a coalition evaporated. In addition, their fear of isolation was assuaged when the Left SRs decided to join the Bolsheviks in a coalition government and when the peasant TsIK joined with the workers' and soldiers' TsIK a few weeks later.

The workers' strong attachment to Soviet power also determined their paradoxical attitude to the Constituent Assembly, which met briefly on 9 January 1918: in their view, the sole legitimate function of the Assembly, a body elected by all the classes of Russian society, was to confer national legitimacy on Soviet power, a dictatorship of the toiling classes that excluded the bourgeoisie and landowners from power. When the election returns made clear that the Constituent Assembly would not support Soviet power, most workers lost interest in it. By all accounts, their participation in the protests against its dissolution was weak. And despite their severe economic problems of the following months, most workers remained convinced that Soviet power was the only real alternative to counterrevolution. And from the experience of the defeat of the Revolution of 1905–6, as well as the defeats of the revolutionary forces in Ukraine and Finland in early 1918, they had no trouble imagining what a victorious counterrevolution would mean.

In writing this book, I tried as far as possible to rely on materials emanating from workers in order to let them speak for themselves. I hoped, in that way, to lend more credence to my contention that the workers were 'conscious' political actors and that the working class as a whole was the central, creative force in the revolution. From that point of view, my most valuable sources were, obviously, statements made by workers as reported in meeting and conference protocols, letters to the press, press reports and memoirs.

In statements of delegates to conferences and workers' letters to the press, one is dealing mainly with the more literate and politically active workers. Nevertheless, they were workers in close contact with the factory masses. Some letters were collectively written and put to a vote at factory meetings. A. Buzinov, a Petrograd worker and member of the SR party, described in the following terms the relationship between worker agitators, the politically active workers, and the factory 'masses' in the years preceding the revolution:

> The 'self-made' agitator said what was in the head of each person but for which the others, less developed workers, could not find expression in words. After each of his words, the workers could only exclaim: That's it! That's exactly what I wanted to say.[5]

Another important source for workers' attitudes are, of course, elections to factory committees, district and central soviets, city and district dumas, union executives, and the Constituent Assembly.

A particularly abundant source for the period covered in this book are resolutions adopted at factory meetings, which were held frequently. The fact that parts of these resolutions might closely follow the wording of party documents limits their value as original formulations of worker attitudes. But several circumstances need to be kept in mind. First, this was a time of broad political freedom and, for the most part, of intense political interest among workers. The typical factory assembly began with a report on the 'current moment' or about a particular problem facing the factory's workers. The report was usually given by one of the delegates to the Soviet or by a member of the factory committee, but sometimes also by party activists from outside the factory. Following this, other points of view were presented by activists of the other parties, local workers or people from the outside. This was followed by a general discussion, often reported as 'lengthy' or 'heated'. The meeting secretaries rarely recorded this part of the meeting. But one can reasonably assume that the whole process left workers with a clear enough grasp of the issues and the different positions. At the conclusion of the discussion, the various party fractions presented their respective resolutions, and the one that gathered majority support would then be sent to the Soviet or to the press.

5 A. Buzinov 1930, p. 103.

Many of the resolutions were clearly composed locally, even if they did reflect party positions. These were sometimes amended from the floor. In other cases, resolutions originated from the floor. Thus, while the resolutions were often written in more literary language, this should not be taken to mean they did not express the attitudes of ordinary workers. One should bear in mind that the relationship between leaders and rank-and-file in this period was far from one-sided. Workers frequently recalled their elected deputies from the city and district soviets and from the factory committees. Local leaders not only had to consider the mood of the rank and file but they were themselves often infected by it, even when it put them in conflict with their party. At the start of the July Days, local Bolsheviks ignored the party's position and led their workers in the demonstrations. In the weeks that followed, most Bolshevik workers refused to abandon the demand for soviet power, although the party had officially done so, albeit temporarily. In the days following the October Revolution, the Menshevik-Internationalists complained that, while the workers were supporting their call for an all-socialist coalition government, they demanded that it be responsible exclusively to the soviets, a position that the Menshevik-Internationalists were firmly rejecting.

And resolutions adopted by worker meetings were taken seriously by contemporary observers as genuine expressions of their positions. In 1918, A.L. Popov, a Menshevik, published a book-length analysis of the workers' attitudes on the question of power based exclusively on resolutions of workers' meetings.[6]

Another important source of information on workers' attitudes are the 'reports from the field' that were a regular feature of worker conferences and party gatherings. Finally, press reports, some written by workers themselves, are an additional, important contemporary source.

Leaving aside contemporary materials, one comes to memoirs. The most valuable belong to workers and were written at or close to the time of the events. Of memoirs by non-workers, those of N.N. Sukhanov, an editor of the Menshevik-Internationalist paper *Novaya zhizn'*, are without doubt the most incisive, although he was more closely familiar with the higher political circles than with the factory rank and file. In the late 1920s under the sponsorship of Maksim Gorky, a series of factory histories was commissioned. They were soon terminated but resumed again in the late 1950s. These works, based on archival and memoir materials, are of very uneven value, but when used in conjunction with other sources can yield useful information.

6 A.L. Popov 1918.

I am well aware of the often partisan nature of the sources used in this book. This, of course, is a problem for any social scientist or historian. But it is especially serious when the subject is a revolution that profoundly divided society and, indeed, the world. I have tried to make allowance for this, pointing out the particular bias of the sources when I cite them. On major questions, I have not relied on any single kind of source.

I did not set out in this study to prove a theory, nor did I select the evidence with a view to validating a *parti pris*. My purpose was to shed light on the nature of the workers' participation in the revolution. I sought to do this on the basis of all the evidence available to me. Of course, it is impossible to write about important historical events, and especially one so controversial as the Russian Revolution, without having a point of view. I have not tried to conceal my sympathy for the workers and their struggles. Nevertheless, I have considered all the data that was available to me. A book that uses the terms 'proletarian' and 'capitalist' is not necessarily less scientific than one that prefers the terms 'worker' and 'entrepreneur', although it may violate the dubious norms of positivist social science.

CHAPTER 1

Types of Political Culture in the Industrial Working Class of Petrograd

Students of the revolution have often approached workers as a homogeneous group, a practice that can yield a rather confused and sometimes contradictory picture of working-class politics. Among Petrograd's workers, one can, in fact, distinguish at least three different, major types of political culture. These coincide roughly with three different groups of workers: the largest part of the skilled workers, especially metalworkers employed in private factories; unskilled and semi-skilled labourers; and a sub-group of skilled workers, mainly printers but also workers with lengthy service in state-owned factories and workers in factories in the semi-rural outskirts of Petrograd, who sometimes owned their own houses and a plot of land. The cultural traits and orientations brought by these groups into the revolution filtered their perceptions and shaped their responses to events. An analysis of their political cultures is, therefore, a logical point of departure for an analysis of their politics in the revolutionary period.

Skilled Workers[1]

John Reed referred to the Vyborg District as the 'Faubourg St-Antoine of Petrograd'.[2] Such was its reputation, earned during the pre-war upsurge of labour militancy, that I.K. Naumov, recalling his arrival from Tula in 1915 as a young worker activist, was moved to write: 'To work in Piter – that is happiness. To work on the Vyborg Side – that is my longstanding dream'.[3]

Statistics on the social and industrial composition of the district give some insight into the sources of this radicalism. Not only did this predominantly proletarian district have the largest concentration of factory workers of any

1 This section deals mainly with metalworkers, who in 1917 accounted for 60 percent of the industrial workforce and the large majority of the skilled workers. Apart from the printers (treated below in the section on the 'aristocracy'), the only other groups in which there was a significant stratum of skilled workers were wood- and needle-workers.

2 This popular district of Paris was the radical heart of the French Revolution.

3 I.K. Naumov 1933, p. 5.

TABLE 1.1 *Literacy among industrial workers in European Russia by industry, August 1918*

Industry	Percent literate workers
Printing	94.7
Machine-construction	83.6
Metalworking	76.5
Clothing	74.9
Chemicals	70.0
Woodworking	69.6
Paper	68.1
Food	66.0
Leather and fur	64.1
Cotton	52.2
All industry	64.0

SOURCE: BASED UPON A.G. RASHIN, *FORMIROVANIE RABOCHEGO KLASSA ROSSII* (M., 1958) P. 601.

district (18 percent of the capital's total industrial workforce), but fully 84 percent of its workers were employed in the metalworking industry. In fact, the number of metalworkers in the Vyborg District alone exceeded the total number of industrial workers in any of Petrograd's other districts.[4]

There were two main types of metalworking: machine construction, which involved much complex, skilled work; and more simple types of metalworking, including metallurgy, founding, pipe-and-wire making, munitions, and the like. In the Vyborg District, 15 of the 21 large factories were engaged in machine-construction. Other districts in which metalworking predominated typically were dominated by one, sometimes two, giant factories that combined both types of production. The journal of the Metalworkers' Union described the giant Putilov Works in the following terms: 'This factory is a universal one, where metallurgy and machine construction are combined ... It is a plant with a high proportion of unskilled labourers ... Metallurgy in comparison with machine construction has an extraordinary percentage of unskilled labour'.[5]

4 See Table 3.4.

5 *Metallist*, no. 3 (1917) p. 3. The relationship between skill and the type of production is indirectly confirmed by a comparison of the sex ratios of the respective work forces. In 1917,

A sociological study of Moscow factory workers conducted in 1924 under the direction of E. Kabo concluded: 'In the worker milieu, skill, literacy and interest in socio-political questions go hand in hand. The greater the skill, the more frequent the attendance of lectures, circles, especially political ones, the greater the number of newspapers read'.[6] The 1918 industrial census, though based on a population smaller than that of 1917, also showed that the highest literacy rates were among workers in printing and machine construction, while the lowest rates were workers in the cotton industry, the least skilled (predominantly female) sector. (see Table 1.1.)

The cultural differences that set skilled workers apart from the unskilled were striking. When he began work as an adolescent in the forging shop of the Nevskii Ship- and Machine-Building Factory, a large mixed (metallurgy and machine-building) plant, A. Buzinov was struck by the cultural abyss separating the metalworkers at this factory from the workers of the nearby textile mills. But he soon became aware that within his own factory,

> the workers of the engineering shop, the machinists and turners, looked down on me from above. I realised the humble position of the hot departments: the founding, rolling and forging shops. In these, I saw people of an uncouth and oafish nature, in both their bearing and their speech. Through their robust ruddiness, one could clearly distinguish in each individual face the coarse features which said that force, not mental agility, predominates in their work. I saw clearly that next to an experienced founder even a shabby machinist seemed an educated, thoughtful person. The machinist held his head higher, was more accurate and forceful in his speech. He could put in a dozen words, including a stinging bit of irony, where the foundry worker found time for only one, and even that would be of a rather simple type. With a machinist you automatically felt like talking about something general and not just about wages. In short, the worker of the engineering shop was no longer the semi-raw material of

in the 31 European provinces of Russia, there were on average 28.4 women workers for every 100 males in metalworking, but only 17.4 per 100 in machine construction. Female workers were almost invariably employed in unskilled work. A survey of the Petrograd metalworking industry found that the average skill level among males was 54.2 (on a scale of 1–100), whereas only 12.1 among women workers. *Ekonomicheskoe polozhenie Rossii nakunune Velikoi Oktyabr'skoi Sotsialisticheskoi revolyutsii* (henceforth cited as Ek. Pol.) (M.-L., 1957), vol. I, pp. 43–4; D.A. Chugaev (ed.) 1967, p. 255.

6 E.A. Kabo 1928, p. 195.

> the founding and forging shops. Indeed, he seemed to have himself undergone the shaping action of the lathes and instruments.[7]

Contemporary observers agreed on what set the more skilled workers apart: a more refined personal culture, greater facility with words and complex ideas, keener interest in broader socio-political issues, and more acute sense of dignity.[8]

As Buzinov indicated, these traits had some relationship to the nature of skilled work itself, which was lighter, less routine, allowed for more autonomy and was more thought-demanding. The wage agreement concluded in July 1917 in the Petrograd metal industry described workers in the highest skill category as independently carrying out particularly complex, exact tasks, guided by drawings and using exact measuring instruments. Workers in category II carried out less complex tasks requiring less accuracy, but nevertheless a quite lengthy learning period and the ability to read drawings. Workers in category III did various uncomplicated but responsible tasks, as well as precise work in mass production that required the use of certain measuring instruments. Workers in category IV minded simple machines – lathes, presses, ovens, etc. This would include most work in ordnance production. A final category, the *chernorabochie* (literally blackworkers), worked at heavy unskilled tasks, such as carrying, washing, loading, sorting.[9] A. Shapovalov, a skilled Petersburg metalworker, recalled that 'work on a turning lathe quite often demands a high level of intelligence,[10] an ability to read technical drawings and knowledge of arithmetic. Some jobs, for example, the turning of cones, also required a certain familiarity with geometry, algebra, and trigonometry'.[11]

The following is a description of the machinist's work before the introduction of Taylorism (which eliminated a large part of the mental component of skilled factory work):

> The machinist of Taylor's day started with the shop drawing and turned, milled, bored, drilled, planed etc. and otherwise machine-and-hand-processed the proper stock to the desired shape as specified in the drawing. The range of decisions to be made in the course of this process ... is

7 A. Buzinov 1930, pp. 20–1.

8 See, for example, V.S. Voitinskii 1923, p. 283.

9 *Metallist*, no. 1–2 (1917).

10 *intelligentnost'* – implying mental and cultural development.

11 A.S. Shapovalov 1934, p. 57.

> enormous ... Taylor himself worked with twelve variables, including hardness of the metal, the material of the cutting tool, thickness of the shaving, shape of the cutting tool, use of a coolant ... etc. Each of these variables is subject to a large number of choices ... But upon these decisions of the machinist depended not just the accuracy of the product, but also the pace of production.[12]

While machine-construction in Russia in this period was on a generally lower technological level than in the West, the relatively weak and fluctuating demand for machinery in Russia made the introduction of batch production and a developed division of labour difficult. This situation placed special demands on workers to show resourcefulness and independence. A student of the pre-revolutionary machine-construction industry found that in Russia 'the basic type of machine builder was not the worker-operator but the so-called broad-profile worker'.[13]

In sum, skilled metalworking involved a high proportion of non-routine tasks, requiring decisions based upon relatively complex calculations with many variables. Executed according to technical drawings, this work fostered a capacity for independent thinking and the ability to move easily between abstract and concrete ideas.

Skilled work required a certain amount of formal education beyond elementary literacy. Shapovalov, for example, decided to attend evening technical school to acquire the knowledge needed to become a skilled worker.[14] And since acquisition of a skill involved several years of apprenticeship, the typical skilled worker, though often born and raised in the village, entered factory life at 14–16 years of age, which meant that by adulthood he was well assimilated into the urban working-class milieu.

With skill came a more developed sense of dignity, fostered by pride of craft and relative material security. After working a few years at the Workshops of the North-West Railroad, the young Shapovalov was offered the following advice by an older worker:

> Go to a factory where they build new machines and do not just repair locomotives. Leave the Varshavka, Sashka. You will learn how to work, gain more experience, become a skilled worker, learn to be bold. You will

12 H. Braverman 1974, pp. 110–11.

13 Ya. S. Rozenfel'd and K.I. Klimenko 1961, p. 54.

14 Shapovalov 1934, p. 57.

> stop being afraid of the foremen, forge freedom for yourself. You will stop fearing being without work. You will gain a broader outlook of life.[15]

S-skii, a liberal journalist writing in 1911, called the Petersburg workers 'the salt of the conscious working people' and he went on to describe the skilled metalworkers:

> Workers in machine production are always in the forefront of every movement ... They are the aristocrats, the progressive ones. Turners, founders, blacksmiths, mechanics and machinists – these are all developed people with a well-formed sense of individuality and rather good wages ... At any rate, this group of workers is able to live without especially burning need, on condition, of course, of continuous employment. They are able to rent a flat, a cheap one, but nevertheless a flat, if they are married ... There is a hearth, something of which many other groups of workers are deprived ...
>
> I was never a worker myself, but it seems to me that work in machine-building factories, despite its burdensome nature, must develop the urge toward individuality in a man. Here there must be room for creativity. The worker must think a great deal, reason in the very process of work. And, therefore, the very essence of his work gives him a push toward self-determination. I have personally had occasion to talk at my home for hours with many workers on various subjects. By the form of their conversation and even by their language, they are almost indistinguishable from our intellectuals. In my opinion, they are more interesting because their judgments are fresher, and their convictions, once established, are very firm. And of late they are developing morally in the purely Russian manner – not by the day but by the hour ... For the most part they are city-born.

The author then described a change of shifts at a machine-building factory:

> A group of workers comes out of the gates. They are wearing work clothes, not exactly in the freshest condition, but undoubtedly well-sewn and of durable quality. Their facial expressions are very serious and concentrated. Through the layer of soot, one can see sullen thought at work. They

15 Ibid., p. 74. 'Varshavka' – the Workshops of the N.W. Railroad linking Petrograd and Warsaw.

> walk unhurriedly and solidly. They talk among themselves – and about matters that generally have nothing in common with the factory they have just left. Over there – one life, the working life; here – another, the public life, with its acute socio-political interests. On the way, they buy newspapers, mainly of a liberal orientation.[16] Once at home, the worker will read his newspaper in his spare time and will, perhaps, disagree with much in it, as liberalism is for the upper classes (*barskii*), and they, the workers, are essentially different.[17]

A. Shlyapnikov, a skilled metalworker and prominent Bolshevik who worked in factories of the Vyborg District during the world war, also drew a connection between militancy and the better material situation of skilled workers. Referring to the Vyborg District, he wrote:

> In pre-war years, when there were large war orders, there was a crying need for working hands. And so employers paid higher wages to attract skilled workers. This contributed to the concentration of the most developed workers in this district. The better working conditions and the militancy gave the district a certain revolutionary reputation, and the 'Vyborzhtsy' maintained it with pride.[18]

Wages in metalworking were the highest in industry, the printers having lost their leading position during their sector's wartime decline (see Table 1.2).

In the Russian context, the emergence of new cultural needs – a developed sense of individuality and dignity and the aspiration towards self-determination – could only intensify hostility to the existing order. As these new needs developed, so did the tension grow between them and a social and political order that stubbornly denied their fulfilment. If the less culturally and politically developed workers were concerned primarily about economic matters, their more skilled colleagues, as Buzinov observed, wanted to talk 'about other, more general things, and not just wages'. For the skilled worker, the struggle was conducted at once on many levels, with the economic often taking a secondary place.

16 Under Tsarism, the socialist press was severely restricted.

17 N. S-skii 1911, pp. 12–14.

18 A. Shlyapnikov 1923, p. 5.

TABLE 1.2 *Average monthly wage of Petrograd workers by industry, in current rubles, 1913 and 1916*

Industry	1913	1916
Metalworking	42.0	51.0
Printing	56.4	38.0
Chemicals	30.0	33.8
Woodworking	41.0	31.3
Leather	36.0	30.7
Minerals	30.7	24.5
Food	28.2	24.5
Textiles	26.0	24.7

SOURCE: P. LEIBEROV, 'Petrogradskii proletariat v gody pervoi mirovoi Voiny', in *Istoriya rabochikh Leningrada*, vol. I, p. 470.

In work and in public life, Tsarist society frustrated these new aspirations. The Russian factory regime was a corrupt and degrading despotism, where any rights had to be wrested by force and were retracted by management at the first sign of weakening. From the Revolution of 1905–6 onward (with a certain pause during the years of political reaction in 1907–11), demands for respect, for polite address (use of the second person plural rather than the singular, reserved for children, animals and intimate acquaintances), an end to searches, decent treatment of women, and the like, became dominant issues in the workers' movement.[19] Shapovalov recalled how painfully he experienced the conflict between his emergent sense of dignity and desire for autonomy, on the one hand, and his subservient, dependent position *vis-à-vis* his boss, on the other.

> From my first days at Olivier's workshop, I felt a peculiar duality. Myself, a revolutionary and Marxist, one who hated the capitalist system and who had set as my goal its total destruction, recognised that capital was pressing on me and subordinating me to the will of the boss to such an

19 Haimson 2005, pp. 179–85.

> extent that I lowered my eyes under his severe gaze, that I was bending over my machinist's lathe more intensely than I needed to when he watched me. Alas, I had to admit that it was as if two men were living inside me: one, who for the sake of the struggle for a better future for the workers, was not afraid of being locked up in the Peter-Paul Fortress and sent to Siberian exile; and another who had not fully liberated himself from the feeling of dependence and even fear. Nevertheless, catching myself on these slavish feelings, I came to hate capitalism and my boss Olivier even more intensely.[20]

The relations in the factories, however, were but a microcosm of the workers' social and political situation in Tsarist society, which was characterised by despotic paternalism that stifled all attempts at self-expression. Here, too, the movement did not limit itself to economic demands, to the struggle for legalisation of trade unions and the like, but fought also for recognition of the workers as citizens, possessing their own economic, cultural and political organisations run by workers.

The emergence of these needs[21] generated a new type of activist: the 'conscious worker'. 'Beyond the Nevskii Gates', Buzinov wrote,

> among the worker masses, one now [1906–7] heard the word 'conscious'. And the emergence of the conscious worker clearly implied that his opposite was also present – the unconscious worker. There were few socialist workers [i.e. party members] and they were supported by the conscious workers. The latter were ten times more numerous than the socialists ... Each was, in a way, a 'legally reasoning individual', capable of understanding everything around him. To a greater or lesser degree, they all understood the situation of the workers and their relations with the factory owners. Life itself transformed them into the vanguard of the worker masses. Their native keen wit and worker sensitivity did not fail them when they exposed the hidden ends behind this or that manoeuvre of management. And they were no longer silent. Somehow in their midst, a special type of agitator was created, a person constantly hammering

20 Shapovalov 1934, p. 618.

21 This topic can only be touched upon here. However, Shapovalov's memoirs offer a vivid and very moving account of the process of gradual awakening of new needs, and with them, a growing commitment to the revolutionary struggle. Buzinov also gives an interesting account of the workers' awakening in the Nevskii District during the Revolution of 1905–6. See also B. Ivanov 1919 and L.M. Kleinbort 1923.

> away at the same point – I would say – of class separation from the exploiters. In the person of these agitators, life had hammered a wedge between workers and owners that no party agitator, not so closely tied to the masses as they were, could have done ... This self-made agitator spoke of that which each worker had in his head but, being less developed, was unable to verbalise. After each one of his words, the workers would exclaim: 'That's it! That's just what I wanted to say!' He would seize upon a subject that could not claim a very wide scope, but rather one of the simplest kind ... It might have to do with a screw and its thread. But the confrontation of a whole series of such details, among which a worker passes his whole life, gave this speech a special persuasiveness. For each worker, be he as benighted as the dark night, it became clear that under his very nose amazing things were going on, and this in itself posed the question: 'And after that, what else is going on that he, like a mole, does not see?'[22]

In this passage, Buzinov refers to 'class consciousness' in the usual sense of a grasp of workers' oppressed economic and political situation. But in the Russian labour movement, the term 'conscious worker' had a much broader meaning that embraced an entire code of conduct, including such varied aspects of social life as male workers' relations with women, attitudes towards the consumption of alcohol, to theft, relations with management, and much else. The 'conscious worker' did not only fight for the economic and political rights of the working class, he was an *intelligentnyi* person, in the broad Russian sense of the term. A. Babytsyn, a skilled mechanic at the New Parviainen Machine-Building Factory in the Vyborg District, recalled:

> On payday the mood among workers was noticeably animated. There would be conversations about how they were going to spend the wage. Certain workers did not go home right away but went to the taverns and tea-houses on Big Sampsionievskii Avenue, where they would get drunk or play billiards amidst the whine of gramophones.
>
> But it was in a different way that the conscious part of the workers spent their leisure time. Many went to the People's House, they attended performances at the Komediya theatre, visited museums. But they did not spend their wages only on distractions. One day, Nikolai Mukhin, a worker in our shop, approached me and, with the caution characteristic

22 Buzinov 1930, pp. 101–3.

> of an underground activist, asked if I could help workers who had been arrested and were suffering for the interests of the working class.[23]

Another worker, expounding on the quality of social relations, wrote: 'Only a conscious working person can truly respect a person's individuality, a woman, cherish the tender soul of a child. We won't learn from anyone but ourselves. We, the conscious working people, do not have the right to be like the bourgeois'.[24] In the autumn of 1917, the workers' committee at the Izhorskii Factory adopted the rule that any worker stealing was subject to dismissal. When that happened the union would be notified of the reason: 'for theft, that disgraces the conscious proletariat'.[25]

Buzinov observed that the conscious workers 'are no longer silent', that is, they actively try to raise up their fellow workers. These 'self-made agitators' were not party people. They were acting on their inner compulsion to bring the others to their level. In the worker, wrote a contemporary observer of the labour scene,

> The spiritual process is an active one. Once the voice of the individual has begun to speak in the worker, he can neither sit under a bush ... nor limit himself to mere words ... The strength of this process is in its dynamism: the upper strata of the proletariat raise up the backward strata to their own level. Questions of honour and conscience are the first small bridges on which the proletarian shakes the hand of the semi-proletarian, opens before him the vista of the complete worker.[26]

This active orientation was crucial to the ability of a comparatively small part of the working class, the skilled workers, to exert its influence over the others. And it helps to explain the relatively rapid integration of large numbers of newcomers from the village into the urban labour movement.

It is remarkable that the Ministry of Trade and Industry, headed by one of Russia's biggest bankers and staffed by former Tsarist officials also referred to skilled workers as the 'conscious' element of the working class. In a survey of Petrograd's factories from soon after the February Revolution, the ministry reported that

---

23 *Vogne revolyutsionnykh boev*, vol. 1 (M., 1967) p. 95.

24 Kleinbort 1923, p. 16.

25 *Rabochii kontrol'i natsionalizatsiya promyshlennykh predpriyatii Petrograda v 1917–1919 gg.*, vol. 1 (L., 1949), p. 226 (henceforth cited as Rab. Kon.).

26 Ibid., pp. 100–1.

> In a whole series of cases, the [factory] committees have been able to introduce a certain order and discipline into the worker masses, and it is generally observed that the influence of the committees and their significance are greater the more the workers are conscious. Therefore, their authority is rather significant, for example, in the metalworking factories. And the opposite is true: it is very insignificant where the majority of workers are relatively uncultured.[27]

The report linked metalworking, consciousness,[28] culture, discipline and organisation. Indeed, although the metalworkers of the Vyborg District were by far the most radical element of the working class, they were far from an 'elemental force' (*stikhiya*), as Bolshevik workers were later often portrayed by Mensheviks and Western historians. In fact, the Vyborg workers took special pride in their discipline and organisation. A report on the demonstration of 18 June 1917 read: 'The Vyborg workers arrived in neat columns on the Plains of Mars. "What district is that?" shouted a voice from the crowd. "You mean you can't see? Perfect order! That means it's Vyborg", proudly answered the column's leader'.[29] V. Malakhovskii, commander of the districts Red Guards, wrote:

> And the people we had there in the Vyborg District were the pick of the crop – everyone was a fine lad. Whomever you chose, he wouldn't let you down. And it's true that we never were let down by them ... Such a gratifying milieu as the workers of the Vyborg District allowed us to organise the Red Guards in such a way that each one of them was put to good use ... While the Red Guards in other districts also numbered in the thousands, they proved much weaker in action. On the day of the uprising, people came from other districts and even from as far as Kronstadt to learn from us how to organise the Red Guards.[30]

---

27 Cited in Sobolev 1973, p. 65.

28 The term obviously involved a value judgment. But in the Russian labour movement and even well beyond there was a consensus on who were the 'conscious' workers. S-skii, a liberal, called the Petersburg workers 'the salt of the conscious working people' and singled out the skilled metalworkers. Buzinov, a Socialist Revolutionary (SR), contrasted the 'backward', unskilled textile workers to the 'conscious' skilled metalworkers. *Novaya zhizn'*, the Menshevik-Internationalist paper, referred to the metalworkers as 'the most conscious masses of Petrograd in the class sense', while the unskilled workers were 'unconscious and uncultured (*neintelligentnye*)' *Novaya zhizn'* (8 and 9 December 1917).

29 *Izvestiya* (20 June 1917).

30 V. Malakhovskii 1925, p. 25.

One of the most important features of the political culture of the skilled metalworkers was what Buzinov termed the aspiration to 'class separateness (*obosoblennost*) from the exploiters'. He noted that the essential thrust of the message of the conscious worker was 'to hammer a wedge between workers and owners'. S-skii similarly observed that the workers would disagree with much that they found in the liberal papers they bought because 'liberalism is for the upper classes, and they, the workers, are essentially different'.

The aspiration towards 'class separateness', or perhaps more accurately 'class independence', from census society (the propertied classes) was more than the desire for self-determination. It stemmed from a deeply held sense of the antagonistic interests that separated workers from the propertied classes. This gave rise to the desire for workers' organisations to be kept under exclusive control of workers, free of intervention or influence from census society. A police survey of the labour movement in Petrograd for November 1915 observed that the most discussed issue in the period was consumer cooperatives, as wartime conditions were already causing food supply problems. At meetings that discussed this subject, workers 'expressed the desire to do without any material aid from the industrialists, who were gladly offering it in the establishment of co-operatives'. Similar attitudes were expressed in regard to the cooperative that had been opened by the Petrograd Society of Factory and Mill Owners (PSFMO). At a meeting of workers of the Erikson factory, for example,

> a majority pointed out that the Society is totally dependent upon the factory owners, and since co-operation is one of the forms of the workers' movement in general, it is necessary to think along lines of our own worker societies that would be independent of the owners.

The report also noted the growth in interest in insurance and sickness funds:

> However, one observes of late in the worker population the tendency towards isolation of their activities from any sort of pressure from the authorities or the entrepreneurs. Here too, one senses the shift toward pure autonomy ... This tendency ... can be observed at all workers' meetings without exception.[31]

---

31 M.G. Fleer 1925, pp. 222–3.

A similar attitude prevailed in the sphere of worker-management relations, where any form of toadying or even socialising was referred to as 'fraternisation'. The ideal was a clean separation.

On the political level, this attitude manifested itself first and foremost in the workers' universal rejection of liberalism. The Constitutional Democrats (Kadets), Russia's liberal party, were unable to attract even a small working-class following. But more than that, the 'conscious' metalworkers rejected any political alliance with the liberal bourgeoisie. This was the fundamental reason for the weak support for the Mensheviks among these workers, particularly in periods of intense labour militancy. Buzinov recalled that even after the revolutionary mood of 1905–6 had passed and the sobered workers became more receptive to the idea of reforms, at their meetings, 'nevertheless, from each word spoken a clear line emerged that separated the workers from the ruling class, and one could feel the spiritual growth of the workers over the past two years'.[32] For this SR activist, too, 'class separateness' meant spiritual growth.

The other side of the coin was the sense of class honour and dignity of the skilled metalworkers, traits that played a very important role in their struggles, turning conflicts that might have begun over wages and other material demands into questions of honour to be won at almost any price.[33] It was class honour that moved Skorinko, a 48-year-old worker at the Putilov factory, to scold his son for 'allowing himself' to be beaten by officers when he defended the Bolsheviks:

> And you tolerated it, you louse!? You should have given them one of the mug. With an inkwell, a revolver, a chair. A worker must not allow himself to be hit by a bourgeois. You hit me? Ok, then take this! Ah, you so and so![34]

This sense of honour lay behind such slogans as 'It is better to fall a pile of bone than live like slaves', or 'We will nevertheless fight and if we perish, then it will be in an honest fight, but we won't retreat for the struggle'.[35]

Some factors that contributed to this value of class separateness readily present themselves. First of all, Russia on the eve of the Revolutions of 1917 was still in many ways a society based on legally defined estates. Elections to the State Duma, for example, were held by curia, based on a combination of

32 Buzinov 1930, p. 126.

33 P.V. Volobuev 1964, p. 238.

34 I. Skorinko 1923, p. 145.

35 *Oktyabr'skaya revolyutsiya i fabzavkomy*, vol. I (M., 1927) p. 208 (henceforth cited as FZK).

estate and property (class) qualifications. This in itself bolstered a sense of class distinction and separateness. Secondly, Russian reality was such that the interests of the propertied classes, as they conceived them, were very obviously deeply opposed to the aspirations of the workers (and peasants). Even the Workers' Group of the War-Industry Committee, one of the most conservative elements of Russian Social Democracy, one that supported the war effort, a group whose chief goal was to promote a political alliance between the workers and the liberal bourgeoisie against the autocracy, could not ignore this reality.

> In its letter to Petrograd's workers in December 1916, the Committee recognised that the propertied classes had always feared the people. But having lost faith in their own forces, they were now turning to the popular movement and wanted the working class to take action in the form of street demonstrations. Of course, they would like this intervention to take place on their own terms, for their own interests – to obtain the most for themselves and to give as little democracy as possible to the workers. But the working class is conscious enough not to let that happen. The bourgeoisie wants political reform, a liberal regime; we will secure our goal – the maximum democratisation of the country. The bourgeoisie wants a government responsible to the Duma [elected by a very unequal suffrage weighted toward the propertied classes]; we – a provisional government based, not on the Duma, but on the organised people. The bourgeoisie will try to maintain the current forms of cruel exploitation; the working class will demand a series of social reforms that will facilitate their struggle against exploitation and the exploiters. The bourgeoisie wants to give freedom to its annexationist appetites; the proletariat and democracy will protest decisively against all military coercion and will strive for a peace acceptable to the workers of all countries.[36]

But there was another, more unconscious factor at work. Shapovalov recalled how deeply bothered he was that he, a conscious, revolutionary worker, cowered before his boss. Catching himself on those slavish sentiments, he came to hate the entire system even more intensely. The aspiration to 'class separateness' was partly a response to the fear that if the workers lowered their defences, if they 'fraternised' with the class enemy, they would yield to these slavish tendencies and allow themselves to be influenced, even dominated by the class enemy.

---

36 E. Maevskii 1918, pp. 96–7.

The opposite side of the coin to 'class separateness' was the strong desire for working-class unity. The 'conscious' workers typically referred to themselves as part of a 'worker family' or as 'a single harmonious proletarian family'.[37] They felt there should be common goals and a common strategy, not division. Workers often expressed impatience with party divisions, sometimes ascribed to the pride of the party leaders. The Menshevik Lev Lande wrote:

> The wish for unity ran strong in the labour movement throughout the February period, and it did not die easily even after October. At bottom, it sprang from the belief that the working class had to remain united if it was to fulfil its historical role. Therefore, though this increasingly conflicted with reality, all parts of Russian social democracy in 1917 paid some lip service to the masses' yearning for a single, united labour party.[38]

Of course, unity and solidarity are key elements in any labour movement, since they are the main sources of workers' power. But in addition, unity filled the same psychological need as 'class separateness': the support of the 'collective' was important in overcoming servile tendencies. Shlyapnikov observed a certain duality among Vyborg metalworkers: they were very militant in the struggle for collective demands, but on an individual level in the factories they would tolerate wage differentials, since to oppose this often meant that the worker had to stand up for himself.

> This occurred quite often because our metalworkers were accustomed to collective struggle, while demands for simple wages and much else in factory life called for a certain amount of personal restraint, persistence and the ability to stand up for oneself, each person alone, sometimes without the common support.[39]

A. Buiko, a Petrograd worker who had grown up in the village, recalled the tremendous strength he drew from his sense of belonging to the collective, once he had been assimilated into the factory milieu:

---

37 Rab. Kon., pp. 152–3; *Velikaya Okeyabr'skaya sotsialisticheskaya revolyutsiya. Dokumenty i materialy. Nakanune Okyabr'skogo vooruzhennogo vosstaniya 1–24 oktyabrya 1917 g.* (M., 1962), p. 311 (henceforth cited as Dok. Nak.).

38 Haimson (ed.) 1975, p. 13.

39 Shlyapnikov 1923, p. 11.

> In the first years before I outgrew my still peasant attitudes, I felt myself alone and I constantly experienced fear in front of other people. But once I grew close to my comrades, I began to feel an unshakeable ground beneath my feet. Confidence and assurance appeared: 'I am not alone – there are many of us. We are all as one!' The consciousness of this imparted so much energy that it lasted for the entire ensuing struggle.[40]

The pressure towards unanimity was strong and in 1917 it often took the form of resolutions adopted unanimously. And an important tool for enforcing labour discipline was to force the recalcitrant worker to answer for his behaviour before a general meeting.[41]

A final element of the political culture of the skilled metalworkers worth emphasising is internationalism – both in relation to ethnic minorities in Russia and in relation to the world war and struggles of the oppressed peoples abroad. Though the Petrograd working class was ethnically overwhelmingly Russian, it had significant minorities.[42] But if ethnic antagonism existed, it played no visible role in the labour movement. One of the most famous strikes of 1912–14 upsurge of labour militancy was a 102-day stoppage at the Lessner Machine-construction Factory, sparked by the suicide of a Jewish worker who had been driven to despair by the taunts of a foreman. In 1917, people with obviously Jewish names, such as Izrailevich or Kogan, were elected by workers as delegates to soviets and other workers' organisations.[43]

The workers' internationalist stance in the world war was forcefully demonstrated in the course of 1917. 'Down with the war!' was a key slogan of the February Revolution. The patriotic wave that swept Russian society when the war began found little echo among Petrograd workers and even that was short-lived. Police reports make clear that no trace remained by the fall of 1915.[44] N.I. Potresov, a right-wing Menshevik and supporter of the war, bitterly lamented in 1915 that, while the 'German invasion' had aroused even the most stag-

---

40 A. Buiko 1934, pp. 94–5.

41 Z.V. Stepanov 1973, p. 129.

42 According to the industrial census of August 1918, 84.2 percent of the industrial working class of Petrograd was Russian. Poles constituted 5.8 percent, Lithuanians and Letts 2.6 percent, Finns 2.3 percent, Germans 0.5 percent and Jews 0.3 percent. Ibid., p. 42.

43 Izrail' Moiseevich Kogan, for example, was elected by the workers of the Skorokhod Shoe Factory to the Petrograd Soviet on 17 December 1917. Tsentral'ni gosudarstvennyi arkhiv Sankt-Peterburga, fond 7384, opis' 7, delo 21, list 80 (henceforth cited as TsGASPb).

44 M.G. Fleer 1925, p. 209. In Moscow, by contrast, when the war broke out, workers participated in a strike against firms with German ties. Shlyapnikov 1923, p. 184.

nant elements of bourgeois society, 'it evoked nothing in the proletarian masses, no response worthy of the most revolutionary class of contemporary society'.[45] In the summer of 1917, the Putilov workers donated 5,000 rubles to make a banner that read: 'We pledge to achieve the fraternity of people. Long live the Russian Revolution as the prologue to Social Revolution in Europe'. It was presented to the Pavlov Regiment in an elaborate ceremony on the Field of Mars. Workers' meetings in 1917 condemned the closing of Finland's parliament by the Provisional Government after the former voted for autonomy in internal affairs. It is worth noting also that a significant part of Petrograd's industry was owned by foreigners, and much of the higher administrative personnel was also of foreign origin.

Unskilled Workers

Unskilled and semi-skilled were generally the least politically active part of the capital's industrial working class. In party circles they were referred to as 'masses of low-consciousness' (*malosoznatel'nye massy*) and sometimes pejoratively as 'the swamp' (*boloto*).

By far the largest group in this category were women workers, overwhelmingly confined to unskilled work. V. Perazich, an activist in Petrograd's textile-workers' union, observed of the sector's overwhelmingly female workforce in the early period after the February Revolution, that 'Our masses in general at that time were still totally benighted … Only very few had managed to become conscious proletarians'. Perazich explained that the problem was compounded by the fact that many of the male workers in this sector who had occupied the relatively few skilled jobs and were generally more active and had provided leadership, had been drafted or had moved to metalworking factories to obtain military deferrals.[46]

Women in industry were almost invariably engaged in menial, unskilled and semi-skilled tasks. In textiles, food-processing, chemicals and shoemaking, they were typically employed in the mostly unskilled production jobs, while men did the skilled tasks in maintenance, set-up, and supervision.[47] Even in the industries that had a bigger proportion of skilled labour, such as metalworking and printing, women were almost always employed in unskilled jobs.[48]

45 N.I. Potresov, *Posmertnyi sbornik proizvedenii*, pp. 230–42, cited in Haimson 1975, p. 13.

46 V. Perazich 1927, pp. 81–2, 86.

47 See, for example, T. Shatilova 1927, p. 10.

48 *Istoriya Leningradskogo soyuza poligraficheskogo proizvodstva*, vol. 1 (L., 1925), p. 48.

If skilled labour fostered the capacity for analytical thought and other intellectual qualities, unskilled work tended to deaden the mind. 'The weaver and spinner', wrote S-skii,

> are workers of a totally different type [than the more skilled metalworkers]. They are slaves of the machines. The machine has devoured them and all their existence. Theirs is stubbornly mechanistic work ... Here the people are numbers. Here, on the faces, is written that which is most terrible in a work atmosphere: the hopelessness of labour. People grow dull, go to seed ... [There is complete] absence of demand for individual creativity.

Women's jobs in metalworking were not much different. A young woman assembling hand-grenades in an exclusively female shop of the Opticheskii Factory left this account:

> My girlfriend Masha and myself worked at the same bench. We sat opposite each other. I remember that I was sitting on a stool with my head bent over a protective glass. Behind it was a sheet of cardboard with tiny slits. From a tin box lined with khaki, I take 40 capsules, instead of the regulation 20, and insert them into the slits. I dip the brush into a bottle and cover the detonator with glue. With the point of a wooden stick, I put a tiny golf leaf circle on it and press it down with a small hammer. My hands more and more quickly repeat these movements, learned by rote, and my body is locked in motionlessness.
>
> At that moment, the foreman, Yanikeev, came up behind me. 'You're breaking the rules, my beauty! Haven't I explained that to you? Or maybe you aren't Russian?' ... Masha tried to joke with him: 'She's not Russian. She's from Tver'. But the foreman turned to her, observed the same violation of the rules, and shouted: 'I've had it playing with you rule-breakers. Collect your pay in two weeks!' I tried in vain to prove to him that there was no defective output ... We were saved from being fired by the revolutionary events that began at the end of February 1917.[49]

There was no room for any initiative or independent thought in this repetitive work of five simple operations.

---

49 *V ogne revolyutsionnykh boev*, vol. II (M., 1971) pp. 34–5.

TABLE 1.3 *Literacy among women textile workers, metalworkers, and all industrial workers, by age, August 1918*

Age	Percent of literate workers		
	Women textile workers	Metalworkers	All industrial workers
To 14	70.0	93.6	80.6
15–19	62.8	92.1	77.1
20–24	51.7	88.6	68.2
25–29	38.6	87.2	66.2
30–34	28.6	86.7	64.2
35–39	19.9	81.1	59.2
40–44	15.1	79.9	58.2
45–49	10.7	72.6	51.9
50 +	7.9 [a]	62.8	42.3
All	37.5	82.6	64.0

[a] 50–54 only.

SOURCE: BASED UPON RASHIN, *FORMIROVANIE RABOCHEGO KLASSA ROSSII* P. 602.

Women were the lowest paid industrial workers: in 1916, the average wage in the textile industry was less than half of the wages in metalworking (see Table 1.2). And women were doubly exploited. Not only did their wages fail to secure anything close to a decent standard of living, but they were subject to the arbitrary rule of unscrupulous managers and foremen who often took advantage of them economically and sexually.[50] The 'decent public' looked upon woman factory workers as little better than prostitutes.

Literacy among women workers was on a low level, although the gap between men and women narrowed considerably in the lower age groups (see Table 1.3). Apart from the rare skilled male workers in the textile mills, it was typically from among the young women that activists were recruited.[51]

50 See, for example, A.E. Suknovalov and A.I. Fomenkov 1968, pp. 98–9; The Bolshevik women's magazine *Rabotnitsa* is replete with such accounts.

51 Suknovalov 1968, pp. 58–80, *passim*.

But more than the mechanical nature of their work and the low level of literacy, it was the overall mode of life of women workers that worked against their active participation in the labour movement. The woman worker typically began to earn a wage at 9 and 11 years of age, sometimes even earlier, putting in endless hours as a nanny or tending a peasant's garden or the local noble's cattle. Later on, she would leave the village to work in the city as a seamstress, mill hand, or salesgirl. Mill work and childbirth, wrote Kabo, led to the early destruction of the women's organism and left them with no energy or time for acquiring basic literacy. As a result, almost all of the textile workers, who averaged 33 years of age (in this sample of Moscow workers from the mid-1920s), were physically exhausted and semi-literate or completely illiterate.[52]

The life of the woman worker was a closed one, an almost unbroken passage between home and the mill that kept her isolated from the larger society and outside the dynamic influence of the labour movement. Her intellectual horizons went scarcely beyond the family and factory shop. 'Working beside a man at the factory for 11–12 hours', wrote the Bolshevik journal *Rabotnitsa*,

> and receiving for her work a significantly lower wage, miserable pennies, is not the woman, whose organism is weaker, also burdened with necessary, heavy housework? Is it easy for her, after endless grinding work at the mill, when a man can relax, to partake in public life, read and converse with comrades about what he has read, when instead of all this, forgetting herself, she gives every free moment to the care of the children? They have to do the washing, and mend the linen, and feed them. And how will you feed them when food constantly grows dearer and wages are so small? ... In this sort of calculation, in these cares and worries about the household, the women worker passes all her free time with the family, and she hardly has any time left for rest, for her personal life. Exhausted, sick from unhealthy, endless mill work, knowing no peace at home, from morning to night, day in and day out, month after month, the worker mother drudges and knows only need, only worry and grief. Her life passes in gloom, with no light. She ages quickly. She is broken. She has suffered her fill in the very years when a person should enjoy the full blossoming of her forces. And she dies having known no happiness in life; she perishes like a broken young tree.[53]

52 Kabo 1928, p. 127.

53 *Rabotnitsa* (19 April 1914).

Little interest in public affairs, weakly developed class consciousness, a tendency to stand aside from the collective struggle, and lack of initiative and perseverance once engaged in it – these were traits of the political culture of unskilled women workers. 'How many times', asked another article,

> have we heard that a strike in this or that enterprise failed ... because 'among the workers there were many women'; that several factories did not support their comrades at work 'because' among the workers employed there are many women; that a strike ended prematurely and was consequently lost 'because' among the workers are many women? ... Why, women are the least conscious group ... They join unions less than men, they attend clubs and lectures less frequently.[54]

'Here, thanks to our disorganization, we have never joined the collective actions of the proletariat', wrote a worker of the Kenig Thread Mill, that employed 2500 women and 80 men.

> And if the women workers in a department declare a strike, the workers in the others don't come to their aid. This, Kenigtsy, is what our disunity and lack of organisation lead to: they exploit our lack of consciousness. And that will continue until we stop regarding our boss as a benefactor and ourselves as slaves ... The majority of the women workers, including those of our mill, drag behind at the tail end of the labour movement. We lack the intensity, the energy required for the struggle against capital.[55]

Among her 30 women respondents, Kabo found that the overwhelming majority were completely uninformed about issues of 'political and cultural life'. Only nine read newspapers before 1917. 'The great majority of women', she concluded, 'are not interested in political and cultural issues; they have no reading habits and cannot remember what they read or when'.[56]

One of the factors holding women workers back was their concern for their families. 'They hold on more firmly to the present', wrote *Rabotnitsa*, 'They are more afraid of taking risks – for themselves, for their children. And it is harder to arouse them to strike, to convince them of the need to hold out to the end'.[57] Although this fear stemmed from a sense of family responsibility and from

---

54 Ibid. (16 March 1914), p. 2.

55 Ibid. (4 May 1914), pp. 12–13.

56 Kabo 1928, p. 132.

57 *Rabotnitsa* (16 March 1914).

material insecurity, it also had roots in the social background and upbringing of women workers. Even younger, unmarried women hesitated to become active. In 1914, when elections were held to the administration of the health-insurance fund at the Laferme Tobacco Factory,

> The older women said: 'What do we need a fund for? They'll dock our pay, and we'll get no help. And anyway, we're too old to give birth'. But even among the young workers many were frightened by the elections. Some even cried when they were elected: 'And what if we get into trouble because of this? What if they arrest us?' [These were legal organisations.] One young worker even said: 'Thank God!' when she learned that she was too young.[58]

Women often exerted a restraining influence on their husbands. A woman worker recalled her relationship before the revolution with her late husband:

> In those days I often became angry at my husband when he would go off to some meeting or as he sat rather often reading a newspaper. 'Is that any business of ours to read newspapers? It's fine for gentlemen to indulge in that, but what can we get out of reading them?'[59]

Of course, it was not gender but the level of skill and the social traits attached to the jobs that women occupied in industry did that were the primary determinants of the political culture of unskilled workers. For women employed in the needle trades, the only skilled industry with a relatively high proportion of women[60] and which typically required two to three years of trade school or apprenticeship, were quite different from the unskilled women workers. The three seamstresses interviewed in Kabo's study were all literate. Two had two years of formal schooling, and one had six. The overall literacy rate for women in the needle trades was 68.2 percent as compared to only 37.9 percent in the cotton industry.[61] Of the other 27 women in Kabo's study, only three had any

58 Ibid. (16 March 1914), p. 10.

59 Kabo 1928, p. 135.

60 About half of Petrograd's 30,000–40,000 needleworkers worked in small workshops sewing underwear and uniforms for the army. The others worked at home in a putting-out system. See Table 3.2 and *Velikaya oktyabr'skaya sotsialisticheskaya revolyulsiya. Dokumenty i materialy. Okiyabr'skoe vooruzhennoe vosstanie v Petrograde* (M., 1957), p. 122, henceforth cited as Dok. Okt.

61 Rashin 1958, p. 601.

formal schooling. All three seamstresses were raised in the city and were daughters of workers. In contrast, seven of the eight textile workers interviewed in the study were born and raised in peasant families. Kabo's interviewers described the latter as 'downtrodden', 'of low culture', 'weakly developed', 'lacking interest in public life'. In contrast, the seamstresses were described as 'energetic', 'intelligent', 'capable'. Two of them were active in public life.[62]

Skilled women workers, in fact, resembled their male counterparts much more than unskilled women workers. And the opposite was true: unskilled male workers, *chernorabochie*, resembled the unskilled women workers both in political culture and in their social backgrounds. Mensheviks and Bolsheviks alike referred to unskilled male workers as 'undeveloped', 'backward', 'unconscious'.[63] Referring to the 1912–14 industrial boom, Kleinbort wrote: 'It was indeed the arrival of the *chernorabochii*, coarse, uncultured, illiterate ... that complicated more than ever the struggle of the working class for its human dignity'.[64] Like unskilled women workers, their male counterparts were engaged in exhausting, repetitive tasks for a bare subsistence wage, though higher than that paid to women.[65]

Unskilled workers were generally recruited from the countryside, and even more so during the war. T. Shatilova, a Bolshevik union organiser in the chemical industry of Petrograd before the revolution, noted that 'in the chemical plants, the majority of workers involved in production jobs were *chernorabochie* ... who had weak ties with the city and lacked proletarian attitudes'.[66] S-skii wrote of a 'huge mass of unskilled *chernorabochie*, of which the majority were newcomers from the countryside'. The Menshevik-Internationalist Bazarov described them as 'casual elements, newly-arrived people turned into workers only for the time of the war'.[67]

---

62 Kabo 1928, pp. 30, 36, 39 and *passim*.

63 See, for example, the editorial by the Menshevik-Internationalist Bazarov (*Novaya zhizn'* 8 Dec 1917).

64 Kleinbort 1923, p. 84.

65 At the 20 March session of the Workers' Section of the Petrograd Soviet, a delegate from the Petrograd district stated:

'You know that there are two categories of workers in the factories: the lower category – *chernorabochie* and women, and skilled workers, who receive a rather decent wage that corresponds to the high cost of living. It is not a question of those workers who receive a good wage; they are secure. But at yesterday's district meeting it turned out that at many plants they receive from between 1.20 rubles and 1.30 rubles a day. In such conditions, it is totally impossible to live in a sort of human fashion'. TsGA SPb f. 1000, op. 73, d. 12, 1.15.

66 Shatilova 1927b, p. 10.

67 *Novaya zhizn'* (8 Dec 1917).

The main difference between men and women workers was that women, regardless of the length of their employment in industry, generally remained stuck in unskilled work, while men could gradually move into semi-skilled or skilled work as they acquired experience. If recent arrival from the village and unskilled work went hand in hand in the case of men, for women these were not necessarily connected. The longer men remained in industrial work, the more they shed their former peasant ways and outlook and became 'proletarianised', whereas Kabo concluded that 'the milieu of their origin and the nature of her work left a more significant imprint on the woman worker [than was the case with men]'. And the reasons were clear: 'Here, all the fundamental characteristics inherited from the recent past that we described are tied up in the tight knot of closed family life and they maintain intact the miserable culture of the urban and rural poor. Life has somehow passed these people by, giving them only small and infrequent joys and leaving as their lot an abundance of deprivations and worries'.[68]

Since newcomers to industry often saw their stay as temporary, or at least had not yet developed any identification with the working class, their commitment to the collective goals of the labour movement, if it existed, was weak, their chief interest being their individual economic improvement and the question of land. The Menshevik-Internationalist paper, comparing the Putilov workers to those at the Trekhgornaya Textile Mill in Moscow, wrote: 'In the first, there is a clear understanding of class interests; in the second, the fundamental issue is land'.[69]

Statistics on participation in strikes show that unskilled workers responded more readily to short-term, economic goals than to the longer-term, mainly political, aims of the workers' movement. In the first half of 1914, a period of intense labour militancy, textile workers were not only less active than metalworkers in the strike movement as a whole, despite their numerical preponderance in Russia, but economic goals played a relatively much greater

68 Kabo 1928, pp. 132 and 223.

69 *Novaya zhizn'* (1 Aug 1917). See also ibid. (8 Dec 1917) for the complaint that the unskilled masses, the war-time workers, failed to see the necessity of raising productivity, in contrast to the skilled workers, the 'genuine proletariat'. According to the August 1918 industrial census, 31.1 percent of all factory workers in European Russia had owned land before the October revolution, with 20.9 percent actually working it through members of their family living in the village. In the more skilled printing and machine-construction industries, these figures were only 17.4 and 9.8 and 24.1 and 13.9 respectively. In needlework, too, the numbers were relatively low – 23.8 and 17.1. By way of contrast, the figures in the cotton sector were 33.6 and 20.4 respectively. Rashin 1958, p. 573.

TABLE 1.4 *Participation in economic and political strikes in 1914, metalworking and textile sectors in European Russia*

	Economic strikes	Political strikes
Metalworking	87,773	661,426
Textiles	115,532	160,336

SOURCE: M. BALABANOV, *RABOCHEE DVIZHENIE V ROSSII V POD'EMA 1912–14* (M., 1927) P. 62.

role in their strikes, as compared to the metalworkers, who by that time were almost completely absorbed by the political movement (see Table 1.4).

Apart from interests and class identity, certain specifically cultural traits also influenced the nature of unskilled workers' participation in the labour movement. Some of these traits had parallels in Russian peasant mentality. One of these was the difficulty in orienting oneself in public issues that were distant from the workers' concrete, personal experience, an ability that the American sociologist C. Wright Mills termed the 'sociological imagination', the capacity 'to grasp history and biography and the relations between the two in society'.[70] Students of peasant culture have often noted the difficulty peasants had in seeing beyond the confines of their own village, a difficulty conditioned by the limited nature of their relations with the outside world.[71] An emissary of the Petrograd Soviet who was sent to work among the peasantry of Yamburg uyezd in the summer of 1917 reported back that all the social questions were being raised at the meetings he organised with the peasants, but 'issues of nation-wide significance were examined very little due to the peasants' lack of preparation, their failure to grasp their importance'.[72]

If the peasants lived in a still significantly natural world where the relationship between family and nature was central, the world of the urban factory workers was predominantly a social one in which the satisfaction of all basic

70 C.W. Mills 1970, p. 6.

71 See, for example E.J. Hobsbawm 1973, p. 13; and B. Galeskii, *Mopi i zawod relnika* (Warsaw, 1963), p. 49, cited in T. Shanin (ed.) 1971, p. 254. Galeskii has observed: 'Because the farmer's produce is essential and, at the lowest level, sufficient for human existence, the labour of the farmer is necessary for the existence of the society as a whole; but the existence of society is not to the same extent necessary for the existence of the farmer'. Ibid.

72 *Izvestiya* (3 Aug 1917).

needs underlined their dependence upon the rest of society: employers for livelihood, landlords for shelter, peasants for food, fellow workers in the production process and in struggle. These differing social situations of workers and peasants found expression in their different reading habits. Kleinbort found that

> The peasant 'who loves to read' ... conducts his farmstead 'more rationally' ... 'is more open to innovation' ... What he finds most valuable in a book is that which is 'useful', that can be put to use here and now in the economy, at the village assembly, in relations outside the village. If, in addition to this practicality, the village discovers some understanding of the book in a sense of general development, it is a very rare book indeed that devours the reader, engrosses him up to such an extent that he forgets his manure, his cattle, the fuss around his home and person ... He is passive, analyses little, looks for sermons, lectures ... [In contrast] the last thing we find in the worker reader is calm. Reading a book, he reacts strongly to this or that part, even more strongly than one might have expected. Accordingly, the book for him is not a sermon or a lecture. Living at the factory, he sees and experiences much. Therefore, the book is the same for him as life. That this is so is shown by his indifference to utilitarian knowledge and the increase in the reading of social books – the opposite of what is undoubtedly taking place in the village.[73]

Not that workers were impractical dreamers. For they read newspapers most of all. And next to fiction, they preferred books on the 'workers'' question, in the same way that peasants asked for books 'on land'.[74] But technical literature, that might have helped workers raise their skill and so also wages, was of little interest to them. As one put it, 'When you put in 12 or 15 hours in a row, it makes you sick to even remember your trade, let alone read about it'.[75]

Unskilled workers, like peasants, had a rather narrow, concrete circle of interests. If Buzinov recalled that with the machinist one felt like talking about something general, and not just wages, and S-skii observed that skilled metalworkers coming out of the factory gates discussed broad socio-political issues, women workers who read newspapers preferred to read 'about our factory ... about accidents and trials ... or about something my husband points out'.[76]

---

73 Kleinbort 1923, pp. 64, 67.

74 Ibid., p. 71.

75 Ibid.

76 Kabo 1928, p. 222.

Unskilled workers' less active participation in the collective labour struggles also had parallels in the oft-observed political passivity or fatalism of peasants, linked by some to the uncertainty that pervaded the peasant economy, subject to the whims of nature.[77] However, it would not be accurate to characterise Russian peasants as passive, as they were capable of periodic outbursts of very militant collective action. These, however, tended to peter out in the absence of concrete results, only to be followed once again by long periods of quiescence. Moreover, these outbursts were not generated from within peasant society, but almost invariably were responses to changes originating outside the village system that somehow challenged the legitimacy of the established order.[78] Lacking a systematic understanding of the functioning and dynamics of society as a whole, peasants exploited opportunities that came from the outside, much in the way they made use of good weather. But once the opportunity had passed, they did not turn to consolidating their movement, to building permanent organisations. Instead, they returned to old patterns and to their preoccupation with local issues and solutions.

The unskilled workers displayed similar patterns of participation in the labour movement. Buzinov recalled how 'the lower stratum of the working class, an essentially inert mass, fell back into a state of lethargy as the revolutionary wave of 1905–6 receded. A kind of indifference to everything that existed and to the future took hold of it'.[79] B. Ivanov, a baker in Moscow, wrote of the 'mass workers', 'tied to the land' and 'with weakly developed consciousness' (*malosoznatel'nye*): 'In moments when his spontaneous energy drives him into battle ... he moves forward with hot determination. But if some obstacle arises in his path, his strength is immediately smashed at the first decisive rebuff by capital'.[80] The bakers conducted two successful strikes in 1907, and the 'mass workers' (*massoviki*) were demanding a third. This was opposed by the 'conscious bakers', the 'proletarianised' ones with no ties to the village. They wanted to postpone another strike in order first to assemble their forces and to deal with organisational issues requiring attention. But the 'mass worker ... took circumstances into consideration very little. His field of vision was limited to

77 Sutti Ortiz, 'Reflections on the Concept of "Peasant Culture" and "Peasant Cognitive System"', in Shanin 1971, p. 330.

78 According to a student of the Russian peasantry, periods of peasant unrest in the second half of the nineteenth and early twentieth centuries clustered around such external events as the tentative agrarian reforms of the late 1840s, the Crimean War, the Russo-Turkish War and the revolutions of 1905 and 1917. R.H. Scott 1973, pp. 10–11.

79 Buzinov 1930, pp. 104–5.

80 Ivanov 1919, p. 83.

the union, and he did not consider the state of the entire movement in the country as a whole.' When the strike failed, the union lost credit in the eyes of these workers. But the other group, which had gained the least, stuck with the union.[81] Similarly, during the period of political reaction in 1907–11, the skilled metalworkers constituted the great majority of the union members in Petrograd. Of 8,459 union members in 1907–8, only 16 percent were unskilled workers. Of the workers who joined the union in 1909 and 1911, only 10 and 5 percent were unskilled.[82]

Yet another characteristic of unskilled workers with an analogy in the peasantry was the dependence upon outside leadership. The Petrograd Soviet's emissary, cited above, observed: 'The peasants still do not understand what has happened and believe that someone will issue them an order "from above" to which they will submit. And when the matter is explained to them, they reply: "He is an anarchist"'.[83] Buzinov wrote of self-made agitators appearing from among the metalworkers. In contrast, Perazich explained the 'backwardness' of the textile workers by the loss of skilled male workers during the war. Despite the severe repression that took thousands of activists out of the factories during the war, Petrograd's metalworkers continuously put forth from their midst new leaders and intensified their economic, and especially political, struggle.

But not all the elements of peasant political culture were inimical to the development of working-class consciousness. The desire for unity was also strong among peasants, whose *skhody* (meetings) also tended to adopt unanimous decisions. As for the valued 'class independence', it was a rare peasant who by 1917 would consider allowing himself or herself to be represented by a big landowner. But for these traits to exert themselves, the newly arrived peasant to industry had to overcome his or her sense of alienation and uprootedness. To cite Buiko once again: 'In the first years before I outgrew my peasant attitudes, I felt myself alone and continually experienced fear before other people'. But in periods of intense labour struggle, the transition could be quite rapid.

Nor can one say that skilled workers completely outgrew their peasant origins. Indeed, one senses that some of the impatience, even scorn, that skilled workers expressed for the 'village' in their midst was to some degree a reaction against the vestiges of peasant culture they were fighting within themselves. This was certainly the case with the tendency to kowtow to authority when confronting it on an individual basis.

---

81 Ibid.

82 F.A. Bulkin 1924, p. 309.

83 *Izvestiya* (3 Aug 1917).

F.N. Samoilov, a Bolshevik worker who had been a deputy in the Third Duma, elected from the workers' curia from the textile centre of Ivanovo-Voznesensk, recalled how he had had to move to a semi-rural suburb of town in 1909 when his wife fell ill. He had been born in the village, but was a skilled textile worker with 17 years of uninterrupted factory work and no economic ties to the land. Nevertheless, the surrounding fields and woods had their effect on him:

> Behind the cottage there was a large level piece of land overgrown with thick grass that seemed like a convenient place to work. When I looked at it, my hands begged for work. At first, I restrained myself but soon I could no longer hold back. The peasant in me finally awoke and the blood of my ancestors, father, grandfathers and great-grandfathers began to boil wildly in my veins. The land attracted me irresistibly to itself ... In the course of many days, I spent all my free hours from work at the mill on the plot ... I experienced the inexpressible pleasure of the muzhik-ploughman, who ploughs his strip with the greatest love and care.[84]

The idyll was cut short, however, when he was arrested and held briefly in connection with his activity in the by then closed textile-workers' union. When he returned, he found the crop destroyed by stray cattle and promised himself 'never again to yield to petty property-owning peasant moods, regardless of the "alluring" situation in which I might find myself'. Yet, he did yield again when he moved to a new working-class district on the edge of town, where he was again eventually arrested. Of course, this was a period of harsh political reaction in Russia, when labour activism was very difficult and bore little fruit. After this new relapse, Samoilov never again yielded to 'peasant moods'.

The 'Worker Aristocracy'

If the two types of worker described above can be seen as more-or-less opposite poles on a series of continua of related social and cultural characteristics, the 'worker aristocracy' was a group apart, sharing many traits of the other skilled workers, but differing fundamentally in some important ways. These were skilled workers (though only a rather small minority of that group) and

84 F.N. Samoilov 1924, pp. 65–88, *passim*.

they, too, were considered 'conscious proletarians',[85] i.e. politically literate, active, culturally developed, class conscious.[86] But they did not share the skilled metalworkers' irreconcilable opposition to census society, their aspiration to 'class separateness' or independence from the possessing classes.

In this group of workers, consisting mainly of printers,[87] skilled veteran workers employed in state-owned factories, and small property-owning workers in the semi-rural outlying districts of the city, the printers formed the largest contingent. Their union had traditionally been led by Mensheviks and remained so into 1920, with the exception of a few months following the October Revolution, when it elected a majority Bolshevik leadership.[88] As skilled workers, the printers were well assimilated into urban life and were nearly all literate. Their work required considerable intellectual skills, and their wages were on a par with those of metalworkers. It was not a privileged material situation[89] but rather the nature of the industry and work, its structure and traditions that muted the antagonism felt by skilled metalworkers towards census society and gave rise among printers to a sense of kinship with the intelligentsia and, through the latter, with the liberal elements of census society.

---

85 Like the term 'conscious worker', 'worker aristocracy' was used by Bolsheviks and Mensheviks alike to denote the same type of worker. For example, the Menshevik-Internationalist Osokin, referring to the printers, wrote of 'the worker aristocracy, to a significant degree detached from the masses, [that] has remained in the ranks of Menshevism'. *Novaya zhizn'* (7 Dec 1917).

86 This is especially true of the printers, who in Petrograd in 1912–14 were second only to the machine-construction workers in their level of participation in the economic and political strike movement. See for example, *Byulleten' Obshchestva zavodchikov i fabrikantov Moskovskogo promyshlennogo raiona, Rabochee dvizhenie yanvar'–mai 1912 g*, pp. 13, 15, 22.

87 The printers were, in fact, not a homogeneous group, neither in terms of their material situation nor their cultural traits. But for present purposes, the term 'printer' is used more or less synonymously with 'type-setter' (in 1905, they were a third of all workers in Petrograd engaged in printing), since this was the dominant group, numerically and ideologically, which set the tone in the printing plants. *Istoriya Leningradskogo soyuza rabochikh poligraficheskogo proizvodstva.* (L., 1925), p. 13.

88 T. Shatilova 1927, p. 187, and *Istoriya rabochikh Leningrada*, vol. 1 (L., 1972), p. 444.

89 By the start of the war, unemployment among printers reached 20–25 percent, and between 1 Jan 1914 and 1 Jan 1917 their numbers in Petrograd declined from 23,000 to 19,000, while the proportion of women in the industry rose from 15.1 percent to 33.7 percent, indicating a decline in the average skill levels. A. Tikhanov, 'Rabochie pechatniki v Petrograde (1904–1914)', in *Materialy po istorii professional'nogo dvizheniya v Rossii*, vol. 3 (M., 1925) p. 114, and Rashin 1958, p. 83.

The printers had a sense of belonging to what the Mensheviks liked to call 'the vital forces of society', a phrase that encompassed the elements of all the classes that, so the Mensheviks argued, were – or could be – interested in democracy.

The work of the typesetter had a strong intellectual element. This was a period when manuscripts were still often untyped, and type-setting required at least a basic understanding of the text in order for work to proceed with sufficient speed and accuracy. In addition, continuous exposure to materials that were at most of a liberal orientation, and often reactionary, could not but leave a trace on typesetters' minds. There was also more direct contact with educated society. According to an early history of the St. Petersburg union, 'type-setters, especially those working on periodical publications, were in direct contact with journalists who, while visiting the composing room, never refused a request by a printer for clarification (given, of course, from their own point of view.)'[90]

The printers tended to set themselves above the mass of workers. Before 1905 at least, they referred to themselves not as *rabochie* (workers), but by the more genteel *truzhenniki* (toilers), 'free artists of the graphic arts', 'literary smithies', even 'commanders of the leaden army'. Their printing establishments were 'temples of art'.[91] As they were drawn into the general workers' movement, these attitudes were attenuated, but they never completely disappeared.

There is evidence also that printers were more frequently recruited from the higher strata of society strata than other workers. According to the above-cited history of the printers' union, while metalworkers almost invariably came from working-class or peasant families, Petrograd's typesetters 'came from all strata, including often very intellectually-developed type-setters from strata that were foreign to the working class, children of the bourgeoisie'.[92] In Kabo's study, of the nineteen printers, six originated in families of white-collar employees (*sluzhashchie*), six in working-class families and another six came from the peasantry. In contrast, only two of the seventeen metalworkers came from white-collar families; six had working-class backgrounds and eight came from the village. This would indicate a higher status in society of printers, since it was apparently not considered so great a step down for an administrative employee, for example, to set his son up as a printer's apprentice.

---

90 *Istoriya Leningradskogo soyuza rabochikh poligraficheskogo proizvodstva*, pp. 13–17.

91 Ibid., p. 17.

92 Ibid., p. 13.

In contrast to metalworking, textiles, chemicals, and other industrial sectors, printing retained many features of a craft industry. To some extent, this was a question of the relatively small size of printing establishments, where the average work force was only 121, as compared to the city-wide average of 409 workers in other industrial enterprises.[93] As in other small plants, relations between the owners and managers, on the one hand, and workers, on the other, tended to be more personal and paternalistic.[94] The direct and informal character of these relations worked against attitudes of class separateness and irreconcilable opposition to census society. Moreover, the small size of the workforce and the economic instability that characterised small enterprises put the workers in a weaker position vis-à-vis the owners and made control of the workers, whom the boss knew by name, relatively easier. In March 1917, the Factory Inspectorate reported:

> It is very important to note that work in the small and medium sized enterprises of Petrograd is proceeding in a relatively normal manner. Work is being conducted in shifts that are longer than eight hours, and although the workers demand higher wages, these claims are very moderate. The reason for this lies in the fact that the workers are less organised and also in the proximity of the owners to the workers, thanks to which they have great influence over the workers.[95]

Workers in small enterprises also lacked the sense of power that their large numbers imparted in the giant factories.

Among the owners of small printing shops, one could find former printers for whom the workers were old acquaintances. During the world war, according to Tikhanov, himself a Petrograd printer, informing and toadying were still quite prevalent among printers:

---

93 *Materialy po statistike truda Severnoi oblasti*, vyp. 1, p. 10. In fact, only 38 factories of over 2,000 workers each employed two-thirds of Petrograd's industrial workers. Stepanov 1965, p. 32.

94 *Istoriya Leningradskogo soyuza rabochikh poligraf*, p. 34.

95 Cited in R.J. Devlin 1976, Chapter 2, p. 9. Most larger factories at that time were in turmoil, the workers pushing for significant economic improvements. The eight-hour day, which was a key economic demand of the February Revolution, was introduced in the larger factories on the workers' independent initiative, once they ended the general strike (see below, Chapter 4).

> An extremely popular manifestation of these slavish sentiments toward the 'father-benefactors' were the anniversary and name-day celebrations, for which the workers would contribute money and then proceed to celebrate together with the boss ... Of course, the administration valued this and encouraged it with sops.[96]

Another element of the structure of the printing industry that worked against class identity and solidarity was the institution of the *kompaniya*. This was an exclusive, cartel-like association of skilled printers who took on work at higher wage rates in return for more rapid executions of orders. The *kompanii* were self-regulating, with an elected elder (*starosta*), who enforced conditions and discipline established by the *kompaniya*. Outsiders were rarely admitted, but they were sometimes taken on at lower wages when there was more work than the *kompaniya* could handle on its own. In this way, some of the printers themselves became employers.

Many of these traits of the printing trade fostered a sense of superiority towards the less 'cultured' workers, as evidenced by the printers' early reluctance to call themselves workers. The 'conscious' metalworkers also manifested a certain disdain for the 'village', but their aspiration to class independence moved them to raise the unskilled masses to their level, to unify the working class around their own standards and goals. This orientation was not nearly so strong among printers, partly because they did not fear or reject cooperation with liberal society and so did not see the same urgency to raise up the others. Moreover, once the unskilled workers were drawn into the workers' movement, they tended to share the metalworkers' irreconcilable attitude to census society.

The printers' identification with the 'vital forces' of society found expression during the world war in the relative strength of 'defencism' (support for the war effort, if not necessarily the state's goals in the war) among them, as compared to the other industrial workers. Tikhanov noted that 'the poison of patriotism was especially potent among the printers, who were in direct contact with it through the press and books'. The journal of the Printers' Union came out in opposition to Karl Liebknecht, the sole Social-Democratic deputy in Germany's Reichstag who voted against war credits. It published the letter of G.V. Plekhanov, Menshevik patriarch and staunch supporter of the war, to the State Duma deputy from the workers' curia A.F. Buryanov, advising

96 A. Tikhanov, 'Rabochie pechatniki v Petrograde (1907–14)', in *Matertialy po istorii professional'nogo dvizheniya v Rossii*, sb. 3, Mocow, 1925, p. 121.

him to vote for war credits.[97] Tikhanov also recalled that 'defencist' attitudes were very strong among printers. Printers also participated in such 'bourgeois' organisations as liberal philanthropies and in the city duma's efforts to alleviate the workers' economic distress. This went counter to the skilled metalworkers' norm of 'class separateness'.[98]

The printers therefore found the Menshevik concept of 'vital forces' – the idea that a coalition of the workers, the intelligentsia and the liberal elements of census society was necessary to bring democratic change – more compatible with their own inclinations. They were more comfortable with that strategy than the Bolsheviks' 'democratic dictatorship of workers and peasants'. The printers tended to view the peasants and the unskilled workers as an elemental, destructive force, a *stikhiya*. At the same time, the Menshevik party, as a workers' party – in contrast to the SRs, identified with the peasantry – but one with a more intellectual following and image than the Bolsheviks, appealed to the printers view of themselves as 'worker-*intelligenty*'.

The other groups of workers in the 'worker aristocracy' shared the printers' readiness to collaborate with liberal society. In state-owned factories, as in the printing shops, this attitude was fostered by the paternalistic nature of relations between workers and management. But unlike the printers, at least a part of the skilled workers of these factories did enjoy a privileged material position. It was that, more than the nature of their work, that fostered more moderate positions and the absence of hostility to census society. A. Anotonov, a worker of the state-owned Obukhovskii Steel Mill, wrote of a stratum of 'highly skilled workers, whom the administration tried to neutralise by giving them apartments in small houses with truck gardens and other small sops'.[99] At the state-owned Military-Medical Preparations factory, many of the highly skilled workers, who lived in state apartments and received relatively high wages and even medals, had refused to strike during the Revolution of 1905–6.[100] According to Tikhanov, the system of sops

> in the state-owned enterprises went as far as the awarding of medals, even gold ones, and hereditary titles. For example, after Easter the workers

97 Ibid., pp. 113,131.

98 Ibid., pp. 115, 131–2.

99 *Doneseniya komissarov Petrogradskogo Voenno-revolyutsionnogokomiteta* (M., 1957), p. 205. Shotman similarly recalled a large number of workers at the Obukhovskii Factory living in state apartments with two rooms and a kitchen. A. Shotman 1935, p. 14. See also L.S. Ganichev 1967, p. 143.

100 Ganichev 1967, p. 128.

> returned to work. Suddenly, in full uniform with crosses and stars, the director appears. He walks up to the nearest worker, greets him with a handshake, and declares: 'Christ has arisen!' and kisses him three times. So he does with all the others.[101]

Such 'fraternisation' was unthinkable in private metalworking factories after the revolution of 1905–6 and especially after the labour upsurge of 1912–14. One should also bear in mind that workers in state factories were part of the state bureaucracy, and skilled workers who had served for many years could not help but be affected by the bureaucratic ethos of state service that pervaded the administration and worked against a clear sense of separateness and antagonism toward management.

There is evidence that in at least some of the state-owned factories wages and conditions were better than in private industry. This was the case, for example, at the Obukhovskii Factory, whose jobs were coveted and could be obtained only through the recommendation of old-timers. Shotman, who had worked at this factory, cited this as one of the reasons it was so difficult to conduct revolutionary work there.[102] At the Government Document Printing Press the eight-hour workday had been introduced even before the Revolution of 1905–6 and the workers elected 'elders' to represent them with management, rights the workers in private industry won only in the February Revolution.[103]

In an article on the state-owned Patronnyi (Ammunition) Factory, which was a rare defencist (war-supporter) bastion in the deeply red Vyborg District, *Izvestiya* offered three reasons for the 'backwardness' of these workers. First, it was a state enterprise and so the workers had been subject to the 'barracks regime' that had prevailed in state-owned factories before the February Revolution and that had made very difficult revolutionary agitation and collective actions. As a result, these workers were not 'propagandised' and lacked a tradition of participation in the labour movement. Secondly, 55 percent of the workers were women, a fact that apparently could speak for itself. In general, during the war state-owned metalworking factories, even more than private industry, were heavily engaged in unskilled ordnance production, employing large numbers of unskilled workers. Finally, this factory was cited as an 'unusual

101 Tikhanov 1925, p. 122.

102 Shotman 1935, p. 14.

103 A. Buntilov 1923, pp. 8–9, 15. See also Stepanov 1965, p. 31, and *Rossiiskii proletariat. Oblik, bor'ba, gegemoniya* (M., 1970), pp. 14–15, note 21.

case' in that its skilled workers were defencists.[104] In state-owned factories, any spontaneously radical tendencies among the unskilled workers had to overcome the moderating influence of the skilled workers, usually the local leaders. For this reason in 1917, even the women of the textile mills were won over to Bolshevik positions well before the workers of most state-owned factories.

An important exception to the generally more conservative outlook of workers in state-owned enterprises was the Sestroretsk Arms Factory, located in a small town not far from the capital and just three miles from the border with Finland. Its workers made rifles for the army and were mostly skilled, unlike the majority in most other state metalworking factories, where the skilled workers were a small, privileged minority. This factory also saw more than its share of political activists, as it served as a haven for worker-revolutionaries from Petrograd who were seeking refuge from the capital's police. It also served as a way-station for smuggling illegal literature and even arms into Russia.[105]

Property, a house and plot of land, exerted a conservative influence on workers. This was particularly evident in the outlying, semi-rural Nevskii District, a SR stronghold for much of 1917 and the centre of the anti-Soviet worker opposition in the spring of 1918. Shotman recalled that

> The main mass of workers consisted of a settled element that had worked continuously at the factory for several years. There were some, for example, who had worked 20 or even 30 consecutive years ... Many workers had their own small houses; there were even those who had several houses which they rented out. Naturally, among this category of worker it was useless to conduct any sort of agitation for the overthrow of the existing order ... Only the youth, and even so, not the sons of the old-timers, but those from outside, were more or less receptive to agitation ...[106]

In times of crisis, this semi-rural factory setting could become the scene of conflict between the settled, local workers and those from outside, since 'the local worker, owning his home, cow, truck, garden and pasture-land, in critical moments for the factory, has the possibility of working for lower wages than the worker from outside, whose entire well-being depends upon the factory wage. The worker from among the local residents, owning private property, is

---

104 *Izvestiya* (27 Oct. 1917).

105 V. Kukushkin 1959; and 'Na Sestroretskom zavode', in *Batsiony revolyutsii*, vol. I (L., 1967).

106 Shotman 1935, p. 14.

also a sort of patriot of his factory and very sensitive to its fate'.[107] Property and cultivation of a plot of land tended to keep workers away from participation in public life. As Samoilov wrote,

> The greatest part of my time away from the factory [was spent] working in the garden … This new situation … began to affect me in a very soporific manner, strongly distracting me from questions of politics … The whole arrangement created the illusion of peace and calm and a certain sense of contentment with one's lot …[108]

Not surprisingly, this type of worker found the SRs' populism, with its emphasis on 'the people' and on land reform, more attractive than social democracy, an urban, working-class movement.

As Shotman hinted, there was also a generational factor at work. Kleinbort described the old-timers (*starichki*) as 'workers who had served 12–15 years in the same place. They are aloof, closed groups that have their privileges. Of course, they fear politics, any sort of questions, aspirations. They live in the past; dream of their little house. They say: We lived better before …'[109] This, of course, did not apply to all older workers, though a more advanced age and family responsibilities tended to foster caution. It was rather the stratum of settled workers, who by virtue of long, continuous and faithful service at the same state factory had acquired certain privileges, amassed a little property, and developed a sense of loyalty. The younger, militant elements, of course, looked on the latter with disgust. 'Try, try you old-timers', wrote a worker at the Russko-Baltiiskii Wagon Factory. 'Soon, for your 25 years of service you will receive a watch and 25 rubles. But remember that if you get sick, they will throw you out like a worthless, squeezed-out lemon, like an old rag'.[110]

The Generational Factor

These varieties of working-class political culture do not constitute a neat set of categories into which one can easily fit all manifestations of workers' politics. They were rather tendencies that could be found in the working class, tend-

107 *Novaya zhizn'* (15 Dec 1917).
108 Samoilov 1924, pp. 66, 89, 90.
109 Kleinbort 1923, p. 80.
110 Ibid., p. 82.

encies that were attenuated, intensified or otherwise modified, depending on local and situational factors. Some of these will be treated in the following chapter that briefly presents Petrograd's districts. Others will be mentioned as they appear in the course of this study. But one that merits some discussion here because of the exceptional role it played is that of age.

While there appears little basis to claim that generational conflict was a major factor in the workers' movement, it is evident that younger workers, regardless of the industrial sector or level of skill, tended to be more active and radical than older workers, who tended to be more cautious. The reputation of younger workers was such that a conference of the Ministry of Internal Affairs with the participation of representatives of the Petrograd Council of Metal Entrepreneurs decided in 1910 that workers under 21 should be prohibited from participating in the general meetings of the Metalworkers' union. Bulkin, who was the union's secretary, explained this decision by the authorities' desire 'to keep out of union affairs the most active, militant workers'.[111] The important role played by young workers in the February and October Revolution is well documented.[112] A worker at the Petrograd Trubochnyi (Pipe) Factory wrote of its Red Guard unit in the weeks preceding the October insurrection: 'As always, the youth was at the front, cheerful and content'.[113] In industries with a less skilled workforce, such as textiles and chemicals, and in the state-owned factories, it was the young workers who formed the militant core and who were most attracted to the Bolsheviks.[114]

The young average age of the members of Petrograd's Bolshevik organisation (28,000 workers in October 1917 – two-thirds of the total membership in the city)[115] is striking. An incomplete but representative list of members of Bolshevik district committees for the first half of 1917 has over a third under the age of 27 years. 60 percent were under 32 years and only 18 percent were over 37. 74.1 percent of these district committee members were workers.[116] Since these were responsible, elected positions, one can assume that the average age of the city organisation was even lower. A.F. Smorodkina, a worker at the Optichceskii Factory, recalled:

111 Bulkin 1924, p. 238.

112 See, for example, Burdzhalov 1967, and Startsev 1962, p. 141.

113 Kudelli (ed.) 1924, p. 112.

114 See, for example, Suknovalov and Fomenkov 1968, pp. 63, 77, 85; Alliluev 1923, p. 327; Shatilova 1927, p. 28; Perazich 1927, p. 91.

115 Stepanov 1965, p. 46.

116 Golovanova 1974, Appendix, Table 7.

TABLE 1.5 *Literacy among Petrograd metalworkers, by age and sex, in early 1918*

Age	Percent of literate workers		
	Male	**Female**	**All**
Up to 20	98	81	94
21–30	95	70	89
31–40	90	47	85
41–50	84	48	82
50 +	51	21	74
All	92	70	88

Note: this table is based on a sample of 10,196 workers.

SOURCE: *METALLIST*, NO. 6 (18 JUNE 1918) P. 10.

> At that time, there was no Komsomol [Communist Youth Organisation] and not even a hint of the youth organisations that later appeared, such as 'Labour and Light'. Youths who had barely turned twenty were, at times, hardened fighters for the revolution. They joined the party at 17–18 or even 16 years, conducted illegal underground activity, often spent time in jail and exile. They had experience in political work among the masses.[117]

I.K. Naumov, a worker at the New Parviainen Machine-construction Factory, was only 22 in 1917. Yet he had already spent time in prison (he was freed by the February Revolution) and was a member of the Bolsheviks' Petersburg Committee, their Vyborg District Committee (this even before the February Revolution), a delegate to all three citywide party conferences in 1917, a delegate from his factory to the Petrograd Soviet, and a member of the Central Soviet of Factory Committees.

The high level of literacy among young workers, a product of the development of the Russian educational system towards the end of the nineteenth century, was an important factor in youth activism. Almost the entire young generation of Petrograd workers was literate. (see Table 1.5)

117 *Vogne revolyutsionnykh boev*, vol. II, p. 37.

Young workers were avid readers. And what they read shaped much of their outlook.[118] Kleinbort found that before the world war over one-half of the members of workers' educational societies were under 23 years of age. One rarely saw older workers there.[119] Similarly, members of workers' clubs were overwhelmingly under 25.[120] Younger workers were, of course, more often single and unburdened with family responsibilities. It was axiomatic in the labour movement that married life discouraged activism.[121]

Of course, young people over the ages have been characterised by enthusiasm, rebelliousness and militancy, and young Russian workers were no exception. Moreover, this was true of all classes of Russian society. A report from Revel in October 1917 stated that the movement to establish soviets among landless peasants was proceeding slowly because the youth, the most active element, had been conscripted into the army.[122] It was also young peasants who led the rural movement during the Revolution of 1905–6.[123] The same was true of the propertied classes: the youth of the Junker (officer cadet) schools of Petrograd were the only element of census society in the capital prepared to oppose the October insurrection with arms.

The rise to prominence of younger workers, like Naumov, was to a large extent facilitated by the departure of older activists from the movement. Of course, many of the old guard did remain. Shlyapnikov and Gvozdev were only among the most prominent of these workers. But even among those who stayed, a significant part tended toward more moderate positions and were out of tune with the militant outlook of the factory youth. The older activists represented a different type of worker-*intelligent* than the generation that reached maturity after the defeat of the Revolution of 1905–6. The older group, despite tensions between them and the intelligentsia, had developed under the latter's guidance and in an atmosphere of sympathy, even if paternalistic, not only on the part of the intelligentsia, but of all of liberal society. These workers learned from the intelligentsia, modelled themselves after it. After the Revolution of 1905–6, however, polarisation along class lines deepened, and the intelligentsia lost its previous enthusiasm for the workers' cause, leaving

118 *Rech'* (3 May 1912); *Pravda* (31 Aug 1912).

119 Kleinbort 1923, p. 30.

120 Levin 1925, pp. 100–2.

121 Shapovalov 1934, p. 121; Tsvetkov-Prosveshchenskii 1933, p. 87.

122 Dok. Nak., p. 306.

123 Scott 1973, p. 20.

the workers' movement to its own resources. This 'flight of the intelligentsia', as the workers saw it, gave rise to a sense of betrayal.[124]

Thus, the new generation of worker activists matured in conditions of relative isolation from educated society. Unlike their 'fathers', they could not feel that they were part of a national movement for democracy. It was these conditions that fostered the irreconcilable antagonism of the 'conscious' metalworkers to census society. Only the printers, in part because of their special relationship with the intelligentsia by virtue of the nature of their work, held onto something of the old image of the worker-*intelligent* as a part of the 'vital forces' of society.

Whether it was fatigue that came with age and the burdens of family life, the experience of defeat of the Revolution of 1905–6 and the harsh political reaction that followed, or apprehension that the workers' movement was developing in isolation from the rest of society, the older workers, though not inactive, tended to take a back seat after 1907. Shlyapnikov, recalling an encounter with old comrades who had left the movement and were 'weighed down by life', wrote of the 'transfer of the red banner from the older to the more energetic generation of workers'.[125] In 1912, the Simens-Gal'ske Electrotechnical Factory opened a new branch in the Moscow District of Petrograd. 'It is interesting', wrote Bulkin

> that the so-called 'old' factory ... where old-timers, settled and highly skilled workers predominated, followed behind and was constantly being pushed forward by the new factory ... where non-local, less skilled and younger workers predominated. At the 'new factory', the workers were both more mobile and more active.[126]

The Siemens Factory was but a microcosm of the shift of the centre of worker activism after the Revolution of 1905–6 from the older factory districts, in particular Nevskii and Narvskii-Petergofskii, to the Vyborg District, with its relatively newer and smaller machine-construction factories.

The Petrograd working class was clearly not all sewn of the same cloth. Though the workers shared a common situation as factory wage labourers, they differed culturally in significant ways, largely as a consequence of the different natures of their work and their social backgrounds and conditions. And yet,

124 Kleinbort 1923, p. 127.
125 Shlyapnikov 1923, p. 188.
126 Bulkin 1924, p. 248.

they did achieve unity at the critical junctures of 1917 – in February and October. To explain how that came about one must examine the interaction between these cultural traits and the evolving socio-political conditions and events of 1917. This is the task of the following chapters.

CHAPTER 2

The Social Composition of the Industrial Working Class of Petrograd and its Districts

On 1 January 1917, there were 392,000 industrial workers[1] employed in Petrograd,[2] whose total population was 2,412,700. In addition, there were some 24,000 workers employed not far outside in factories that were economically and politically connected with the capital.[3] These 416,000 workers represented 12 percent of Russia's three and a half million industrial workers, in the country's total population of 134 million.[4]

Over 60 percent of Petrograd's workers were employed in metalworking (see Table 2. 1), a fact that left a decisive imprint on the course of the labour movement not only in Petrograd, but in Russia as a whole. In the Central Industrial Region (Moscow and five surrounding provinces), by contrast, metalworkers made up only 18.6 percent of the industrial workforce (192,000 of 1,030,000). There, the textiles industry dominated: 42.7 percent of all workers were employed in the cotton sector alone.[5]

The average concentration of the workforce (number of workers per factory) was also much higher than in the rest of Russia – as much as 40 percent above the average.[6] The concentration of large masses under one roof – in Petrograd 38 factories each employing over 2,000 workers accounted for over two-thirds of the total industrial workforce[7] – facilitated communication, political education and lent particular force to workers' collective actions.

---

1 The category 'industrial worker' includes non-managerial personnel employed in factories, mines and quarries (excluding transport, construction, etc.) employing over 10 workers or not less than 10 horsepower of mechanical energy.

2 *Materialy po statistike truda Severnoi oblasti*, vyp. I (1918), p. 18. Estimates of the total vary slightly. Another figure often cited is 384,000. Since the difference is not very significant, depending on the source, both figures will be used here.

3 *Materialy po statistike truda*, vyp. V, p. 43.

4 Gaponenko 1963b, p. 51.

5 Trukan 1967, pp. 16–17.

6 Stepanov 1965, p. 32.

7 Ibid.

TABLE 2.1 *Distribution and average concentration of Petrograd workers by industry, 1 January 1917*

Industry	Number of factories	Number of workers	Percent of all workers	Average number per factory
Metalworking	379	237,369	60.4	626.3
Textiles	100	44,115	11.2	441.2
Chemicals	58	40,087	10.2	691.2
Paper, printing	218	26,481	6.7	121.5
Food-processing	70	15,773	4.0	225.3
Woodworking	81	6,754	1.7	83.4
Leather, shoes	50	12,627	3.2	252.5
Mineral-processing	32	3,900	1.0	121.8
Others	23	5,722	1.5	248.8
All	1011	392,828	99.9	388.5

SOURCE: *MATERIALY PO STATISTIKE TRUDA*, VYP. I, P. 10.

TABLE 2.2 *Change in the number of workers employed in Petrograd by industry between 1 January 1914 and 1 January 1917*

Industry	Numbers of workers					
	1914		1917		Change 1914–17	
	In 1000s	%	In 1000	%	In 1000	%
Metalworking	100.6	41.5	235.9	61.3	+ 135.3	+ 134.5
Chemicals	21.6	8.9	42.9	11.2	+ 21.3	+ 98.6
Textiles	40.1	16.5	36.2	9.4	− 3.9	− 9.7
Food processing	22.7	9.4	15.5	4.0	− 6.8	− 30.5
Printing	23.1	9.5	19.4	5.0	− 3.7	− 16.0
Clothing	10.2	4.2	14.7	3.8	+ 4.5	+ 44.1
Woodworking	5.0	2.1	5.2	1.4	+ 0.2	+ 4.0
Paper	4.4	1.8	3.6	0.9	− 0.8	− 18.2
Other	14.9	6.1	8.6	2.2	–	–
All	242.6	100.0	382.0	99.2 [a]	+ 139.4	+ 57.5

[a] Less than 100 percent due to rounding.

SOURCE: RASHIN, *FORMIROVANIE RABOCHEGO KLASSA ROSSII*, P. 83.

Wages in Petrograd were also higher than elsewhere, though this was partially offset by the higher cost of living. The *Bulletin of the Society of Industrialists of the Central Industrial Region* observed in 1912 that economic motives alone could not explain the greater intensity of the strike movement in Petrograd province, since the wages of metalworkers and printers were much higher there than elsewhere in the empire.[8]

A third of Petrograd's workers were employed in state-owned factories, a fact that reflected the historic dependence of Russia's metalworking industry on state support (as well as on foreign capital). In all, 134,414 workers were employed in 31 state factories, and another 6,768 in two large state railroad workshops.[9]

Petrograd's industry underwent tremendous expansion during the war, in particular in the war-related branches – metalworking, chemicals, and, to a lesser degree, apparel (see Table 2.2). Most striking was the growth in metalworking. It alone accounted for 83 percent of the new jobs. The relative weight of metalworking in the total industrial workforce grew from 42 percent in 1915 to over 60 percent in 1917.

Women workers made up a disproportionate part of the new workers (see Table 2.3). Although in absolute terms the increase in number was about the same for both sexes, the relative increase in the female labour force exceeded that for men by over 50 percent, bringing the adult female component to 33.2 percent, from 25.7 percent on the eve of the war. In metalworking, woodworking and printing, sectors with the largest proportion of skilled workers, despite a significant increase in the number of women, men continued to predominate. But in textiles and food-processing, whose workforces were mainly unskilled and where women had long since been prominent, they now formed the majority. In both industries, the absolute number of male workers declined, due to the decrease in the overall number of workers but also to the widespread movement of men of draft age into defence-related industry to obtain deferments. In the leather and chemicals industries, the number of men and women was more or less evenly balanced, the latter experiencing the largest decline in the proportion of men, since shoe-making still employed a significant proportion of skilled workers and leather-processing involved heavy physical work that could not be easily done by women.

8 *Byuleten' obshchestva fabrikantov i zavodchikov Moskovskogo promyshlennogo raiona*, no. 16 (1912).

9 Stepanov 1965, pp. 31 and 42.

TABLE 2.3 *Changes in number of industrial workers in Petrograd, by age and sex, 1914–17*

Year	Number of workers					
	Adult men		Adult women		Under 16 years	
	1000	Percent of workforce	1000	Percent of workforce	1000	Percent of workforce
1914	158.4	65.2	61.6	25.4	22.9	9.4
1917	231.2	58.5	129.8	32.8	33.8	8.6
% increase	46.0		110.7		47.6	

SOURCE: BASED ON STEPANOV, *RABOCHIE PETROGRADA*, PP. 34 AND 36.

There were four principal sources of recruitment into the industrial workforce during the war:

1. peasants, mostly women, but also adolescents and men above draft age
2. the wives and children of workers, craftsmen, workers in small workshops and other non-industrial forms of working-class employment
3. evacuees from factories in Poland and the Baltic provinces
4. urban petty-bourgeois and bourgeois elements seeking to avoid the draft.

A. Anikst, who headed the Labour Section of the People's Commissariat of Labour, reported that there had been at least 170,000 'wartime workers' in the factories of Petrograd in 1917 – 150,000 in metalworking and 20,000 in chemicals.[10] A. Antonov, a Petrograd metalworker who was involved in industrial management during the civil war, gave similar figures.[11] Soviet historians, using archival materials, calculated that about 70 percent (116,000) of the male workers of Petrograd were of draft age in 1914. Of these, no more than 15,000–20,000 were drafted, the others receiving deferments for war-related work, health or other reasons. They thus concluded that 200,000–220,000 or 52–7 percent of the industrial workers of January 1917 had been employed in the city's factories

10 Anikst, *Organizatsiya raspredeleniya rabochei sily* (M., 1920), p. 51, cited in Shkaratan 1959, p. 25.

11 N. Antonov, *Dva goda diktatury proletariata v metallopromyshlennosti Petrograda* (1920), p. 15, cited in Shkaratan 1961.

when the war began,[12] approximately the same figure (about 55 percent) cited by Anikst and Antonov.

Among the newcomers, peasants were by far the most numerous element. *Novaya zhizn'*, citing the Commissariat of Labour, reported that about 150,000 workers were in one way or another tied to the village and were employed in factories mainly in order to obtain military deferments.[13] This is supported by evidence from individual factories. At the Sestroretsk Arms Factory, for example, of the 3,286 workers hired between January 1914 and July 1917, the majority were peasants. Among the new men, 1,875 came from the countryside.[14] A. Smirnov, a worker of the Skorokhod Shoe Factory, recalled that the workers hired in 1915–16 were predominantly women from the village.[15] The Petrograd Trubochnyi Factory saw such an influx of peasants that it was given the nickname of 'the peasant factory'.[16] Even at the Phoenix Machine-construction Factory, which had a much more skilled workforce, 20 percent of the male newcomers were peasants.[17]

Despite this wartime influx from the countryside, economic ties to the land among Petrograd's industrial workers were much weaker than elsewhere. According to the August 1918 industrial census, 19.5 percent of those employed in Petrograd at the time the data were collected had owned land before the October Revolution, and 7.9 percent had worked it through members of their family. In European Russia as a whole, the corresponding figures were 30.0 percent and 20.9 percent; in Moscow – 39.8 percent and 22.8 percent; and in Ivanovo – Voznesensk, the 'Russian Manchester' – 35.7 percent and 22.6 percent.[18]

Data for the other categories of newcomers are more limited. An estimate of the number of evacuees from factories to the western regions, based upon figures for a 10-day peak period, put them at 15,000–20,000.[19] The other sources of new workers were the urban poor, and, to a much lesser degree, people from the middle and upper strata of society seeking deferments. At Phoenix about 23 percent of the newcomers were former artisans.[20] Among the new workers

12 Leiberov and Shkaratan 1961, p. 52 and pp. 42, 58, *passim*.

13 *Novaya zhizn'* (27 Dec, 1917).

14 Tsybul'skii 1959, p. 143.

15 Smirnov 1935, p. 8.

16 Arbuzova 1923, p. 175.

17 Stepanov 1965, p. 42.

18 Rashin 1958, p. 575, Table 143.

19 Leiberov and Shkaratan 1961, p. 51.

20 Stepanov 1961, p. 43 and Ek. Pol. vol. 1, p. 43.

were also significant numbers of former janitors, doormen, cabbies, etc., as well as the wives of industrial workers. In January 1917, 33,800 youths under the age of 16 were working in the factories. As for the well-off, some reportedly coming to work in cabs, a commission of the Putilov Works reported in the autumn of 1917 that 7 percent of its approximately 36,000 workers were elements 'foreign to the working class'.[21] At other factories, these appear to have been purged by the workers soon after the February Revolution.

In sum, although very significant changes occurred in the social composition of Petrograd's industrial working class during the war, there remained a very considerable, urbanised core that had participated in one of the most intense periods of labour struggle in Russia's history, the upsurge of 1912–14, an upsurge that only the start of the war and intensified repression had temporarily cut short. As an industrial centre, Petrograd in 1917 retained the characteristics that had traditionally set it apart from other industrial areas of Russia and that had made it the vanguard of the workers' movement: predominance of the metalworking sector with a large machine-construction component and a high degree of concentration of a more urbanised, skilled and better-paid workforce.

The Social Composition of Petrograd's Districts

It is not always possible fully to account for the particular positions and attitudes that predominated in a given factory solely on the basis of the social composition of its workers or the conditions prevailing there. The social geography also played a role in shaping attitudes and influencing actions. This, as well as the fact that much data on working-class consciousness focuses on the district level, call for a brief survey of the social composition of Petrograd's districts.

This geographical factor asserted itself in various ways in 1917–18. For example, the location of most printing shops, not in the predominantly industrial, working-class outlying districts, but in the city centre that was populated by more affluent and educated elements, undoubtedly reinforced the ties that printers felt towards 'society' and also their perception of the relative strength of the propertied classes as compared to the workers. On the other hand, new workers immersed in the militant atmosphere of the Vyborg District, with its large cadre of skilled metalworkers, its homogeneous proletarian population, and revolutionary reputation, were more quickly assimilated into the prevailing radical spirit of the labour movement.

---

21 Leiberov and Shkaratan 1961.

The geographical proximity of a militant, predominantly skilled workforce to one that would normally be inclined towards moderation and passivity often had a powerful effect on the latter. The Treugol'nik Rubber Factory in the Narva District, for example, whose workforce was overwhelmingly female and unskilled, struck before 1917 only when 'taken out' by the more militant workers of the relatively nearby Putilov Works or some other metalworking factory. This was true even during the mass poisoning at Treugol'nik in 1913.[22] This widespread tactic of 'taking out' (*snyatie*) involved the arrival of a group of already striking workers to a still working factory, who with shouts, occasionally stone-throwing, breaking down of locked gates, and, if it came to it, physical threats, persuaded the frightened or reluctant workers to join the strike. Sometimes these scenes were prearranged to allow the workers to later claim they had been coerced into the strike. The workers of the quiescent Kersten Knitwear Mill, mostly women of recent peasant origin, were called *kolbasniki* (from *kolbasa* – sausage) by the other workers because of the boss's custom of treating them occasionally to sausage and tea while he kept them overtime. Because the few Bolsheviks who worked here were poor orators, reinforcements from the neighbouring Vulkan Machine-construction Factory would be called in when meetings were held.[23]

In districts dominated by one or two giant factories (5,000 workers or more), workers of the smaller plants tended to look to them for guidance. The authority of the Putilov Works, to cite the most striking example, went far beyond its own Petergof District and even the city. Its participation in any collective action, by virtue of its numbers alone, reinforced the confidence of the others. When the February Revolution began, a meeting of the workers of the main workshops of the N.W. Railroad first sent a delegation to the Putilov Works before deciding on their path of action.[24] Similarly, the workers of the James Beck Textile Mill in the Vyborg District traditionally sought the advice and support of workers of the nearby New Lessner Machine-construction Factory.[25]

A long distance from the centre of the city tended to isolate workers from political life, and it made it difficult for socialist agitators to reach the workers. This was a particularly important factor when the workforce was mostly unskilled work and unable to supply its own left-wing (internationalist) leaders. In these factories, the local 'intelligentsia', which consisted of the clerical

22 *Krasnyi Treugol'nik na putyakh Oktyabrya* (L., 1927), p. 9.

23 Suknovalov 1968, p. 7.

24 Frantishev 1962, p. 59.

25 *Vyborgskaya storona* (L., 1957), p. 181.

and technical employees, the foremen, and the like – people who were almost invariably defencists – had little trouble in influencing the workers, at least in the early months of the revolution. Such was the case, for example, in the Porokhovskii district, which was dominated by two very large, state chemical factories. The delegate from this district to the Bolsheviks' Petersburg Committee reported in October 1917: 'Until the Kornilov Days [end of August 1917], the Mensheviks and SRs predominated. Now the mood is ours ... Distance from the centre hurts our cause'.[26] The Left SR paper *Znamya truda* similarly wrote:

> The district, thanks to the absence of convenient communications, finds itself in especially unfavourable conditions. It is very hard to tear our speakers away [from the centre] ... Despite the lack of homogeneity (many peasants that have been hired because of the war), interest in the political life of the country continues to grow ... We especially feel the absence of intellectual forces [favourable to us]. But thanks to this, one notes an extremely gratifying fact: the appearance of agitators and propagandists from among the workers themselves. There is a collegium of orators – 17 workers. In the near future the district will be able to conduct party work by its own forces.[27]

This was written in August. By way of contrast, the Vyborg District from the very start of the revolution had been supplying not only its own workers, but other districts of the city and even nearby towns with worker agitators and organisers.

Finally, one should bear in mind that these districts were not only administrative units but also – and this was especially true for the working-class districts – social entities. One need only recall the pride of the Vyborg District workers in their revolutionary reputation. Buzinov's memoirs of the Nevskii District in the Revolution of 1905–6 are imbued with 'Nevskii patriotism', to such a degree that it appears as the epicentre of that revolution. Workers marched in demonstrations in 1917 with their comrades from work in columns organised by district. This identity was greatly reinforced by the role played in 1917 by the district soviets.

Map 2.1 and Table 2.4 show that industrial enterprises were generally located in the outlying districts, away from the city centre, where the well-off population lived and where government and major commercial and financial institutions were located.

---

26 *Pervyi legal'nyi peka*, p. 315.

27 *Znamya truda* (24 Aug 1917).

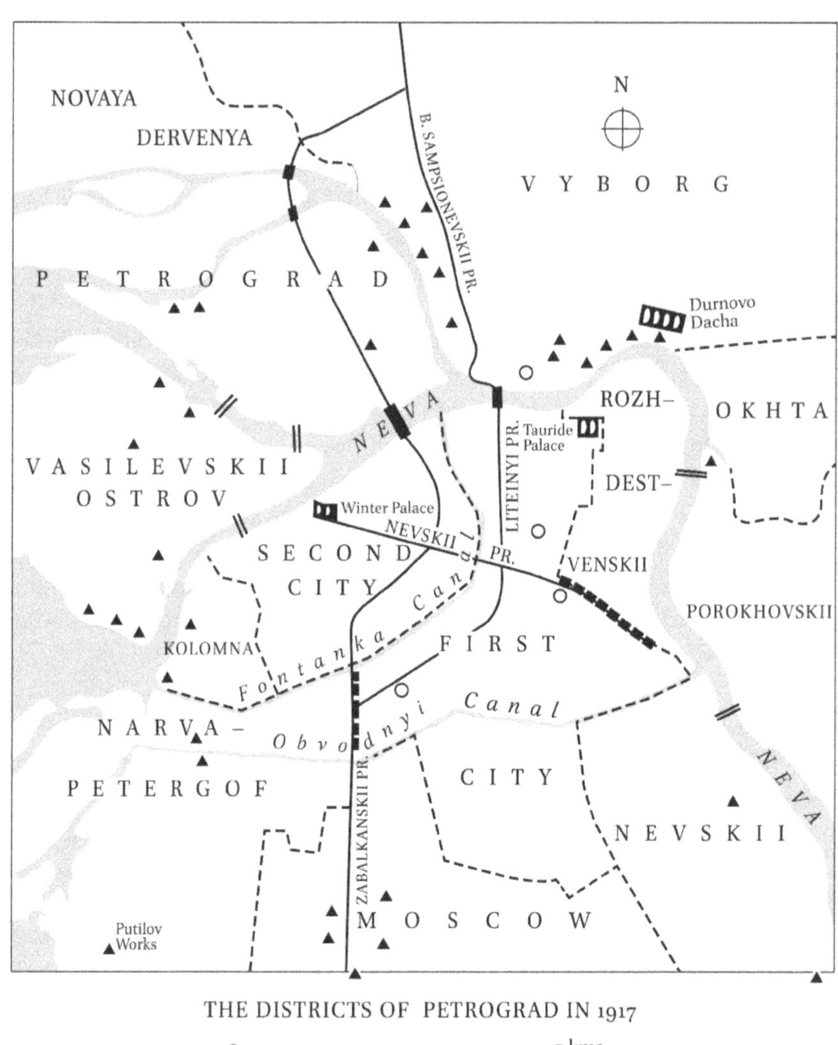

MAP 2.1 *The districts of Petrograd in 1917*

TABLE 2.4 *Distribution of industrial workers and metalworkers by district, 1 January 1917*

District	All industries		Metalworking		
	Number of workers	Percent of all workers	Number of workers	Percent of district's workers	Percent of all metal workers
Vyborg	68,932	17.9	57,978	84.1	24.5
Vasilevskii ostrov	51,876	13.5	37,530	72.3	15.9
Narva	38,784	10.1	6,549	16.9	2.8
Nevskii	38,208	9.9	26,641	69.7	11.3
Petrograd	37,840	9.8	24,444	64.6	10.3
Petergof	36,148	9.4	37,753	93.4	14.3
First City	32,769	8.5	13,299	40.6	5.6
Moscow	21,079	5.5	11,012	52.3	4.7
Polyustrovo-Porokhovskii	18,931	4.9	1,262	6.7	0.5
Kolomna	10,480	2.7	9,237	88.1	3.9
Rozhdestvenskii	10,233	2.7	2,063	20.2	0.9
Lesnoi	6,811	1.8	6,015	88.3	2.5
Admiralty, Kazan', Spasskii	5,660	1.5	1,865	32.9	0.8
Okhta	4,273	1.1	3,110	72.8	1.3
Novaya derevnya	3,083	0.8	1,631	52.9	0.7
Total	385,107	100.1	236,389	–	100.0

SOURCE: STEPANOV, *RABOCHIE PETROGRADA*, P. 30.

The Vyborg District[28]

The relationship between the level of worker activism and the size and concentration of the working-class population, especially metalworkers, of a given district has already been noted. And in both respects the Vyborg District, described by a Menshevik paper as 'our exclusively proletarian district',[29] surpassed all others (see Table 2.5). Here the workers easily provided their own

28 In common usage 'Vyborg District' usually also included Novaya derevnya and Polyustrovo. Some of the general sources for this section are: *Raionnye sovety Petrograda v 1917 g.*, 3 vols (M.-L., 1966–8); Golovanova 1974; and Stepanov 1965.

29 *Iskra* (3 Oct 1917).

TABLE 2.5 *Industrial workers employed in districts as percentage of total district population*[30]

District	Number of workers	District population	Workers employed as percentage of district population
Vyborg	68,932	150,465	45.8
Petergof [a]	36,148	91,000	39.7
Nevskii	38,208	190,000	20.1
Vasilevskii ostrov	51,876	268,000	19.4
Narva [a]	38,784	208,900	18.6
Kolomna	10,480	96,000	10.9
Moscow	21,079	194,000	10.8
Petrograd	37,840	360,000	10.5
First City	32,769	414,600	7.9
Okhta	4,273	60,789	7.0
Rozhdestvenskii	10,233	166,000	6.2
Admiralty, Kazan', Spasskii	5,660	311,590	1.8

[a] Separate figures for Narva and Petergof were not available and were calculated on the basis of the 1915 *uchet* in *Statisticheskii spravochnik po Petrogradu* (1921) Table 1.

SOURCE: BASED ON *VEDOMOSTI OBSHCHESTVENNOGO GRADONACHAL'STVA PETROGRADA*, 17 APRIL 1917, CITED IN GOLOVANOVA 1974, PP. 41–57; AND STEPANOV 1965, P. 30.

leaders and did not depend on central party organisations. A report from the district's Bolshevik committee on the first five months of legal activity following the February Revolution stated:

> The esteemed task of being the initiator of the revolution fell upon the Vyborg District. But this task also carried with it many obligations: for lack of an organised central apparatus, the Petrograd Committee, the district had to meet the very numerous requests for agitators and organisers not only in Petrograd but also in the provinces.

30 Although these figures indicate concentration by place of employment rather than habitation, given the poor state of municipal transport, one can assume that workers did often live close to where they worked.

As for the district's party committee, continued the report, its organisers and agitators were needed mainly by the military units. On the other hand,

> many factories manage well on their own, and often days go by without requests ... That indicates that new capable activists have grown who are able to manage without outside support. And life required much of them. We needed representatives to the district and central Soviets, as well as to the district and central Dumas. And the district was able to supply them.[31]

In the Vyborg District 51 of 56, or 89 percent, of the members of the Bolshevik district committee were workers. The proportion for the city as a whole was 74.1 percent.[32]

The proletarian character of the district and the large size of its working-class population favoured the aspiration to 'class independence', as did its location, separated by the Neva River from the well-off districts, but nevertheless close to them.

This district was the main Bolshevik stronghold from the very outset of the February Revolution. The moderate socialists, who favoured an alliance with the liberal elements of census society, found much less support here than anywhere else. Even social-democratic internationalist groups, whose positions were close to those of the Bolsheviks but who called for unity of all social-democratic tendencies, aroused little interest. L. Leont'ev, a member of one such internationalist group, the 'mezhraionka', which eventually merged into the Bolshevik party in the summer of 1917, recalled that although his group had considerable appeal for Petrograd's workers, Mensheviks and Bolsheviks, 'on the Vyborg side it developed weakly'.[33]

In October 1917, too, the district's workers demonstrated little concern over the fact that the Congress of Soviets had, initially at least, produced an exclusively Bolshevik government, whereas workers in the other districts overwhelmingly supported the call for an all-socialist coalition government, a demand that expressed the workers' fear of political isolation, especially in regards to the intelligentsia (issues to be discussed in detail in later chapters). But in the Vyborg District, the prospect of isolation was clearly less frightening.

---

31 *Revolyutsionnoe dvizhenie v Rossi v avguste 1917 g.* (M., 1967), pp. 94–6. (Dok. Aug.).

32 Golovanova 1974, appendix, Table 7.

33 Leont'ev 1924, p. 131.

Certain other characteristics also contributed to the level of organisation and activism. Almost all the factories were relatively large (with well over 500 workers each) and were situated along the banks of the Neva or Bol'shaya Nevka Rivers or along the parallel Bol'shoi Sampsionievskii Prospekt, the main thoroughfare. This made for easy communication between the factories. Secondly, as the map shows, although the district was separated from the centre by the river, it was close enough – as long as the bridges were not lifted or the ice melted – for news to reach factories quickly. In most other districts, the principle factories were on the periphery and so much farther from the centre.

Petergof and Narva Districts

The Petergof District was next only to Vyborg in concentration of workers in large enterprises. It consisted of two sub-districts. One was dominated by the Putilov, Til'mans and Langezipen factories. The other was the site mainly of small commercial enterprises and was populated by small shopkeepers and white-collar employees. The Putilov Works dominated both districts. (In popular usage Narva District included Petergof.)

Except for a relatively brief period in June and early July 1917, the workers here were not at the forefront of the movement, a fact that surprised many observers, since the Putilov workers had been in the van during the 1912–14 labour upsurge. But the factory had experienced a mass influx of peasants and non-working-class urban elements during the war to meet the expansion of ordnance production. The Bolsheviks won firm control of the district soviet only after the July Days in 1917, although on purely economic matters they were often able to gather considerable support from the start.[34]

The Narva District to the northeast of Petergof had a much smaller working-class population and was much less active. It had the smallest proportion of metalworkers of any industrial or semi-industrial district of the city, the only large metalworking enterprises being the workshops of the Baltic and N.W. Railroads. The two largest factories here were the Treugol'nik Rubber Factory with 15,000 workers, overwhelmingly women, and the Government Paper Printing Plant with about 8,000 workers, one of the most conservative factories of the city. The rest of the workers were employed in factories with predominantly unskilled work forces.

34 *Raionnye sovety Petrograda v 1917 godu*, vol. II (L., 1967), p. 91 (henceforth cited as Raisovety).

Vasilevskii ostrov

This island in the estuary of the Neva River was the second largest industrial district, though its population was very mixed. Its industrial areas were situated around the port to the south and on Golodai Island in the north, far away from the 'Point', which was part of the city's centre, just across the bridge from the Winter Palace, the Admiralty, Army Headquarters and other key government buildings. Nearby was the Stock Exchange. On the eastern part of the island, along Bol'shoi and Srednyi Prospekts and the intersecting 'lines', lived members of the nobility, merchants and high state officials. The district was also the centre of higher education, with the Russian Academy of Sciences, St. Petersburg University, the Mining Institute, the Academy of Arts, the Bestuzhev Women's Higher Courses, as well as several secondary schools.[35]

There were 16 large factories, with the Petrograd Trubochnyi Factory itself employing a third of the entire workforce. Along with the other large metalworking factory, the Baltic Shipbuilding Factory (8,000 workers), it employed large masses of unskilled workers in the production of ordnance. In addition there were several smaller electrotechnical enterprises, five textile mills, several leather factories, and a few tobacco-processing plants. Next to the Vyborg District, Vasilevskii ostrov became one of the Bolsheviks' main strongholds in 1917. They formed a bloc with the other international fractions and took control of the district soviet as early as mid-May.[36]

A significant factor in the district's politics was the large number of educational institutions. The more radical students supplied many of the agitators and organisers for the district's workers, who were not always able to provide them on their own. 30.6 percent of the members of the Bolshevik district committee in the period from February to July 1917 were, in fact, *intelligenty* – the highest proportion of any industrial district. 57.6 percent were workers – the lowest proportion (see Table 2.6).

Another consequence of the presence of radical intellectuals was the relatively strong degree of support for the various groups of Internationalists. This was one of the few districts where the Menshevik-Internationalists enjoyed significant influence among workers. (In September, the district's Menshevik-Internationalist organisation merged into the Bolshevik party, practically en masse.) In contrast to the Vyborg District, the question of the relations between the workers and the intelligentsia was a prominent issue here.

---

35 *V ogne revolyutsionnykh boev*, vol. II, p. 102.

36 *Raisovety*, vol. I, p. 123.

TABLE 2.6 *Social background of identified Bolshevik district committee members March–June 1917*

District	Percent workers	Percent *intellegenty*	Percent others	Total identified members
Vyborg	89.5	8.8	1.7	57
Narvskii-Petergofskii	85.7	10.7	3.6	28
Nevskii	83.4	16.6	0	12
Petrograd	82.1	10.7	7.2	28
Second City	76.7	13.3	10.0	30
Porokhovskii, Liteinyi, Okhta and Railroad	64.3	28.6	7.1	14
Moscow	63.6	18.2	18.2	11
Vasilevskii ostrov	57.6	30.6	11.8	26
First City	50.0	50.0	0	16
Rozhdestvenskii	35.7	28.6	35.7	14
All districts	74.1	18.2	7.7	236

SOURCE: GOLOVANOVA 1974, APPENDIX, TABLE 7, P. 13

Petrograd District

This district (in popular usage, it sometimes included Novaya derevnya) consisted of seven islands sandwiched between the Vyborg District, the city centre and Vasilevskii ostrov. It, too, was socially heterogeneous, with only a relatively small worker population. The population of southwest and central sections was quite well-off, while the workers, as usual, lived in the outlying areas toward the west and northeast shores. Several large factories (averaging 1,500 workers)[37] were situated here. The machine-construction factories included Langezipen, Vulkan, Shchetinin and Lebedev, as well as a tram depot. But these skilled factories were not predominant. There were in addition three textile mills – Kersten, James Beck and Leont'iev Brothers, the state-owned Factory for Military-Medical Preparations (about 3,000 workers, mostly women),[38] and some of the city's largest printing plants, including the State Printing Plant, Pechatnyi Dvor and the Otto Kirkhner Printing House and Bindery.

37 Stepanov 1965, p. 33.

38 *Bol'sheviki Petrograda v Oktyabr'skoi revolyutsii* (L., 1957), p. 33.

The workers here were generally less radical than in the three aforementioned districts. Bolsheviks won control of the district soviet only at the start of August, while the Mensheviks and SRs maintained a strong oppositional presence right up to the October Revolution, when they were finally dislodged. The political mood in the district was uneven, a reflection of the presence of very radical metalworking factories along with a large number of conservative printing establishments.

Moskovskaya zastava

The majority of this district's 11 large factories were located at its southern end, where Zabalkanskii Prospekt became the Moscow Highway. Its industrial workforce was evenly split between metalworking and other sectors. Leatherworking was strongly represented by the Skorokhod (6,500 workers – Russia's largest shoe factory) and the Nevskii Shoe Factory (1,600). Together they accounted for almost a third of the district's workers.[39] Among the electrotechnical plants were Dinamo (2,300 workers of which 1,000 were women)[40] and Siemens-Shukkert. There were also two wagon-building plants – Rechkin and Artur-Koppel – a tram depot and the city-owned 1886 Electric Lighting Society. Even farther to the south were a dozen or so small factories and hundreds of workshops with few hired workers.[41]

Workers made up only a relatively small part of the district, which had a large well-off population closer to the city centre, and an even larger population of white-collar employees and petty bourgeois (shopkeepers, artisans, etc.). This was one of Petrograd's four districts, along with Nevskii, Okhta and Porokhovskii, where the SRs enjoyed particularly strong support. Even as late into the revolution as September 1917, the SRs held eight of the district soviet's 20 seats. The outlying, semi-rural location of many of the factories and workshops helps to account for this.

39 *Moskovskaya zastava v 1917 godu* (L., 1957), p. 128.

40 Stepanov 1965, p. 35.

41 *Vogne revolyutsionnykh* boev, vol. II, p. 217.

Nevskii-Obukhovskii District

Located in the southeast extremity of the capital at a considerable distance from the centre – to reach it from the centre, one took the train that ran between Tsarskoe Selo and Nikolaevskii Station – the Nevskii District consisted of two sub-districts, each dominated by a very large mixed metalworking plant – the Nevskii Shipbuilding and Machine-construction Factory and the Obukhovskii Steel Mill, each with over 10,000 workers. The two other large metalworking enterprises were the Aleksandrovskii Locomotive Factory and the repair shops of the Nikolaevskii Railroad. The latter three were state-owned. In addition, there were four large textile mills, two paper mills, a soap factory, a wax factory, the State Porcelain Factory, and a number of smaller enterprises that also employed mainly semi-skilled or unskilled workers.

The Nevskii District was the most moderate of all the industrial and semi-industrial districts, the main bastion of the SR defencists. Some of the reasons for this moderation have already been mentioned. Three of its four largest factories were state-owned, and the two largest were located in villages well outside the city. For example, the address of the Nevskii Factory was 'selo Smolenskoe' (Smolenskoe village). Many of its workers were recruited from the neighbouring villages of Rogatkovo, Lesnozavodskaya and Murzinskaya.[42] Those of the workers of the Obukhovskii Factory who owned plots of land and kept cattle were nicknamed 'the cowherds of Rybtskoe', Rybatskoe being the village in which it was located.[43] Before and during the Revolution of 1905, the district had been a centre of worker militancy, but it had been relatively quiescent during the new labour upsurge of 1912–14. By that time the workers' movement was processing in isolation from, and in opposition to, census society. But these workers became active again in the spring of 1918, when they supported the Menshevik-SR opposition to Soviet power, calling for the formation of an 'all-national' (in fact 'all-class') government to be created by the Constituent Assembly.

Kolomna District

Officially a sub-district of the Second City District, Kolomna had its own district soviet in 1917 and was treated as a separate entity by the left parties. It

42 *V boyakh za oktyabr'* (L., 1932), p. 27.

43 Rozanov 1938, p. 354.

was the only industrial area in the Second City District, with three large shipbuilding factories: Franko-Russkii (6,500 workers), Admiralty, and New Admiralty (together with 2,500 workers). Franko-Russkii, a privately-owned factory, was the more radical of the three and dominated the district politically. The Bolsheviks were the predominant party in the soviet from the middle of May, when it called for the transfer of power to the soviets.

Second City District

This central district included the Admiralty, Kazan and Spasskii (and, officially, Kolomna) sub-districts. Commercial enterprises, army barracks and state institutions dominated, with no large-scale industry. Here were located many of the central government's institutions, bank headquarters, theatres, museums, libraries and palaces. This was socially hostile territory through which workers had to pass to reach Nevskii Prospekt, their protests.

First City District

The Nikolaevskii Railroad Station (connecting the capital to Moscow and the rest of Russia) was located in the centre of this district, from which Nevskii Prospekt began. Occupying about a quarter of the city's total land area (before the incorporation of the outlying districts in 1917), it had three sub-sections: Liteinyi, with luxurious homes of the nobility and the big bourgeoisie; the Moscow section, with its large number of printing establishments; and the Aleksandr-Nevskii section, where workers of the Nikolaevskii Railway Workshops and the nearby Novaya Bumagopryadil'nya, Kozhevnikovskaya and Aleksandr-Nevskaya textiles mills and a few other factories lived. The Liteinyi District had two large, state-owned ordnance factories – Orudiinyi and a branch of Patronnyi (together with 6,000 workers), but the main sources of employment here were the many commercial establishments. The principal inhabitants were white-collar employees, professionals and property-owners.

Rozhdestvenskii District

This was the location of the Tauride Palace and Smol'nyi Institute. There were three large industrial enterprises here: the Nevskaya Bumagopryadil'naya and Nevskaya Nitochnaya textile mills (together with about 4,000 workers) and a tram depot, as well as several small electrical and metalworking factories, the largest being Ouf, Shpigel' and Opticheskii. The district also had many military units stationed there. A local Bolshevik characterised it as mainly 'petty bourgeois and semi-intelligentny', with few workers.[44] Only about one-third of the Bolshevik district committee members here were workers, the lowest proportion of any district.[45] Menshevik-defencists had strong support in the district soviet well past the July Days, after which the internationalist fraction gradually gained strength.

Okhta and Porokhovskii Districts

These isolated, semi-rural districts were situated across the river on the right bank of the Neva. Along with the Nevskii District, they were the main bastions of the SRs. Ohta had only small, semi-artisanal workshops and no large-scale industry.[46] The Porokhovskii District, on the other hand, was dominated by two very large, state-owned chemical factories, whose 18,000 workers maintained strong ties to the peasantry.

This completes the outline of the major social and economic influences on working-class consciousness in Petrograd. The resulting picture is admittedly not a simple one but, as the following pages will show, it provides a framework that allows for a coherent analysis of the evolution of working-class attitudes and action in 1917–18.

---

44 Peka, p. 194.

45 Golovanova 1974, appendix, Table 1.

46 *Derevoobdelochnik*, no. 20 (Mar 1908).

CHAPTER 3

The Honeymoon Period – From the February to the April Days

For workers, the dominant political question of this period was their relationship to the propertied classes. The February Revolution left them ambivalent on this score. Their historical experience had bequeathed them a deep and pervasive distrust of the bourgeoisie, which, especially after the defeat of the Revolution of 1905–6, had shown itself deeply hostile to their aspirations. But that mistrust was balanced now by two new factors: census society's belated rally to the revolution, once it had become a fait accompli, and the workers' reluctance to assume responsibility for running the state and the economy.

This ambivalence found political expression in the system of dual power. State power formally resided in the provisional government, which consisted exclusively of representatives of the propertied classes. But it was to govern according to the platform agreed upon with the Soviet, or so the workers believed. At the same time, the Soviet reserved for itself the right to 'control' (monitor) this government and to intervene, if necessary. Meanwhile, as far as the workers were concerned, the Soviet was the sole source of legitimate authority in Russia, the Provisional Government being merely the executor of its will.

In the economic sphere, the workers were at once more and less radical. While they refused to yield on their social expectations for the revolution, regardless of the threat they might pose to the political alliance with census society, they nevertheless showed no intention of challenging the economic dominance of the bourgeoisie. At the same time, already in the early weeks of the revolution, they began to voice doubts regarding the good will of the factory owners and their managers, and there were the first signs that workers would not stop before direct intervention in the sphere of management if they felt that the interests of production and of the revolution required it.

In this way, a hesitant alliance was established between the working class and census society, each side eyeing the other with unconcealed suspicion.

The Labour Movement during the War

The February Revolution in Petrograd occurred against the background of growing economic dislocation, military reverses and deepening alienation of all classes of society from the Tsarist regime.

At the root of the economic problems lay the war and the backwardness of the Russian economy, which was unable to meet the needs of the front and the rear in a prolonged war. Moreover, the state proved incapable of organising even the limited economic base that was at its disposal. Russian military reverses were in large part a result of these factors. While census society was turning away from the regime (without, however, daring to break with it) for its inability successfully to prosecute the war and to keep the increasingly restive workers in check, the workers' anti-government mood was intensified by deterioration of their economic conditions as a consequence of a war that most of them considered imperialist, and so criminal, as well as by the intensely repressive nature of the regime.

During the winter of 1916–17 workers experienced the effects of the war and the economic crisis in the form of production stoppages due to shortages of fuel and raw materials, declining living standards resulting from galloping inflation and the repression of strike action, and scarcity of consumer goods, with long queues forming before bakeries and food shops. Work conditions had deteriorated, with no limits on overtime and the abrogation of laws protecting female and child labour. Management, now virtually freed of legal constraints and zealously supported by the state's repressive apparatus, replied to workers' demands with the very real threat of the front, jail or exile. The labour press, trade unions and most other forms of worker organisation had been shut down soon after the start of the war. The Bolshevik deputies in the State Duma were in Siberian exile for their anti-war agitation. So efficient was state repression that the average career of any underground worker activist lasted only three months before he or she was arrested.[1]

To many observers, the political scene in Petrograd on the eve of the world war had already exhibited all the signs of a revolutionary situation, bringing back memories of 1905.[2] The strike of 6–12 July 1914, culmination of a powerful new labour upsurge that had begun in 1911–12, had started as a protest against a police attack against Putilov workers and soon escalated into a general political strike, with the construction of barricades and pitched street battles between the strikers and the 'forces of order'.

---

1 Shlyapnikov 1923, vol. II, p. 104.

2 See, for example, ibid., vol. I, pp. 13–19.

The outbreak of war, mobilisation and intensified repression put an abrupt end to this movement. The anniversary of Bloody Sunday, 9 January, and May Day 1915, unlike previous years, were not marked by strikes or street demonstrations. But the spring and summer of 1915 already witnessed the resurgence of strike activity, though at first predominantly economic in its demands, except for the strike of 30,000 workers protesting against the bloody repression of a textile strike in Ivanovo-Voznesensk.

But if less than a third of the 180,864 worker-days lost were due to political strikes in the first year of the war, in the second year already half of the 596,039 worker-days lost were in political work stoppages.[3] On 9 January 1916, 100,000 workers downed tools in Petrograd to mark the anniversary of Bloody Sunday. In February, the Putilov workers began an economic strike, to which they soon added the political demands of the social-democracy's minimum programme. Before long, over 100,000 workers were on strike in solidarity with them.[4]

The strike movement continued to gather momentum in the autumn of 1916, as its political character became increasingly pronounced. It culminated in a protest strike involving 120,000 workers against the court martial of Baltic sailors, accused of membership in an underground Bolshevik organisation. Locked out, the workers responded by declaring a new strike. The largest wartime strike before the February Revolution occurred on the anniversary of Bloody Sunday, 9 January 1917. Estimates range from 200,000 to 300,000 participants. But no one foresaw that the revolution was a mere six weeks away. Nevertheless, the potential of so powerful a mobilisation was not lost upon the workers' leaders. The Executive Committee of the Bolsheviks' Petersburg Committee (PC) reported: 'The success of the demonstration of January 9 raised very much the spirits of the masses. In the factories, the mood is very buoyant and politically aware; this opens up broad revolutionary possibilities'.[5] In the six months between September 1916 and the start of the revolution, a little over one million worker-days were lost in collective actions in Petrograd, three-quarters of these in political strikes.

---

3 Leiberov 1964, p. 65.

4 Burdzhalov 1967, pp. 32–3.

5 *Proletarskaya revolyutsiya*, no. 11 (13) (1923), pp. 265–6.

The February Revolution – The Birth of Dual Power[6]

The general strike that resulted in the overthrow of Tsarism grew out of two separate collective actions of workers. On 17 February, one of the shops of the Putilov Factory struck for higher wages and for the reinstatement of several dismissed activists. Other shops soon joined, and when the administration locked the workers out on 22 February, the entire workforce of 36,000 went on strike. A strike committee was formed, and delegations were dispatched to other factories to drum up support. One of the delegates met with Kerenskii, then a Trudovik (right-wing populist) deputy of the State Duma, and prophetically mused that this could be the beginning of a major political offensive.[7] No one, however, guessed how near the dénouement really was.

International Women's Day fell on 23 February.[8] The mood among women workers was very angry against the background of high prices, food queues, and the recent disappearance of bread from a number of bakeries. The day began with meetings in the factories that featured anti-war speeches, but no other actions were planned. Among the Bolsheviks, the most militant political group, the strategy was to accumulate forces with a view to a decisive general strike on May Day.[9] Nevertheless, in the Vyborg District women workers struck in several textile mills. Gathering outside nearby metalworking factories, they easily persuaded the men to join them. I. Gordienko, a worker at the Nobel Machine-construction Factory, recalled:

> On the morning of February 23, one could hear women's voices in the lane which the windows of our shop overlooked: 'Down with the war! Down with high prices! Down with hunger! Bread for the workers!' In a flash, several comrades and myself were at the windows ... The gates of No. 1 Bol'shaya Sampsionievskaya Manufaktura were wide open. Masses of women workers filled the lane, and their mood was militant. Those who caught sight of us began to wave their arms, shouting: 'Come out! Quit work!' Snowballs flew through the window. We decided to join the

6 There are a number of useful general accounts of the February revolution from different political points of view: Burdzhalov 1967; Sukhanov 1919; Shlyapnikov 1925; Trotsky 1965, vol. 1, Chapters 1–15; Chamberlin 1935, vol. 1, Chapters 1–4; Mstislavskii 1932. Specific events will be mentioned here only insofar as they touch directly on the main issue: working-class attitudes.

7 Cited in Burdzhalov 1965, p. 117.

8 The Russian (Julian) calendar was 13 days behind the Gregorian, used in the West.

9 Ibid., p. 120.

> demonstration ... A brief meeting took place outside the main office near the gates, and we poured out into the street ... The comrades in front were seized by the arm amidst shouts of 'Hurray!', and we set off with them down Bol'shoi Sampsionievskii Prospekt.[10]

That day the demonstrators concentrated efforts on 'taking out' other factories. Singing revolutionary songs, a crowd of strikers would stop at the gates of a factory and call on those inside to join them. If no response followed, some of the strikers would steal inside to agitate, and that failing, to threaten. At the Metallicheskii Factory, the administration had taken the precaution of locking the gates. But the crowd broke them down. Along their way to the city centre, the workers disabled trams and attacked isolated policemen. Several bakeries and food shops were ransacked. The geographical goal from the outset was Nevskii Prospekt, Petrograd's main thoroughfare. But the police were still able to keep most demonstrators from crossing the river. According to the Okhrana (Tsarist political police), 87,534 workers from 50 factories struck on that day.[11] Although anti-war and anti-government slogans were heard from the start, the most popular by far on that day was 'bread!'

On the morning of 24 February, workers appeared at their workplaces as usual but, after brief meetings, again took to the streets. Events followed the pattern of the previous day, and clashes with the police became increasingly frequent. Bread was still the most widespread slogan, but anti-war and anti-government cries were gaining in prominence. The strikers now numbered about 200,000[12] and they came from all districts of the city. Now students began to appear in significant numbers. The demonstrators were also more successful in getting across to the city's centre. Among certain regular army and Cossack units, there were signs of favourable disposition towards the demonstrators. The next day the City Governor's office reported 240,000 striking workers (another estimate is 305,000).[13] For all practical purposes the strike had become general. Besides the industrial workers, artisans, white-collar employees, members of the intelligentsia joined in larger numbers. This created an atmosphere of general sympathy to the movement that further raised workers' spirits. The police were on the run, moving on the street only in groups. Anti-war and anti-government slogans predominated alongside calls for a demo-

10 Gordienko 1957, pp. 56–7.

11 'Fevral'skaya revolyutsiya i Okhrannoe otdelenie', *Byloe*, nos. 7–8 (1918), p. 162. Another estimate, based on more complete data, puts the figure at 128,000. Leiberov 1964, p. 65.

12 Burdzhalov 1967, p. 143; Leiberov 1964.

13 Leiberov 1964, p. 65.

cratic republic and the other social-democratic programmatic demands: the eight-hour workday, land reform, and a Constituent Assembly. Nevskii Prospekt belonged to the demonstrators.

It was at this point that people began to sense that the movement would end in victory, that this was a revolution. A police informer reported on that day:

> Since the military units did not hinder the crowd and in individual cases even took measures to paralyse the initiative of the police, the masses have acquired a sense of certainty that they will go unpunished, and now, after two days of unhindered marching about the streets, when revolutionary circles have put forward the slogans 'down with the war' and 'down with the government', the people have become convinced that the revolution has begun, that success is with the masses, that the government is powerless to suppress the movement, since the military units are not on its side, that victory is close since the military units will soon openly cross over to the revolutionary forces, that the movement that has begun will not die down and will grow continuously until the final victory and the overthrow of the state.[14]

A police official reported the words of a cabbie on that day: 'Tomorrow the cabbies will not drive members of the public as usual, only the leaders of the disorders'.[15] Petrograd's cabbies were not a radical group.

On Sunday 26 February, the number of strikers was about the same as the previous day. The police began to retaliate by firing into the crowds, especially on Nevskii Prospekt. But the crowds scattered only to reassemble as soon as the shooting ceased. The sacking and firing of police stations began. There were isolated cases of mutiny in the garrison.

27 February marked the victory of the revolution. All of Petrograd's industrial working class was out in the streets. From the morning, crowds approached the barracks to persuade the soldiers to join the movement. By afternoon, the mutiny was a mass phenomenon. The rest of the day was spent burning down police stations and liberating political prisoners.

Meanwhile, at the Tauride Palace, seat of the State Duma, the two social-democratic deputies still at liberty, N.S. Chkheidze and M.I. Skobelev, both Mensheviks, along with the recently freed Menshevik-defencist leaders of the 'Workers' Groups' of the Military-Industrial Committee and several independ-

14 *Byloe*, nos 7–8 (1918), p. 174.

15 Ibid., p. 169.

ent social-democratic intellectuals (including N. Sukhanov and N. Sokolov), seized the initiative in organising a Soviet of Workers' Deputies to take charge of the movement. Declaring themselves the Soviet's Provisional Executive Committee, they set up military and food commissions and invited the factories to send delegates to a meeting of the Soviet that evening.

In another section of the palace, the State Duma, recently dissolved by the Tsar, met in 'private session' – the census deputies were still reluctant openly to defy the will of the autocrat – and formed a Provisional Committee of Members of the State Duma for the Restoration of Order and for Contacts with Persons and Institutions.

On the night of 28 February–1 March, these two groups, one speaking for 'revolutionary democracy' and the other for census Russia, reached an agreement on the formation of a government consisting exclusively of census deputies of the Duma. The Duma Committee, for its part, agreed to the Soviet's programme, which included, among other things, full political freedoms, political amnesty, immediate measures for the convocation of a Constituent Assembly. But nothing was decided in regards to the war or the eight-hour day, the long-standing demand of the workers' movement. On 2 March, the Soviet plenum (both workers' and soldiers' sections) overwhelmingly approved this arrangement, but premised its support for the Provisional Government on the latter's conscientious adherence to the Soviet's programme. The plenum also decided to establish an 'observation committee' to monitor (*kontrolirovat'*)[16] the activities of the government. Thus was born the system of dual power.

Attitudes Regarding State Power and the Relationship to Census Society

The idea of a soviet of workers' deputies, a legacy of the Revolution of 1905–6, was close to workers' hearts, and the question of its election was raised in some factories as early as 25 February, well before the formation of the Provisional Executive Committee of the Soviet.[17] At the same time, there can be little doubt that the overwhelming majority of the workers were not prepared for the Soviet itself to take power and that the dual power arrangement corresponded to their understanding of the situation and the tasks at hand.

16 This word in Russian means 'to monitor', but, depending on the context, it can shade over to imply actively control.

17 *Byloe*, nos 7–8 (1918), p. 174.

At the 2 March Soviet plenary meeting, the formula of conditional support, 'inasmuch as' (*postol'ku-poskol'ku*), was approved by a vote of 400 to 19. But the establishment of an 'observation committee', something that had not figured among the Executive Committee's recommendations, indicated a greater level of distrust toward the census government among the rank-and-file delegates than among the Soviet's leaders.

Some Bolsheviks and the Menshevik-Internationalist V.A. Bazarov spoke out against the executive's proposal. The meeting's protocols note that 'in the course of the discussion, a current emerged that rejected any possibility of contact with the Duma Committee and demanded the creation of a Provisional Revolutionary Government by the Soviet of Workers' and Soldiers' Deputies'.[18] But as Shlyapnikov, a member of the Russian Bureau of the Bolshevik Central Committee and of the Soviet's Executive Committee, recognised, even among the Bolshevik delegates many voted with the majority.[19] A majority of the Bolsheviks' Petersburg Committee also rejected the slogan of a Provisional Revolutionary Government that would be created by the Soviet. Instead they adopted a somewhat more guarded formula of conditional support for the government than that of the Soviet: 'The Petersburg Committee of the RSDWP(b) ... will not oppose the Provisional Government as long as ...'[20]

Attitudes in the factories regarding the Soviet's position were also overwhelmingly favourable. Many of the resolutions of factory meetings closely echoed the Soviet's wording. A meeting on 8 March of the some 8,000 workers of the Izhorskii Factory, a mixed-production metalworking plant in Kolpino, not far from Petrograd, resolved: 'All measures of the Provisional Government that destroy the remnants of the autocracy and strengthen the freedom of the people must be fully supported on the part of democracy. All measures that lead to conciliation with the old regime and that are directed against the people must meet with the most decisive protest and counteraction'. The meeting went on to affirm the necessity of defending by all means the social-democratic minimum programme, the so-called 'three whales': democratic republic, eight-hour workday and confiscation of landlord, Church and monastery lands and their transfer to the peasantry. It also called upon the Soviet to appeal to the working classes of the world to rise up against their governments and to conclude a democratic peace without annexations or reparations.[21] Despite the

18 *Izvestiya Petrogradskogo soveta rabochikh i soldatskikh deputatov* (3 March 1917).

19 Shlyapnikov 1923, vol. I, p. 240.

20 Peka, pp. x–xi.

21 *Revolyutsionnoe dvizhenie v Rossii posle sverzheniya samoderzhaviya* (henceforth: Dok.

expression of support for the Provisional Government, mention of the possibility that it might turn against the people betrays the workers' basic distrust of census society. The resolution was at once an expression of support and a threat.

Yet even this guarded formulation appears relatively positive when compared to many others. A meeting of leatherworkers in early March expressed support for the Soviet's position on political power but omitted any direct expression of support for the government. It added: 'Even now, when all the classes are swept up in the powerful revolution created by the workers and soldiers, we must not completely trust the bourgeoisie. We must establish unremitting control over it on the part of the Soviet of Workers' and Soldiers' Deputies'.[22] Even more explicit was the resolution of the general assembly of the Petrograd Cable Factory on 3 March. After having heard a report from the factory's delegate to the Soviet, it resolved (by a vote of some 1,000 to 3):

> We consider that the most essential question of the current moment is the establishment of strict control over the ministers who were appointed by the State Duma and who do not enjoy popular confidence. This control must be constituted by representatives of the Soviet of W. and S.D.[23]

Similarly, on 3 March a meeting of about 2,000 woodworkers at the Chinzelli Circus adopted a resolution that declared: 'We have confidence in the Soviet of Workers' and Soldiers' Deputies'. And it went on to call the Soviet to exert vigilant control over every step of the Provisional Government and to inform the workers and soldiers and the whole population of any retreat on the part of the Provisional government from its promises and, in that case, to call the people out to battle.[24]

Workers' resolutions in March 1917 point to a conclusion that was obvious to the political leaders of census society: the Provisional Government had little legitimacy in workers' eyes. And the support that they did give it was a function of the Soviet's legitimacy and the control that it was to exert over the government. Well aware of this, the Duma Committee had, in fact, tried

---

Feb) (M., 1957) p. 475. For similar resolutions, see *Pravda* (17 Mar 1917) (from Nobel', Vakuum and others); *Pravda* (23 Mar.) (Sestroretsk Arms Factory); *Izvestiya* (4 Mar.) (Petrograd Union of Woodworkers); (8 Mar.) (a meeting of printers).

22 *Pravda* (19 Mar. 1917).

23 Ibid. For similar resolutions, see Dok. Feb., p. 478 (Sestroretsk Arms Factory); *Pravda*, no. 3 (1917) (tavern and hotel workers), Shlyapnikov 1923, vol. II, p. 292.

24 Izvestiya (4 Mar 1917).

to persuade the more moderate leaders of the Soviet's Executive Committee – Skobelev, Chkheidze and Kerenskii – to join the government. Having failed, P.N. Milyukov, the leader of the Kadet party who became Minister of Foreign Affairs, insisted that the Soviet at least make a public declaration of support.[25] It was the Soviet, not the government, that issued the call to the workers to end the general strike that had grown into the February Revolution.

All this was an admission that the government lacked authority among workers. Nor was this the case only in Petrograd. Workers' resolutions adopted in provincial centres were typically addressed either to the Petrograd Soviet or to Kerenskii,[26] not to the Provisional Government.[27]

By their actions, too, workers demonstrated that they considered the Soviet to be the real source of authority. For example, the workers of several state-owned factories turned to the Soviet, not the government, to approve changes they had made in their administrations.[28] Others asked the Soviet to enact various reforms. When the general assembly of the Patronnyi Factory decided on 4 March that alcoholic beverages should go the way of the old regime, it mandated its deputies to work out a decree with the Soviet to prohibit alcohol.[29] Many factories petitioned the Soviet to enact a law establishing the eight-hour workday.[30] And it was to the Soviet that they turned to issue an appeal to the peoples of the other countries at war, calling on them to exert pressure on their governments to conclude a democratic end to the conflict.[31] When suspicions or open conflicts arose between workers and management, it was again to the Soviet that workers appealed to investigate.[32]

The only working-class elements that directly expressed support for the government were white-collar employees (*sluzhashchie*) and railway line workers. The latter, especially outside the big cities, constituted a large semi-proletarian

---

25 Sukhanov 1919–23, vol. 1, p. 210. See also Rosenburg 1974, p. 178.

26 Although the Soviet Executive Committee had decided against participation in the government, Kerenskii, a member of the Executive, unilaterally decided to join the government. In a typically theatrical and emotionally charged performance before the 2 March plenum of the Soviet, he was able to win approval 'by acclamation' for this move (without any discussion or vote). I found no expression of workers' attitudes toward this decision, which seems to mean it made little difference to them.

27 Ferro 1967, p. 178.

28 Dok. Feb., pp. 543–4; Rab. kon., p. 42.

29 TsGA SPb f. 24602, op. 7, d. 7, 1.68.

30 Ibid., f. 7384, op. 9, d. 293, 1.3.

31 Dok. Feb., p. 446.

32 TsGA SPb f. 4601, op. 1, d. 10, 1. 9 ob.; Rab. kon., p. 57.

mass with strong peasant ties and they were subject to the influence of the higher administrative personnel, generally Kadets or right-wing socialists.[33] The white-collar employees of the Russian Joint-Stock Company of United Mechanical Factories pledged 'to give full support to the Provisional Government and the Soviet in their responsible work to create a new organisation of society and to summon the Constituent Assembly'.[34] Similarly, a joint meeting of workers and employees of 26 railway lines jointly resolved to 'support the Soviet and the Provisional Government'.[35] According to an early history of the railroad workers, these workers did indeed view the Provisional Government as a popular democratic government: 'No other part of the working class put such store in it'.[36]

On the other hand, despite their misgivings and expressed qualifications, few industrial workers in Petrograd rejected dual power as a viable political arrangement. The main exceptions were in the Vyborg District. A large meeting on 1 March at the Sampson'evskii Brotherhood was extremely hostile to the State Duma and its Provisional Committee and voted by a large majority to subordinate that Committee to a Provisional Revolutionary Government.[37] Another meeting in the same place on 3 March, attended by approximately a thousand people, called on the Soviet immediately to remove 'the provisional government of the liberal bourgeoisie' and to proclaim itself a Provisional Revolutionary Government.[38] According to the Bolshevik worker A.I. Sudakov, meetings in this hall were famous for their anti-Duma and anti-Provisional-government sentiment.[39] The Mensheviks' Vyborg District organisation indirectly confirmed this, when it reported: 'With the exception of the attitude to the Provisional Government, all the issues – land and the future political system – are being decided clearly and categorically'.[40] The Mensheviks' newspaper reported that 'The calls to overthrow and even to arrest the Provisional Government that we heard from irresponsible street orators in the first days of the revolution evoked applause but led to no practical results'.[41]

33 Tanyaev 1925, pp. 3–4.
34 *Izvestiya* (8 Mar 1917).
35 Ibid. (9 Mar 1917).
36 Tanyaev 1925, p. 16.
37 Dingel'shtedt 1925, p. 193.
38 *Pravda* (9 Mar 1917).
39 Burdzhalov 1965, p. 286.
40 *Rabochaya gazeta* (17 Mar 1907).
41 Ibid. (9 Apr 1917).

Within the Petrograd Bolshevik organisation itself, apparently only the Vyborg District (with a predominantly working-class membership of 50–600 in March 1917) called for a Soviet government. In fact, the Bolsheviks' Petrograd Committee had to forbid distribution of the Vyborg district organisation's leaflet containing the resolution of its general assembly of 1 March demanding the resignation of all the members of the State Duma, that 'bastion of the old regime', and the formation of a Provisional Revolutionary Government.[42] Shlyapnikov commented that the Vyborg Bolsheviks 'were somewhat inclined to force events, calling for an immediate, even armed, struggle by all means against the Provisional Government'.[43]

There was some support outside the Vyborg District for that position, since before the formation of the Provisional Government and its endorsement by the Soviet on 2 March, workers of several factories apparently assumed the Soviet would form the government. The mandate presented by the delegate to the Soviet of the Shchetinin Aircraft Factory in Novaya derevnya, adjacent to the Vyborg District, read: 'The general assembly ... has elected the deputy Grachev to the Provisional Revolutionary Government – the Soviet of Workers' Deputies'.[44] Similarly, the Schlusselburg Powder Factory on 1 March mandated its delegates to the Soviet to 'enter into relations with the Provisional Revolutionary Government [meaning here the Soviet] in order to obtain information and directives'.[45]

Moreover, immediately upon Lenin's return to Russia in early April (before the April crisis that marked the first street protests against the government), several Vyborg metalworking factories passed anti-government resolutions. Perhaps Lenin's authority – he called for Soviet power as soon as he reached Petrograd – facilitated open expression of views that had been suppressed when it became evident that they were not widely supported. Party discipline was also a factor for the Bolshevik workers. On 4 April, before Lenin's return, a general assembly of workers of the Nobel Machine-construction Factory resolved:

> 1) that the liberation of the working class is the affair of the workers themselves; 2) that the way of the proletariat to its final goal – socialism – lies not on the path of compromises, agreements and reforms, but only

42 *Pravda* (8 Mar 1917).

43 Shlyapnikov 1923, vol. 1, p. 225.

44 Burdzhalov 1965, p. 223.

45 Shlyapnikov 1923, vol. 1, p. 222.

> through merciless struggle – revolution; 3) that the bourgeoisie is aware of the danger that threatens it from the proletariat and from time to time has arranged a blood-letting of the working class: in 1905 we had January 9; 1912 – Lena; after Lana – Kostroma (June 1915) and Ivanovo-Voznesensk (August 1915); 4) that the working class cannot trust any government composed of bourgeois elements and supported by the bourgeoisie; 5) that our Provisional Government, composed almost completely of bourgeois elements, cannot be a popular government to which we can entrust our fate and our great victories. This meeting of workers of the Novel Factory demands: 1) that procedures to call the Constituent Assembly begin at once; 2) that the Provisional Government officially address all the warring states – both allied and hostile – with the proposal to immediately start peace talks, while repudiating all annexations and reparation and granting the right of self-determination to every nation.[46]

This resolution bases its antagonism to the bourgeoisie on the past experience of the workers' movement. That antagonism was not softened for these workers by the atmosphere of national reconciliation and unity following the February Revolution. But they held back from calling the Soviet to take power.

Another meeting of 5,000 workers and soldiers went only somewhat further. Its unanimous resolution began by demanding legislation on the confiscation of land in favour of the people, the introduction of the eight-hour work day, a war tax on the capitalists, arming of the workers, the issuance of a joint declaration with the Allies rejecting annexations and reparations and calling for immediate peace talks, and the publication of all secret treaties. And it went on:

> These five main demands of the people, of course, will not please the bourgeois-aristocratic government, by which we mean the Provisional Government. Putting forth these demands, we will let all those parts of the people that are wavering and trusting the Provisional Government know that the existence of such a government is unacceptable.
>
> In the event of the inevitable refusal by the Provisional Government directly and unconditionally to satisfy these basic demands of the people, the Soviet of Workers' and Soldiers' Deputies must declare itself the unique supreme power and publish in its name these and other laws that are needed by the people.

46 *Pravda* (7 Apr 1917).

> Such a second stage of the revolution will by its example (and not by declaration) have an effect on the toilers of the other countries and, in particular, Germany. The German people, seeing against them a workers' government, will more boldly turn against their own oppressors, against Wilhelm and the bourgeoisie. That is when a truly defensive war will begin ... Until then the war will be one of plunder.[47]

About this time, two other Vyborg District factories, the Old Parviainen Foundry and Mechanical Factory and Russian Renault, also called directly for Soviet power.[48] But the arguments they put forth were always based on an analysis of the bourgeoisie as demonstrated by past experience. For most workers, and especially the newcomers to industry, this argument was not sufficiently convincing. Some perceived it as dangerous. The workers needed current, concrete proof that the current political arrangement could not work before they would change their minds. The above-cited resolutions appear to have understood that.

Besides the large number of workers' resolutions supporting the Soviet's position on power, worker support for it is also clearly indicated by their 'revolutionary defencism': they continued to condemn the world war as imperialist but they now recognised the necessity of military defence, since it was defence of the revolution. A typical resolution of the period declared: 'We will not under any circumstances allow Wilhelm and his underlings to fill the place left by Nikolai the Last. We want peace without annexations and retributions, peace that the toiling masses of the warring countries will sign. The Soviet of Workers' and Soldiers' Deputies and the Provisional Government must facilitate the conclusion of such a peace'.[49] Since the imperialist aspirations of the bourgeoisie and its unflinching support for the war effort under the old regime were well-known, worker support for a defensive war under the Provisional Government indicates either that they felt the bourgeoisie had undergone a change of heart since the Revolution, or, much more likely, that they were confident that the Soviet could act to ensure the government's adherence to its peace policy. Even more radical workers, like those of the Franko-Russkii Shipbuilding Factory, shared this belief. A meeting at that factory called on the people to exert

47 *Soldatskaya pravda* (18 Apr 1917).

48 *Izvestiya Petrogradskogo soveta r. i s.d.* (15 Apr. 1917), *Pravda* (21 Apr. 1917).

49 Dok. Feb., p. 546.

> energetic influence on the Provisional Government with the aim of forcing it to issue a categorical declaration on the war in the sense that Russia in this war no longer pursues annexationist goals. On the other hand, we consider it extremely necessary that the Provisional Government immediately press the states allied with Russia to make similar declarations.[50]

On the question of the war, the Bolsheviks defended a different position. But it made little sense to workers and even aroused considerable hostility. The party retained its pre-revolutionary slogan of 'down with the war', arguing that the 'bourgeois government' was imperialist, but at the same time it expressed conditional support to this government. As a result, many workers saw 'down with the war' as a threat to the revolution, and the Bolsheviks had considerable trouble explaining this contradiction. At the First City Conference of the party in early April, Naumov, a worker from the Vyborg District, complained:

> The masses do not understand our calls to end the war. Something here is missing. They are right those who ask: 'So that means sticking the bayonets into the ground?' That's what the masses are saying. A situation is being created in which we have to clarify this thought for ourselves and for the masses. Otherwise, when we explain the essence and character of the war to the masses and call on them to understand that it has to be ended, one feels that, all the same, something is missing.[51]

Given the Bolsheviks' stand on the war, the consistent position would have been to call for the soviets to replace the liberal government. Only then would revolutionary defencism be justified, since the workers' and peasants' government would actively pursue a democratic peace policy. It is not surprising, then, that it was mainly in the Vyborg District where the Bolshevik position on the war was supported.[52] For it was mainly here that workers wanted to replace the census government with the soviets. After the Bolshevik Central Committee members Stalin and L.B. Kamenev returned from Siberian exile in the middle of March, they changed *Pravda*'s editorial policy, taking a sharply defencist turn, which brought the policy on the war and on state power in line with that of the Menshevik-SR majority of the Soviet. The party's position on the question of

---

50 Ibid., p. 554.

51 *Pervaya Petrogradksaya obshchegorodskaya konferenstiya RSDRP(b) v aprele 1917 g.* (M., 1925), pp. 16–17. See also Mitel'man, Glebov and Ul'yanskii 1961, p. 574.

52 Shlyapnikov 1923, vol. II, p. 142.

power and the war would change again only in late April, following the April Days and Lenin's return to Russia.

But if the vast majority of workers supported the Soviet leadership's position on dual power, they nevertheless did not really see things in the same way as the leaders. And the disagreement revealed itself first in relation to the war. Workers took for granted that the Provisional Government, willingly or under pressure from the Soviet, agreed to the latter's policy in support of diplomacy aimed at a rapid, democratic peace. But the social democrats who negotiated the dual power arrangement, had, in fact, been far from convinced of that. M. Rafes, a Bundist (right Menshevik), reported that Sukhanov, who had a major hand in the negotiations, argued 'that there can be no question of participation of democracy [socialists] in the provisional government, since that would mean participation in the war they are conducting'.[53] In his memoirs, Sukhanov writes that both sides in the negotiations studiously avoided the question of the war, since they knew it would lead to a collision.[54] The Soviet plenary meeting that voted to support the Provisional Government was apparently unaware of this conscious omission. That helps to explain why no one apparently objected to Kerenskii's unilateral decision to participate in the government, even though he was a representative of 'revolutionary democracy'.

These differences soon came to the surface, however, around the 'liberty loan' that was launched by the government at the beginning of April.[55] On 7 April, the Executive Committee of the Soviet endorsed it by a vote of 21 against 14 with 7 abstentions. But the Soviet itself decided to withhold support until the government took concrete action toward securing a democratic peace. However, it finally endorsed the loan on 22 April, with only 117 Bolsheviks and Internationalists voting against.[56] But almost everywhere in the factories opinion was strongly opposed to the loan and very critical of the Soviet Executive Committee, and later of the Soviet itself, for endorsing it. The most common worker reaction to the Soviet's appeal to support the loan was to demand instead a special tax on capital and on war profits and initiative from the government to press the Allies to renounce all annexationist war aims. On 10 April, the mechanical department of the Russko-Baltiiskii Wagon-construction Factory, by a vote of more than 400 to 7, resolved:

53 Rafes 1922, p. 194.

54 Sukhanov 1919–23, vol. I, p. 127.

55 The Provisional Governement issued the loan in March in an effort to replenish the state's empty coffers. The left socialists, notably the Bolsheviks, considered the loan a mesure of support for the imperialist war, a form of war credits, and called to boycott it.

56 Ibid., vol. III, pp. 217, 223, 310, 313.

> Recognising that the 'Liberty Loan' was adopted with the aim of continuing this fratricidal war, which benefits only the imperialist bourgeoisie, we do not consider it possible for the socialist proletariat to take part in that loan.
>
> At the same time, we recognise that the cause of supplying the army with all it needs requires financial resources and we point out to the Soviet that this money should be taken from the pockets of the bourgeoisie that instigated and continues this slaughter and is making millions in profits in this bloody frenzy.
>
> We energetically protest against the conduct of the 21 members of the Executive Committee of the Soviet of workers' and soldiers' deputies, who accepted the 'Liberty Loan', and we consider such an attitude to the cause of the proletariat is a betrayal of the International.[57]

The vote in the Soviet in support for the loan was the first occasion that prompted the recall of their deputies by workers. At the Novaya Bumagopryadil'nya Mill, both delegates, Menshevik sympathisers, were censured and recalled for agitating in favour of the loan.[58] At the Skorokhod Shoe Factory, the four delegates to the district soviet, all SRs, ignored the decision of the workers' general assembly to reject the loan, and voted to support it. The workers recalled three of them and replaced them with Bolshevik deputies. The fourth deputy was forgiven, after making a public recantation.[59]

But despite this reaction to the 'Liberty Loan', it did not produce a perceptible shift in the workers' position towards dual power or toward the Menshevik-SR leadership of the Soviet, although this episode undoubtedly sowed the first seeds of doubt. Once again, it was mainly from the Vyborg District that there were heard calls for the Soviet to take power.

Dual Power in the Light of Attitudes before the Revolution

The workers' reaction to the 'Liberty Loan' underlines a problem implicit in the preceding analysis: given that support for the Provisional Government was so guarded, that mistrust of census society was so deep, and that workers' willingness to make concessions for the sake of that political alliance was so

57 *Pravda* (11 Apr 1917).

58 Perazich 1927, p. 28.

59 Smirnov 1935, pp. 39–40.

limited, why, in fact, did they give their support to dual power rather than opt in the February Revolution for a government of 'revolutionary democracy' in the form of the soviets? Before attempting to answer this, it is useful to examine whether the position after the February Revolution represented continuity or a break with pre-revolutionary attitudes.

From the start of the revolution on 23 February and until 2 March, when work in the factories began to resume, there is little evidence that workers held concrete ideas about the nature of a provisional government to exercise power until convocation of a constituent assembly. The slogans of the revolutionary workers were 'down with the war' and the traditional social-democratic 'three whales'. These said nothing about the nature of an interim government. Nor did the socialist parties offer much guidance. Sukhanov writes that their leaders did not raise the issue. When the Soviet met for the first time on 27 February, this seemingly most urgent question was not discussed.[60] A police report about a meeting that took place with 26 Bolsheviks and Menshevik-Internationalists on 26 February on Vasilevskii ostrov cites the resolution adopted, which was limited to questions of tactics for street fighting.[61] At this point, all attention was focused on the aim of overthrowing the autocracy. Only on 27 February did the Bolshevik Central Committee issue its call to establish a provisional revolutionary government with its organising centre at the Finland Station in the Vyborg District. And by that time, the Soviet had already been formed.

But if the workers did not express views on the provisional organisation of power, their attitudes toward the State Duma and to census society in the period preceding the insurrection can be established. These found their clearest expression in the debate on participation in the War-Industry Committees and on the tactics of the 'workers' group' attached to these committees. The War-Industry Committees were established in the summer of 1915 by the Congress of Representatives of Trade and Industry to help in organising Russia's military industry. In the autumn of that year, the leadership of the Central War-Industry Committee, which included such prominent capitalists as A.I. Guchkov (future Minister of War in the first Provisional Government) and A.I. Konovalov (future Minister of Trade and Industry), obtained permission to organise two-stage elections to 'workers' groups' that would be attached to the committees. This electoral campaign was the first legal opportunity since the outbreak of war for workers openly to discuss the government's domestic and foreign policies.

60 Sukhanov 1919–23, vol. 1, pp. 22 and 96.

61 *Byloe*, nos. 7–8 (1918), p. 171.

Three main political views emerged in these discussions. The Bolsheviks and Left SRs opposed participation in the committees, since that would mean participation in the war effort. However, they were in favour of participating in the first stage of the elections to the 'workers' group' in order to exploit this legal opportunity for anti-war and revolutionary agitation. Menshevik-Internationalists (left Mensheviks), such as N.S. Chkheidze, who were opposed to the war, nevertheless supported participation in the committees as a tool for organising anti-government forces and obtaining improvements in workers' conditions.[62] Finally, Menshevik-Defencists (right Mensheviks), such as K.L. Gvozdev, recognised that the government's war aims were imperialist, but nevertheless called to defend the country against Germany, even while advocating the overthrow of Tsarism as the main means of the country's defence.

The electors' meeting took place on 27 September 1915. The Bolshevik position carried by a vote of 90 to 81. However, Gvozdev disputed the validity of the elections on the grounds that a Bolshevik worker had substituted himself for an elector from the Putilov Works who had declined to participate.[63] A second electors' meeting took place on 29 November, in the course of which the Bolsheviks and Left SR electors walked out in protest. Those who remained voted unanimously (with some abstentions) to participate.

On the face of it, the issue was the attitude toward the war. But in fact, both Bolsheviks and Menshevik-Internationalists opposed participation in the war effort, even under the guise of defence, although the latter opposed the Bolsheviks' call to boycott the committees. Even the Defencists equivocated on the war. As E. Maevskii, a Menshevik-Defencist member of the Workers' Group wrote: 'Defence of the country was understood by the Workers' Group, despite what the anti-defencists said, not as the establishment of civil peace or reconciliation with the old regime, but first and foremost as an irreconcilable struggle against the Tsar and autocracy'.[64] Only towards the end of 1916 did the defencism of Gvozdev's group clearly emerge, prompting Chkheidze and other Menshevik-Internationalists finally to disown the Workers' Group.

What was really at issue – and what had always been the fundamental bone of contention within Russian social democracy – was revolutionary strategy and, specifically, the relationship between the working class and census society in the revolutionary struggle. The war, which was wholeheartedly supported

---

62 Shlyapnikov 1923, pp. 103–4.

63 Ibid., p. 115.

64 Maevskii 1918, p. 5.

by the bourgeoisie, was only one aspect of this more general issue debated at the electors' assemblies. Speaking before the first assembly in November 1915, Emel'yanov, a Menshevik-Defencist worker at the Trubochnyi Factory, argued:

> This war, as any other, is conducted only in the interests of the bourgeoisie, and not of the workers. Such is our principled view of the war … And still our opponents call us nationalists … And yet … following the Zimmerwald Conference, we merely repeat: 'peace without annexations and retributions'. We strive for this peace in union with all of revolutionary democracy. How can we achieve such a peace? Our opponents do not march together with other classes. They are thinking of a revolutionary overthrow that they will achieve solely by their own forces. However, the achievement of this goal and of peace is possible only through the mobilisation of all the vital social forces of the country around these slogans … The only salvation for the country lies not in technical defence, not in participation in committees and commissions on defence, but in the radical transformation of all our life in the interests of democracy … If you adopt this point of view, then the mobilisation of all vital forces of the country is necessary for the democratisation of the public order. We disagree with our opponents in our evaluation of the active forces: they rely uniquely on their own forces in the revolution; we strive to rally all the strata of Russian society that are able to strive for the democratisation of the public order and that want to fight … The political struggle isn't a call to strike, not a meeting in front of a factory, not a loud resolution or outcry, but long preparation for battle … Our adversaries say that we betray the interests of the revolution and they say that mainly because of our evaluation of the bourgeoisie. Our bourgeoisie cannot reconcile itself to the rule of autocracy and itself is striving towards power, but in a cowardly and slavish manner. We will criticise and push it toward a decisive battle with the obsolete regime. In the final battle [i.e., for socialism] we must depend on our own forces, but in the struggle for political freedom we must march in contact with the bourgeoisie.

Emel'yanov added that questions of labour policy could also be raised in the committees. He observed that the laws protecting female and child labour had been abrogated and that low-paid Chinese and Persian workers were being brought into the country. Participation in the committees would open legal possibilities for organising the working class. He concluded: 'Our aim is victory over the internal enemy, repulsing the German army, and peace without annexations or retributions'.[65]

Dunaev, a Bolshevik worker, answered him:

> The Military-Industry Committees are an institution of the liberal bourgeoisie – say our opponents. We can march arm in arm with them. It follows that Guchkov[66] will march hand in hand with us against the contemporary Stolypins.[67] This same Guchkov, who together with the late Stolypin, hanged our comrades? Chinese, Persians and Koreans are being brought in. To listen to Gvozdev and Emel'yanov it would seem that it is the government that is bringing them in, while the industrialists have nothing to do with it. But comrades, tell me, who is it that needs these coolies and Persians? ... The coolies are being imported by the liberal industrialists, the same industrialists with whom you are about to enter into an alliance against the yellow peril. Female and child labour is widely being used now. Who sought the abrogation of the miserable rights of the women and children? The aristocracy? They already were exploiting their labour from dawn to dusk. No, this was sought by the Guchkovs, Konovalovs and Ryabushinskiis. The factory owners pressed the buttons, and the rights of the workers were abrogated. This is whom you call revolutionary elements and invite to march arm in arm with you. All the attempts of the workers to improve their situation have ended in their being sent to the front at the word of the factory owners. Where are our comrades from Lessner, Phoenix and the other factories? They were sent by messieurs the liberal factory owners to the front and to the jails. This is honoured company! And with its help they want to create the organisation of the working class. Our opponents say that we depend solely on our own forces, and you, messieurs liquidators,[68] desire to conduct the struggle in union with all revolutionary forces. Fine. Where, then, do you seek your allies? Did you go to the peasantry? No, you need something else. You go to the Military-Industry Committee and act in the backyard of a bourgeois organisation. (noise, protests) This is where you seek allies for yourselves, in the organisations of the bosses, who before the war organised lockouts and are now stuffing their pockets on war orders. (noise,

65 Shlyapnikov 1923, vol. I, pp. 116–19.

66 A big industrialist and landowner, chairman of the Central War-Industry Committee.

67 Minister of Internal Affairs who put down the Revolution of 1905–6 with extreme cruelty.

68 Reference to Mensheviks who wanted to liquidate the underground organisation after the defeat of the Revolution of 1905.

> agitation) You used the occasion with Kudryashev and decided to arrange new elections. To whom did you appeal? To the worker masses? Did you go to the factories and mills and conduct agitation among the workers? No, you went to Guchkov and, somewhere behind the scenes, hidden from the workers, you conducted some sort of shady negotiations. In union with Guchkov, you want to overturn the will of the entire Petrograd proletariat … (The chairman cuts Dunaev off.)[69]

These two speeches are a graphic expression of the fundamental issue that divided the Bolsheviks and the Mensheviks: the relationship of the working class to the bourgeoisie. The Bolsheviks and their supporters were irreconcilable on this question, and their position was based on the long history of intimate collaboration of the bourgeoisie with the Tsarist state against the labour movement and its goals. The Bolsheviks concluded that the bourgeoisie would not willingly give up the repressive apparatus of the Tsarist state. It needed this state to keep in check a working class that it feared to face alone in a democratic regime. The Mensheviks, on the other hand, argued that at least a part of the bourgeoisie was of a liberal frame of mind and that, with nudging from the workers' movement, these 'vital forces' of census society would break with the autocracy. As a corollary, they argued, largely in vain, for workers to separate the economic struggle against the industrialists – here they should not be too radical, so as not to frighten the liberals – from the political struggle to overthrow the autocracy.[70]

Maevskii nicely summed up the basic differences underlying the debate about participation in the War-Industry Committees:

> The Workers' Group saw the coming revolution not only as a bourgeois one but also correctly evaluated the role that could be played by such distorted representation as that of the Fourth Duma. Fighting the Bolsheviks and the semi-Bolsheviks, the Workers' Group often had to stress that, whatever the Duma was now, in the context of an upsurge of revolutionary activity of the masses, it could and would be transformed into one

69 Ibid., pp. 119–20.

70 In a sense, the Mensheviks were driven to insist on the existence of a progressive, potentially revolutionary segment of census society, since they were convinced that the working class alone could not succeed in carrying through and consolidating a democratic revolution. As for the peasants, on whom the Bolsheviks counted as allies for the workers, the Mensheviks considered them a largely benighted mass, an elemental force that could not be relied upon and that was potentially counterrevolutionary.

> of the stages or supporting points of the future revolution. At the same time, the representatives of the Group had to fight intensely against boycottist attitudes and indifference toward the Duma and its activity, that were being bolstered and intensified among workers by Bolshevik agitation ... The supporters of the Group tried to convince workers of the need, in the name of the revolution, to coordinate their efforts with the efforts of certain circles of the progressive bourgeoisie and to use the Duma as a national centre, which, in its confrontations with the government, could focus the attention of the entire nation ... Already then, in their criticism of the Workers' Group, we saw the Bolshevik and semi-Bolshevik argument opposing the internationalism of the proletariat to the task of national defence, opposing the proletariat to all other classes, portrayed as a single, solidly reactionary bourgeois mass.[71]

There was, in addition, a third, intermediate position, that of the Menshevik-Internationalists. The worker Kuz'min stated at that meeting that, while he put no faith in 'Guchkov and Co.', the legal opening provided by the 'workers' group' should be exploited to support and organise workers. He cited the example of his own factory, Trubochnyi, where under the guise of presenting reports on the activities of the War-Industrial Committee, the activists had been able to organise meetings and conduct agitation.[72]

The result of the voting did not, therefore, necessarily signify that workers accepted the defencists' position in regards to the bourgeoisie. Even so, the vote was close at both meetings. One can conclude that at least a half of Petrograd's workers opposed even the Menshevik-Internationalist position of 'non-organic' participation in the committees. This was a rejection of even the appearance of collaboration with the bourgeoisie and the war effort. Given the extremely limited opportunities to organise openly during the war and the workers' deteriorating economic situation, this principled support for the Bolsheviks' boycottist position is quite remarkable.

But what best demonstrated the predominant attitude among workers was their failure in practice to support the tactics promoted by the Workers' Groups. Maevskii wrote that the defencists' efforts to mobilise workers to exert pressure on the Duma by sending delegations to its chairman or to the heads of the various different Duma factions

---

71 Maevskii 1918, pp. 5–8.

72 Shlyapnikov 1923, vol. 1, p. 126.

> enjoyed little success, coming up against in broad worker circles the old Bolshevik, boycottist prejudices, embellished with verbal radicalism … The only form of movement that certain circles of the Petrograd working class had long mastered, with the aid of the Bolsheviks and their semi-Bolshevik followers, was 'strikism', which in the opinion of the Workers' Group and its supporters was the least active and effective form in conditions of war. The representatives of the Workers' Group spared no effort to make the masses, infected by Bolshevik maximalism, understand the simple revolutionary truth – that not every measure, even if externally super-radical, is really revolutionary in substance.[73]

Striking, as opposed to the tactics advocated by the Workers' Group, was, of course, an independent form of working-class action.

Despite the continuous growth and politicisation of the strike movement, none of the workers' collective actions before 1917 had anything to do with the State Duma. Sukhanov confirms that the '[Workers'] Group did not enjoy any popularity among the worker masses. The overwhelming majority of the conscious proletariat of the capital and also in the provinces adhered to a strongly anti-defencist position and were deeply hostile towards the cooperation with the plutocracy on the part of a small group of Social Democrats led by K.A. Gvozdev'.[74]

When a group of the Duma census deputies came out with strong oppositional statements at its October 1916 session – it was there that the Kadet leader Milyukov challenged the government, asking: 'What is it, stupidity or treason?'[75] – the Workers' Group decided that 'they could not wait until the working class realized the revolutionary significance of organised intervention into the clash of bourgeois society with the autocracy' and decided to strike on 14 February, the opening of the Duma session. The strikers were to march to the Tauride Palace.[76] (Not that the Kadets were grateful for this help. *Rech'*, their party paper, labelled the rumours of a workers' demonstration a provocation.)[77]

73 Maevskii 1918, pp. 7–8.

74 Sukhanov 1919–23, vol. 1, p. 15.

75 Pearson 1977, p. 114. Even at this point, however, the census opposition dared only to call for the formation of a 'government of confidence', rather than a responsible government. As for concrete, practical action, that was entirely out of the question.

76 Maevskii 1918, p. 10. Grave 1927, p. 181; Maevskii 1918, p. 11.

77 Grave 1927, p. 181; Maevskii 1918, p. 11.

The Bolsheviks and Menshevik-Internationalists, on their part, supported the call to strike but urged the workers not to go to the Duma.[78]

According to police reports, 90,000 workers struck on that day, but only two small groups, a few hundred, were reported in the vicinity of the Tauride Palace and they were quickly dispersed.[79] Maevskii claims that the movement was prevented by extreme police measures.[80] But even on the first day of the February Revolution the police were not able to keep determined demonstrators from reaching the city's centre.

In fact, the workers began to show interest in the Duma only after the victory of the Revolution on the afternoon of 27 February, the day that the soldiers mutinied en masse. But for the first four and a half days, when it had been predominantly a working-class movement, the Duma was ignored. The common goal of the demonstrators had been Nevskii Prospekt, with gathering points at Kazan' Cathedral, Znamenskaya Square, and the corner of Liteinyi and Nevskii prospekts.

Why Dual Power?

But it was not the case, as both Trotsky and Sukhanov claim, that only or mainly soldiers went to the Tauride Palace on 27 February.[81] The Soviet historian E.N. Burdzhalov found that among the crowds there were many workers, including members of the Bolshevik party.[82] Several of the latter, on being freed from jail, stopped only long enough to remove their chains and to find arms before setting off at the head of a Cossack regiment for the Tauride Palace.[83]

Clearly, something had changed with the victory of the Revolution, and Maevskii appears justified in his claim that the strategy of the Workers' Group, 'after certain errors', was finally adopted by the working class in the February Revolution.[84] Certainly, the Bolsheviks were genuinely surprised to find themselves suddenly in a minority in the Soviet, since they had been by far the strongest underground organisation among the workers.[85] At the time, they

78 Grave 1927, p. 184.

79 *Byloe*, p. 160.

80 Maevskii 1918, p. 12.

81 Trotsky 1965, vol. 1, pp. 134–5; Sukhanov 1919–23, p. 63.

82 Burdzhalov 1967, vol. I, p. 203.

83 Ibid., p. 68.

84 Maevskii 1918, p. 12.

85 Shlyapnikov 1923, vol. I, p. 203.

tended to explain this citing technical and organisational factors: the Bolsheviks, being largely an underground organisation, were not so well known to broader circles of workers; the Mensheviks and SRs were better orators; the Bolsheviks were engaged in street fighting when the elections to the Soviet took place, while the Mensheviks and SRs were in the factories, etc.

But to Shlyapnikov, at least, these arguments were one-sided. The revolution had created a new situation. 'The revolution shook awake even the sleepiest of the lower elements of society, summoned them to action and pulled into battle the soldier masses, the intelligentsia of common birth, and even the philistine man in the street. In this way, what had begun as a proletarian movement under proletarian and revolutionary "populist" slogans, took on, as it broadened, an increasingly "all-national character" … We had to … evaluate our slogans and agitation tactics in completely different circumstances than only two days before'.[86] Shlyapnikov hints here at a crucial shift in the workers' view of the political situation that had been created by the revolution: on the one hand, the revolution had assumed the appearance of a national (all-class) movement; on the other hand its victory in the capital gave rise to an intense longing for national unity among workers which predisposed them not to examine too critically the depth of the shift that had occurred in census society. 'The February events', wrote the Left SR paper *Znamya truda*, 'made people forget what only a few days ago had been their irreconcilable differences with the landowners and capitalists. It seemed that everyone was united'.[87]

There was much at the time to support the impression of national unity. After all, had not the Duma finally adhered to the revolution, a shift that made its victory, especially outside the capital, so much easier, since the Duma alone could command the allegiance of the state and military bureaucracies and of census society generally? And had not the Duma Committee accepted the Soviet's programme (or at least so it seemed)? Was not the entire population in the capital out in the streets sporting red ribbons?[88]

86 Ibid.

87 *Znamya truda* (17 Nov 1917).

88 V.B. Stankevich, a Popular (right) Socialist, put the apparent national unity into clearer perspective in his memoirs: 'Officially, they celebrated, blessed the revolution, shouted "hurray" for the fighters for freedom, decorated themselves with ribbons and marched around sporting red banners. Everyone said "we", "our" revolution, "our" victory, "our" freedom. But in their hearts, in intimate conversation, they were horrified, they shuddered and felt themselves captives of a hostile elemental milieu that was travelling along an unknown path'. Stankevich 1926, p. 33.

The political representatives of census Russia were also preaching national unity and reconciliation. On 3 March, the Central Committee of the Kadet party proclaimed:

> The old regime has disappeared. The State Duma, having forgotten party differences, united in the name of the salvation of the Fatherland and took upon itself the creation of a new government ... Let all differences of party, class, estate and nationality be forgotten in this country ... Let the hope burn strong in all hearts that this time we will be able to avoid ruinous disunity [an allusion to 1905–6].[89]

The February Revolution could thus appear as vindication of the strategy of the Workers' Group. This was no doubt not lost upon the workers. All the same, in view of the unhappy history of relations between the working-class movement and the bourgeoisie, one can understand Shlyapnikov's surprise at 'how easily the worker masses were taken in by the trap of "all-national unity" and the unity of a "revolutionary democracy," in which were included also the Petersburg industrialists and the Moscow merchants'.[90]

Part of the answer lay in the atmosphere fostered by the victory of the revolution: it was a mixture of euphoria and disbelief, but also anxiety at the precariousness of the victory, all of which pushed workers toward welcoming the proposed alliance with census society.

Their mood was exalted once workers realised they had won. Some described it in dream-like terms, as a state of intoxication, like being swept up by an irresistible force. N. Tolmachev, a Bolshevik worker at the Nobel Machine-construction Factory, wrote to his family at the end of the first week:

> My dears ones, allow me congratulate you on this joyous holiday of Russian liberation. In these days of general amnesty, please grant me an amnesty for my criminal silence. Caught up in the revolutionary movement, I could think of nothing and of no one; I forgot everything and everyone ... On February 22 on my way to work, I found myself in a demonstration of 20,000 persons and I was unable to regain my senses until the last few days. I was everywhere, of course: in the first demonstrations and during the shooting, and when the troops rose up, then together with the soldiers I was in the arsenals of Peter-Paul, I stole revolvers, rifles, rode

89 Dok. Feb., p. 420.

90 Shlyapnikov 1923, vol. 1, p. 224.

> around in a car to arrest police, attended meetings, assemblies, spoke there myself. In days such as these, one cannot stand aside. And I have sobered up only in the last few days. Having fallen into the whirlwind of events, one becomes a chip of wood that is swept along, turned and spun.[91]

A woman worker at the Treugol'nik Rubber Factory recalled her exhilaration and sense of empowerment:

> I can't express my joy … I thought I was lost forever at the boss's factory. And suddenly, I was resurrected, I grew up. That night, I put on Russian boots and my husband's cap, a worker's overcoat, I said goodbye to my children and left. I didn't appear at home for four days, until March 2. My family thought I had been killed …[92]

And Rafes: 'There were no trams running in those days. We had to walk for miles but felt no fatigue. Everyone was experiencing such a mood of exhilaration that the distance did not tire them'.[93]

The Bolsheviks and Left SRs, believing that the struggle had really only begun, could only let matters take their course. 'The people are expressing a state of intoxication with the great act that has been accomplished', Kollontai wrote to Lenin and N. Krupskaya. 'Amidst the feverish commotion, amidst the desire to create, to build something new, something different from what went before, the note of the already-achieved victory rings too loud, as if everything has already been done, already completed'.[94] S.D. Mstislavskii, a Left SR, described his feelings at the plenary session of the Soviet on 2 March that overwhelmingly ratified the dual power:

> The most sensitive [of those opposed to endorsing the liberal Provisional Government] refrained from speaking. For was this the place, at the matins, to preach one's disbelief? Not to convince anyone but only to darken their human joy, joy that for many was the first they had known … I envied these people, who believed so sincerely that it was all over, that

---

91 Burdzhalov 1967, vol. 1, pp. 380–1.

92 Shabalin, 'Ot fevralya k oktyabryu – iz istorii zavoda "Krasnyi Treugol'nik"', in *Bastiony revolyutsii*, vol. 1, p. 269.

93 Rafes 1922, p. 187.

94 *Novyi mir*, no. 4, 1967, p. 237, cited in Sobolev 1973, p. 110.

> the revolution was completed – the last bullets will have been shot, and a whole new way of life will begin to flow in a broad powerful current, and we will gather in the fruits of the February exploit … But I could not help feeling that it was not so, that ahead lay a difficult path through a thicket of contradictions, through which it would not be so easy to cut with a single blow, as the first knot had been cut by the February insurrection.[95]

Another powerful factor that argued in favour of the alliance with census society was fear of counterrevolution and civil war. Although the Soviet was in control of Petrograd, no one had a clear idea in the early days of the revolution of the mood in the rest of the country, and in particular the army at the front. Rumours were circulating that troops loyal to the Tsar were headed for the capital. And, indeed, troops had been called in but they were won over to the revolution before reaching the capital.[96] Rafes recalled that 'there was no certainty in the durability [of the victory] in any district of the capital … The mood of the outsider elements, the public, was the same – they ran for the gates at every shot'.[97]

Given this uncertainty, workers in some factories were reluctant to accept election to the Soviet. At the James Beck Mill, the workers elected I.A. Tikhonov, a spinner on 28 February. He was well-known as a political activist going back to the Revolution of 1905–6. But with tears in his eyes, he pleaded to be let off the hook, explaining that he was married now, that he had been sentenced in 1906 to exile to his native Tver Gubernia, and that if the old regime were to return, he would be in for a very hard time. He finally relented. But the story repeated itself when the meeting tried to elect his substitute.[98] At the Thornton Mill, too, no one wanted to be a deputy. The decision was finally adopted to send the most active people in the factory committee to the Soviet, since 'they are all single'.[99]

Upon returning to the factories after the revolutionary days, workers immediately set to destroying management's 'black books', which contained the names of 'troublemakers' who had been blacklisted by the Society of Factory and Mill Owners. The workers at the Thornton mill burnt all the personnel

95 Mstislavskii 1922, p. 65.

96 Burdzhalov 1967, vol. 1, pp. 244–5.

97 Rafes 1922, p. 187. In these words one can also see the strange coexistence of anxiety and elation.

98 Perazich 1927, p. 23.

99 Ibid., p. 19.

cards, despite the director's assurances that they contained no political information. But the workers saw English words next to the names and so burned them just to be sure.[100]

Given the uncertainty as to the state of the revolution, it seemed important not to alienate the propertied classes. For the latter's deputies, a majority in the State Duma, were much more capable than the workers of commanding the allegiance of the officers' corps, the state bureaucracy, and the 'captains of industry'. To alienate the propertied classes by excluding them from power would have created great difficulties for the revolution and could have provoked a civil war, something workers desperately wanted to avoid.

S. Skalov, a Bolshevik worker, explained why he led a group of insurgents to the Duma on 27 February rather than taking them to the Finland Station to set up a provisional revolutionary government, as a Bolshevik leaflet had proposed:

> I felt that I acted correctly when I did not agree to go to the Finland Station to gather our forces there separately. (And there were such proposals). On our way to the Tauride Palace, on the corner of Shpalernaya and Liteinyi Prospekt, we saw a note – I can't remember from which organisation it came – inviting all workers to gather at the Finland Station. By such self-isolation, we would immediately have opposed our own, very weak, organisational forces to those of the State Duma, and by that we would have untied its hands, giving it full freedom of action and independence, something that could have been pregnant with consequences …
>
> We could not go against the Duma on 27 February 1917, nor was there any reason to. We were organisationally too weak, – our leading comrades were in jail, exile and emigration. Therefore, it was necessary to go to the Duma, to pull it into the revolutionary current … It was necessary to create revolutionary chaos, to terrorise any initiative of the Duma directed against the revolutionary actions. And that could be done only by being inside the Duma, filling up all its pores, so to speak, with revolutionary reality.[101]

In similar fashion, participants in the Bolsheviks' First City Conference on 14 April explained how the representatives of census society ended up in power as a result of the revolution:

---

100 Ibid., p. 22. See also Smirnov 1925, p. 29.

101 Skalov, '27 fevralya 1917 v Peterburge', *Krasnaya nov'*, 1931, Book 3, p. 118, cited in Burdzhalov 1967, pp. 203–4.

> When the Soviet of deputies was formed – state power was then proposed, but the workers did not consider it possible to take power into their hands ... Did the Soviet of Workers' Deputies act correctly in refusing power? I consider that it did. To take power into our hands would have been an unsuccessful policy, since Petrograd is not all of Russia. There, in Russia, the correlation of forces are different. Given its relative weight in society, the proletariat in Russia could not take power – that would have provoked a counterrevolution.[102]

The Mensheviks' argument in favour of dual power was similar. They warned that to breach the united national ranks of the revolution by attempting to take power from the Provisional Government would only play into the hands of the forces of the past that had not yet been completely destroyed. 'The Soviet cannot enjoy authority in broad strata of the bourgeoisie. Yet, at the given stage of our economic development, the leading role in economic life cannot but belong to the bourgeoisie ... If the Soviet Workers and Soldiers' Deputies took power, it would be an illusory government, one that would lead to the outbreak of civil war'.[103]

Here was a key reason for the workers' endorsement of dual power: except for a small minority, concentrated mainly in the Vyborg District, workers were not prepared to assume responsibility for running the state and the economy. And that is what Soviet power meant. Moreover, in the minds of most workers, including Bolsheviks,[104] this was a bourgeois-democratic, not a socialist, revolution: none of the popular expectations and demands linked to the revolution were intended to threaten capitalism, nor did they in any direct sense, as will be seen in the following chapter.

As for the minority of workers that did not believe in the loyalty of the propertied classes to the revolution and that wanted the Soviet to take power, they yielded to the overwhelming majority, once they saw how isolated their own position was. They, too, were concerned with unity, though not the national unity that the Mensheviks and Socialist Revolutionaries claimed and in which they had absolutely no confidence – but the unity of 'revolutionary democracy', of the toiling classes.

---

102 *Pervaya Petragradskaya*, pp. 13.

103 *Rabockaya gazeta* (7 Mar 1917). See also 12 Mar, and *Izvestiya* (2 Mar 1917).

104 Few Bolsheviks inside Russia were apparently aware that Lenin had changed his position on this sometime after the war broke out.

CHAPTER 4

The February Revolution in the Factories

Although most workers lacked any clear idea of the political arrangements that should follow immediately upon the overthrow of the autocracy, they had quite definite views about the social and economic benefits the revolution should bring them. In their minds, the establishment of democratic freedoms was integrally bound up with socio-economic reform. 'Will political freedom [by itself] aid workers to live in a human fashion?' asked a worker delegate at the 5 March meeting of Petrograd's Soviet. '[It is necessary] to secure the minimum conditions of existence, the eight-hour day, a minimum wage. With the old conditions still in existence, freedoms are useless'.[1]

This social dimension of workers' conception of the revolution consisted of three basic elements: the eight-hour day, a significant improvement in wages, and 'democratisation of factory life'. These, however, were seen as part of the democratic revolution and not as a challenge to the capitalist system and to private property.

The industrialists, however, did not see things in the same way. To them, 'social' demands, besides threatening their profits, raised the spectre of 'socialism'. They were inclined to see workers as a basically anarchist force that would move onto 'socialist experiments', given the opportunity. The French ambassador, Maurice Paléologue, recalled a conversation in June 1915 with the prominent banker and industrialist A.I. Putilov. The latter described the coming revolution as 'horrifying anarchy, endless anarchy, anarchy for 10 years'.[2] Indeed, fear of the unleashed masses had been the major reason for the weak, indecisive opposition to the autocratic regime even on the part of the more liberal fringe of the bourgeoisie. In a speech to a conference of the Council of Private Railroads a few weeks after the February Revolution, N. Nekrasov, Minister of Railways, a man who enjoyed a 'leftist' reputation among liberals, admonished the industrialists not to fear social reform:

> There is no need to be frightened by the fact that social elements are now beginning to appear. One should instead strive to channel these social elements in the appropriate direction ... The essential thing is the rational

1 TsGA SPb f. 1000, op. 73, d. 7 cited in Sobolev 1973, p. 58.
2 Cited in Mitel'man et al., *Istoriya Putilovskogo*, p. 487.

> combination of the social moment and the political, and by no means to deny the social moment, to fear it … What we have to achieve is not social revolution, but the avoidance of social revolution through social reforms.[3]

The industrialists initially appeared to heed this advice. But given the correlation of class forces immediately following the February Revolution, they had little choice but to make concessions to the workers. They did so, however, not so much because they agreed with Nekrasov but more to gain time until the workers' revolutionary ardour subsided and made possible a successful counter-offensive.

The Mensheviks and SRs, on their part, issued warnings to the workers that echoed Nekrasov's advice to the members of his class. An editorial in the Menshevik *Rabochaya gazeta* a few days after the revolution explained to workers:

> Our revolution is political. We are destroying the bastions of political authority, but the foundations of capitalism remain in place. A battle on two fronts – against the Tsar and against capital – is beyond the forces of the proletariat. We will not pick up the glove that the capitalists are throwing down before us. The economic struggle will begin when and how we find it necessary.[4]

But such advice was completely out of tune with workers' thinking. They had suffered under the heel of the autocracy with which the industrialists had been closely allied. They, along with the soldiers, had made the revolution. It was not up to them to make concessions to the bourgeoisie but quite the opposite.

The Eight-Hour Day

The eight-hour day had long been a central demand of the workers' movement. On the face of it an economic measure, workers considered it to be an integral part of the democratic revolution. A resolution adopted on 24 March 1917 by a conference of worker representatives of factories of the Artillery Authority declared: 'We have secured the eight-hour workday and other freedoms'.[5]

---

3 *Rech'* (29 Mar 1917).

4 *Rabochaya gazeta* (7 Mar 1917).

5 TsGA SPb, f. 4591, op. 1, d. 1, l. 26.

The question of ending the general strike that had led to the victorious revolution was first raised in the Soviet on 5 March. Its chairman, Chkheidze, stated in his report that, although Tsarism had not yet been completely destroyed, it was sufficiently beaten to allow work to resume in the factories. The workers should do that, however, with the understanding that, if the need arose, everyone would come out in the streets again. He recognised that workers could not continue living under the same conditions and he promised that the Soviet would begin work on changing them as soon as production had resumed.

Chkheidze's report provoked 'passionate debate',[6] in the course of which five worker deputies and five soldiers spoke. The workers insisted that the strike had to continue until the eight-hour day and better work conditions were secured. One of them complained: 'Many have forgotten many promises – they do not speak of the longstanding slogan of the proletariat, the eight-hour day'. In the name of the world proletariat, he called upon the assembly to introduce that reform.[7]

But the soldier deputies expressed concern about the army that was short of supplies and demanded an immediate end to the strike. The vote was 1,170 against 30 to return to work. The size of the majority, at least in part, is explained by the Soviet's expressed commitment immediately to formulate demands and to present them to the factory owners. But it also reflected the worker delegates' concern not to endanger the unity of 'revolutionary democracy', the workers' alliance with the soldiers.

But it soon became clear that the Soviet's decision was out of step with the dominant mood in the factories. One of the Soviet's agitators reported back: 'When I told them [the workers in the factories] of this decision, in my heart I felt that we could not do that: workers cannot win freedom without using it to ease the burdens of their labour, to fight capital'.[8] In a series of factories, workers refused to obey the Soviet's decision to end the strike and protested against what they considered its undemocratic character. A meeting on 7 March of the organising committee of the Moscow District Soviet resolved (27 votes in favour, one opposed, two abstentions):

> Considering the decision of the Soviet of Workers' and Soldiers' Deputies in favour of the immediate return to work, a decision adopted without

---

6 *Izvestiya* (6 Mar 1917).

7 TsGA SPb f. 1000, op. 73, d. 7, ll. 10–11, cited in Sobolev 1973, p. 58.

8 *Pravda*, (17 Mar 1917).

> preliminary discussion locally by the workers and soldiers themselves, we find this resolution to be incorrect, and, therefore, we have decided to postpone the return to work for two days and immediately to raise the matter for its re-examination by the Soviet. In addition, the Moscow District Committee finds it necessary to begin immediately the reorganisation of the Soviet Workers' and Soldiers' Deputies.[9]

A meeting of the workers of the Factory of Military-Medical Preparations similarly called the decision 'premature and autocratic' and decided to continue the strike.[10] At a meeting of workers of the Novaya Bumagopryadil'naya textile mill, a Menshevik worker suggested a ten and a half hour workday, asking: 'What would our English comrades say about the eight-hour day?' To this a woman worker retorted: 'We have already sacrificed so much. Do you really mean to say that we have to await instructions from abroad?' The meeting decided to continue the strike until management accepted the eight-hour day.[11] Of the 111 factories reporting to the Petrograd Society of Factory and Mill Owners, only 28 had resumed work by 7 March, the date set by the Soviet.[12]

Nor was it the workers of the traditionally more radical factories who most strongly opposed the Soviet's decision. On 7 March at a meeting of the Bolsheviks' Petersburg Committee, it was reported that a majority of factories in the Vyborg district, 18 in all, had resumed work.[13] At a meeting of some 7,000 workers of the New Lessner Machine-building Factory in this district, only six workers voted in opposition to the Soviet's decision. While criticising it as premature, the meeting declared that

> for the sake of the coordination and unity of all revolutionary forces of the country, we submit to the decision of the Soviet Workers' and Soldiers' Deputies and declare that at the first call of the representatives of the workers and soldiers we will leave work to continue the struggle for the fundamental slogans of the proletariat and peasantry: the eight-hour day, a republic, and the confiscation of all land for the benefit of the peasantry.[14]

---

9 TsGA SPb, f. 7384, op. 9, d. 293,1.5.

10 Dok. Feb., p. 230.

11 Perazich 1927, p. 32.

12 Dok. Feb., pp. 569–77.

13 Ibid., p. 39.

14 *Pravda* (9 Mar 1917), p. 88.

This was a manifestation of the discipline of the more skilled metalworkers and of their concern for the unity of revolutionary forces. On the other hand, among less skilled workers, militancy in regard to economic questions often contrasted with their more moderate positions on political matters. These latter often aroused less interest, as they were more distant from the workers' immediate experience. Thus, in the Moscow District, which remained an SR bastion well into 1917, workers expressed much stronger opposition to the Soviet's decision to return to work than in the Vyborg District, although many of the Vyborg workers had supported the call for the Soviet to take power back in the February Days.[15]

In most factories, the workers eventually heeded the Soviet's decision to resume work, but only after they had introduced the eight-hour day without waiting for management to agree – they either left work after eight hours or else demanded extra pay for overtime. On 8 March, after hearing reports from the factories, the Soviet of Petrograd District concluded

1. that the decision of the Soviet of Workers' and Soldiers' Deputies to return to work met with strong resistance from the proletariat of the Petrograd Side and that this decision was carried out in a very inharmonious manner;
2. that the resumption of work in the majority of cases was and is being accompanied by the introduction of the eight-hour day and a number of other improvements in work.[16]

In only a handful of factories did workers, in fact, agree to forego the eight-hour day. At the state-owned Promet Pipe Factory, they decided that the eight-hour day could be introduced only gradually.[17] The workers of the Nevskii Machine and Shipbuilding Factory in the Nevskii District also decided not to introduce the reform 'because of the circumstances of the present period'.[18] Both factories would remain SR strongholds well into 1917.

---

15 See, for example, the strongly worded resolution of the Dinamo Electrical Factory (about half of its workers were women), that roundly condemned the Soviet and flatly refused to end the strike. TsGA SPb, f. 7384, op. 9, d. 293, 1. 5.

16 Dok. Feb., p. 231.

17 *Izvestiya* (10 Mar 1917). However, not long after, the factory's general assembly decided against overtime work, as that violated the eight-hour day established by the 10 March agreement between the Society of Factory and Mills Owners and the Soviet (see ahead). Dok Feb. p. 511.

18 TsGA SPb f. 1000, op. 73, d. 9, l. 7–8.

The matter was finally put to rest when the Petrograd Soviet and the Petrograd Society of Factory and Mill Owners agreed on 10 March to introduce the eight-hour workday. That the industrialists saw this as merely temporary and hoped to reverse the reform at a later date was made amply clear a few days later at a meeting of representatives of Petrograd-based companies with A.I. Konovalov, Minister of Trade and Industry, himself a major industrialist. The meeting's formal agenda had to be put aside, since discussion of the reform took up so much of its time. B.A. Efron, chairman of the Society, stated plainly that 'the agreement reached in Petrograd is a real concession aimed at regulating work life in the capital, and the workers themselves [!] consider it only a temporary concession in the present circumstances'. He affirmed that an eight-hour work day was not possible, since employers simply could not afford to pay workers time-and-a-half for overtime. The participants, supported by the minister, adopted a resolution that declared: 'This is not the time to introduce the eight-hour day. One must approach this question very carefully'.[19]

The Mensheviks' paper, reflecting the position of the moderate socialists, who were a majority in the Soviet, warned workers not to heed those calling for the eight-hour day. It reminded them that this very demand put forth by the workers of the capital in November 1905 had frightened the bourgeoisie back into the arms of the Tsar. The industrialists responded to the general strike for the eight-hour day with a general lockout organised in collaboration with the administrations of the state enterprises, dealing a decisive blow to the revolutionary movement. Again, the paper advised workers first to consolidate the democratic revolution before engaging the economic struggle.

But most workers did not share this view. To them, a revolution stripped of its social content, even as a tactical concession to secure the allegiance of census society, was not worth the candle. On that level, at least, the Bolsheviks, who urged the Soviet immediately to enact the eight-hour day, were from the start more in tune with the workers' mood.[20]

Wages

Following the victorious revolution, workers expected 'to live in a manner worthy of a worker and a free citizen', wrote the journal of the Textile Work-

19 *Torgovo-promyshlennaya gazeta* (17 Mar 1917).

20 *Pervyi legal'nyi Peka*, pp. 27–8.

ers' Union.[21] 'The conditions of predatory exploitation that existed under Russia's feudal system cannot exist in the new Russia', declared the Nevskii District Soviet.[22] A decent wage was thus another social reform that workers considered part of the democratic revolution. Although the eight-hour day increased hourly wages between 20 and 28 percent, it was not enough to satisfy many workers, whose wages had been severely eroded by wartime inflation. Only a week after the 10 March agreement, the Petrograd Society of Factory and Mill Owners observed that it had not calmed the workers: they continued to make demands, and first of all for wage increases.[23]

According to the 1918 Industrial and Professional Census, the average wage in 28 of Petrograd's factories in continuous operation in the years 1913–17 rose by 120 percent between 1913 and 1916. But the Soviet economist S.G. Strumulin calculated that the real average wage on January 1916 amounted to only 84 percent of the pre-war average wage; and the real average wage in February 1917 was only 55 percent of the pre-war level.[24] Another Soviet historian cites estimates by workers' organisations in 1917, which initially went undisputed by the industrialists, to the effect that the cost of living in current rubles had quadrupled during the war. From this he concluded that, despite the near tripling of nominal wages compared to the pre-war level, even after the February increases, real wages were on average still 25–30 percent below pre-war levels.[25]

Moreover, these were only average figures. Unskilled male workers in February–March 1917 were earning 2.25–3.5 rubles a day. In March 1917, a representative of the owners of the Langezipen Factory admitted that to live 'on three rubles calls for extreme ingenuity'.[26] The plight of the unskilled workers was, indeed, very dire, and they were pressing hard. Petrov, a worker from the Treugol'nik Rubber Factory (two-thirds of its 15,000 workers were women)[27] reported to the Soviet on 20 March:

> Work conditions at the Treugol'nik Factory are terrible – wages don't correspond to the quality of work. The women received 1.35 rubles a day – the majority are married, soldiers' wives, and it is hard to live on that.

21 *Tekstil'nyi rabochii*, no. 2, 1917.

22 Cited in Selitskii 1963, p. 17.

23 Volobuev 1964, p. 126.

24 G. Strumilin, *Problemy ekonomii truda*, 1925, p. 488, cited in Volobuev 1964, p. 90.

25 Volobuev 1964, p. 91.

26 *Gosudarstvennyi arkhiv Rossiiskoi Federatsii* (GARF), f. POFZ, op. 1, d. 21, l. 110, cited in Volobuev 1964, p. 91.

27 Ek. pol., vol. I, p. 45.

> Men received 2.40 rubles – very low. During the revolution we presented demands, and the administration seemed ready to make concessions. But wages did not improve. Women – 2.35, and men – 3.35 ... Now, I'd like the Soviet to ask the Executive Committee immediately to begin work on an economic reform. Comrades, we can't live like this any longer. The high cost of living is terrible, and a family can't live on 3.35 rubles. To calm the workers we had to tell them that reforms are being drawn up. But I don't know whether that's true or not.[28]

At the Putilov Shipyard the relationship between the victorious revolution and wage demands was especially clear, as pointed out by the factory's delegate at the same meeting of the Soviet:

> With each passing day, the economic situation grew worse, and life became simply impossible. And then at the start of the revolution, that is, precisely in mid-February, workers at the shipyard had become so hungry that they had no energy left. They presented economic demands, that is, they decided to join battle, saying: We will defend our demands at any price, since we can't go on living like this. But it turned out suddenly that all of Petrograd joined the struggle ... The government was overthrown ... So the question arose: to return to work or to continue to strike? The Soviet of Workers' and Soldiers' Deputies instructed us to start work. We obeyed and at the same time presented our demands.[29]

The situation was particularly volatile where wages were lower. A Bolshevik worker from the state-owned Admiralty Shipbuilding Factory reported:

> You know the anarchy that reigns there. You know how until now the workers there were squeezed, and then, having won certain political freedoms, they are now making use of them to the fullest extent ... They tell the director: Either you agree to what we say, do what we demand, or you get out ... One day we decide one thing. The next day they learn that another factory has decided something else, and they present the same demand ... In one day there are five or six changes, and each day work almost stops, and not infrequently it does stop, as the workers gather to discuss ... Do the workers have grounds to be agitated? Yes. At the

---

28 TsGA SPb, f. 1000, op. 73, d. 16, l. 4.

29 Ibid., ll. 9–10.

> Admiralty Shipbuilding Factory a good half of the workers earned 1.18 rubles for a nine-hour day. There can be no doubt that no one can live on that wage; and so they are forced to work 16 hours a day and they are so exhausted and drained that they are ready to quit any day. During the war, they say, they already went on strike two times, and many of the activists have already been sent to the front. But now they are ready for a third time.[30]

All the speakers asked the same thing: enact a minimum wage. The delegate from the Putilov Shipyard concluded:

> And now it is the duty of the Soviet of Workers' and Soldiers Deputies to understand our situation and examine all the rates, to change them so that we have a tolerable existence, and not be surprised that we make such demands. And so we want a commission to be elected here, that it investigate the situation and begin negotiations with management, who, together with the entrepreneurs under the flag of patriotism, stripped the workers naked, since they all believed that a worker is created only for them to drink his blood drop by drop and squeeze out all his juices and then to throw him overboard like a useless object. Now, comrades, it isn't so: when the workers have awoken from their sleep of toil, they demand a just wage and make just demands, and the entrepreneurs shout: 'Help, they're robbing us!' Comrades, no doubt you do not share their horror. You understand the situation of all workers and you will no doubt tell them: 'No. You oppressed the workers, you fleeced them, and from now on must pay what their labour is worth'.[31]

To workers, the February Days that ended in the victorious revolution were not only a political uprising against the autocratic state but at the same time an economic strike against the employers. This fusion of economic and political struggles was in direct continuation of the workers' movement of 1912–14, when strikers regularly included political demands alongside their economic demands. The most striking expression of this tendency was the widespread demand for 'polite address', that is for workers to be addressed by managers in the polite second person plural.[32] The pre-war Minister of Trade and Industry

---

30 Ibid., ll. 26–8.

31 Ibid., l. 11.

32 In Russian, the first person singular is reserved for close friends, children, and animals.

of V.I. Timiryazev, an industrialist and banker, himself recognised this as a political demand.[33]

Immediately upon returning to the factories after the February Days, workers presented wage demands to management. Unskilled workers were the most uncompromising. At the Kersten Knitwear Mill (2,193 women and 335 men), where wages were low even by standards of the textile industry, some 2,000 workers assembled in the yard on 9 March and adopted the following demands:

(1) immediate removal of the manager of the knitwear department as a person 'who does not correspond to the demands of his position; he is rude to women workers'.
(2) immediate introduction of the eight-hour day and a general increase of 50 percent, pending a review of wage rates
(3) immediate payment of wages for the revolutionary days up to 7 March
(4) regular fortnightly payment of wages
(5) defective output to be sold at cost in limited quantities to the workers
(6) overtime to be made voluntary and paid at time and a half
(7) the right to hold meetings without permission and without the presence of foremen or other representatives of management.

These workers decided not to resume work and to declare an economic strike and remain out until their demands were met in full. Work resumed on 15 March after most of the demands had been granted.[34]

At the Skorokhod Shoe Factory (3,242 women of 4,900 workers), work resumed on 10 March after the administration promised a quick response to the workers' economic demands. The average wage was 5.72 rubles for men and 2.95 for women. The workers were asking for 10 and 7 rubles respectively and for work materials to be supplied at the factory's expense. When management offered only a 20 percent increase and refused to supply materials, the conflict went to arbitration. But the sides remained deadlocked. The administration then offered an additional twenty percent and a 10,000-ruble donation to the Leatherworkers' Union. The majority of the workers' delegates in the arbitration committee were inclined to accept the offer, but the rest of the workers would not hear of it. On 20 March an angry crowd of about 500 workers gathered in front of the director's office and refused to leave until their

33 Kleinbort 1923, pp. 76–9.

34 Suknovalov and Fomenkov 1968, p. 63.

demands were met. The director telephoned the Petrograd Society of Factory and Mill Owners, which authorised him to accept the demands.[35]

On wages, too, workers were clearly not in the mood for concessions.

The Press Campaign against 'Worker Egoism'

As noted earlier, the political alliance that concerned the workers most was not the one with census society but rather the alliance with the soldiers (and through them, with the peasants, as the vast majority of soldiers were young peasants). The test of this alliance came early in the revolution. In the second half of March, the 'bourgeois' (that is, non-socialist) press, in particular *Rech'*, the newspaper of the liberal Constitutional Democrats (Kadets) and *Russkaya volya*, started to accuse workers of pursuing narrow, egoistical interests at the expense of the poorly supplied soldiers in the trenches. Workers saw in this a campaign of census society aimed at turning the soldiers against them. And they were genuinely alarmed.

In many factories, including some of the most radical, meetings affirmed the workers' readiness to work overtime, the eight-hour workday notwithstanding. At the Old Parviainen Factory in the Vyborg district (at the start of April, and probably even before, the workers here demanded the transfer of power to the soviets) it was resolved:

> Taking into account the seriousness of the current situation, we consider it necessary to carry on work at full capacity. No negligence or excessive wage demands. At the same time, we must say that socio-economic problems, for example, shortages of raw materials, are a serious brake on production.[36]

Many similar resolutions were adopted at this time. At the end of March, the workers' committee of the state-owned Patronnyi Factory drew up a report on the factory's operations since the revolution for the soldiers of the 25th Infantry Regiment. Output was down by 2.5 percent but, the committee explained, that was temporary and inevitable, given the revolutionary situation. It continued:

35 Smirnov 1925, pp. 24–6.

36 *Izvestiya* (24 Mar 1917).

> The workers of the Petrograd Patronnyi Factory, as genuine patriots of their fatherland, which is living through a difficult war, and who also cherish the freedom that has been won, having frequently discussed the question of production at their general assemblies and in order to refute the false rumours being spread by unknown persons with provocative aims, have mandated the provisional executive committee [of the factory's workers] to declare that, the workers, having adopted the eight-hour day as the basis, are conscious of the approaching danger and will nevertheless strive by all means to support their brethren-soldiers at the front who, together with the workers, have won freedom in Russia, freedom which the workers protect with all their might, [and they will] work unswervingly – if necessary, more than eight hours – up to twelve hours, and more. But workers cannot by any means assume responsibility for stoppages due to lack of fuel, metals or other materials or for other reasons that do not depend on them. Dark slander against the workers emanates from henchmen of the old regime who seek to undermine the unity of workers and soldiers, to destroy the freedom we have won with our blood.[37]

Soon workers became more specific about the nature of the 'dark forces spreading false rumours'. 'Comrade soldiers!' began the declaration of workers' committee of the Aivaz Machine-building Factory

> We, workers, have been hearing rumours that someone is spreading slander to the effect that the workers are allegedly concerned at present only with increasing their wages and that they are neglecting the production of artillery shells, that they are striking.
>
> We remained silent as long as we thought these were merely idle people wagging their tongues. But now we see that landowners, afraid for their land, and [capitalists] protecting their profits, want to sow discord among us; they want to weaken the alliance of soldiers and workers, who shoulder to shoulder overthrew the autocracy and placed Russia on the democratic path of life.
>
> Comrades. The enemies of democracy are spreading discord among us, since they fear the combined strength of the workers and soldiers in the form of the Soviet of workers' and soldiers' deputies. You, who have left our ranks, the lathe and the hammer, for the barracks, and you, all

37 TsGA SPb, f. 4602, op. 1, d. 3, ll. 83–4.

> the conscious soldiers, declare to all those slanderers that the conscious workers are applying all their energy so that work on defence proceeds at full steam. We, workers, know of no factory in Petrograd that is presently on strike.[38]

In the long run, despite some initial success, the press campaign backfired against its initiators, as it served to bind workers and soldiers more closely in opposition to the propertied classes. *Izvestiya*, the organ of the Petrograd Soviet, commented on the 'campaign of the bourgeois press' in its editorial of 11 April: 'You are trying to frighten us with the spectre of civil war. But it is you who have initiated it'.[39] It was not yet civil war but it was the end of the Revolution's 'honeymoon period', soon to be definitively buried by publication of the note of the Minister of Foreign Affairs, Milyukov, assuring the Allies of Russia's support for the war.

The press campaign also had the effect of arousing suspicions among workers of possible malicious intent on the part of management when problems arose in the factories that held up production.

This episode revealed a considerable degree of political sophistication among workers, who were able to appreciate the larger political issues beyond their immediate economic interests. And despite the disruption to production caused by the February Days and the continuing supply problems, productivity in many factories did, in fact, increase in the weeks following the February Revolution. N.N. Kutler, a member of the Kadet Party's Central Committee and a leading industrialist, observed a certain 'enthusiasm for work' in the weeks following the revolution.[40] A conference of representatives of workers and management of the factories of the Artillery Authority reported in early April that productivity was rising where supply problems were under control. At the Patronnyi Factory, whose administrative personnel had fled during the February Days, production had fallen only two percent. At the Okhta Powder Factory, production was at 900 puds and defective output at 15 percent, as compared to the pre-revolutionary output norm of 800 puds and 30 percent defective output. At the Orudiinnyi Factory, output was up by 28 percent; at Opticheskii – 11 percent; at Trubochnyi it was normal; and the Sestroretsk Arms Factory was producing 600 rifles per day as compared to 450 before the Revolution. On their part, the worker delegates to this conference harshly criticised the incompet-

38 *Pravda* (29 Mar 1917).
39 *Izvestiya* (11 Apr 1917).
40 Volobuev 1964, p. 157.

ence of the administration of the Artillery Authority and demanded its abolition.[41] At the end of March, the Petrograd Committee of Intermediate and Small Industry reported that 'in many small enterprises of Petrograd labour productivity has not only not declined but has even risen, despite the introduction of the eight-hour workday'.[42] And in mid-April, the director of the Schlusselburg Powder Factory reported to the Ministry of Trade and Industry that, although the first week had been difficult, production was proceeding more or less satisfactorily. 'The workers show a completely conscious understanding of the current conjuncture' and were cooperating energetically to increase production.[43] The Mensheviks' *Rabochaya gazeta* reported the results of investigations by soldiers' delegations from the front that met with both workers and management: in some places productivity had risen since the Revolution; in others it had declined, but the latter was a consequence of the lack of fuel and materials and not the fault of the workers.[44]

Worker-Management Relations: 'Democratisation of Factory Life'

The workers' conception of the democratic revolution also included an end to 'factory autocracy' or, as they sometimes expressed it, the 'democratisation of factory life'. In part, this meant elimination of those elements of the Tsarist regime that had penetrated the factories, since the relations between factory managements and the state authorities had been a symbiotic one in which managers served as police informers and the police and army violently suppressed economic strikes. This relationship became especially intimate during the war, when protesting workers risked immediate loss of military deferment, jail or exile. Police and troops were stationed on a permanent basis at or near many large factories.

This situation was underlined in the report of an inquiry into the strike movement conducted by the left fractions of the State Duma in the summer of 1916:

> A strike usually ends in a lockout, and this lockout occurs with the closest participation and closest support of both civil and military authorities … Just as soon as the factory closes, the military authorities immediately

41 TsGA SPb, f. 4601, op. 1, d. 10, 1. 33.

42 Volobuev 1964, p. 157.

43 Dok. Apr., p. 468.

44 *Rabochaya gazeta* (7 and 16 Apr 1917).

> begin to take workers into the army. For example, at the Putilov Factory several hundred youths were sent to disciplinary battalions ... Because of the shortage of workers, soldiers are being sent [to work in this factory], and they often lack skills ...

At the Baltiiskii, Obukhovskii and other factories there are increasingly frequent cases in which workers who are past military age, often 42–5 years old, are sent to the military-naval barracks, where they are locked up for various periods and put on bread and water.

> These interventions on the part of military authorities in support of the entrepreneurs, which characterise the workers' economic movement during the war, have by no means weakened the old, traditional method of regulation of conflicts between labour and capital, in which our civil authorities have been involved for a very long time.
>
> All the conflicts of late have been accompanied by incessant repressions. Searches and arrests have not ceased for a single day. Workers are afraid to elect representatives for fear of losing their best people ...
>
> Sensing the weight of the civil and military authorities behind them, the entrepreneurs have been conducting an exclusively insolent and provocative policy towards the workers with particular confidence and calm ... During the war, the entrepreneurs are using 'military methods' to enslave the workers. The strongest weapon is to deprive workers who are subject to military service of the right to move freely from one enterprise to another ... The threat of the front – the last word in entrepreneurial tactics – is a threat they carry out in the end willingly, transforming the front into a place of exile and forced labour.[45]

In the workers' view, the democratic revolution was to sweep away the despotic absolutism of the Russian factory system. In 1912, the Petrograd Society of Factory and Mill Owners had adopted a Convention that, among other things, prohibited toleration of workers' collective representation in the factories.[46] During the war, this rule was enforced even more strictly. Now that the revolution had made the workers free citizens, the political equals of the administrators, workers wanted to be treated as such at work. This did not involve incursion into the administration's prerogatives in managing the technical and financial

45 Fleer 1925, pp. 298–304.

46 Kruze 1961, p. 99.

sides of the enterprises. But workers wanted a voice in the conditions under which they worked. (As shortly will be seen, workers in state-owned enterprises initially saw a much greater role for themselves but soon retreated from that position.)

At the same time, the revolution gave rise among workers to a sense of responsibility for production. Although this found strongest expression in state-owned factories, it was not entirely absent in private enterprises. It reflected, in part, workers' new-found sense of citizenship, but even more their concern for the revolution in the face of the external military threat and their latent doubts as to management's good faith, doubts that were intensified by the press campaign against 'worker egoism'.

Purge of the Factory Administrations

Upon returning to their factories after the February Days, workers set at once to ridding them of administrators who had been particularly oppressive. At the first general assembly of the workers of the ordnance department of the state-owned Patronnyi Factory, it was unanimously decided 'to filter management from foreman to general'.[47] At times this purge assumed a dramatic character: the meeting would discuss the merits and faults of various administrators and then vote on their fate. If the vote went against the individual, workers might toss a sack over his head and ride him out through the gates in a wheelbarrow. This action, frowned upon by 'conscious' workers, was a mark of special disgrace. At the Putilov Factory, 40 managers were removed in the course of three days, many of them in wheelbarrows.[48]

Women workers in the textile mills were often more magnanimous toward their former oppressors. In a typical scene from early March, the assembled workers of the Thornton Mill called out the foremen, one after the other, demanding them to give an account of their past behaviour. They would shout: 'Foreman of such-and-such department onto the table!' And the individual was pushed forward. Sweating profusely, he would desperately try to justify himself, arguing that he had merely been transmitting pressure from above. After he promised to change his ways, the meeting decided he could remain. This ordeal was particularly stressful for the British foremen, whose mastery of Russian was too rudimentary for them fully to understand what was happening. As

47 TsGA SPb, f. 4602, op. 7, d. 7, l.68.

48 Mitel'man et al. 1961, p. 567. See also Sergeev 1967, p. 374.

for the 30 policemen that were on the factory's payroll and the members of the administration whose counterrevolutionary views were well-known to the workers, they were escorted to the local militia (the new police), although some of the workers had wanted to deal them a good thrashing.[49]

In the factories with more skilled workforces, the workers were generally better organised and the process took on a more orderly character. In the larger enterprises, meetings were held in individual shops. They compiled lists of undesirable administrators, which were then transmitted to the factory committee for its approval.[50] This purge of the administrations was not an anarchist-inspired revolt against authority as such, as it has sometimes been portrayed in the literature. Workers made a genuine effort to weigh the evidence. For example, in the pattern shop of the Baltiiskii Factory, a meeting on 9 March voted 56 against 23 (with three abstentions) to dismiss the manager Sadov. But another meeting two days later allowed Sadov to make his case, after which he was reinstated by a vote of 46 against 12 (7 abstentions).[51] On the other hand, once workers felt they had weighed all the evidence, they refused to take back administrators they had purged, even when arbitration chambers decided that they should.[52]

The reasons given for dismissing administrators shed light on the workers' conception of the changes that the democratic revolution should introduce into factory life. The general assembly of the submarine department of the Baltiiskii Factory discussed the case of foreman Stesyura and his activity under the old regime:

> 1. The first question raised was political, and no basis was found to fault him.
>
> 2. Secondly, the question was posed: Did he exploit labour? It, too, was examined by the general assembly and the result was the following: he liked to push the work, but he paid more for work than other administrators ...
>
> 3. The third question was whether he is fit for his job. We examined that question from the time the ship 'Bars' was being built and found that there were no major misunderstandings or damage to work on his part.

49 Perazich 1927, p. 20.

50 See Sergeev 1967, p. 374; and Mikhailov 1932, p. 189.

51 TsGIA SPb, f. 416, op. 25, d. 5, ll. 2–3.

52 See, for example, Sergeev 1967; and TsGA SPb, f. 4601, op. 1, d. 10, l. 33.

> And so we found that on the three main questions there were no major disagreements and also on the smaller questions he was found not guilty …[53]

The clearest grounds for a decision to purge administrators were political. The workers of the boiler-making shop of the same factory explained their decision to dismiss its supervisor:

> We find that he fulfilled more the functions of a purely police administrator than those of a foreman or shop manager, striving to turn the above-named shop into a house of silence or a disciplinary department, where with aching hearts one would hear his answers: 'I'll send you off to the front! I'll use martial authority!' He sent away … [four names of workers] and others. From the above, one can see his devotion to the old reactionary regime. We add to this the fact that his removal has caused no harm to the shop.[54]

Another issue considered was 'exploitation'. This was broader than the level of payment for work, an area in which foremen had enjoyed broad arbitrary power.[55] 'Exploitation' could include any manner of mistreatment, but in particular affronts to workers' dignity. Often mentioned were 'coarse (impolite) relations', foul language, arbitrary and oppressive fining, assignment of workers to particularly hard jobs as a punishment, the playing of favourites, and the like.[56] 'Exploitation' had thus an important moral dimension, beyond the economic. According to his accusers at the Baltiiskii Factory, the foreman Morozov was of a 'primitive, unfeeling nature that was used to having its own way, refusing to consider anything else … He often resorted to insults, trampling upon a person's dignity. He inflicted abuse worthy of the gutter … Down with this painful burden of our oppression!'[57]

Workers often had long memories. A meeting of the paint shop of the Baltiiskii Factory gave the following reasons for dismissal of foreman Volkov:

> This is the chief culprit of the oppression and humiliation that we experienced over the last years … Let us recall the first days of his rule. Of

53 TsGIA SPb, f. 416, op. 25, d. 5, l. 12.
54 Ibid., l. 19.
55 Shlyapnikov 1923, vol. 1, p. 11.
56 See Sergeev 1967, p. 379; and Rab. Kon., p. 45.
57 TsGIA SPb f. 416, op. 5, d. 30, ll. 67–8.

course, not many of us experienced them. But the voices of our comrades that he humiliated call out to us and beg for revenge. Comrades! From the very first days of his rule, when he put on his idiot's mittens of violence, he displayed his base soul. In 1909, many of our comrades suffered in their self-respect and because of his contrivances were thrown out of the factory in the most shameless manner … From that year began the era of our oppression. He forgot 1905 … From 1909, he began his disgraceful programme of reducing rates to an impossible 8–9 kopeks without any consideration for the work conditions … We all experienced that until the final days of his arbitrary rule …[58]

But accusations were rarely of a single nature. The following resolution includes accusations that were political, economic and moral:

> We, the workers of the riveting shop have unanimously resolved at our general assembly that each member of the administration who has received an order from us to immediately leave the plant is removed by us, so that he, because of his past criminal activity and in the future, will not be able to enter the factory, and therefore we ask to pay special to these people, since while they stood at the head of the shop they were mainstays of the autocracy. They were exclusively occupied with the oppression of our comrades. In the pre-revolutionary period, they decided the 'fate' of workers. Many of our comrades were handed over to be judged by higher authorities for a conversation about the freedom that has just now triumphed; and these authorities immediately dismissed them and contacted the Military Commander to have them shipped off to the front. Besides that, his coarse language, our miserably paid work, thanks to them, [all these] in our common opinion are weighty accusations against them and they arouse in us, not charity towards them, but a feeling of extreme contempt. On the basis of what we have presented, we ask the Executive [workers'] Committee of the Baltiiskii Factory to immediately dismiss them. For there is no room here for condescension.[59]

The accusation of incompetence was also sometimes made. But as a rule it did not stand alone but was added to bolster political and economic arguments. A resolution from this factory began with the observation that department

58 Ibid., f. 416, op. 5, d. 30, 1.64.

59 Ibid., f. 416, op. 25, d. 5, 1.6.

supervisor Lyashchenko was a 'man whose technical qualifications for his job were weak. In all, we would spend a mere two or three hours a day in the shop and sometimes would not appear at all'. But his main crime was 'unlimited exploitation' and 'cruel treatment' of workers. Before the war, he would answer any requests from workers with the threat of jail. During the war, he threatened them with the front. Besides that, he 'managed a network of spies among the workers and made sure that there should be no organization except monarchist among his subordinates'.[60] In similar fashion, the general assembly of workers of the First Electric Station decided to remove the board of directors as 'appointees of the old government, and in recognition of their harmfulness from an economic point of view and uselessness from a technical one'.[61]

The Factory Committees

If the purge of administrations was the negative side of democratisation of the factories, the positive side found its expression in the workers' demand for a role in setting and enforcing internal work rules (*vnutrennii rasporyadok*). The vehicle for this was their elected factory committees.

The workers' demand for elected representatives in the factories had a long history, and, despite the 1912 convention of the Petrograd Society of Factory and Mill owners that prohibited permanent worker representation, several large factories, in fact, had tolerated semi-official 'elders' councils' before the revolution.[62] The 10 March agreement that provided for elected factory committees assigned them the following functions: (1) representation of workers in dealings with government and public institutions; (2) voicing of workers' opinions on issues of public and economic life; (3) resolution of issues regarding relations among workers themselves; and (4) representation of workers in dealings with management and owners on matters pertaining to their mutual relations.[63]

Where the workers' practice overstepped the bounds of the agreement was on the third point, which was in any case quite vague. Everywhere workers demanded control over internal work rules, a demand that had been made

60 Ibid., f. 416, op. 25, d. 5, l. 155.

61 Rab. Kon., p. 42.

62 Shlyapnikov 1923, vol. 1, p. 167.

63 *Izvestiya* (11 Mar 1917). One should note the political functions assigned to the factory committees in the second point. The committees regularly organised meetings on political issues. They also organised a workers' militia and led workers in political actions.

in the years before the February Revolution and which was a key element of workers' conception of the new democratic order, as it pertained to the factories. This was not, for the most part, a claim to the right unilaterally to establish norms, but rather to the right to negotiate them and to oversee their application. In the words of the Menshevik Maevskii, it meant 'the establishment of a constitutional regime' in the workplace.[64]

On 13 March, the provisional factory committee of the Radiotelegraph Factory affirmed

> the need to create a permanent factory committee that will be responsible for (*vedat'*) the internal life of the factory ... What should that committee decide? To that aim the committee adopted thirteen paragraphs, which, after reporting to the general assembly of the Radiotelegraph Factory, it undertook to elaborate:
>
> (1) The length of the workday
> (2) The minimum worker's wage
> (3) The payment for labour
> (4) Immediate organisation of medical aid
> (5) On labour insurance
> (6) On the establishment of a mutual aid fund
> (7) On hiring and firing
> (8) The investigation of various conflicts
> (9) Labour discipline
> (10) On rest time
> (11) On the factory's security
> (12) On food
> (13) The rights, duties, election and existence of a permanent factory committee.[65]

At the Phoenix Machine-building Factory, the committee's areas of concern were to include the following: security of the plant, regulation of wages, norms, and the determination of rates, resolution of labour conflicts, food supply, healthcare, and cultural and educational work.[66] A meeting of representatives of 8,000 workers of eight tobacco factories drew up the following list

64 Maevskii 1918, p. 34.
65 ЦГАСПб, f. 4605, op. 1. 15; see also Dok. Feb., pp. 491–2.
66 Borisov and Vasil'ev 1962, p. 80.

of demands which, taken together, constitute a comprehensive statement of the workers' idea of the new order in the factories. Besides purely monetary demands, they called to

(2) abolish overtime and authorise it on an individual case basis on permission of the central organ
(3) destroy the black book of the entrepreneurs
(5) oblige the administration to use polite address in addressing workers
(7) oblige the administration to deal with the workers through the latter's representatives
(8) remove elements from the factory that the workers consider undesirable
(9) hire and dismiss workers only with the agreement of the workers' committee
(10) abolish searches and transfer responsibility to protect the integrity of material to the workers themselves and to their representatives
(12) abolish fines; the choice of means of influence should belong to the factory committee
(20) elect elders at work by the workers themselves.[67]

The factory committees were thus meant to correct the worst pre-revolutionary abuses of managerial power, including arbitrary dismissals, the hiring of 'foreign elements' seeking to evade military service, the playing of favourites, arbitrary assignment of workers to skill categories, arbitrary payment for work, arbitrary and despotic use of fines, and others. But they assumed functions that also went beyond the correction of abuses. Taken together, these constituted what workers termed 'control over the internal life' of the factories. This, they felt, was their right as free citizens. And although it clearly went beyond what private employers were prepared willingly to accept, workers in private factories, and soon also in state-owned enterprises, did not want to participate in managing the technical and financial sides of the enterprises, which they considered management's exclusive spheres of competence.

But although the demand for 'workers' control' of management was not raised in private factories, there were already signs of what might lay ahead. In March, the Minister of Trade and Industry reported that workers in the capital 'suspect the administration of holding up production of goods destined

67 *Izvestiya* (Mar. 11, 1917).

for defence'.[68] These suspicions were rooted in doubts about the owners' good faith. After all, until very recently they had closely collaborated with the Tsarist police. Nor had workers forgotten the industrialists' fondness for lockouts. In only the six months preceding the outbreak of war, the owners in the capital, in concert with the administrations of state-owned factories, had organised no less than three general lockouts, firing in the process a total of 300,000 workers.[69] These lockouts were responses to strikes for economic and political demands. Workers with longer memories could also recall the general lockouts of November and December 1905 in St. Petersburg that had dealt a major blow to the revolution.[70] In the weeks following the February Revolution, the owners were, of course, in no position to make use of such tactics. But the campaign in the 'bourgeois' press against workers' alleged laziness and egoism made the latter wonder if the problems in the factories that were holding up production were really due to objective causes, as management claimed, rather than to sabotage, possibly with the aim of conducting a 'hidden lockout'.

A meeting on 22 March of representatives of workers of the Moscow District of Petrograd that discussed the bourgeois press campaign made the following proposal to the capital's workers:

> To convene district meetings to clarify the reasons for the industrial breakdown (*razrukha*) in their various districts, and then to convene a city-wide meeting of representatives of all the districts to clarify and publish the true causes of the industrial breakdown and to expose those who are holding back the fixing of this breakdown.[71]

The assembly did not apparently feel the need to specify who the suspects might be.

Similar suspicions were voiced at the 20 March session of the Petrograd Soviet. The delegate from the Metallicheskii Factory stated:

> We are getting reports to the effect that, although there is work in certain shops, this work is not being set in motion for unknown reasons. We are told that its turn has not yet come, and the shops are idle. We had a meeting of elders at our factory which decided to elect a commission

---

68 Sobol'ev 1973, p. 82.

69 Kruze 1961, p. 328; Balabanov 1927b, p. 31. Most were obviously rehired eventually, after undergoing 'filtration'.

70 Shuster 1976.

71 *Pravda* (8 Apr 1917).

> of three people to investigate if there are not abuses on the part of management in favour of the old regime and of the Germans, and if it turns out that the work can begin, then immediately to demand that the administration begin it. Perhaps the administration will not want to listen; so it is desirable that this originate from the Soviet Workers' and Soldiers' Deputies in order that such a commission be immediately formed from [representatives of] the factories of all of Petrograd, just as previously there was one of the Central War-Industry Committee. True, that commission was bourgeois, and only a small group from the workers participated in it. But it is now desirable that such a commission be created with a view to control and that it conduct an inspection of all factories in order to make sure there are no abuses on the part of the administration in holding up work. Are the declarations of management that they do not have metal, coal and oil correct?[72]

Here, in effect, was already a call for workers' control, in the sense of oversight, monitoring of management. But it was a call for control by the Petrograd Soviet, since the workers did not feel that they could obtain access to the necessary information if they acted in an atomised fashion in the separate factories.

But it is also important to understand what was not being proposed. The motive behind this proposal was practical, not in any sense 'ideological': it reflected the workers' desire to ensure the functioning of the factories so that the latter could continue to produce their goods and to provide employment. It did not arise from an abstract conception of 'industrial democracy'. Workers considered the revolution bourgeois-democratic, not socialist. They were not demanding participation in management, let alone responsibility for it, but rather access to information to allow them to verify the good faith, and perhaps also the competence, of management.

At the same meeting of the Soviet, another delegate recounted how the workers of his factory had returned after the February Days to find that they could not resume work because materials were lacking. They searched the factory but found nothing. A few days later, however, the administration discovered a small amount of tin in one of the factory's shops, and that allowed production to resume. He commented:

> But they could have done that two days earlier, that is, we could have worked three days. But instead of going to the trouble, either out of care-

72 TsGA SPb, f. 1000, op. 73, d. 16, 1.6.

> lessness or maybe with the intention of holding up production, they didn't inquire in the respirator department ... This general shortage is their fault, since they don't want to bother about [supply] in good time. In view of this, I would ask that they be obliged to conduct matters properly.[73]

This worker was asking for management to be obliged to do its job. He was not suggesting that the workers do it.

Nevertheless, as early as the beginning of April, isolated incidents occurred during which factory committees intervened directly into the running of factories, moving beyond their role in setting and monitoring the application of internal work rules. These incidents involved mainly the shipment of goods and materials. At the Kebke Canvas Factory, after the workers' committee presented a report to the general assembly about a production stoppage, the workers decided to ask the Petrograd Soviet to investigate. Production was being held up despite earlier assurances from management that the factory had orders to produce goods worth ten million rubles and at least a year's supply of materials. When the administration was asked about this now, it was evasive. In the meanwhile, the workers learned that canvas was being hastily packed and that loaders were being paid a special bonus to do that work. When asked for an explanation, the administration would answer only that it was a matter of military security. And when the trucks arrived for the goods, instead of loading the canvases that had already been packed, others were taken right off the looms.

The factory committee then issued an order to stop loading and it detached the factory's telephone line.[74] On 7 April, several days after these events, at a meeting of the Petrograd Society of Factory and Mills Owners, a representative of the factory stated that management had documents from the military about the shipment of the canvasses. But he did not explain why the director had refused to show them to the factory committee. Others remarked about similar incidents that had occurred in other factories, including at the United Cable Factories and the Paramanov Leather Factory.[75]

Nevertheless, cases of direct intervention beyond the area of internal work rules were very rare at this time. There was no general demand for workers' control. Nor did the Bolsheviks, who later became its champions, propose it. Nevertheless, it was already evident how it might arise given the appropriate conditions.

---

73 Ibid., l. 30.

74 Rab. Kon., p. 57.

75 Ibid., pp. 58 and 53.

Such, at least, was the situation in private enterprises. In state-owned factories, on the other hand, workers initially did consider that they should participate in management well beyond the sphere of internal work rules. That did not last long, however, and after a few weeks, the committees limited their claims to the right of oversight, in the sense of access to information, explicitly rejecting responsibility for managing production.

Events at the Patronnyi Factory were typical. The following is from the report of the factory committee prepared for the 265th Infantry Regiment in the context of the bourgeois press campaign:

> Upon receiving the order of the Soviet of Workers' and Soldiers' deputies to resume work from 7 March, the workers met on the morning of 6 March in their general assembly and, in view of the fact that no one from the higher ranks was present at the factory, although they could not help but know of the Soviet's call to resume work at the factory, as it was published in all the papers, the workers at their general assembly decided to start work independently from 8 March of this year.
>
> At the general assembly of 7 March, after preliminary discussion of the matter in the separate shops, it was decided not to take back the majority of the ranks [officer-managers], but to begin work on the morning of 8 March.
>
> To deal with current, and at times very complex and responsible matters relating to the factory, a provisional executive committee was elected from representatives of the shops, who until then had been responsible for the application of internal work rules ... After concluding an agreement with General Orlov, the representative of the Main Artillery Authority, concerning the election of a factory administration and upon the arrival of Major-General Doronin, who had been elected by the workers as director of the factory, the last friction was eliminated ... The provisional executive committee of the Petrograd Patronnyi Factory, having fulfilled the task conferred upon it as best it could, is now reorganising itself on a new basis, having transferred all executive authority to the administration of the factory in the person of the director, Maj.-General Doronin, elected by the workers, and it retains the functions of an observing and consultative organ ...[76]

76 TsGA SPb, f. 4602, op. 1, d. 3, ll. 83–84. For the provisional constitution of this factory committee, see Dok. Apr., 358–60.

The takeover of management is presented here as a matter of necessity, although the refusal to allow back the old administrators was asserted as a right. It should be kept in mind, however, that those administrators were army officers and so literally servants of the old regime. And, in this state-owned factory at least, the workers elected the new director.

The director at the state-owned Okhta Powder Factory reported that in the first days after the revolution the workers there felt that they 'must and can manage all the affairs of the factory'.[77] The factory committee, for its part, reported that

> in view of the novelty of the work of the factory committee, it lacked a clear orientation, since the direct functions of the factory committee had not been spelled out. For example, it not only took upon itself control [monitoring of management] but also the responsibilities of management. Similar things happened, of course, in other enterprises, too.

However, a conference of the factories of the Artillery Authority held in early April adopted 'Guidelines for Factory Committees' that limited their sphere of competence to internal work rules and control (monitoring).[78]

The protocols of the general assembly of the Admiralty Shipbuilding Factory shed some light on the reasons for this retreat from responsibility for management. Here it was originally decided that the workers' committee should exercise 'control'. But this 'control' was interpreted so broadly as to effectively include its direct participation in management. For example, the factory committee's 'technical commission' was assigned responsibility for examining the need to improve equipment and make repairs, for establishing conditions for receiving and placing production orders, for deciding matters relating to the size of the administrative staff, and so forth. Its 'control-finance commission' was put in charge of the movement of orders from the moment an offer was made, as well as the transfer of orders to other factories, the receipt and pay-out of funds, and so forth. On 15 March, it was given additional responsibility for the purchase of metal, instruments, and other materials.[79] But less than two weeks later, the factory committee decided to limit its activity to control (monitoring), retaining the right to demand the removal of administrative staff through arbitration. And on 7 April, a general assembly of workers further decided that the

77 Cited in Sobolev 1973, p. 66.
78 Rab. kon. i nats. pp. 178–9.
79 TsGA SPb, f. 9391, op. 7, d. 8, ll. 7 and 12.

election of administrative personnel by the workers was not desirable.[80] At a general assembly on 27 April, the chairman of the factory committee explained the situation to the workers. He began with the difficulties that the factory committee had encountered:

> In the confused conditions that existed when the committee was formed and in view of the difficulty of adapting this institution to both management and control, the committee found itself in a contradictory situation. For in issuing orders to the corresponding organ of administration, it would limit itself in the area of broad control, inhibiting both the initiative of the factory's director and undermining the efficiency and orderliness of execution. Practice and common sense told us we had to transfer the functions of management to the factory's director and, in that way, to unite the entire personnel into a single, integrated organisation. The committee retains the full right of control [access to information] of all the actions of the director of the factory and of individuals and institutions of the factory administration through the conciliation board, including the right to initiative in reorganising and dismissal of personnel.[81]

Workers in state-owned factories initially felt they should assume responsibility for management. This seems to have stemmed from their conception of the democratic revolution as it pertained to state-owned enterprises, which now belonged to the people. Such views were definitely widespread among railroad personnel. An early history of their union observed that, since the workers considered February a popular revolution, they could not imagine it without their close and active participation, and in particular in the area of management: 'Seventy percent of the railroads belonged to the Tsar. He was overthrown. The railroads naturally now belong to the people. They should be entrusted to the workers, as part of the people. Such ideas of primitive democracy were widespread among the railway personnel'.[82] Similar syndicalist attitudes were common also among employees of the Ministry of Posts and Telegraph.[83]

But in state-owned industrial enterprises workers soon reached the conclusion that they did not want, at least at the present stage, to assume responsibility for management, not least because they lacked the necessary skills and

80 Ibid., f. 9391, op. 7, d. 8, l. 30.

81 Ibid., f. 9391, op. 1, d. 11, l.4.

82 Tanyaev 1925, p. 53.

83 Bazilevich 1927, p. 40.

expertise. Worker management, they decided, had to await the advent of socialism, which lay somewhere in the undefined future. Moreover, in conditions of economic dislocation caused by the war, the factory committees realised that there was a very good chance they would fail at the task of running the factories and be discredited in the eyes of the workers. The Guidelines for the Activity of Factory Committees adopted by the Conference of State Enterprises of Petrograd on 15 April were quite clear: 'Not wishing to assume responsibility for the technical and administrative organisation of production in existing conditions until the full socialisation of the economy, the representatives of the main factory committee participate in administration with the rights of only a consultative voice'.[84]

Despite this retreat, workers of state-owned enterprises did adopt a more radical position than workers in private industry. From the start, they asserted the right to control, in the sense of oversight, a claim that was made as a right and was not a response to a perceived threat to production (although in many cases the top administrative personnel had abandoned the factories when the revolution broke out). In private enterprises, as already noted, the right to control was very rarely asserted at this time. And that happened only where workers perceived a direct threat to the enterprise's operation.

As for the owners, in their hearts they had not abandoned the position of their 1912 convention, article 7 of which rejected permanent worker representation in the workplace and any interference in managerial prerogatives. That article also specified that 'in particular, no interference is to be tolerated in matters of hiring and dismissal of workers, in the setting of wages and conditions of employment, and in the elaboration of internal regulations'.[85] These were precisely the areas in which the factory committees were now claiming rights.

Of course, in the absence of support of the Tsar's repressive apparatus, the owners now had to show more flexibility. The more enlightened among them went so far as to argue that, given the revolutionary situation, it was in their interest to deal with organised workers, since Western experience showed that organisation and recognition acted as restraining factors on workers' radicalism. In this spirit, the managing director of the Nev'yansk Mining Factories wrote from Petrograd on 9 March to his manager:

> I consider it superfluous to linger on these [events of the February Revolution]. I will only point out that the first act of this Russian revolution,

84 Dok. Apr., pp. 383–5.

85 Balabanov 1927b, p. 38.

> unprecedented in the history of peoples, bore a purely political character. On this platform, full unanimity and unity was possible of all strata and masses of the Russian people, who toppled to dust with such dizzying speed the disgraceful old government. But now the second act is opening – and in that act a socialist platform is being put forward. Of course, there can be no question of that platform. There is no doubt that under the influence of socialist ideas and propaganda many excesses are occurring in the factories, directed chiefly at participation of the worker masses in the management of affairs.
>
> At the [state-owned] Izhorskii Factory such an excess has already occurred – a soviet of workers consisting of 50 people was elected, including six engineers, to manage the factory. Having removed the factory's director, Admiral Voskresenskii, it began to manage the factory. The soviet held out for several days, but now the factory has returned to its normal management.
>
> In this regard, today at a closed meeting of the Council of Congresses of Mining Industrialists of the Urals, opinions were exchanged. The conclusion was reached to go to meet any wishes of the workers in the sense of their organisation (the election of elders, arbitration boards, and the like), but under no conditions to tolerate intervention in management of the factory, and that this position must be firmly and stubbornly defended.[86]

The industrialists were at least as wary of the workers' intentions as the workers were of theirs. In fact, none of the socialist parties with any influence among workers was proposing socialism, even as a mid-term goal, let alone as an immediate perspective. (Lenin's position on the nature of the coming revolution in Russia, which had evolved during the war, was apparently not widely known within the country. In any case, it does not appear to have influenced party policy before his return in April 1917.) Nor is there evidence that ordinary workers considered socialism as a proximate goal of the revolution.

But while the above letter might appear quite liberal when compared with the 1912 convention, it is clear that the workers' conception of 'internal work rules' (*vnutrennii rasporyadok*), which they claimed the right to supervise (*vedat'*) through their elected factory committees, went considerably beyond anything the employers, even under the impact of the revolution, were really prepared to tolerate. This, in itself, bore the seeds of a spiral of reaction and

86 Dok. Feb., pp. 479–80.

counter-reaction. But the potential for such conflict was greatly enhanced by workers' doubts, which often enough turned out to have a real basis, about management's good faith whenever threats arose to continued production. It was the workers' desire to verify the reasons given by management for these problems that was at the origins of the movement for workers' control that arose in the following weeks. The owners, for their part, tended to see in this movement a confirmation of their worst fears of the workers' socialist intentions.

CHAPTER 5

From the April to the July Days

On 18 April, Russian workers celebrated May Day for the first time in conditions of broad political freedom. Even Lenin, who was calling for the soviets to take power, described Russia as the freest of all the countries then at war. It was early spring in Petrograd, and it was the spring of the revolution. The atmosphere surrounding the demonstrations was one of enthusiasm and hope. In Russia's capital, May Day 1917 was celebrated not only as a workers' holiday but as a national holiday of the revolution. The number of demonstrators exceeded even the turnout on 23 March for the funeral of the fallen in the February Revolution.

'In general', recalled Sukhanov, 'the entire city, from large to small, if not at some meeting, was out in the streets'.[1] The Menshevik Internationalist newspaper *Novaya zhizn'* remarked on how different Petrograd's May Day was from those celebrated abroad, which were demonstrations of the proletariat against the bourgeoisie: 'The [Russian] proletariat can say with legitimate pride that on that day the whole of democracy of the country was to a greater or lesser extent an active participant in its proletarian socialist holiday'.[2]

Of course, by that time the strong sense of national unity that had characterised the first days after the Revolution no longer existed. The campaign against the workers' alleged egotism had driven a wedge of bad feeling between the workers and census society. But all the same, workers could feel that much had been achieved and that the alliance with census society was generally holding up. Few suspected that May Day would be the last public event characterised by a sense of national unity. For on that very day, events were being set in motion that would bring down definitively the curtain on the 'honeymoon period' of the revolution.

The April Days

The workers' 'revolutionary defencism' during this period was premised upon the assumption that the Provisional Government, prodded by the Soviet, would

1 Sukhanov 1919–23, vol. III, p. 244.

2 *Novaya zhizn'* (20 Apr 1917).

adopt an active foreign policy aimed at securing a rapid, democratic peace. And in the meanwhile, the government's military policy would be purely defensive. (A de facto cease-fire reigned on the Eastern front.) Yet almost at once, the workers were given grave cause for concern. On 7 March, the government newspaper wrote:

> The government believes that the spirit of lofty patriotism that the people has shown in its struggle with the old regime will also give a boost to our valiant soldiers on the battlefield. The government, on its part, will do all in its power to provide our army with everything necessary for pursuing the war to a victorious conclusion. The government will religiously respect and consistently fulfil the treaties concluded with its allies.[3]

A few days later, P.N. Milyukov, the Minister of Foreign Affairs and leader of the Kadet party, told an interviewer that what Russia needed was a 'decisive victory'.[4]

Workers, however, were of quite a different opinion, which was clearly reflected in the resolution of a general assembly of workers of the Dinamo Factory, adopted a few days after the Revolution:

> The people and the army went into the street not to replace one government by another but to realise our slogans. And these slogans are: 'Freedom', 'Equality', 'Land and Liberty' and 'an end to the bloody war'. The bloody slaughter is not needed by us, the classes without property.[5]

Although workers enthusiastically welcomed the Soviet's 14 March appeal 'To the Peoples of the Entire World' to combat the annexationist policies of their governments, they were unsettled by statements on the war made by the Provisional Government and by articles on that topic in the bourgeois (non-socialist) press. On 19 March, a general assembly at the Pechatkin Paper Factory, after hearing reports from its workers' committee and from representatives of the Menshevik party, unanimously adopted the following resolution:

> We, workers of the Pechatkin Mill, salute the Soviet of Workers' and Soldiers' Deputies for its internationalist position in relation to the war.

3 *Vestnik Vremennogo pravitel'stva* (7 Mar 1917).

4 *Rabochaya gazeta* (14 Mar 1917).

5 Dok. Feb., p. 465.

> But we consider it totally insufficient on the part of the Soviet of Workers' and Soldiers' Deputies to limit its efforts for peace to publishing manifestos. To end the war quickly, it is necessary immediately to put pressure on the Provisional Government so that, obeying the will of Russian democracy, it will also declare its rejection of annexations and reparations and its readiness to begin peace talks at any time on the conditions announced in the Manifesto of the Soviet of Workers' and Soldiers' Deputies.
>
> At the same time, this meeting protests against the slogan 'War to Total Victory', that is presently being unfurled on the banner of the Provisional Government and is being promoted by the entire bourgeois press. For behind this slogan are concealed the annexationist aspirations of the capitalist class of Russia and of the whole world.
>
> The path to peace is not through bloody war but through the revolutionary pressure of the popular masses of Europe on their predatory ruling classes and governments.[6]

Under pressure from the Soviet, on 27 March the government finally issued a declaration to the citizens of Russia that renounced any annexationist aims. But, implicitly contradicting itself, it reaffirmed at the same time Russia's determination to respect all her treaty obligations with the Allies. These secret treaties provided for a new division of the colonial world in which Russia would obtain, among other prizes, Constantinople and the Dardanelles. Milyukov later admitted publicly that the declaration was worded in such a way as to appear the opposite of what it was, in fact, affirming.[7]

At the same time, the Kadets' Central Committee and Milyukov himself continued to speak out in favour of the annexation of the Dardanelles.[8] As a result, the Bolsheviks' demand for publication of the Entente's secret treaties was gaining support. In mid-April, a meeting of 3,000 workers of the Skorokhod Shoe Factory, after hearing a report from their delegate to the district soviet, voted unanimously to support the latter's demand for the immediate publication by the government of all the treaties, a proposal of peace terms, and the convocation of a peace conference. 'We don't want to find ourselves in the position of conducting an annexationist war'.[9]

---

6 *Rabochaya gazeta* (21 Mar 1917).

7 Ibid. (6 May 1917).

8 Ibid. (12 Apr 1917); *Pravda* (13 Apr 1917).

9 *Rabochaya gazeta* (15 Apr 1917).

After more prodding from the Soviet, Milyukov finally agreed to transmit to the Allied governments his declaration from 27 March, which had been intended only for the Russian public. But he posed a condition: the declaration would be accompanied by a note of clarification. These were transmitted 18 April, and on 20 April the note appeared in the press: it affirmed Russia's firm determination to prosecute the war in full accord with the Allies and in respect of all the treaty obligations. It also declared that the revolution had strengthened the popular will to prosecute the war to a victorious conclusion.

Publication of the note immediately provoked a spontaneous explosion of popular anger that took the form of workers' and soldiers' meetings and demonstrations on 20 and 21 April. For the most part, these were not directed against the Provisional Government and the dual power arrangement. They demanded only the resignation of Milyukov, and, somewhat less insistently, of A.I. Guchkov, Minister of War. Only a relatively small number of workers marched behind banners with the inscriptions 'Down with the Provisional government' and 'Power to the soviets'.[10]

Rabochaya gazeta published the following account of the events of 20 April.

> Petrograd reacts with unusual sensitivity and nervousness to the burning political issues of the day. Milyukov's note, published yesterday, provoked strong agitation on the streets. Everywhere there were groups of people, meetings, which of late have become habitual sights, but they were in immeasurably larger numbers. Everywhere, at street meetings, in trams, passionate, heated disputes take place about the war. The caps and kerchiefs stand for peace; the derbies and bonnets – for war.
>
> In the working-class districts and in the barracks, the attitude towards the note is more defined and organised. A strong protest is expressed against the politics of annexation, against the challenge to democracy from the government in its note.

---

10 A group of left Bolsheviks in the Petrograd Committee, led by a S. Ya. Bagdat'ev, published a leaflet calling for the soviets to take power. They were subsequently taken to task by Lenin and the party's Central Committee, which accused them of adventurism. V.I. Lenin, *Polnoe sobranie sochinenii*, vol. 31, pp. 319–20. These Bolsheviks were apparently from the Vyborg District. At the session of the First Petrograd City Conference of Bolsheviks on 22 April, one of the delegates observed: 'Yesterday we didn't take into account the circumstances of the situation and put forth unsuitable slogans. The Vyborg comrades understand this especially keenly'. *Pervaya petrogradskaya obshchegorodskaya konferentsiya* RSDRP(b) (M.-L., 1925), p. 59.

> The Finland Regiment was out from the morning. Carrying red flags bearing the inscriptions: 'Down with annexationist politics', 'Milyukov and Guchkov to resign', and so forth, they moved toward the Mariinskii Palace, where the Provisional Government was in session ...
>
> After the Finland Regiment, come other regiments. Towards evening, workers' demonstrations make their appearance. The banners, for the most part, are old ones, left over from May Day. But there are also some new ones that protest against the policy of annexations, demand peace without annexations or indemnities, hail the Soviet of Workers' and Soldiers' Deputies. A part of the demonstrators moves to the building of the Morskoi Korpus on Vasilevskii ostrov, where a general assembly of the Soviet is in session.
>
> From time to time counter-demonstrations appear. Small, disorderly crowds of the petty bourgeoisie, among which one can also see officers, but especially many women. They run along Nevskii Prospekt with posters, shouting 'Long live the Provisional Government', 'Down with Lenin'.
>
> By evening, the atmosphere becomes even more agitated. And just as the mood reigning in the working-class districts and in the barracks is sympathetic to the Soviet of Workers' and Soldiers' Deputies, to the same degree an attitude hostile towards it predominates on Nevskii Prospekt.[11]

The next day the demonstrations recurred, only on a much larger scale and with more serious consequences. Again, the Menshevik *Rabochaya gazeta* reported:

> Yesterday on the streets of Petrograd the atmosphere was even more agitated than on 20 April. Everywhere small meetings occurred, everywhere demonstrations. In the [working-class] districts a whole series of strikes occurred ...
>
> The inscriptions on the banners were of a most varied nature, but one could nevertheless observe a common feature: in the centre [of the city], on Nevskii, Sadovaya and other streets, slogans in support of the Provisional government predominate: in the outlying districts – it is the opposite. There one sees only strong protests against the foreign policy of the Provisional Government and its author, Mr. Milyukov ...
>
> Clashes between demonstrators of the two groups are frequent. The initiators are defenders of the Provisional Government. They often charge at the banners bearing protests against Milyukov. The demonstrators from

---

11 *Rabochaya gazeta* (21 Apr 1917).

> the other side repulse them. But this often takes the most unfortunate forms. There are many rumours of shooting. But who is to blame – that still has to be clarified.
>
> After midday, when the Executive Committee [of the Soviet] published its order to the soldiers not to go into the streets armed, one began to observe curious scenes in which soldiers tried to persuade their comrades to refrain completely from participation in the demonstrations, regardless of their nature [that is, armed or otherwise]. Soldiers also often appealed to civilians for calm …
>
> In the evening the situation in the streets became more acute. The gunfire was very intense.[12]

As this report indicates, when they learnt of the Soviet's order, the soldiers generally refrained from demonstrating, entrusting resolution of the conflict to the Soviet's leaders. But the workers were not so trusting. They came out in even larger numbers than on the previous day. And as usual, the Vyborg District's workers were in the fore. But there were also many workers from factories with less skilled workforces, including several thousand from the Petrograd Trubochnyi Factory, from the Putilov Works, and even from two or three textile mills.[13] The various strata of the working class were all united in their opposition to the imperialist war.

On 21 April, the Kadet Party organised counter-demonstrations in support of Milyukov. On that day, several workers and soldiers were killed or wounded in street clashes. This was the first bloodshed since the revolution. By all accounts (official hearings were held on the April Days), the authors were provocateurs hiding amidst the 'proper public'.[14] One of the clashes involved textile workers.

> On 21 April, the women of these mills [Novaya Bumagopryadil'nya, Kozhevnikovskaya, and part of Okhtenskaya Bumagopryadil'nya] moved with the demonstrators along the odd-numbered side of Nevskii. The other crowd moved in parallel fashion along the even side: well-dressed women, officers, merchants, lawyers, etc. Their slogans were: 'Long live the Provisional Government', 'Long live Milyukov', 'Arrest Lenin'. A clash occurred at Sadovaya. A hail of curses descended upon our workers: 'Trollops! Illiterate rabble! Filthy scum!' P. Romanova couldn't contain

12 Ibid. (22 Apr 1917).
13 Sobolev 1973, pp. 223–30.
14 Dok. Apr., pp. 740–50.

> herself: 'The bonnets you're wearing are made from our blood!' And a fistfight broke out. The bearer of Novaya Bumagopryadil'nya's banner was knocked off her feet and the banner torn. The same thing occurred to the Kozhevnikovskaya banner. In response, our workers tore some of the opponents' banners and in the scuffle they tore off the fancy bonnets of the bourgeois women and scratched their faces. At that moment, a detachment of sailors, led by an orchestra, approached, and the Kadet demonstration retreated. After this, the workers moved with the remainder of the red banners onto Vasilevskii ostrov to the Morskoi korpus, where the Soviet was in session. From there, our demonstrators were accompanied by a detachment of Putilov workers to Ekaterinov Prospekt.[15]

These clashes left a deep and lasting impression. 'That day opened everyone's eyes. The repressed hatred toward the bourgeoisie grew stronger', recalled a Vyborg-district worker.[16] It was the news of street clashes that finally brought the Putilov workers out in the street on the second day. According to one of the participants of the strike, workers from the nearby Treugol'nik Rubber Factory, marching behind a red banner, arrived that afternoon at the Putilov Factory. A joint meeting was organised.

The mood was indecisive. Some spoke in favour of joining the street demonstrations; others against. It was decided to await a decision from the Soviet. But before that could arrive, individual workers returned from Nevskii, all telling of the violence on the part of the bourgeoisie against workers, of the tearing of red banners, of arrests for shouting against the Provisional Government. At that moment, someone read a Kadet leaflet that called people out into the streets. The crowd's mood shifted sharply. 'What?! They're chasing us from the streets, tearing our banners, and we're going to watch this from a distance? Let's move onto Nevskii!' An overwhelming majority voted to go.[17]

This was not merely a response to the government's betrayal. It was a matter of class honour.

The April Days provided a strong impulse for the organisation by workers of their own armed force. On 22 April, the general assembly of the Skorokhod Shoe Factory decided, in view of the 'dark forces … that are threatening the foundation of order of free Russia … and wanting, therefore, to defend interests

---

15 Perazich 1927, p. 42.

16 Kudelli 1924, p. 15.

17 *Delo naroda* (25 Apr 1917).

of the toiling masses and the general interests of the country', to request from the Soviet 500 rifles and 500 revolvers for its Red Guard.[18] At a meeting of factory delegates, convened on 23 April to discuss the organisation of Red Guards, one of the speakers explained:

> The bourgeoisie attacked on the streets. 21 April was a regrettable day. One can draw many conclusions from it ... The Soviet put too much trust in the Kadets. The Soviet of Workers' Deputies lost that day. The Soviet did not go into the street. The Kadets went into the street. Despite the Soviet of Workers' Deputies, the workers went into the street and saved the situation. If we had a Red Guard, they would pay attention to us ... Then they wouldn't tear down our red flags.[19]

The Menshevik and SR majority in the Soviet opposed the formation of a workers' armed force, arguing that there was no need of it, as the soldiers were revolutionary. Moreover, the soldiers might see a Red Guard as a threat.[20] But despite the Soviet, a citywide conference of Red Guards was convened on 28 April. Factories, employing in all some 170,000 workers, sent 158 delegates. F.A. Yudin, a member of the Mensheviks' Central Committee, came from the Soviet's Executive Committee to dissuade the meeting from going ahead. And he did not spare his words: 'As a genuine friend of the working class, I must say openly to you that our worker lives in ignorance. One can hold a rifle firmly in one's hand, when one is strong in the head'. These words caused such an uproar that the meeting voted, albeit by a narrow margin, to stop him from continuing. However, the assembled were not prepared to defy the Soviet's authority. They merely asked it to reconsider its position. After all, had not the Soviet itself distributed arms to the workers in February? It could find itself faced with the necessity of disarming them. The conference decided to suspend temporarily the formation of a city-wide organisation of Red Guards.[21] But workers continued to organise Red Guards locally. In the Vyborg district, the district soviet decided the very next day to transform the district's militia, which had been created after the February Revolution to replace the Tsarist police, into a Red Guard.[22]

---

18 Kudelli 1924, p. 23.

19 Dok. Apr., p. 167.

20 Startsev 1962, p. 111.

21 Dok Apr. p. 438.

22 Startsev 1962, pp. 116–22; *Pravda*, Apr. 29, 1917.

The April Days went far to restoring the class polarisation that had characterised society under the Tsarist regime. But that polarisation did not yet express itself politically among workers. Resolutions adopted by factory meetings from this time still expressed support for dual power. They limited themselves to demanding Milyukov's and Guchkov's resignation and to urging the Soviet to firm up its control over the Provisional Government. They still believed that the Soviet was able and willing to do that. For example, a meeting of 2,000 workers at the Siemens and Gal'ske Electrotechnical Factory demanded 'reinforced control' over the government and the removal 'of all the supporters of the annexationist war, in particular Milyukov and Guchkov, and the inclusion of elements who can guarantee the most democratic defence of the interests of the broad popular masses'.[23] At the Baltic Shipbuilding factory, the workers demanded the repudiation of Milyukov's note and expressed 'full confidence in the Soviet. We are certain that the Soviet of Workers' and Soldiers Deputies, supported by our confidence in it and that of organised revolutionary democracy, will be able to force the Provisional Government to consider the wishes of the revolutionary people and the revolutionary army'.[24]

What workers, in fact, really meant was clearly expressed in a resolution adopted by the workers of the Cotton-Printing Mill of Voronin, Lutsh and Chesher: 'Full power must belong to the Soviet of Workers' and Soldiers' Deputies, and the Provisional Government must carry out the will of the Soviet'.[25] Indeed, that is how the workers had viewed things from the start. In some resolutions adopted at this time, the workers stated that they were giving the bourgeoisie a last chance. The general assembly of the Nevskaya Thread Mill declared:

> The bourgeois government, in the persons of Milyukov, Guchkov and Co., is not making errors but is following a conscious plan to dupe the people of Russia and other countries ... Therefore, we ask the Soviet of Workers' and Soldiers' Deputies 1) to watch every step of the Provisional Government; and 2) We demand that the Soviet of Workers' and Soldiers' Deputies force the Provisional Government to publish all the secret treaties and to issue an appeal to all the warring states immediately to end the war ... 3) At the first anti-revolutionary step by the Provisional Government, the Soviet of Workers' and Soldiers' Deputies must take energetic measures up to the seizure of power'.[26]

---

23 *Rabochaya* gazeta (22 Apr 1917).

24 Grebach 1959, p. 115; Dok. Apr., p. 733.

25 *Izvestiya* (27 Apr 1917).

26 Dok. Apr. p. 773.

Workers at the Dinamo Factory called directly to remove the entire government, if it did not dismiss Miliukov and Guchkov.[27]

Most of the demands to abandon dual power, to break politically with census society and for the soviets to take power, came from the Vyborg district's machine-building factories and a few similar enterprises elsewhere in the city.[28] For example, the general assembly of the Opticheskii Machine-building Factory stated:

> The Provisional Government, by its composition, does not represent the majority of the population of Russia. Milyukov and Co., who represent a band of capitalists and landowners who made up the Fourth State Duma, having seized the power won by the people, have unmasked themselves. We declare that we do not want to shed our blood for the interests of Milyukov and Co. in agreement with the capitalist oppressors of other countries. Therefore, we consider that the Milyukov-Guchkov company not corresponding to its function and we recognise that the sole government in the country must be the soviets of the workers', soldiers' and peasants' deputies, which we will defend with our lives.[29]

But the call for the soviets to take power was beginning to gather support now in other sectors of the industrial working class. The workers of the Nevskii Mechanical Shoe Factory called to 'reorganise both the Executive Committee of the Soviet of Workers' and Soldiers' Deputies and also the Soviet itself, as they are unable to adopt a decisive revolutionary class position of a break with bourgeois policy, and to replace them with representatives who stand for a decisive path of struggle, for the full transfer of power into the hands of the proletariat and the peasantry'.[30] Similar resolutions were adopted by the Needleworkers' Union[31] and the Delegates' Council of the Upholsterers' Section of the Woodworkers' Union.[32]

---

27 *Rabochaya gazeta* (22 Apr 1917).

28 Among these were: Rozenkrants Copper Foundry (*Pravda* (28 Apr 1917)); Old Parviainen (Kudelli, *Leningradskie rabochie*, p. 24); Russkii Renault, Langezipen Machine-construction Factory, Puzyrev Auto Factory, New Lessner Machine-construction Factory, Russko-Baltiiskii Wagon-construction (Dok. Apr., pp. 732–68, *passim*); Sestroretsk Arms Factory (*Bastiony revolyutsii*, vol. 1, p. 236); and others.

29 *Pravda* (11 May 1917).

30 *Soldatskaya pravda* (26 Apr 1917), cited in Sobolev 1973, p. 237.

31 Ibid.

32 *Pravda* (26 Apr 1917). These two unions represented relatively skilled groups of workers.

Despite the predominance there of Bolsheviks, the Vyborg District soviet did not yet call directly for the soviets to take power. This was possibly because that was not yet the policy of the Bolsheviks. Instead, the soviet's resolution, adopted on 20 April, declared that 'such actions by the Provisional Government, that are a betrayal of the interests of democracy, must receive the most energetic rebuff. To inform the Soviet of Workers' and Soldiers' Deputies of our attitude to the Provisional Government's note and to call on the latter to take the most decisive action, pledging it our full support in that'.[33] The 'decisive action' was left undefined, but the meaning was clear.

Most of the workers who at this time called for the soviets to take power had already been inclined in that direction even before the April Crisis. But the majority of workers did not change their position as a result of the crisis. Their reaction was clearly expressed by a Putilov worker, when he was asked by someone during the April Days if the Soviet had sanctioned the strikes and demonstrations: 'He answered in the negative and added that the workers do not want a civil war but will show the bourgeois that they have to take us into account'.[34] Most workers still believed that they could force the representatives of census society to adhere to the programme of the revolution. There was, therefore, no need for a break with census society that threatened civil war.

The fear of civil war, a major factor in workers' initial support for dual power, continued to influence their politics. On the eve of the April Days, a general assembly of workers of the Leont'ev Textile Mill declared:

> We fully support the tactics of the Soviet that are directed at preserving the unity of the revolution and at energetically repelling any attempt to divide the revolutionary forces ... This meeting rejects Lenin's anarchistic call to seize state power that can only lead to civil war, which in the current situation would threaten the cause of freedom, which is far from consolidated, with ruin.[35]

Sukhanov confirms that, even after the April Days, relatively few workers were convinced by the Bolshevik argument 'that there is nothing to fear from civil war, since it has already arrived and only through it can the people achieve their liberation'.[36] Most workers continued to support the moderate socialists.

---

33 Dok. Apr., p. 733.

34 Ibid., p. 749.

35 *Rabochaya gazeta* (14 Apr 1917).

36 Sukhanov 1919–23, vol. III, p. 276.

V.B. Stankevich, an SR, addressed the following words to the 20 April meeting of the Petrograd Soviet:

> So what do we do now? ... Certain people decide the question very simply: they say that we have to overthrow and arrest the Provisional Government ... But why, comrades, do we have to 'take action'? ... At whom should we shoot? At the masses who support you? Why, you do not have a worthy opponent: against you, no one has any power. As you decide, so it will be. It is not necessary to 'take action', but rather to decide what to do ... Decide that the Provisional Government should not exist, that it should resign. We will inform them over the telephone, and in five minutes they will hand in their resignations. By seven o'clock it will not exist. What is the purpose here of violence, demonstrations, civil war? ...

This speech provoked 'stormy applause, enthusiastic cheers'.[37] To most workers, who shared Stankevich's view of the political situation, the conclusion from the April Days was to call on the Menshevik and SR leaders of the Soviet to tighten their 'control' of the Provisional Government to make sure it adhered to the Soviet's programme.

The crisis ended formally with the government's agreement to dispatch a new explanatory note to the Allies, reiterating its original 'Declaration to the Citizens of Russia' and explaining that Milyukov's call for 'sanctions and guarantees of a firm peace' meant, in fact, arms limitation, the establishment of international tribunals, etc. This 'clarification' was, of course, in complete contradiction with Milyukov's original note, which, moreover, the government did not bother to repudiate. Nor were Milyukov or Guchkov forced to resign, as the demonstrators had demanded, although they did leave the government within a week or so.

This solution to the crisis was approved by the Soviet's Executive Committee on 21 April by a vote of 34 against 19. It also passed by a large majority of the plenum (combined workers' and soldiers' sections) of the Soviet. In sum, despite the crisis provoked by the Milyukov note, the moderate socialist, 'defencist', majority of the Soviet still appeared to be riding high on the wave of popular support.

---

37 Ibid., pp. 275–6.

The First Coalition Government

It was only natural at this point for the members of the government again to raise the question of the socialists entering a coalition. For the crisis had dramatically demonstrated that the census government lacked both popular authority and coercive force. The Soviet, on the other hand, had both but did not share responsibility for government. Accordingly, the government, supported by the bourgeois press, pressed for the Soviet to delegate its representatives to the government. Kerenskii threatened to resign if the Soviet refused.

The initial reaction of the Soviet's Executive Committee was unanimously to reject the idea. But only two days after that decision, on 28 April, a joint meeting of the Executive Committees of the Petrograd and Moscow Soviets barely missed reversing that position. Guchkov's resignation as Minister of War on 30 April, forcing a reorganisation of the government, added a new urgency to the situation.

Until then, I.G. Tsereteli, a moderate Menshevik and undisputed leader of the Petrograd Soviet's majority, had opposed a coalition. The Mensheviks' newspaper argued that socialists who entered the government would soon find themselves compromised in the eyes of the masses, the targets of 'anarchist demagogues'. They would lose all influence among workers.[38] It also argued that the Soviet could more effectively pressure the government from the outside. If its representatives participated in the government, sharing responsibility for its actions, this would be more difficult. Nevertheless, on 1 May, Tsereteli came out in favour of a coalition, and the Soviet's Executive Committee supported him by a vote of 44 against 10 (with 2 abstentions). The Bolsheviks, Menshevik-Internationalists and Left SRs opposed.[39]

In the negotiations that followed, Milyukov was forced out of the government by his own party colleagues, despite a threat from the Kadets' central committee to call out all of its other ministers from the government. As a result of the agreement, six representatives of the Soviet, a sizeable minority, entered the government. On 13 May, a plenary session of the Soviet overwhelmingly expressed its full confidence in the coalition. The former position of only conditional support for the government was abandoned. A resolution proposed by Trotsky opposing the government gathered only 20–30 votes.[40]

Izvestiya, the Soviet's paper, explained the Soviet's new position in the following manner. First of all, the uniquely census government had been unable

38 *Rabochaya gazeta* (25 Apr 1917).

39 *Novaya zhizn'* (2 May 1917).

40 Ibid. (14 May 1917).

to govern and to stave off the ruin that was threatening Russia, since its ministers were not trusted by the masses, who would not obey them. On the other hand, if the Soviet took power on its own, that would unleash a civil war, and the Soviet already had enough enemies. The 'broad masses' would not follow the Soviet in such a move. Finally, with the Soviet's representatives now inside the government, the latter would more decisively carry out the programme of revolutionary democracy.[41]

On a superficial level, the Soviet's decision appeared to correspond to the will of the majority of workers, even if the Soviet's vote in favour of the coalition clearly exaggerated the strength of that position among the workers. Indeed, a process of recall and replacement of deputies originally elected in the February Days was picking up speed. But aside from that, workers who supported the formation of a coalition government did so because they believed that the presence of the Soviet's representatives inside the government would permit the Soviet more firmly to exert its influence over the 'bourgeois ministers'. As a result, manoeuvres, such as the Milyukov note, would no longer be possible.

Meanwhile, the workers' mistrust of census society had only grown deeper. At their meetings, rather than express confidence in the new coalition government, as the Soviet had done, workers typically voiced support uniquely for the socialist ministers. The general assembly of workers and employees of the Factory of the Russian Society of Wireless Telegraphs and Telephones promised 'full support for our comrades in the government'. The workers of the Ust'-Izhorskaya Shipyard sent 'a warm greeting to the socialist ministers' only. A meeting at the Zigel' Iron Foundry and Machine-building Factory declared: 'Having heard a report on the coalition from our representatives to the Soviet … we pledge full support for the Soviet and its representatives in the Provisional Government … We are certain they will honestly carry out their obligations to the people'.[42] Even workers who did voice support for the coalition government made it clear that they considered legitimate only the Soviet and its representatives in the government. A meeting of 7,000 workers at the Admiralty Shipyards resolved

> to support the Provisional Government and to rally around the Soviet of Workers' and Soldiers' Deputies, which must serve as the centre of revolutionary democracy, consciously and unswervingly striving to increase socialist influence over the organs of power. We approve of the entrance of our comrade socialists into the government. We welcome their inten-

41 *Izvestiya* (3 May 1917).

42 *Rabochaya gazeta*. (12 May 1917).

> tion to carry out the financial programme developed by the Economic Department of the Soviet of Workers' and Soldiers Deputies.[43]

Most of the opposition to the formation of a coalition government came from workers who were already opposed to the dual power. They argued that the socialist ministers would merely serve as a screen for the continued machinations of the bourgeoisie, that the only real solution to the crisis of power was a uniquely soviet government.[44]

There were, thus, two conflicting interpretations of the Soviet's decision to participate in the government. A minority of workers, convinced that census society opposed the revolution's programme, felt that the Soviet's representatives would become hostages of the census ministers. Most workers, however, did not yet feel that cooperation with census society was impossible. But at the same time they felt it necessary to strengthen the Soviet's control of the census representatives and they believed the coalition would achieve that.

However, that was not the reasoning that had moved Tseretelli to change his mind about the formation of a coalition. He, along with his Menshevik and SR colleagues in the Soviet's leadership, were moved above all by their concern to maintain the political alliance between revolutionary democracy and census society. They believed that to be absolutely essential to the revolution's survival. 'We must by all means keep the liberal bourgeoisie in the government', admonished *Rabochaya gazeta*.[45] Most workers also desired cooperation with the bourgeoisie, but not at the price of renouncing or even diluting the revolution's goals. If they became convinced that they had to choose between the two, they would choose the revolution. It soon became clear to the workers, however, that the moderate socialists would choose cooperation with census society over the revolution's goals, since they argued, paradoxically to the workers, that the revolution was doomed without the cooperation of census society.

---

43 Ibid. (15 May 1917).

44 Among factories supporting this position were United Cable (Dok. Apr., p. 895), the Military Horseshoe Factory (ibid., p. 844), 1,250 workers of the new machine-building shop of the Putilov Works (*Pravda* (9 May 1917)), the Tseitlin Machine-building Factory (ibid. (18 May, 1917)); and the Nevka and Nevskaya Nitochnaya textile mills (Perazich, *Tekstili Leningrada*, p. 42).

45 *Rabochaya gazeta* (3 May 1917).

The Break with Census Society

In the weeks that followed the April crisis, the euphoria of the first period of the revolution was completely forgotten by workers, amidst a growing sense of political cul-de-sac and approaching economic crisis. The guarded *rapprochement* with the bourgeoisie gave way to increasingly bitter polarisation in the social, economic, and now also the political spheres.

Perhaps the most striking indicator of the shift in political views that occurred in May and June was the vote in the Workers' Section of the Petrograd Soviet. Immediately after the April crisis, the Bolsheviks, having rallied to Lenin's April Theses that called for the soviets to take power – which, at that time, Lenin believed could be done peacefully – launched a recall campaign of delegates to the Soviet. On 1 July, V. Volodarskii, a leading Petrograd Bolshevik, told the party's city conference that it now held a majority in the Workers' Section of the Soviet.[46] Two days later, less than two months after Trotsky's resolution calling to oppose the formation of a coalition government had gathered a mere 20–30 votes, a majority of the worker delegates supported a resolution that called for the transfer of power to the soviets.[47]

The earliest and strongest support for this position came from the metalworkers. In May, the soviets of the two districts with the largest concentrations of metalworkers, Vyborg and Vasilevskii ostrov, already had left socialist, mostly Bolshevik, majorities, as did the soviet of the small Kolomenskii district, dominated by three large shipyards.[48] In other districts, the 'defencists' retained dwindling majorities in the soviets until the July Days.

On 3 May, an electoral meeting at the Sestroretsk Arms Factory overwhelmingly voted for Bolshevik candidates to the Petrograd Soviet.[49] A few weeks later the workers of the Phoenix Machine-building Factory, who had originally sent two Mensheviks and one Bolshevik to the Soviet, replaced the Mensheviks with Bolshevik deputies.[50] In May, a general assembly at the New Baranovskii Machine and Pipe Factory that lasted five hours finally gave an overwhelming endorsement to the Bolshevik position in favour of a soviet government.[51] In June, the workers of the Nobel Machine-building Factory recalled their SR

---

46 *Vtoraya i tret'ya obshchegorodskie konferentsii bol'shevikov v iyule i sentyabre 1917 g.* (M.-L., 1927), p. 26.

47 *Novaya zhizn'* (4 July 1917).

48 *Raisovety Petrograda* v 1917 g. (henceforth: Raisovety) (M.-L., 1966) vol. I, pp. 71, 123.

49 *Bastiony revolyutsii*, vol. I, p. 131.

50 *Stankostroiteli imeni Sverdlova* (L., 1962), p. 76.

51 Ek. Pol., vol. I, p. 42.

deputy after he voted against the Bolsheviks' position on power.[52] On 9 May, a meeting of 1,250 workers of the machine-building shop adopted the Putilov Factory's first resolution in support of soviet power.[53]

The following report from the Vulkan Foundry and Machine-building Factory offers some insight into the political thinking of the skilled metalworkers:

> The Vulkan Factory was under intense influence of the Mensheviks. Well-known speakers came to the workers' general assemblies. Menshevik members of the Soviet Executive Committee would visit us. But despite this, their work did not produce the desired results. The Menshevik current did not grow but, on the contrary, it declined. On the other hand, the Bolshevik current began from the start to win a strong position for itself. This was evident not only from the opinions expressed by individuals but also from speeches made by comrade workers and their common demands. And gradually this turned into the workers' strong dissatisfaction with their Menshevik representatives in the Soviet of Workers' and Soldiers' Deputies. And so it was decided to hold new elections.
>
> Before these elections, the Bolshevik faction and the United Mensheviks [Internationalists] decided to work together and began their pre-election activity. From that moment onward, our work proceeded smoothly and quickly. The comrade workers united around the slogans expressed in the mandate to their delegates to the Soviet of Workers' and Soldiers' Deputies. At the pre-election meeting, the talented speakers, Kamenev and Lunacharskii, conclusively rallied almost everyone present, and our above-mentioned mandate was supported by the vote of the entire assembly. As a result of the new elections, all four delegates proposed by the Bolsheviks and the united faction were elected overwhelmingly.[54]

Commenting on that meeting, Lunacharskii wrote: 'I now know that it is possible in the course of a half hour to leave not even the vaguest trace of the most empty defencism'.[55]

'Conciliationist' attitudes were still strong among the less skilled groups of workers. But even there they were eroding, in particular in factories that were the scene of economic conflicts. (See below). At the Petrograd Trubochnyi

52 *Pravda* (16 June 1917).

53 *Putilovtsy v trekh revolyutsiyakh* (L., 1933) p. 338.

54 *Pravda* (27 June 1917).

55 *Literaturnoe nasledstvo* (M., 1971) no. 8, p. 341.

Factory, which employed a vast number of recent arrivals from the countryside, the SRs enjoyed great influence after February and reported carrying away membership dues 'by the sackful'.[56] In new elections to the Petrograd Soviet in June, they received 8,552 votes and the Menshevik-Defencists 1,067. But a bloc of Bolshevik and Social-Democratic Internationalists already managed to win 5,823 votes.[57] SR support was still very strong among textile workers and would remain so for considerably longer in some mills.[58] At the Kersten Knitwear Mill, all the delegates to the Soviet were SRs, until new elections in mid-September gave the Bolsheviks 965 votes to the SRs' 1,340.[59] At the Treugol'nik Rubber Factory, with a mostly female work force, the SRs lost their majority only following the July Days.[60]

Competition for worker support was confined mainly to the Bolsheviks and SRs. The Mensheviks, perceived by workers as an urban, proletarian party, were unable to withstand competition with the Bolsheviks for the support of more skilled workers, the natural base of Russian social democracy. They retained significant influence only among printers.[61] The Menshevik-Internationalists enjoyed some strength in the Vasilevskii ostrov district, thanks to the large concentration of students there. But a proposal for the Bolsheviks to form a bloc with them in the elections to the city duma was not warmly received at the Bolshevik's Petrograd conference in the middle of July. One delegate said: 'We should be cautious about a bloc, since the Menshevik-Internationalists are so unstable and numerically insignificant that a bloc has little meaning. If they are consistent internationalists they should break with the [Menshevik-Defencist] organisation'. A delegate from the Vyborg District observed that 'there are almost no Menshevik-Internationalists, perhaps a few hundred'. 'They are too few to help us, and there is no sense in helping them', added a third.[62]

The weakness of the Menshevik-Internationalists was due to their ambiguous position on power. They opposed the coalition government but they did not

56 Bortik, 'NaTrubochnom', p. 269.

57 Arbuzova 1923, p. 175.

58 Perazich 1927, p. 42.

59 Suknovalov and Fomenkov 1968, pp. 62, 79; Ek. Pol, vol. I, Table 7.

60 Shabalin, 'Ot fevralya k oktyabryu', pp. 278–9.

61 At their All-Russian Congress in December 1917, of the 95 delegates, 48 were Mensheviks and 6 Menshevik sympathisers, 15 were Bolsheviks and 4 sympathisers. There were only 5 SRs and 5 Left SRs (*Znamya truda* (19 Dec 1917)). In Petrograd itself, the Bolsheviks briefly controlled the Printers' Union in the October 1917 period.

62 *Vtoraya i tret'ya obshchegorodskie konferentsii bol'shevikov v iyule setnyabre 1917 g.* M.-L., 1927., pp. 93–4.

support a soviet government, something workers had trouble understanding. Nor did it help that they refused to break organisationally with the defencist wing of their party, which supported the coalition government.

Thus, by the end of June, the large majority of the urbanised, more skilled workers had been won over to the Bolsheviks. The struggle for the others continued between the Bolsheviks and SR-defencists. In particular, for workers with strong ties to the land, the SRs continued to exercise strong attraction. Commenting on the big SR victory in the Moscow municipal elections in June, *Rabochaya gazeta* noted that 'the masses support the simplified slogan "Land and Freedom", especially those who have not broken their ties with the village'.[63]

The soviets were not the only forum that registered the growing worker support for soviet power. In elections to the twelve district dumas (representative assemblies) at the end of May, of the total of 784,910 votes cast (about 75 percent of all eligible voters), the Bolsheviks won 20.4 percent and the moderate socialists (mostly SRs) 56.0. The rest went mainly to the Kadets (see Table 5.1). The electoral campaign was run both on municipal and national issues. Most of the Bolshevik support came from the working-class districts. Thus, in the Vyborg district, they won an absolute majority of 58.2 percent. The moderate socialists won 34.9 percent there, and the Kadets a mere 6.9. In Vasilevskii ostrov, Petrograd and Narva districts, all of which had a significant amount of industry, the Bolsheviks also did relatively well.[64]

But the most dramatic expression of the growth of support for soviet power was the vote at the First Petrograd Conference of Factory Committees in 30 May–3 June, which was attended by 568 delegates from 367 factories, together employing 337,000 workers.[65] A resolution calling for measures to combat the deteriorating economic situation concluded with the following words: 'The coordinated and successful execution of the above measures is possible on condition of the transfer of power into the hands of the Soviet of Workers' and Peasants' Deputies'. 297 delegates supported that resolution. The resolutions proposed by the moderate socialists and Menshevik-Internationalists, which called for 'state regulation' of the economy without, however, defining the nature of the government – though clearly not a soviet one – together received only 85 votes. The anarchists who, like the Bolsheviks, opposed the Provisional

63 Cited in *Novaya zhizn'* (28 June 1917).

64 Some districts with a significant amount of industry, such as Petergof, Nevskii and Novaya derevnya, were not incorporated into the city until the summer.

65 *Revolyutsionnoe dvizhenie v Rossii v mae-iyune* (henceforth: Dok. May) (M., 1959), p. 293.

TABLE 5.1 *Petrograd district duma election returns (number of votes cast)*

District	Bolshevik	%	Moderate socialist [a]	%	Kadet	%	All parties [b]	%
Admiralty	2,983	15.8	11,105	58.7	4,503	23.8	18,931	100.0
Aleksandr-Nevskii	8,737	12.8	49,891	73.0 [c]	9,116	13.3	68,318	
Kazan'	2,219	10.1	9,253	41.9	9,382	42.5	22,077	
Kolomna	6,035	14.9	23,724	58.4	10,241	25.2	40,626	
Liteinyi	5,085	8.6	30,583	51.5	22,507	37.9	59,423	
Moscow [d]	6,758	9.7	41,517	59.4	21,667	31.0	69,942	
Narva	18,202	17.1	73,293	68.9	12,625	11.9	106,392	
Petrograd	30,348	22.6	72,750	54.2	29,323	21.8	134,345	
Rozhdestvenskii	2,944	5.0	37,671	63.5 [e]	18,126	30.5	59,358	
Spasskii	4,945	13.2	20,210	53.8	10,885	29.0	37,581	
Vasilevskii ostrov	37,377	34.3 [f]	49,293	45.2	19,299	17.7	108,975	
Vyborg	34,303	58.2	20,568	34.9	4,071	6.9	58,942	
Total	159,936	20.4	439,858	56.0	171,745	21.9	784,910	

[a] Includes Mensheviks, SRs, Trudoviks and Popular Socialists, the latter two with about 1 percent of the vote.
[b] Not included in the breakdown are the minor non-socialist parties which took about 1.7 percent of the vote.
[c] The Mensheviks and SRs ran separately here, the former taking 10.6 percent, and the latter 60.5 percent of the vote.
[d] Known to be incomplete.
[e] The Mensheviks and SRs ran separately here, the former taking 32.1 percent of the vote, and the latter 15.4 percent.
[f] This was a Bolshevik-Menshevik-Internationalist bloc. As the majority of the Menshevik organisation here was internationalist, the defencists did not run candidates.

SOURCE: BASED ON W. ROSENBERG, *LIBERALS IN THE RUSSIAN REVOLUTION* (PRINCETON: PRINCETON UNIVERSITY PRESS, 1974), P. 162.

Government, presented a resolution that characteristically did not mention the state. It attracted 44 votes. But even if one excludes the anarchist vote, almost two-thirds of the delegates supported the transfer of power to the soviets.[66]

66 FZK, Vol. I, p. 107.

This vote did not, of course, accurately reflect the distribution of positions among the mass of Petrograd's workers. These delegates had been selected by the factory committees and not by general assemblies. However, the factory committees were the worker organisations closest to the rank and file. They were in constant contact with the workers, and recall elections were frequent. At the very least, one can say that the vote at the conference reflected the position of the most active and trusted of the workers' local leaders.

A most striking manifestation of the shift in political attitudes was the demonstration of 18 June. The Bolsheviks' Central Committee, responding to pressure from the factories and from certain military units of the garrison, decided to call a demonstration on 10 June. But the All-Russian Congress of Soviets, then meeting in Petrograd, feared a repeat of the April Days. Tsereteli even made the unfounded claim that the Bolsheviks were planning a coup d'état. And so the Congress decided to ban the demonstration. But the Menshevik-SR majority of the Petrograd Soviet wanted to provide an outlet for the pent-up popular energy and so decided to call a demonstration for 18 June as a show of the unity of revolutionary democracy and of its support for the soviets. To avoid any discordant notes, only slogans acceptable to all party fractions of the Soviet were to be allowed, slogans such as a universal peace, the rapid convocation of the Constituent Assembly, a democratic republic, and the like. The issue of state power was studiously avoided.

The demonstration was, nevertheless, a resounding triumph for the Bolsheviks' position demanding the transfer of power to the soviets. All accounts concurred that only a small number of banners carried by the crowd, estimated at between 300,000 and 400,000, bore inscriptions with the neutral slogans proposed by the Soviet.[67] Sukhanov gave the following account:

> 'All power to the Soviets!' 'Down with the 10 capitalist ministers!' 'Peace to the hovels, war to the palaces!'
>
> Thus firmly and forcefully did the vanguard of the Russian and the world revolutions, worker-peasant [that is, soldier] Petrograd, express its will ... The situation was completely clear and unambiguous.
>
> Here and there, the chain of Bolshevik banners and columns was interrupted by specifically SR and official soviet slogans. But they were drowned in the mass; they seemed exceptions that forcefully confirmed

---

67 *Rabochaya gazeta* (20 Apr); *Pravda* (20 Apr); *Novaya zhizn'* (20 Apr); *Izvestiya* (20 Apr 1917). See also Chamberlin 1965, vol. 1, p. 162.

> the rule. And again and again, like a stubborn call from the very bowels of the revolutionary capital, like fate itself, like the fateful Birnam Wood, they moved toward us. 'All Power to the Soviets!' 'Away with the Ten Capitalist Ministers!'[68]

Some workers refrained from participation. This was especially the case in the Nevskii district, an SR stronghold. Only 800 of the Obukhovskii Steel Mill's 15,000 workers took part. But the abstention of the others was in itself telling of their doubts. After all, the demonstration had been called by the Soviet, in which the SRs and Mensheviks still held a majority.

The Mensheviks' *Rabochaya gazeta* explained away the Bolsheviks' triumph with the claim that the Bolshevik party was the only one that had taken the demonstration seriously. The Mensheviks and SRs had been indifferent and did not mobilise their partisans. Besides, every little Bolshevik group carried a banner, sometimes several. But the newspaper did not attempt to explain why the workers who supported the SRs and Mensheviks had, as the paper admitted, remained indifferent to the Soviet's call to demonstration. The author was, of course, not oblivious to this problem but instead of trying to explain it, merely ended sourly with the comment that it would have been better for the Soviet not to have called the demonstration at all and to have left the Bolsheviks to demonstrate alone.[69]

Pravda, on its part, observed how deeply society had become polarised since March:

> What strikes one in surveying the demonstration is the complete absence of the bourgeoisie and its fellow travellers. In contrast to the day of the funeral [of those who had fallen in the Revolution] ... when the workers were engulfed in a sea of philistines and petty bourgeois, the demonstration of 18 June was a purely proletarian affair: its main participants were workers and soldiers. Already on the eve of the demonstration, the Kadets declared a boycott, proclaiming through their Central Committee the need to 'abstain' from participation – they literally hid. Nevskii [Prospekt], usually bustling and full of people, was absolutely empty on that day of its usual bourgeois habitués.[70]

---

68 Sukhanov 1919–23, vol. IV, pp. 339–40.

69 *Rabochaya gazeta* (20 June 1917).

70 *Pravda* (20 June 1917).

Izvestiya, the official organ of the Central Executive Committee (TsIK) of Soviets[71] and of the Petrograd Soviet, observed similarly that 'the bourgeoisie and the petty bourgeois, frightened to death, were almost completely unseen that day'.[72]

The Underlying Causes of the Shift to Soviet Power

The groundswell of worker support for soviet power was based upon the conclusion that census society and 'its' government – the socialist ministers were seen as mere hostages of the 'capitalist ministers' – were counterrevolutionary. Alarm over the growing outspokenness of well-known census politicians against the soviets and in support of the war only reinforced this perception.

The Spectre of Counterrevolution

On the eve of the demonstration of 18 June, the workers of the Russko-Baltiiskii Wagon-building factory passed the following resolution by an overwhelming majority:

> Having discussed at the general assembly … of 9 June the appeal of the Central Committee of the RSDWP (Bolshevik) to all workers and soldiers of Petrograd to participate in a peaceful demonstration against the counterrevolution that is raising its head, we found this call to be timely and in accord with the interests of the toilers.
>
> Now when the need for a demonstration against the counterrevolutionary bourgeoisie and other dark forces has been finally recognised by the All-Russian Congress of Soviets of Workers' and Soldiers' Deputies, and since the call to demonstrate is supported also by the Central Committee of the RSDWP [the Bolsheviks], we too, as on 9 June, have decided to join that demonstration …
>
> We demand that the most decisive measures be taken against the Black Hundred[73] forces, and that the State Duma and State Council, those centres, around which counterrevolutionaries of all sorts and hues are grouping, be immediately dispersed.

---

71 This TsIK was elected at the All-Russian Congress of Soviets in June and took over from the old Executive Committee that had been made up by the Executive Committee of the Petrograd Soviet with the addition of some delegates from the provinces.

72 *Izvestiya* (29 June 1917).

73 A proto-fascist antisemitic organisation that had enjoyed the patronage of the Tsar.

> We demand the removal from the Provisional Government of the ten ministers of the bourgeoisie, appointees of the Third and Fourth Dumas.
> We demand a decisive struggle against the capitalist-lockouters and against anarchy in industry.[74]

This resolution makes clear that these workers had a very different idea of the aims of the 18 June demonstration than its sponsors in the Soviet. Of interest also is the reference to the Bolshevik Central Committee's endorsement of the demonstration as one of the reasons to participate. In fact, many factories refrained from demonstrating on 10 June only because the Bolshevik Central Committee, not the Soviet Congress, decided to cancel it (see below). The fears voiced by Menshevik leaders in February, and which had caused them to refuse Milyukov's insistent proposal to participate in the provisional government, had been well-founded: their 'conciliationism' with the bourgeoisie was fast compromising them in the eyes of workers.

For rapidly growing numbers of workers, the situation was clear: since the bourgeoisie opposed the aims of the revolutionary people, it should not have representation in government. This was the meaning of the demand to transfer power to the soviets. It was the call for the formation of a government exclusively of representatives of the toiling classes, the overwhelming majority of Russian society. A meeting of 2,000 workers of the Old Parviainen Machine-building Factory on 8 June decided that 'the only correct way to stop the advancing counterrevolution is for the All-Russian Soviet of Workers, Soldiers' and Peasants' Deputies to take power'.[75]

The Bolsheviks' Petersburg Committee met on 6 June to discuss the advisability of the demonstration that the party had called for the 10th. The immediate pressure for some action had emanated from the garrison: soldiers were angered by the government's preparations for a new offensive on the eastern front, where a de facto cease-fire had been in effect since February, and by measures in preparation for that offensive that curtailed their rights. Several of the participants argued that if the party did not organise the demonstration the soldiers would come out on their own and would be armed. I.N. Stukov, a delegate from the Kolpino organisation, presented the following arguments in favour of a demonstration:

> An objective evaluation of the current situation gives us hope of success. A demonstration on the widest possible scale is needed, because, on the

74 *Pravda* (1 July 1917).

75 Dok May, p. 492.

> one hand, the counterrevolutionary movement is growing; on the other hand, we have to oppose it with the organisation of revolutionary forces ... As far as the workers of Kolpino are concerned, they are downright dismayed, [asking] how long the party is going to put off joining battle with the counterrevolutionary movement.

Tomskii, a trade-union leader, added: 'The mood of class antagonism is so intense – just take a look in the trams – that one can't assume the demonstration will occur peacefully'.[76]

For workers, one of the most provocative signs of census society's counterrevolutionary turn of mind was the resurrection of the State Duma, which they considered a completely discredited Tsarist institution, dominated by representatives of the propertied classes, and with no legitimate place in a democratic society. Yet not long after the April Days, the State Duma met in anniversary session, during which prominent leaders of census society denounced the soviets in unadorned terms, bringing those assembled to raptures.

Widely reported in the socialist press were the words of the V.V. Shul'gin, a political figure close to the Kadets. He expressed his 'weighty doubts' about the course the revolution had taken and decried the fact that the 'honest and talented' Provisional Government lacked 'full authority'.

> It is placed under suspicion. A guard has been posted beside it and has been instructed: 'Be careful – these are bourgeois, and so watch them closely. And if anything happens, then know your duty'. Gentlemen, on the 20th you were able to see for yourselves that the guard knows his job and carries out his duty honestly. But it is a big question whether those who posted that guard are acting correctly ...

Turning to the leftist agitation critical of the Provisional Government, he echoed Milyukov's famous speech of 1916, which had been made in the State Duma against the wartime Tsarist government: 'Is it stupidity or treason?' And Shul'gin replied: 'It is stupidity. But all considered together – it is treason'.[77]

The ovation that followed was deafening. 'They had clearly been hurting', remarked Sukhanov.

---

76 *Peterburgskii komitet* R SDRP(*b*) *v 1917 g.*, SPb, 2003, pp. 265–6.

77 Sukhanov 1919–23, vol. III, pp. 347–8; *Novaya zhizn'* (28 Apr 1917); *Rabochaya gazeta* (29 Apr 1917).

> True, in essence there was nothing new here compared to what the bourgeois papers were repeating each day. Still, a public declaration about all this in front of people, at a large assembly of like-minded people and in the very face of the enemies that were besieging you – that filled the bourgeois souls with enthusiasm.[78]

The State Duma continued to meet in 'private session' throughout May and June. In one of his speeches, M.V. Rodzyanko, Chairman of the Fourth Duma and a big landowner, went so far as to imply that the State Duma was the unique source of legitimate power in Russia.[79] In a letter to Duma deputies, he called on them to 'be at the ready, since the time will soon come for your intervention into the life of the country'.[80]

For their part, workers demanded the immediate abolition of the State Duma and State Council, which they saw as rallying centres for the counterrevolution. In addition, the Petrograd Union of Woodworkers mandated its delegate to the Third All-Russian Conference of Trade Unions to demand the immediate arrest of all open counterrevolutionaries,[81] a demand that also figured prominently on banners of the June 18 demonstrators.[82]

But this outspokenly aggressive tone was not limited to meetings of the State Duma. In May, at a congress of the Kadet Party, which had become the main political party of census society after the February Revolution, Milyukov was given a standing ovation when he declared that 'possession of the strait [of the Dardanelles] is the most essential vital necessity for our country'. Nor did he stop there:

> We are told that you cannot conjure up a revolution. That is not true. I think one can, if that is necessary for the well-being and salvation of the fatherland. But if you can call forth a revolution, then you can also stop it if that is for the good of Russia.

The Menshevik-Internationalists' *Novaya zhizn'* remarked about that speech: 'The party's physiognomy is now clear: hatred of the "red rag"'.

This was the background to workers' reaction to the 'Durnovo incident' that occurred on the morning after the 18 June demonstration. The dacha (summer

78 Sukhanov 1919–23, vol. III.

79 *Novaya zhizn'* (9 June 1917).

80 Dok. May, p. 187.

81 Ibid., p. 311.

82 *Izvestiya* (20 June 1917).

residence) of this former Tsarist Minister of Interior, merciless architect of the bloody suppression of the Revolution of 1905–6, was located next to the Metallicheskii Factory in the Vyborg District. After the February Revolution, it had been occupied by local workers' organisations, and its shady park was often visited by workers' families of this industrial district. But the entire ground floor of the building had been taken over by anarchists, who were armed to the teeth. On 7 June, the Minister of Interior ordered the unlawful occupants to vacate the building. In response, the workers of 28 factories immediately went on strike, causing the order to be hastily rewritten to target only the anarchists. In the meanwhile, the Congress of Soviets, which was then in session, had the order fully rescinded. But during the 18 June demonstration, the anarchists decided to raid the local jail, freeing seven of their comrades, whom they brought back to the dacha. Early next morning, government troops raided the building and arrested 70 of its occupants, including members of the Metallicheskii factory committee and trade-union activists. One anarchist was killed in the gun battle, and the building was left in a shambles.[83]

On learning of this, the entire Vyborg District went on strike. In other districts, workers awaited only the signal to take to the streets against the government.[84] The Executive Committee of the Petrograd Soviet at once established a commission to investigate and report back the next day. On 19 June, the Congress of Soviets discussed the incident and approved the Soviet Executive Committee's handling. But many workers were not satisfied. According to Sukhanov,

> Workers from Petrograd's factories, from different parties, appeared [before the Congress] to express their attitude to the events of the night, marching one after the other onto the stage. In unadorned, sincere fashion they bitterly reproached the government for the raid on the dacha, for the senseless killing. Some were indignant; others mocked the grandiose military operation against a group of people who had never shed a drop of blood even then, when defending themselves from this military pogrom.
>
> The Congress listened silently and sullenly. Maybe the workers were wrong. But in a single voice, without party distinction, they were living testimony to the fact that an unbridgeable abyss separated the capital's workers from the congress, that the two were speaking different languages. No one could miss that.[85]

---

83 Sergeev 1967, pp. 391, 398; Dok. May, p. 493; *Novaya zhizn'* (9 June); *Izvestiya* (19 June 1917).

84 Latsis 1923, p. 107.

85 Sukhanov 1919–23, vol. III, pp. 357–8.

Resolutions adopted at factory meetings support Sukhanov's assessment. The general assembly of the Aivaz Machine-building Factory declared:

> Despite pressure from the entire proletariat of Petrograd on the Soviet of Workers' and Soldiers' Deputies for it to take measures to suppress the reaction that is raising its head, the Soviet's inactivity, on the one hand, and the support of the bourgeois government, on the other, have provided the counterrevolution with the opportunity to make great strides.
>
> On the day of the greatest solidarity of the proletariat, the government mobilised the new 'revolutionary gendarmerie' for a violent operation against anarchist groups at the Durnovo dacha. Instead of an open struggle with word and reason against these ideological opponents who disorganise the proletariat, the government resorts to mass arrests without trial and investigation, provoking a violent counter-reaction that divides the forces of the proletariat.[86]

A meeting at the New Lessner Machine-building Factory resolved:

> We recognise that the tactics of our comrade anarchists are unacceptable and harmful. But the causes that create such conflicts are rooted in the counterrevolutionary policies of the bourgeoisie, acting behind the back of the Socialist ministers. These policies, based very nearly on the old foundations, cause agitation among the masses. This sort of phenomena can be eliminated only by the transfer of power to the Soviets of Workers' and Soldiers' Deputies (example: Kronstadt [where power was effectively in the hands of the local soviet]. There the anarchists have made no seizures and will not attempt them).[87]

One of the 'counterrevolutionary policies of the bourgeoisie' alluded to in the resolution and that was causing much agitation among workers in the spring of 1917 was the plan for the so-called 'unloading' (*razgruzka*) of industry from the capital. While the government was moving at a snail's pace on the matter of regulating the economy, which was seriously faltering under the crushing burden of war, already in April it began work on a plan to evacuate Petrograd's industry to the provinces, arguing that there it would be closer to sources of food and raw materials. This plan immediately aroused workers'

86 *Pravda* (24 June 1917).

87 Dok. May, p. 567.

suspicions. There was broad agreement across the soviet political spectrum that the economic basis of the plan was seriously faulty. After all, the major cause of the impending economic crisis was the disorganisation of transport. Yet, it was estimated that 200,000 railroad cars would be required to move the factories. Surely, it was argued, it made better sense to use those cars to bring materials to the factories, rather than to tie up transport for shipping the factories around the country. Besides that, the owners refused to commit themselves to a date for resuming production. Some even stated that it could not happen before January 1919. Yet, Petrograd was Russia's principle centre of military production.[88]

Workers were convinced that the plan was politically motivated by the census politicians' desire to rid the capital of a political threat. Prince Lvov, the Prime Minister, told one of the 'private' meetings of the State Duma:

> All of Russia has been handed over to that idol, Petersburg, that even under the old regime sucked the juices from the people and continues to suck them now. Russia is being sacrificed to that loud-mouthed insolence, to that chaos, that is called Petersburg.[89]

A meeting of 700 workers of the Kozhevnikovskaya textile mill adopted the following resolution:

> After hearing and discussing a report on the unloading of Petrograd ... [we] protest against the malicious intentions of the factory and mill owners and of our coalition Provisional government. We find that the factory and mill owners intend by this unloading to exile part of the revolutionary proletariat beyond the Urals so that it will be easier for them to assume the leadership of the counterrevolutionary movement.[90]

Another meeting suggested that it would be more advisable 'to unload the city, not of its workers, but of its stock-market speculators, bureaucrats and idle strollers along Nevskii Prospekt'.[91]

---

88 FZK, vol. II, p. 31, and Sukhanov 1919–23, vol. VI, p. 64.

89 *Novaya zhizn'* (1 July 1917). *Novaya zhizn'* correctly pointed out to the Prince that, to the degree that such chaos did exist in Russia – pogroms, lynching and other lawless acts – it was to be found almost exclusively in the provinces.

90 Rab. Kon., p. 83.

91 *Rabochaya gazeta* (26 May 1917).

In was, in fact, on the issue of the 'unloading' that the Bolsheviks won their first major victory in the Workers' Section of the Petrograd Soviet on 31 May. According to a report in *Izvestiya*, in the course of a debate on that day on the 'unloading', the government and the Executive Committee of the Soviet in particular were subjected to harsh criticism on the part of the Central Bureau of Petrograd's Trade Unions, the Metalworkers' Union, and the Bolsheviks, all of whom called for power to be transferred to the soviets and for the immediate conversion of military industry to peacetime production. All these critics portrayed the 'unloading' as a move on the part of the bourgeoisie against the political and social aspirations of the proletariat. A resolution proposed by the Central Bureau of Trade Unions declared that what was needed was not the 'unloading' of Petrograd, but an end to the war and a serious struggle against the advancing economic breakdown. This demanded regulation of the economy and control over production by a state, in which power would be in the hands of the Soviet of Workers', Soldiers' and Peasants' Deputies. 173 deputies supported this resolution, whereas 144 supported the position of the Soviet's Executive Committee that defended the Provisional Government.[92]

Faced with this opposition, the Provisional Government discreetly set the plan aside, at least for the moment.

The 18 June Military Offensive

Soon after the April crisis, the Provisional Government began to prepare a summer military offensive, which would put an end to the de facto ceasefire on the Eastern front. In connection with these preparations, Kerenskii, Minister of War, rescinded many of the rights that had been won by rank-and-file soldiers in the February Revolution. Officers were given authority to use force against insubordinate troops under battle conditions, and the soldiers' elected committees lost the right to remove commanders or to interfere with battle orders. These measures, if they could be applied, would have in practice annulled Order no. 1 of the Petrograd Soviet that had broken the power of the officers' corps, a fundamental act of the February Revolution.[93]

Although most workers still supported a position of 'revolutionary defencism', they saw these measures as a threat to the revolution. They had no

---

92 *Izvestiya* (2 June 1917).

93 The Soviet's order no. 1 provided for the immediate election of committees by rank-and-file soldiers and sailors in all military units and ships. In all political actions, the soldiers were to obey, not their officers, but these committees and the Soviet. All arms were to be under the control of the committees. The lower ranks were accorded equal civil and political rights in private and public life with other citizens. *Izvestiya* (2 Mar. 1917).

illusions about the counterrevolutionary frame of mind of the officer corps, especially its higher ranks. In some factories, workers openly expressed their sympathy for soldiers of the regiments that were being disbanded as punishment for insubordination. The general assembly of the Nevskii Shoe Factory unanimously adopted the following resolution on 6 June:

> Having learnt of the disbandment of five regiments, we angrily protest against such measures. Insubordination has as its source the justified indignation of the soldiers against the tactics of offensive. The disastrous tactic of conquest cannot help but be resisted by conscious soldiers. We express our solidarity with the soldiers of the disbanded regiments.[94]

Workers were also alarmed at the government's announced intention to send part of Petrograd's garrison to the front. This violated an agreement concluded during the February Revolution between the Soviet and the Duma Committee to keep intact the capital's garrison in order to defend the centre of revolution.

Under the impact of these policies of the Provisional Government, 'revolutionary defencism' was eroding quickly among workers. This position had been premised on the assumption that the government would seek a speedy, democratic and universal peace. Preparations for a new offensive left little doubt that this was not the government's policy. It was no secret that, despite its poor morale, Russia's ill-equipped army was being prepared for a new offensive under intense pressure from London, Paris and, not least, Washington. These allies had responded to the Soviet's appeal for a general peace and for the rejection of annexations and reparations with their own call for the overthrow of 'Prussian militarism', for 'just reparations for losses' and for the restoration of Russia's military capacity.[95]

It is therefore not surprising that workers were unconvinced by Kerenskii's efforts to portray the offensive as merely a tactical operation, not a political decision.[96] They felt the offensive would hurt chances for a speedy and just peace by damaging the international authority of the Russian Revolution in the eyes of workers of the other warring countries. Even the Menshevik *Rabochaya gazeta*, which supported the offensive, recognised the popularity of the slogan of an 'immediate general ceasefire'. It reported that a mass meeting at the

94 Dok. May, p. 301.
95 Kochan 1970, pp. 218–20.
96 *Rabochaya gazeta* (25 May 1917).

end of May of workers and soldiers on the capital's Plains of Mars broke into thunderous applause at every mention of the word 'ceasefire'.[97]

The Provisional Government's foreign policy was widely discussed at factory meetings, which more and more often adopted resolutions demanding the transfer of power to the soviets. A joint meeting on 5 June of the foundry, tool-making and pattern-making shops of the Putilov Factory sent greetings to the Congress of Soviets and added:

> We hope that foreign policy, which now stands frozen in place on the issue of peace without annexations ... will immediately begin to move off that spot ... and we similarly hope that the All-Russian Congress of Soviets will decide the fate of domestic policy, in particular of the dual power and the lack of authority of our coalition Provisional Government, and the congress must henceforth say that power should be transferred to the hands of democracy.[98]

On 15 June, a joint meeting of two shifts of the Old Parviainen Machine-building Factory unanimously adopted the following resolution:

> We ... consider the politics of conciliation with our capitalists and, through them, with the capitalists of the entire world, to be ruinous to the cause of the Russian and international revolutions, to the cause of the world unification of the proletariat.
>
> We call all our comrade proletarians and rural semi-proletarians to break decisively with the policy of imperialism and appeasement of imperialism – a policy directed at reducing the Russian Revolution to the role of obedient servant and executor of the will of international capital.
>
> The Russian Revolution, which summons the toilers of the wide world to a struggle against capitalism, must offer a worthy example of this struggle in a disciplined and thought-out form. Down with the power of the capitalists! Long live the revolutionary proletariat and peasantry! Down with the politics of powerlessness, the politics of appeasement of worldwide plunderers! Long live the politics of force, the politics of decisive struggle for the freedom of the toilers of the entire world! Peace to the hovels, war to the palaces! In the name of this great struggle, we consider it necessary to carry out immediately a series of measures that are expressed

97 Ibid. (28 May 1917).

98 Ibid., (18 June 1917).

> in the following slogans: Down with the counterrevolution, down with the ten capitalist ministers, down with the 'Entente imperialists', who stand behind the counterrevolution that is being organised, down with the capitalists who are organising an Italian [go-slow] strike and hidden lockouts. All power to the workers' and peasants' deputies ... Neither a separate peace with Wilhelm, nor secret treaties with English and French capitalists! Immediate publication by the Soviet of genuinely just peace terms. Against the policy of offensive. Bread. Peace. Freedom.[99]

The Provisional Government launched the offensive on 18 June, the very day tens of thousands of workers and soldiers were in the streets of the capital expressing their lack of confidence in that government. Nevertheless, a joint meeting of the workers' and soldiers' sections of the Petrograd Soviet on 20 June approved the offensive by a vote of 472 against 271 (39 abstentions). This followed a similar vote by the Congress of Soviets a day earlier.[100] But the vote in the Soviet owed much to the soldier deputies, who tended to be more conservative than the workers (and who were heavily overrepresented in relation to their numbers). The attitude of most of Petrograd's workers to the offensive is reflected in the following resolution of the New Lessner Machine-building Factory:

> On the issue of the offensive, we declare that this offensive has dealt a blow to the Russian Revolution and to the International and that the entire responsibility for that policy falls on the Provisional Government and the parties of Mensheviks and Socialist-Revolutionaries that support it. We are convinced that only through the revolutionary efforts of the toiling masses and of all peoples is it possible to end the war, and for that we need, not an offensive on the front, but an offensive against the bourgeoisie inside the country for the transfer of power to the hands of the Soviet of Workers' and Soldiers' Deputies.[101]

Economic Regulation

The demand for state regulation of Russia's faltering economy arose in the latter part of April. It marked, on the workers' part, a deepening of the social content of the revolution. Until then, they had been mainly concerned with

99 Kudelli 1924, pp. 34–5.
100 *Izvestiya* (23 June 1917).
101 *Pravda* (22 June 1917).

eliminating the remnants of the old regime and dealing with grievances that it had bequeathed. Economic regulation was a new issue that arose out of the conditions of the revolution itself.

But it, too, was linked to the perception, increasingly widespread among workers, that the bourgeoisie wanted to overturn the revolution and that one of its means to that goal was to sabotage the economy. Workers increasingly suspected that this strategy lay behind cutbacks in production in the factories. It also explained why the industrialists were so firmly opposed to reinforcing state economic regulation. Workers suspected, in fact, a hidden lockout aimed at weakening the proletariat, the vanguard of the revolution. 'Of late', wrote the Menshevik-Internationalists' *Novaya zhizn'* in mid-May

> one observes in a whole series of enterprises the reduction of production. So far, this phenomenon has manifested itself only in medium and small enterprises. But all the same, it is beginning profoundly to alarm the worker masses. The more conscious workers are beginning to make the connection between their new economic gains and the curtailment of production that follows.[102]

In June, the conservative daily *Novoe vremya* observed that owners were selling their factories, sending their money abroad and then following it, in accordance with the old Russian saying: 'Where my fortune lies, there too lies my heart'.[103] Similarly, the Petrograd Textile Workers' Union observed a tendency among the sector's owners, who were mostly British, to close their current accounts and to ship finished and semi-finished goods, and, if they could get away with it, even raw materials and machine parts, across the border to Finland. In some mills, the workers were already on a reduced week. The union's journal reported that, in one of the mills, management told the workers it had to reduce production because of a shortage of raw cotton, while at that very time raw cotton was being taken out of the mill and loaded onto barges for destinations unknown. Another English entrepreneur, Charles Munken, left Petrograd in May for Finland, ostensibly to buy spools. But he ended up in England and was soon followed by his partners and by the mill's English managerial staff, who had emptied the mill's safes before leaving. Even Percy Thornton, an industrial of liberal reputation, was threatening to pack it in.[104]

---

102 *Novaya zhizn'* (10 May 1917).

103 *Novoe vremya* (20 June 1917).

104 Perazich 1927, p. 85.

Before the February Revolution and during the first months of the new regime, capitalists and census politicians had attributed the economy's serious problems to the incompetent management of the Tsarist government and to the impact of the war. Never did they mention the workers as a factor in this. But all that soon changed. In May, N.N. Kutler, industrialist and prominent leader of the Kadet party, depicted the economic situation in the following terms: Russia's economic mechanism had been destroyed by the workers' purge of managerial personnel; productivity had fallen by 20–40 percent; anarchy and disorganisation ruled. And the main problem was the 'inordinate demands' of the workers that were making the enterprises unmanageable.[105] Commenting on this speech, *Rech'*, the Kadets' paper, made an ominous prediction: 'Two or three weeks will go by, and the factories will begin to close one after the other'.[106]

As for state regulation, this was blocked by the firm opposition of the capitalists. In mid-May the Executive Committee of the Petrograd Soviet adopted a plan, drawn up under the leadership of Menshevik economist V.G. Groman, for broad state regulation of production, distribution and finance. Two days later, A.I. Konovalov, Minister of Trade and Industry, a wealthy Moscow industrialist, resigned, citing this plan as his reason. In his letter of resignation to Prime Minister Lvov, he explained that he had no quarrel on most issues with the Minister of Labour (the Menshevik-Defencist M.I. Skobelev, who was also a member of the Soviet's Executive Committee), not even on the matters of financial reform and labour relations. But he was sceptical about the form of public control and regulation of the economy that Skobelev was proposing. And he added: there would be hope of averting a crisis only if the 'Provisional Government at least demonstrated genuinely full authority; if it at least took the path of restoring the discipline that has been undermined and if it showed energy in the struggle against the inordinate demands of the extreme leftists'.[107] His solution to the country's economic woes was simple: rein in the workers. At the Congress of War-Industry Committees a few days later, he again railed against the 'inordinate demands of the workers' and warned that, 'if there is not a sobering of minds in the nearest future, we will witness the closure of tens and hundreds of factories'.[108]

105 *Rabochaya gazeta* (14 May 1917); Sukhanov 1919–23, vol. III, p. 109.

106 *Rech'* (13 May 1917).

107 *Novaya zhizn'* (20 May 1917).

108 Ibid. (19 May 1917).

Konovalov was considered on the extreme left wing of his class.[109] If he opposed economic regulation, there was little hope for the others. Indeed, a major theme of the All-Russian Congress of Representatives of Trade and Industry on 1–2 June was opposition to economic regulation by the state in any form.[110] P.P. Ryabushinskii, a banker and industrialist who also enjoyed a liberal reputation, explained to the assembled why state regulation of the economy was possible in the other warring countries but not in Russia:

> In Europe, when the state intervenes in the sphere of national [economic] life, it has full control, something to which we do not object. But we fear that such control is impossible in Russia as far as its usefulness and advisability for the state as a whole is concerned, so long as the government itself is in a situation of being controlled.[111]

Translated into direct language, Ryabushinskii was objecting to the influence of the Soviet on the government. Things were different elsewhere, where the capitalists could ensure economic regulation would be in their interests. But in Russia, the correlation of class forces favoured the workers. And so, state regulation of the economy was unacceptable.

There was broad agreement at this time across the soviet political spectrum about the bourgeoisie's position on the economy. The Mensheviks' *Rabochaya gazeta*, although it supported a political alliance with the liberal bourgeoisie in the form of the coalition government and firmly opposed the growing chorus calling for the soviets to take power on their own, clearly stated that the industrialists were organising a hidden lockout. An editorial from mid-May on this subject is worth quoting at length:

> In the industrialists' camp there is animation. The brief stupor that seized them in the first days of the Revolution has passed. No trace remains now of their recent confusion and of their panicky willingness to make concessions. If during the first month of freedom, the united industrialists, without almost any resistance, acquiesced to workers' demands, now they have decisively shifted to the defensive and they are quickly preparing an offensive along the entire front …

---

109 Ibid. (21 May 1917).

110 Ibid. (2 June 1917); Dok. May, p. 197.

111 *Izvestiya Moskovskogo Voenno-promyshlennogo komiteta*, no. 13 (1917), p. 15. cited in Volobuev 1962, p. 35.

> They do not decide to declare open war at once on the workers. The volcanic soil of the Revolution is still too red-hot, the working class still too threatening in its revolutionary enthusiasm for the industrialists, at least at the present moment, to decide on a frontal assault and to smash the adversary with a counter blow.
>
> But intensification of the general course of economic ruin, the advancing spectre of mass unemployment, the social fright of the possessing classes – all this will create favourable ground for carrying out the offensive designs of the entrepreneurs. And so, not deciding to advance openly 'down the middle', they are attempting an encircling movement around the flank in order to attack the enemy from the rear. Of late, more and more frequently one hears of an 'Italian strike' [slowdown strike] practised by the entrepreneurs now here, now there. The plants are not being repaired, worn parts are not replaced, work is conducted in a slipshod manner. The entrepreneurs shout on all crossroads that the 'excessive demands' of the workers cannot be met and are directly disastrous to the enterprises. They generously propose, or at least pretend to propose, that the government lift from them the unbearable burden of running the enterprises.
>
> In other cases, they cut back production, dismiss workers under the pretext of lacking metal, fuel, orders, or the competition of imports. Here, we have before us a different means of struggle – the hidden lockout.
>
> In the Labour Department of the Soviet of Workers' and Soldiers' Deputies, one daily encounters facts that confirm the existence of a definite plan of the industrialists.[112]

This analysis might easily have appeared in the Bolsheviks' *Pravda*. Only the latter would have drawn from it the conclusion that, since the bourgeoisie was counterrevolutionary, it should be excluded from government: the soviets should take power on their own. M.N. Zhivotov, a Bolshevik delegate from the 1886 Power Co. to the First Conference of Petrograd Factory Committees in early June, made precisely that argument:

> To us workers, it is clear that the bourgeoisie is organising its counterrevolutionary offensive against democracy and especially against its van-

112 *Rabochaya gazeta* (20 May 1917). After the October Revolution, however, the same newspaper would change its view, arguing that the Bolsheviks' accusation of sabotage by the owners was 'demagogic fantasy' (Ibid., 12 Nov. 1917).

> guard detachment, the working class ... It has been conducting its counterrevolutionary attack very skilfully, and, at first glance, imperceptibly, intensifying the economic dislocation and, with it, the shortage of food ... It is even prepared to provoke hunger revolts and anarchy in order then to declare a dictatorship and, with the aid of military force, to settle accounts with that anarchy and at the same time with the Revolution, since, to the bourgeoisie, it is the same thing as anarchy.
>
> You have to be blind or mentally immature not to see this counterrevolutionary work of the bourgeoisie. Sabotage on the part of the coal industrialists in the Donbass, sabotage in the textile industry, and the same organised sabotage by the entrepreneurs in a whole series of Petrograd factories – this demands the organised intervention of the working class in the form of the immediate establishment of workers' control, which alone can erect a barrier to the counterrevolutionary designs of the capitalists.
>
> If we don't conduct a struggle against the disorganising work of the capitalists, it will destroy all our proletarian organisations, since the fall in production and the closure of factories are daily increasing the army of unemployed, and a hungry and unemployed person does not have any thought for organisation. And if the organisations lose their worker masses, if the latter are beyond their influence, then we will see real anarchy that will not be so easily controlled ...
>
> It would be naïve to think that the coalition government, with the bourgeois brotherhood assembled there, will design and carry out control over its very own capitalists and industrialists. All the more insistently, therefore, should we, workers, strive for the establishment of control with the participation of representatives of the workers and workers' organisations locally, in our factories.
>
> In the not distant future, life will undoubtedly put forth the workers' demand for control over production, but it will not be fully realised by a bourgeois government, but by a government of revolutionary democracy that will take its place.[113]

Zhivotov was supported by other delegates. Tseitlin, from the Kersten Knitwear mill, addressed the following words to the 'conciliators' (Mensheviks and SRs), who argued that the very survival of the revolution required that it retain the support of the liberal bourgeoisie:

---

113 FZK, vol. I, pp. 105–6.

> Anticipating unemployment, we can't allow it to ruin us. You [Menshevik leaders M.I. Skobelev and F. Dan] say that we can't take power into our hands now because the masses aren't organised. But when these masses are hungry, we won't be able to do anything. We need to create now a government that will avert hunger. We have to create that organ that was proposed during the revolution. We need to create a strong centre of factory committees that will be the Ministry of Labour of the proletariat of all of Russia. It will, of course, act more decisively than the ministry of Skobelev.
>
> We need immediately to regulate all of production, immediately to convert a whole series of factories from military production to production of goods of prime necessity needed by the whole country. And workers must show initiative in that direction, not pinning their hopes on those who occupy ministerial chairs. We need to produce agriculture machines and other necessary goods.
>
> You will ask: 'But where will the money come from?' It has to be taken from the plunderers who shout hypocritically about the 'Liberty Loan' that exists only on the posters. We should take the money and not behave like artists, begging on the streets for a 'Liberty Loan' of pennies from the bourgeoisie. The factory committees should inspect the factories that are closing in order to adapt them for other goals.
>
> We have to look at things as they really are, and not as they are portrayed by the [Menshevik and SR] conciliators with the bourgeoisie. We must demand categorically. You'll achieve nothing with appeasement.[114]

The Menshevik leader D. Dalin replied for the Executive Committee of the Petrograd Soviet, completely rejecting those arguments: 'To say that workers should take upon themselves management of production means that they must take power. But I protest against raising any sort of political questions at a conference of this kind, a conference of factory committees'.[115] But Dalin protested in vain, since the very logic of their situation was driving workers to embrace the demand for soviet power. And this logic was most acutely felt by the activists in the elected factory committees who were closest to the problems of production.

That logic did not, of course, really escape the Menshevik and SR leaders of the Soviet. When the Soviet's own Economic Department, consisting mainly

114 Ibid., p. 123.

115 Ibid., p. 100.

of moderate Mensheviks and SRs, presented its plan for state regulation of the economy to the Soviet's Executive Committee, Skobelev, Menshevik Minister of Labour, exclaimed: 'You want to take power!'[116] He understood only too well that even this modest plan for state regulation would be unacceptable to his census partners in the government, that it could be adopted and carried only by a government in which the industrialists had been deprived of influence, a government of 'revolutionary democracy', in sum, a soviet government.

Factory committee activists with 'conciliationist' political attitudes were naturally driven leftward by the problems they faced daily. An activist at the Admiralty Shipyards recalled: 'I was a delegate to the First Conference of Factory Committees together with a Menshevik and an SR. But my opponents voted with me on all the basic questions … Our [Bolshevik] resolutions were adopted. One of my opponents tore up his membership card at his party meeting and joined ours several days later'.[117]

The issues examined here – the government's war policy, the increasingly aggressive tone of prominent census politicians and of the census press, the government's inactivity in face of the looming economic crisis, the suspicions concerning a hidden lockout by industrialists, the government's plan to 'unload' Petrograd of its industry – these by the end of May had convinced a majority of the more urbanised, skilled strata of workers of the need for the soviets to exercise power on their own. This was confirmed by the first vote in the Workers' Section of the Soviet at the end of May in favour of soviet power.

As for the less skilled workers and those with ties to the countryside, they mostly still supported the SRs, and, to a much lesser extent, the Mensheviks. These were, on the whole, less politicised people, and the above-mentioned issues were still too distant from their concrete, everyday experience. Perazich, a Bolshevik leader in the textile workers' union, observed that workers in the mills might turn away from their local Menshevik and SR activists when conflicts arose over cutbacks to production. These workers would then condemn their local Mensheviks and SRs as 'bosses' stooges' for refusing to confront management. Yet these same workers would listen approvingly to activists of these same parties who came from the outside to speak to them. 'Most of our masses at that time were politically still quite benighted and followed the Mensheviks and SRs.' At Thornton, for example, when the Left SR

116 Sukhanov 1919–23, vol. IV, p. 110.

117 'Petrogradskie rabochie ob iyul'skikh dynakh', *Krasnaya letopis'*, no. 9 (1924), p. 33.

Marusya Spiridonovna spoke, proclaiming the slogan 'All power to the soviets', the workers didn't let her finish, shouting: 'Scram! ... Hard labour convict! ... Murderer!'[118]

A.I. Slutskii, who was working in the Nevskii district, still firmly under the influence of SRs, reported at the end of May to the Bolshevik Petersburg Committee that 'the situation in the Nevskii district is such that Bolsheviks can't speak at meetings – they are whistled down',[119] He made the same observation as Perazich:

> Listen to what the workers say after the meetings, where they possibly applauded speakers who defended the platform of the Soviet of Workers' and Soldiers' Deputies [i.e. support for the coalition government]. But when it comes to their essential needs – wage rates, inflation, raises, the unloading [of Petrograd's factories] – if these issues have touched this stratum of workers, then their agitation is great.
>
> You can observe the same thing among peasants: peasants are very weak when it comes to orienting themselves in political questions. But when it comes to resolving the land issue, they are very radical. You need only look at the sixth clause of their resolution [adopted at the First All-Russian Congress of Peasant Representatives on 25 May], where they clearly state that the appointed government has to be kicked the hell out.[120]

A classic case of this period in which an economic conflict radicalised a group of unskilled and semi-skilled workers occurred at the Putilov Factory. Its 30,000 workers were a microcosm of Petrograd's industrial proletariat. During the labour upsurge of 1912–14, Bolsheviks had the undisputed lead here. The factory's workers struck a total of 102 days in 1913 and 145 in the first six months of 1914, mainly in support of political demands or to protest political repression.[121] During the war, however, the factory lost its leading role in the capital's labour movement. According to a police report from February 1916,

118 Perazich 1927, p. 81. Mariya Spridinovna had assassinated a colonel of the Tsarist political police, the commander of a punitive detachment that was putting down peasant uprisings in Tambov guberniya in 1906. Sentenced to life imprisonment at hard labour, she was freed by the February Revolution.

119 *Peterburgskii komitet RSDRP(b) d 1917 g.*, SPb, 2003, p. 230.

120 Op. cit., p. 265.

121 *Putilovtsy v trekh revolyutsiyakh*, p. 236.

> Before the war, they stood at the head of the Petrograd workers. A radical shift occurred from the start of the war among the factory's workers and patriotic sentiment predominated over socialist. In the course of time, this patriotic sentiment declined significantly, but justice requires one to note the unconditional loyalty and restraint of the Putilov workers, who did not participate in such traditional time-honoured labour demonstrations as 1 May and 9 January.

During the entire previous year, continued the report, the workers remained mostly calm, despite the Bolsheviks' efforts to draw them into the general movement.[122] What the report did not mention was the rapid expansion of the factory's military production at the start of the war that more than doubled its workforce with the hiring of a mass of unskilled and semi-skilled workers, many fresh from the village. On the other hand, some 6,000 workers (the factory had employed 16,000 in 1913), who had participated in the intense pre-war labour struggles, were drafted into the army. In February 1917, there were no less than 10,000 unskilled labourers (*chernorabochie*) employed at the factory.[123]

Back in 1916, after failing to persuade the workers to strike to mark the anniversary of Bloody Sunday (9 January 1905), the Bolsheviks decided to change tactics and began to emphasise economic demands. The results were not long in coming. On the very date of the above-cited police report, the factory's workers were on strike for economic demands.[124] In the three months following the February Revolution, most workers here supported the Mensheviks and SRs. In the first elections to the Petrograd Soviet, the factory sent only nine Bolsheviks among its 45 deputies. The only exceptions were the shops with concentrations of skilled workers, such as instrument-making. The latter's workers declared themselves for soviet power very early.[125] But when it came to economic issues, the Bolsheviks had more reason to celebrate. Their candidates did very well in elections to the Metalworkers' and Woodworkers' Unions, and Bolsheviks were a majority from the very start in the factory committee – out of a total of 22, six were Bolsheviks and seven sympathisers.[126]

The shift in the political attitudes of the mass of the factory's workers began in earnest at the end of May. The catalyst was the festering 'conflict of March'.

---

122 Ibid., p. 291.

123 Kruze 1961, p. 72; Stepanov 1965, p. 27; Mitel'man et al. 1961, p. 631.

124 *Putilovtsy v trekh revolyutsiyakh*, p. 236.

125 Mitel'man et al. 1961, p. 577.

126 Ibid., p. 590.

On 19 April, management had agreed to new wage rates that were to be introduced retroactively from 7 March. But weeks passed, and the retroaction was not paid. The administration remained silent. 'Italian' strikes began. Finally, the board of directors announced that the director had overstepped his authority in agreeing to the retroaction, which would not be paid. The factory committee sent delegates to various government ministries (the factory had been sequestered by the state in 1915) but to no avail. On 8 June, some shops went on strike, and it was only with great difficulty that the Bolsheviks kept the workers from taking their protest to the streets. On 13 June, K.A. Gvozdev, the Menshevik assistant Minister of Labour, came to the factory and promised the workers that he would fight for their demand, which he recognised as just. But at the insistence of the factory's board of directors, he agreed to postpone any action until the Petrograd Society of Factory and Mill Owners and the Petrograd Metalworkers' Union completed their negotiations of a general wage agreement for the entire metal sector. This delay so angered the Putilov workers that they participated en masse in the 18 June demonstration behind a banner that read: 'We have been cheated! Comrades, prepare for battle'.

The inscription on the banner was referring to the promised retroaction but undoubtedly also to the policies of the Provisional Government. D. Yu. Gessen, a Bolshevik worker at the Putilov Factory, reported to the Bolsheviks' Petersburg Committee on 20 June:

> In the Narva District, there has been a radical change of mood in our favour, as the new elections have shown and in which Bolsheviks were chosen. The Putilov Factory, that defines the mood of the whole district, has clearly shifted to our position with the adoption of the resolution of comrade Trotsky.
>
> The militant mood of the Putilov Factory has deep economic causes. The issue of wage increases is very acute there. The workers' demands for increases have not been answered from the very start of the Revolution. Gvozdev came to the factory. He promised to satisfy the demands that have been made but he didn't fulfil his promise. In the 18 June demonstration, the Putilov workers also carried this poster: 'We have been deceived!' This Monday, the factory decided to strike. The Metalworkers' Union suggested to postpone the strike for three days in order to notify the other factories. The Putilovtsy agreed to work these three days, although certain shops decided to conduct an Italian strike. The masses consider the strike political. On Thursday, the workers decided to arm themselves by Wednesday.

> The Putilov workers were not at the fore of the movement before this. They are now being pushed there by economic causes.[127]

The SR paper similarly reported at this time that 'the mood is tense. Meetings are being held in the shops and they call for an immediate armed demonstration, not only in defence of the [economic] demands, but against the general direction of the Provisional Government'.[128]

Discontent over wages was growing among all the workers who still supported the position of the Mensheviks and SRs.[129] And although it did not yet find expression in their politics, the glaring absence of banners on 18 June in support of the Petrograd Soviet's 'conciliationist' leadership clearly indicated that this was not far off. After all, the Soviet's leaders had themselves called the demonstration as a show of support for its policies.

It is striking that both the radical and the moderate elements of the more politically aware stratum of workers shared the same evaluation of the bourgeoisie as a class hostile to the Revolution. But the moderates did not consider soviet power a viable alternative. They feared that the workers would be isolated and so crushed. Tkachenko, one of the relatively few Menshevik delegates to the factory committee conference in early June, sent from the Electric Lighting Factory, gave eloquent expression to that view:

> We have here two competing world views, two currents of social thought that view very differently the question of how we, workers, can avert the approaching crisis of production that is preparing to swallow up, along with the revolution, all our conquests in the sphere of rights and in the

127 *Peterburgskii komitet RSDRP(b)*, pp. 329–30. At the Second Factory Committee Conference, in August, Ivanov, a delegate from the Putilov Factory, told the assembly that 'when you discuss the current situation, you have to tell the entire people in full voice how the bourgeoisie wants to saddle and ride us. In discussing the current situation, consider how we, the Putilov workers, have been led around by the nose, not being able to work calmly. And yet, they heap all the blame on us, the workers. If our masses are upset, it is because they are half-starved, and as workers yourselves, you know the condition in which the Putilov workers find themselves and you will tell all of Russia so that the deception that the administration has committed against this vanguard fighter of the working class, the Putilov workers, is known to all. FZK, vol. I, pp. 209–10.

128 *Delo naroda* (20 June 1917).

129 Perazich 1927, pp. 69–73; *Rabochaya gazeta* (6 June 1917). According to *Novaya zhizn'*, in the first two and a half months following the revolution, prices rose more than in the previous two and a half years (16 May 1917). For a lower estimate of the rate of inflation, see *Istoriya SSSR*, no. 3 (1959), p. 224.

economic realm. The signs of the coming catastrophe can already be seen, and energetic measures are needed on the national level to avoid this catastrophe.

Comrade Zinoviev [who spoke for the Bolsheviks] calls on us to concentrate all our energies in order to seize power from the hands of the capitalist-lockouters and to transfer it to the Soviet of Workers' and Soldiers' Deputies. I am certain that any efforts to compel Comrade Zinoviev to examine the question in light of the real correlation of forces in the country will be in vain. In the attempts by Western-European workers to protest, he sees worker battalions already advancing to storm the bastions of capitalism.

Comrade Lenin ... spoke to us of our age-old hatred of the capitalist predators, of our class hatred of the capitalist-aggressors. He spoke of the millions that the lockouters have made from our blood, of the hourly insults from our enemy exploiters, of the oppression that we experience daily on our hides. He pointed out to us that our socialist ministers are being led around on a leash by the bourgeois plunderers and that we should expect nothing from them, because they are finished people.

But neither Lenin nor Zinoviev showed us who in the final analysis will accompany us, the workers, in the struggle for power. Alone, we workers do not have the strength to retain power in our calloused hands without the direct cooperation of the peasants, without the sympathy of the petty bourgeoisie.

You all know whom the peasants said they would support at their congress and with whom they will build a new state in the country. For twenty years comrade Lenin wrote and told us of the need for a dictatorship of the proletariat and the peasantry to seize political power in the state. In those days, he convincingly showed us that the peasantry, being in essence a petty-bourgeois class, will solve its problems in common struggle [with the workers] only up to the point when we will have resolved the land question and the question of political power in the country and that it will decisively part ways with us as soon as it becomes a question of expropriating private property, of realising socialism. And what has changed since ten years ago? Can it be that the peasantry has begun to sense the coming inevitability of socialism and that it has decided to act together with us? ... No, the situation has not changed.

We should never forget that we are living and acting in a period of bourgeois-democratic revolution; we are conducting a struggle with the colossal exertion of all the material and spiritual forces of the people, in the midst of a world slaughter that has gone on forever and that has totally

> exhausted the state organism. In so critical a situation of the country, we, workers, having become the builders, the architects of the new life, must act with the greatest circumspection and not attempt to take too risky steps, so as not to add new, irreparable misfortunes to the devastation that already exists ...
>
> Control of production and distribution is not frightening. State control and regulation of production and distribution are as necessary as bread and air, and we will realise them locally. What is frightening is when they link control to the transfer of power to the soviets. They want to convince us that without the transfer of all power in the country to workers and to democracy it is impossible to realise genuine control of production, the uniform distribution of food among the population. And in doing so, they would have us believe that the workers will be able to manage that task without the cooperation of all of democracy and in face of the open opposition of the bourgeoisie and the intelligentsia.
>
> I am concluding, comrades, and I ask only one thing: that before you set out on the decisive seizure of power, you carefully weigh the circumstances, you clarify in detail who else together with you, workers, will carry out this transfer of power. Fear more than death to remain alone in battle. For as soon as you are left alone, you will be defeated, and then the captains of industry will climb onto the ship of state over our bodies and seize the wheel of power.[130]

Tkachenko said nothing in defence of the coalition government. Nor did he deny the bourgeoisie's counterrevolutionary frame of mind and its decisive influence over the government. That was the fundamental weakness of his argument. The position of the Mensheviks and SRs, which played so heavily on fear – fear of the workers' political isolation, of the workers' inability to deal with the country's problems, and fear of civil war within revolutionary democracy – left their activists in a difficult position when they spoke to workers, since they could not deny that to leave the coalition government in power meant the continued pursuit of the imperialist war, economic collapse (since the bourgeoisie opposed regulation and blocked workers' control) and massive loss of jobs, and, with the resulting weakening of the workers' movement, the prospect of a victorious counterrevolution. But while the radicalised workers were acutely aware of the risks and dangers involved in taking power

130 FZK, vol. I, pp. 102–4.

through the soviets, they were convinced that to leave the coalition government in power would quickly lead to a victorious counterrevolution. The choice was obvious.

In a report on the Food Congress, which had been convened to discuss the increasingly serious food situation, the Menshevik-Internationalist *Novaya zhizn'* presented the moderate socialists' position in much the same light. The left wing of the congress, consisting mostly of workers and a part of the peasant delegates, argued for measures that would encroach on the rights of private property. The right wing, which was much smaller, argued that the capitalists were playing a positive, organising role and that their support was vital. As for the majority, they were simply paralysed by fear.

> They too have no faith in the capitalists. But they fear any decisive measures aimed at the liquidation of the privileges of property. To them, the path of Russia's future development appears as a struggle against insurmountable obstacles. Every now and then, they evoke the 'greyness' and ignorance of the masses, their anarchistic tendencies, the lack of firm government, the stubbornness of the merchants and industrialists.[131]

It is telling that resolutions adopted at workers' meetings in this period in support of the Menshevik-SR leadership of the Soviet very rarely expressed support for the coalition government. Instead, they called for the unity of revolutionary democracy and criticised the Bolsheviks for provoking a split within its ranks. Thus, on the eve of the demonstration of 18 June, the printers of the Otto Kirkhner Printing House, after a prolonged debate, resolved:

> We consider that the Bolsheviks are making a gross mistake in their evaluation of the conditions of the current situation, which calls for the unity of the forces of revolutionary democracy, and that they are harming the cause of the revolution, introducing disorganisation into the midst of the working class. We printers propose to the entire proletariat of Petrograd to demonstrate on 18 June against their capitalist classes, as the main culprits who engineered this war.[132]

---

131 *Novaya zhizn'* (28 May 1917).

132 *Rabochaya gazeta* (18 June 1917). For similar resolutions, see in ibid., 5 July 1917 (Kibbel' printing plant); 8 July 1917 (general delegates' assembly of Petrograd printing plants); and 14 Apr 1917 (Leont'ev Textile Mills).

At a meeting of the Bolshevik Petersburg Committee on 20 June, a delegate from the Moscow district reported that 'until now, the SRs dominated. The Soviet's policy of marking time and our [cancelled] demonstration of 10 June marked a shift in the workers' attitudes in our favour. The events that followed woke up the non-party masses, too. The SRs were at a loss before the 18th and didn't know what slogans to put forth. The masses took note of this wavering and shifted to us'. The delegate from the Nevskii district, another SR stronghold, likewise reported: 'Until the demonstration, we were, at least so it appeared, very weak. The Mensheviks and SRs were totally at a loss and did not put forth any slogans. Before the demonstration, they busied themselves with frightening people, and so not many came out for the demonstration'.[133]

In less than four months of the Revolution, the political attitudes of most of Petrograd's workers had undergone a major shift. The experience of those months had clarified the political situation, dispelling the illusion of national unity born of the February Revolution. Lenin summed this up when he compared the demonstration on 18 June with those of 23 March (the funeral of the fallen in the February Revolution), and 18 April (May Day):

> Then, it was a universal *celebration* of the first victory of the Revolution and of its heroes, a backward glance by the people at the first, very successfully and rapidly executed stage toward freedom. 1 May was a holiday of the aspirations and hopes tied up with the history of the worldwide labour movement, with its socialist ideal.
>
> Neither demonstration set as a goal to indicate the direction of the continued movement of the Revolution, nor could they not have shown it. Neither posed to the masses the concrete, specific and burning questions about whether and how the Revolution should proceed.
>
> In this sense the 18th of June was the first political demonstration of action, a clarification – not in a pamphlet or a newspaper, but on the street; not through leaders but by the masses – a clarification of how the various classes are acting, want to act, and will act in order to carry the Revolution further.[134]

Izvestiya, controlled by the Menshevik-SR majority in the Soviet, made essentially the same observation:

133 *Peterburgskii komitet RSDRP(b)*, pp. 322 and 338.

134 Lenin, *Polnoe Sobranie*, 5th ed., 1962, vol. XXXII, p. 361.

> The characteristic difference between the present demonstration and those of 23 March and 1 May was the abundance of banners and the precision of slogans. If the former unity no longer exists, now at least everyone is more acutely aware of what he is struggling for and what the next tasks of the struggle are.[135]

135 *Izvestiya* (20 June 1917).

CHAPTER 6

The Struggle for Power in the Factories in April–June

The demand for government regulation of the economy, one of the focal points of the intensifying struggle around the question of political power, had its analogue in the factories during this period in the unfolding movement for workers' control.

The conflict that arose at the Langezipen Machine-building Factory is an example. At the end of April, the Senior Factory Inspector for Petrograd Guberniya reported:

> Guards posted by the workers on 27 April refused to allow the administration to leave before the end of work. As a result, the factory director was forced to remain in his office until 4:00 p.m. The factory's workers suspect the administration of holding up defence production. Accordingly, the issue is being discussed by a mixed commission of the Soviet of Workers' and Soldiers' Deputies, the Society of Factory and Mill Owners, the Union of Engineers and the Central War-Industry Committee.[1]

The conflict came to a head on 2 June when the director announced his intention to close operations, citing a 33 percent drop in output, 10 million rubles of losses on state orders, and a lack of funds. This situation he attributed to the introduction of the eight-hour day, a 50 percent decline in labour productivity, constantly rising prices, and shortages of fuel and raw materials. At the request of the factory's workers, the Central Soviet of Factory Committees, which had been elected just a few days earlier at a city-wide conference of factory committees, conducted an inquiry into the factory's ownership. Although the director refused to cooperate with the inquiry, it was finally established that the original owner, the Azov-Don Bank, had transferred its shares to a certain Zhivotov, who in turn transferred them to the Siberian Bank of Commerce, which in turn registered them in the name of a certain Kislyanskii. By that time, however, the director informed the workers that he had unexpectedly come up with the

1 Dok. Apr., p. 444.

450,000 rubles, borrowed from an acquaintance, and that production could proceed at full speed.[2]

In the meanwhile, however, the workers had moved to establish control over management. On 5 June, the factory committee reported:

> The situation of late at the factories of the Langezipen Co. Inc., i.e. 1) the refusal of the factory administration to recognise the workers' and [white-collar] employees' control commission 2) the administration's violation of the decision of the arbitration chamber from 6 May 1917 concerning the amount of wages of employees, and 3) the latest declaration of the administration on the closure of the plant – have placed us before the necessity of taking the following measures: 1) No goods or raw materials may be shipped out from the factory without the permission of the factory committee; in addition, manufactured goods ready for shipment must be registered by the factory committee and are shipped out by it. 2) All orders issued by the factory committee are binding on all workers and employees, and no order from the administration is valid without the sanction of the factory committee. 3) No documents or correspondence relating to the factory can be destroyed without the factory committee having reviewed them. 4) To carry out the above tasks, the elected control commission will assume its duties beginning today. 5) The firemen and guards are duty-bound to keep watch over the factory's buildings against fire.[3]

Two weeks later, the control commission asked the government to hold up payment of dividends by the enterprise, pending a complete state investigation. The commission itself began work on a counter-report to the one produced by management and it requested that the Ministry of Labour obtain for it the necessary documents. Finally, it turned to the Central Soviet Factory Committees for help in drafting regulations and procedures for the factory committee.[4]

Izvestiya, the newspaper of the Soviet, described this conflict as characteristic of a 'whole series of declarations of closure by the owners' that were being received by the Central Soviet of Factory Committees. The paper observed that despite the variety of reasons offered, in most cases they boiled down to a lack of funds and financial losses. 'However, at the first attempt by workers' organ-

2 FZK, vol. I, p. 148; *Izvestiya* (17 June 1917); *Novaya zhizn'* (19 June 1917).

3 Rab. Kon., pp. 104–5.

4 Ibid., p. 111.

isations to verify the reasons offered by the entrepreneurs, the most complex and crafty machinations aimed at a lockout by the capitalists are very often uncovered'.[5]

This conflict was also characteristic in that the workers' actions were essentially defensive in motivation: they wanted to prevent any further decline in production and a possible closure. These, they suspected – and in this case, their suspicions were clearly not without foundation – were the result of management's passive or active sabotage. The above-cited declaration of Langezipen's factory committee stated that the owner's expressed intention to close 'has placed us before the necessity' of establishing control. The motive for infringing on managerial power was the workers' desire to defend production, their jobs, and, in the final analysis, their revolution.

The same attitude was evident in the move to establish control by the workers of the Voronin and Co. Cotton-Printing Mill:

> The general assembly of workers and employees ... having heard the report on the systematic contraction of production at the factories of Voronin and Co, adopted the following resolution:
>
> The observed contraction of production of late at the factory is the conscious activity of the mill owners, that is aimed at bringing the country to ruin and thus destroying freedom.
>
> Considering the very seriousness of the consequences of this attempt at counterrevolution, the general assembly mandates the factory committee, together with the committees of workers and employees of the other mills belonging to the given company, to elect a central committee that must control the activity of the company in the production of goods. Insofar as a desire to disorganise production in the enterprises is discovered, to inform the Soviet of Workers' and Soldiers' Deputies and the Provisional Government.[6]

While it is difficult to know what proportion of similar conflicts in fact involved malevolent intentions or incompetence on the part of management, as opposed to difficulties that were beyond its control, *Torgovo-promyshlennaya gazeta*, the newspaper of the industrialists, reported the results of an inquiry in the spring of 1917: of 75 (mostly smaller) plant closures in Petrograd in the previous

5 *Izvestiya* (17 June 1917).

6 Rab. Kon., pp. 74–5.

weeks, 54 were motivated by management's desire to resist workers' pressure in favour of their economic demands and 21 were related to supply problems.[7] *Den'*, a liberal paper, wrote in mid-June that 'If in some cases these closures are motivated by the lack of raw materials, in many others the aim is to intimidate the workers and the Provisional Government'.[8] In any case, the workers' suspicions often enough had a real enough basis[9] to raise doubts in their minds when they were faced with threats to production. Moreover, workers viewed these problems against the background of the government's announced plan to 'unload' Petrograd of its industrial enterprises and the industrialists' oft-used pre-revolutionary practice of lockouts as a weapon against workers' economic and political demands.

The basically defensive motivation of the movement for workers' control explains why it did not arise before May. For it was then that the situation became really alarming. Even so, the demand for control – in the sense of access to documents and the comprehensive monitoring of the administration's activity – was still quite rare. A Soviet study of what it called 'cases of control' in May and June in 84 Petrograd factories (employing together 230,000 workers) found that in 24.5 percent of the cases the demand was for control (monitoring) of production, and in 8.7 percent for control of finances and sales. For the rest, 24.6 percent concerned 'control over conditions of work', 24.1 percent hiring and dismissals, and 7.5 percent the physical protection of the plant. These latter three areas were all part of what the workers called the 'internal regime' (*vnutrennii rasporyadok*) which the committees had asserted their right to 'regulate' already in the first days after the revolution.[10]

V.M. Levin, a left SR activist elected to the Central Soviet of Factory Committees, told their first conference at the end of May:

> The intervention of the working class into the bourgeois economy with a bourgeois government in power was not foreseen by any party pro-

---

7 Cited in Ferro 1967, p. 400.

8 *Den'* (17 June 1917).

9 See, for example, the cases of the Soikin Printing Press (*Rabochii put'*, 7 Sept 1917); Russkaya Univernil' (*Rabochaya gazeta*, 2 July 1917); unnamed (ibid., 18 May 1917); Brenner Factory (*Novaya zhizn'*, 22 July 1917; FZK, vol. I, p. 147; *Revolyutsionnoe dvizhenie v Rossii v iyule 1917 g.* (henceforth: Dok. July) (M., 1959) p. 341); Aerowheel Factory (Rab. Kon., pp. 112–14); Petichev Cable Factory (FZK, vol. II, pp. 54–5); Nevskii Shoe Factory (ibid., p. 57); Promet Pipe Factory (*Izvestiya*, 17 June 1917); (*Novaya zhizn'*, 19 June 1917). These are only a sample of such cases.

10 Selitskii 1971, p. 200.

> gramme ... But the factory committees were not afraid of intervening in the economic life of the country. True, they were forced to do it, since the factories would have closed long ago, and a mass of working people would have found itself on the street, adding to the army of unemployed that, even so, is beginning to grow.[11]

The Petersburg Committee of the Bolshevik Party first issued an appeal to workers to establish control in the factories only on 19 May. And the wording is significant: 'In response to a series of declarations from factory committees concerning the need for control and its establishment, it was decided to recommend to comrade workers to create control commissions in the enterprises from representatives of the workers'.[12] The movement for workers' control thus originated 'from below' as a response to the threat to production and jobs. This was made very clear in a summary report of the activity of the committee of the Putilov Factory from the end of 1917:

> When the factory committee arose, it was given neither a programme of action nor a charter that could guide its work. The programme and charter were composed and written by real life itself. Its practical instructions, as the functions of the committee developed, formed the basis, the guiding principles. In that way, the factory committee had the best teacher – life.[13]

The initiative for the creation of a city-wide and then national organisation of factory committees was also based upon practical needs. Osipov, a delegate from the Benoit Machine-building Factory, told the first conference of factory committees at the end of May:

> The organizing committee has done a great service to the workers' movement in gathering all the representatives of the factory committees at a general conference to discuss such a burning issue as control in production ...

---

11 FZK, vol. I, p. 112. In his 'April Theses' Lenin did in fact write: 'Not the "introduction" of socialism, as our direct task, but only the transition to control of social production and the distribution of goods on the part of the Soviet of Workers' Deputies'. Here Lenin was referring to control, again in the sense of regulation and oversight, but on the part of the state.

12 *Pravda* (24 May 1917).

13 *Putilovtsy v trekh revolyutsiyakh*, p. 431.

> The workers of the Benoit factory sent me to this conference. The owner has announced that there is no money and he is throwing out 500 workers. The owners are placing us on the knife's edge. They are putting Russia in an even worse situation in their desire to test our force. We won't allow that …
>
> In response to the administration's announcement of the layoff of hundreds of workers, the factory committee adopted a resolution that it sent around to the ministries. In it, it pointed out that production is being managed in an abnormal way. It pointed out the entrepreneur's incompetence. The figures show that production is rising. Yet the entrepreneur has no money, no materials either. Yesterday, workers from the factory spoke with the assistant Minister of Trade and Industry, Pal'chinkii. He sent them to the military authority. There they said they could not help. All this shows that it is not individual groups but the entire proletariat that must work in the given direction and move things forward.[14]

As soon as the Central Soviet of Factory Committees, established by the conference, began to work, it was inundated with requests for help from the factories.

The pragmatic motivation of the movement for workers' control explains why the demand for 'control' and, even more so, the attempts to establish 'control' in practice were at this point still far from universal. When the first conference met at the end of May, what was referred to as 'workers' control' ranged from attempts fully to subordinate management to the factory committee, as at Langezipen, an extremely rare occurrence, to the committees' search for raw materials and fuel. And at the Second Petrograd Conference of Factory Committees in August it was observed that some of the smaller factories had still not even elected committees.[15]

Since the most urgent problem was the shortage of fuel and raw materials, supply issues were usually the first, and certainly the most widespread, grounds of worker intervention into what were normally managerial activities. Indeed, a workers' conference on the problems of fuel and raw-material supplies preceded the First Conference of Factory Committees by several weeks.[16] That spring, many factory committees sent delegations to the Donbass and other regions to seek out or accelerate the delivery of supplies.[17]

---

14 FZK, vol. I, pp. 122–3. See, in this respect, the speeches of Fokht, Vakkhanen and Tseitlin, ibid., pp. 123–4.

15 Ibid., p. 183.

16 Rab. Kon., p. 75.

17 Ibid., pp. 70, 80; *Putilovtsy v trekh revolyutsiyakh*, p. 337.

The Factory Committee of the Rozentrantz Copper-rolling Mill produced the following report of its activities in the spring of 1917:

> The first steps of the committee were the struggle to improve wage rates, and we achieved that. Then the factory committee had to undertake decisive measures to supplement the work force. The factory was very poorly supplied with fuel, and only a trip by representatives of the factory committee was able to resolve that problem. The factory committee had to put pressure on the administration to fulfil urgent production orders. On the other hand, there were whole piles of finished orders that our clients were refusing to accept. The factory committee took upon itself the resolution of that matter and achieved positive results. The furnaces in the foundry shop were stopping because of a lack of bricks, and only thanks to the intervention of the committee were we able to obtain everything that was needed.[18]

At the first conference of factory committees, Levin spoke of an 'Italian (slow-down) strike' by the industrialists:

> The fact is that after the first weeks of the revolution a strange thing was observed. First in one factory, then in another, there was no anthracite coal, no oil, kerosene, raw materials, orders, and even money. But the main thing was that the administration is taking no active steps to obtain all that is needed for the normal course of work.
>
> Everything points to the fact that the administration of the factories is conducting an Italian strike, which in the present situation is tantamount to sabotage. Workers are faced at any moment with the threat of being thrown out into the street, and for that reason they don't trust the administration and they are scurrying, seeking a way out of the dead-end, into which *messieurs* the capitalists are determinately driving our industry.
>
> And the factory committees are sending their representatives all over the city in search of fuel. They borrow it temporarily from factory committees of other factories. They send representatives to railway junctions, too, where fuel delivery is being held up, to places where fuel is being stored, to where oil and coal are extracted, in order to learn the causes of their absence ...

---

18 *Nakanune Oktyabr'skogo vooruzhennogo vosstaniya, 1–24 oktyabrya* (henceforth: Dok. Nak.) (M., 1962), p. 288.

> All this the factory committees are trying to clarify. They are trying to establish the connection between one thing and another and to avert many problems. The members of the factory committees are conducting negotiations with government representatives about production orders, about the financial situation of the enterprises, etc. And as a result, oil and coal appear, orders and money are found ...
>
> Why, it is no secret that it not only is not in the interests of our country's capitalists to put an end to the economic dislocation, but that it is even contrary to their interests. To end the economic chaos would mean to strengthen the young, growing organism of our revolution – and no one knows how it will end for the capitalists. In the best case for them, the developing revolution will deprive them of only a part of their advantages. And in the worst? Who can guarantee that from a Russian revolution it will not become a world revolution, an international revolution?[19]

Workers showed willingness to cooperate with management in seeking solutions to production problems. They were even prepared to make sacrifices. But they demanded proof of management's good faith. And for that they needed 'control' – access to information. For example, the administration of the Baltic Wagon-building Factory announced in June that it was winding up the production of automobiles because it was unprofitable. When the factory committee presented figures that cast doubt on that claim, management offered to continue production, if the workers could guarantee profitability. The workers agreed to that but in return they demanded control, in particular access to all of the factory's accounts. Management rejected this as being 'without precedent'.[20]

At the Second Factory Committee Conference in August, N.K. Antipov, a delegate from the Vyborg district, explained that he was not opposed in principle to worker participation in government economic commissions with representatives of capital. But given the industrialists' lack of interest in resolving the economic problems, such collaboration was useless:

> Can our comrades achieve anything by participating in these conferences with the industrialists? It would be possible to liquidate the economic

19 FZK, vol. I, pp. 113–14.

20 *Izvestiya* (17 June 1917). See also the case of the Brenner factory. *Novaya zhizn'* (22 July 1917); FZK, vol. I, p. 147; Dok. July, p. 342.

> breakdown by such means, if the owners were really unable to manage production correctly. But here it is a matter of lack of desire on the part of the owners, and we won't be able to force them by means of these conferences. They aren't willing to make any concessions, and, therefore, we have no reason to go there.[21]

Although anarchists, with their anti-state and direct-action orientations, were naturally attracted to the factory committees, their influence in them was limited, as evidenced by the small number of votes their position gathered at the factory-committee conference at the end of May. And there were very few cases before the October Revolution of the takeover, or attempted takeover, of factories, a policy that at least some anarchists advocated. Those that did occur were responses to the imminent threat of closure.[22] And even in those cases, the workers turned to the state for sequestration. There was no slogan 'factories to the workers', akin to the rural demand of 'land to the peasants'.

The goal of the movement for workers' control was to monitor management's activity, which meant above all access to documents. The question of what should be done if monitoring revealed sabotage was not really confronted. At the Second Conference of Factory Committees in August, Levin stated that the Central Soviet of Factory Committees had always taken the position that the takeover of factories was unacceptable:

> We demanded control over production from the ministries. But in that matter, we were met with indecision and a reluctance to act on their part; and, on the part of the industrialists – with anger and fear for their property. Many consciously or unconsciously confuse the concept of 'control' with the concept of 'seizure of the factories and mills', although the workers are decidedly not adopting the tactic of seizures. And if any do occur, they are isolated, exceptional cases.[23]

While voices calling for the workers to assume managerial functions could already be heard at this time, they were very rare. When the Central Bureau of Petrograd Trade Unions met on May 11 to discuss the factory-committee con-

---

21 FZK, vol. I, p. 181.

22 For a case of takeover (the Brenner factory) before October, see *Novaya zhizn'* (22 July 1917); FZK, vol. I, p. 147; Dok. July, p. 342. For cases of takeover before October, see Selitskii 1971, p. 200.

23 FZK, vol. I, p. 171.

ference planned for the end of the month, some union activists argued that the workers should demand the socialisation of production by the factory committees. But others, 'an incomparably larger group', defended control, arguing that one had to be realistic and not be led by subjective desires.[24]

When management of the Lebedev Aircraft Factory at the end of May rejected the workers' wage demands, some union activists convinced the workers to take over the plant. The factory committee threatened collectively to resign if that occurred. And it put some tough questions to the workers at their general assembly on 3 June: Where would they get money to pay wages? Would the technical personnel agree to work under the workers' direction? No one had satisfactory answers. Some argued that the decision had been misinterpreted, that the intention was not to take over the factory but only to establish control. The assembly finally decided to take the wage conflict to arbitration, and the question of a takeover was forgotten.[25]

On a more theoretical level, too, workers did not equate control with socialism, when, in their understanding, workers would themselves manage the factories. Naumov, a worker from the Vyborg district, explained this to the First Conference of Factory Committees:

> As Marxists, we must view life as constantly moving forward. The revolution continues. We say: our revolution is a prologue to the world revolution. Control is not yet socialism and not even taking production into our hands. But it already moves beyond the framework of the bourgeois order. It is not socialism that we are proposing to introduce. No. But having taken [state] power into our hands, we must direct capitalism along such a path that it will outlive itself. The factory committees should work in that direction. That will lead to socialism.
>
> Our task in the present moment is the organisation of production that will put workers in the best hygienic conditions. We have to put production in order out of the present chaos. For that we need to have moral influence over the worker masses. Their factory committees, therefore, have to organise clubs, lectures, cafeterias and the like. All this will occur if we have organization ... The factory committees have to take in hand any flare-ups that are unorganised and therefore destructive and direct them along a correct path of class struggle. Having strengthened ourselves in the sphere of production, having taking control into our hands, we will

24 *Novaya zhizn'* (13 May 1917). See also Perazich 1927, p. 80.

25 *Rabochaya gazeta* (6 June 1917).

> learn in a practical way how to work actively in production and we will lead it in an organized manner to socialist production.[26]

In a report from April 1917, the committee of the Putilov Factory presented its activity in much the same way:

> The workers are preparing for the time when private ownership of the factories and mills will be abolished and the means of production, along with the buildings, erected by the hands of the workers, will be transferred to the hands of the working class. Therefore, in doing a small thing, one must continually bear in mind the great and main aim towards which the people aspire.[27]

This committee, as will be seen later, was in no rush to assume responsibility for running the factory. At the same time, workers' control, while it was fundamentally a practical response to a perceived threat, was also seen as a school for workers' management, a step toward the socialist goal.

This period thus saw the emergence of two parallel, mutually reinforcing, power struggles – one on the state level, the other in the factories. But whereas the workers in the factories demanded only 'control', on the state level most already wanted to exclude the propertied classes from participation and even indirect influence in government. On both levels, in the factories and in the political arena, the workers' radicalisation occurred essentially as a defensive response to perceived threats to the revolution, which workers continued to view as fundamentally bourgeois-democratic. Most workers had not yet grasped that the logic of their struggle was leading them beyond that framework and toward another, much more radical revolution. The July Days, the subject of the next chapter, would be a painful step towards that realisation.

---

26 FZK, vol. I, p. 126.

27 *Putilovtsy v trekh revolyutsiyakh*, p. 333.

CHAPTER 7

The July Days

The Workers and the Menshevik-SR Soviet Majority

The demand 'All power to the soviets' that the radicalised workers adopted indicates that they still considered the moderate socialists at the head of the Petrograd Soviet and the Central Executive Committee of Soviets (elected by the Congress of Soviets of 3–24 June) as a legitimate part of 'revolutionary democracy'. The goal of the workers who participated in the demonstration on 18 June had been to impress upon these leaders the need for them to take power on their own, to the exclusion of representatives of the propertied classes. For the workers to break with the 'conciliators' would have meant to break with the broad popular masses who still supported them: most of the peasantry and the soldiers, most workers in the provinces, and the democratic (left-leaning) intelligentsia. The capital's workers were sensitive to the danger of their isolation and of civil war within the ranks of revolutionary democracy, and the Mensheviks and SRs never tired of warning them of it. But unlike the leaders of those two parties, the fear of isolation did not stop these workers from demanding an end to the alliance with census society (or with its purported liberal elements) and the formation of a government based exclusively on the soviets of workers', soldiers' and peasants' deputies, that is, on the toiling classes.

At the same time, however, anger among these workers, and in particular metalworkers, toward the 'conciliators' was reaching a boiling point. When the Congress of Soviets decided to prohibit the demonstration planned for 10 June, it sent its emissaries to the factories to explain the decision. In some districts, the emissaries were met with understanding, even warmly. The Nevskii district, for example, was completely calm, since workers there had not intended to demonstrate on the 10th. But in other districts, the reception was very hostile. An emissary who went to the Vyborg district on 10 June sent back the following report:

> Vyborg District. June 10. 1) Nobel Factory 2) Old Parviainen 3) New Parviainen 4) New Lessner. Everywhere the attitude is profoundly hostile to the Congress of Soviets of Workers' and Soldiers' Deputies, that is [said to be] 'tagging behind the bourgeoisie and is [itself] petty bourgeois in essence'. Nowhere do they intend to demonstrate on the 10th, but not because the

> Congress of Soviets is calling not to; only because the Central Committee of the RSDWP (Bolshevik) is suggesting not to demonstrate today.
>
> The impression is such that one can expect a demonstration in the nearest future, if only the [Bolshevik] Central Committee calls for it. At the Nobel and Old and New Parviainen Factories, I had to limit myself to speaking only with the council of elders [the factory committee], since it was not possible to hold a meeting, as work was in progress. At the New Lessner Factory there was a workers' meeting, but it was impossible to speak, since they would not let me finish my speech.[1]

Novaya zhizn' published a similar report from the Vyborg District:

> At some factories, for example Parvianen, Rozenrantz, Lessner, Phoenix, Koenig, the Society of United Machine-building Factories, Promet, the attitude to the orators, delegates of the Congress, is hostile. Protests ring out against the declarations of the Provisional Government. They refused to listen to the orators and interrupted them with shouts: 'We're not comrades to you' … In the Vyborg district, it was decided not to demonstrate until a new call from the Central Committee of the RSDWP(b).

At the Gvozdil'nyi Factory in the Vasileostrovskii district, the emissaries were interrupted with shouts of 'bourgeois!'[2] Those sent to the Putilov Factory reported:

> Near the shops where work was in progress, we met some 300 people. They greeted our automobile with extreme hostility: 'Two of you people were already here. Even so, we barely managed to keep the people at work. And then you show up to take them away from their work, etc.'. There were no meetings at the factory. Work was proceeding.
>
> Workers' statement about the All-Russian Congress [of Soviets]: 'Some types arrived from the boondocks to instruct us; we know everything already without you; we won freedom here with our blood, and where were you?'
>
> They would not let me speak and asked me to leave. Our car left amidst whistling and angry rumbling. A Bolshevik who made a speech waved his revolver. They asked to see our mandates, although in their great state of

1 Dok. May, p. 500.

2 *Novaya zhizn'* (June 10, 1917).

agitation they forgot to look at them. The attitude to the Soviet Soldiers' and Workers' Deputies is hostile, a series of ironic remarks about the army at the front and about Kerenskii.[3]

Resolutions adopted at factory meetings expressed the same hostility to the Soviet's leaders. A general assembly of workers of Aivaz Machine-building Factory, reacting to the government's raid on the Durnovo dacha, protested

> against the Soviet's inactivity in the struggle against the counterrevolution, and [we] demand that the Soviet authoritatively affirm the rights of all revolutionary groups to free revolutionary activity and take decisive steps to end the world slaughter. This meeting declares that, as long as power is in the hands of the bourgeoisie and it, under the cover of the Soviet, digs the grave of the proletarian revolution, the workers will not hesitate to adopt any means of struggle for the sake of victory of the cause of the people.[4]

On 19 June, a meeting of the workers of the Baranovskii Factory sent the following message to the Soviet leaders: 'We are horrified by the thought, that involuntarily creeps into our minds, that this blow [the attack on Durnovo] was intentionally directed, with eyes closed to reality'. They demanded that the Soviet immediately re-examine its policy, since the Provisional government was organising the counterrevolution. The resolution ended with a pledge of support for the Soviet, 'if the latter will express our will and carry out our wishes'.[5] Here we find an expression of conditional support for the Soviet, reserved in the early days of the revolution for the Provisional Government. A week earlier, it was reported that this factory had ceased to pay dues to the Soviet.[6]

Such expressions of hostility did not, however, mean that these workers were ready to act against the Soviet. That question arose at a meeting of the Bolsheviks' Petersburg Committee on 20 June. It was clear that the massive protest of 18 June against the Soviet's support for the coalition government and against its foreign policy – the military offensive, perceived by workers as a blow against the revolution, was launched on the day of the demonstration – had not moved the Soviet leaders. One of the participants at the meeting,

3 Dok. May, p. 501. *Rabochaya gazeta* claimed that these 300 workers were Bolsheviks.

4 Dok. May, p. 560.

5 Mikhailov 1922, p. 198.

6 Ibid., p. 200.

citing the agitated mood in the districts, argued that the party should abandon 'parliamentary methods of struggle'. The fact that the Congress of Soviets and the Petrograd Soviet had, in effect, sanctioned the raid on the Durnovo dacha, he argued, proved that they were prepared to use force against the left. This effectively ruled out the peaceful path.

The others, however, rejected that idea. M.O. Pletnev, a young worker from the Nobel Factory in the Vyborg district, where anger was boiling over, responded:

> I'll tell you how the workers at the Nobel Factory reacted to events. When the question arose at the meeting – What, then, should we do?, the workers answered: 'The situation is complex. We have to wait, to analyse our forces, and to be ready'. The question of parliamentarism is a serious one. When the masses are straining to act, they have to explain to themselves against whom exactly they wish to act. Why, we can't act against our own comrades who haven't yet understood what we understand. We have to tear those comrades away from the politics of conciliation with the capitalists and nudge them towards the politics of a break. Only then, when we have used all means, when everyone has developed a conscious attitude toward events, we won't repeat the experience of the Paris Commune. To impose our understanding – that is adventurism. The anarchists say: 'Strike while the iron is hot'. And we won't be any different from them, if we lead the masses into the street at this time. Our task is to go to the workers and soldiers who still haven't understood what we have understood and to ask them to understand us. You can't force understanding. We will call to the masses: 'Rid yourselves of your trust in the parties that are conducting the erroneous policy of conciliation with the capitalists'.

Naumov, a worker at the Old Parviainen Factory in the Vyborg district, suggested that the Bolsheviks' Petersburg Committee immediately inform the Soviet's Executive Committee of the profound dissatisfaction and the explosive mood among the capital's workers and soldiers, who were pressing for immediate action; that it inform the Soviet that it could no longer postpone taking power, 'as, otherwise, the Petersburg Committee cannot assume responsibility for any possible actions [by workers] …' The same position was defended by M.I. Latsis, a party organiser in the Vyborg District: 'When you enter the worker milieu, you feel how everything is churning and boiling. For now, we are holding the masses back. But others could call them out. What should we do, if they come out? Leave them in the streets on their own, or lead the movement? Both options are frightening. I think we should tell the All-Russian Congress [of Soviets]: take power into your hands, or we cannot be responsible for what will happen'.[7]

That was the position finally adopted by both the Bolsheviks' Central and Petersburg Committees: try to prevent a new demonstration; but if it happens, direct it towards pressuring the Soviet leaders to take power.[8] Neither the Bolsheviks nor the radicalised workers were prepared to act against the Soviet leaders or the masses who supported them. As a result, any new demonstration of workers and soldiers could only be a repeat of June 18, at least on the part of the demonstrators. But, to the workers' surprise, the government and the moderate leadership of the Soviet were, for their part, prepared to react differently, and that would create an entirely new situation for the workers, one that left them deeply perplexed.

The July Days[9]

From the workers' point of view, the 18 June demonstration had indeed changed nothing. In fact, the situation had become even more alarming: the raid on the Durnovo dacha,[10] the launching of the military offensive, patriotic demonstrations during which workers and soldiers were assaulted and even arrested for refusing to remove their caps, sometimes even for no reason at all. In the economic sphere, there was no movement on regulation on the part of the government. Instead of regulation, the workers received this message from the socialist Minister of Labour:

> Comrade workers, remember not only your rights, not only your desires, but also the possibility of their realisation; not only your welfare, but also sacrifices in the name of consolidating the revolution and the victory of our ultimate ideals.[11]

---

7 *Pervyi peterburgskii* komitet, pp. 327, 332, 338.

8 Latsis 1923, p. 106.

9 Among historical monographs on the July Days, one should mention especially Rabinowitch 1968 and Znamenskii 1967.

10 'We see', a worker told the Soviet Congress, 'that the government of capitalists desires from time to time to let some workers' blood flow', cited in Znamenskii 1964, p. 22.

11 *Rabochaya gazeta* (28 June 1917).

Workers' wage demands, spurred by the galloping inflation, were meeting with growing intransigence from the owners.[12] And the food situation, though not yet desperate, was again deteriorating. Bread rations were reduced by 15 percent on 26 June; the same occurred with meat and butter on 1 July.[13]

Although the workers reacted to the military offensive with a profound feeling of betrayal, among the soldiers of Petrograd's garrison the anger was even more intense. This was especially the case when various units, including the very militant First Machine-gun Regiment, learned they were to be disbanded and sent to the front.[14]

When the factory horns sounded on 3 July, workers needed little coaxing to lay down their tools. '"Finish up! ... Into the yard!" – shouts rang out from all the shops. We already knew the meaning of those shouts and whistles', recalled A. Metelev, a worker in one of the Vyborg district factories.

> Always in such cases, the workers would quickly put their tools away in the boxes, dress, and go into the yard or to the large-calibre turning shop, where a general assembly was held. On hearing these shouts, no one, except for the administration and the firemen, could think of remaining in the shops. That would be worse than strike-breaking ... A work stoppage at that time, when there were usually no meetings, had to mean that the cause was some extraordinary political event outside the walls of the factory.
>
> In the narrow factory yard ... a representative of the machine-gun regiment and several workers from other factories were waiting for all the workers to assemble. News was circulating in the crowd that the machine-gun regiment was already in marching formation, that some of the automobiles with machine guns mounted had left for the city, that the Lessner and Erikson workers were also coming out into the streets.
>
> One could see the excitement in the workers' faces. Everyone wanted to hear something new, something good. Hearts beat with excitement.
>
> 'Our regiment with several dozen machine guns', began the representative of the machine-gun regiment, 'has decided to march to the Tauride Palace ... It is already on Sampsionievskii Prospekt ready to march, waiting for the factories to come out in order to march to the palace together with the workers'.

---

12 'Petrogradskie rabochie ob iyul'skikh dnyakh', *Krasnaya letopis*, no. 9 (1924), pp. 19–41 *passim*.

13 Latsis 1923, p. 111.

14 Znamenskii 1964, pp. 16–17.

> Amidst the general noise and the voices, a worker from some factory reported that they, too, regardless of the absence of any instructions, were coming out to march with the machine-gunners. The admonitions of a member of the factory committee to hold back and to await specific instructions from the Bolsheviks' Central Committee provoked even more noise among the workers and the insistent demand to open the factory gates.
>
> To discuss: 'Why come out? Where to go? With whom to fight?' – that was completely unnecessary. Everyone understood exactly the meaning of the action. It had been ripening for a long time in the profound depths of the toiling masses …
>
> Ten minutes later, having drawn up ten abreast in the narrow factory lane, we went out onto Sampsionievskii Prospekt. The red guards marched behind the first banner 'All Power to the Soviets', after which came unarmed workers, women, juveniles …
>
> The streets of the Vyborg district filled with flowing humanity. This was the first time the district had taken on such an aspect, when beneath the red banner were marching only workers and soldiers … The badges of government functionaries, the shiny buttons of students, the bonnets of 'sympathetic ladies' – all that was in February, four months ago. There was nothing of that in today's movement.[15]

Across town in the Petergof district, in the cannon shop of the Putilov Factory, rumours had been circulating since the morning of meetings to be held in the street. The workers learned of the resignation of the 'capitalist ministers' the previous night (ostensibly over concessions that the government had made to the Ukrainian Rada, that was demanding autonomy for Ukraine) and of the government's intention to send more troops from the city's garrison to the front. The workers' mood was very angry. Around 2 p.m. they learnt that a delegation from the Second Machine-gun Regiment was asking to assemble the workers for a meeting, but that the factory committee, with its Bolshevik majority, was refusing, since the party's position was to dissuade workers from coming out. But the workers gathered on their own in front of the main office, demanding to open the meeting. A soldier confirmed that his regiment had received orders to leave for the front the next day. But the regiment had decided to fight their own capitalists rather than the German proletariat. By this time, about 10,000 workers had assembled. When the machine-gunners announced they

15 Metelev 1922, pp. 159–61.

would start marching at 4 p.m. with their machine-guns mounted on trucks, the crowd roared: 'Let's move! Let's move!' In vain did the factory committee try to persuade them of the need to act in a more organised manner. The workers had already begun to form ranks in the street.

Efimov, a Putilov worker, ran to inform the Bolsheviks' district committee. The consensus was that, despite the party's decision to keep the workers from demonstrating, it was impossible to leave them on their own to the whims of fate. The Bolsheviks had to march with them. By this time, they learned that the entire city was on the move. An immense crowd had assembled at the Narva Gates, not far from the factory. Some women were shouting: 'Everybody has to go. No one should stay back. We'll watch the homes'.

When the Putilov column reached Nevskii Prospekt on its way to the Tauride Palace, it was met by *intelligenty*, students, and officers, who tried to block the way. Some even tore down the workers' banners, telling them that it was all the work of German spies who wanted to open the way for their army to crush Russia's revolution, won so cheaply, with so few sacrifices. To this a worker replied: 'The victory came cheaply for you, but it was won on the back of the people'. And the column moved on.

It arrived at the Tauride Palace, seat of the Central Executive Committee of Soviets (TsIK), at 2 a.m. The workers camped in the adjoining park, declaring that they would not move until the TsIK took power. A representative of the TsIK came out to inform them that the question would be decided later that day or the next. And at 4 a.m. the workers began to file back to the factory. After more meetings, around 10 a.m., they went home.[16]

The initiative for the demonstration that day had been entirely the workers', prompted by the machine-gunners. The TsIK had expressly forbidden any action. All the socialist parties, including the Bolsheviks, had opposed it, although the latter yielded to the workers' initiative. The greatest number of demonstrators were from districts with the largest concentrations of industrial workers – Vyborg, Petergof, Vasilevskii ostrov.[17]

The next day, after considerable hesitation, the Bolsheviks' Central Committee called to continue the demonstrations, stressing the importance of preserving yesterday's peaceful character. In the vast majority of factories, the workers' meetings decided to take part. Between two-thirds and three-quarters of the capital's industrial workers participated that day, ignoring the TsIK's explicit prohibition. The exceptions were mainly workers in factories still under

---

16 'Petrogradskie rabochie ob iyul'skikh dnyakh', *Krasnaya letopis'*, no. 9 (1924) p. 19.

17 Znamenskii 1964, p. 55.

SR influence – in the Nevskii, Okhta and Moscow districts, and most of the textile mills and printing establishments. On the other hand, many of the soldiers who had come out the previous day now refrained. Only about half of the 100,000-strong garrison took part on the second day.[18]

The July Days were one paradox within another, something that was most graphically manifested in a scene at the Tauride Palace, when a worker ran up onto the stage, shaking his fist in the face of Viktor Chernov, the SR Minister of Agriculture, and shouted: 'Take power, you son of a bitch, when it is given to you!'[19] Workers and soldiers marched in their thousands to demand that the leaders of the Central Executive Committee of Soviets, who were already quite compromised in their eyes, assume power. This same TsIK, however, showed itself to be willing sooner to commit political suicide than to take power on its own, without representatives of census society. Yet, it told the demonstrating workers that it, and it alone, would determine the composition of a new government (the 'capitalist ministers', it will be recalled, had resigned) at its next session. It thus acknowledged that it already held power. At the same time, the TsIK declared counterrevolutionary the thousands of workers and soldiers who were demanding that it take power. And when 'loyal' troops arrived on the night of July 4–5 to put down the 'insurgents', who were demanding that the TsIK take power, the commanders of these troops solemnly declared that the TsIK was the only authority that the army would unconditionally obey and that the TsIK alone would decide the fate of the revolution.

The workers had one goal in the July Days: to press the Soviet to take power on its own, without 'capitalist ministers' – in other words, to form a government responsible exclusively to soviets of workers', soldiers' and peasants' deputies. To that end they ignored the Mariinskii Palace, the seat of the Provisional Government, and went directly to the Tauride Palace. They had no intention of using force, except to defend themselves against 'bourgeois' elements in the city centre. There were women and children among the demonstrators. An orchestra marched at the head of Kronstadt sailors. The demonstrators' conviction, a naïve one, as it turned out, that the leaders of the TsIK would be unable to resist the masses' moral pressure, was evident throughout. There was no intention of exerting anything more than moral pressure.

---

18 Ibid., pp. 84, 106; *Rabochaya gazeta* (6 July 1917); Perazich 1927, p. 81; *Krasnaya letopis*, no. 9 (1924), p. 31.

19 Milyukov, *History of the Second Russian Revolution*, vol. I, p. 244., cited in Chamberlin 1975, vol. 1, p. 171.

One of the four workers' delegates (in all, 54 factories sent 90 delegates) who were allowed on 4 July to address the joint session of the TsIK Workers' and Soldiers' Deputies and the Executive Committee of the All-Russian Soviet of Peasants' Deputies, told the meeting:

> Representative of 54 factories are here. There is no sense talking about what has happened. It's strange to read the appeal of the Central [Executive] Committee: it calls workers and soldiers counterrevolutionaries. We demand that all the land be seized immediately, that control over production be instituted immediately! We demand a struggle against the hunger that is threatening us.
>
> Our demand – it is the common demand of the workers – is all power to the Soviets of workers' and soldiers' deputies. You must consider this.

Another delegate stated:

> I am also the representative of 54 factories. You see what is written on the banners. The same question has been discussed in all the factories. These are resolutions adopted by workers. You know these resolutions. Hunger is threatening us. We demand the resignation of the ten capitalist ministers. We trust the Soviet but not those whom the Soviet trusts. Our comrade socialist ministers have taken the road of conciliation with the capitalists. But these capitalists are our blood enemies.[20]

'We trust the Soviet, but not those whom the Soviet trusts'. Or rather: We want to trust the Soviet but it keeps yielding to our enemies.

Of course, there were various shades of attitude. At the same meeting, a worker from the Putilov Factory, rifle in hand, leaped onto the stage:

> Comrades! How much longer have we workers to endure treachery? You have assembled here, you deliberate, you make deals with the bourgeoisie and with the landowners ... You are busy betraying the working class. You must know that the working class will not stand for it! We Putilov workers are here 30,000 strong, every one of us. We will achieve our will! There should be no bourgeois! All power to the soviets! We grasp our rifles firmly in our hands. Your Kerenskies and Tseretelis will not fool us.[21]

20 Dok. July, p. 21.

21 Sukhanov 1919–23, vol. iv, p. 430.

This sounded threatening. But when Chkheidze passed the worker a note in which he stated that the TsIK was currently discussing the matter and that he should advise his comrades to go back to their factories, all the bewildered worker could do was meekly walk off the stage. In his memoir, Metelev, a Bolshevik worker who was in the thick of the events, makes no mention of even the suggestion of using force against the TsIK.[22] He himself was one of the delegates sent from the Putilov workers into the Tauride Palace. There he waited patiently through the night. When the 'loyal' troops arrived at dawn, he had finally to leave.[23]

By the evening of 4 July, the streets around the Tauride Palace were empty. The movement had ended. But in the course of those two days, an estimated 400 had been killed or wounded, the victims of clashes between the demonstrators and provocateurs. Criminal elements had also taken the opportunity to loot shops.

Once the demonstrations ended and the workers and soldiers had returned to their home and barracks, the situation took an ominous turn. On the night from 4–5 July, while Tsereteli was addressing the assembly in the Tauride Palace, the sound of marching boots threw the hall into a panic. But F. Dan, the Menshevik leader, reassured them: 'Comrades ... calm down! There is no danger. It is regiments loyal to the revolution that have arrived to defend its authoritative organ, the Central Executive Committee ...' Sukhanov recalled the scene:

> At that moment in the Ekaterinskii hall, rang out a powerful refrain of the 'Marseillaise'. There was enthusiasm in the hall. The Mamelukes' faces were glowing. Casting jubilant, dirty looks in the direction of the leftists, they seized each other by the hands and in an effusion of sentiment, their heads bared, belted out the 'Marseillaise'.

'A classic scene of the start of counterrevolution', Martov [Menshevik-internationalist leader] spat out.

Sukhanov commented that there really was no need of troops, since no one was threatening the TsIK.[24] But troops did arrive, some from outside the capital, others from regiments of the garrison that had been opposed to the

---

22 It is true that V. Chernov, the SR Minister of Agriculture, was arrested by a group of sailors and was rescued by Trotsky. But Trotsky implies that the sailors were, in fact, provocateurs. In any case, anarchist influence was quite strong among sailors.

23 Metelev 1922, p. 171.

24 Sukhanov 1919–23, p. 440.

demonstration. This, in turn, influenced other army units of the garrison that had been neutral or were wavering.

But another factor in the sudden shift in the balance of class forces was the rumours, followed by the publication the next morning in newspapers, of forged documents purporting to show the complicity of Lenin and the Bolsheviks with the German General Staff. The documents, leaked by the Minister of Justice, were calculated with a particular view to influence the garrison.[25]

For the workers, the 'debauch of counterrevolution' had begun.

Reaction Unleashed

To understand workers' reactions to the July Days and particularly to their aftermath, it is important to appreciate the scale of bloodshed that occurred on 3 and 4 July and of the repression in the weeks that followed. This for workers was a first real taste of civil war. And it was not civil war between census society and revolutionary democracy, something those who had been demanding soviet power had come more or less to face. It was civil war within revolutionary democracy. For the repression received the sanction, active or passive, of the moderate socialist leaders of the TsIK of Soviets. This deeply shook workers, disoriented them and blocked their path to further action. Before long, however, the shock wore off and gave way to rage, and it was no longer directed only at census society but increasingly also at the 'conciliators' within revolutionary democracy, a concept that itself was now put into question. Two competing emotions, fear and anger, coexisted, neither able to gain the upper hand. For most workers, only the October insurrection would resolve the conflict.

Most of the casualties that occurred on 3 July resulted from clashes between armed demonstrators and provocateurs in the hostile crowds and in buildings lining the route of the workers and soldiers. On 4 July, however, regular government troops began to fire into the workers' columns, often at point-blank range.[26] Civilians also got into the act. D. Afanas'ev, a worker at the New Lessner Factory, related the following incident, by no means isolated:

> At the Tauride Palace, the Putilov workers declared they would stay until the Soviet took a decision, one way or the other. When I learned of the Soviet's decision not to adopt a decision under pressure from the

25 Chamberlin 1975, p. 177.

26 'Petrogradksie rabochie ob iyul'skikh dnyakh', *Krasnaya letopis'*, no. 9 (1924), pp. 25, 34.

street, I went to a relative's place nearby. The next day, I went home with two comrades, arguing on the way with anyone who was insulting the Bolsheviks.

At Shchukin Market we came across a well-dressed nanny in the midst of a crowd, who was announcing that Trotsky and Lunacharskii had been arrested, that Lenin and Zinoviev were in hiding, that they had taken money from Wilhelm, and so forth. She called mercilessly to kill the Bolsheviks. We asked: Who gave you money to slander the Bolsheviks and the workers? We argued for ten minutes, exposing her lies. Then some twenty merchants, probably butchers, arrived and began to swear at the Bolsheviks: 'Beat the Jews and the Bolsheviks! Into the water with them!' And the crowd soundly thrashed us. One comrade ran away; another died in hospital two weeks later from the beating. They took away my pistol, threw it into the canal, and began throwing stones.

Six sailors arrived and dispersed the crowd. They pulled me, covered in blood, from the canal. I dragged myself towards home but I couldn't keep myself from cursing two bourgeois who were talking among themselves and calling Lenin a provocateur. I called them provocateurs. They dragged me to the Aleksandr-Nevskii militia station, where there were already many arrested workers. I was there until 7 July. Three Don Cossacks and two sailors gave me something to eat and released me. I was sick for about a month.[27]

On 14 July the general assembly of the Langezipen Factory unanimously decided:

To bring to the attention of the TsIK of the Soviets of Workers' and Soldiers' Deputies that a worker of the Langezipen Factory, T. Sinitsyn, was murdered at the Vologda Station for verbally defending the Bolsheviks. We draw the TsIK's attention to the fact that this is the complete destruction of freedom of speech and a victory of the counterrevolution …

We demand that the TsIK take decisive measures against the counter-revolution that is openly raising its head. We demand that the TsIK cease to abet the counter-revolution, whose foundation and basis are the State Duma, the State Council and the Kadet party.[28]

---

27 Ibid., pp. 30–1.

28 Tomkevich 1972, p. 40. On beatings and arrests of activists of the Textile Workers' Union, see Perazich 1927, p. 86.

Reports poured into the TsIK of violence against workers, Bolsheviks and their sympathisers. In some districts, crowds pushed their way into trams, searching out 'Leninists'. Once again, Petrograd's jails were filled with political prisoners. On the night of 4–5 July, government troops raided and ransacked the premises of the Bolshevik Central and Petersburg Committees. Nearly the entire leadership of the party was put out of action for the rest of July and for most of August. But the middle and lower levels of the party were also hard hit. The Petersburg Committee reported that it had not been able to conduct agitational work during the month of July.[29] The recently purchased printing shop of the party was completely demolished, and *Pravda* was shut down, along with various provincial Bolshevik papers. The Minister of the Interior was authorised to close any publications that called for insubordination to military authorities or for violence and civil war, concepts that the minister interpreted very liberally.[30]

The government immediately undertook the disarming of workers and the military units that had participated in the demonstrations.[31] At Sestroretsk, near the border with Finland and where the local soviet had been long running affairs – much to the disgust of the non-socialist press that railed against the 'Sestroretsk Republic' – the time had come for revenge. A full-scale military operation was mounted, including several hundred Cossacks, Junkers (cadets of the officers' school), and six armoured trucks. The commander was authorised to shoot resisters and, if need be, raze the town. However, he met no resistance. The troops indiscriminately searched workers' homes and ransacked the premises of the workers' organisations and the Bolshevik party. They left with the entire factory committee as prisoners.[32]

On 11 July, *Novaya zhizn'*, the daily of the Menshevik Internationalists that would itself soon be closed by the government, appeared with an editorial entitled 'The Flowers' – from the Russian saying: 'These are merely the flowers; the berries are still to come'.

> The counterrevolution is making great strides, not by the day but by the hour. Searches and arrests. And what arrests! Even the Tsarist political police did not permit itself the sort of insolent conduct that the bourgeois

29 *Vtoraya i tret'ya obshchegorodskie konferenstsii bol'shevikov v iyule i sentyabre 1917 g.* (henceforth: *Vtoraya I tret'ya*) (M.-L., 1927), p. 83.

30 Sukhanov 1919–23, vol. v, p. 20.

31 See, for example, Dok. July, pp. 161–4; Peka, pp. 211–14; *Istoriya Leningradskogo ordena Lenina i ordena Krasnogo znameni obuvnoi fabriki imeni Ya. Kalinina* (L., 1968), p. 171.

32 'Petrogradksie rabochie ob iyul'skikh dnyakh', pp. 36–41.

> youth and Cossack officers have displayed in their effort to 'restore order' in Petrograd.

Various other repressive measures that were adopted, although they were not directed at workers, angered them deeply, including the reintroduction of the death penalty for soldiers at the front; the dissolution of the Finnish Parliament (whose Social-Democratic majority had voted for Finland's autonomy in internal affairs); and the government's failed attempt to arrest the Central Committee (Soviet) of the Baltic Fleet for refusing its order to send ships to the capital to put down the demonstrations of 3–4 July.[33] Somewhat later, it was revealed that the ships were to be scuttled in case they proved unreliable.

While the TsIK of Soviets protested against the government's repressive 'excesses' and somewhat restrained its zeal, for example, obtaining the release of a delegation from the Baltic Fleet's Central Committee and blocking Kerenskii's attempt to outlaw the entire Bolshevik Party,[34] it was clearly complicit in the repression. For after the Kadet ministers resigned on 1 July, the ministers who had been delegated by the TsIK constituted an absolute majority in the government, six of the eleven ministers. And the new, second coalition government, formed on 7 July, was in fact, if not officially, a 'soviet' government in the sense that its Prime Minister and several key ministers, including the Minister of Internal Affairs, I.G. Tsereteli, were members of the TsIK. This new cabinet had been formed on the decision of the socialist ministers, who formally adopted the TsIK's programme. As the Mensheviks' own paper commented: 'Formally, a dictatorship of the Provisional Government has been declared. But in fact the TsIK of Workers' and Soldiers' Deputies is participating in this dictatorship'.[35] In response to the protests from Yu. O. Martov, prominent Menshevik Internationalist, against the arrest of workers and Bolsheviks, Tsereteli replied: 'I take upon myself these arrests'.[36] The TsIK also endorsed the reintroduction of the death penalty at the front.

The apparent assumption of control of the government by the TsIK was, in reality, only a prelude to more far-reaching concessions to the census politicians. After a brief scuffle between the centre-left in the TsIK and the census

33 *Novaya zhizn'* (18 July 1917); Sukhanov 1919–23, vol. iv, p. 501.

34 Sukhanov 1919–23, p. 486.

35 *Rabochaya gazeta* (11 July, 1917).

36 Sukhanov 1919–23, p. 506. It should be noted, however, that on this matter Tsereteli was acting independently of the Menshevik CC, where Dan's position had officially won out, namely, that the major threat to the revolution was from the right.

political leaders, a third coalition was put together, which included five Kadet ministers. For the first time, the government did not announce a programme or seek endorsement from the TsIK. Tsereteli openly acknowledged that this represented a major surrender of power by the TsIK. He explained to the Petrograd Soviet that 'workers are a huge part of the population, but they are not the whole country. And we must march under the banner of an all-national platform. The powers of revolutionary organisations have to be limited ...'[37] No protest from the TsIK majority was forthcoming.

A minority of workers, mostly in the Vyborg district, wanted to take action in face of the government's offensive. A number of factories went on strike on 5 July. There were even some abortive attempts to organise new demonstrations.[38] Metelev recalled Red Guards and young workers stuffing explosives into their shirts and boots and crossing the Neva River, some in boats. They wanted to free the Kronstadt sailors, who were being besieged in the Peter-Paul Fortress.[39] Latsis recalled that 'the Vyborg committee [of the Bolshevik party] instinctively mobilised the whole district. I personally went to all the factories and asked the Red Guards to be at the ready. A plan to defend the district was even drawn up'. But his proposal for a general strike was rejected by a close vote in the executive of the Bolsheviks' Petersburg Committee. Lenin, now in hiding, was vehemently opposed to the idea.[40]

The mood among most of the capital's workers, however, was not nearly so militant. Workers who had participated in the demonstrations were stunned: a peaceful demonstration had resulted in massive bloodshed. Overnight, the correlation of class forces had shifted against the workers. Nor was it clear how far the reaction would go. For the first time, the workers had really to confront the extent of their political isolation.

Izvestiya reported that some factories in the Vyborg district resumed production on 5 July, although not all the workers appeared at work. Those who did come had trouble getting back into the routine. 'My hands are shaking from emotion; my hands won't hold the tools, say the workers'. Despite the appeals for calm from the various local socialist party organisations, the workers were so agitated that many of the factory committees sent them home after lunch.[41] In the Vasilevskii ostrov district, went one report, the dominant

37 Ibid., vol. v, p. 115.

38 Ibid., vol. iv, p. 474; Tomkevich, '*Znamya oktyabrya*', p. 20.

39 Metelev 1922, p. 172.

40 Latsis 1923, p. 114; Rabinowitch 1968, p. 211.

41 *Izvestiya* (6 July 1917).

emotion among women workers was fear.[42] Once the initial shock wore off, depression set in. Naumov described the mood at Lessner:

> We felt inexpressibly sad. At the factory, the workers were gloomy. They don't believe the slander, but not all of them were sufficiently armed to repel the poisonous, choking slander that was seeping into the workshops ... Not a day went by without the publication of some new 'revelation'. Rather than allow us to present our own point of view, they were transmitting our view in distorted fashion, in their own words. And repression, repression from all sides.[43]

Workers were emotionally drained. Some observers noted a tendency to withdraw from politics. At a meeting of the Bolshevik Petersburg Committee on 10 July, the delegate from the Narva district reported that 'the mood among the worker masses is sluggish, apathetic. This especially strikes the eye at the Putilov Factory ... It is to be explained by fatigue from the exertion of the last days'.[44] At the Second Factory Committee Conference in early August, V. Ya. Chubar, a worker from the Orudiinyi factory, stated that 'our nearest task is to shake the broad masses out of the temporary apathy into which they have fallen as a result of fatigue'.[45]

Shocked by the sudden rightward shift of the correlation of class forces, workers desired to restore the fractured unity of revolutionary democracy. They could not conceive of a break with the moderate socialists, who formed the majority in the TsIK and most local soviets. 'Among workers', observed Latsis in the middle of July, 'the question of unity with the SRs and Mensheviks is being raised. This is based on the assumption that by now everyone's eyes have been opened to the counter-revolution and to the need for unity to combat it'.[46] In some factories, including Metallicheskii, New Parviainen, Orudiinyi, Promet, Dinamo and others, failed efforts were made to overcome party differences among workers.[47]

42 *Vtoraya i tret'ya*, p. 60.

43 Naumov 1933, p. 32.

44 *Pervyi legal'nyi Peka*, pp. 370–1.

45 FZK, vol. I, p. 192.

46 *Vtoraya, i tret'ya obshchegorodskie konferetsii bol'shevikov v iule i sentyabre 1917 g.*, M-L. 1927, p. 61. The same was noted by several Bolshevik and non-Bolshevik observers. Ibid., p. 69; *Novaya zhizn'* (11 July 1917).

47 *Vtorayai i tret'ya*, pp. 61–2; *Pervyi legal'nyi*, p. 370; *Novaya zhizn'* (13, 19, 20 July 1917).

But the desire to restore unity of 'revolutionary democracy' went beyond the factory level. Speaking on 10 July for the Bolshevik fraction of the Petrograd Soviet, the worker G.F. Fedorov appealed for unity of all revolutionary forces against the danger from the right. When the Menshevik leader F.I. Dan proposed the TsIK's resolution, calling to support the new coalition government – which had formally adopted the programme proposed to it by TsIK, the socialist ministers promising to report to the TsIK at least twice a week – it passed almost unanimously. A quarter of those present, no doubt Bolsheviks and sympathisers, merely abstained.[48] Sukhanov commented that in the prevailing circumstances, even the hated Kerenskii, who headed the new government, seemed preferable to much else that could happen.[49]

For now, the workers, and this included many Bolsheviks, remained wedded to a strategy of pushing the moderate socialists in the TsIK to the left. This was reflected in factory resolutions at the time that often adopted a defensive tone and limited themselves to protesting against the repression and to demanding action by the TsIK. But the issue of power was passed over in silence. A general assembly of workers of the Old Parviainen Factory, after strongly condemning the rising tide of counterrevolution, concluded only with an appeal for 'the necessary unity of all revolutionary forces to repel at any moment actions of the counter-revolution against the Soviet of Workers' and Soldiers' Deputies and against the further development of the revolution'.[50]

But despite the fear, fatigue and the desire to restore the unity of revolutionary democracy, workers who had participated in the July Days did not change their view on the need to exclude the propertied classes from representation in the government. The Mensheviks and SRs made very energetic efforts to lay the blame for the bloodshed at the feet of the Bolsheviks, but the latter did not lose the support they had won among workers before the July Days. Korotkov, a Bolshevik worker at the Admiralty Shipyards, described the scene he found at his factory after returning from jail a few days after the July Days. A meeting was in progress.

> The SRs had come with their 'big guns'. The mood was depressed among the workers, and the SRs wanted to exploit that to the fullest extent against the Bolsheviks. When they demanded that the instigators of the factory's demonstration be turned over to the police, only a few voices supported

48 Sukhanov 1919–23, vol. v, pp. 20–2.
49 Ibid., p. 23.
50 *Izvestiya* (14 July 1917). See also, e.g., Tomkevich 1972, p. 40.

> them, shouting 'Pakhomov, Korotkov and the other Bolsheviks – into the Neva!' That provocation fell flat. Pakhomov responded well, calling them cowards covered with workers' blood. After that, the workers would not let the SRs speak, telling them firmly not to come back to the factory. And the workers kept their word.[51]

From Kolpino, a town several kilometres from the capital, the local Bolsheviks sent the following report:

> The Izhorskii Factory participated in the demonstration, in accordance with the decision of the Workers' Section of the [Petrograd] Soviet of Workers' and Soldiers' Deputies. Their participation took the form of a delegation (of 25 people) to the Tauride Palace, and [the factory] stopped work. During the days of the events in Piter, Kolpino lived mainly from rumours, and the mood shifted according to the nature of the rumours. However, that does not apply to workers who are [Bolshevik] party members, as they were generally well-informed, thanks to organised information. (Two comrades were dispatched daily, morning and evening, to Piter.) From the moment the demonstration was liquidated, the mood among the workers clearly shifted not to our favour. Accusations, the authors of which were the SRs, were levelled against us to the effect that we duped the workers of the Izhorskii factory when we said that the factories in Piter were striking (they cited the Nevskii district [whose workers did not participate in the July Days]). On the evening of 5 July, the SRs organised a meeting of some five to six thousand that gave us the chance to turn the mood around in our favour. After that, the attempts to try our comrades for allegedly reporting false information on the events in Piter fell through completely. There were cases of workers leaving our organisation, but they were isolated and for the most part they were motivated by fear. On the other hand, there were cases (also isolated) of people shifting to us from the SRs. The mood in general has stabilised as relatively calm, and if there were small excesses, their object was the SR's leaders.[52]

The situation was similar at the Putilov factory.[53]

---

51 *Krasnaya letopis'*, no. 9 (1924), p. 35. See also Temkin 1958, p. 12.

52 Dok. July, p. 103.

53 Dok. July, pp. 162–3; *Vtoraya*, p. 63.

Bolshevik support among workers continued to grow after the July Days. At the Treugol'nik Rubber Factory, which employed mostly women, new elections to the city Soviet elected a majority of Bolshevik delegates – two thirds – putting an end to the SRs' predominant influence.[54] V. Volodarskii, a popular Bolshevik tribune, reported to the Bolshevik' Petrograd Conference on 16 July that the mood everywhere was positive toward the party among workers.[55] This was an exaggeration, but the attitude to the Bolsheviks was changing quickly even in those factories where most workers were still hostile.

A Putilov worker penned the following letter, which was endorsed on 11 July by a workers' assembly of the cannon shop, a Menshevik bastion until the July Days. It gives eloquent expression of the mood among the workers who had taken part in the demonstrations.

> Citizens!
>
> Like an ancient oak amidst the forest, the giant Putilov factory stands amidst the nation's industry, shaking the earth with the heavy blows of its hammers. Here are workers from all corners of Russia, and working, they think their thoughts. Amidst the whistling of the saw, the howl of the wires, under the depressing gaze of gun carriages and cannons, gloomy thoughts creep into their minds. In toil, as under a forced-labour regime, mothers and fathers who bore us are dying. We, too, are dying here in hopeless estrangement from the enviable joy, from the security and culture that the wealthy, carefree, 'educated' minority are enjoying not far from us, separated only by that bold monument of antiquity – the Narva Gates.[56]
>
> Where is justice? Where are the results of the blood and lives of the fighters who fell in the revolution? Where is the new life? Where is that sublimely joyous, green-red bird that so temptingly flew over our land and disappeared ... as if to deceive us?
>
> Citizens! This was not the first time the Putilov workers shed their blood for the common interests of the working class. Remember January 9 [1905] and refrain from those sweeping accusations now being heard on the streets of Piter. In those days, on July 3–4, we went with the pure hearts

---

54 *Vtoraya*, pp. 61–4, 92; Shabalin, 'Ot fevralya k oktyabryu', in *Bastiony revolyutsii*, vol. I, p. 293.

55 *Vtoraya*, p. 57.

56 Triumphal gates, not far from the factory, erected in 1827–34 to commemorate the victory against the Napoleonic invasion of 1812.

> of loyal sons of the revolution. We went not against the Soviet of Workers' and Soldiers' Deputies, but to support it. That is why we had inscribed on our banners: 'All Power to the Soviets!'
>
> When we come out – they shoot us. That is why some of us took arms with them for the purpose of self-defence. On 9 January, the loyal servants of the House of Romanov shot us. Now it has been precisely established that the first shots, and also part of the returning fire, were organised by provocateurs – enemies of Russian freedom, enemies of the workers.
>
> Citizens! The renewed life cannot wait. With the iron logic of all the events that have occurred, it inexorably pushes the revolutionary people forward into the streets, forward, and it is often the street that decides the question. But to our sorrow, we are alone and we often lack organised forces. The developed workers are too dispersed and often do not live by the interests of the class as a whole, but in numerous factions and sects that do us harm. We are left to our own resources. The 'Soviet of Workers' Deputies' has begun, so it seems, to do without workers, and its membership, increasingly isolating itself, has become lost in tedious work of an administrative nature. And the Provisional Government has already completely congealed in dead bureaucratic forms.
>
> It is in that light that the economic and political situation appeared to us, workers, on the eve of the events of July 3–4.
>
> Citizens! Look with confidence on the black, smoking chimneys that rise out of the earth. There, at their foot, creating new values that you need, the same sort of people as yourselves, suffer and agonise in the bondage of perfected, ferocious exploitation. Slowly, consciousness is ripening there. In our hearts hatred is accumulating, and the gentle conditions of another life for all of humankind are being lovingly written on the bloody banner. Down with fratricidal strife!
>
> All citizens! To the active support of the 'Committee for the Salvation of the Revolution',[57] repeating its words directed at the workers: 'Neither under the boot of Wilhelm nor backward under the vile yoke of Nicolas the Bloody'.[58]

These lines expressed the disappointment with the results of the February Revolution, the workers' hatred of privileged society, and their desire for a new

---

57 This was apparently formed at the factory to defend workers and their organisations against the wave of repression.

58 Dok. July, pp. 71–2.

life, one for which their movement had sacrificed so much. But the overall tone of the letter is sad, even somewhat apologetic. There are bitter words for the Soviet and the government, but the author proposes no alternative. Instead he writes that the worker leaders are divided among the various parties, leaving the others to their own resources. And so 'Down with fratricidal strife'. Confronted with the prospect of civil war within the ranks of revolutionary democracy itself, these workers could only call to restore unity against the threat of counterrevolution from the propertied classes. For their part, following the July Days, the Mensheviks and the SRs waged an aggressive campaign aimed at pinning responsibility for the bloodshed on the Bolsheviks. 'The blood is on the head of those who called out armed people', declared the TsIK, which expelled Lenin and Kamenev pending an investigation into the charges that Bolsheviks had accepted German gold. 'This demonstration is a knife in the back of the revolution'.[59] 'The Bolsheviks are friends of Nikolai and Wilhelm', declared *Izvestiya*, organ of the TSiK.[60] The reaction against the Bolsheviks in the Nevskii district, the SR's main stronghold among workers, was especially strong. On 10 July, the delegate from the district to the Bolsheviks' Petersburg Committee reported:

> The factories did not participate in the demonstration and kept on working. The mood in relation to the Bolsheviks has a pogrom tinge. The SRs are actively fanning that mood. They are drawing up a list of Bolsheviks [at the Aleksandrovskii Machine-building factory] for the purpose of repression. They are searching out the district's better-known comrade Bolsheviks. Crowds are milling about the street, threatening a pogrom against our district committee. The workers are for the most part fed with rumours and with what they read in the boulevard press. A meeting yesterday at the Obukhovskii Factory was a failure for us. Our main adversaries are the SRs. All the same, considering everything, there is hope that we will soon be able to repair things.[61]

The delegate from the Porokhovskii district, which like Nevskii, was semi-rural and far from the centre, painted a similar picture:

> The worker milieu in our district resembles a stagnant swamp. Following 5–6 July, this manifested itself clearly. The Bolsheviks are being vilified

59 *Izvestiya* (5 July 1917).
60 Ibid. (12 July 1917).
61 *Pervyi legal'nyi*, p. 371.

> and persecuted. We, six people, were thrown out of the factory with the blessing of the [district] soviet. Our soviet and the Mensheviks are working for the counterrevolution. They are behaving in a vile manner.[62]

According to Perazich, a leader of the textile workers' union, only two textile mills had participated in full force in the demonstrations. He understated the reaction in writing that the campaign in the bourgeois press, supported by the defencists at workers' meetings, 'temporarily in some places confused our women workers'. At the Thornton Mills, for example, the Bolsheviks were recalled from all their elected positions, after they refused to repudiate their party.[63]

A meeting of delegates from the capital's printing establishments on 7 July placed the entire blame for the crisis on 'the left wing of revolutionary democracy, that is a significant irresponsible minority trying to impose its will on all of revolutionary democracy. We will obey only the slogans and appeals that are shared by revolutionary democracy of all of Russia'.[64]

The Bolsheviks even had trouble printing their newspaper, since the printers refused to do the work.[65] In one state-owned printing establishment, according to one of its workers, 'it reached the point where a non-party worker who shared the Bolsheviks' views was put on trial by the general assembly to decide whether to revoke his military deferment and send him to the front'.[66]

But their experience over the next few weeks – the continued deterioration of the economic situation and the increasingly tangible and immediate threat of counterrevolution – would force these workers to rethink their position. With the partial exception of the printers, the anti-Bolshevik reaction to the July Days soon yielded to a rapid shift in favour of the Bolsheviks, which also had its parallel among workers in Moscow and the provinces.

As for the majority of Petrograd's workers, those who had participated in the July Days to press for Soviet power, they were forced to rethink their strategy, now that the Mensheviks and SRs in the leadership of the TsIK and of most local soviets had turned against them and, consciously or otherwise, had sided with the counterrevolution. For the most part, these workers could not envisage

62 *Pervyi lega'lny* Peka, p. 372.

63 Perazich 1927, p. 86.

64 *Novaya zhizn'* (8 July 1917).

65 *Vtoraya i treti'ya*, p. 95.

66 'Petrogradskie rabochie', *Krasnaya letopis'*, no. 9 (1924) p. 32.

abandoning the soviets. That would have meant to isolate themselves from the workers, soldiers and peasants in the rest of Russia who continued to support the moderate socialists. It would have threatened civil war within revolutionary democracy.

Most workers did not support the new slogan that Lenin proposed to his party in the weeks following the July Days: a dictatorship of the proletariat and poorest peasantry. No mention was made of the soviets. The workers did not see this as a way forward. In fact, they saw no way forward. The political situation appeared to them a dead-end. A way forward would open up again only several weeks later in the late summer and early fall, when the soviets in the rest of Russia rallied to the goal of Soviet power. But even then, the traumatic experience of the July Days would continue to weigh upon workers and to hold most of them back from the kind of political initiative they had shown in the first six months of the revolution. For in the February, the April and the July days the initiative had come 'from below'; the Bolshevik party had followed. After the July Days, however, the party would have to take the initiative, and the workers would follow. The party, however, was the boldest, most determined section of the working class.

In contrast to the situation on the political level, the rank and file held onto the initiative in the factories. Even though the factory-committee activists, most of whom were Bolsheviks or Bolshevik sympathisers, continued to insist that workers' control was not socialism but only a school for socialism and that they could not accept responsibility for running the factories, the rank and file and the very logic of the situation were forcing them increasingly to abandon their initially bourgeois-democratic conception of the revolution.

CHAPTER 8

Rethinking the Revolution: Revolutionary Democracy or Proletarian Dictatorship?

Census Society on the Offensive

While workers, chastened by their defeat in the July Days at the hands of the Provisional Government, supported by the moderate socialist leaders of the TsIK, took up defensive positions, the forces of the political Right moved to the offense, hoping to cash in on this breach in the unity of the popular classes. As the Menshevik *Rabochaya gazeta* had foreseen back in May, the 'revolution's volcanic soil' had by then cooled sufficiently for the propertied classes and the allied intelligentsia to decide upon a frontal attack.[1]

At 'private' meetings of deputies of the State Duma, which continued to offer a quasi-official forum for political representatives of census society, despite workers' insistent protests, Aesopian language about 'the evils of dual power' was no longer considered necessary. 'The revolution was victorious thanks to the Duma', declared A.M. Maslennikov, a liberal deputy, in a typically brazen revision of recent history.

> Skobelev, Chkheidze and Kerenskii came and begged us to assume leadership of the uprising. But at that moment, a band of crazy fanatics, imposters, and traitors, calling themselves the Executive Committee of the Soviet of Workers' and Soldiers' Deputies, latched onto the Revolution.[2]

Well-known, respected orators now spoke openly of the need for a bourgeois dictatorship, for dispersal of the soviets, for a *coup d'état*, insisting at the same time that the Constituent Assembly could not possibly be convened during wartime. One of the most striking symbols of the period was the re-emergence from self-imposed seclusion of the notorious Tsarist reactionary and anti-Semite, V.M. Purishkevich, who at one of these meetings bluntly demanded suppression of the soviets and imposition of martial law.[3]

---

1 *Rabochaya gazeta* (May 20, 1917). See also Sukhanov 1919–23, vol. v, p. 8.

2 *Novaya zhizn'* (July 19, 1917).

3 Sukhanov 1919–23, vol. 5, p. 55; Price 1921, pp. 64–5; *Revolyutsionnoe dvizhenie v Rossii v iyule 1917 g.* (henceforth cited as Dok. July) (M., 1959), pp. 294–5, 318–19; *Rabochii put'* (20 Aug 1917).

On 3 August, at the Second All-Russian Commercial and Industrial Congress, P.P. Ryabushinskii, a liberal banking and industrial magnate, made a particularly vitriolic speech in which he bitterly attacked the soviets and other popular organisations and described the Provisional Government as a mere facade. 'In fact, a gang of political charlatans has been running everything'. These words evoked a storm of applause from across the hall. 'The soviet pseudo-leaders of the people have directed it onto a path of ruin, and the entire Russian state stands before a gaping abyss'. Decisively rejecting any new role for the state in regulating economic life, Ryabushinskii declared the revolution to be 'bourgeois' and called on those standing at the helm of the state to act in a 'bourgeois manner'. These words evoked shouts of 'correct!' from across the hall. And he concluded ominously:

> Therefore, our task is an extremely difficult one. We must wait. We know that the natural development of life will take its course and, unfortunately, it cruelly punishes those who violate its laws. But it is bad when we must sacrifice state interests in order to convince a small group of people ... Unfortunately, the long, bony hand of hunger and national impoverishment will have to seize those false friends of the people, members of the various committees and soviets, by the throat for them to come to their senses ... In this difficult moment, when new waves of unrest are approaching, all vitally important, cultural forces of the country must form a united harmonious family. Let the steadfast merchant's nature manifest itself! Men of commerce! We must save the Russian land![4]

There followed thunderous applause, as the assembled leaped to their feet to hail the orator. *Russkoe slovo*, a pro-government Moscow newspaper, commented on the mood at the congress: 'A rustle of hatred, anger and scorn flew across the hall at the mention of each socialist minister, including A.F. Kerenskii'.[5]

In the days that followed, Ryabushinskii's graphic metaphor would be repeatedly cited at workers' meetings and in the socialist press as evidence of the industrialists' intentions, with Ryabushinskii personifying the 'capitalist-lockouter'. 'Thanks for the truth', commented the Bolsheviks' paper *Proletarii*. 'The conscious workers and peasants can only be grateful to Ryabushinskii. The only question is: whose hand will do the grasping by the throat?'[6]

---

4 *Ekonomicheskoe polozhenie Rossii nakanune Velikoi oktyabr'skoi sotsialisticheskoi revolyutsii* (henceforth cited as Ek. Pol.), (M.-L., 1957) vol. I, pp. 196, 200–1.

5 Cited in *Novaya zhizn'* (Aug. 8, 1917).

6 *Proletarii* (Aug. 10, 1917).

After the July Days, the spectre of counterrevolution began to assume for the first time the more concrete outline of a military dictatorship. Addressing one of the gatherings of State Duma deputies in July, the Kadet-party leader Milyukov was strikingly frank on this matter:

> I must say that, shaken by recent events, by our failures at the front and by the revolt of the Bolsheviks in Petrograd, the members of the government have understood the need for a radical change of course. The death penalty has been restored; perhaps other measures will soon be adopted. But we feel that it is absolutely necessary that the Minister-Chairman [Kerenskii] either yield his place or, in any case, take on as aides authoritative military men and that these authoritative military men act with the necessary independence and initiative.[7]

On 22 July, General L.G. Kornilov accepted from Kerenskii the supreme command of Russia's armed forces. While he did this, he presented an 'ultimatum', demanding complete freedom in issuing operative orders and in making appointments. And he declared that he considered himself responsible only to his own conscience and to the whole people – he made no mention of the government.[8] This Cossack general was already well-known to Petrograd's workers. While in command of the capital's garrison during the April Crisis, he had ordered artillery fire against the demonstrating workers and soldiers. A massacre was averted only thanks to the gunners' insistence on having the Soviet countersign the general's order.

While the bourgeois press touted Kornilov as the 'strong man' who would save Russia – his biography was being distributed in vast numbers – rumours were rife in soviet circles of a military conspiracy. There was talk of removing the general. Meetings of such far-right organisations such as the Union of Twelve Cossack Armies, the League of Cavaliers of St George, the Conference of Public Figures, sternly warned the government against taking any such action.[9]

Meanwhile, the government pursued its repression of the Left. After a brief reappearance, the Bolsheviks' main newspaper was again shut down on 10 August. Political arrests also continued, including those of prominent Bolsheviks, like Trotsky and Lunacharskii. But lesser figures were also swept up. On 28 July at the Tsirk Modern, a popular venue for public meetings, a worker was arrested

7 Cited in Tsvetkov-Prosveshchenskii 1933, p. 133.

8 Sukhanov 1919–23, vol. 5, p. 110.

9 Ibid., p. 131; *Revolyutsionnoe dvizhenie v Rossii v avguste 1917 g.* (henceforth cited as Dok. Aug.), (M., 1959), p. 360.

for denouncing Kerenskii. Another was taken in for condemning the Liberty Loan.[10] On 6 August, the Minister of Internal Affairs was empowered to arrest and hold people indefinitely without trial.

The government had by now abandoned even the pretence of a peace policy. On the third anniversary of the outbreak of the war, Kerenskii wired King George, assuring him of Russia's ability and will to 'pursue the world war to the end'. When the Prime Minister Lloyd George refused to issue passports to the British delegation to the socialist Stockholm Conference – it was the cornerstone of the peace strategy of Russia's moderate socialists – he cited a note he had received from Kerenskii, who gave a negative opinion of the conference and reduced it to a 'private affair'.[11] The Provisional Government closed down the Menshevik-Internationalists' newspaper *Novaya zhizn'* for exposing Kerenskii's role in the conference's failure. And in connection with this, it adopted a law that made it a criminal offence to insult in print a representative of a friendly state.[12]

As workers saw it, the moderate socialist majority in the TsIK had capitulated to the propertied classes. This view received symbolic support at the Moscow State Conference in mid-August. The conference was Kerenskii's initiative. He hoped to obtain from the gathering an expression of support for the government from all the classes of society. But even though the Bolsheviks boycotted the conference, the assembly was so polarised that on almost every question the representatives of census society were irreconcilably opposed to those of the popular classes. 'That which gladdens the one side', commented *Novaya zhizn'*, 'meets with icy cold from the other'.[13] The conference very nearly ended in a brawl when a young Cossack delegate declared that the toiling Cossacks had no confidence in their leaders.[14] Against the background of this polarisation, workers were appalled to learn that Tsereteli had demonstratively offered his hand in front of the entire assembly to the representative of the Council of the Congress of Trade and Industry, A.A. Bublikov.[15]

In the factories, the industrialists were now determined to withdraw the concessions they had been forced to make earlier in the revolution. They concentrated particular fire on the elected factory committees. A circular from

---

10 *Novaya zhizn'* (July 29, 1917). For a more detailed account of the repressive measures, see Rabinowitch 1976, Chapter 3.

11 Price 1921, p. 66.

12 Sukhanov 1919–23, vol. 5, p. 135.

13 *Novaya zhizn'* (Aug 13, 1917).

14 Trotsky 1967, vol. II, p. 181.

15 Dok. Aug., p. 370.

the Council of United Industry dated 22 August declared that management alone had the right to make decisions concerning hiring and dismissal. It rejected any financial obligation to the factory committees – most notably the payment of wages to their full-time members – other than to provide a space for their meetings. The committee of the Skorokhod Shoe Factory issued the following declaration to the workers in August:

> In order to consolidate our economic and political gains, which we have won at the price of our many fallen comrades, we must adopt a particularly serious attitude in the current situation, after all the events that took place on 3 and 4 July. Comrades, you see that in all the factories and mills the bourgeoisie has undertaken an offensive against your economic gains. They are acting openly and conducting a struggle against your organisations. Comrades, we have to unite around our organisations and support them with all our strength.
>
> Comrades! The administration of our factory is already beginning to intervene in the internal rules of our factory, that until now have been in our hands. The administration has declared to us that it will conduct hiring and firing independently. Comrades, you know [what this means] from bitter experience under the old regime, when they threw us out of the gates for every word spoken for justice and in our place hired people who suited them ...[16]

'Every day we hear of new attacks against the rights that we have won', declared a rapporteur at the Second Petrograd Factory Committee Conference in August.[17] Another speaker, a member of the Central Soviet of Factory Committees, observed:

> When the Central Soviet of Factory Committees began to work, the entrepreneurs were open to our influence in direct negotiations with representatives of the Central Soviet. But now they are becoming less and less flexible. In their stubbornness, they cite the Society of Factory and Mill Owners and refuse to recognise the Central Soviet, since it is not a government institution.[18]

---

16 *Rabochii kontrol' i natsionalizatsiya promyshlennykh predpriyatii Petrograda v 1917–1919 gg.* (henceforth cited as Rab. Kon.), (L., 1949) vol. 1, pp. 152–3.

17 FZK vol. I, p. 191.

18 Ibid, p. 173.

The government took an active part in this counteroffensive against the factory committees. M.I. Skobelev, the Menshevik Minister of Labour, issued a series of circulars on 28 August, upholding the industrialists' position on the rights of factory committees. In the meanwhile, the government made no move to implement the plan for economic regulation that had been drawn up in May by the economic commission of the Petrograd Soviet. When the government's Economic Council finally began to meet in July, it merely heard reports without making any action proposals.[19] 'Not one serious reform has been adopted, neither in the social sphere nor in that of the national economy', concluded a resolution of the Conference of Factory Committees in August.[20]

On the other hand, the government dusted off its plan for 'unloading' Petrograd of its factories. Although ostensibly an economic measure aimed at moving the factories closer to their sources of fuel and raw materials, the plan's political motives were barely concealed. A government resolution from 8 August called to evacuate medical and educational institutions along with 'other institutions ... and to elaborate a plan to expel people, who present a threat in the counterrevolutionary sense'. In fact, the original version of the resolution had been even more explicit, calling 'to liberate the capital of elements that create a danger of a repetition of the events of 3–5 July'.[21]

Towards the end of August, a list of 47 factories to be given priority in the evacuation became public. It included all the state-owned plants, most large private metalworking factories, and a number of chemical works. To add insult to injury, only a small part of the workers employed in those factories were to accompany them to the new locations. The rest would be dismissed with two weeks' severance pay. On the other hand, the state was to assume the entire cost of moving the private factories.[22]

But even without that plan, the threat to industry and to employment was growing more serious each day. By early August, 43 factories, mostly small and medium-sized, had closed. Although these closures affected relatively few workers, the psychological impact was great. Around that time, Petrograd's Metalworkers' Union reported that 25 other factories were slated to be closed soon and production was to be reduced in another 137.[23] These factories

19 Sukhanov 1919–23, vol. 5, p. 129. See also the critical assessment of government economic policy by the Menshevik economist V.A. Bazarov in *Novaya zhizn'* (Dec. 30, 1917).

20 FZK, vol. I, p. 217.

21 Dok. Aug., pp. 177 and 614.

22 Stepanov 1965, p. 96.

23 *Izvestiya* (Aug, 18, 1917).

included some of the largest, both state and private, in the city.[24] 'The storm has broken out over all our heads', declared a representative of the Central Soviet of Factory Committees at the conference in August.[25]

Although unemployment was still low,[26] the trend was alarming. Industrial employment had expanded by 10–12 percent in the first half of 1917. But in July, it declined for the first time since the end of 1911. And if employment at the moment of the October Revolution had not yet fallen significantly below February's level,[27] that was largely due to the efforts of the factory committees.

The employers' position also hardened on wages. The Petrograd Society of Factory and Mill Owners issued a directive forbidding its members from concluding separate agreements. A fine of 25 roubles per worker was set for recalcitrant members.[28] On 12 July, negotiations for a collective agreement between the Society and the Metalworkers' Union broke down. The main stumbling point was the union's wage demand for unskilled workers.[29] On their part, the owners demanded the introduction of obligatory minimum output norms. The union finally decided not to join battle over this latter question and accepted a government-proposed compromise that introduced minimum output norms. The union felt that the industrialists wanted a strike in order to open the way for a lockout along the lines of the one in late 1905 that had contributed to the defeat of the 1905 revolution. But despite the union's concessions, the implementation of the new wage rates was marked by endless disputes and haggling on management's part.[30]

At this time, the Textile Workers' Union was being deluged with complaints about the improper calculation of its members' wages. Despite an agreement with the Society of Factory and Mill Owners that granted a 25 percent, across-

---

24 Stepanov 1965, pp. 140–1; *Revolyutsionnoe dvizhenie v Rossii v sentyabre 1917 g.* (henceforth cited as Dok. Sept.), (M., 1962) p. 197; FZK, vol. II, 1928, pp. 57–8; Perazich 1927, pp. 75, 90.

25 FZK, vol. II, p. 190.

26 *Znamya truda* (6 Oct 1917).

27 Stepanov 1927, p. 27.

28 Perazich 1927, p. 87.

29 The demand for a minimum wage was made at the start of the revolution under strong pressure from the unskilled workers, whose wages – and even the entrepreneurs admitted this – were below the subsistence level. Although the unskilled workers' situation improved after February, a minimum wage was never enacted, and inflation soon ate up what had been won. The low wages of unskilled workers and the difference in their wages with those of skilled workers – a difference that the union was able to close with only limited success in negotiations – was a constant source of tension between the two categories of workers. TsGA SPb f. 1000, op. 73, d. 16, *passim*; f. 4591, op. 1, d. 1, l. 40.

30 Stepanov 1965, p. 81; S. Bruk, in Anskii 1927, pp. 127–8; *Rabochaya gazeta* (6 Aug 1917).

the-board raise, many owners claimed to know nothing of the agreement; others said that wages were already too high; and still others raised wages selectively. Negotiations toward a new collective agreement, begun on 27 June, dragged on for more than two months, the owners fighting tooth and nail over each demand. For example, it required two days of hard bargaining for them to agree to provide the workers with boiling water for tea. And even then, they insisted on inserting the words: 'Only in view of extraordinary circumstances'.[31]

Meanwhile, workers were reading reports in the press about the industrialists' war profiteering. One particularly scandalous case was that of M.V. Rodzyanko, Chairman of the State Duma, who had been supplying the army with defective rifle butts at highly inflated prices during the entire course of the war.[32]

August was also the beginning of the decline of real wages, following the increases the workers had won in the spring. According to one estimate, the cost of living in Petrograd rose by approximately 70 percent in the months of January–June 1917 but by 75 percent in July and August alone.[33] Data from a limited, but fairly representative, sample of Petrograd factories indicate that real wages after the February Revolution reached their apogee in May and June, after which they began to fall, although nominal wages continued to rise, though at a slower pace than before. For example, real wages at the Obukhovskii, Parviainen, Baltiiskii (metalworking), Kersten, Novaya bumagopryadil'nya (textile) and Shaposhnikova (tobacco) factories rose on average 110 percent in the first six months of 1917.[34] But in July and August, the average nominal wage in these factories increased only 12 percent, which meant a dramatic fall in real wages, in most cases to below the level of February 1917. The collective agreements of mid-August and early September in the metal and textile industries allowed workers temporarily to recoup only some of the lost buying power, but real wages continued to fall.[35]

Food shortages began to be seriously felt in the summer months, for the first time since the previous winter.[36] At one point, the capital had only a two-

31 Perazich 1927, pp. 64–9.

32 *Novaya zhizn'* (12 and 23 Aug 1917).

33 Stepanov 1965, pp. 53–4.

34 Although if Moscow is any guide, real wages still failed to catch up to their pre-war level. Government figures for Moscow show a rise in wages of 515 percent between July 1914 and July 1917, while the prices of food staples in the same period rose by 566 percent, and of other basic necessities by 1109 percent. *Znamya truda* (17 Oct 1917).

35 Stepanov 1965, pp. 53–4.

36 Sukhanov 1919–23, vol. 5 p. 173.

day supply of grain. The irregular food shipments caused serious distribution difficulties. The Food Authority of the Vyborg district reported that 'queues have in fact turned the eight-hour day into a twelve and thirteen-hour day, since women and male workers go from their factories and other work places directly to the queues, where they spend four to five hours, sometimes up to their next work day'.[37]

At the factory-committee conference in August, V.P. Milyutin, a Bolshevik economist, presented the following summary of the economic and political situations, subsequently incorporated into a resolution that was passed overwhelmingly:

> One is forced to note a changed situation of late in the economic and political spheres.
>
> In the economic sphere, the particular character of the current situation is that Russia has already entered a period of genuine catastrophe, as the economic breakdown and the food crisis have reached extreme limits. We are already experiencing an acute shortage of grain, and the picture of genuine hunger looms before us in all its immensity. The papers report that the ration in Astrakhan has been cut to half a funt [0.2 kg] and that it might have to be cut even more.
>
> A similar crisis has hit industry: in metallurgy, production is down by 60 percent; the textile industry barely exists. The coal industry is shrinking daily, and it is possible that by the fall the railroads will not be able to function because of the shortage of coal and fuel. And the state's debt grows daily, amounting at present to 60 billion [rubles], almost exclusively expended on the war, since only five billion are being spent on the country's other needs …
>
> The Provisional Government, thanks to the conciliatory policy of the petty-bourgeois [moderate socialist] parties, has done absolutely nothing to restrain the industrialists' predatory sabotage … The Provisional Government has done absolutely nothing to avert the advancing catastrophe.
>
> In this atmosphere of approaching economic disaster the country's political life has been evolving for the past while. The distinctive trait of the current political moment is the open organisation of counterrevolution.

37 Stepanov 1965, p. 67.

> The disgraceful legacy of the past is being restored: capital punishment, administrative exile and arrests, attacks on workers' organisations and their press – these are the striking manifestations of counterrevolution that are occurring in plain view.
>
> Parallel to this are the fanning of the war and the distinct influence of international capital, especially English, on the entire internal life of the country.
>
> All power has in practice passed now into the hands of the counterrevolution, despite the fact that half of the cabinet consists of 'socialists'.[38]

Final Rejection of 'Conciliationism'

Toward the end of August, only a small minority of workers still supported the coalition government and the moderate socialists. Radicalisation among workers before the July Days had affected disproportionately the more urbanised, skilled stratum, especially those employed in the metal and woodworking sectors. For that reason, most of the shift in political allegiance took place among supporters of social democracy – these workers abandoned the Mensheviks and shifted support to the Bolsheviks. The SRs, on the other hand, although they were weakened, still had many supporters, notably among the semi-skilled and unskilled workers. All the more dramatic, therefore, was the decline in their support in the weeks following the July Days. Some of these workers shifted to the party's left wing, which, like the Mensheviks-Internationalists, opposed the coalition but without embracing the demand for soviet power. But most of them turned to the Bolsheviks, whose position appeared more coherent and who were not tainted by organisational links to the 'conciliators'.

Elections to the city duma on 20 August registered the remarkable increase in Bolshevik support since the spring (see Table 8.1). The Bolsheviks' share of the vote rose from 20.4% of the total vote in the district duma elections of early June to a third. The Bolsheviks were the only party that increased its absolute number of votes, this despite a 30 percent drop in voter turnout since June.[39] The Bolsheviks drew their principal support from workers, with absolute majorities in the heavily working-class Vyborg and Petergof Districts and pluralities in the Vasilevskii ostrov and Petrograd Districts, which also had siz-

38 FZK, vol. I, pp. 200–1.

39 The relative turnout was, in fact, lower, since new districts had been incorporated into the city boundaries in May.

TABLE 8.1 *Returns in Petrograd elections to district Dumas (27 May–5 June), to the city Duma (20 August), and to the Constituent Assembly (12–14 November 1917) (number of votes cast, in 1,000s)*

Election date	Bolshevik		SR		Menshevik		Kadet		All parties	
	Number	%	Number	%	Number	%	Number	%	Number	%
May–June	160	20.4	431[a]	55.0[a]	–	–	172	21.9	785	100
August	184	33.4	206	37.4	24	4.3[b]	114	20.8	549	100
November	424	45.0	152	16.1	29	3.0[c]	247	26.2	942	100

[a] These figures include both the SR and Menshevik votes, as the two parties ran a joint list.

[b] The Menshevik list in the August election was exclusively Internationalist.

[c] Includes votes for both Menshevik defencists and Internationalists: 1.8 percent and 1.2 percent respectively.

SOURCES: MAY – W. ROSENBERG, *LIBERALS IN THE RUSSIAN REVOLUTION*, P. 162; AUGUST – *DELO NARODA* (23–4 AUG 1917); NOVEMBER – *NASHA RECH'* (17 NOV 1918).

able worker populations, as well as in Lesnoi District and Novaya derevnya, adjacent to the Vyborg District (see Table 8.2).[40] The strong vote for the Bolsheviks in some of the central districts is explained by the presence of military units. For example, in the Admiral'teiskii District, 86 percent of the votes cast for Bolsheviks came from soldiers.[41]

The vote for SRs declined everywhere in the city, although the party retained significant support in the outlying Nevskii, Moscow and Polyustrovo-Porokhovskii Districts. These had some industrial enterprises, as well as significant numbers of white-collar employees, petty bourgeois and soldiers.

The low turnout hurt the Kadet party most: the well-off residents of the city did not heed the Kadets' plea to return from their summer homes to vote. The party also suffered from the recent incorporation of six outlying districts, whose population was of modest means.

The Kadets won pluralities in two central districts – Liteinyi and Admiralty – and managed to increase their share of the vote since the spring elections by

40 For the social composition of the districts, see Chapter 3.

41 *Delo naroda* (Aug. 23, 1917).

TABLE 8.2 *Breakdown by districts of Petrograd Duma election returns, 20 August 1917 (percent of total district vote)*

District	Bolshevik %	SR %	Menshevik %	Kadet %	Total number vote cast [a]
Admiral'teiskii	35.7	35.8	2.2	21.3	11,865
Aleksandr-Nevskii	28.0	52.4	3.4	12.8	43,552
Kazanskii	17.1	29.9	3.5	41.0	13,375
Kolomenskii	29.7	38.3	2.3	26.2	23,609
Lesnoi	36.5	29.3	5.3	24.6	15,830
Liteinyi	16.9	35.2	4.0	38.5	31,236
Moskovskii	21.3	34.8	4.5	33.0	39,967
Narvskii	33.3	50.2	3.2	11.3	69,621
Nevskii	20.1	66.8	2.8	8.5	30,812
Novaya derevnya	37.5	28.1	4.3	28.5	9,825
Petergofskii	61.7	31.5	1.6	3.4	27,949
Petrogradskiii	38.0	25.9	5.4	26.3	70,515
Polyustrovo-Porokhovskii	34.5	55.0	2.3	6.8	19,690
Rozhdestvenskii	15.5	39.3	4.9	33.9	34,287
Spasskii	16.8	39.7	3.6	33.0	17,970
Vasilevskii ostrov	38.1	32.9	8.2	17.7	64,726
Vyborgskii	63.0	23.9	3.5	7.6	35,711

[a] Includes votes for several minor socialist and non-socialist parties that together received 4.0 percent of the vote.

SOURCES: ROSENBERG, *LIBERALS IN THE RUSSIAN REVOLUTION*, P. 220; *DELO NARODA* (23–4 AUG 1917).

three to four percent in four other districts (Moskovskii Spasskii, Petrogradskii and Rozhdestvenskii).[42] This is explained by the rightward shift of the middle strata, many of whom had supported the moderate socialists in the earlier days of the revolution but had since moved to the right, as the middle ground crumbled.

Among the district soviets that had any significant working-class constituency, only those in the Narvskii, Nevskii and Porokhovskii Districts still had

42 Rosenberg 1974, p. 220.

moderate-socialist majorities at the end of August.[43] But, in fact, they no longer reflected the prevailing sentiment, and new elections would soon register the workers' radicalisation.

In the factory committees, which the Bolsheviks had dominated from the start, the latter further consolidated their position. At the Second Conference of Factory Committees on August 7–12, their resolution received 82 percent of the votes, with only ten percent opposing and eight abstentions.[44] The Bolsheviks also held majorities in the executives of all the industrial trade unions, with the exceptions of the Printers and the Paper Workers. Seventeen of the twenty-three members of the Petrograd Trade-Union Council were Bolsheviks.[45]

The reaction against the Bolsheviks caused by the bloodshed of the July Days had thus proved short-lived. It had affected mainly workers who had not participated in the demonstrations. Less than a month after the workers of the Thornton Knitwear Mill recalled their Bolshevik delegates from the Petrograd Soviet, they restored them all in new elections.[46] The shift in the political mood was especially striking in the textile industry, with its largely unskilled, female workforce.[47] Before the July Days, only two or three mills had adopted resolutions calling for soviet power. But on 13 August, a meeting of 80 Textile-Union delegates from 24 mills for the first time adopted that position.[48] A worker at the Skorokhod Shoe Factory (4,900 mostly unskilled workers) recalled that 'even the most backward workers turned away from the SRs' in the weeks following the July Days.[49]

The same occurred at the large state-owned factories, which had before been defencist bastions. At the Trubochnyi Factory (20,000 mostly unskilled workers),[50] a factory-wide meeting of delegates on 17 August adopted the Bolshevik-sponsored resolution, condemning the 'counterrevolutionary essence' of Ker-

43 Stepanov 1965, p. 169; *Raionnye sovety Petrograda v 1917 g.* (henceforth cited as Raisovety) (M.-L., 1968), vol. III, p. 179.

44 FZK, vol. I, p. 215. At the first conference at the end of May, the Bolshevik resolution calling for soviet power garnered only 63 percent.

45 Shatilova 1927, pp. 179–88.

46 Perazich 1927, p. 91.

47 See above, Chapter 2.

48 Perazich 1927, pp. 79–82, 87.

49 'Piterskie rabochie ob iyul'skikh dnyakh', *Krasnaya letopis*, 9 (1923). pp. 21–2.

50 M. Bortik, 'Na Trubochnom zavode', in Anskii 1928, p. 208.

enskii's 'government of salvation'.[51] The Patronnyi and Arsenal factories, defencist exceptions in the Vyborg District, elected their first Bolshevik delegates to the Petrograd Soviet in August.[52] The Bolshevik paper reported that month a dramatic shift in the political mood at the Obukhovskii Steel Factory in the Nevskii District. Before the July Days, these workers had held the distinction of having formed the only volunteer military unit for the government's June military offensive.[53] Immediately following the July Days, the local Bolsheviks here had been terrorised. But all that changed in the following weeks.

> Was it not that recently that the defencists ruled undividedly at the huge Obukhovskii Factory that sets the tone for all the proletariat and semi-proletariat of the Nevskii District? Not long ago Deich and Aleksinskii [prominent Mensheviks and SRs] were welcomed guests here, and a Bolshevik could not show his face. But in the elections [to the district duma in mid-August], the defencists won only one mandate. The SRs, to hold on to their following, had to hastily recast themselves in a protective internationalist hue. Of the 38 mandates [out of 52] that the party obtained, 26 consider themselves as belonging to the left wing of the SR Party.[54]

The paper went on to report that Bolshevik speakers had enjoyed the most success at a recent meeting and were repeatedly interrupted by applause. In this semi-rural district, the SR label retained its attraction, winning 74.4 percent of the vote in the district duma elections.[55] But support for the Provisional Government was rapidly fading among the workers.

And the SR party organisation in the city was suffering from mass defections. At the 23 August meeting of its Petersburg Committee, reports from the districts all told of declining influence among workers. Rank-and-file members complained about the party's right-wing policies and were leaving in droves to join the Bolsheviks. The only exceptions to this general picture were in the outlying Nevskii, Porokhovskii and Moskovskii district organisations, where the party's support, though declining, remained significant.[56] In contrast, membership

---

51 Notman 1932, pp. 249–50.
52 Stepanov 1965, p. 68.
53 Raisovety, vol. II, p. 81.
54 Proletarii (17 Aug 1917). See also Antonov 1957, p. 211.
55 *Proletarii* (13 Aug 1917).
56 Znamenskii 1964, p. 260.

in the Bolsheviks' Petrograd organisation (excluding soldiers) increased from 30,620 to 36,015 in the month of July alone.[57]

As for the Menshevik organisation, which by this time was extremely weak, it was now controlled by the internationalist wing, which opposed the coalition government. At the party's Petrograd conference in early August, the internationalists had a fifteen-person majority among the hundred or so delegates (although the defencists had slightly more support among the city's electorate).[58] In the district duma elections of mid-August, rank-and-file pressure blocked the leadership's attempt to run a joint slate with the defencists.[59] Nationally, too, support for the defencist wing of the party was declining. At the party's national congress on 19 August, Tsereteli prevailed over Martov (leader of the internationalist wing) by an unprecedentedly narrow margin of 115 to 79.[60]

The political evolution of the Rozhdestvenskii District Soviet after the July Days illustrates well the thinking of workers who had supported the coalition government still at the beginning of July and who had initially blamed the Bolsheviks for the bloodshed of the July Days. This district was located in the 'bourgeois' centre and counted only some 10,000 factory workers, almost half of which were employed in two textile mills, the rest being scattered among small metalworking and electrical factories, printing plants and a tram depot. Several military units were also barracked there.[61] On 6 July, a plenary meeting of the soviet condemned the Bolsheviks as an 'irresponsible minority, blindly leading benighted masses to civil war within revolutionary democracy and threatening to divert the revolution onto the path of reaction and counterrevolution'.[62]

But under the impact of the right-wing reaction and the government's repressive measures, the soviet's attitude toward the Bolsheviks softened. A week later, another meeting again condemned the 'irresponsible agitation of anarcho-bolshevik elements'. But this time it added that, 'as a result of the defeat of the irresponsible counterrevolution from the left, the counterrevolution from the right has raised its head and is shifting to active operations'. Calling on the workers to rally behind the TsIK (which supported the coalition government),

57 *Vtoraya i tret'ya petrogradskie obshchegorodskie konferentsii bol'shevikov v iyule i sentyabre 1917 g.* (henceforth cited as Vtoraya) (M.-L., 1927) p. 14; *Shestoi vserossiiskii s'ezd* RSDRP(*b*) (M., 195 8), p. 44.

58 *Novaya zhizn'* (Aug. 8, 1917).

59 Sukhanov 1919–23, vol. V, p. 190.

60 *Rabochii put'* (Aug. 28, 1917).

61 Raisovety, vol. I, pp. 80, 89; vol. II, p. 199.

62 Ibid, vol. III, p. 201.

the soviet called on the TsIK to take measures against the increasingly militant counterrevolution from the Right. And it protested against the biased nature of the commission investigating the July Days, in which workers and soldiers had inadequate representation and which was focusing exclusively on the 'anarcho-Bolshevik' organisations, without trying to get to the real root of the counterrevolution, which was on the Right.[63] Four days later, the soviet forcefully declared its opposition to a special military unit that had been sent to disarm the district's workers, declaring that it would itself investigate if there were illegal arms. To the soldiers of that unit it pointed out the necessity of disarming 'supporters of the counterrevolution among the bourgeoisie of all ranks and stations'.[64]

When the Provisional Government, with the TsIK's blessing, restored the death penalty at the front, a longstanding demand of the Right, the district soviet finally broke with the defencists, voting thirteen against five (with five abstentions) to condemn the measure, which had heavy symbolism for workers, many of whom could recall the mass executions that followed the defeat of the Revolution of 1905.[65]

> One of the most valuable achievements of the Great Russian Revolution – the abolition of the death penalty – has been destroyed with a single stroke of the Provisional Government's pen.
>
> Already under Nikolai II, in the period of the cruellest and darkest reaction, the death penalty called forth the unanimous indignation of toilers, on the one hand, and a feigned squeamish attitude on the part of the bourgeoisie, on the other; and a rumble of anger rolled across Russia from one end to the other.
>
> Victorious people, having overthrown the autocracy, first of all abolished the death penalty, as a barbarism that is unworthy of a free country.
>
> Now the Provisional Government, on the demand of the generals and of people incapable of appreciating this great achievement, and also on the request of the Minister of War [Kerenskii], who has adhered to these demands, has again restored this legalised murder ... Soldiers, appointed to the role of executioner, will hastily drag their comrades, exhausted and driven senseless by the savage, three-year-old slaughter, and sentenced to the death penalty ... They will shoot them like dogs only because they

63 Ibid., p. 202.

64 Ibid., pp. 203–4.

65 See, for example, Mikhailov 1932, pp. 205–6.

> did not self-sacrificingly give up their lives in the interests of their own class enemies – the imperialist bourgeoisie, which has thrown the toilers of one side against the very same toilers of the other side ...
>
> A great absurdity has occurred: a free country abolishes the death penalty for highly placed criminals, all the Nikolais, Sukhomlinovs, Stürmers and Protopopovs [Tsarist ministers], etc. but retains it for soldiers, exhausted by the senseless three-year-old slaughter and whom the base and cowardly bourgeoisie now slanders with the undeserved title of cowards and traitors ...
>
> It is a crime to remain silent at this attack on the part of the Provisional Government against the achievements of the Revolution. Nowhere and at no time will the toilers reconcile themselves to this disgrace and they will never calmly accept that form of murder called capital punishment ... Down with the death penalty! ... Down with the war as the cause of this horrible result that disgraces humanity! Long live the revolutionary International![66]

(A month later, a plenary session of the Petrograd Soviet (both workers' and soldiers' sections), which met after a four-week recess (testimony to the soviets' atrophy under the moderate socialists), broke dramatically with the TsIK by voting 900 against four in favour of abolition of the death penalty. The four who opposed the resolution were the Menshevik leaders of the TsIK – Tsereteli, Dan, Liber and Chkheidze.[67])

This same meeting of the Rozhdestvenskii soviet adopted another resolution, demanding that the TsIK undertake a serious struggle against the 'counterrevolution, grown bold, which now openly shows its face, having found its leader in the [State] Duma, in the clergy, the landowners, and the capitalists'. It called on the TsIK to 'put an end to the comedy' and finally to disperse the State Duma,

> that insignificant group of counterrevolutionaries and ultimate toadies of the autocracy who claim to speak for Russian people, which has never authorised them for anything, who allow themselves intolerable insults and call for the dissolution of the legitimate organs of revolutionary democracy ... The TsIK must direct the most serious attention of the government and especially of its socialist ministers to the need for full-

66 Raisovety, vol. III, p. 204.

67 Sukhanov 1919–23, vol. V, p. 180.

> scale repression of the counterrevolution from the right, which is growing more insolent with each day.

The resolution was now completely silent on the 'anarcho-Bolsheviks' and the 'counterrevolution from the Left'.[68]

A similar shift of position occurred in Moscow, whose industrial working class in many ways resembled those workers in Petrograd who had refrained from participation in the July Days.[69] There had been no July Days in Moscow. At that time, even the factory committees were largely dominated by defencists.[70] 'I'm very struck that the Moscow organisation is so weak', observed a Petrograd Bolshevik at a meeting of the Moscow's Bolshevik Committee in July. 'In Piter, we are always holding back the masses. Here we have to intensify our agitation to get action'.[71] Sukhanov also observed that 'many [on the Right] had put their hope in the patriarchal humility' of Moscow.[72] All the more startling, then, was the practically general political strike that met the opening of the State Conference on 11 August. Kerenskii had chosen Moscow for this conference precisely with a view to avoiding the capital's social polarisation and embattled atmosphere. But not only did Moscow's workers bring the city to a standstill, they did so in defiance of the Moscow Soviet, which had voted 354 to 304 against a strike.[73] (It was, however, supported by the Central Council of Trade Unions, with only the Printers' and the White-collar Employees' unions dissenting.)[74]

The rapid radicalisation of Moscow's workers (as well as those in most provincial towns) after the July Days is explained by the increasingly tangible nature of the threat of counterrevolution and of the looming economic crisis, the two being closely connected in the workers' view. Even the least politicised

---

68 Similar shifts occurred in other districts that had condemned the Bolsheviks immediately after the July Days. *Vtoraya*, pp. 62–3.

69 37 percent of all industrial workers in Moscow were employed in the textile industry and 26 percent in metalworking. Moscow's workers also had stronger ties to the land. According to the 1918 industrial census, 39.8 percent of those employed in August 1918 had owned land before the October Revolution; in Petrograd the figure was only 16.5 percent. Moscow's workers were also employed in much smaller factories: average concentration was only 159 workers as opposed to 389 in Petrograd. Grunt 1961, pp. 200–2; *Materialy po statistike truda severnoi oblasti*, vyp. 1 (1918), p. 10.

70 Trotsky 1965, vol. II, p. 257.

71 Dok. July, p. 110. See also Dok. Sept., pp. 28, 95.

72 Sukhanov, *Zapiski o revolyustii*, vol. V, p. 154.

73 Ibid.

74 *Izvestiya* (Aug. 13, 1917).

workers had come to see that the Bolsheviks' arguments against the coalition government and in favour of soviet power made sense. Addressing the All-Russian Conference of Factory Committees in October, B.D. Kamkov, a prominent left SR, explained the late radicalisation of the peasantry, soldiers and also 'that significant part of the proletariat' with strong ties to the peasantry, in the following terms:

> Only the sad experience of the past seven months of the revolution could create the conditions for the final elimination, for the liquidation of the politics of conciliationism and for the transfer of power to the hands of revolutionary democracy. Right away, during the first governmental crisis [the April Days], the broad masses were not able to understand the slogan 'All power to the soviets' that the left wing of revolutionary democracy put out to them. These masses turned out to be too backward; they had not developed sufficiently to be able to accept that slogan without [direct] experience. Artificially – if one can express it that way – through the technical means of the actions of a minority, it is not possible to convince the masses of that slogan. But now the sad experience of all the coalitions has graphically, concretely proven the bankruptcy of the principle of coalition and now almost all soviets, both of workers' and of peasants' deputies, have spoken in favour of the organisation of a homogenous [socialist] government. The unsoundness of the principle of coalitions was proven concretely ...
>
> The issue of peace evolved in the same way. Posed abstractly at the start of the revolution, the issue of peace could not be mastered sufficiently by the peasantry, by the army and by a significant part of the proletariat. Now all understand concretely that the government has not only done nothing to bring nearer a democratic peace but that it has even created all sorts of obstacles to it.[75]

Kamkov's analysis sheds light on the role played by political parties, and, more generally, by political leadership, in the radicalisation of workers. The less-skilled workers had difficulty in orienting themselves in political questions that were distant from their concrete personal experience.[76] By themselves, the Bolsheviks' arguments could not convince them of the error of 'conciliationism', especially since its rejection meant that civil war in some form

75 FZK, vol. II, p. 161.

76 See Chapter 1 above.

lay ahead, something no one wanted. These workers needed more concrete, personal experience. But it was just at that point that the role of the party became so important. Without its leadership, the mass radicalisation would have expressed itself in 'spontaneous', uncoordinated protests that would easily have been suppressed. Despite a widely-held view, acute material need and economic insecurity – the situation of the unskilled workers – do not favour political radicalism. Workers in that situation cannot afford to take risks. They must wait for the bolder elements of their class to take the initiative and open the perspective of a victorious outcome to the struggle. In 1917, that role was played by the skilled metalworkers, and, in the first place, the members of the Bolshevik party. These workers were materially better off than the rest. They had greater confidence in their own abilities and had a stronger sense of dignity. They could imagine their class providing the society with leadership. That, after all, was the practical meaning of soviet power.

Thus, toward the end of the summer, as in February 1917, Petrograd's working class was again politically united. What united it was a common analysis of the counterrevolutionary intentions of the propertied classes. And the social polarisation was tangible. 'And when you encounter the street [i.e. the masses], what do you observe there?' asked A.I. Shingarev, a Kadet party leader, at a meeting of his party's Central Committee on 20 August.

> Yesterday in Novaya derevnya [adjacent to the Vyborg District], they simply would not let Milyukov speak … [I myself] was able only with difficulty to finish a meeting at Goryachee pole in the building of the Labour Exchange, at which only Kadets and Bolsheviks [!] and a few curious onlookers were present. While searching for common concepts, common terms, … [I] mentioned the fatherland. And a worker with a savage expression on his face shouted spitefully: 'A worker has no fatherland – he has a fist!' When I reminded them that that kind of mutual bitterness in France led to people chopping of each other's heads, a sailor shouted: 'And your heads should be chopped off!' At the Chinzelli circus, a soldier declared that 'we need equality of purses! And the bourgeois should have their necks twisted!' Benighted, embittered people, having thrown aside their recent leader, Tsereteli, are taking to rebellion. It is reaching the point of shooting, since words are helpless.

Although Shingarev quite accurately caught the popular mood, he was wrong to say that workers were taking to rebellion. The term he used was *buntarstvo*, which implies unorganised, direct action. But there was little sign of that among workers in Petrograd in August 1917. On the other hand, the mood among the propertied class was becoming very restless, to say the least. The protocols of the above meeting are replete with hints of an imminent 'surgical intervention' – the meeting took place a week before the Kornilov uprising. Shingarev himself stated that 'a dictator in the perspective is already in view'. This led him to ask if the Kadet party should not abandon the coalition government. He replied in the negative, reasoning that even if the dictator later turned power over to the Kadets, the origins of such a regime would be tantamount to political suicide for the party. But he admitted that the dilemma tormented him.[77]

Buzinov, a worker at the Nevskii Factory, gave the following example of the changed political atmosphere since the spring. When in April a worker who was known to have been a Black Hundred (member of a reactionary, anti-Semitic organisation) resurfaced in the district and began conducting his agitation openly, the other workers let him be, since 'in those days of universal intoxication with the young freedom, workers showed a striking tolerance toward alien convictions'. But in the summer of 1917, 'when the political atmosphere had already become incandescent, an SR worker at the Nevskii Factory gunned him down in broad daylight'.[78]

There was more to this hostility toward the propertied classes than the workers' perception of the opposing economic and political interests. Their class honour was also in question. The resolution adopted by the Rozhdestvenskii District Soviet and cited earlier referred to the 'pretentions … of this insignificant group of counterrevolutionaries … who allow themselves intolerable insults … [and] who are becoming more insolent with each day.' The words 'insolence', 'contempt', 'mockery' and the like were constantly repeated at workers' meetings and in their resolutions in reference to the politics of the propertied classes. Under the threat of mass job cuts at the beginning of August, a meeting of the workers of the Pulemet (machine-gun) Factory protested against

> the hidden lockout by the factory and mill owners, who cite the government and enjoy its support while they fire workers and close factories, each day throwing thousands of our worker comrades into the street. By these hidden lockouts, the capitalists put the army at the front and the peasants without agricultural implements in an impossible position, even while they shout about the salvation of the fatherland. Is this not mockery of the working people?[79]

77 Dok. Aug., p. 373.
78 Buzinov 1930, p. 92.
79 Dok Aug. 198.

'The current situation finds the revolution in extreme danger', declared a resolution adopted overwhelmingly by the workers of the Anchar Factory on 25 July.

> And all the compromising of the Mensheviks and SRs with the bourgeoisie will not succeed in leading the country out of its dead-end but will only increase the disorganisation ... We workers declare that the fear of the Soviet majority to take power into its hands proves the bankruptcy of its policies and allows the right-wing counterrevolution to grow in strength. Conciliation with the bourgeoisie allows it to mock the working class ... We ... see salvation in the transfer of power to the hands of the soldiers, peasants, and workers in the form of the soviets, whose basis will be the people. For only the entire people, united around a revolutionary government, will be able to save the country and the revolution ...[80]

In his memoir, I. Skorinko, then a sixteen-year-old worker at the Putilov Factory, offered the following account of the 'charged atmosphere' in Petrograd in the late summer. In the long summer evenings, he and his comrades had the habit of meeting after work at the Bolsheviks' district headquarters to discuss politics, collectively imagine a future socialist society, sing, and tell jokes. One of those evenings, a young worker arrived from the city's centre after having been beaten up for defending Lenin against accusations of spying for the Germans. Hearing this, the young workers hopped on a tram and headed for Nevskii Prospekt. There they came upon a truck full of high-school students. The truck carried the banner: 'war to a victorious conclusion'. The young workers began to whistle in derision and were attacked by a crowd. Skorinko was beaten up and left on the ground, where he remained until helped to his feet by two passing prostitutes. But on his way home, he was drawn into another argument and was again beaten, after which the police arrested him for speaking out against Kerenskii. When he was released in the morning and returned home, he had to explain what happened to his father, a 48-year-old worker at the same plant and a veteran of the Revolution of 1905–6.

> While telling my story, I closely followed the frame of mind of my father, as a revolutionary worker. (On previous occasions when I landed in trouble,

80 *Rabochii i soldat* (Aug. 5, 1917).

as a father, he would add a little trouble of his own – a beating.) This time he grew furious and broke into uncontrolled abuse directed at the bourgeoisie, at Kerenskii, and the police. Then he became bellicose and swore that the Putilov Factory on its own would scatter the entire bourgeoisie and grind Nevskii into dust for insulting comrade Lenin. When I told him about the two prostitutes, tears welled in his eyes, even though he tended to view them from the 'social' point of view.

But when I mentioned that I had been punched in the face at the Spasskii police station, he leaped up, knocking over his chair and shouting, to my mother's horror: 'And you just took it, you good-for-nothing? You should have given him one in the mug with an inkwell, a revolver, a chair. A worker should not tolerate a blow from a bourgeois. He hit you? Then give it back. Ekh, you worthless lout!'

'Look at the old fool', my mother jumped in. 'He's gone off his mind and now he wants to drive his son mad, too. Bolsheviks? You'll soon see your son without a head, thanks to his father. The officers will rip it off'.

I strongly doubted that I would show up in that form, as it was 'technically' impossible. But my father, ignoring her, stamped his foot and let loose a barrage of abuse addressed at my head, saying that I was good even without it. 'To hell with it!' (Actually, it was said rather differently.) 'For Lenin, for the Bolsheviks, let them tear it off. But we'll tear off a hundred for that one'.

After that, he dashed about the apartment, swearing and mumbling something to himself. And when our lodger, a baker at a large bakery, an SR, entered the room, he ran up to him and shouted at the top of his voice: 'Out of this apartment, the devil with you, damned SR! Go to Kerenskii [a right SR] for whom they beat up children! Get out!'

The lodger left that very day. And my father, jubilant, declared that from now on he was a Red Guard, despite his forty-eight years. As two Red Guards, we shook each other's hand and embraced. This created an unusual closeness between us.[81]

The Question of 'Revolutionary Democracy'

Despite the atmosphere of class hatred, it was one thing for workers to demand an end to 'conciliation' of the propertied classes, but quite another to envi-

81 Skorinko 1923, pp. 144–5.

sion an acceptable path forward after the experience of the July Days. The TsIK's repeated capitulation to the census politicians and its toleration, if not always outright approval, of repressive measures against workers and the political Left, cast doubt on the very concept of 'revolutionary democracy' and on the demand for soviet power. For the SRs and Mensheviks in control of the TsIK, the Central Executive Committee of Soviets, and of the Executive Committee of Peasants, still enjoyed the support of a large part of the peasantry, of the soldiers, and of most of the left-leaning intelligentsia. All these, together with the workers, constituted 'revolutionary democracy'. And although the moderate socialists were seen as abetting the forces of counterrevolution, few workers were prepared to write them off as themselves counterrevolutionary. The July Days, therefore, posed very difficult questions for workers: If 'revolutionary democracy', as the basis of a new government, was no longer possible, on what social forces could a revolutionary government rely? Would such forces be capable on their own of saving the revolution? And if so, how would that affect the social nature of the revolution?

The discussion at the conference of Petrograd's Bolsheviks in mid-July illustrated the complexity of these questions. It is worth recalling that two-thirds of the party's membership in the capital (including in the total the party's military organisation) were workers,[82] and so too were three-quarters of the members of the party's district committees.[83] The central debate at the conference revolved around the following question: should workers abandon the demand to transfer power to the soviets, since the TsIK, the Central Executive Committee of Soviets, was in the hands of the 'conciliators'? For to abandon that demand meant to break with the 'petty-bourgeois' elements of revolutionary democracy that supported the TsIK. In that case, a new revolutionary regime would not have 'revolutionary democracy' as its social basis, but only the workers and the poorest peasantry. In other words, it would be a dictatorship of the proletariat.

Two basic positions emerged. One argued in favour of retaining the demand 'all power to the soviets'; the other supported the position put forth by Lenin – a government of the workers and the poorest peasants. At the base of this disagreement was the political assessment of the peasantry: were the TsIK

82 Stepanov 1919–23, pp. 46–7. This may be an underestimate. The registration book of the Second City District, an area with relatively little industry, showed that 86.4 percent of the 913 new members who joined in the months March–June were workers. Golovanova 1974, p. 196, table 6.

83 Ibid., appendix 13, table 17. The figures are from the period between February and July 1917.

and petty bourgeoisie (the peasantry) appendages of the counterrevolution, or were they wavering between revolution and counterrevolution? If the former evaluation was true, then 'in the future we are alone'.[84]

The partisans of retaining the demand for soviet power recognised that the peasantry at that moment clearly supported the SRs. But they pointed out that workers were a small minority of Russia's population. Without a revolution in developed Western states, an isolated Russian working class would not be able to exercise and hold on to power. A proletarian dictatorship could not 'support itself on bayonets'. To write off the petty bourgeoisie into the camp of the counterrevolution would, therefore, be a mistake and mean the ruin of the revolution. The key issues of the revolution – land and peace – had not been resolved for the peasantry. Events would inevitably move them leftward. The petty bourgeoisie is benighted and vacillates, but its own interests will drive it to the side of the working class and against census society.[85]

The opponents of that position argued that the peasantry represented by the Executive Committee of the Peasant Congress were the better-off peasants. Together with the right SRs, they were thirsting for workers' blood and they would not follow the workers. The working class could ally itself only with those rural elements that shared its interests – the poorest peasantry. The July Days did not cause a mere wavering of the soviet. They produced a radical shift in the correlation of political forces, and the counterrevolution emerged victorious. This ruled out peaceful, parliamentary means of struggle for power. Among other things, the warrant for Lenin's arrest that prevented him from addressing the conference was proof of this. Indeed, after the July Days, even if the soviets wanted to take power, they could not, since they no longer wielded the power they once possessed.[86]

To these arguments, the supporters of the old strategy responded that the concept 'poorest peasantry' was not a Marxist concept and did not correspond to any real social category. Indeed, it sounded more like some lumpen element. Besides, it was wrong to claim that the counterrevolution was victorious as long as it was unable to shut the mouths of the workers and soldiers, something it clearly was not able to do. The peasants willingly supported the soviet majority, but their concrete experience would soon teach them better. An insurrection directed against the present leadership of the TsIK and against the peasantry was uncalled for. In the meanwhile, 'our presence in the soviet prevents it [the

84 *Vtoraya i tret'ya petrogradskie*, p. 80.

85 Ibid., p., 80.

86 Ibid., p. 74.

TsIK] from making a deal with the bourgeoisie. Our duty is to remain in it and conduct our former decisive line'.[87]

By a vote of 28 against 3, with a full 28 abstaining, the conference adopted the compromise position that had earlier been adopted by the party's central committee, in opposition to Lenin's position.[88] The resolution called both for a government based upon the 'proletariat and poorest peasantry' and for the transfer of power 'to revolutionary soviets of workers' and peasants' deputies'.[89] The concession to the advocates of abandoning the soviets was thus the insertion of 'revolutionary' before 'soviets'. Another concession was the resolution's call for a 'decisive battle', a euphemism for insurrection. The resulting resolution was, thus, very ambiguous, referring at once to workers and peasants and also to workers and poorest peasants, to soviet power and to an insurrection. It offered no clear answer to the critical question of the party's attitude towards the peasantry.

Retention of the demand for the transfer of power to the soviets meant that Lenin's position, in fact, received the short end of the compromise. Nevertheless, supporters of Lenin's position were a very sizeable minority. Their resolution was defeated by a vote of 22 to 15. Moreover, most of the 28 who abstained in the vote for the victorious resolution leaned toward Lenin's position. This group included the entire delegation from the Vyborg district, eleven people in all, who indeed pointed out that the victorious resolution was ambiguous and complained that Lenin's theses had not been read to the conference.[90]

The fundamental question was thus left open. The majority wanted to continue to try to win over the rest of revolutionary democracy, even while paying

---

87 Ibid., p. 71.

88 Lenin explained his position in three articles: 'Three Crises', 'Toward Slogans', and 'On Constitutional Illusions', *Polnoe sobranie sochinenii* (M., 1962), vol. XXXII, pp. 428–32; vol. XXXIV, pp. 10–17, 33–47. In these articles he argued that there was no choice but for the workers, supported by the poorest peasants (the village, according to Lenin, was undergoing a process of differentiation), to take power, even against the will of the soviet majority. The new government would adopt a revolutionary policy and thus win over, or at least isolate, the peasants from 'conciliationist' influence. Lenin rejected the view that the moderate socialist leaders could still adopt a revolutionary policy. Nor did he deny that the new slogan meant civil war under very difficult conditions. But he was not writing off the peasantry. He argued rather that the workers could not afford to wait, that it was futile to hope to win over the peasantry before seizing power and proving to the peasants through concrete revolutionary measures that it was in their interest to ally themselves with the workers.

89 *Vtorayai tret'ya*, p. 88.

90 Ibid., p. 80.

lip service to preparation of an insurrection. Although two weeks later, the party's Sixth All-Russian Congress adopted a resolution calling for a government of workers and poor peasants, without mentioning the soviets, many factory meetings and worker organisations continued to call for the transfer of power to the soviets or for the formation of a government of revolutionary democracy.

The issue was clearly unresolved for many workers, including many Bolsheviks. This emerged very clearly at the Second Petrograd Conference of Factory Committees on August 12–14. If the debate at the Bolsheviks' conference centred on the peasantry, the more immediate concern of the factory committees was another part of revolutionary democracy – the left-leaning, socialist intelligentsia.[91] The factory-committee activists felt particularly keenly the need for the economic, technical and administrative knowledge and skills of that group.

Before the July Days, when they called for the transfer of power to the soviets, the more politically conscious workers understood that they were writing off the support of the largest part of the intelligentsia, those who identified with the propertied classes. But in the wake of the July Days, they grasped the full extent of the workers' isolation from educated society, since the left-leaning intelligentsia almost unanimously supported the 'conciliators', and these had turned against the workers.

The conference delegates realised that the industrialists' successful opposition to reinforced state regulation and the advancing economic crisis were pushing them toward the assumption of responsibility for managing the factories, and that, in doing so, they would not be able to count on the support of the intelligentsia. G.D. Vainberg, a type-setter and member of the Central Soviet of Factory Committees, told the conference:

> Just as the bourgeoisie, with its association of zemstvos and municipalities[92] was fully armed for the moment when Tsarism fell, so we must approach the moment of capitalist collapse with a ready apparatus. We must exert all our strength in this work-struggle. Especially as class contradictions emerge with increasing clarity and the intelligentsia moves

91 Here we use the term 'intelligentsia in a sociological sense, the one used in everyday language at the time, to refer to people who earn their living in occupations that require a diploma of higher, or at least secondary, education, or the equivalent. This definition would also include students, since they looked forward to working in such occupations.

92 Local self-government institutions.

> away from us, we are forced to rely only on ourselves and to take all our organisations into our own workers' hands.[93]

The delegates were acutely aware of the immense difficulty of the task before them in their isolation. 'Throughout all the reports, the howl about the shortage of qualified people runs like a read thread', observed one speaker.[94] 'Tsarism did everything possible to leave us unprepared', lamented another, 'and, of course, everywhere, in both political and economic organizations, we don't have enough qualified people'.[95]

This was, in fact, a main argument put forth by the Mensheviks and SRs against any attempt by the workers to take power. These parties constantly emphasised the numerical and cultural weakness of the Russian working class, its poor organisation, its ignorance and isolation. 'We are alone', declared one of the few Menshevik delegates to the conference.

> We have few workers who are capable of exercising control. We have to organise courses to prepare rank-and-file workers for government affairs and for the exercise of control in production. If we took power into our hands, the masses would crucify us. The bourgeoisie is organised and has a mass of experienced people at its disposal. But we don't and we, therefore, won't be able to hold onto power.[96]

But these warnings had little effect, since those who made them were unable to refute the validity of the Bolsheviks' assessment of the economic situation, which called for urgent action. Meanwhile, the coalition government, supported by the 'conciliators', took no action to stem the deepening economic crisis. Therefore, it was not surprising that the vast majority of delegates were in agreement with the response offered by Maksimov, a delegate from Grebnoi Port:

> The bourgeoisie knows its interests better than the petty-bourgeois parties [i.e. the Mensheviks and SRs]. The bourgeoisie fully understands the situation and has expressed itself very clearly in the words of Ryabushinskii, who said that they had to wait until hunger grabs the working class by the throat and destroys all its gains. But while they are grabbing our

93 FZK, vol. I, p. 189.
94 Ibid., p. 188.
95 Ibid., p. 189.
96 Ibid., pp. 206–7.

> throats, we will still be fighting and if we perish, then it will be in an honest fight. But we will not back away from that fight.[97]

'The working class has always been isolated', argued N.I. Derbyshev, a Bolshevik type-setter and member of the Central Soviet of Factory Committees.

> It always has to conduct its politics alone. But in a revolution the working class is the vanguard. It must lead the other classes, including the peasantry. Everything depends upon the activity of workers in various organisations, commissions, and the like, where workers must be a majority.
>
> Against the approaching hunger and unemployment, we must pit the activity of the masses. We have to shed the Slavic spirit of laziness and together cut paths through the forest that will lead the working class to socialism.[98]

Again and again, delegates appealed for self-reliance. When it was suggested to limit the number of working sections at the conference, since the issues to be discussed were complex and the number of 'active forces' was limited, S.P. Voskov, a carpenter, chairman of the committee at Sestroretsk Arms Factory, retorted:

> The absence of *intelligenty* in no way impedes the work of the sections. It is already time for workers to shed the bad habit of constantly looking over their shoulder at the *intelligenty*. It is necessary for all participants at the conference to participate in some section and work there independently.[99]

V. Ya. Chubar', a mechanic at the Orudiinyi Factory and member of the Central Soviet of Factory Committees, similarly admonished the gathering: 'The hopeless condition of industry forces the workers to assume the full burden of the economic crisis. We must take part in the organs that regulate industry and distribution. But we have become so used to tutelage that it is extremely hard to free ourselves from that habit'.[100]

---

97 Ibid., p. 208.

98 Ibid., p. 206.

99 Ibid., p. 167.

100 Ibid., p. 191.

These workers were struggling to throw off the legacy of their subordinate position in society. People who their entire lives had been on the receiving end of commands did not find it easy to envision themselves in the role of a governing class, all the more so without the support of the educated elements of society.

Many observers in that period commented on the alienation of the intelligentsia from the working class. At a conference on extra-school education, A.V. Lunacharskii, a Bolshevik intellectual who was active in cultural affairs, provoked heated controversy when he stated that the workers' great thirst for knowledge was not being satisfied

> because at the present time one can observe that the proletariat is itself isolated from the intelligentsia ... Even the ranks of the worker-intelligentsia have grown significantly thinner, thanks to the fact that the proletariat in its overwhelming majority has passed under the banner of the extreme left of democracy, while the intelligentsia finds itself to the right.[101]

To those who objected to his statement Lunacharskii answered that 'it is not the proletariat that is to blame, but the intelligentsia, which has adopted a radically negative attitude to the political tasks put forth by the proletariat'.[102]

This rift was evident within the ranks of the socialist parties themselves. Both Russian populism (the SRs) and social democracy were split in 1917 between a 'defencist' right wing and an 'internationalist' left wing. The vast majority of the socialist intelligentsia adhered to the right wing, while the left consisted almost exclusively of workers, peasants and soldiers. The American historian O. Radkey pointed out in his study of the SRs that when the party formally split in the fall of 1917,

> it is clear ... that nearly all the sailors and a large majority of the workers and the army went with the L[eft] SRs, most of the intellectuals and white collar workers stayed where they were, and the peasantry divided into two camps, the larger loyal to the PSR, but the lesser one already sizeable and steadily growing ... From every quarter came complaints of a dearth of intellectuals which seriously impeded the activity of the new party.

101 Lunacharskii was referring to the older generation of worker-intelligenty who had been formed in close contact with the intelligentsia before and during the revolution of 1905.

102 *Novaya zhizn'* (Oct 18, 1917).

> Sukhanov termed it the party of the rural plebs and ranked it even lower on the cultural scale than the Bolsheviks, the party of the urban plebs.[103]

A similar process occurred within the ranks of Russian social democracy. Although the historical literature often depicts the Bolsheviks as a sect of ideologically driven intellectuals, in fact the party, with some notable exceptions to be sure, was shunned by the left-leaning intelligentsia. At the Bolsheviks' Petrograd Conference in July, a delegate complained of the 'universal flight of the intelligentsia'. L.V. Volodarskii, who headed the party's agitation department in the Petrograd and was a tailor by profession, added:

> The intelligentsia, in accord with its social composition, has crossed over to the defencists and does not want to take the revolution farther. They don't come to us and everywhere they adopt a position of resistance to the steps taken by the workers.[104]

He repeated this complaint a few weeks later at the Party's national congress in a report on the Petrograd organisation:

> Our work is being conducted by local forces from the ranks of the worker masses. There are very few intellectual forces. All the organisational work, and a significant part of the agitational work, is conducted by the workers themselves. The members of the Central Committee [in the majority *intelligenty*] took little part in our organisational work. Lenin and Zinoviev – very rarely, as they were busy with other work. Our organisation grew from below.[105]

In the provinces, where there were even fewer educated people and where the cultural level of workers themselves was lower, the absence of educated people was felt even more acutely. The Bolsheviks' Central Committee was bombarded with urgent requests to send 'literary forces', 'at least one *intelligent*'. But the Central Committee's secretary, Ya. M. Sverdlov, almost invariably answered that the situation was little better in Petrograd and that no one could be spared.[106]

---

103 Radkey 1963, p. 159.

104 *Vtoraya*, p. 28.

105 *Shestoi vserossiiskii s'ezd* RSDRP(*b*), p. 45.

106 See *Perepiska sekretariata TseKa* RSDRP(*b*) *s mestnymy organizatsiyamy, mart-okiyabr' 1917 g.* (M., 1957) *passim*.

Workers came increasingly to identify the Mensheviks, and to some degree the SRs too, with *intelligenty* and the Bolsheviks with workers. Walking through a working-class district during the July Days, the Menshevik Andreev came upon a worker making a speech in support of the Bolsheviks. Andreev told the speaker the Bolsheviks were in practice facilitating the counterrevolution. Upon hearing that, 'a worker standing next to me shouted angrily: "You're a nice one with your eye-glasses to talk of counterrevolution!"'[107] A Menshevik from Petrograd reported on his visit in June to a Moscow tea-packing factory, where all the members of the factory committee, except one, were Mensheviks. When he asked about this exception, the worker answered that although he belonged to no party, he voted for the Bolsheviks because 'their electoral list contained workers. The Mensheviks are all gentlemen – doctors, lawyers and the like'. He further stated that Bolsheviks stood for workers' control and soviet power.[108] Speaking in the autumn of 1917 to the soviet of the town of Orekhovo-Zuevo not far from Moscow, a certain Baryshnikov stated:

> Due to the fact that the ideology and politics of the working class call for the immediate radical transformation of the current system, the attitude of the so-called intelligentsia to the workers has become strained. And therefore, there already exist no ties between us, and in the eyes of the working class they have finally defined themselves as servants of bourgeois society.[109]

This rift, although it never had been so deep, traced its origins to well before. Memoirs of worker-activists about the period following the defeat of the Revolution of 1905–6 are full of complaints about the 'flight' and the 'betrayal' of the intelligentsia, which occurred against the background of the deepening class polarisation of Russian society. The radical intelligentsia was frightened by a workers' movement that directed its struggle not only against the autocracy but also against the bourgeoisie, who had allied itself with the autocracy.[110]

The February Revolution, which appeared to have the support of the entire society, had temporarily papered over this polarisation. A certain *rapprochement* took place between the workers and the left-leaning intelligentsia on the basis of a shared 'revolutionary defencism' and support, albeit guarded on the

---

107 *Rabochaya gazeta* (July 7, 1917).

108 Ibid. (30 June 1917).

109 *Revolyutsionnoe dvizhenie v Rossii nakanune Oktyabr'skogo vooruzhennogo vosstaniya* (henceforth cited as Dok. Nak.), (M., 1962), p. 152.

110 For more on this see Mandel 1982, pp. 67–87.

workers' part, for the liberal government. But this rapprochement turned out to be merely a brief interlude in the mutual alienation, and by late summer nothing remained of it.

The Bolsheviks could, therefore, with much justice depict themselves as the party of the proletariat. By the fall of 1917, they enjoyed the support of a large majority of workers. And workers were a majority of the Bolshevik party members, which they to a very large extent ran themselves. *Intelligenty* were prominent on the national level. But the party was a democratic organisation in 1917. If Lenin and Trotsky were able in October to sway the more moderate majority of the Central Committee to organise the insurrection, it was thanks to the pressure of the party's lower and middle ranks. Had it been otherwise, there would have been no October Revolution.

As the Bolshevik party conference made clear, a central issue after the July Days was the danger presented by the political isolation of workers from the peasants and the left-leaning intelligentsia. Yet defence of the revolution against the threatening counterrevolution called for action against the TsIK and Executive Committee of Peasants, which were supported by a majority of peasants and by the socialist intelligentsia. The delegates to the factory-committee conference in August at first seemed prepared to take up the challenge of their isolation. At the end of the discussion on workers' control, a resolution calling for the transfer of power to the 'proletariat and those strata of the peasantry adhering to it' was adopted overwhelmingly by a vote of 198 to 13 (with 18 abstentions).[111] A proposed amendment calling for the 'transfer of power to revolutionary democracy' received a mere 23 votes.[112]

But the debate flared up again when Yu. Larin, who had recently joined the Bolshevik party after leaving the Menshevik-Internationalists, gave a report on unemployment. He concluded by proposing a resolution that called for the transfer of power to 'revolutionary democracy'. Not surprisingly, an amendment was immediately proposed: to change 'revolutionary democracy' to 'the proletariat and poorest peasantry' or to 'proletariat supported by the poorest strata of the peasantry'. But Larin replied that the amendment was unacceptable, and in particular the second variant that gave preference to the workers. It would only play into the hands of the forces that were trying to bait the peasantry against the workers. But Evdokimov responded that this was not simply a question of the choice of words. Larin's formulation had a concrete political intention. But 'the proletariat is the revolutionary vanguard. Hegemony fully

111 FZK, vol. I, p. 218.

112 Ibid., p. 216.

belongs to it, and it will be able to draw behind itself various strata of the peasantry'. To this Larin countered that the amendment would mean the ruin of the revolution. Lunacharskii supported Larin's position, stressing that the peasants had to be part of the movement and should not be pushed aside or given the impression that their role was subordinate to that of the workers. And besides, there was no clear line demarcating the poor from the non-poor peasantry, and one could not predict which elements would adhere to the workers. It was better, therefore, to leave the question open.

At this point, N.A. Skrypnik intervened to remind the conference that it had already adopted a position and could not reverse itself only a few minutes later. And yet, that is exactly what the conference did when it adopted Larin's resolution. This moved Evdokimov to comment that the conference did not know what it was voting for and that it had 'whipped itself'.[113]

But Evdokimov was undoubtedly wrong in saying that the conference did not understand what it was doing. These were among the most politically sophisticated workers in the capital. Moreover, the adoption of opposing formulas repeated what had happened three weeks earlier at the Bolshevik party's Petrograd conference, which had adopted an internally contradictory resolution on the issue of power along very similar lines. Rather, the lack of coherence reflected the workers' reluctance to accept the political conclusions that flowed from their analysis of the post-July situation. Workers had much trouble confronting their political isolation and the prospect of civil war within the ranks of revolutionary democracy that it raised. The conference's first resolution made these things appear inevitable. But Larin's resolution left open the possibility of restored unity of revolutionary democracy and avoidance of civil war, at least on a large scale.

The mood of the conference was defiant, but the delegates could not suppress their doubts about the workers' capacity to go it alone. Judging by discussion at the conference of the need for legislation to entrench the rights of factory committees and also by the debate over whether or not to participate in government-sponsored economic organisations, it would appear that the delegates did not see an end to the coalition government as an immediate prospect.

To be sure, as noted earlier, many factory meetings adopted resolutions calling for a government of 'workers and the poorest part of the peasantry'. But given the wavering even among Bolsheviks, one cannot take those resolutions in themselves as evidence that these workers were prepared to seize power

113 FZK I, pp. 221–3.

against the opposition of the TsIK and those who supported it. Even in the Vyborg District, according to the commander of the local Red Guards, one observed at this time a certain 'political lull, and even a certain cooled attitude' toward training in the Red Guards.[114]

Nevertheless, there was even at this time a part of the workers prepared to act in accordance with the Bolsheviks' new slogan. Some factory resolutions leave little doubt that the workers who adopted them had written off the moderate socialists as enemies of the revolution and were prepared to act against them. At Voenno-podkovnyi factory, which had consistently adopted radical positions, being one of the first to call for soviet power in 1917, the workers' general assembly adopted the following resolution in the first half of August:

> Only the poorest classes of the population with the proletariat at their head can decisively suppress the greedy appetites of the predators of world imperialism and lead this long-suffering country onto the wide road, bring peace, bread and freedom, and liberate humanity from the bondage of capitalist slavery.
>
> We declare that, having thrown aside all the turncoats, who hide their betrayal of socialism behind defencist phrases, we will support only those who hold high and bear honestly the banner of revolutionary internationalism.[115]

A resolution adopted by the young workers of the Putilov Factory, no doubt friends of Skorinko, was formulated along similar lines:

> We, the young people, having learnt from the bitter experience of our fathers how dangerous it is to fraternize with the bourgeoisie, declare that hour will be a fearful one when we, the young people, come out into the streets for the salvation of the revolution to destroy with our young hands those parasites who live off the blood and sweat of the toilers ...
>
> [We express] our profound contempt for the SRs and the Mensheviks, who continue to cohabit with the bourgeoisie and allow themselves to be led on a leash by Kerenskii and Tsereteli.[116]

114 Malakhovskii 1925, pp. 13–14.

115 *Proletarii* (Aug 18, 1917). It is worth noting that, contrary to what is often claimed in the historical literature, the workers' demands were not 'peace, bread and land'. They were deeply concerned with political freedom throughout the revolution.

116 *Rabochii i soldat* (Aug, 2, 1917).

When on 18 August the Petrograd Soviet voted for repeal of the death penalty, Tsereteli exclaimed to the delegates: 'But your resolution means that you express non-confidence in the Provisional Government! And what if repeal of capital punishment does not follow? Will you continue to seek repeal of the death penalty or the overthrow of the government?' At these words, all hell broke loose in the hall. Sukhanov recalled:

> Shouts rang out: 'Yes! yes! We will again take to the streets!' Others shouted about Bublikov and the handshake [with Tsereteli at the Democratic conference]. Still others whistled and stamped their feet. Others madly applauded ... But Tsereteli just waved his hand: he did not believe they would take to the streets again to overthrow the coalition.[117]

If some workers were ready to act, despite the danger of isolation, theirs was not the dominant mood. Kerenskii's diplomatic notes in this period, which by comparison made Milyukov's note in April seem almost inoffensive, provoked no strike or demonstration among Petrograd's workers. True, all the socialist parties, Bolsheviks included, were constantly appealing for calm and restraint. But such appeals had not stopped the workers in the April or July Days.

This decline of political activism did not, however, signify a weakening of the workers' opposition to the coalition government and to the policies of the TsIK. In an article on the Rozhdestvenskii District in late August, the Left SR newspaper *Znamya truda* summarised a series of reports from the district's factories and military units: 'It appears that in all these places the mood among the workers and soldiers is one of perplexity and apathy, on the one hand, and dissatisfaction with the general direction of domestic and foreign policy, on the other'.[118] The perplexity was over how to move ahead on the question of state power. Most workers did not have an acceptable answer.

Moscow's workers, on the other hand, who had only recently abandoned 'conciliationism' and had not experienced the defeat of the July Days, defied the leaders of their Soviet and organised a general strike on 11 August to protest the opening of Kerenskii's State Conference. The workers in Petrograd, for their part, did nothing, since the only mass action that made sense after the July Days would have been an insurrection to overthrow the government. And most workers were not prepared for that. Nor did they have a clear idea of what would replace the overthrown Provisional Government.

---

117 Sukhanov 1919–23, vol. v, p. 180. On Bublikov, see p. 220 above.

118 *Znamya truda* (Aug, 27, 1917).

It was in this rather confused context that news of General Kornilov's march on Petrograd broke at the end of August. The workers reacted to it with a paradoxical mixture of alarm and relief.

CHAPTER 9

From the Kornilov Uprising to the Eve of October

The Kornilov Uprising

Speaking before the Moscow State Conference in mid-August, General Kornilov had warned lest it require the shock of the fall of Riga (about 500 km from Petrograd) for order to be restored in the rear.[1] A week later, on 21 August, news of a broad breach of the front near Riga reached the capital. Soon after, Riga fell, threatening Petrograd. At once, the 'bourgeois' press and the census politicians joined in a chorus of condemnation of the army ranks, blaming their demoralisation on the Bolsheviks, on the soviets and on revolutionary democracy in general. Yet V.B. Stankevich and B.C. Voitinskii, government commissars at the front and moderate socialists, each independently reported that the soldiers were retreating in an orderly manner and giving battle to the enemy. The decisive factor in the failure of the 18 June offensive was the overwhelming numerical superiority of the enemy's artillery. And both commissars singled out the very radical Lettish Riflemen (they would later become Red-Army shock troops during the civil war) for their discipline and valour.[2] By 25 August, the German offensive had been halted, and Petrograd was out of danger.

Following Kornilov's abortive coup, it was widely believed in left circles that Riga's fall had been planned or, at least, not prevented in order to discredit the soldiers and the soviets, as a prelude to the coup.

Meanwhile on 24 August, even as such Bolshevik-led organisations as the Central Soviet of Factory Committees, the Petrograd Trade-Union Council, and the Workers' Section of the Petrograd Soviet were feverishly organising the capital's defence, Kerenskii again shut down the Bolshevik press. Events moved swiftly from there. Cossack units were summoned to the capital, allegedly for its defence. Insistent provocative rumours of an impending Bolshevik 'action' on the half-year anniversary of the February Revolution were being circulated. On 26 August, the Commander of the Petrograd Military Region, who was under Kornilov's direct command, placed the capital on a military footing, positioning troops in the working-class districts. The next morning, the Kadet ministers resigned en masse from the government, State Controller F.F. Kokoshkin

---

1 Chamberlin, vol. I, p. 204.

2 Sukhanov 1919–23, vol. V, pp. 198–204.

declaring a coalition to be no longer feasible.[3] Stock prices soared on 28 August, when Kornilov's fortunes seemed to be riding high.[4]

On 30 August, when Kornilov's failure had already become evident, the front page of the Kadet party's central newspaper, *Rech'*, appeared completely blank. Two weeks later, the contents of the hastily deleted editorial were revealed to the Democratic Conference by the Bolshevik D.B. Ryazanov. The editorial declared that Kornilov's aims are identical to those that the party felt necessary for the country's salvation. Indeed, the party had advocated the same programme well ahead of the general. 'True, it is a conspiracy and illegal. But it is not counterrevolutionary'.[5] As for Kerenskii, head of the government, he later admitted to the Democratic Conference that he had known about the conspiracy long before it occurred and that he had even been offered the role of dictator. He did not explain why he apparently did not feel it necessary to take preventive measures. The Left SRs' *Znamya truda* summed up the thinking on the left: the conspiracy had not been directed against the Provisional government but against the revolutionary-democratic organisations. It was to be carried out 'legally' on the part of the Provisional Government, which had already begun to execute some of its measures. But a chance dispute within the government's ranks prevented its realisation.[6]

On the night of August 27–8, the news of Kornilov's march on Petrograd exploded like a bomb in the working-class districts. In the prevailing atmosphere of pent-up frustration and rage that had been unable to find any acceptable outlet in action, the response was the farthest thing from panic. The howl of factory whistles announcing the emergency at once dispelled the sluggish, depressed mood of the two preceding months. The capital had not witnessed a like display of frenzied activity and enthusiasm since the February Days. For Kornilov's uprising offered workers a way out of the political impasse, the opportunity to strike a decisive blow against the counterrevolution, and not in opposition to the rest of revolutionary democracy, but in unison with it. It was widely believed among workers, left party activists included, that since census society had literally taken up arms against the revolution, the moderate socialists would have no choice but to abandon 'conciliationism'. Here at long last was a way to move forward without the risk of isolation and civil war within the ranks of revolutionary democracy.

3 Ibid., pp. 207–15.
4 *Znamya truda* (Sept. 1, 1917).
5 *Novaya zhizn'* (Sept. 19, 1917).
6 Ibid. (Sept. 16, 1917).

Reports from the factories to the Central Soviet of Factory Committees on 29 August all told of high spirits and feverish activity among the workers: meetings, the searching for arms, the organisation of Red-Guard units, the building of fortifications. 'Everywhere the picture is the same', the Bolsheviks' *Rabochii* summed up these reports: 'everywhere energy, restraint, organisation'.[7] Reports received by the SR party committees of the Petrograd and Kolpino Districts read the same way: 'The mood is cheerful, unanimous, full of determination'.[8] A Soviet historian estimated that between 13,000 and 15,000 workers signed up for the Red Guards in those days.[9] The Soviet's paper *Izvestiya* put the figure at closer to 25,000.[10] In any case, the shortage of arms restricted the numbers. The TsIK was deluged with demands from the factories to distribute arms. One district reported that it had only 420 rifles for 4,000 workers who had signed up.[11]

Sukhanov's reaction to the news paralleled that of the workers:

> Both of us [he was at the time with Lunacharskii] gave a singular, deep sigh of relief. We felt excitement, uplifted, and a kind of joy of some sort of liberation ... Yes, this was the storm that would clear out the unbearably stifling atmosphere. It was, perhaps, the gates wide open to resolving the revolution's crisis. It was the starting point for a radical change in the conjuncture. And in any case, it was complete revenge for the July Days. The Soviet can be reborn! Democracy can spring forth, and the revolution can quickly find its way back to its legitimate, long-lost, path ...[12]

The TsIK's role in the workers' mobilisation was minimal. In fact, it advised the district soviets to calm the workers and to refrain from taking any independent measures without orders from the centre. It agreed to distribute a mere 300 rifles to each district. Yet, the Petergof district alone was asking for 2,000.[13] The real organising centres of the defence were the Military-Revolutionary Committee (it had been established by the Executive Committee of the Petrograd Soviet, including representatives of the Soviet, of the Petrograd Trade-Union Council, and of the three main parties – Bolsheviks, Mensheviks and SRs), the

---

7 *Rabochii* (Aug 31, 1917).

8 *Znamya truda* (Sept. 3, 1917).

9 Startsev 1965, p. 164.

10 *Izvestiya* (Sept, 5, 1917).

11 Dok. Aug., p. 510.

12 Sukhanov 1919–23, pp. 216–17.

13 Stepanov 1919–23, p. 175.

district soviets, and above all the factory committees and their Central Soviet. Trotsky remarked that the role of the Military-Revolutionary Committee was limited, since the workers were always two steps ahead of its orders.[14]

The Putilov Factory, whose workers had shown signs of political fatigue after the July Days, set the tone. *Izvestiya* reported that 'it was as if it were reliving the revolution'.[15] Working around the clock, the factory's cannon department in three days produced over a hundred artillery pieces, usual output for three weeks. In all, this factory dispatched some 8,000 workers, including eight Red Guard units, detachments for constructing fortifications and agitators to work among Kornilov's troops.[16] Even the hitherto sleepy Nevskii District came to life. Its district soviet of factory committees demanded 10,000 rifles and urged all the committees 'more firmly to take the initiative into their hands, to oppose the counterrevolutionary plans of the bourgeoisie with your might'.[17]

As the latter declaration makes clear, workers needed no convincing of the bourgeoisie's complicity in the counterrevolutionary uprising. 'In view of this counterrevolutionary bourgeois movement', declared the workers of the Trubochnyi Factory, 'and also the assaults of the former Tsarist *oprichniki* [political police of Ivan the Terrible] on the freedom and the democratic achievements of the proletariat of Russia … all power must pass to the Soviet of workers', soldiers' and peasants' deputies'.[18] An assembly of 8,000 workers at the Metallicheskii Factory unanimously 'expresses its lack of confidence in the socialist ministers and demands the creation of a unified, decisive, revolutionary government for the struggle against the counterrevolutionary clique organised around Kornilov and the General Staff and inspired by the traitors to the revolution, the Kadets, who call themselves the Party of Popular Freedom'.[19]

The resolutions adopted by workers reflected the emotive depth of their response to the coup but also their relief at the apparently restored unity of revolutionary democracy. In another unanimously-adopted resolution, the workers of Shop no. 6 of the Trubochnyi Factory demanded arms, a trial of the conspirators, and the release of the political prisoners arrested in the aftermath of the July Days.

---

14 Trotsky 1965, vol. II, p. 226.

15 Cited in *Rabochii put'* (Sept. 5,1917).

16 M. Mitel'man, B. Glebov and A. Ul'yanskii 1961, pp. 650–1.

17 Dok. Aug., pp. 485–6.

18 Ibid., p. 488.

19 Ibid., p. 487.

> On our part, we swear to die in the name of the liberation of the class of toilers. And let the whole bourgeois clique not think that we have forgotten our tasks, that we are preoccupied with our party disputes. No, when self-sacrifice is required, let that vile clique know that we are ready to die or gain victory.[20]

A meeting of 3,000 workers at the Old Baranovskii Machine-Building Factory addressed the following resolution to the TsIK:

> Recognising that the workers in the factories have always marched at the head of the revolutionary-democratic movement against the age-old oppression of the toilers and that the bourgeoisie has always tried to direct the point of the sword against the workers, and, not disdaining any methods, it has attacked and baited the working class in an attempt to cut off the head of the revolutionary movement in order to crush the workers, as the most united and organised proletariat ... [we have] resolved:
>
> In this grave moment, when ... the clouds of counterrevolution hang over us, ready at any moment to choke us with their poisonous fumes, we, the revolutionary proletariat, cannot passively stand aside as that pack of scoundrels and traitors moves against revolutionary Petrograd ... We demand that the TsIK arm the workers, who, not sparing their lives, will stand as one in defence of the just rights of revolutionary democracy and, together with our brethren soldiers, we will erect an impassable barrier to the counterrevolution and we will rip out the poisonous fangs of the snake that has dared to poison the Great Russian Revolution with its lethal venom.

The resolution went on to demand the liberation of the political prisoners of the reaction that followed the July Days and abolition of the death penalty, retaining it as a last exception only for Kornilov, 'who preached its reintroduction'. And it concluded:

> Believing in our bright future, we raise high the banner of freedom – long live the Great Russian Revolution: to the defence, comrade workers and soldiers, of the Freedom that is so dear to us, against the butchers

---

20 *Rabochii put'* (Sept. 5, 1917).

> who would lead it to slaughter, who are determined to drink our fraternal blood. To the defence, comrades! All as one![21]

This resolution, adopted by one of the most consistently radical groups of workers in Vyborg District, illustrates important aspects of the political thinking among the more skilled metalworkers. They, too, were worried about the workers' possible political isolation, but they nevertheless considered the workers the vanguard of the revolution. More importantly, despite the deep class polarisation, they continued to view their revolution in essentially bourgeois-democratic terms. In the resolution, they are defending their freedom – there is no mention of socialism. While the fact that the bourgeoisie had turned against the revolution and was sabotaging the economy called for new, radical measures – Soviet power and workers' control – their immediate motivation was to defend what had been won in February against the threat of counterrevolution.

As it turned out, the workers did not have to join battle with Kornilov (although their military efforts were not in vain: they would be put to use in the October Insurrection). Since Kornilov could offer nothing to his overwhelmingly peasant troops but their continued oppression, they melted away en route, when they came into contact with worker-agitators, who had come from Petrograd and had infiltrated the echelons. The railway workers also played a key role in sabotaging the lines and diverting the trains.

In some ways, the reaction to the Kornilov uprising paralleled the workers' response to their defeat in the July Days. Confronted with the threat of counterrevolution, in both cases they rallied even more strongly to the Bolsheviks and the demand for a government without representation of the propertied classes. On the other, the counterrevolutionary threat strengthened the desire for unity within revolutionary democracy, and first of all, within the working class. 'We recognise as the most important thing that all workers act in unison', read one resolution.[22] The left SRs' *Znamya truda* reported that the mood in the factories was 'everywhere cheerful and unanimous'. At the Langezipen factory, 'the situation has brought together all the party groups. The bickering has died down'. At the Lorents factory, 'a rapprochement has occurred between the SRs and Bolsheviks'. At Dyuflon, 'one observes unified action. One can sense the responsibility of the moment'.[23]

---

21 Mikhailov 1932, pp. 205–6.

22 Dok. Aug., p. 486.

23 *Znamya truda* (Aug. 31, 1917).

M. Zhdanov, a worker, wrote to the Left SR paper:

> The slogan of the day has become – unite! Only in complete unity is there strength, and only in an organised rebuff is there defence of the revolution. Until Kornilov, it seemed that this most needed slogan, the slogan of unity, was buried by the prideful leaders. It rose again to the surface only in the moment of grave danger to which the Russian Revolution has been subjected. It rose up and seized the masses, those benighted masses, as the 'political leaders' have grown accustomed to calling them.
>
> But unity had to be based upon the platform of the left. He concluded: 'There can be no question of a coalition. Only democracy. No bourgeoisie whatsoever'.[24]

The Kornilov affair raised hopes among workers that the moderate leadership of the TsIK would finally reject an alliance with the bourgeoisie. This seemed only logical to the many workers who considered that the moderate socialists were misguided, but they were not prepared to write them off as counterrevolutionaries. On 28 August, a Bolshevik carpenter in the port told the Soviet of Kronstadt (an island naval base not far from Petrograd):

> If the TsIK wants to represent democracy, then it has to understand that until now it has been mistaken in its analysis of the political situation and it must recognise that it now has to correct its errors. Kronstadt has always been on the right path, and, in view of the recent events, from this moment on our differences and disagreements will not be so deep.[25]

Sukhanov remarks that the 'abyss separating the proletariat and petty-bourgeois democracy was filled in by the *Kornilovshchina*'.[26] Even Lenin, who after the July Days had relegated the defencists into the camp of the counterrevolution, during a brief period following the Kornilov affair proposed a compromise to the TsIK: take power at the head of the soviets, and the Bolsheviks, while retaining their full political freedom, would act as a loyal opposition.[27]

But many workers needed convincing the moderates had indeed undergone a change of heart. A meeting of delegates of the factory committees of the

24 Ibid. (Sept. 7, 1917).

25 Dok. Aug., p. 491.

26 Sukhanov 1919–23, vol. V, p. 319.

27 Lenin, *Polnoe sobranie sochinenii*, vol. XXXIV, pp. 133–9.

Nevskii district declared: 'We express our full confidence in the Soviet of Workers' and Soldiers' Deputies [i.e. the TsIK], inasmuch as it expresses the political will of the workers and peasant masses'.[28] So here was the old formula of conditional support, but now applied to the moderate leaders of the TsIK. The workers of the Langezipen machine-building factory were even less sanguine, adopting unanimously the following resolution at the start of September:

> 1. Freedom is threatened, and we are prepared to defend ourselves to the last drop of blood, regardless of who is in power ...
>
> 5. We demand that the Soviet of Workers' and Soldiers' Deputies, as well as the Provisional Government, cease their criminal bargaining with the bourgeoisie. If, however, the Soviet cannot change the direction of its policies, then we demand that its members resign at once and yield their places to more worthy representatives.
>
> 6. We declare that the Kornilovite experiments carried out on our backs, thanks to the criminal accommodation [to the bourgeoisie], have cost us dearly and we suppose that the Kornilov rebellion has washed your sleepy eyes clear and allowed you to see the situation in its true light.
>
> 7. We declare that you have long spoken for us, but not to our way of thinking, and we demand that you start to speak the language of the proletariat. Otherwise, we reserve for ourselves complete freedom of action.[29]

In fact, the TsIK did appear to veer to the left in the wake of the Kornilov Affair. It finally demanded the release of workers and party activists arrested following the July Days. And it clashed sharply with Kerenskii over the composition of a new government (following the Kadets' resignation during the uprising). On 31 August, the Menshevik Party's Central Committee declared unacceptable the participation of Kadets in the government.[30] The SR Central Committee did the same the next day.[31] To exclude the Kadets was to exclude representation of census society, since the Kadets had become the hegemonic party of the propertied classes in 1917. The TsIK decided temporarily to fill the vacant ministerial portfolios itself, pending convocation of a 'preparliament' that would

28 Dok. Aug., p. 227.

29 *Rabochii put'* (Sept, 3, 1917).

30 *Rabochaya gazeta* (Sept. 1, 1917).

31 *Revolyutsiya 17-go goda: Khronika sobytii* (M.-L., 1926) vol. IV, p. 143.

be elected by revolutionary democracy. The government would be responsible to this preparliament until the Constituent Assembly met. Nevertheless, Kerenskii insisted on his right to form a new government and began to negotiate with the Kadets.

Another dispute arose over Kerenskii's appointment of B.V. Savinkov to the post of Governor of Petrograd. Savinkov had been Kerenskii's military commissar and had so completely compromised himself in the Kornilov affair that the SR Party had to expel him. Kerenskii soon replaced him with P.I. Pal'chinskii, a figure even more odious to workers, who, while acting Minister of Trade and Industry, had consistently sided with the industrialists. Upon assuming his new post, Pal'chinskii immediately shut down the Bolshevik and Menshevik-Internationalist press – this at a moment when the capital's workers were busy organising its defence against Kornilov.

Sukhanov also confirms that the attitude in TsIK was hostile toward a new coalition government.[32] But that did not last, and TsIK finally approved Kerenskii's new cabinet, his 'directorate of five', in return for a few concessions: dissolution of the State Duma, proclamation of a democratic republic (the Provisional government had refused this under the pretext that it was the prerogative of the Constituent Assembly) and the pledge that the 'directorate of five' would resign once the preparliament was convened. On 2 September, the TsIK adopted a resolution to the effect that the events at the front and the civil war provoked by the counterrevolution called for a strong government to carry out the programme of revolutionary democracy. And this government, to be created by a conference of revolutionary democracy, the preparliament, should be free of any compromise with counterrevolutionary elements.[33]

In sum, while the Menshevik and SR leaders of the TsIK seemed to shift to the left, their concessions to Kerenskii and the vagueness of their declarations left room for doubt. How were the counterrevolutionary elements going to be excluded from power? And why call a preparliament to represent revolutionary democracy, when the Second Congress of Soviets was supposed to meet in mid-September, according to the decision of the first congress?

These questions would soon find answers, and they would not please the capital's workers. In the meanwhile, a joint meeting of the workers' and soldiers' sections of the Petrograd Soviet on 31 August adopted a Bolshevik-sponsored resolution on the question of political power for the first time, demanding a government of 'the revolutionary proletariat and peasantry'. The mod-

32 Sukhanov 1919–23, vol. v, p. 337.

33 *Izvestiya* (3 Sept 1917).

erate socialists' resolution, calling for support of the Provisional Government, gathered a mere fifteen votes. The Menshevik and SR leaders then demanded a roll-call vote in order to force their parties' deputies to either support their resolution or openly to defy them. Faced with this choice, many delegates left the hall. Even so, the resolution was rejected by a vote of 279 against 135.[34]

Since many of the Soviets' delegates had been busy on that day with the defence of the capital against Kornilov, the real test came on 9 September, when the delegates were present in full force. The Soviet's Executive Committee, still in the hands of the moderate socialists (thanks to the overrepresentation of the generally more moderate soldiers in relation to their real numbers), challenged the vote taken on 31 August. They presented a motion of support for the Soviet's praesidium. During the debate, Trotsky asked the moderate leaders if they still considered Kerenskii a member of that praesidium. When the reply came in the affirmative, the fate of the motion was sealed: the vote was 519 to 414 (with 67 abstentions) to dismiss the current praesidium.[35]

On 5 September, it was the Moscow Soviet's turn to adopt a Bolshevik-sponsored resolution on the question of power. By the end of that month, practically all soviets in towns with any industry or with a garrison had rejected a coalition government and had voted for one or another version of the Bolsheviks' position.

In Petrograd, the SRs were the only party still seriously competing with the Bolsheviks for support among workers, though with rapidly declining success. And when the SRs met on 10 September at their city conference, nearly all the delegates adhered to the party's left, internationalist, wing, which by now had its own newspaper and was about to formally split from the SR Central Committee.[36]

What distinguished the Bolshevik position from that of the Left SRs and the Menshevik-Internationalists was not their rejection of a coalition government with representatives of the propertied classes, with all three opposed. The question was the nature of the government to replace the coalition. After the Kornilov uprising, the Bolsheviks again brought out the demand for the transfer of power to the Soviets. But the Left SRs and Menshevik-Internationalists considered the soviets to be too narrow a base for a viable government. On the other hand, they failed to make clear to workers what social groups they wanted to include that were not represented in the soviets. And so, even Left-

34 Trotsky 1965, vol. II, p. 265; Sukhanov 1919–23, vol. IV, p. 28.

35 Ibid.

36 Stepanov 1965, p. 193.

SR workers often supported the Bolsheviks' demand for Soviet power. The Left SRs' paper never tired of criticising the Bolshevik formula of a 'dictatorship of the proletariat and poor peasants', in particular arguing that 'poor peasants' was a meaningless economic and political category. But it admitted that 'workers adopt that demand, and that SRs vote for it'.[37] A Left SR leader reported that several workers and soldiers, members of his party, had asked him why the SR fraction in the Soviet had voted on 31 August against the Bolshevik resolution on power.[38]

As for the Menshevik and SR defencists, the Kornilov affair virtually eliminated all that had remained of their support among workers. In Petrograd's Moscow district, formerly an SR stronghold, new elections to the district soviet in early September gave fourteen Bolshevik delegates and six left SRs but no defencists.[39] The workers of the Obukhovskii factory in the Nevskii district, another long-time SR bastion, replaced all the SR delegates to the Soviet with eleven Bolsheviks and two syndicalists. The Bolsheviks' paper commented: 'Who could have imagined this a month ago? Thus falls the last bastion of defencism'.[40] Meetings in this district during the Kornilov rebellion witnessed some dramatic scenes. At one assembly, a former defencist worker mounted the rostrum and, with tears in his eyes, begged forgiveness from his comrades, promising personally to wring Kornilov's neck. Another appeared with a huge portrait of Kerenskii, which he proceeded to tear up.[41] A worker at the Patronnyi Factory sent the following report to the Bolshevik *Rabochii put'*:

> Our factory (8,000 workers) was the nucleus of the petty-bourgeois bloc (of Mensheviks and SRs) in the red Vyborg District. Only the brass shop invariably supported the Bolsheviks, but its support was submerged in the factory mass.
>
> As delegates to the Soviet, the factory sent Mensheviks and SRs and one or two Bolsheviks ... Just a month and a half ago, the Bolsheviks couldn't speak at meetings. Now the circumstances have changed dramatically. A trifling thing happened. On 4 September, at the general assembly of our factory, first an SR and then a Menshevik delegate to the Petrograd Soviet spoke openly of things about which they had until then been silent. They told the meeting what they had voted for and what against

37 *Znamya truda* (Sept. 6, 1917).

38 Ibid. (Sept. 2, 1917).

39 Stepanov 1965, p. 184.

40 *Rabochii put'* (Sept. 22, 1917).

41 *Batsiony revolyutsii*, vol. 1, p. 168.

> at the Petrograd Soviet. Thus, on the issue of land [very important to this contingent of workers], they voted against its immediate transfer into the hands of the people, and on the secret treaties – against violating them. And they advised the workers to await the Constituent Assembly to decide these matters. And that was enough. It has become clear to the workers that to wait on these matters for the Constituent Assembly and to postpone convocation of the Constituent Assembly means to leave the decision up to the landowners and capitalists; it means to leave the peasants without land and endlessly to drag out the war.[42]

An even more critical consequence of the Kornilov affair was the definitive shift to the left of the soldiers, both in the capital and the provinces and at the front, to the side of the workers. This helped to allay workers' fears of isolation.[43] Indeed, workers and soldiers in the provinces were in some ways moving past the capital, since in many towns the soviets refused to relinquish the power they had assumed during the emergency.

The downfall of the Menshevik-SR majorities in the soviets meant that the opposition to the coalition government could again find expression in the demand for transfer of power to the soviets. Although the workers' fear of isolation and of civil war did not vanish – there was no assurance that all the peasants or the left-leaning intelligentsia would support Soviet power – workers were relieved to be able to restore the demand to transfer power to the soviets. The latter had atrophied under the leadership of the defencists, but these popular organisations had deep roots in workers' consciousness.

The Democratic Conference

But after the defeat of the Kornilov uprising, the immediate issue was not a congress of soviets that would take power, but rather the TsIK's decision to convene a Democratic Conference to decide the question of power. On 3 September, the TsIK announced the mode of representation, conceived with a view to assuring a disproportionate presence of defencist supporters. Thus, the soviets were allotted 300 delegates, but most of these were, in fact, allotted to the

42 *Rabochii put'* (Sept. 8, 1917). See also the meeting at the Orudiinyi factory, also ibid. (Sept. 19, 1917).

43 At the same time, it is important to emphasise that the Kornilov affair merely accelerated a process that had began at least at the beginning of August. See *Perepiska sekretariata TseKa RSDRP(b)*, pp. 133–303, *passim*.

TsIK and to the Peasant Executive Committee, both elected back in June. The Soldiers' Committee, which had also been elected in the spring, were allotted 150 delegates; the trade unions – 100, with an additional 35 going to the railroad and post-telegraph unions, dominated by Mensheviks and SRs; dumas and zemstva (local governments elected by universal suffrage, and not, in fact, organs of revolutionary democracy) – 500; co-operators – 150 (about them, Lenin remarked that they represented the members of cooperatives to the same degree as postmen represented those who sent and received letters); organisations of national minorities – 100. Finally, doctors, journalists, and even the Orthodox clergy were allotted delegates. (The Kadet newspaper *Rech'* was indignant that midwives had been left out.) Aside from the fact that the resultant body could in no way claim to be a valid representation of 'revolutionary democracy', there was much overlapping representation, so that some of the delegates could cast as many as four votes.[44]

The defencists had organised the conference in this way because they remained convinced that the revolution was doomed without the support of the liberal elements of the propertied classes. The problem was that the Kornilov uprising had quite conclusively demonstrated that a liberal, in the sense of democratic, bourgeoisie did not really exist: the propertied classes were firmly in the camp of the counterrevolution. Following Kornilov's defeat, the Left SR Kamkov wrote:

> The 'liberal bourgeoisie' about which comrades Tsereteli, Dan, Liber and Gots have sighed so much, has turned out to be a figment of their imaginations. The urban bourgeoisie, as a class, could not only not be interested in 'deepening' or even in consolidating the gains of the revolution already achieved, but the entire course of events has thrown it into the camp of the enemies of the revolution. It has more and more clearly become a counterrevolutionary force.[45]

The defencists were therefore forced to sneak representatives of census society through the back door, so to speak – by giving representation to local governments elected by universal suffrage, to peasant co-operators, who were mostly well-off peasants, and to various conservative professional groups, such as doctors and lawyers, not to mention the clergy, that identified with the propertied classes.

44 Sukhanov 1919–23, vol. VI, pp. 84–5.

45 *Znamya truda* (Sept. 14, 1917).

A conference of Petrograd's factory committees in September discussed the question of its participation in the Democratic Conference. The attitude toward the defencists was extremely hostile. The conference had been convened to discuss the circulars issued by the Menshevik Minister of Labour, M.I. Skobelev, at the end of August, abrogating the main rights of the factory committees. 'Comrade Kolokol'nikov [the Ministry of Labour's representative at the conference, also a Menshevik] believes that only minor reforms are needed, a certain house-cleaning', stated Rovinksii, a delegate from the Langezipen factory. 'But you are cleaning up by putting down new garbage, and the workers themselves will have to clear out institutions like the Ministry of Labour'.[46]

Despite the angry mood, the proposal to boycott the Democratic Conference unless the factory committees were allotted 100 delegates was rejected overwhelmingly. D. Evdokimov, a Bolshevik typesetter, expressed the workers' ambivalence toward the defencists:

> Our enemies are strong, they are organised, they will bring forth new Kornilovs and will find support in the person of Kerenskii. But even that wouldn't be frightening if the conciliators could understand the current situation. If the Democratic Conference really reflected the mood of the broad masses, it could play a great role. But, unfortunately, the odds are strong that the Democratic Conference will be a revised edition of the Moscow Conference.[47]

Why, then, participate? Because there were still wavering masses who continued to support the 'conciliators' and could still be won over. To boycott the conference would mean to write-off the 'conciliators', to accept a permanent split in revolutionary democracy. It meant giving up the idea of a peaceful transition of power and setting the course for insurrection. Despite everything that had occurred since the July Days, the delegates still hesitated.

In this, the conference reflected the dominant mood in the factories. Despite their widespread scepticism, most workers were willing to give the Democratic Conference a chance, since it held out the prospect of a peaceful transition with a united revolutionary democracy taking power. At a meeting at the Admiralty Shipbuilding Factory, Belov, a delegate to the factory-committee conference stated that he considered the Democratic Conference 'bourgeois'. But Levit-

46 FZK, vol. II, p. 21.

47 Ibid., p. 40.

skii, who had also been a delegate to the conference, took a different position: 'All the same, the left wing at the conference will have enough presence to outweigh the representatives of the bourgeoisie'. The meeting decided to send a delegation to the conference to read out a declaration with the workers' demands. The meeting ended with the cry: 'Hurray for the continuation and flourishing of the revolution!'[48] The Bolshevik paper observed that 'the Democratic conference has evoked strong interest in broad worker and soldier masses of the capital', though it added that the mode of representation was a source of serious concern. Many factories, it continued, were sending delegates to the conference to express their views on the question of power, and in the overwhelming majority of cases, these views coincided with the position adopted by the Petrograd Soviet on 31 August.[49]

To fully evaluate workers' attitudes to the Democratic Conference, however, one has to consider the fact that the Bolsheviks were not putting forth any alternative. And after the traumatic experience of the July Days, the workers were not about to take the initiative on their own. The party's failure to show workers a clear way forward after the Kornilov affair, was, in fact, a source of much discontent among the party's rank and file, many of whom considered its policy hopelessly muddled. The 31 August resolution of the Petrograd Soviet, subsequently endorsed by many factory meetings, had called for a 'government of the revolutionary proletariat and peasantry'. That position, when it had been adopted in August by the Bolshevik party, was meant to signify a practical orientation toward insurrection. But after the Kornilov affair, the party's leadership returned again to the idea of a peaceful transition, one that would put power in the hands of the defencist-dominated TsIK.

At a meeting of the Bolsheviks' Petersburg Committee on 7 September, A.I. Slutskii, who gave the report for the city executive committee, observed that the correlation of forces had shifted to the left as a result of the Kornilov uprising and its defeat. The soviets had regained their former power, and events were leading to a major confrontation between the Provisional Government and the TsIK, a confrontation that would open the way for a peaceful transition of power. And though he added that one should not expect the Mensheviks and SRs to take the lead in this, he warned specifically against any 'action' (*vystuplenie*), as that would only play into the hands of the bourgeoisie, which wanted nothing more than for the petty bourgeoisie and the defencist parties to be frightened away from the proletariat.

48 TsGA SpB. f. 9391, op. 1, d. 11, l. 31.

49 *Proletarii* (Sept. 16, 1917).

Slutskii's report immediately drew fire from many of those present. They criticised it for offering nothing 'that could guide us in our internal organizational life'. 'I demand', declared one delegate, 'that the PK [Petersburg Committee] lay out all the information about what is being done and in what direction we should act.' 'Comrade Slutskii', complained another, 'gave us neither old nor new slogans. Our central paper does not sufficiently clarify our position. And for that reason our entire party finds itself in a state of uncertainty and our comrades in the localities are confused'.

Slutskii's supporters countered that the situation did not allow for a more defined position on the issue of power. One argued:

> I consider that explanation given by the Executive Committee to be correct, although one might see in it a lack of clarity. We are now offering a programme for whose realisation we will fight. But to say what bodies will form the government and to indicate a concrete path to it – that we cannot do.

The demand for a clearer position reflected a deep division in the committee on the evaluation of the political situation. Those who demanded a clear position wanted to maintain the party's post-July orientation toward armed insurrection. This meant writing off the moderate socialists and the TsIK which they still led. The partisans of this view considered the TsIk's shift to the left during the Kornilov affair to be ephemeral. As one of them argued:

> We have to change something in relation to the Soviets. Their composition has not yet changed. They were merely frightened and shifted a little to the left. But that doesn't exclude a shift back to the right, since they are petty-bourgeois in composition. That shift doesn't yet allow us to conclude that the Soviet will take a revolutionary path ... Our goal is not to march arm in arm with the leaders of these Soviets but to try to tear the more revolutionary elements away from them and to draw them behind us.
>
> Our Central Committee has lost its head ... The contemporary situation is one of the radical polarisation of the proletariat and the bourgeoisie. Both in the factories and among the poorer peasants, we observe a shift to the left. To think of compromises now is funny ... No compromises! ... We are frightened, we are rushing about. The counterrevolution has taken its first step, but we can't forget that it is preparing its second. Our revolution isn't the same as in the West [i.e. France's bourgeois-democratic revolution]. Our revolution is proletarian. Our task is to consolidate our position

> and unconditionally to prepare for a militant confrontation. I propose that the Central Committee more clearly, more definitively present the current situation in its press.

But the defenders of the party's vague position on power were not prepared to write off the Mensheviks and SRs and the social forces that supported them. The issue was, thus, not a new one: it was the fear of the workers' isolation and the desire to avoid a civil war within revolutionary democracy. 'Compromise is not at all a rejection of Marxism. But one must always take into account the situation. Isn't the Democratic Conference a compromise? But we are attending it with the defencists. But if they decide there that the proletariat should hold power, then that will be an all-Russian [national] decision. After that the Democratic Conference will perhaps fight tooth and nail'. Another added:

> The masses are themselves seeking a way. When the counterrevolution came to crush the Soviet, they felt that they were perishing. Now even Chernov [SR leader] is forced to oppose Kerenskii. The Soviets are now ambivalent. But on the other hand, they are clearly taking the path of civil war. The Soviets are hesitating when they see that the brain of the proletariat mistrusts them. And it is possible, therefore, that the circumstances will stack up in such a way that the forces that support the conciliators will have to make concessions in the interests of the proletariat.

The meeting took no vote. But the course of the debate indicated that the partisans of the vaguer position were in a majority. This position could best be described as one of 'wait and see', or as one put it: 'accumulation of forces'.[50] In the meanwhile, the party continued to appeal to the workers for restraint, vigilance and to avoid yielding to provocations.

The same uncertainty and dissatisfaction could be observed among the Left SRs, the party closest to the Bolsheviks. A meeting of the (by now left) SR organisation of the Moscow district of Petrograd on 14 September adopted the following resolution: 'We find that the articles in our paper do not at all satisfy the workers. And we ask that the articles take a clear and more definite position in their evaluation of the current moment'.[51]

---

50 *Peterburgskii komitet RSDRP(b) v 1917 g.*, pp. 429–37, *passim.*

51 *Znamya truda* (Sept. 16, 1917).

One of the consequences of the Bolsheviks' indeterminate position was dissipation of the energy and enthusiasm that had been generated by the Kornilov uprising. Workers sank back into what some observers described as apathy. The Left SRs' *Znamya truda* wrote in mid-September that when news of Kornilov's uprising reached the capital,

> the working class amazed many people with its energy, restraint and determination to repulse the usurper. The working class armed itself, sent out several thousands for trench work, and took upon itself the creation of a militia to which it entrusted the protection of the factories.
>
> But the immediate danger has passed ... and in the worker milieu a certain apathy has appeared. They refuse to do guard duty at night, refuse to attend military training, although they demand universal arming, and factory meetings are again attended by small numbers, and you have to lock the gates to keep them from leaving, and even that does not help, since they find ways to leave before the whistle blows.[52]

Although the article stated that it was referring in particular to the craft industries, whose workers were employed in small workshops, a similar, though less pronounced, phenomenon could be observed in many of the larger factories. 'We have about 4,000 armed people', read a report from 24 September to the Bolsheviks' Petersburg Committee. 'But those are the people who signed up. And we could find 40,000 who are asking for arms. That's how it was during the Kornilov days ... At present, one observes a cooling off – first of all, because the mood has already passed, but secondly – and this is the main reason – because there are no arms'.[53]

The apparent decline in interest for politics was also related to the increasingly alarming economic situation (see below, Chapter 10). Workers were growing tired of meetings that did not lead to action. Reporting for the Central Soviet of Factory Committees in mid-October, N.A. Skrypnik told the Bolshevik Central Committee that 'one observes everywhere a yearning for practical results; resolutions no longer satisfy'.[54] A resolution adopted by workers of Moscow's Dinamo Factory at the end of September made the same point more forcefully: 'We need decisive measures and their realization in practice. For playing with

52 Ibid.

53 *Peterburgskii komitet*, p. 463.

54 *Oktyabr'skoe vooruzhennoe vosstanie v Petrograde* (henceforth cited as Dok. Okt.), (M., 1957), p. 53.

words destroys everything that remains and only irritates the hungry, proletarian working class'.[55]

But if the alternative to the Democratic Conference was insurrection, the workers were not actively pressing for that. This, of course, is not surprising after the traumatic experience of the July Days and in view of the Bolsheviks' constant calls for restraint, their warnings not to yield to provocation. But as economic collapse loomed ever larger, the Bolsheviks' temporising carried the danger of workers' demoralisation, undoubtedly the gravest threat to the revolution.

As it turned out, even the deeply biased representation at the Democratic Conference strongly favouring the 'conciliators' produced a surprisingly close vote on the question of power. This was testimony that the social polarisation had spread to all of Russia. On 19 September, the conference voted 766 against 688 (with 38 abstentions) in favour of a new coalition government with representatives of the propertied classes. The delegates from the urban soviets voted overwhelmingly against a coalition. Those from organisations of national minorities vote equally strongly for a coalition. But only relatively small minorities of delegates from other groups supported a coalition. As it turned out, the votes of the co-operators (140 for a coalition, 23 against, one abstention; and following Kerenskii's example, they declared from the start that they would not recognise the conference's decision as binding) and the zemstvos (local rural governments – 80 for and 30 against, with one abstention) made the difference.[56] Were it not for these delegates, whose presence at the conference was highly questionable, the conference might well have decided to form a government without representation of the propertied classes.

But then came the surprise. An amendment to exclude the Kadets from any future coalition government was adopted by a vote of 595 against 493, with 72 abstentions. Yet it was obvious that, apart from the Kadet party, there were no significant political forces that represented census society, except for the generals, who wanted a military dictatorship. Adoption of this amendment thus rendered meaningless the prior resolution in favour of a new coalition government. As a consequence, the amended resolution was rejected by a vote of 183 against 813, with 80 abstentions.[57]

This vote graphically illustrated the moderate socialists' dilemma. They insisted that the survival of the revolution depended on the inclusion in power

55 Dok. Sept, p. 342.

56 *Izvestiya* (20 Sept 1917).

57 Sukhanov, *Zapiski o revolyutsii*, vol. VI, pp. 135–6.

of all the 'vital forces' of society, a concept which, for them, included the bourgeoisie. But society was so deeply polarised that a coalition of representatives of the toiling classes with those of the propertied classes was impossible. All the same, the defencist leaders of the TsIK remained undaunted. They proposed to enlarge the conference's presidium and to mandate it to come up with an acceptable solution. But to Tsereteli's consternation and chagrin, when that body met on 20 September, it voted 60 against 50 against the inclusion of representatives of census society in a new coalition government.

The machinations undertaken by the defencist leaders in the following days need not detain us further here. Suffice it to say that they gave the workers an abject lesson in the Mensheviks' and SRs' professed attachment to democratic principles, as the latter tossed aside the decisions of the Democratic Conference and of its enlarged presidium. It all ended with Kerenskii once again unilaterally forming a government which included not only his former 'Directorate of Five' but also a series of census politicians extremely odious to the workers: A.I. Konovalov, the industrialist who had resigned in April as Minister of Trade and Industry to protest against plans for a reinforced state regulation of the economy; the textile magnate S.A. Smirnov, who had recently locked out 3,000 workers, an act that several government commissions had found unjustified, prompting the Ministry of Internal Affairs to ask for the mills' sequestrations;[58] N.V. Kishkin, a prominent Kadet politician, who had been forced to resign as government Commissar in Moscow because of his less than ambiguous role in the Kornilov affair; and S.N. Tret'yakov, Chairman of the Moscow Stock Exchange.

This was obviously not a government designed to inspire workers' confidence. And yet, the TsIK agreed to support it in return for Kerenskii's support for the creation of a 'pre-parliament', which was to be made up of fifteen percent of the delegates to the Democratic Conference and 156 delegates from census society. Kerenskii accepted, but only on condition that the 'pre-parliament' be given only a consultative role.[59]

And so, by the time the Democratic Conference closed on 23 September, the worst fears of workers had been confirmed: nothing remained of the TsIK's shift to the left during the Kornilov affair, nothing of its 2 September declaration in favour of a strong government free of compromises with counterrevolutionary elements. After this demonstration of contempt for the will of the Democratic Conference (itself a profoundly biased expression of the will of revolutionary

58 Dok. Sept., pp. 279–80.

59 Sukhanov, *Zapiski o revolyutsii*, vol. VI, pp. 140–62.

democracy), it is little wonder workers later showed little sympathy for the defencists' explanation of why they walked out of the Second Congress of Soviets at the end of October, namely that the insurrection, organised by the Petrograd Soviet, had taken place a few hours before the Congress opened and was, therefore, an usurpation of its authority, this even though the congress overwhelmingly endorsed the insurrection.

Setting Course for Soviet Power

On the same day that the Democratic Conference closed, the TsIK, under strong pressure organised by the Bolsheviks, reluctantly agreed to convene a Second Congress of Soviets of Workers' and Soldiers' Deputies on 20 October (later postponed to 25 October). This was more than a month past the date that had been decided by the First Congress. From that moment onward, the future congress became the unique focus of the workers' political interest and hopes. Despite the Bolsheviks' decision to participate in the pre-parliament – against Lenin's strong objections – most workers paid no attention to it, regarding it as an illegitimate offspring of a discredited Democratic Conference. The Menshevik-Internationalists' newspaper *Iskra*, which had been urging workers to make use of the pre-parliament to form a united revolutionary-democratic government, had to recognise that 'the workers are deeply indignant at the outcome of the Democratic Conference', and that this indignation made them all the more firmly embrace the Bolshevik slogan 'All power to the soviets'. 'To the broad masses, it seems as obvious and as clear as day. The majority say: "The Democratic Conference disappointed. The Soviets are the true representatives. Let the Congress meet and take power"'.[60]

From the moment the date of the congress was announced, almost every factory meeting, after declaring its irreconcilable hostility to the new coalition government, called for the Soviet Congress (or simply 'the soviets') to form a new government. On 24 September, the general assembly of Voenno-podkovnyi factory, after hearing a report from one of its deputies to the Petrograd Soviet, resolved:

> The general assembly warmly applauds the Petrograd Soviet's final shift to a revolutionary line of conduct ...

60 *Iskra* (17 Oct 1917).

> We regard with scorn the pitiful conciliators, who, through diversions and manipulations, are trying to avert the approaching new wave of the revolution, to distort the firmly expressed will of the masses, to hide the failure of their entire policy of conciliations.
>
> We declare that you won't fool us with any democratic conferences, with any pre-parliaments. We believe only in our Soviets, for whose power we will fight to the death.
>
> Long live the immediate All-Russian Congress of Soviets of workers', soldiers' and peasants' deputies!
>
> All power to it!
>
> Long live revolutionary democracy!
>
> Long live the earliest peace among the peoples and the Third International!
>
> Long live the final decisive battle and our victory![61]

Similarly, the workers of the New Admiralty Shipyard, after hearing a report on the Democratic Conference, resolved that

> [the conference had been convened] by the leaders of the TsIK in a such a composition so as to completely distort the true will and face of Russia's revolutionary democracy.
>
> This distortion, this fraud, was needed by the leaders of the petty bourgeoisie for a new attempt to save the government of open and hidden Kornilovites, shielding it from the workers and peasants of Rus' with the screen of a pseudo-popular Democratic Soviet or pre-parliament.
>
> Recognising that this fraud failed and that the defencists fooled no one but themselves ... the workers once again decisively declare that a coalition government is completely unacceptable, that it can only bring the country new catastrophes and civil war, and we demand the establish-

61 Dok. Okt., pp. 98–9.

> ment of a truly revolutionary government, a government of the Soviet of Workers', Soldiers' and Peasants' Deputies that must consolidate and deepen the gains of the revolution through the immediate convocation of a Constituent Assembly, which must reverse the economic collapse, establish workers' control of production and distribution without consideration for the interests of a band of bandits, bring an end to the war by announcing democratic peace conditions and renouncing the Tsarist treaties, give land to the peasants and bread to urban democracy. To that government the workers will give their deepest confidence and full support ...
>
> Only such a government that has as its base the workers and poorest peasants can sincerely offer its hand to the oppressed of all countries with the certainty that they will respond with the cry: Long live Revolutionary Russia! Long live the social revolution![62]

When the Bolshevik leadership, under strong pressure from the party rank-and-file and middle-levels, as well as from Lenin, inundating it with angry letters from across the border in Finland, decided demonstratively to walk out of the opening session of the pre-parliament, workers reacted with relief. They saw this as a sign that the party was moving from words to concrete deeds. That act gave a sharp boost to the workers' flagging political interest.

On 9 October, the plenary session of the Petrograd Soviet met 'amidst great animation', according to the Menshevik-Internationalists' paper.[63] The object of discussion was a proposal to boycott the pre-parliament. Almost all the thousand delegates were in attendance – a striking contrast to the absenteeism that had plagued the Soviet in September. According to the same paper – which opposed a boycott – the excitement was reminiscent of the Soviet's sessions of the first days of the revolution. Trotsky's speech, in particular, was repeatedly interrupted by stormy applause from almost all the delegates. 'We walked out', he concluded, 'in order to say that only a government of soviets can raise the slogan of peace and hurl it over the heads of the international bourgeoisie to the proletariat of the whole world. Long live the direct and open struggle for revolutionary power in the country!'[64]

---

62 *Znamya truda* (Sept. 30, 1917).

63 *Novaya zhizn'* (Oct. 11, 1917).

64 Ibid.

After Trotsky, the Menshevik-defencist M.I. Liber spoke. He observed that even the Bolsheviks were not unanimous about leaving the pre-parliament, that, in fact, the leadership had taken the decision by only a narrow majority. When he began the next sentence with the words: 'Let Trotsky, Kamenev, Zinov'ev and Lenin take power', he was cut short by applause, and was unable to conclude with 'they won't be able to solve the problems'. And he accused the Bolsheviks of breaking the united front of revolutionary democracy – a charge that would be thrown back at the defencists when they walked out of the Congress of Soviets a few weeks later. But it was Yu. O. Martov, leader of the Menshevik-Internationalists, who, with real or feigned naiveté, hit the nail squarely on the head, when he said that he could not understand why the Bolsheviks had walked out of the pre-parliament. The only conceivable reason would be to form a government through the force of arms. But that, he declared, was unthinkable now. The Bolsheviks' policy was objectively aiding the counter-revolution. 'They must remember that the masses in their majority are disillusioned with the revolution'.

But that assessment did not at all correspond to the mood in the Soviet. Only 146 delegates voted against the Bolsheviks' resolution. The resolution presented by Liber, calling to support the pre-parliament, received only some 100 votes. Since the Bolsheviks' fraction was not nearly as large as the vote in support of their resolution (800 votes),[65] most of the Menshevik and SR deputies must have voted against their parties' proposed resolutions.

Factory meetings also strongly supported the boycott. On 8 October, a general assembly at the Old Parviainen factory warmly hailed the walk-out from the pre-parliament and called

> on all genuine representatives of the soldiers, peasants and workers to walk out in the same manner. We declare that we unanimously and completely will support, both materially and morally, the Soviet of workers', solders' and peasants' deputies and, at its first call, we are ready to rise up in defence of the gains of the revolution.[66]

The meeting decided to donate 3,000 rubles to the Bolshevik Party Central Committee in preparation for the Constituent Assembly and another 2,000 to the Petrograd Soviet.

---

65 Ibid. The meeting elected a delegation to the Congress of Soviets of the Northern Region on a proportional basis: 15 Bolsheviks, 10 SRs and 5 Mensheviks.

66 *Rabochii put'* (Oct. 11, 1917).

Around this time, the general assembly of the Factory of Armour-Piercing Shells (about 700 workers) resolved:

> We congratulate the Bolshevik fraction that has left that market place, 'Soviet of the Russian Republic' [pre-parliament], where, alongside enemies of the revolution, inspirers of Kornilov, fraternisation is being conducted behind the back of the people by representatives of the Menshevik and SR Parties. Those who have joined the Soviet of the Republic have abandoned the soviets of workers', soldiers', and peasants' deputies, and, we think, for good ...
>
> Only the Congress of workers', soldiers' and peasants' deputies called for 25 October, having taken power into its hands, can give the Constituent Assembly, land and a democratic peace to the exhausted peoples.[67]

Petrograd's workers impatiently awaited the Soviet congress and its decision to take power. This does not mean that they no longer had doubts about what lay ahead or that they were brimming with optimism. As we shall, this was far from the case. But the economic and political situations grew more alarming with each passing day. Too much time had been wasted. The rapid transfer of power to the soviets appeared as the only viable alternative to economic collapse and counterrevolution.

The walk-out from the pre-parliament set the stage for the final act. There were no more distractions or straws to cling to that might paralyse the will. The same session of the Petrograd Soviet that overwhelmingly acclaimed the Bolsheviks' decision to boycott the pre-parliament also decided, again by an overwhelming majority vote, to form a committee for the defence of the revolution. The proposal came from the Menshevik-Internationalists. The committee's mandate was to gather data with a view to defending the approaches to Petrograd from the advancing German troops (which had just captured the Moon-sund Archipelago in the mouth of the Gulf of Finland), to arm the workers, and to secure the capital against any new counterrevolutionary sorties. In those defensive terms did the Soviet formulate the mandate of that body that would two weeks later overthrow the Provisional Government.

67 Ibid. (21 Oct. 1917).

CHAPTER 10

Class Struggle in the Factories – September–October

The period from July to October was one of profound contrasts in the workers' movement. On the political front (with the notable exception of the workers' response to the Kornilov affair), one could observe a certain lassitude, a marking of time. On this level, workers left the initiative to the Bolshevik party. But in the factories, the workers' struggle for power with the administration only intensified, as rank-and-file workers pushed their committees toward bolder intrusions into managerial prerogatives. It was on that level that workers' main energies were concentrated in a desperate effort to avert mass unemployment and to keep intact the working-class vanguard of the revolution.

Factory Committees under Attack

The workers' defeat in the July Days had encouraged the industrialists to adopt a more aggressive policy in the factories. Nor did their political defeat in the Kornilov affair change that. In fact, they became more aggressive. Having played the military card and lost, they concentrated on their economic power as a last line of defence.

In early September, immediately following Kornilov's defeat, the industrialists launched a full-scale offensive against the factory committees. Buoyed by Skobelev's circulars denying the factory committees the right to meet during work hours and to be paid for that time, as well as their right of 'control' over hiring and firing, the Committee of United Industry decided to end, as of 15 September, the payment of wages to factory-committee members and to delegates to the Soviet. In doing so, they abrogated the agreement reached in March between the Petrograd Soviet and the Petrograd Society of Factory and Mill Owners. They even tried to have lifted the military deferments of the factory-committee members, arguing that they were not engaged in production. This threatened even the members of the Central Soviet of factory committees.[1]

1 FZK, vol. II, pp. 7–9.

At this time, the Committee of United Industry laid out its 'Conditions for the Restoration of Industry' in a note to the Minister of Labour. It demanded the following measures: the power to hire and fire must be the exclusive prerogative of management; management must have unilateral power to impose disciplinary measures up to and including dismissal; factory committees, soviets or any other organisations must be prohibited from any interference in management, while management should be freed of any responsibility to these organisations; finally, workers who failed to maintain the productivity levels of the previous year should be fired. And the note concluded with the ominous warning that without these measures, industry was threatened with a complete shutdown.[2]

From the workers' point of view, this assault on the rights of factory committees had only one aim – to remove the last obstacle preventing a massive shutdown, in essence, a lockout. This conviction was only reinforced by the plan to 'unload' Petrograd's industry that resurfaced at this time. As the socialist press pointed out, the industrialists' note was based upon the claim that the chief cause of the fall in productivity was workers' abuse of their new freedom. But they conveniently forgot all the blame the census politicians had heaped upon the tsarist government for the growing economic dislocation in the months before the February Revolution. Productivity had been declining since 1915. The chief causes were shortages of fuel and raw materials, the failure to replace worn-out machinery, the physical exhaustion of workers, and the influx of large numbers of new, inexperienced workers to the expanding military industry.[3]

The cure that the industrialists were proposing for what ailed the economy boiled down to one thing: put a leash on the workers. Meanwhile, they continued to oppose any new state regulation of the economy. In August, when the reorganised Factory Conference (*Zavodskoe soveshchanie*), a state body charged with oversight of the economy, finally began to function, the Central Soviet of Factory Committees was able to request that it act to prevent unjustified plant closures, and the conference could and did, as a last resort, sequester factories. But the industrialists disregarded the law and boycotted the conference, appealing against it to the notorious Pal'chinskii, now in charge of the Special Conference on Defence.[4]

As workers saw it, the employers' recommendations, rather than a formula for restoring industry's health, amounted to a *carte blanche* for its shutdown. And they were determined to prevent that.

---

2 *Rech'* (Sept. 13, 1917).

3 See, for example, the report of the Director of the Baltic Shipbuilding Factory in Stepanov 1965, p. 126.

4 FZK, vol. I, p. 186; Rab. Kon., pp. 216–17.

The Struggle for Production – Workers' Control Checked

The mood in the factories was increasingly desperate. The gnawing sense of impending disaster became all-pervasive, as workers engaged owners and management in a dogged holding action to save the factories.

The prospects of success did not appear particularly bright. Experts told the Second Petrograd conference of factory committees in mid-August that Petrograd's industry could at best expect in the coming year only two-thirds of the quantity of fuel that the city had received in the current year, itself a period of acute shortage. As for the Ministry of Railroads, it was as disorganised now as before the revolution. Without immediate emergency measures, one could expect the railway system to collapse by the end of September.[5] All the speakers warned the meeting against optimism: 'In figuring out how to get out of the disaster that is threatening, we can speak only of making it less painful'.[6] 'We see hunger approaching', said a delegate from the Orudiinyi factory. 'Unemployment is growing, and all measures to regulate economic life meet with opposition. Attempts to carry out control also meet with resistance on the part of management ... The country is heading towards ruin, the people are exhausted, labour productivity is falling. We must take measures'. At the Fourth Conference two months later, on the very eve of the October Revolution, N. Skrypnik reported: 'We are no longer standing in the antechamber of economic collapse; we have entered the zone of collapse itself'.[7]

The atmosphere in the factories became so tense that violence threatened to erupt over any minor conflict. In a report to the Central Soviet of Factory Committees dated 12 October, the Putilov factory committee complained of management's 'provocative' attitude. It cited the following incident by way of illustration. In early September, the workers learned that lathes that had been stored at the factory were being readied for shipment and that the administration was taking inventory in the artillery shops as part of a plan for evacuation.

All this coincided with publication in the press of information and entire treatises on the evacuation of Petrograd's industrial enterprises. Extremely attentive to anything that concerns the condition of the industrial enterprises, the factory's workers immediately grew alarmed, seeing in the shipment of the aforementioned lathes and machines (which at that time were being loaded

5 FZK, vol. I, p. 269.

6 Ibid., p. 186.

7 Ibid., vol. II, p. 119.

onto barges) the start of the evacuation of the Putilov Factory, and they came to their organisation, the factory committee, for answers.

To clarify the question that was agitating the workers and threatening to upset the normal work process, the factory committee immediately asked the factory's administration who owned the items that were being loaded and what was their intended destination. The committee could not obtain an answer that it considered satisfactory.

Nor did the Main Artillery Authority give an answer to help to clarify things. The report continued:

> Considering futile any further quest for 'the truth' about the shipment, the committee, in order to calm the excited workers and avoid excesses during the loading, informed the factory administration and the factory-wide conference that the shipment would be held up by the factory committee unless documented facts about who owned the lathes and machines that were being loaded and where they were being shipped to was provided by the morning of 25 September.

Since no reply was forthcoming, the committee refused to release the barges. On 6 October, the administration sent the factory committee the copy of a letter from the Artillery Authority, warning that the delay threatened irreparable harm to the cause of national defence.

> Knowing only too well of what consists this 'national defence' and from what quarter it is being threatened with irreparable harm, the workers' committee, precisely to avoid real harm to national defence (the workers' agitation could have erupted in the form of a work stoppage), continued to insist on seeing real facts about the items being loaded onto the barges.

Finally, after more lengthy negotiations, documents were produced, showing that the machinery did not belong to the factory. The loading was allowed to proceed.

The report concluded:

> In this way, a matter that could have been put to rest in an hour dragged on for a whole month, only because the 'bosses' wanted to demonstrate their autocratic inclination and refused to deal with the workers' controlling organisation on this matter in the required way.[8]

8 Dok. Nak., pp. 275–6.

Workers were incensed at the policies of the industrialists, who enjoyed the government's support. On 8 July, in the presence of a government commissar, the administration of the Lebedev Aircraft Factory informed the factory committee that the plant would have to close unless output reached a specified level by 15 August. That target was reached and even surpassed. Then in September, the administration announced that it was evacuating the factory to Yaroslavl' on the Volga and that it could take only half of the current work force. The following day, in a resolution adopted by the workers' assembly, the factory committee outlined the various aspects of the economic crisis, placing ultimate blame on the war. But it went on:

> Meanwhile, of late messieurs the factory and mills owners, and together with them our boss, V.A. Lebedev, with the help of the Provisional Government, have taken to curing the country after their own fashion. A radical measure has been devised: to evacuate the factories and mills to the materials, and the workers to the food. For this the government is allocating vast sums from its devastated coffers.
>
> But we know that messieurs the industrialists are not capable by these methods of curing the country of all the ills that it is suffering from as a result of the war. These 'doctors' are capable only of stuffing their already bulging purses with millions in subsidies that are being allocated by the government for the evacuation of the factories and workers. We know that it is better to bring food to the population rather than the population to the food; it is easier to ship materials to the factory than the factories to the materials. We are certain that the time of miracles has passed, that the mountain should not go to Mohamed, but Mohamed himself to the mountain. We are certain that these methods are not intended to heal the country but only to aggravate the industrial crisis, since, under the guise of an evacuation, mass dismissals of workers are being organised and the army of unemployed is growing.
>
> The factory-owner Lebedev is frightening us, saying that there might soon be Zeppelin raids on the airport and that, in any case, we won't be in a position to continue work here in Petrograd.
>
> But we ask: who allowed the Germans to advance so near to Petrograd? Will Lebedev guarantee us that the Germans will not be allowed to advance to Yaroslavl', Penza and Taganrog, and that we won't be forced, like a cat and her kittens, to be carried away from there too? Can Lebedev assure us that there is, in general, a threat of 'German' attacks rather than attacks of the Lebedevs, Ryabushinskiis and the whole capitalist class on the working class? The facts of the last few days have clearly shown that

> the external German is not more dangerous than the internal 'Germans' in the person of Kornilov and his class.
>
> All the above leads us to the following conclusion that, as long as the Provisional Government connives with the internal enemies, opens the way into Russia to the external enemies, as long as the industrialists conduct a policy of sabotage, unemployment and imaginary shortages of materials and food, as long as this war continues, no measures will help this country get out of the critical situation in which it now finds itself, and the war and other aforementioned delights will continue as long as our government lets itself be led around on a leash by the Lebedevs and Ryabushinskiis, and the Lebedevs and Ryabushinskiis by the English and French governments.[9]

The resolution concluded with the demand to transfer power to the workers and poorest peasantry, to immediately propose democratic peace terms, publish the secret treaties and to establish full workers' control of the country's industry.

These workers also took issue with the position adopted by the Central Soviet of Factory Committees in regards to the proposed evacuation: the Central Soviet had decided to allow evacuations in individual cases, if they could be justified and were conducted under the supervision of the workers.[10] The Lebedev workers argued that this lent credibility to a plan that served only the interests of the owners and the counterrevolution. Of course, it did not help that Lebedev's workers who were to accompany the factory were being offered temporary lodgings in Yaroslavl's jail.[11] At the All-Russian Conference of factories of the Artillery Authority in the beginning of October, one of the speakers observed:

> One can read reports in the papers that jails are being adapted for workers of factories that are being evacuated. But, comrade workers, you have spent too much time in prisons under tsarism to again go to the jails. Or there is a report that two houses of ill-repute have been requisitioned as lodging for workers. This is a mockery of the workers that should be rejected with indignation.[12]

9 Ek. Pol., vol. I, pp. 414–15.
10 FZK, vol. II, p. 102.
11 *Rabochii put'* (13 Sept. 1917).
12 FZK, vol. II, p. 102.

Most factories, however, did agree with the Central Soviet and sent out delegations to inspect the proposed evacuation sites. But in very many cases they found conditions completely unsuitable for a quick resumption of production. And that, after all, was the official justification for the operation – to keep the war industry going. At the Third Conference of factories committees in September, Nikitin, a worker from the Parviainen Machine-building Factory, reported on the findings of the delegation sent from his factory that was slated to be evacuated to the south:

> Our delegation that returned from Yuzovka [in the Donbass] reported that fourteen totally unfinished structures had been readied for the factory. Only one is more or less ready, but even there the floor hasn't been laid. Small houses were also being built for the workers that you could puncture with an iron rod. Some have already collapsed. Wages are low. The workday is ten hours. The food situation is about the same as in Piter; clothing is more expensive than here. The construction is poorly organised; they bring in cement on horses. They asked to ship presses from here, but the foundations for them have not been readied. The administration shows complete negligence, as with the whole of production, when mountains of already manufactured shells lie around, but without copper rings, and one can't find copper anywhere.[13]

At the Treugol'nik Rubber Factory, management would not even give workers the assurance that the machines and materials destined for evacuation would, in fact, reach their destination. As a result, the workers stopped the evacuation.[14] The same occurred at most factories, since the workers did not believe the economic and defence reasons that were cited for the evacuation.

At this time, many of the factories resembled besieged fortresses, their worker-defenders rushing from breach to breach. The situation at the Vulkan Machine-building factory and foundry was by no means unique. John Reed in his celebrated *Ten Days that Shook the World* mentions a conversation he had on 15 October 1917 with one of the owners, S.G. Lianozov, an oil baron known as the 'Russian Rockefeller', and a Kadet party supporter:

> 'Revolution', he said, 'is a sickness. Sooner or later the foreign powers must intervene here – as one would intervene to cure a sick child and teach it

---

13 Ibid. p. 34. See also pp. 33–4; Stepanov 1965, p. 96; *Rabochii put'* (Sept. 12, 1917).

14 Rab. Kon., p. 175.

> how to walk. Of course it would be more or less improper, but the nations must realise the danger of Bolshevism in their own countries – such contagious ideas as 'proletarian dictatorship', and 'world social revolution' … There is a chance that this intervention may not be necessary. Transportation is demoralised, the factories are closing down, and the Germans are advancing. Starvation and defeat may bring the Russian people to their senses …'
>
> Mr. Lianozov was emphatic in his opinion that whatever happened, it would be impossible for merchants and manufacturers to permit the existence of the workers' shop committees, or to allow the workers any share in the management of industry.
>
> 'As for the Bolsheviks, they will be done away with by one of two methods. The Government can evacuate Petrograd, then a state of siege declared, and the military commander of the district can deal with these gentlemen without legal formalities … Or if, for example, the Constituent Assembly manifests any Utopian tendencies, it can be dispersed by force of arms …'[15]

Vulkan employed some 2,900 workers, overwhelmingly men. In June, the administration announced that it was forced to cut production and possibly close the factory because of the drastic fall in productivity. The factory committee reacted by constituting a commission to investigate the causes of the productivity problems. At the conclusion of its inquiry, the commission drafted a series of recommendations that were endorsed by a workers' assembly on 14 July. These included measures to reduce the proportion of defective goods and also measures aimed at strengthening work discipline, including strict enforcement of the eight-hour day, an end to lateness, and similar behaviour. Overtime would be allowed when production required for it. The workers' assembly established a commission, consisting of production workers and office employees, and mandated it to ensure that these measures were enforced.[16]

Productivity did rise significantly. But the administration resisted the proposed technical improvement, arguing that they fell outside the factory committee's sphere of competence. Meanwhile, it announced a planned cut of 640 jobs, with more to follow shortly, citing supply problems and financial difficulties resulting from the decline in productivity, the high wages, and the rising cost of raw materials. The factory committee countered by pointing out that the

15 Reed 1960, p. 8; see also V.I. Startsev 1968, pp. 40–2.
16 Stepanov 1965, p. 126.

main cause of the delays in production was the factory's practice of subcontracting the production of parts for shrapnel shells. The subcontractors were consistently late. If Vulkan installed the appropriate machinery, it could produce in eight hours the same output that now took ten hours. As for the claimed supply problems, the factory was fully supplied for up to a year of continuous production.[17]

On 9 August, following a lengthy debate about the announced job cuts, the factory committee adopted the following decision, which was presented to the director:

> Having exhausted all possible peaceful means available to the working class and having achieved no result on the matter of the layoff of our comrade workers and office employees, the factory committee of the Vulkan Factory, after all the conflicts, both with the ministries and with the capitalists, has come to the conclusion that all the job cuts are closely linked to the 'unloading' of Petrograd. Therefore, standing on guard for the Revolution, we find it necessary to demand from the ministry, through the united forces of all the factories in which production is being cut back, to immediately transfer all such factories where production is being cut back to management of the state. We further pose the following conditions as an ultimatum: if the ministry refuses this demand of the entire proletariat, we declare ourselves to be standing on guard of the revolution's interests and in no way will we allow dispersal of the revolutionary forces through the unloading of the revolutionary centres and layoffs, until the conference of factory committees has taken a decision.[18]

On 16 August, following the intervention of the Ministry of Labour and lengthy negotiations over the conditions of layoffs, 633 jobs were cut.[19]

But as soon as this crisis ended, a new one arose. After publication of Skobelev's circulars, management at Vulkan decided to halve the wages of members of the factory committee and of delegates to the Soviet and to other workers' organisations.[20] The workers evaluated this move as an attempt to undermine their resistance. And, indeed, a few days later, management announced that the plant would close because of financial difficulties. But the

---

17 *Novaya zhizn'* (4 Aug. 1917).

18 Dok. Aug., p. 208.

19 FZK, vol. II, p. 588; Stepanov 1965, p. 152.

20 Ibid., p. 153.

factory committee discovered that the difficulties were due to the administration's failure to press the Naval and Artillery Authorities to revise prices to bring them in line with inflation.[21]

A general assembly was convened on 6 September to discuss the situation. The speakers noted the director's offensive against the factory committee: besides his refusal to pay full wages, he had forbidden office employees from giving out any information. He was also resisting the introduction of necessary technical improvements and he ignored recommendations for the more rational deployment of technical personnel. It was clear to the workers that the owners had decided to shut the factory and were fishing for a justification. But what particularly enraged them was the lack of respect the administration showed for the workers' elected representatives: at meetings, the director permitted himself expressions such as 'keep your tongue between your teeth'.[22]

This set the assembly seething. A worker proposed that the director, in the interests of the factory, be given 48 hours to clear out. If he refused, the assembly would absolve the factory committee of responsibility for any actions that the workers might take against the administration. The secretary of the factory committee pleaded for cooler heads: such an ultimatum could have very serious consequences. He proposed that the workers first consult their competent organisations, notably the Central Soviet of factory committees. But the meeting all the same adopted the ultimatum, with the factory-committee members opposing or abstaining.[23] When the owners responded that the director was staying at his post, the factory committee resigned as a group, but not before it had contacted the Petrograd Soviet and other workers' organisations. In the meantime, the party organisations in the factory (Bolsheviks were by far the dominant group, but there were also Mensheviks and SRs), appealed jointly for restraint and sent their members to the most volatile shops to calm spirits down. And they succeeded.

After a meeting with the members of the factory committee (who had formally resigned), a commissar of the Ministry of Labour, accompanied by representatives of the Factory Conference [*Zavodskoe soveshchanie*], presented the workers with the following proposal: (1) immediate establishment of state control over the factory by a commission made up of representatives of government and management; (2) the establishment of a 'workers' bureau', consisting

21 Rab. kon., p. 174.

22 FZK, vol. II, p. 58.

23 *Rabochii put'* (Sept. 24, 1917).

of representatives of the workers and management on a parity basis; and (3) an inquiry into the director's activity by an inter-ministerial commission with the participation of representatives of the Metalworkers' Union. If the commission found the director was obstructing production, he would be dismissed. On their part, the workers insisted that the proposed control commission include representatives of the workers' organisations. As for the 'workers' bureau', they wanted it renamed 'control and conflict commission'. With these changes, the proposal was accepted.[24]

In an article published in the Bolshevik *Rabochii put'*, the factory committee's secretary explained that the workers had little confidence in this 'state control' that would be exercised by the current government, one that was not democratic, and in the absence of workers' control at the level of the national economy. All the same, this could be considered a 'victory for life'. The factory committee had by that time developed its own excellent technical-control apparatus and had established strong ties with the central workers' institutions.[25]

But the Vulkan workers' troubles were not over. Soon after, the administration announced it would no longer pay wages to the members of the factory committee. A report from the factory committee to the Central Soviet of factory committees summed the matter up:

> As you know, the factory committee has twice already defended the factory's existence in relation to matters of finances and raising productivity. But the administration's sabotage continues. It finds expression both in the extremely defective state of the basic shops and in the extreme difficulty with which the factory committee must see to the application of the sectorial wage agreement at the factory. But now the administration is adopting new measures of sabotage. It has decided to withhold completely the money to pay wages to the factory committee, in all eleven people, including the technical-control commission, the wage commission, the investigation commission, and the arbitration chamber. This measure is not only a general offensive against factory organisations (the administration cites Skobelev's circular) but it strikes at the very existence of the factory itself. For as it is, it is only with great difficulty that the factory committee exists at present, overburdened with work in the midst of extremely tense workers, who stand at defective lathes and who are

24 *Rabochii put'* (Oct. 8, 1917); *Znamya truda* (Sept., 30, 1917).

25 *Rabochii put'* (Oct, 8, 1917).

> poorly paid, and while the factory administration constantly threatens to shut the factory and dismiss the workers.[26]

This was not the last conflict at Vulkan. But thanks to the efforts of its factory committee, prodded by the workers, the factory survived well past the October Revolution, which, it goes without saying, these workers supported wholeheartedly.

Vulkan was characteristic of the situation in Petrograd's factories in several respects. First, in the course of the escalating struggle for power between the workers and management, the factory committee was being drawn from its original function of control, as 'passive' monitoring and oversight, and was being increasingly pushed toward direct assumption of managerial functions, among other things, in its efforts to raise productivity. Secondly, in contrast to their relative (at least internal) passivity on the political front, the rank-and-file workers continued to hold the initiative in the factory and were pressing their often reluctant factory committee to bolder measures. Finally, as before, the struggle for production led inexorably to the struggle for political power. Vulkan's workers called on the state to assume responsibility for all factories in which production was being cut. But at the same time, the secretary reminded the workers that effective control would be possible only under a 'truly democratic state' and with workers' control established on the national level.

The discussion that follows examines these three aspects of the factory-committee movement in this period.

From Workers' Control towards Workers' Management

Workers first began to intervene into areas that directly concerned the management of production already in the spring, when the factory committees began to look for fuel and raw materials and for new orders. But that limited activity, to which management generally did not object, was not enough to ensure that production could continue. The committee of the Parviainen Machine-construction Factory achieved notoriety for action it took in August that saved 1,630 jobs, slated to be cut because of a shortage of fuel. The factory committee, with the support of its Central Soviet, formed a commission to investigate the problem. It concluded that the factory was using fuel irrationally and that fuel consumption could be reduced by up to 30 percent with no reduction of

26 Dok. Sept., pp. 326–7.

output. After offering some resistance, the administration agreed to apply the commission's proposals. Meanwhile, the factory committee worked out rules for stokers, machine operators and other workers with a view to eliminating wasteful fuel consumption. Writing this up, *Rabochii put'* offered the following comment:

> Here the factory committee has already taken the path of technical improvement of production. It would be interesting to hear what former Minister of Labour and former social democrat Skobelev has to say: can a factory committee during work hours work out rules for fuelling machinery? ... The workers are creating a new life, and the ministers, past and present, on their knees before the capitalists, are only hindering this creative activity.[27]

In August, fuel ran out at the state-owned Sestroretsk Arms Factory, located sixteen kilometres from Petrograd. The alternative energy source, water power, was also running low. With the help of technicians, the factory committee took upon itself the excavation of a canal to the water-power source of a closed cardboard factory situated on a nearby estate, ignoring the protests of its owner. Thanks to this measure, the factory kept running. The left SR *Znamya truda* wrote up this story under the title: 'What Would Happen to the Factories Without the Factory Committees?'[28]

It needs to be emphasised that these encroachments on managerial prerogatives were not manifestations of a thirst for power for its own sake or the expression of anarchist leanings, as a number of historians have argued.[29] The activity of the factory committees was indeed evolving in a more radical direction. But the basic motivation had not changed: the workers wanted to keep their factories running, to save jobs and to defend the revolution. Workers' control in its initial conception of monitoring bore a resemblance to dual-power in the political sphere. Both arrangements were born of mistrust of the capitalists. But workers' control, as originally conceived, was based upon the assumption that the capitalists would cooperate or at least tolerate control. The workers wanted to leave the administration in charge of running the basic financial and productive dimensions of the enterprises, while reserving for themselves the

---

27 *Rabochii put'* (Sept. 8, 1917).

28 *Znamya truda* (Oct. 1, 1917). See also FZK, vol. II, p. 68.

29 For some Western interpretations of the factory committees as expressions of anarchist tendencies, see Keep 1976, especially ch. 5, 'Drift Toward Industrial Anarchy'; Avrich 1973b: Lewin 1975, pp. 7–8, 126; Carr 1966, vol. II, pp. 63–4.

right to monitor this activity and to intervene in cases of abuse. But that was the problem: workers' control came up against the same obstacle as dual power in the state: the party to be 'controlled' was not obliging. On the political level, the workers soon concluded that the bourgeoisie wanted, in fact, to reverse the revolution. And they were reaching the same conclusion in regards to the owners' interest in keeping their factories running.

'They tell us that we have to control', complained a delegate from Dinamo to the Second factory committee conference in August. 'But what will we be controlling, when only walls, bare walls remain?'[30] And Left SR V.M. Levin, a member of the Central Soviet of factory committees, warned:

> It is very possible that we stand before a general strike of capitalists and industrialists. We must be prepared to take the enterprises into our hands to render harmless that hunger that the bourgeoisie counts on so heavily as a counterrevolutionary force.[31]

It should be noted that Levin himself was far from anarchist leanings. After the October Revolution, he consistently opposed requests from workers for state takeover of their enterprises when that was not justified by sabotage or the flight of the administration.

Not surprisingly, it was during this period that the demand to remove the owners was first seriously raised. The workers of the Vulkan Factory demanded that the state take over all the enterprises in which productivity was declining. A report in *Rabochii put'* on sabotage at the Soikin Printing House also ended with the proposal that the state requisition and confiscate factories that were being sabotaged or closed. An investigation had revealed that the owner of this printing establishment was not making necessary repairs or replacing worn-out parts and that he was selling off the machines piece by piece to speculators.[32] The Kolpino and Obukhovskii district branches of the Metalworkers' Union both proposed that the unions take over enterprises, 'as the only radical means of struggle'.[33] The Textile Workers' Union also raised the question of confiscation or nationalisation of factories.[34]

But these were still relatively isolated proposals. The workers' movement as a whole had not yet come around to the demand for nationalisation. Attention

30 FZK, vol. I, p. 211.
31 Ibid., p. 250.
32 *Rabochii put'* (Sept. 20, 1917).
33 Dok. Aug., p. 219.
34 Perazich 1927, p. 80; A.E. Suknovalov and I.N. Fomenkov 1968, p. 105.

was still focused on control, though its meaning was expanding beyond 'passive' monitoring. At the same time, it was already clear that the workers would not hesitate before that measure if their jobs and the revolution required it.

Factory Committees under Pressure 'from Below'

In his report on the factory committees to the Bolshevik Central Committee on 16 October, Skrypnik stated: 'One observes everywhere an attraction for practical results; resolutions no longer satisfy. One senses that the leaders no longer fully express the mood of the masses; one observes a growth in the influence of anarcho-syndicalists, especially in the Narva and Moscow Districts'.[35] The conflicts at the Vulkan and Putilov factories were examples of rank-and-file pressure on the factory committees. So too was the rejection by the Lebedev workers of the Central Soviet's position on factory evacuations, considered too conciliatory. In a report from this period, the director of the Admiralty Shipyards wrote that 'one observes, under pressure from the workers, a deviation of the activity of the committees from their direct and fruitful activity directed at preliminary control of management, in other words – in the direction of management of the factory'.[36]

The factory committees, finding themselves under pressure 'from below' to intervene more forcefully into the managerial sphere, were not by any means always enthusiastic about such radicalisation of their activity. The anarchists, on the other hand, advocates of 'direct action' and takeover of the factories, were. Hence, their growing attraction for workers in some districts. The source of this mounting pressure on the factory committees was, of course, the workers' disappointment with the limited success of workers' control, as initially conceived. In retrospect, it is clear that the movement for workers' control, by helping to forestall mass unemployment, played an important role in the victory of the October Revolution, which would not have been possible with a demoralised and dispersed working class. However, despite the slogan's popularity and the energetic efforts of the committees themselves, effective control, in the sense of access to documents and systematic monitoring of managerial activity, largely eluded the workers before the October Revolution. The above-cited report from the Putilov Factory expresses well that frustration: a matter that could have been put to rest in an hour dragged on for a month,

35 Dok. Okt., p. 53.

36 Stepanov 1965, p. 134.

enervating the workers and wasting their energy, simply because 'the "bosses" wanted to demonstrate their autocratic power to the end'.

Nor did the factory-committee activists hide their disappointment. On 26 September, during a discussion of the upcoming layoff of 5,000 workers at the Putilov Factory because of a shortage of fuel, N.N. Glebov told his colleagues in the factory committee:

> The administration has given up and it is hardly likely to take the dismissals upon itself, and in all probability we will have to take on this dirty work ourselves: to blame in all this, of course, are the representatives of the higher ups [*verkhy*] who have refused to let us get close to control.[37]

Another member of the committee, M.A. Voitsekhovskii, urged the others: 'We must gain the right to control, and it's about time we put an end to our traipsing about the shops of the factory'.[38] E.N. Surkov, a delegate to the second conference of factory committees in August stated: 'At the first conference [end of May] we expected to greet the second one among brilliant successes. But the revolutionary wave has stopped. And those for whom it is profitable were able to exploit that, and as a result our activity has to a significant degree been paralyzed. We are being told that the factory committees have lost their authority'.[39] At the Fourth Conference on the eve of the October Revolution, I.P. Zhuk, a delegate from the Schlusselburg Powder Factory, was still trying to fight this disappointment:

> Many take a sceptical attitude toward the coming [All-Russian Factory-Committee] conference, but workers can't adopt that kind of attitude. The conference must give us, not vague resolutions, but concrete answers to all the cardinal questions that arise in connection with the unprecedented anarchy that has seized hold of all of industry. The conference must resolve the question of the factories that are closing and in which sabotage is discovered ... We must carry all this out not in words but in deeds.[40]

In private factories, effective control in the sense of 'passive' monitoring more often than not proved unattainable because of the strong resistance of the owners, who had government support. But in the state factories, the workers

---

37 *Putilovtsy v trekh revolyutsiyakh* (L., 1933), p. 388.

38 Ibid, p. 390.

39 FZK, vol. I, p. 188.

40 FZK II, p. 120.

had more success.[41] Given the approaching crisis, it is easy to understand why workers were pressing for more militant action, for a more active and direct role of the committees. But in the existing circumstances, most factory committees and their Central Soviet were reluctant to assume responsibility for management of the factories. A conference of representatives of Petrograd workers' organisations in October discussed the offers that were being made by some factory administrations for the workers to delegate representatives to participate in management. These offers were evaluated as an attempt on the part of management to shift the blame for the condition of the factories onto the committees. The conference decided to reject these proposals.[42] The Conference of Factories of the Naval Authority and the All-Russian Conference of Factories of the Artillery Authority adopted similar positions. The latter's decision read:

> Having discussed the question of control of the economic, technical and administrative aspects of production by the factory committees, and considering that responsibility for production lies exclusively with the administration of the factories, [the Conference] recognises the right of the factory committees through their control commissions to be present at all meetings of the administration and to demand exhaustive explanations to questions and to receive them.[43]

This was control still in its original sense.

Around the same time, the Putilov factory committee, supported by the workers, rejected a proposal made by Pal'chinskii to participate in a standing conference of representatives of workers and management 'to regulate the entire work of the factory'. It was decided that the factory committee could participate but only for the purpose of control, assuming no responsibility for management of the factory.[44]

There were several interconnected reasons for this position. In part, it expressed the committees' reluctance to assume responsibility for something they were not at all confident they could handle, and particularly in the difficult economic conditions of the period. The resolution on Pal'chinksii's proposal, dated 28 September, explained:

---

41 *Pervaya vserossiiskaya tarifnaya konferentisya soyuza rabochikh metallist每stov, Protokoly*, Petrograd, 1918, p. 4.

42 FZK, vol. II, p. 177.

43 Dok. Okt., pp. 127. See also, pp. 116–17.

44 Rab. Kon., p. 205; *Putilovtsy v trekh revolyutsiyakh*, pp. 386–91.

> Having discussed the matter of participation in institutions regulating the entire life of the Putilov Factory and considering that the present situation of the factory, which is the result of [specific] causes, has to be recognised as catastrophic and that reorganisation of the factory's administration and regulation of its production are an extremely complex matter and demand time, the joint conference of the factory committee, the Petergof district soviet of workers' and soldiers' deputies, in the presence of a representative of the centre of factory committees, resolve:
>
> 1. The workers cannot assume responsibility for the course of production in the factory in the near future.
>
> 2. Representatives of the workers should participate in the council that is being formed with the goal of actively participating in control and regulation of the entire production activity of the factory and to counteract any attempts to hold up the proper work in the factory, chiefly on the part of external forces.[45]

If their understanding of the complexities of the task made factory committees refuse responsibility for managing the factories, the rank-and-file workers sometimes reacted with less circumspection, as they were farther from the complexities. A situation similar to Vulkan's arose at the Petrov Mill in late September. The owners, citing the Skobelev circulars, refused to pay wages to the workers' delegates for time away from work. After trying to resolve the matter peacefully, the workers invited representatives of management to their general assembly on 30 September and demanded recognition of the factory committee, of their deputies to the Soviet and of the worker militia guarding the plant. The director, however, repeated his refusal and did so 'in a rude form'. According to the account of a worker, a crowd then threatened to ride the administration out in wheelbarrows. But the managers still did not budge. One announced his resignation, asking to be left in peace. At this, the meeting broke up. The prospect of losing the entire administration had evidently sobered the workers.[46]

And that threat was at times very real. In a few cases, the workers accepted the challenge. On 19 October, the general assembly of workers of the Aivaz machine-building factory decided to dismiss the engineer Abratanskii for his

---

45 Ibid.

46 *Znamya truda* (4 Oct. 1917).

oppressive behaviour towards workers. The engineer, however, did not accept the decision and, in the course of an argument, struck one of the workers. In reaction, a group of angry workers beat him and rode him out of the gates in a wheelbarrow. The other engineers then went on strike in protest (though the foremen and clerical employees remained solidary with the workers). The factory committee, while condemning the workers' action, judged the managers' strike as sabotage and decided to continue production under its own supervision, asking support from the Metalworkers' Union. It also raised the issue of the factory's transfer to the state. The next day, a general assembly was convened to discuss what had happened. The assembly condemned the violence committed by the workers but approved the decision to pursue production under the factory committee's leadership. It adopted a resolution that stressed the need, now that the factory committee was in charge, for the strictest labour discipline, conscientiousness and a 'decisive struggle against all phenomena that disorganise our midst and throw shame on the name of the conscious workers'.[47]

Concern for their lack of competence in the technical and economic problems facing the factories was not the only consideration in the factory committees' refusal to assume responsibility for management. Although there was widespread recognition that the owners' 'Italian strike' would sooner or later leave no alternative, the committees feared that under the coalition government and in the absence of workers' control on a national level, they would serve as shields for the administration and end up being compromised in the eyes of the workers. These concerns were clearly expressed in the course of the Putilov committee's discussion of Pal'chinskii's offer of a joint worker-management commission. In the first place, Pal'chinskii was offering the committee only five places and was refusing any participation to representatives of the broader workers' organisations, like the Central Soviet of Factory Committees. With this kind of 'sawed-off' control, there was every likelihood the administration would merely exploit the committee to deflect workers' anger from itself for its actions against the workers' interests. N.S. Grigor'ev, a committee member, summed up this argument:

> The entrepreneurs at present are seeking any means by which the workers might whip themselves. Without the function of real, factual control, we should not enter that organ. When it turned out that the Government [the factory had been sequestered in 1915] could not do without us and that it

47 Dok. Okt., pp. 132, 928.

> was having a hard time, it came to us for help. But we will help it only when it gives us a guarantee that we are real controllers, and otherwise we should not let ourselves be caught by the bait that they are tossing.[48]

Similar views were expressed at the All-Russian Conference of factory committees in mid-October in the discussion of a proposal that factory committees delegate one member to each department of the factory administration. The delegates would have a consultative voice, and their task would be to ensure that management followed a general plan to be drawn up by some future national economic organ in which workers' representatives would be a majority. V. Ya. Chubar', a member of Petrograd's Central Soviet of factory committees, argued that the proposal's formulation was unfortunate, 'since it assigns workers the role of some sort of adjutants to generals'. And he cited the recent decision of the Conference of Factories of the Artillery Authority that opposed workers' delegating representatives to the administration:

> The members of the factory committee could turn into pushers [*tolkachi*], whom the administration will use as extra help, while itself remaining outside of active work. Such phenomena have already been observed in the practice of state factories. Besides, if the workers enter the factory administration, be it only with a consultative voice, in a critical moment (and that can be any time at present), the worker masses will direct all their discontent at the factory committee, blaming it for not having taken measures to prevent the interruption of production. In that way, members of the factory committee entering management will sow discord in the workers' own midst.[49]

He recommended that control be exercised by a workers' control commission that was separate from management.

N.K. Antipov, another member of Petrograd's Central Soviet of factory committees, added that if one of late could indeed observe a tendency among management to offer a place to the factory committees, their real aim was to foist upon them responsibility for its own failures:

> Of late one observes in Petrograd that the entrepreneurs themselves are trying to draw the factory committees into management in order after-

---

48 *Putilovtsy v trekh revolyutsiyakh*, p. 389.

49 FZK, vol. II, pp. 174–5.

> wards to pin all the responsibility for all kinds of shortcoming on the workers' representatives. Such pitting of undeveloped masses against their factory committees can be successful, and in some cases one can already observe a certain straining of relations between worker masses and their elected organs. Recently in Petrograd there was a meeting of representatives of all the workers' organisations that discussed the question of workers entering the factory administration and it decided it negatively.[50]

The All-Russian Conference voted 83 against 4 for a resolution calling for control through workers' commissions separate from management.[51]

Besides these concerns, there was also a closely related 'ideological' motive in the refusal to take responsibility for management: since the factories were still under capitalist control, the committees would be participating in exploitation of the workers, even if their motive was to prevent the collapse of industry and mass unemployment. Speaking at the First Petrograd conference of factory committees in the spring, Lenin had, in fact, reproached the committees for acting as the 'errand boys' for the capitalists in seeking out supplies of fuel and orders for their factories.[52] At the time, a delegate from the Novyi Arsenal Factory replied that the workers had no choice but to engage in such activity in order not to find themselves out on the street. 'The factory committees had to find raw materials for production. This is not being "errand boys." If we did not support the factories and mills in this way, there is no telling what would have happened'. Lenin, of course, was not opposed to workers' control. He was arguing rather that only with state power in the hands of the soviets and the establishment of workers' control on the national level could the factory committees ensure that their efforts would benefit the workers and not the capitalists.

Some union leaders voiced apparently similar criticism. D.B. Ryazanov told the All-Russian conference of factory committees that 'the union movement does not carry the stain of the entrepreneur, and it is the bad luck of the committees that they seem to be component parts of the administration. The union opposes itself to capital, while the factory committee involuntarily turns into an agent of the entrepreneur'.[53] Similarly, A.K. Gastev, a leader of the Petrograd Metalworkers' Union, noted the 'touching solidarity [of the

50 Ibid., p. 177.

51 Ibid., p. 186.

52 FZK, vol. I, p. 92.

53 FZK, vol. II, p. 192.

factory committees] with the administration'. Factory committees from the provinces were sending their representatives to the government in Petrograd to praise their factories in support of the owners' requests for orders and subsidies. Gast'ev said that such collaboration with management had forced his union to adopt a series of resolutions aimed at curtailing this independent activity of the factory committees or at channelling it in a more acceptable direction.[54]

But the criticism of these union leaders was based on different considerations than Lenin's. These union leaders were worried by the competition of the factory committees, seeing them as usurping union functions. They accused the committees of anarchism, of concern only for their own factory at the expense of the working class as a whole. As will be seen later, this criticism was largely unfounded. The union leaders' critical attitude really had deeper roots. These were moderate Bolsheviks and Mensheviks who feared that the activity of the factory committees was taking workers beyond the limits of the bourgeois-democratic revolution, something that would, in their view, doom the revolution to defeat, since Russia lacked the conditions for socialism.

Although circumstances themselves were forcing the factory committees beyond control in the sense of 'passive' monitoring, the committee activists were not immune to the criticism that they were participating in the exploitation of workers. For it hit at a core value of the 'conscious workers' – class independence from the exploiters.[55]

The Struggle for Production and the Question of State Power

The search for solutions to the problems facing the factory committees on both the practical and 'ideological' levels inevitably led them to the problem of state power. At the Fourth Petrograd Conference of factory committees in mid-October, Skrypnik had harsh words for the delegates who expressed their disappointment with the meagre results of the activity of the factory committees:

> They apparently flattered themselves with illusions. But our conference from the start said that under a bourgeois government we will not be able to carry out consistent control. The future centre [of factory committees,

54 *Pervaya vserossiiskaya tarifnaya konferentsiya soyuza rabochikh metallistov* (L., 1918), p. 7.

55 See Chapter 2 above.

> to be established at the All-Russian Conference of factory committees the following week] will find itself in the same conditions, and to speak of a control board under a bourgeois government is impossible. Therefore, the working class cannot bypass state power, as comrade Renev [an anarchist] proposes.[56]

A delegate from the Putilov factory, E.I. Egorov, concurred:

> We are only too well acquainted with life in the factories to deny the need for the [all-Russian] Conference. We know how often the factory committees turn out to be helpless, knowing how to avert a production stoppage in the factories but lacking the possibility to intervene. The conference can give valuable directives. But we should not fool ourselves that the conference can lead us out of the dead-end. Both private and state administrations are sabotaging production, referring us to the Society of Factory and Mills Owners. They are still strong. The conference must first of all point out out those obstacles that prevent people of action from saving the country. These obstacles are placed before us by the bourgeois government. Only the reorganisation of state power will give us the possibility of developing our activity.[57]

It will be recalled that the First Conference of factory committees that met at the end of May was the first major gathering of workers' representatives in Petrograd to support the demand for soviet power. For that demand arose directly out of the problems the factory committees encountered in their efforts to support production. The position of the anarchists, on the other hand, that called the workers to take over management of the factories but remained silent on the question of power, did not find significant support among the factory committees. At the Second Conference in August, the anarchist V.M. Volin proposed an amendment to the resolution on workers' control that would have omitted the demand to transfer power to the proletariat and poorest peasantry. Replying for the Bolsheviks, V.P. Milyutin stated: 'I decisively disagree with the amendment, because it would mean to cross out the very essence of our resolution. We are not anarchists, and we recognise the need for a state apparatus and it must even be developed further'. The amendment was rejected overwhelmingly.[58]

---

56 Ibid., vol. II, p. 123.

57 Ibid., p. 122.

58 Ibid., vol. I, p. 216.

But if the anarchists did not have much influence in the factory committees themselves, their influence among rank-and-file workers was growing in certain districts in the weeks preceding the October Revolution.[59] S.M. Gessen, a worker at the Putilov Factory, told the Bolshevik Petersburg Committee on 15 October that in the Narva District, 'where our influence is strong, the mood is cheerful, expectant [*vyzhidatel'noe* – wait-and-see]. Among the backward masses there is an indifference to politics. But there has been no decline in the influence of the party. The independent activity of the masses is declining'. M.S. Gorelik from the same factory added: 'One has to observe that the anarchists are working energetically at the Putilov factory, so that it is difficult to restrain the workers in an organised framework'. Similarly, from the Rozhdestvenskii district: 'The mood is expectant ... The mood has declined in connection with the layoffs due to the evacuation of the factories. The influence of the anarchists has grown significantly'.[60]

The anarchists' advocacy of 'direct action' was attracting workers, particular the less skilled ones who had grown disillusioned with the lack of movement on the political level. Nevertheless, the Bolsheviks maintained their predominant positions in practically all the workers' political and economic organisations in Petrograd.

Despite growing tension in the factories, there were still very few cases of takeover by workers. And when they did occur, it was in response to the plant's closure or to the flight of the administration. At the Respirator factory, the workers detained several administrators for a few hours. Although the circumstances of the conflict are not completely clear, it is known that the workers were demanding retraction of an administrative order issued on 31 August, possibly related to the Skobelev circulars. In response to this 'arrest', the entire administration resigned. The workers decided to continue production on their own, asking the government to appoint a neutral commissar as the factory's legal representative in obtaining raw materials from the client factories that had ceased their production as a result of the conflict. The workers also demanded that the administration be charged and tried for 'desertion of the rear'. (The factory was producing gas masks.) The workers' request for the state to take over the factory was typical of such conflicts. This, of course, was far from an anarchist-inspired demand.

As before, workers' control remained primarily a practical response to real problems. Even in the state-owned factories, where the workers had asserted

59 Dok. Okt., p. 52.

60 *Peterburgskii komitet*, pp. 505–6.

their right to control from the start of the revolution and where control had, indeed, made more progress, the factory committees and the rank-and-file workers continued to recognise the administration's authority. On 3 October, a joint meeting of the factory and shop committees of the state-owned Izhorskii factory adopted a resolution calling for cooperation with the director. The workers were urged to carry out unswervingly the orders of the foremen and senior workers. Where doubts arose over the propriety of an order, the workers were told to notify the shop committee at once, but not on their own to refuse to obey the order or to prevent its execution.[61]

Regulations governing worker-management relations at state-owned Orudiinyi factory, adopted on 28 August, affirmed the factory committee's right to control but made clear that control was to be understood as monitoring the activity of the administration. And appointment of higher administrative personnel was left to management. The regulations further stated:

> Each skilled tradesman and worker is obliged to execute the legitimate demands of administrative personnel who are their direct supervisors … maintaining polite address throughout. The skilled tradesman or workers, in a case of a disagreement with representatives of management on one or another matter, take it to the shop committee, which sorts the matter out. In extreme cases, the local committee passes the matter onto the central factory committee or to the conciliation chamber.[62]

The authority of management was thus recognised, but it was subject to oversight (control) by the workers' representatives.

Quiet on the Wage Front

The understanding that there was no salvation from economic collapse without taking political power away from the propertied classes and the workers' growing concern for the fate of their factories explain the surprising calm that reigned in Petrograd in this period in the traditionally conflictual area of wages. Meanwhile, the rest of Russia was experiencing a powerful economic strike wave.[63]

---

61 Stepanov 1965, p. 130.

62 FZK, vol. II, pp. 67–8.

63 P.V. Volobuev 1964, p. 239. According to one estimate, 1.1 million workers in Russia took

The Third Conference of factory committees in Petrograd on 10 September issued a warning to workers 'to refrain from dispersed and premature actions that can only be useful to the counterrevolution. On the contrary, it is necessary to concentrate all the workers' energy on organisational efforts toward the impending solution of the questions that are being raised by the unloading [of Petrograd] and the evacuation, of the question of construction of state power and a rapid termination of the three-year-old world war'.[64] And the workers heeded these warnings. There were only two major industrial strikes in Petrograd in the months of August to October: 7,000 workers of the railroad workshops, part of a nationwide railway strike on 24 September–7 October, and 25,000 woodworkers, who struck from 16 October to 28 October. Besides these, there were a few small strikes, the most notable being that of workers of 21 printing plants on August 12–22 and 2,500 paper workers from 21 September to 4 October. In all, no more than ten percent of Petrograd's 417,000 industrial workers took part in strikes in the three months preceding the October Revolution.[65] In contrast, in Russia's Central Industrial Region, if one counts only the sector-wide strikes, well over 40 percent (and nearer to 50 percent if one includes smaller strikes) of the 1,030,000 workers took part in economic strikes in this period, including 110,000 leatherworkers, 300,000 textile workers and 15,000 rubber workers, in addition to the workers of the railway workshops and in individual metalworking factories.[66]

---

part in strikes in September and 1.2 million in October (A.M. Lisetskii 1968, p. 42, cited in L.S. Gaponenko 1963a, p. 436). In the strike wave of January–February 1917 'only' 700,000 had participated (G.A. Trukan 1967, p. 217). Gaponenko presents the following aggregate statistics for strikes in March–September 1917:

	March	April	May	June	July	August	September
Number of Economic Strikes	27	42	78	76	73	109	117

There was also a growing tendency for strikes to embrace entire sectors within regions (Gaponenko 1963a, p. 386).

64 FZK, vol. II, p. 36.

65 Official strike statistics for 1917 do not exist, since the Factory Inspectorate fell into disuse after February and the Ministry of Labour published only aggregate data. The estimate of 10 percent, which probably exaggerates the proportion of industrial strikers that struck, is based on press reports and published archival material.

66 G.A. Trukan 1967, pp. 203–17; P.A. Nikolaev 1960, pp. 96–9.

It was not as if reasons to strike were lacking in Petrograd. Between the start of negotiations in the metal sector at the end of June and the conclusion of an agreement six weeks later, the Metalworkers' Union had to intervene in some 180 factories to prevent conflicts from becoming strikes.[67] At a meeting of the union's central and district executives on 1 July, the Bolshevik members argued against a sector-wide strike and in favour of a compromise on wages. Their main argument was that the economic demands were covered in the demand for soviet power and that the workers should preserve their energy for that goal. That position received majority support.[68]

Three weeks later, the Petrograd Society of Factory and Mills Owners broke off negotiations, rejecting the union's wage demands for unskilled categories. On their part, they insisted on including output norms in the agreement. The union's delegates' assembly responded by voting their executive a strike mandate to be used as a last resort.[69] But a few days later, the delegates' council decided to accept a government-sponsored compromise on wages and also the inclusion of output norms, 'taking into account the serious economic situation of the country'. It observed that, in the existing conditions of inflation and economic breakdown, only an end to the war, genuine control over production, and the transfer of power to the working class and its allies could spare the workers from 'unbearable conditions of existence'.[70]

But that was not the end, as the introduction of the new rates was resisted by some of the owners and even more stubbornly so by managers of state-owned factories, who were not members of the Society of Factory and Mill Owners. Moreover, it soon became evident that inflation had already eaten most of the wage increase.[71] Many disputes arose also over the classification of jobs. There were some isolated strikes, but the great majority of workers, though sympathetic to the strikers, did not support them. At the end of September a group of workers of the Putilov factory struck in protest against their job classification. A meeting of 5,000 workers of the Cannon Department adopted the following resolution:

> To call the above-mentioned comrades back to work immediately, as their strike is in the interests only of the entrepreneurs and it disorganises the close ranks of the Putilov workers … In summoning the striking workers

67 Stepanov 1965, p. 80.
68 Ibid.
69 S. Bruk, 'Organizatsiya soyuza metallistov v 1917 g.', in Anskii 1928, pp. 127–8.
70 Stepanov 1965, pp. 80–1; Volobuev 1964, p. 233.
71 Stepanov 1965, p. 182.

> back to work, the factory and shop committees will strive to satisfy their just demands.[72]

In a similar manner, a general assembly of the workers of the Parviainen machine-building factory on 12 October refused to support 200 striking mechanics and turners:

> We, workers, feel the grasping hands of hunger. We see perfectly well that the capitalist factory owners, grown insolent, are trying at every opportunity to wrest from workers whatever they can, that they artificially swell the ranks of the unemployed, provoking strikes by their refusal to meet their most essential demands. But we firmly declare that we will go into the streets only when we find it necessary. We are not afraid of the coming battle that draws near and we firmly believe that we will emerge victorious from it.
>
> Long live power in the hands of the Soviets of workers' and soldiers' deputies![73]

72 *Putilovtsy v trekh revolyutsiyakh*, pp. 384–5.

73 *Rabochii put'* (Oct. 18, 1917).

CHAPTER 11

On the Eve

At a meeting of the Bolsheviks' Central Committee on 16 October, Zinoviev, who belonged to the moderate wing of the leadership opposed to an insurrection, stressed that 'the mood in the factories is not what it was in June. It's clear that there is not the mood that there was in June'.[1] The day before, at a closed session of the Bolsheviks' Petersburg Committee, M.I. Latsis, a party organiser in the Vyborg District and on the left of the party, reported: 'One observes serious concentration and work among the masses. In our district, in addition to the district [party] committee, a centre has been organised. It was organised from below. In an action [*vystuplenie* – here a euphemism for 'insurrection'], the organised apparatus must be in the fore, and the masses will support us. It is completely different from before'.[2]

On this point, at least, there was some agreement between the two wings of the party: in contrast to the period before the July Days, one could not now expect initiative on the political front from the rank-and-file workers. It was now the party's turn, which, as Latsis put it, had grown accustomed to acting as a 'fire extinguisher', itself to light the fuse.

In evaluating the workers' state of mind on the eve of the insurrection, it is important first to identify the issues as they were actually being debated at the time (and not as historians have often mistakenly portrayed them). The first problem facing the workers as the date of the Congress of Soviets neared was whether the soviets should, in fact, take power or whether it made more sense to await the Constituent Assembly, elections for which had finally been set by the government, after three postponements, for mid-November. If the elections yielded a majority in favour of a government responsible exclusively to the toiling classes, to 'revolutionary democracy', then a peaceful transition of power might be possible. This would avert, or at least lessen, the danger of the workers' political isolation and civil war, posed by a soviet seizure of power. On the other hand, to wait several more weeks meant to stand by helplessly while the economic and military[3] situations continued to deteriorate.

---

1 Dok. Okt., p. 55. For a rather different evaluation of the workers' mood on the eve of October than what is presented in this chapter, see Rabinowitch 2007, ch. 12.

2 *Peterburgskii komitet*, p. 504.

3 At the beginning of October, the Germans occupied the Moon-sund archipelago in the Gulf

The question, in essence, was whether bloodshed and civil war could be avoided or at least minimised. The right Bolsheviks, the Left SRs and Menshevik-Internationalists (the defencists, who supported the coalition government but whose influence among workers was by now negligible, can be ignored) argued that the violent seizure of power by the soviets was unnecessary. And in any case, it was unlikely to succeed. It would only alienate potential allies within the camp of revolutionary democracy, creating a social basis for civil war. To this, the Bolsheviks' left wing replied that civil war, at least at some level, was unavoidable and, in fact, it already existed. Even if a majority in the Constituent Assembly declared itself for a government of revolutionary democracy alone, Kerenskii would not hand over power without a fight. Besides, what guarantee was there that the Constituent Assembly, already thrice postponed, would ever meet? Decisive action, not continuing to mark time, would win over the wavering elements of revolutionary democracy.

These issues emerged clearly in the political debate at the All-Russian Conference of Factory Committees that met in Petrograd a week before the insurrection. Trotsky's report on the current moment was received with enthusiasm. Not surprisingly, the major part of his speech was devoted to demonstrating why civil war was unavoidable. Those who compared Russia in 1917 to France of 1789 and its bourgeois-democratic revolution, he argued, were blind. France then only had the embryo of a proletariat. But in Russia

> The extreme poles dominate ... Our working class represents a developed, organised type of revolutionary class and is far superior to the proletariat of the French revolution ... On the other, we have organised capital. That has determined the high degree of class polarisation. Conciliationism would have a basis if class antagonisms were not so acute ... There are two extreme wings, and if the revolutionary parties were to draw back from civil war now, the right wing would all the same carry out its offensive against the revolution and all its achievements. Desertion by the party would not avert the civil war – it would merely unfold in an unorganised way, in a haphazard and dispersed manner, and, one can assume, to the

---

of Finland, forcing the Russian Baltic Fleet to retreat, after offering stiff resistance. Citing the threat to the capital, the Provisional Government announced its intention to evacuate Moscow. Facing a barrage of criticism from the Left, which saw in the evacuation another move directed against Petrograd's revolutionary workers, the government abandoned the idea. But it was widely believed among workers that the government was scheming to let the German army through to pacify the capital. Sukhanov 1919–23, vol. VI, pp. 218–19, 235–6.

> greatest benefit of the propertied classes. Civil war is imposed on us by the economic situation and by economic and historical development.

Trotsky then turned to the threat of the workers' political isolation, observing that 'there is already a civil war between the peasants and the landowners'. Peasant emissaries were coming to the Petrograd Soviet to ask it not to allow the government to send soldiers to shoot the insurrectionary peasants. At the same time, the soldiers were unambiguously calling the Soviet to take power and to avert spontaneous mass desertion at the first snowfall. The bourgeoisie, for its part, had blocked the Constituent Assembly by all means available to it.

> The genuinely revolutionary masses, the proletariat, and the army and insurrectionary peasants that were drawn to it, can fight for the Constituent Assembly only by taking power.
>
> You cannot direct historical development artificially along a peaceful path. You have to recognise that and openly say to yourselves that civil war is inevitable. But we must organise it in the interests of the worker masses. That is the only way to make it more bloodless, less painful. You can achieve that result not by hesitation and wavering but only by a stubborn and courageous struggle for power. Then, perhaps, there will still be a chance that the bourgeoisie will retreat. We cannot allow demoralisation of the working class by wavering.[4]

B.D. Kamkov, speaking for the Left SRs, recognised that the workers, soldiers and peasants all wanted to replace the coalition government with one consisting exclusively of representatives of the toiling classes, of revolutionary democracy. But the question was how to achieve that. Is it possible, he asked, is it permissible to achieve that through the revolutionary pressure of a single city? He reminded the delegates of what had occurred on 3–5 July.

> We consider an action [*vystuplenie*] in the present circumstances to be the greatest political mistake. The conditions now are unfavourable for an open battle with the bourgeoisie. If we felt that all that was left was to lose everything or to perish with dignity, then, following the example of the Paris Commune, we would not refuse to write that heroic page of history. But the situation is exactly the opposite. The masses are uniting more and more around the revolutionary vanguard. The revolutionary cavalry,

---

4 FZK, vol. II, pp. 156–9.

> the proletariat, is more and more closely united with the revolutionary infantry, the toiling peasants, and the final victory seems assured to us ... Power will not slip away; there is no one from whom to take it.

And he concluded that, instead of taking power, the workers should use the Congress of Soviets, which had been finally convened, despite the TsIk's sabotage,[5] to ensure convocation of the Constituent Assembly.

Fifty-three delegates to conference voted in favour of the following resolution, with only five opposed and nine abstentions:

> The government of the counterrevolutionary bourgeoisie is destroying the country. Having demonstrated, and itself having understood, its total inability to conduct the war, it is dragging out the war for the sole purpose of smothering the revolution. It does nothing to fight against the economic dislocation. On the contrary, its entire economic policy is directed at aggravating the disorganisation with the aim of starving the revolution to death and burying it under the debris of universal economic ruin. The salvation of the revolution and achievement of the goals posed by the toiling masses in this revolution lie in the transfer of power to the hands of the Soviets of Workers', Soldiers' and Peasants' Deputies.[6]

This conference was representative of the prevailing sentiment in Petrograd's factories. On 21 October, a general assembly at the Admiralty Shipyard was convened to discuss the current situation. Pakhomov, a Bolshevik worker and one of the factory's delegates to the Soviet, gave the report:

> We should not, at this time, at any price support the Government which tries only to deceive the people and to destroy the revolution by all means, [a government] thanks to whose efforts the army and the revolutionary navy, in an unequal battle with the German navy, are perishing, and that is trying to hand over the Petrograd workers to the apprenticeship of the German capitalists ... [We must demand] the transfer of power to the Soviet of Workers' and Soldiers' Deputies.

---

5 Even after the TsIK finally set a date for the congress, it urged local soviets not to send delegates. At the same time, the defencist parties played down the significance of the soviets for Russia's political life. The TsIK's organ, *Izvestiya*, went so far as to call for their disbandment, arguing that they had outlived their useful function. *Izvestiya*, no. 195, 1917.

6 FZK, vol. II, p. 167.

On the question of an insurrection:

> All this talk of an action by the Bolsheviks is being circulated only for the reason of testing the faint-hearted and so that it will be possible to send a new Kornilov against Petrograd to put down the Bolsheviks, who will have taken the action. But we have to take power.

Therefore, he concluded, he was not calling the workers to come out into the streets. Instead, he was telling them to be ready 'to die with honour or live in disgrace. That means that if an action is necessary, it will be criminal to stand aside'.

After Pakhomov, Zakharenko, a defencist worker, took the floor. The meeting protocols report:

> He expressed doubt as to why the extreme leftists are acting in such a risky manner. For his part, he proposes to be cautious, and if the leftists speak of socialism, then let them say what socialism is. On peace, he said that they are waiting for it more in the trenches than they are here, and if the soldiers are brought to that point, they will no longer be soldiers but gangs that shoot peaceful citizens. About the action, comrade Zakharov spoke of about how unarmed crowds [would] face the army in a duel that will certainly destroy us. On land, he said that anarchy has begun in the villages, but he did not explain why, because land is not evenly distributed in the different regions of our Russia and you can't give power to the soviets because they are representatives of a minority, since only the Petrograd proletariat supports the soviets, but the village does not have any consideration for them.

As Zakharenko's speech indicates, the defencists were playing on workers' fear of political isolation and warning that an attempt by the soviets to seize power would be decisively crushed. On the other hand, they had nothing to offer that could counter the Bolsheviks' devastating criticism of the coalition government. Another worker, Kharitonov, replied to Zakharenko with a question: 'Since when have we had in Russia a majority composed of capitalists and landowners, who have been in the government all this time and from whom the Bolsheviks are now proposing that the entire people free itself and transfer power to the soviets, as elected by the people?' He went on to speak of the bourgeoisie's intention to surrender Petrograd to the Germans.

There followed a discussion, which ended with the unanimous adoption of the following resolution:

> We, the workers of the Admiralty Shipbuilding factory on Galernyi ostrovok … having heard a report on the current situation, declare that the government of Kerenskii, of the bourgeoisie and landowners, is the government of bourgeois-landowner dictatorship and civil war and is conducting a policy of betrayal of the revolution and deception of the people. This government is preparing to desert Petrograd for Moscow … and with that, together with Rodzyanko,[7] to surrender Petrograd to the Germans. In this counterrevolutionary design we see an insolent challenge to the workers and a new conspiracy against the revolution, one more dangerous than Kornilov's.
>
> We declare we will all, to the last man, fight for the power of the Soviets of Workers', Soldiers' and Peasants' Deputies. For in that alone lies the path to peace, land and freedom.[8]

Similar resolutions adopted at other factory meetings on the eve of the insurrection leave little doubt that in the choice between waiting for the Constituent Assembly and the immediate seizure of power by the soviets, workers almost unanimously supported the latter position.[9] Even workers who elected Left SRs to represent them in the various workers' organisations often voted in favour of the Bolshevik position, rather than support the Left SRs' call to wait for the Constituent Assembly. Thus, the Admiralty factory's resolution was adopted unanimously, although the Left SRs had received more than a quarter of the votes in recent elections at the factory.[10] Defying the official position of their party, the SR – by now Left SRs – organisations of the Petergof district and of the Sestroretsk Arms Factory themselves called for the Soviet Congress to take power.[11] The leaders of the Menshevik-Internationalists and of the Left SR admitted that the workers did not want to wait any longer. 'Our speeches seemed "doomed" to us ourselves', recalled S.D. Mstislavskii, a prominent Left SR.

---

7 Big landowner and prominent politician.

8 TsGA SPb f. 9391, op., 1, d. 11, l. 43.

9 For a sample of other resolutions, see Dok. Okt., pp. 92–135 *passim*; Dok. Nak pp. 277, 295, 325; *Revolyutsiya 1917-go goda* (M.-L., 1926), vols. 4 and 5, *passim*. I found only one resolution clearly supporting the internationalists' position that called to use the Soviet Congress, not to take power, but to prepare the Constituent Assembly. It was adopted by a meeting of the Obukhovskii factory, whose workers had been strong supporters of the SRs. This was the Left SRs' position. *Znamya truda* (Oct. 3, 1917).

10 Dok. Okt., p. 162.

11 *Znamya truda* (Oct. 17, 1917).

> True, at meetings, workers and soldiers applauded our orators. But we felt that they were applauding the voice, the sound, but not the significance of the words – they kept on thinking their own thoughts, as before. And in the face of this 'their own', what force could our ideas about a 'system of power', 'priority of the social', 'a transitional period' have when compared with the militant cries of Lenin, so resonant and comprehensible to the excited masses?[12]

Only a few days before the insurrection, Mstislavskii wrote in the Left SR paper:

> Of course it is hard for the masses, exhausted by the sense of 'dead end', to withstand the lure of a slogan that so simply and radically, with one wave of the hand, resolves all our difficulties, the economic ruin, the 'accursed questions'. To all wishes, one answer – rise up! In a word, one brief moment of decision, a new upsurge of energy, intense street fighting – and we will have crossed the line, before which we have been lingering for eight months.[13]

Any doubts about the workers' position on this question were laid to rest on the 'Day of the Petrograd Soviet', Sunday 22 October. To mark the occasion, the Petrograd Soviet called for a peaceful review of Soviet forces in mass meetings. Eye-witness accounts concur that the response was overwhelming. 'The day surpassed all our expectations', recalled M.M. Lashevich, a Bolshevik delegate from the garrison to the Petrograd Soviet. '30,000 showed up at the People's House. Whoever was at the meeting, will never forget it. The enthusiasm of thousands of workers and soldiers was so great that it would have taken only a single direct call for that entire human colossus to go barehanded to the barricades, to death'.[14] While Lashevich was no doubt exaggerating the general readiness to man the barricades, there can be no doubt that the mood was very positive, even enthusiastic at the prospect of the transfer of power to the soviets. Pestovskii, a Bolshevik who spoke on that day at two factory meetings in the Vasilevskii ostrov district, recalled: 'We spoke openly to the masses about the coming seizure of power by us and we heard nothing but approval'.[15]

---

12 S. Mstislavskii 1922, p. 116.

13 *Znamya truda* (Oct. 21, 1917). See also Martovs statement, in *Iskra* (Oct. 17, 1917).

14 P.F. Kudelli (ed.) 1924, p. 104.

15 Trotsky 1965, vol. III, p. 113.

Non-Bolshevik observers, opposed to an insurrection, concurred. Once again Mstislavskii:

> The Day of the Soviet took place in numerous meetings in the midst of a tremendous upsurge of enthusiasm. At the People's House, Trotsky so electrified the crowd with his speech that thousands of hands rose in a common outburst of emotion, when he called to swear loyalty to the revolution, to fight for it – to the mortal end.[16]

Sukhanov similarly recalled:

> The cyclopean building of the People's House was packed to the brim with an innumerable throng. It overflowed the theatrical halls, awaiting the meetings. But there were also crowds in the foyers, in the buffet, and in the corridors ... The mood of the three thousand plus people who filled the hall was distinctly elated ... Trotsky at once began to heat up the atmosphere – with his art and polish. I remember that he described at length and tremendous extreme force the difficult (in its simplicity) picture of life in the trenches. The essence was entirely in the mood. The political conclusion had been known for a long time ...
>
> The mood around me was close to ecstasy. It seemed as if the crowd would spontaneously, without anyone having given the direction, break out in a religious hymn ... Trotsky composed some brief, general resolution or declared some general formula, such as 'we will stand for the worker-peasant cause until the last drop of our blood'.
>
> 'Who is for?' The thousand-strong crowd, as one person, raised its hands. I saw the raised hands and the burning eyes of the men, women and adolescents, workers, soldiers, peasants and typically philistine figures. Were they spiritually transported? Did they see through the slightly lifted curtain the corner of some 'promised land', for which they had been longing? Or were they imbued with the consciousness of the political moment under the influence of a socialist's political agitation? ... Don't ask! Accept it as it was ...
>
> 'Let this vote be your oath – with all your force, through any sacrifice, to support the Soviet that has taken upon itself the great burden of pursuing

16 Mstislavskii 1922, p. 117.

> to the end the victory of the revolution and giving the earth, bread and peace!'
>
> The innumerable throng kept their hands in the air.
>
> Approximately the same thing was taking place all across Petersburg. Everywhere, there were final reviews and final oaths. Thousands, tens of thousands, hundreds of thousands of people ... Strictly speaking, this was already the insurrection. It had begun already ...[17]

Even the Menshevik-defencist *Rabochaya gazeta*, which for months had been writing about the masses' 'disillusionment' and 'apathy', could not deny the reality:

> And so it has begun. The Bolsheviks gave the signal for the 'insurrection'. At the Sunday meetings, the masses of soldiers and workers, electrified by the 'revolutionary' speeches of the Bolshevik leaders, vowed to 'come out' [*vystupat'*] at the first call of the Petrograd Soviet.[18]

It might seem difficult to accord this assessment of the popular mood with the earlier-mentioned opinions of left and right Bolsheviks to the effect that the mood was very different from that of June, that the masses were not rushing into the streets, could not be expected to take the initiative. But, in fact, there is no contradiction. Rather, the circumstances at the end of October were very different from those of the start of July, when workers imagined that pressure on the Mensheviks and SRs on its own would bring about the peaceful transition of power to the soviets. All the TsIK had to do, workers thought, was to declare itself the legitimate government. As the SR leader V.B. Stankevich had told the Petrograd Soviet in April, all that was needed was a phone call from the Executive Committee, and the Provisional Government would be no more.[19] But after the July Days no one could have illusions about a peaceful transfer of power. No one could doubt that Kerenskii would resort to force, as he had done in July and August, if he felt the Provisional Government threatened.

---

17 Sukhanov 1919–23, vol. VII, pp. 89–92.

18 *Rabochaya gazeta* (25 Oct. 1917). Not long after, the paper would claim that the worker masses had not supported the insurrection.

19 Sukhanov 1919–23, vol. III, p. 276.

The transfer of power would require armed force, and that required planning and leadership. In the July Days, the worst that the workers imagined was that they would have to return to the factories empty-handed. In October, all the cards were being played. It was civil war, at least on some level of intensity, and failure would mean that revolution would be drowned in the people's blood.

For their part, the Bolsheviks were doing everything in their power to dissuade the workers from independent political initiative. They warned at every turn against premature, unorganised action. That was why the Petrograd Soviet had decided that 22 October should take the form of indoor meetings, fearing that even peaceful street demonstrations could turn into a premature, bloody confrontation.

But this still was not the complete picture. The Bolsheviks were clearly not complacent about the workers' mood. Otherwise, why bother to report that the mood was 'not like in June'? On the one hand, Petrograd's working class was as united as it had been only at the time of the February Revolution in its firm wish for the Soviet Congress to take power. But that wish was not enough. Its realisation would require force. A closer analysis reveals that behind the apparent unanimity of the 22 October meetings, there were different shades of attitude toward the transfer of power to the soviets and that the issues posed by the July Days had not been resolved for all workers.

One can discern at least four different 'moods' among workers in relation to the insurrection. The Menshevik Internationalists' *Novaya zhizn'* captured something of this in an editorial comment on Bolshevik agitation in the factories that was asking workers to be ready to take action in support of the soviets:

> The mood of the masses, in so far as one can judge it, is not characterised by certainty. Some part is apparently prepared to act. The frame of mind of another part is not particularly militant and is inclined to refrain from taking action. Finally, there is another group, whose attitude to an action is either a negative or completely passive one. It is hard to say what the correlation is among these three groups. But the active group hardly constitutes a majority.[20]

The largest group was, it seems, the hesitators. Although they strongly desired soviet power, they had painful memories of the July Days and feared bloodshed and defeat. They would take action, but only if the situation left them no alternative. Hence Trotsky's assertion that civil war could not be avoided, that it was

20 *Novaya zhizn'* (Oct. 15, 1917).

on some level inevitable. Hence the Bolsheviks' generally defensive framing of their assertion that the insurrection, or 'action', was necessary. On 21 October, Sukhanov was called to speak at a workers' meeting in the Petergof district. He found some 4,000 workers standing in the yard of the Putilov factory under an autumn drizzle, listening to a succession of orators. A comrade of Sukhanov's, a Menshevik-Internationalist, told him that the crowd had barely let him finish his speech. 'The mood is very strong', he said. 'Of course, only a minority are active, but that's enough to disrupt the meeting'.

While I was waiting, I myself saw that the mood was strong. An SR, true, a totally inept one, was not allowed to pronounce two consecutive words. But it was undoubtedly the case that a minority was acting, and even so not a large one: the local Bolshevik youth. The majority stood silently with a 'vigilant [*vyzhidatel'noe* – wait and see] and concentrated' look. The bearded ones, puzzled or sad, were shaking their heads.

These were the same Putilovtsy who had 'come out' 30,000 strong on 4 July to give power to the soviets. All without exception hated and despised the *Kerensh-china* [Kerenskii regime]. But they knew how the July Days had ended. Power to the soviet – an excellent idea. But an insurrection?

Sukhanov was known to the workers from his articles in *Novaya zhizn'* and his speeches at their meetings. He began cautiously with a fierce attack on the coalition government. But no sooner had he said that an insurrection was unnecessary, than pandemonium broke out, and he was forced to stop.

> Yes, I confirm that the mood was conditional, ambivalent. The majority were ready 'in their hesitation to abstain'. But the minority, capable of putting together an impressive fighting force, was undoubtedly eager for battle. At any rate, the fruit was ripe. No reason to wait more and more, not to speak of there being a possibility of doing so. The mood would not be better but it could weaken. A ripe fruit has to be picked. At the first success, the sluggish mood would firm up. If it doesn't end up in wild scenes of senseless bloodshed, everyone will support.[21]

At the meeting of the Bolsheviks' Petersburg Committee on 15 October, reports from the districts presented a similar picture of a large group of indecisive workers. Several speakers began their reports with phrases such as 'the mood is extremely complex', or 'it is hard to judge the mood'. The delegate from the Narva District (which included Petergof) supported Sukhanov's assess-

---

21 Sukhanov 1919–23, vol. VII, pp. 87–8.

ment: 'The general picture is that there is no strong urge to come out. Where our influence is great, there the mood is good. Among the backward masses, there is indifference to politics. But there is no decline in our influence. The level of autonomous activity of the masses is falling'. In the Petrograd district: 'Where our influence is strong, the mood is temporising. And where it [our influence] isn't strong, there is apathy and a struggle with the factory committees'. From the Rozhdestvenskii district: 'The mood is temporising. If there is a sortie on the part of the counterrevolution, we will repulse it. But if there is a call to action, then I don't think the workers will come out. The mood has declined in connection with the job cuts due to the evacuation of the factories. There has been a significant rise in anarchist influence'. From Vailevskii ostrov: 'As regards military training, instruction is being conducted in the factories and mills. There is no mood for an action'. And from the trade unions:

> There is practically not a single union where the mood has not become stronger in our favour. There is no clearly militant mood among the masses. If there is an offensive on the part of the counterrevolution, then it will be repulsed. But the masses themselves won't take the offensive. If the Petrograd Soviet calls for action, the masses will follow the Soviet.[22]

Of course, as several reports indicated, it was not easy to gauge the mood. This was in part because the Bolsheviks were not directly asking the workers to participate in an insurrection. Indeed, until the Bolshevik Central Committee's meeting of 16 October, the party had not yet taken the decision to organise an insurrection. And even after it had been decided, a significant part of the party's membership was apparently not informed. The leaders continued to speak in defensive terms of a possible action in response to a very likely attack on the soviets and their congress by the Provisional Government. Of the national leaders, only Lenin did not mince words, calling directly for an immediate insurrection in his letters that were published in the Bolsheviks' central paper on 19–21 October.[23] As Mstislavskii aptly put it, where Lenin (still underground) said 'necessary', Trotsky said 'inevitably', that is, while Lenin called for insurrection at the most opportune moment, without reference to the Soviet Congress, Trotsky, and Bolshevik agitation generally, presented the armed action as necessary since the government and other counterrevolutionary forces would not toler-

22 *Peterburgskii komitet*, pp. 504–7.

23 *Rabochii put'* (Oct. 19–21, 1917).

ate the Soviet Congress, which was to decide to take power. The defensive tone of the Bolsheviks' agitation was undoubtedly influenced by their sense of the workers' hesitant mood.

The trauma of the July Days, the bloodshed and the repression that followed, and the associated fear of isolation and civil war, were the major factors in this indecisive mood. Sukhanov recalled:

> … In those weeks more than ever … I visited the factories and spoke before the 'masses'. I formed a definite impression: the mood was ambivalent, conditional. The coalition and the existing situation could no longer be tolerated. But should we take action and should it take the form of an insurrection? They did not know for sure … Many remembered well the July Days. It should only not happen again! …[24]

The left of the Bolshevik Party was, therefore, at pains to stress how much the situation had changed since July: all the major urban soviets had been won over to the demand for soviet power; the soldiers were thirsting for peace at almost any price; the peasant war against the landlords was shifting into high gear. In sum, the 'conciliators' were suspended in air without significant popular support.

The moderate Bolsheviks, for their part, and the Menshevik Internationalists and left SRs, emphasised the workers' isolation within the ranks of revolutionary democracy. The rest of revolutionary democracy was indeed moving to the left, but premature action could frighten it again into the arms of reaction. Responding to rumours of an impending insurrection, *Novaya zhizn'* warned the workers that the counterrevolution would be even bloodier than it had been in July. Indeed, one could expect a repeat of the Paris Commune. There would be no food. And a civil war would make it impossible to resolve the problems facing the revolution.[25] Mstislavskii in *Znamya truda* similarly warned that an insurrection would lead to the same result as in July: workers would be shot, and the revolution would be set back.[26] Meanwhile, the defencist and bourgeois papers were expressing confidence that an uprising would be easily crushed, and editorialists even dared the Bolsheviks to try.[27]

These articles took their toll on worker confidence. Sokolov, commander of a unit of Red Guards at the Trubochnyi factory, certainly not one of the waverers,

---

24 Sukhanov 1919–23, vol. VII, pp. 36–7.

25 *Novaya zhizn'* (Oct. 13, 1917).

26 *Znamya truda* (Oct. 15, 1917).

27 Sukhanov 1919–23, vol. VII, pp. 44–6.

recalled the night of 23–4 October, when the Red Guards were placed on alert and decided to spend the night at the factory.

> Many perhaps slept that night. But the one writing these lines did not feel like sleep. Various thoughts overwhelmed the night. Much at that time was still not clear that has since become clear. The July Days stood out too vividly before my eyes; the hissing of the philistines shook my certainty in victory.

The previous afternoon they had held a review of Red Guards at the factory. Among the speakers was a Menshevik who called the insurrection untimely. This time, recalled Sokolov, the workers listened to him with more patience than usual. Encouraged, the speaker declared that the workers would not come out. It was only at that point that he was finally cut off by shouts of 'enough!'[28]

Apart from the trauma of the July Days, the dire economic situation also weighed heavily on the workers' resolve. Naumov, the young worker from the Vyborg district, told the Bolsheviks' Petersburg Committee on 15 October that 'one observes dissatisfaction among the masses. The mood is depressed; there is latent indignation with the wage rates, with the evacuation, the job cuts. The mood is extremely complex'.[29] V.V. Schmidt made the same point in his report on the trade unions to the Bolsheviks' Central Committee on October 16:

> The overall number of organised workers is 500,000. Our party's influence predominates ... The mood is such that one should not expect active sorties [*vystupleniya*], especially in view of the fear of job cuts. That is a restraining element up to a certain point. In view of the specific economic conditions, one can expect colossal unemployment in the near future. In this connection, the mood is one of wait-and-see. Everyone recognises that there is no way out of the situation except in the struggle for power. They demand all power to the soviets.[30]

The impact of the looming economic collapse was thus twofold: it lent great urgency to the need for soviet power but it was also the source of insecurity that inclined workers to caution.

---

28 Kudelli 1924, p. 113.

29 *Peterburgskii* komitet, p. 565.

30 Dok. Okt., p. 53.

Apart from the temporisers, another section of the working class, particularly among the less skilled workers (which included most women) and those who had only recently come to industry, was withdrawing from political life, as it seemed to be leading nowhere. These workers were falling under the influence of anarchists, advocates of direct action in the factories. In a report from the end of September, the Menshevik organisation of the Narva district observed:

> In the worker milieu, interest in political matters declined. Something resembling disillusionment is setting in. Bolshevism no longer satisfies the masses. One observes the rise of influence of the maximalists and the anarchists. There is not a hint of discipline among the worker masses.[31]

Alexandra Kollontai, who was active among women workers, warned the All-Russian Factory Committee Conference in October:

> I considered it my duty to tell you here what is taking place among the women workers of Piter, as the most backward and undeveloped part of the working class … You have to come to their aid. Otherwise, their passivity will deal us ourselves a serious blow, since they are unable to see clear among the various party lists [in elections to the Constituent Assembly] … Fear the indifference that now exists among women workers. Organise rallies for women workers in your towns … Comrade men, make your best effort![32]

In fact, the situation was even more complex. For other reports from factories and districts where SR (defencist) support had been particularly strong, told of an increase in political interest and activism. The representative of Petrograd's Moscow district, whose workers had sat out the July Days, told the Bolsheviks' Petersburg Committee that 'the mood in the factories is restless [*besshabashnoe*]. The masses will come if the Soviet summons them. Few will come out at our party's call. The organs created during the Kornilov days have been maintained'. Similarly, from the Nevskii district: 'The mood is in our favour. The masses are attentive'. And from the Obukhovskii factory in that same district: 'The factory was previously a defencist stronghold. A shift in mood has now taken place in our favour. At the meetings that we organize, 5,000–7,000 people come … 200 have signed up to the Red Guards … The factory will without doubt

31 *Rabochaya gazeta* (Sept. 29, 1917).

32 FZK, vol. II, p. 192.

come out on the summons of the Petrograd Soviet'. And the Kapsiul'nyi factory in the Porokhovskii district: 'Until the Kornilov uprising ... the Mensheviks and SRs predominated. Now the mood is ours ... The factory committee is fully prepared to take action on the call of Petrograd Soviet'.[33]

These were workers who had not participated in the July Days and had not directly experienced the defeat. They were recent converts to the demand for soviet power and so had not had time to be disappointed with the lack of results from political activity. This also explains why Moscow's workers seemed more decisive than those in the capital. In Moscow, workers' meetings regularly adopted resolutions that presented the 'action' in offensive terms, not as a necessary response to an inevitable attack by the government and other counterrevolutionary forces. Some resolutions did not even link the 'action' to the Congress of Soviets. A delegates' meeting of the Moscow Textile Workers' Union with representatives of the factory committees on 9 October decided on a general textile strike, after which the assembled walked together to the Moscow Soviet, where they declared they were prepared to do battle for soviet power at the Soviet's first call.[34]

On 15 October, a delegates' meeting of the Moscow Metalworkers' Union adopted a resolution, stating that, since the bourgeoisie wanted to crush the revolution by means of an economic crisis, the workers had to assume the task of organising the economy on a national scale. 'Taken together, all this has placed the following task before the proletariat: to take power by means of an organized insurrection [*vystuplenie*] through the soviets, together with the poorest strata of the village, and the immediate creative work to organise the production and the distribution of goods'. The meeting then called on the Moscow and Petrograd Soviets to exert their revolutionary authority to immediately end all strikes, to meet the workers' demands by decree, and to legislate the right of workers' control over hiring and dismissals.[35] This accurately reflected the mood among Moscow's rank-and-file workers. A delegate from the Gyubner factory in Moscow told a meeting of union delegates on 15 October that the workers had mandated him to declare that 'they do not want an economic strike. But they are unanimously prepared to take action for political goals'. Another delegate proposed that the union break off negotiations at once with the owners and, if necessary, the workers should 'defend our rights on the barricades'.[36]

---

33 *Peterburgskii* komitet, pp. 504–6.

34 Dok. Nak., p. 505, note 143.

35 Ibid., p. 296.

36 Ibid., pp. 297–8. See also Sukhanov 1919–23, vol. VII, p. 69, on Moscow's militancy in October.

Another reason for the difference in moods between Moscow and Petrograd, but also a reflection of that difference, was the different ways the respective Bolshevik party organisations were talking to the workers. Moscow's Bolsheviks were much more direct in speaking about the insurrection, presenting it as a planned, offensive action. This might also partly be explained by the fact that Moscow's Bolsheviks were less affected by the wavering of the Bolshevik Central Committee, located in Petrograd. But it is also the case that events in Moscow did not have the same national significance as those in Petrograd – the local Bolsheviks might not have felt the same need for caution. At the same time, the hesitant mood in Petrograd should not be exaggerated. Among the more skilled elements, the metalworkers in particular, a sizeable group was prepared to take offensive action. As noted earlier, Latsis told the Bolsheviks' Petersburg Committee that in the Vyborg district 'one observes in the masses serious concentration and work. In our district, besides our district committee, a centre has been organised. It was organised from below'.[37] With only 18 percent of the city's industrial workers, the district gave a third of the city's Red Guards.[38] In the Kolomenskii district, with its three big shipyards, 'the mood is even better than on July 3–5'. Among workers of Lettish origin, mostly skilled workers who had been evacuated from Riga, 'the mood is enthusiastic. At the call of the [Bolshevik] Petersburg Committee, and not of the Soviet, the masses will come out. Our line was left in the July Days'. And the Finnish workers, several thousand in the capital: 'Their mood is: the sooner the better'.[39]

Some workers, in fact, demanded from the Congress of Soviets of the Northern Region (which included Petrograd, Moscow, Kronstadt, the Baltic Fleet and other northern towns) that met on 11–12 October that it immediately take power. Thus the Kolomenskii district soviet on 12 October:

> We consider the immediate transfer of power to the hands of the Soviet of Workers and Soldiers' Deputies a task that cannot be postponed. [The district soviet] considers any delay a most serious crime against the revolution and proposes that the Congress of Soviets of the Northern Region put this slogan into practice.[40]

37 *Peterbutgskii komitet*, p. 504.

38 Stepanov 1919–23, pp. 30 and 245. See also Dok. Okt., p. 871, note 30.

39 *Peterbutgskii komitet*, p. 504, 507.

40 Raisovety, vol. 1, p. 356.

This soviet sent three delegates to that congress to tell it 'not to leave for home but to take power into your hands'.[41] On 11 October, a meeting of the workers of the Baranovskii machine-construction factory in the Vyborg district demanded that the Petrograd Soviet 'immediately take full power into its hands and declare the conspirators, with Kornilov, Kerenskii and Co. at their head, to be outside the law and arrest them'.[42]

There was, therefore, a significant number of workers prepared to take the offensive. These included many of those who had been among the first in 1917 to demand the transfer of power to the soviets. The single largest group was undoubtedly the members of the Bolshevik party, some 28,000 workers at the end of September. (The total membership in the capital was 43,000, including 6,000 soldiers).[43] In the Petrograd Committee of the party, opinion had completely changed since the beginning of September, when a majority had felt the situation called for a peaceful transfer of power. M.I. Kalinin, who chaired its 5 October meeting, observed that 'there is a clear orientation of the majority [in the party] in favour of the seizure of power'. Even those who were opposed, admitted that there was no alternative. But they argued that the time was not yet ripe, that the chances of success at the moment were not great, especially since the economic and military crises would make it impossible for the new government to improve the situation of the masses. To this Latsis replied: 'They consider only the second factor – the economic disorganisation. But they forget the counterrevolution ... We must say that if we let the moment pass, there will not be another. They [the forces of counterrevolution] are active. We must choose the moment that suits us, and not the one that suits them.' 'I thought we were revolutionaries here', said Rakh'ya. 'But I had doubts when I heard comrades Volodarskii and Lashevich'. 'The opinions expressed by comrades Volodarskii and Lashevich are valuable but they are negative', stated M.M. Kharitonov. 'They have been infected by the atmosphere of the Smolny Institute [seat of the party's central committee, whose majority was opposing Lenin's call for an insurrection]'. The representatives from the Vasilevskii ostrov district summarised the majority position in favour of an insurrection:

> We cannot say that we are in some sort of indeterminate situation. Our task is to find that line along which we can proceed with unfurled banners ... We are taking course for a socialist revolution. I remember the opinions

---

41 *Novaya zhizn'* (Oct. 13,1917). See also *Novaya zhizn'* Oct. 3 for a similar position adopted by the workers of the Russko-Baltiiskii wagon-construction factory.

42 *Soldat* (Oct. 19, 1917).

43 Stepanov 1919–23, pp. 46–7. See also above, p. 232.

> at the [July] Petrograd Conference, where it was said there would be other attempts and even other defeats. We have built our entire tactic on the enthusiasm of the worker masses. Remember how, relying on the workers, we overthrew the [Tsarist] yoke ... You close your eyes to that ... You speak of Lenin forcing events. You are wrong. Our aim is neither conspiracy nor forcing events, but, in any case, we can achieve nothing through passivity ... It would be forcing to say: we will do it on the 20th. [Lenin was calling for the insurrection at the most opportune moment, without mentioning dates.]
>
> The greatest mistake is not to pay attention to the counterrevolution. The most serious thing is that the counterrevolution is consciously trying to provoke a spontaneous movement against us. We are sitting here and we can't decide whether or not to enter the pre-parliament; [meanwhile] they are conducting pogrom agitation ... Events have unfolded in a historically inevitable manner ... Our task is once more to raise high the banner and go into battle. Otherwise, they will summon us to battle, and then the result is unknown.[44]

The resolution adopted by the Bolsheviks' Third Petrograd Conference of 7–11 October leaves no doubt as to where the majority of the city's organisation stood. The resolution concluded with the words: 'All these circumstances speak clearly to the fact that the moment of the final decisive confrontation has arrived, the one that will decide the fate, not only of the Russian Revolution, but of the world revolution'.[45] A meeting of the city's party activists [*aktiv*] at the time of the Congress of Soviets of the Northern Region, declared:

> To continue the policy of 'accumulating forces' [an allusion to the Central Committee] ... would lead to disillusionment of the masses in the party of the revolutionary proletariat and would lead not only to their refusal to further support the Bolsheviks ... but also to spontaneous actions [*vystupleniya*] on the part of the masses, and, moreover, in conditions of extreme dispersal of the movement and general disorganisation that would not only put in doubt the victory of the movement but that would expose the masses to the bloody vengeance of the bourgeois counterrevolution ...

44 Ibid., pp. 486–91 *passim*.

45 *Rabochii put'* (Oct. 14, 1917).

> Hopes attached to the Congress of Soviets are unfounded, since that means one expects a solution to the basic tasks of the revolution from resolutions and not from the struggle of the masses ...
>
> The hope that the Constituent Assembly will solve the fundamental questions are illusory, since ... the convocation of the Constituent Assembly is in doubt (attacks from the right-wing of the coalition) ... [and] even a Constituent Assembly with the most leftist composition cannot change anything significant without direct and active support from the proletarian-peasant revolution, whose delay becomes more and more dangerous ...
>
> A defensive policy at present is incorrect. [It has become clear that] a shift to the offensive is needed for the rapid rooting out of the hotbeds of counterrevolution and for the creation of a revolutionary government.[46]

Thus, while as late as 16 October the Bolshevik Central Committee was still debating the issue, Petrograd's party organisation had for some time already been urging an immediate insurrection. In theses prepared for the Petrograd party conference, Lenin noted that 'unfortunately, one observes a wavering in the leadership of the party, a "fear" of the struggle for power, a tendency to substitute resolutions, protests, congresses for this struggle'.[47] And he appealed to the *nizy*, the 'lower' levels of the party, to exert pressure on the Central Committee. He had copies of his letters to the Central Committee, which the latter itself wanted to keep secret, sent to the Petersburg Committee, the Vyborg district and other local party organisations. Moscow's party organisation was of the same mind as Petrograd's. The Moscow city conference of the Bolsheviks on 10 October instructed the Moscow Committee to bring the revolutionary forces into battle readiness.[48]

Of course, the rank and file of the party were not free of doubt. They were also worried about the chances of victory and about the tremendous difficulties that a revolutionary government would face. Their support for an insurrection did not arise out of some chiliastic fervour. Instead, they saw in it the only hope of saving the revolution. They too were apprehensive, but their fear did not paralyse their will to act.

The other organisation that was solidly in favour of an insurrection was the Red Guard. Sukhanov, who repeatedly insists in his memoir on the state of indecision among rank-and-file workers, had this to say:

46 *Petrogradskaya pravda* (Nov. 5, 1922).

47 V.I. Lenin 1958–67, p. 34, p. 343.

48 Dok. Nak., p. 68.

> That did not mean that the Bolsheviks were not able to put together, summon and send into battle as many revolutionary battalions as were necessary. On the contrary, they undoubtedly had that ability. They had sufficient number of vanguard, active cadres, ready for sacrifice. The most dependable were the workers and their Red Guards. After them, the sailors were a fighting force. Worse than the others were the garrison soldiers ... There was enough fighting material. But only a small part of those who followed the Bolsheviks at that time were good quality fighting material. On the average, their mood was strongly Bolshevik, but rather sluggish and unsteady as applied to an action or insurrection.
>
> They had to place their hopes to a large degree on the worker Red Guards. But one could really depend only upon their spirit. The fighting ability of that army, that had never smelled powder, that had never seen a rifle until the last few days, that had no conception of military operations and discipline, was more than doubtful.[49]

The young Putilov Red Guard, Skorinko, is emphatic about the militant spirit of those workers:

> The conduct of the Red Guards was above any criticism. It is a lie and insolent slander that the Red Guards got drunk and looted during searches. That did not happen. For in those days, being a member of the Red Guards promised no material benefits. Just the opposite – given the growing strength of the reaction, it threatened serious unpleasantness. Only conscious workers, dedicated body and soul to the interests of the revolution, joined its ranks.
>
> How highly the workers of the factories and mills valued their Red Guards and cared about the purity of its ranks is shown by the fact that in certain shops of the Putilov factory workers were elected to the Red Guards by the general assembly. The author of these lines, not without pride, recalls how he was one of the delegates from the turret shop to the Red Guards.
>
> And if a comrade was found whose presence in the Red Guards or whose casual conduct shocked everyone, he was expelled from their ranks in disrepute. Of course, I will not speak of the conduct of the Red Guards afterwards, when a mass of [politically] foreign elements wormed their way into its honest ranks.[50]

---

49 Sukhanov 1919–1923, vol. VII, pp. 234–5.

50 Skorinko 1923, pp. 137–8. The remarks at the end refer to the often undisciplined char-

Skorinko awoke on the morning of 23 October to find his father, who had just come home from his shift at the factory, sitting on the floor, cleaning his rifle. There were tears in his eyes. The mother exploded:

> In his old age, your father has signed up with the wind-chasers ... He won't beat his son for doing that. And now look what he's up to! Cleaning his rifle ... What are you going to do, kill somebody? ... Everyone in the courtyard is laughing at you.
>
> Paying no attention to his wife, my father angrily informed his son that Kerenskii had just outlawed the Bolshevik press and was threatening to disarm the workers. Accompanied by the weeping and admonitions of my mother and the ironic looks of the other tenants, my father and I, our rifles slung over our shoulders, set off for headquarters, where we found extraordinary animation.
>
> At the headquarters, under the tables, on the tables, and next to them, we saw a mass of workers, whose interests before had been limited to their families, now fondly cleaning their rifles, barely keeping themselves from going to the [city] centre to conquer their workers' power.
>
> Everywhere people were talking, but there were no arguments. To argue in such moments, when unification was occurring on the other side of the barricades, this the workers instinctively assumed was dangerous. Among the hundred-odd Red Guards, among whom there were both SRs and Mensheviks, there was such a communality of interests on that day that my father, embracing me, remarked: 'Today I feel especially brave. And if everyone feels like me, then tomorrow there will be soviet power, that is – ours'.
>
> 'And if the day after we have to give it up?' jokingly remarked a company commander, as he ran past.
>
> 'Never! But damn it, even for a day, but it will have been ours', shouted my father, shaking his rifle and evoking enthusiasm from those present. 'Let us have it for only a day, and we will show them how we care for our property'.
>
> After the training, news arrive that Junkers [officer cadets], Cossacks and shock troops were moving towards Piter, and all of us, with only rare exceptions, stayed overnight at the headquarters. On the morning of

---

acter of the soldiers recruited into the rapidly created Red Army in February 1918, when Petrograd appeared under imminent threat of German occupation (*Peterburgskii komitet RKP(b) v 1918 g.*, SPb, 2013 p. 23). For the moral quality of the Red Guards of the October period, see also the testimony of G. Georgievskii 1919, pp. 76–7.

> 24 October, we were informed by a member of the district committee … of the bourgeoisie's attempt that night to postpone its downfall by making arrests among the workers' leaders. The appeal of the Piter Soviet was read at once, calling for revolutionary restraint and enjoining the revolutionary units to be in full battle readiness. When the appeal was being read, I knew that as a sign of our readiness to fight for a communist society, we, the armed workers, would do anything. We were high-spirited then and madly bold. Who can doubt that now?[51]

A Soviet historian analysed 3,500 dossiers of Petrograd Red Guards that were compiled in 1930 for pension purposes. Although the sample is far from perfect,[52] it offers an approximate idea of the social composition of the Red Guards. About three-quarters were male metalworkers. Women who joined served mainly as medics. 44.3 percent were Bolshevik party members, as were 69 percent of the commanders. Thus, although Bolsheviks were prominent, participation in the Red Guards was by no means a strictly Bolshevik affair, something that is confirmed by memoirs. Three-quarters were under 31 years of age; 52.2 percent were under 26, and 26.4 were under 21.[53] As usual, youth was in the fore. But there were older workers too. I. Peskovoi, a metalworker from the Vasilevskii ostrov district, recalled that 'it was interesting to look at the composition of our unit – it had young workers about 16 years old and old ones about 50. Such a mixture boosted our morale and fighting spirit'.[54]

V.F. Malakhovskii, a soldier and organiser of the Vyborg district's Red Guards, paid tribute to their spirit and daring, which in turn infected the soldiers, on the whole less enthusiastic about an insurrection. But they were poorly trained as soldiers. For example, when attacking, many did not crouch down. When the soldiers pointed this out to them, they answered that 'to bend over while running and to fight lying down is a disgrace for revolutionaries, it displays cowardice'. The soldiers had to explain that there was no honour in offering one's forehead to the enemy.[55] The workers' sense of class honour might have been a military liability, but without it, it is unlikely that there would have been an October Revolution.

---

51 Ibid., pp. 145–7. See also I. Peskovoi 1923, p. 317.

52 Some of the Red Guards had died; others joined only after the October Insurrection; still others, who had been members of parties other than the Bolsheviks, might have reported themselves as unaffiliated.

53 V.I. Startsev 1962, pp. 137–41; Stepanov 1919–23, pp. 29, 34, 36.

54 Peskovoi 1923, p. 316.

55 Kudelli 1924, p. 117.

Estimates of the number of Red Guards in Petrograd on the eve of the insurrection vary, but on the basis of archival and memoir materials, the historian Stepanov places the figure at 34,000.[56] This tends to be supported by reports from the districts read at the Bolsheviks' Petersburg Committee.[57] But that figure does not represent all the workers who were prepared to take arms. The scarcity of rifles was a serious problem and source of much complaint.[58] In addition, as Skorinko notes, the workers in some factories were careful about whom they allowed to serve in the Red Guards. At the Admiralty shipbuilding factory, for example, they adopted a charter that stated that members of the Red Guards could not have criminal records, had to be literate, of irreproachable conduct, not younger than 18 years old, and, as far as possible, have some familiarity with military matters.[59]

The mood among the workers on the eve was thus complex. There was a virtually universal, strong desire for the soviets to take power to rid the country of the coalition with the representatives of the propertied classes. But the advancing economic crisis was weighing down spirits. Among the less skilled elements, there was a certain fatigue with politics. The apparently poor odds of victory and the spectre of a civil war caused many to hesitate.

In these circumstances, the role of the resolute minority that was prepared to take the initiative became critical. They had to start, to force the issue, to make further procrastination impossible, and the rest would rally. Sukhanov's assessment proved correct: 'It was all a matter of mood. The political conclusions had long been known … At the first success, the flabby mood would become firm'.

But without the initiative of the decisive minority, Bolshevik workers in the first place, and despite the common yearning for the transfer of power to the soviets, the economic crisis and the political stagnation would have very probably led to demoralisation and opened the way for a successful counterrevolution. The role of the party, therefore, was critical in October. But it could not have played that role had it not been a democratic organisation, 'flesh of the flesh' of the working class.

---

56 Stepanov 1965, p. 245.

57 *Peterburgskii komitet*, pp. 523–5.

58 Ibid., pp. 462–5.

59 Dok. Sept., pp. 375–6.

CHAPTER 12

The October Revolution and the End of 'Revolutionary Democracy'

Formally, the insurrection began on the morning of 23 October in response to repressive measures taken by the Provisional Government against the Petrograd Soviet and the Bolshevik Party. The immediate reason for the government's action was an order of the Military-Revolutionary Committee of the Petrograd Soviet placing the city's garrison under its command. On the night of 23–4 October, the government shut down the Bolshevik newspapers *Rabochii put'* and *Soldat* for inciting insurrection. It ordered the arrest of Bolsheviks involved in anti-government agitation and opened criminal proceedings against the Military Revolutionary Committee. At the same time, Kerenskii summoned troops from outside the capital (since the garrison was fully under Bolshevik influence), posted Junkers (officer cadets) at strategic points, ordered the bridges linking the centre to the working-class districts raised, and sent the destroyer Aurora, docked for repairs at the Franko-Russkii shipbuilding factory, out to sea, supposedly on a training exercise. Telephone lines to Smol'nyi, seat of the Petrograd Soviet and the Bolsheviks' Central Committee, were cut.

The Military Revolutionary Committee, acting in the name of the Petrograd Soviet, immediately went into action, beginning with the reopening of the newspapers that had been closed. By the afternoon of 25 October, the entire capital, with the exception of the Winter Palace, seat of the Provisional Government, was in its hands. At 2.35 p.m., Lenin made his first public appearance since the July Days, addressing the plenary session of the Petrograd Soviet.

> Comrades! The workers' and peasants' revolution, about whose necessity the Bolsheviks have spoken all the time, has taken place ...
>
> We will have a Soviet government, our own organ of power, without any participation whatsoever of the bourgeoisie ...
>
> The third Russian revolution must in its final analysis bring the victory of socialism ...
>
> To end this war, closely linked with the present capitalist system, it is clear to everyone that we must overcome capital itself. In that cause, we

> will have the help of the worldwide workers' movement, which is already beginning to develop in Italy, England and Germany ...
>
> We must immediately publish all the secret treaties ...
>
> We will gain the confidence of the peasants by a single decree that will destroy the landed property of the aristocracy ...
>
> We will establish genuine workers' control over production ...[1]

These words were received with a long ovation, after which the Soviet adopted a resolution of full support for the 'workers' and peasants' revolution'.[2] V.K. Arsen'ev, a Menshevik-Internationalist delegate from Crimea who had arrived in Petrograd for the Soviet Congress, recalled that session of the Soviet:

> When Trotsky informed the Soviet that 'power had passed to the people', there followed a thunder of applause. Then Lenin and Zinoviev came out. Such a triumph. Trotsky's speech in particular carved itself into my mind ... It was some kind of molten metal – every word burned the soul ... And I saw that many people were clenching their fists, that a definite, unshakeable determination was being formed to fight to the end.[3]

The insurrection ended with the seizure of the Winter Palace and the arrest of the ministers of the Provisional Government after a siege that had lasted late into the night. It was during that siege that the Congress of Soviets opened. Shortly thereafter, the Menshevik and SR (defencist) delegates demonstratively walked out, ostensibly in protest over the insurrection, which, they claimed, had been carried out 'behind the back of the Congress'. They proceeded to the City Duma, around which a Committee for the Salvation of the Revolution and the Country had been formed, which included deputies of the City Duma, members of the outgoing TsIK that had been elected at the Soviet Congress in the spring, the Executive Committee of Peasant Soviets, also elected in the spring, the two defencist parties, members of the pre-parliament, and representatives of certain army committees from the front. This became the principal centre of organised resistance to the new regime.

---

1 Lenin 1958–67, vol. 35, pp. 2–3.

2 *Novaya zhizn'* (Oct. 26, 1917).

3 Kudelli 1924, p. 121.

While the insurrection had indeed begun before the Congress could adopt its decision to take power, the reason given by the defencists for leaving was hardly credible, given that the outgoing TsIK, which they controlled, had gone to such great lengths to avoid a new congress, in violation of the decision of the First Congress. Moreover, once the date for the new congress had finally been set, the defencists practically disowned it before it could meet. Already on 12 October, they had walked out of the Congress of Soviets of the Northern Region in protest at its resolution calling for the transfer of power to the soviets. There was, therefore, no question that that walkout was not motivated by a concern over legality but was a politically-motivated refusal of the very idea of a government responsible to the soviets.

On the other hand, it is plausible that one of Lenin's reasons for insisting that the insurrection begin before the congress opened was his desire to present the delegates with a *fait accompli* that would avert the kind of wavering which he had only with great difficulty been able to overcome in his own party's Central Committee. As for the possibility that this might upset the defencists, not only did that not bother Lenin – he wanted a decisive split with them, since he was convinced their presence would paralyse any new government, even in the very unlikely eventuality that they agreed to one based on the soviets.

At the same time, it was undoubtedly military-tactical considerations that were paramount in the insurrection's timing. Everyone, and certainly Kerenskii, knew that there would be a Bolshevik majority at the congress and that it would decide to take power. If the Provisional Government was still in existence, the congress would be a sitting duck for the mass arrest of its members. In retrospect, the Provisional Government appears practically helpless. But that was not the perception in Petrograd on the eve – there was a widespread belief that an attempted insurrection would be crushed in a bloodier version of the July Days.

In any case, it was a relatively small minority of the 650 delegates that walked out of the congress. In all, there were approximately 80 Menshevik delegates of various tendencies and 60 SRs. Those who remained were approximately 390 Bolsheviks, 90 Left SRs, some 25 Menshevik Internationalists grouped around the newspaper *Novaya zhizn'* and a few smaller groups. A group of Menshevik Internationalists that followed Martov voted 14 against 12 to leave the congress.[4]

After a recess, the congress reconvened on the evening of 26 October and adopted a 'Decree on Peace', that proposed an immediate, democratic peace to

---

4 Chamberlin 1965, vol. 1, p. 320; *Novaya zhizn'* (Oct. 20 and 26, 1917); *Znamya truda* (Oct. 27, 1917); Sukhanov 1919–23, vol. VII, p. 216.

all governments, while at the same time summoning the workers of the warring countries to action, and a 'Decree on Land', abolishing private landed property and transferring it to the exclusive use of the actual cultivators. Finally, the congress established a government, the Soviet of People's Commissars (*Sovnarkom*), which consisted exclusively of Bolsheviks, as the Left SRs and the remaining Menshevik-Internationalists refused to participate in a government without the defencists. The latter, for their part, wanted no part in any government that included Bolsheviks. The congress closed in the early morning of 27 October.

Workers' Attitudes towards the Insurrection

Once the insurrection became an accomplished fact, Petrograd's workers gave it their overwhelming support. Their previous doubts and hesitations had not been over the principle of a violent seizure of power. They had their source, rather, in the fear of bloodshed and defeat. But once the insurrection was underway, there was no doubt about the outcome that the vast majority of workers desired.

Opposition to the victorious insurrection and to the establishment of a government based on the soviets was very limited. (The issue of the party composition of the government that arose on 27 October will be treated presently.) Not unexpectedly, the main opposition came from printers. The immediate issue for them was freedom of the press, since the Military-Revolutionary Council had closed the non-socialist papers. But behind the protest over these closures was, in fact, a rejection of the legitimacy of the insurrection itself. On 27 October, the Delegates' Assembly of the Union of Typographical Workers adopted the following resolution by a vote of 173 to 60:

> Considering that freedom of the press is an inalienable right of the proletarians and of all citizens, that freedom of the press was won by the entire Russian people, that restriction of freedom of the press deprives other parties, including socialists, of the right of freedom of expression of their views, that abolition of freedom of the press by alleged representatives of the working class opens the way to counterrevolutionaries of all shades and makes election campaigning for the Constituent Assembly impossible, the delegates' assembly mandates the executive to defend freedom of the press by all available means up to and including a general strike.[5]

5 *Delo naroda* (Oct. 28, 1917).

Other resolutions refusing to recognise the 'Bolshevik government' were adopted by the workers of the State-Document Printing House, the printing offices of the Ministry of Internal Affairs, the Bulletin of the Provisional Government, the SRs' *Delo naroda*, the Ekateringof Printing House, as well as by the Executive Committee of the Union of Cardboard Workers[6] and the workers of the Municipal Power Station on the Fontanka Canal.[7]

The significance of these resolutions was, however, limited. This was clearly demonstrated by the brief strike at State-Document Printing House, which, besides skilled printers, employed a large number of paper workers. S. Arbuzov, a carpenter and Bolshevik, was sent there on 26 October by the Military-Revolutionary Committee to replace the commissar who had been appointed by the Provisional Government. A general assembly of all the employees was convened, at which Arbuzov presented himself. According to his report, a minority of workers, led by the office employees, refused to recognise him. The factory committee suggested that he leave until it could resolve the conflict and promised to call him back the next day. When he called the next day, someone grabbed the phone from the chairman of the factory committee, declared that he was the legitimate commissar and that he would have nothing to do with representatives of the Military-Revolutionary Committee. Meanwhile, the Military-Revolutionary Committee learned that an appeal to the population issued by Kerenskii against the Soviet government was being printed at this plant. Arbuzov arrived with a detachment of armed men to find 23 workers and the former commissar, a Menshevik, with the stereotypes of the appeal and 600 printed copies. When Arbuzov's men proceeded to destroy these, a strike broke out, involving, according to Arbuzov, 60–90 employees of the total of 965.[8] A meeting of those on strike adopted the following resolution:

> Not to consider this government a government of revolutionary democracy but one only of the Bolshevik Party of the Petrograd Soviet. Considering this government illegitimate, we will support with all our might the Committee for the Salvation of the Fatherland and the Revolution, in which all of revolutionary democracy is participating.[9]

6 Popov 1918, pp. 362–3.

7 'V Oktyabre v raionakh Petrograda' (henceforth cited as V Oktyabre), *Krasnaya letopis*, no. 2 (23) (1927), p. 178.

8 Dok. Okt., pp. 855–6.

9 Popov 1918, p. 362.

On 28 October, the workers who had joined the strike dropped out but the technicians and office employees continued to strike. The workers held a meeting that adopted the following resolution:

> We, workers, find the strike of the employees unacceptable and disastrous, since the lack of trust will call forth anarchy in the country, further aggravate the economic disorganisation and accelerate the country's ruin, and we, therefore, mandate our presidium to inform the Union of Technicians and Office Employees that they should resume work on 30 October on a common basis.[10]

Novaya zhizn' reported on this conflict:

> As is known, [the printing house], dissatisfied with the insurrection, decided to strike. One of the shifts on Saturday evening ended work early. The engineers decided not to work at all on Monday. After listening to speeches from various orators, calling not to intensify the split within democracy through isolated strike actions, both meetings [of the factory committee and of the paper workers] rejected the strike as a means of struggle against the adventurists ...
>
> The attitude towards the government is most varied. There is no unity in this opportunist plant.[11]

Those still on strike returned to work on 30 October.

As this incident shows, the more educated elements of 'revolutionary democracy' (office employees, engineers, state functionaries, but also teachers, doctors, and others) were prepared to strike against the new government. But among workers who opposed the new regime, there was a reluctance to do so, since they considered the deposed government a much worse option. And at that very moment, Kerenskii was on his way to Petrograd with an army of Cossacks led by General Krasnov, a known 'Kornilovist'.

The same logic could be observed among railway workers, especially the line workers (to be distinguished from the industrial workers in the depots and workshops), many of whom also opposed the new government. At a conference of the main railroad committee in Moscow in mid-November, the delegate of the Samara-Zlatoust Railroad reported: 'I won't say that our line consisted of

10 Dok. Okt. p. 890. *Novaya zhizn'*.

11 *Novaya zhizn'*, Octo. 30, 1917.

Bolsheviks. In its majority, it is against the Bolsheviks. But a collision is taking place – those who are against the Bolsheviks have to defend a government which does not satisfy us'. The delegate from the Libavo-Ramenskaya Railroad similarly reported that the first news of the insurrection was met with great hostility. 'To put down the Bolsheviks, we were ready to rise up, arms in hand. But at the same time, a new government was being constructed, and we were not at all sure that the Committee of Salvation represented an organ that would save the revolution rather than the counterrevolution. If Kerenskii had obtained reinforcements and made war on Petrograd, we would not be meeting here now – we would be at home working in blood up to our knees'.[12]

Sukhanov's reaction was similar. He was opposed to the new government but he considered the alternative, the Committee of Salvation created by the defencists, incomparably worse. One of the latter's more 'reasonable' members, who had been a member of the old TsIK, proposed 'to assemble troops and scatter that scum [*svoloch'*]' – a reference to the Congress of Soviets.

> It was not just a mood. It was the programme of the Menshevik-SR wreckage of those days. Under the banner of the 'Committee of Salvation', the Mensheviks, in coalition with the almost-Kadets, the [right-wing SRs] Avksent'ev and Shreider, began work on restoring the *Kerenshchina* [the Kerenskii regime] ... In reality, all these elements – a microcosm of the Democratic Conference but without the Bolsheviks – were loyal allies of Kerenskii, who was marching on Petrograd in a Kornilovist crusade ... The *Kerenshchina* now was impossible, except as a *Kornilovshchina*. For it was impossible to resurrect it except by a successful, victorious *kornilovshchina*. And that would lead to the total defeat of the revolution – not to the sham dictatorship of Kerenskii, but to a genuine Kornilovist dictatorship of the stock exchange and the bayonet ... But the debris of the former, once all-powerful, Soviet bloc refused to understand this at the time.[13]

The main opposition within the ranks of 'revolutionary democracy' came from the 'democratic intelligentsia' and elements socially close to it. The vast majority of bank employees and state functionaries went on strike when Military-Revolutionary Committee commissars appeared at their places of work. This was the first ever strike of employees of government institutions. Also opposed to the government were the Union of the Toiling Intelligentsia, the Union of

12 A. Tanyaev 1915, pp. 141–2.

13 Sukhanov 1919–23, vol. VII, pp. 230–1.

Engineers, the Union of Judges, the Council of the Petrograd Society of Journalists, the Executive Bureau of the Socialist Group of Engineers, the All-Russian Society of Editors, the Union of Democratic Clergy, the office workers of the Baltic ship-building factory and of the Dyuflon factory, the General Assembly of Teachers and Students of the Petrograd Teachers' Institute, The Union of Pedagogical Councils, the Socialist Collective of the Nikolaev Engineering Institute, the Students of the Higher Women's Courses, and the United Petrograd Students.[14]

The following resolution adopted by the Executive Bureau of Socialist Engineers gives a clear sense of the depth of hostility to the October Insurrection within this social stratum:

> A band of utopians and demagogues, exploiting the fatigue and dissatisfaction of the soldiers and workers, by means of utopian appeals to social revolution, through deliberate deceit and slander of the Provisional Government, has drawn behind it benighted masses and, against the will of the vast part of the Russian people, on the eve of the convocation of the Constituent Assembly, has seized power in the capitals and in certain cities of Russia. With the aid of arrests, violence against the free word and press, with the aid of terror, this gang of usurpers is trying to hold onto power. The Bureau of the Socialist Group of Engineers, decisively protesting against the seizure that has taken place, against the arrest of the people's ministers, against the order to arrest Kerenskii, against murders, violence, against the closure of newspapers, persecutions and terror, declares that the acts of the usurpers have nothing in common with socialist ideals and that they destroy the freedom won by the people. The Bureau of the Socialist Group of Engineers warns the workers and soldiers against the continuing attempts to deceive their trust with utopian, borrowed, paper decrees and against the baiting of all of democratic Russia, and it declares that genuine socialists cannot give the slightest support either to the usurpers of power or to those who do not decisively and firmly break with them.[15]

Such deep hostility could not be found among the small minority of workers who still supported the defencists. The call to break with those who refused to

14 Popov 1918, pp. 363–78, *passim*.

15 Ibid, p. 372.

break with the Bolsheviks, with the 'dark masses', was in fact a call to break with the vast majority of workers and soldiers. In many public institutions, lower-level white-collar employees refused to support their higher-ups that struck and they condemned their action as sabotage. Such was the position that was adopted, among others, by the Union of Junior Employees of State, Educational and Other Organisations, the workers and office employees of the City Duma, the Union of Trade and Industrial (white-collar) Employees, the Junior Employees of the Ministry of Education.[16]

It would be wrong to attribute the hostility among the left-leaning intelligentsia to the way in which the transfer of power occurred. Like the defencists who walked out of the Congress of Soviets, most of the 'democratic intelligentsia' was opposed to the very idea of a government based upon the soviets. And the sources of this opposition predated the October Insurrection. The Menshevik-Internationalist historian and critic, V.P. Polonskii, himself hostile to what he called the 'craziness [*sumsbrodstvo*] of Bolshevism', wrote the following end-of-the year survey of Russian journalism, 'that collective physiognomy that until recently reflected the soul of our so-called intelligentsia, our spiritual aristocracy':

> One would be hard pressed to find another group of people, apart from the intelligentsia, in whose thinking and moods the revolution has wreaked more cruel havoc.
>
> I have before me a pile of newspapers, magazines, brochures. Amidst the current material, one most often encounters the old, most sensitive theme of our intelligentsia's consciousness – the theme of 'the intelligentsia and the people'.
>
> And as one reads, a picture emerges that is most unexpected. Until recently, the predominant type of *intelligent* was the *intelligent-narodnik* [populist], the well-wisher, kindly and sympathetically sighing over the lot of our 'younger brother'. But, alas, this type is now an anachronism. In his place has appeared the malevolent *intelligent*, hostile to the *muzhik*, to the worker, to the entire benighted, toiling mass.
>
> The contemporary ones are no longer striving, as before, to fill in some sort of abyss that separates them from the *muzhik*. On the contrary, they want to demarcate themselves from the *muzhik* with a clear and impassable line …

16 Dok. Okt., pp. 368, 574, 575; S. Volin 1962.

> Such is the emerging, portentous confusion. It manifests itself with great clarity in the literature. In a great number of articles devoted to the people and the intelligentsia, the people is treated as a benighted, brutalised, grasping, unbridled mass, a rabble. And its present leaders – as demagogues, worthless nullities, émigrés, careerists, who have adopted the motto of the bourgeoisie of old France: Après nous, le déluge …
>
> If you will recall what yesterday's sympathizers and advocates for the people have written of late about 'mob rule', the extremely alarming fact of our present existence will appear indisputable: the intelligentsia has completed its leave-taking from the people. The *intelligenty* had just enough powder left to bid good night to the 'one who suffers all in the name of Christ, whose stern eyes do not weep, whose hurting mouth does not complain'.
>
> And that one, the eternal sufferer, had only to rise to his feet, to mightily straighten up his shoulders and take a deep breath for the intelligentsia to feel disillusioned.
>
> And it is not the excesses of the October Days, nor the craziness of Bolshevism that are the reason for this. The departure of the intelligentsia, the transformation of the 'populists' into 'evil-wishers', began long ago, almost on the day after the [February] revolution …
>
> Writers and poets, essayists and artists (not all, of course, but many, many) have turned their backs on the people. 'You have stood up on your feet too soon. You are a rank barbarian. Your path is not ours'.[17]

In contrast to the intelligentsia, the vast majority of Petrograd's workers enthusiastically welcomed the insurrection. Resolutions were adopted by every type of factory and among every stratum, from the metalworkers in the Vyborg district to the textile workers in the Nevskii district and also most workers in the printing trade. Typical of the position of the 'conscious metalworkers' was the following unanimous resolution:

> We, the workers of the Rozenkrantz factory numbering 4,000, send our greetings to the Military-Revolutionary Committee of Petrograd Soviet of Workers' and Soldiers' Deputies and to the All-Russian Congress of Soviets, who have taken the path of struggle, and not accommodation, with the bourgeoisie – the enemies of the workers, soldiers and poorest

17 *Novaya zhizn'* (Jan. 4, 1918).

> peasants, and with that we declare: Comrades, continue along that path, as hard as it might be. On that path, we will die together with you or be victorious.[18]

More interesting, however, are similar resolutions adopted by the workers of the state-owned factories that had long been defencist strongholds.[19] At the Promet pipe factory, whose workforce was mostly female, elections to the Petrograd Soviet on 17 October gave the Bolsheviks 963 votes, the Mensheviks 309 and the SRs 326. But the general assembly of the day shift on 27 October adopted the following resolution unanimously (with 18 abstentions):

> We, workers of the Promet factory ... numbering 1,230 people, having heard the report of comrade Krolikov on the Second All-Russian Congress of Workers' and Soldiers' Deputies and on the formation of a new people's socialist government, send it our greetings and express to it our full confidence and promise our full support in its difficult task of fulfilling the mandate of the congress.
>
> We protest against the formation by the S.D.-Mensheviks and the SR-Defencists of the national Committee of Salvation, [seeing it] as an obstacle to the implementation of the measures that the broad masses of workers, soldiers and peasants are awaiting with growing impatience.[20]

---

18 *Pravda* (Oct. 28, 1917). Similar resolutions from this stratum of workers were adopted by the Sestroretsk Arms Factory (*Znamya truda*, Oct. 28, 1917), the Schlusselburg Soviet and the Schlusselburg Powder Factory (Dok. Okt., p. 566), the Number 2 Dept. of the Putilov Works (*Znamya truda*, Oct. 28, 1917), the Staryi Baranovskii machine-construction factory (Stepanov 1965, p. 274), the Parviainen machine-construction factory (ibid.), the Petrograd Metalworkers' Union (Dok. Okt., p. 346), the Central and District Strike Committees of the Woodworkers' Union (*Znamya truda*, Oct. 28, 1917), the Petrograd Council of Trade Unions (*Novaya zhizn'*, Oct. 27, 1917), the Skorokhod shoe factory (*Triumfal'noe shestvie sovetov* (M., 1963) vol. I, p. 205) (henceforth cited as Dok. Nov.), the Nevskii shoe factory (*Izvestiya*, Nov. 3, 1917), the Needleworkers' Union (*Pravda*, 2 Nov. 1917), and many others.

19 Such resolutions of support were passed by Patronnyi (Dok. Okt., p. 564), Promet (ibid., p. 514), Obukhovskii steel mill (*Pravda*, Nov, 6, 1917), Aleksandrovskii locomotive factory (*Izvestiya*, 1 Nov. 1917) – both in the Nevskii District – and the Soviet of the Kolpino District, site of the Izhorskii factory (TsGA SPb f. 171, d. 1, l. 11).

20 *Pravda*, (28 Oct. 1917).

The workers of the railway workshops, also long-time supporters of the SRs, responded in similar fashion,[21] as did the (mainly women) workers of textile mills, the food and rubber factories.[22]

Even more telling was the rank-and-file opposition among printing workers to the position of their union's executive. The resolution of a joint meeting of workers of the Orbit and Rabochaya pechat' printing houses on 28 October stated:

> We, the workers of these printing houses, having heard the report of comrade Venediktov about the meeting of delegates on 27 October, in which he said that the Executive had poorly informed the printers of the meeting that has taken place and where, thanks to the incomplete representation, a vile resolution, proposed by a certain Rubin, was incorrectly adopted, which censured the Revolutionary committee for its having allegedly shut down the socialist press.

After a discussion of the report, the following resolution was adopted:

> We, the workers of the given printing houses, protest against the actions of the Executive of our union that poorly informed the workers of the forthcoming delegates' meeting, and for that reason, we, certain printing establishments of the Petrograd district, not knowing about the meeting, could not attend it, and therefore we do not assume responsibility for the decision of the delegates' council. Further, having heard the resolution adopted at the delegates' meeting and printed in the paper *Delo naroda* on 28 October, we declare that we are deeply angered by it and we consider it unworthy of worker-printers and we protest against it in the most forceful fashion. We declare that the sort of delegates' council that adopts similar resolutions cannot express our will, but only the will of the bourgeois assassins of the people. Therefore, we express our complete lack of con-

21 Locomotive Workshops of the Nikolaevskii Railroad (Popov, *Oktyabr'skii perevorot*, p. 314) and Main Workshops of the North-West Railroad (ibid.).

22 Union of Textile Workers (Perazich 1927, p. 97), the Nevka textile mill (*Pravda*, Oct. 30, 1917), Schlusselburg cotton-printing factory (Dok. Okt., p. 560), Novaya bumagopryadil'nya textile mill (*Izvestiya*, Nov. 2, 1917), Leont'ev Brothers (*Pravda*, Nov. 3, 1917), Voronin and Co. textile mills (ibid., 31 Oct 1917), Kozhevnikovskaya textile mill (*V Oktyabre*, p. 178), Shaposhnikova tobacco factory (Dok. Okt., p. 346), the food-processing factories of the Petrograd Food Authority (Popov 1918, p. 309), the Treugol'nik rubber factory (*Znamya truda*, Oct, 28, 1917) and others.

> fidence in the Executive of the union, which purposely poorly informed of the meeting, and also in the delegates' council for its resolution, and, addressing the proletarians of Petrograd, we declare that we are marching together with them and not with the likes of this executive and delegates' council.
>
> Long live the Soviet of workers' and soldiers' deputies!
>
> Long live the revolutionary people!
>
> Down with traitors of the working class, like the Rubins and his like![23]

A revealing incident took place at the press where the Menshevik-Internationalists' paper, *Novaya zhizn'*, was printed. The 29 October edition of the paper printed a protest on the part of the editors against the typesetters who had refused to print a number of documents, including one of Kerenskii's orders, General Krasnov's appeal to the Cossacks, and a report from the City Duma. The Menshevik-Internationalists had adopted a neutral position in the incipient civil war, but the editors had been absent when the typesetters, who had summoned the district commissar for support, opposed the technicians, who demanded that the documents be printed.[24] The next day, the workers met in a general assembly that decided, with only one opposing vote and five abstentions, to condemn the majority of the executive of the Printers' Union, whom they accused of spreading false information about the actions of the Military-Revolutionary Committee among the city's printers and were calling to sabotage the decision 'of the revolutionary government of workers and peasants regarding the prohibition on printing appeals that are of a purely pogrom nature and false information that provokes panic and, as a consequence, bloodshed'.

> We denounce as disgraceful this criminal activity of a part of our 'executive', which is leading to a split in our proletarian ranks and will be of service only to our class enemies. We loudly declare that we will with all our might support the revolutionary government of workers and peasants that will lead to peace and the Constituent Assembly.

23 *Pravda* (Nov. 4, 1917).

24 *Novaya zhizn'* (Oct. 29, 1917).

> At a moment when the people is destroying the rotten roots of the capitalist system and giving power to its genuine representatives, we, printers, cannot use our labour to print the 'orders' of Kerenskii, who has been overthrown by the people, and, therefore, we recognise the actions of our comrade type-setters as correct. And if in the future our support is required by the Revolutionary Committee, then we will always be prepared to give it.[25]

Only one person voted against the resolution and five abstained. The dissatisfaction with the defencist majority of the union executive soon led to a Menshevik-Internationalist majority and, for a brief period after that, to a Bolshevik majority in the leadership.[26]

After the October Revolution, the Mensheviks and SRs, and following them many Western historians, emphasised the fact that in October, in contrast to February, the masses were not in the streets. This was cited as proof that the October Revolution was not a popular revolution, but a military coup lacking popular legitimacy. 'Look at the streets', wrote the Menshevik-defencists' *Rabochaya gazeta*. 'They are empty in the working-class districts. There are no triumphal marches, no red banners going to meet the victors ... The Bolsheviks will barely hold out a week'.[27] S.P. Melgunov, a right-wing populist and historian, similarly observed that the factories kept working on 25 October. 'Mass participation of genuine workers in the actions of 25 October cannot be claimed, even though, in theory, the factory committees were supposed to organise the insurrection. Work in the factories and mills was not stopped on the morning of the day'.[28]

But the comparison with February wilfully ignores the very different circumstances of October. The February Revolution was a spontaneous movement that pitted masses of unarmed workers against a regime that had vast repressive forces at its disposal. The workers' strike and demonstrations played a decisive role, but as a *moral* force that allowed the workers to draw the soldiers to their side. The mass strikes and street demonstrations created an atmosphere in which the soldiers could feel that their participation in the movement could end in the overthrow of the regime rather than a military tribunal and executions. The street battles in which workers participated took place for the most part on the last two days of the revolution and their main goal was to disarm the

---

25 *Pravda* (Nov. 2, 1917).

26 *Iskra* (21 Oct 1917); Popov 1918, p. 315.

27 *Rabochaya gazeta* (Oct. 27, 1917).

28 S.P. Melgunov 1953, p. 106; S.P. Melgunov 1972, p. 65.

police. By contrast, in October, the main armed forces in the city had already been won over before the uprising. The insurrectionists' task was to occupy strategic buildings and disarm the last supporters of the old regime. There was no call for mass actions.

But more to the point, after eight months of disappointment and frustration, and in the face of the advancing economic catastrophe and the threatening military situation, is there any wonder that workers did not pour into the streets in triumphal processions? The October Revolution without doubt raised the workers' hopes. They would not have supported it otherwise. But at the same time, it was an act of desperation to save the February Revolution from the looming threat of counter-revolution. And the workers were aware that the odds of success were not good.

Finally, those who insist on the lack of mass participation in the October Revolution with the aim of denying it popular legitimacy ignore the fact that the insurrection's leaders did not want the masses in the streets. Trotsky writes that after the traumatic experience of the July Days, the leaders feared that any unnecessary bloodshed would have a demoralising effect on workers.[29] Indeed, the Bolsheviks went to great efforts to persuade workers to stay at work. An appeal to the workers signed jointly by the Petrograd Soviet, the Petrograd Trade-Union Council and the Central Soviet of Factory Committees appeared in bold type on the front page of the 27 October edition of *Pravda*:

> Strikes and demonstrations on the part of the worker masses in Petrograd only do harm. We ask you immediately to end all economic and political strikes. Everyone should be at work and producing in full order. The new government of Soviets needs the work of the factories and all enterprises, since any disruption of work creates new difficulties for us, and there are enough of them as it is. Everyone at his place! The best way to support the new government of Soviets in these days is to do one's job. Long live the firm restraint of the proletariat![30]

The delegates' assembly of the Petrograd Woodworkers' Union, whose members were on strike on 25 October, voted unanimously to end the action, declaring that 'every worker in these days must be at his place and, by that, prove his support for the new government. Order, restraint, calm and vigilance'.[31]

---

29 Trotsky 1965, vol. III, ch. VI.

30 *Pravda* (Oct. 27, 1917).

31 Ibid.

Sukhanov, who had opposed the insurrection and was a severe critic of the new regime, recalled that 'the Mensheviks and SRs comforted themselves for several months afterward with this idea of a military conspiracy, poking it into the eye of the Bolsheviks'.

> Apparently, in the view of these witty people, an insurrection of the proletariat and of the garrison necessarily required the active participation and mass action in the streets of workers and soldiers. But there was nothing for them to do in the streets. They didn't have an enemy that required their mass action, their armed force, battles, barricades, etc. This was an especially happy circumstance of our October insurrection, for which afterwards they brand it a military conspiracy, almost a palace coup.
>
> These witty people would do better to look and ask: Did the Petrograd proletariat sympathise or did it not with the organisers of the October insurrection? Were they with the Bolsheviks, or did the Bolsheviks act independently of, and against, their will? Were they on the side of the victorious insurrection, were they neutral, or were they against it?
>
> There can be no two answers here. Yes, the Bolsheviks acted on the mandate of the Petersburg workers and soldiers. And they carried out the insurrection, throwing into it as many (very little!) forces as were necessary for its successful realisation. No, pardon me: through carelessness and clumsiness, the Bolsheviks threw into it many more forces than were necessary. But that has no relationship whatsoever to the understanding of the insurrection itself.[32]

Some authors point out the absence of any kind of ferocity and even the presence of a certain gentle attitude on the part of the workers' Red Guards towards their adversaries. This, they argue, indicated that support for the uprising even among its active participants was rather half-hearted. This mildness was, indeed, a rather remarkable characteristic of the workers who took part in the insurrection. An army officer, one of the defenders of the Winter Palace, gave this account of the 'storming':

> Small groups of red guards began to penetrate the Winter Palace [to agitate among its defenders] ... While the groups of red guards were not yet numerous, we disarmed them, and this disarming was done in an amicable way, without any conflict. However, the red guards became

32 Sukhanov 1919–23, vol. VII, p. 224.

> more and more numerous. Sailors and soldiers of the Pavlov Regiment appeared. Disarming began in reverse – of the Junkers, and, once again, it was done in a rather peaceful fashion ... [When the actual storming began] large masses of red guards, sailors, Pavlovtsy, etc. penetrated into the Winter Palace. They did not want bloodshed. We were forced to surrender.[33]

Skorinko, the young Red Guard from the Putilov factory, recalled the lenient treatment by the Red Guards of the White prisoners they had captured in the fighting outside of Petrograd at the end of October:

> Executions were something alien to us. We regarded with disgust the soldiers who were demanding them. Because of that, later the workers and peasants would pay with their own blood. General Krasnov, who was released on his word of honour, ran off to the Don and repaid our nobility in a manner befitting a general. [He organised a White Army there.][34]

Melgunov also noted a rather gentle attitude, even a certain embarrassment, in the relations between the arrested ministers and the Red Guards and sailors who were escorting them to jail. They exchanged comments on the way and these developed into conversations. 'How will you manage without the intelligentsia', Tereshchenko, a big capitalist, asked one of the sailors.[35] Both Sukhanov and Melgunov interpreted the lack of ferocity as a lack of determination and fighting spirit. But that is to misread the atmosphere of the period. The main argument of the defencists to workers had been that the insurrection would lead to bloodshed and civil war, as in the July Days, but only much worse. The participants in the insurrection, therefore, had every reason to avoid unnecessary violence in order not to frighten away the wavering elements of revolutionary democracy. In their speeches on 25 October, both Lenin and Trotsky emphasised the 'exclusively bloodless' character of the insurrection. I.P. Flerovsky, a Bolshevik sailor on the battleship *Aurora*, recalled how on the fateful night of 25 October, the crew 'decided to wait out just another quarter of an hour [before firing on the Winter Palace], sensing by instinct the possibility of a change of circumstances'. Trotsky commented on this: 'By "instinct",

33 Dok. Okt., pp. 426.

34 Skorinko 1923, p. 152.

35 Melgunov 1972, pp. 90–1.

one should understand the stubborn hope that the matter would be settled uniquely through demonstrative methods'.[36]

The savagery and the terror of the civil war were still ahead. Despite the acute social polarisation, on the personal level, the workers' attitude was often surprisingly tolerant. An incident from Moscow, where the fighting in October was more prolonged and much bloodier than in Petrograd, illustrates this well. A delegate sent by hospitalised Red Guards read the following message to the Moscow Soviet in early November:

> [Our group of wounded] ... thanks the military-aviation school for the wine it sent us and which is being distributed, [and] although it was meant only for the fighters for freedom, but since Junkers and officers are also lying among us and we say in the hospital that there can be no party distinctions, we decided among ourselves to share the wine and we showed the Junkers that the Bolsheviks are not so terrible. And when the doctor came and asked: Should I give some to the Junkers? – we decided to give it to them, and in case the Aviation school makes inquiries, it should not have complaints against the hospital for giving a portion to the Junkers.[37]

The Question of a 'Homogeneous Socialist Government'

If there were illusions that the transfer of power would allow the new government immediately to tackle the economic and political crises, they were soon dispelled. On the morning of 27 October, General Krasnov's armoured train mounted with artillery reached the town of Gatchina in the approaches to Petrograd. Meeting no resistance there, he proceeded the next day to Tsarskoe selo, less than an hour from the capital. There his forces easily scattered the Red Guards who had come out from Petrograd to confront him. The local garrison, 16,000 soldiers with no will to fight, remained neutral. That night, timed with Krasnov's advance, the Junkers in Petrograd rose up. That same day, on 28 October, Vikzhel, the All-Russian Executive Committee of the Railway Union, which was led by Menshevik-Internationalists, presented the Soviet government with an ultimatum: it would call a general railway strike unless a 'homogenous socialist government' was formed, that is, a coalition government

36 Trotsky 1965, vol. III, p. 250. See also Sukhanov 1919–23, vol. VII, p. 202.

37 S.A. Piontkovskii 1928, p. 53.

of all the socialist parties from Bolsheviks on the left to Popular Socialists on the right. Meanwhile, reports were coming from Moscow that the insurrection there was in serious difficulty and that much blood was flowing.

The fortunes of the October Insurrection seemed to be hanging on a thread. Malakhovskii recalled the mood among the Vyborg district Red Guards:

> From the morning of the 28th, news of our defeats began to arrive. The Junkers rose up in Petrograd. For several minutes, there was despondency at our headquarters. The spectre of defeat rose up before us. Then we shook it off. It was – it wasn't. There will be something to remember: if only for four days, but we chased out the capitalist ministers.[38]

It was at that moment that the issue of the political isolation of the exclusively Bolshevik government formed by the Soviet Congress and the need for a coalition of the socialist parties, a 'homogeneous socialist government', became the subject of lively discussion in the factories. That formula had long been the Menshevik-Internationalists' position, and now, together with the Left SRs, they were energetically organising workers' meetings with the aim of pressing the Bolsheviks and the defencists to reach an agreement.[39]

The Bolsheviks, including Lenin and Trotsky, who were the leaders of the party's left wing, were not insisting on an exclusively Bolshevik government, although the latter without doubt wanted nothing to do with the defencists, who, in their view, would only paralyse the new government. The Bolsheviks had, in fact, invited the Left SRs, the only party that did not walk out of the Soviet Congress, to join in a coalition government. But the latter rejected the offer, insisting, along with the Menshevik-Internationalists, on an all-socialist coalition.[40] But, regardless of what Lenin and Trotsky might have thought, a socialist coalition was also the position of the Bolshevik party. All the major workers' organisations in Petrograd – the Soviet, the Central Soviet of Factory Committees, the Petrograd Council of Trade Unions – that by then were firmly under Bolshevik leadership, came out publicly in favour of a unified socialist government.

On the other hand, the Bolshevik party was firm that it would not concede the principle of soviet power, i.e. a government created by and responsible to the soviets. And that was the problem with the formula of a 'homogeneous

38 Malakhovskii 1925, p. 26.

39 *Znamya truda* (Oct. 29, 1917).

40 Popov 1918, p. 386.

socialist government': it left open the central question – on what basis? There were only two positions that had any significant support among workers. One, which was promoted by Mensheviks-Internationalists and Left SRs, called for a 'homogeneous revolutionary-democratic government' from Bolsheviks on the left to the Popular Socialists on the right. The other, defended by the Bolsheviks, insisted that any coalition be responsible to the soviets, in the form of the newly elected TsIK, the Central Executive Committee of Soviets. That meant that the Bolsheviks would be a majority in the government, as they had been a strong majority at the Soviet Congress.

There was also a third position, defended by the SR and Menshevik defencists, but with no perceptible worker support. These parties were opposed to the very principle of a government responsible to the soviets and to a Bolshevik majority. At most, the soviets could be one institution among others that constituted the basis of the government. But at one point, these parties were even insisting on the transfer of power to the Committee of Salvation or to the Petrograd City Duma, both of which included representatives of the propertied classes. That, of course, would have been a complete negation of the October insurrection.

Thus, while the Bolsheviks' position was clear to workers, that of the Menshevik-Internationalists and Left SRs was the source of considerable confusion. Workers who pronounced themselves in support of the demand for an all-socialist coalition understood that to mean a coalition government responsible to the soviets. But the Menshevik-Internationalists and Left SRs who were promoting that demand saw it as an alternative to soviet power, which they considered to be too narrow a base for an effective revolutionary government. They argued that the soviets represented only a part of revolutionary democracy, that there were significant elements that were not attached to the soviets but organised around other institutions, such as cooperatives, municipal dumas, and their like. As a result, a government responsible exclusively to the soviets would be a dictatorship of one part of democracy against the other.[41]

This explains the opposition of these parties to a Bolshevik majority in the proposed coalition. At one point, the TsIK (with its Bolshevik majority) invited the parties that had left the congress, as well as Vikzhel, the Post-Telegraph Union (also led by Menshevik-Internationalists) and the socialist fractions of the Moscow and Petrograd Dumas, to join an enlarged TsIK. But the Menshevik-Internationalists rejected this proposal since it did not change the fact that

41 See, for example, *Iskra* (Oct. 31, 1917).

the government was responsible uniquely to the TsIK, in which the Bolsheviks would still be a majority. An editorial by B.V. Bazarov in *Novaya zhizn'* made the following comment on this proposal: either the present government was strong enough to govern along the lines that the Bolsheviks desired – and if so, why dilute it with 'petty-bourgeois' elements? – or else, it was not strong enough (as the Menshevik-Internationalists argued). In that case, the other parties had to participate at least on an equal basis with the Bolsheviks.[42]

Bazarov's thinking was based on the following considerations. The Bolsheviks really represented only the urban workers. Even if they could obtain the passive support of the peasants, such a regime could not survive. Moreover, its exclusively working-class base would inevitably move it to adopt socialist measures, which would be disastrous, given Russia's socio-economic backwardness. This, of course, posed the question: if a government responsible to the soviets could count on the active support of workers and possibly the passive support of the peasantry, what other social forces were missing? Missing, in the view of the Menshevik-Internationalists and Left SRs, were the 'middle strata' – the urban petty-bourgeoisie, the wealthier peasants, and above all the 'democratic intelligentsia'. These supported the defencists.

And so, the defencists feared a break with the bourgeoisie, and that made them deny the latter's counterrevolutionary position. The internationalists, on their part, while agreeing with the Bolsheviks that the propertied classes wanted to crush the revolution, feared a break with the defencists, around whom, so they argued, the 'middle strata', and above all the left-leaning intelligentsia, were grouped. An editorial in *Novaya zhizn'* entitled '2 × 2 = 5' observed that in some factories the workers' meetings were adopting resolutions that called for a coalition of all socialist parties and at the same time insisted that it be responsible to the new TsIK elected at the Congress of Soviets. But such a government, observed the editorialist, would have a Bolshevik majority. And yet, this government based upon the TsIK shows daily that it cannot govern. It issues decrees 'like pancakes' and they have no practical effect. One might ask, continued the editorialist, why a government that is supported by broad masses of workers and soldiers cannot govern effectively. The Bolsheviks explain the government's difficulties by the sabotage of the intelligentsia, the educated elements, who support the defencist parties. But, continued the editorialist, even if one ignores the government's incompetence and accepts the Bolsheviks' explanation, even if one concedes that the defencists do not have the support of the popular masses, but only of intellectual forces, even then concessions

42 *Novaya zhizn'* (Nov, 3, 1917).

would be necessary, since 'the proletariat cannot govern without the intelligentsia'. And for that reason, the TsIK can be only one of the institutions to which the government must answer.[43]

Among Bolsheviks, there was no disagreement that the government should be responsible exclusively to the soviets and on the need to vigorously prosecute the civil war being waged in Moscow and outside Petrograd. But while the left wing of the party considered that the participation of the defencists in a government would only block necessary revolutionary measures, the centrists and moderates wanted to give an all-socialist coalition, if it was possible, a chance.

The internationalists' position in favour of a homogeneous socialist government, but one not responsible uniquely to the soviets, and their neutrality in the incipient civil war, for which they blamed both sides equally, had limited support among workers: mostly workers of small metalworking and printing plants, of large state enterprises producing ordnance; and some large private factories also employing mostly unskilled labour.

Workers in small factories, and the same was true for most printers, did not share the same attachment to the value of 'class independence' as did the 'conscious' metalworkers. They lacked confidence in the potential of the working class and could not see themselves as the leading force in society, especially in the face of the hostility of the 'middle strata'. At the end of October, the general assembly of the Atlas foundry and pipe factory (about 400 workers) adopted the following resolution with only five abstentions:

> 1. We demand an end to this fratricidal war that is continuing thanks to inter-party disagreements, which are leading the revolution to ruin.
>
> 2. We demand the immediate creation of a homogeneous socialist government from Bolsheviks to Popular Socialists.
>
> 3. We protest against the seizure of power by the one party of Bolsheviks, whose tactics, along with those of the defencist parties that support a coalition with the bourgeoisie, have brought the country to civil war ...
>
> We adhere to the position, adopted by the Left SRs and the Menshevik-Internationalists.[44]

---

43 Ibid. (Nov. 4, 1917).

44 *Znamya truda* (6 Nov. 1917). Similar resolutions from small factories were passed at

The large state-owned factories that supported this position all belonged to the Main Artillery Administration: Arsenal,[45] Orudiinyi,[46] Patronnyi[47] and Kapsyul'nyi.[48] Their workers had only relatively recently adopted the demand for soviet power. The resolution adopted by the Kapsyul'nyi workers, which was proposed jointly by the local Bolsheviks, Left SRs and Menshevik-Internationalists, demanded a united socialist government and the end to civil war within the ranks of democracy. At Arsenal, the workers declared that they would consider counterrevolutionary any party that refused to participate in an all-socialist coalition government. A meeting at Patronnyi on 30 October elected a delegation to go to the Vikzhel negotiations and demand an end to the fighting and immediate agreement on an all-socialist government. The Bolsheviks at this meeting tried in vain to convince these workers that they had to specify the basis of the government they wanted: to whom should it be responsible? The Patronnyi workers had avoided the main bone of contention at the Vikzhel negotiations. Similar resolutions were adopted by the workers of Vargunina, Shapovskaya and the Belgian Paper Mills,[49] the Pal' Textile Mill,[50] the Nevskii Stearine Works[51] and the Siemens-Shukkert Electrotechnical Factory[52] (mostly ordnance production). Vargunina, Pal' and Nevskii Stearine, as well as the Atlas factory, were all in the Nevskii District, which would become the centre of opposition to the Soviet government in the spring of 1918.

All in all, worker support for the Left SR-Menshevik-Internationalist position (but not simply for a socialist coalition) was weak. And even the workers who supported it could not accept neutrality in the armed conflict that these parties were advocating. For example, while a meeting of workers and office employees of the Odner mechanical factory called for a government of Bolsheviks, Mensheviks and SRs, they insisted that 'a victory of Kerenskii's troops would have disastrous consequences for the gains of the revolution'. The resolution adop-

---

Reikhel' (*Novaya zhizn'*, Oct. 30,1917), Odner (ibid., Nov. 1, 1917), Ekval' (Popov 1918, pp. 396–7), the Central Power Station (*Znamya truda*, 3 Nov. 1917), and a joint meeting of Brenner, Bruk, Butt, Aleksandrov and Trainin (*Znamya truda*, Nov. 5, 1917).

45 *Znamya truda* (Nov. 3, 1917).

46 Popov 1918, p. 395.

47 *Iskra* (Nov. 5, 1917).

48 *Novaya zhizn'* (Nov. 3, 1917).

49 Popov 1918, p. 39.

50 *Znamya truda* (Nov. 5, 1917).

51 Ibid.

52 Ibid.

ted at Arsenal (cited above) concluded: 'Considering the advance of Cossack troops on Petrograd, and fearing the violence of reactionary forces that want to suppress the revolution, we consider it necessary to take measures to ensure the most energetic defence of Petrograd'.[53]

The main reason for the relatively weak support for the Left SR-Menshevik-Internationalist position was its rejection of soviet power. Workers had difficulty understanding that. When the Bolshevik Central Committee discussed the demand to allow representation in an enlarged TsIK of groups that had not been represented at the Congress, the representative of the Petersburg Committee made clear: 'That question has already been decided for the masses, and there is no need to speak about some kind of broadened soviets'. He called on the Central Committee to heed the will of the masses and to reject any changes to the TsIK.[54] The Left SR P.P. Proshyan made a similar observation when his fraction in the TsIK met to discuss the Vikzhel's proposal, which would have given the defencists a majority in the new institution to which the coalition government would answer. He argued to reject that proposal out of hand: 'The whole scheme is the result of intellectuals' flabbiness [*intelligentskaia rakhlyabannost'*], a retreat in the face of the horrors of civil war, which they want to end at any price'. In a social revolution, he continued, civil war is unavoidable, and even if it could be temporarily halted, it would inevitably flare up again and in more terrible forms. A socialist coalition government was still possible, he argued, but only on the basis of a government responsible uniquely to the soviets, 'as the workers' mood should make even the defencists more conciliatory'. He was seconded by V.M. Levin: 'The masses would view such an agreement as a rejection of their slogans and would have the impression that all the gains that they are fighting to defend are being yielded without a fight by the leaders of the movement'.[55]

Bazarov, the Menshevik-Internationalist, also had to admit that workers most often coupled their demand for a socialist coalition with the insistence on soviet power. But he attributed this to a lack of political sophistication:

> At some factories at the present time, resolutions have been adopted that demand at the same time a homogeneous democratic government, one based upon an accord of all the socialist parties, and recognition of the current TsIK as the organ to which the government should answer .

53 *Znamya truda* (Nov. 3, 1917).

54 Dok. Nov., p. 23.

55 *Znamya truda* (Nov. 2, 1917).

> The Bolsheviks, who have overwhelming influence among Petrograd's proletariat, never bothered to teach them political arithmetic. The basic rule of parliamentary arithmetic is that the executive power belongs to the predominant party in that organ to which the government is responsible, or else it is formed by all the parties in proportion to their representation in it … But at present, such a government can only be Bolshevik.[56]

There was sometimes an element of confusion among workers who were demanding a socialist coalition. But this was not what Bazarov thought. Some workers wanted to believe that the divisions among the socialist parties were the result of personal and organisational ambitions, rather than differences of principle. In early November, a worker at the Schlusselburg Powder Factory wrote to *Znamya truda*:

> Our socialists are still haggling about who should be in power – the Bolsheviks or the SR-defencists – refusing to see what is happening around them, how the best forces of the vanguard of workers and soldiers, who are decided to die or win, are perishing, while you 'leaders' of the Russian revolution are busy haggling. It is time to come to your senses and end the division … Where is the rest of revolutionary democracy, where is that revolutionary proletariat, the toiling peasantry and soldiers, who sit exhausted in their dugouts? … That is where power should be, but not in the present parties, not in the discord among their 'leaders'. And you should recognise this, if you are genuine socialists, and openly say to the people: 'Yes, we were wrong. The Soviet of workers', soldiers' and peasants' deputies should take power' … And you should fulfil their will in the direction they have designated.[57]

This worker was directing his criticism at all the party leaders. But, in fact, without realising it, he was supporting the Bolsheviks' position.

A similar misunderstanding was in evidence at the Obukhovskii Factory, whose general assembly on 21 October, convened jointly by all the local party groups, decided to send a delegation to the Vikzhel negotiations to demand that the socialist leaders end their squabbling. According to the Left SR B.D. Kamkov, who witnessed the scene, the delegation warned the negotiators: 'If by the morning an agreement has not been reached, the workers will start fighting

56 *Novaya zhizn'* (4 Nov. 1917).

57 *Znamya truda* (Nov. 7, 1917).

among themselves, but first they will finish off all the leaders'. It then read out the workers' resolution:

> The meeting considers that there can be absolutely no return to the former coalition government.
>
> We have resolved: to consider as criminal this state of affairs [the split in revolutionary democracy] and we propose to all workers, regardless of their party affiliation and political convictions, to apply pressure on their political centres in favour of an immediate agreement of all the socialist parties and to form a socialist government on a proportional basis responsible to the Soviets on the basis of the following platforms:
>
> 1. the immediate proposal of a democratic peace.
>
> 2. land to the land committees and abolition of private property of the landed estates.[58]

This, too, was the Bolshevik position. Lenin and Trotsky may not have wanted the defencists in the government but they knew they were in a minority in the party and so did not participate in the Central Committee meeting that accepted Vikzhel's proposal to negotiate an all-socialist coalition. Kamenev gave the following reply to the Obukhovskii delegation:

> Inform the Obukhovtsy that the TsIK stands on the same platform that you are proposing. The TsIK stands on the ground of an agreement and, therefore, it has sent its representatives to the Vikzhel commission. And if the right[-wing] groups will accept that the government should be responsible to the TsIK of the All-Russian Soviet, then an agreement will be reached.[59]

Besides the workers' strong attachment to the soviets as the only legitimate basis of revolutionary power, the other problem with the Left SR and Menshevik-Internationalist position was their neutrality in the incipient civil war. For that position, which Vikzhel had adopted, the workers in Petrograd's railroad workshops and depots condemned their union executive (Vikzhel) as

58 Ibid. (Nov. 2,1917).

59 *Znamya truda* (Nov. 3, 1917).

counterrevolutionary. A meeting of 1,090 workers of the locomotive workshops of the Nikolaevskii Railway resolved unanimously:

> To express our non-confidence in Vikzhel for its openly counterrevolutionary policy. To express confidence in the All-Russian Congress of Soviets of Workers', Soldiers' and Peasants' Deputies that truly expresses our interests and strongly defends the happiness and power of the people. The meeting calls on all our comrade railway workers to rally around their proletarian organisations and it sends greetings to the Petrograd proletariat, which is shedding its blood, and says: 'Comrades! We are with you!'[60]

Some railway workers even prepared to take action against Vikzhel and its supporters. At the Conference of Railway Committees mid-December 1917, which was on the whole hostile to the Bolsheviks, a delegate from the Niloaevskii Railway reported on a meeting of workers of the First and Second Districts of that railroad. It had adopted the following resolution at the end of October:

> Upon full clarification, we recognise the activity of the main railroad committee as supporting Vikzhel and hence Kerenskii ... If in its activity it does not take up the struggle against Kerenskii's troops, then we will arrest it.

This delegate reported that when some of those present at that meeting nevertheless defended Vikzhel, explaining that it wanted to spare the fatherland bloodshed, the workers arrested them.[61] At the same conference, a delegate from Moscow similarly reported:

> In the workshops and among the workers we saw a force such that if we did not adhere to the Bolsheviks, then there would be a settling of accounts with the main railway committees. On some lines, there was an attempt on the part of workers, who had organised into Red Guards, to take active steps to make arrests and even executions.[62]

---

60 Popov 1919, p. 315.

61 Tanyaev 1925, p. 147. See similar reports on the First and Ninth Districts of the railroad at p. 153.

62 Ibid., p. 155.

But there was no violence. In Petrograd and Moscow, the general railway strike that Vikzhel called found very little support, not least, according to the delegates, because the railway committees were afraid of workers of these cities' depots and the workshops.

The main and most coherent support for the Left SR-Menshevik-Internationalist position came not from workers, but from soldiers, office employees and technical personnel. Toward the end of October, a strong movement arose in Petrograd's garrison to force an end to the civil war outside the capital through negotiations. Various army units urged the Military-Revolutionary Committee to allow them to send delegations to talk with General Krasnov's troops.[63] Except for the Guards regiments, there was little stomach in the garrison for fighting. And the following resolution of the draughtsmen of the Putilov factory is consistent with the internationalists' position:

> As unwilling witnesses to the seizure of power by the Bolsheviks and to the fratricidal war that is occurring … [we express] our strong protest against that party that has reached the point of shedding fraternal blood and we adhere to those socialist parties that stand for an immediate end to the civil war and the formation of a socialist government on an equal basis of all socialist parties.[64]

But the vast majority of Petrograd's workers rejected neutrality in the incipient civil war and supported the new Soviet government, even while calling for a coalition with the other socialist parties. But whereas the more moderate workers called for an all-socialist coalition, the more radical ones tended to direct their appeals only to internationalist parties.

Judging from reports to the Bolsheviks' Petersburg committee on 29 October, the more moderate position had strongest support in the Nevskii, Porokhovskii and Narvskii districts, which had long been SR strongholds. Here, according to the reports, workers favoured an agreement of all socialist parties – but in proportion to their representation in the TsIK. They insisted that the government be responsible exclusively to the soviets – no concessions from Soviet power.

---

63 Dok. Okt., p. 758.

64 Popov 1918, p. 399. Similar resolutions were adopted by the office employees of the Putilov Works and Shipyard (*Novaya zhizn'*, Nov. 1, 1917), the Central Committee of the Petrograd Port (ibid., Nov, 3, 1917), All-Russian Post and Telegraph Union (Popov 1918, p. 393), the office employees of the Treugol'nik Rubber Factory (ibid.), and the All-Russian Union of Workers and Employees of the Waterways (*Znamya truda*, Nov. 3, 1917). This was also, of course, the position espoused by Vikzhel.

And they called to defend the revolution against the troops that had been led astray by Kerenskii, although they urged to try to end the civil war by peaceful means. In the meanwhile, they supported the Soviet government as it existed.[65]

But the more radical position definitely had the most support. Typical was the resolution of a meeting of 3,600 workers of the Putilov shipyard, which called for an agreement of the socialist parties and for a merciless struggle against the counterrevolution led by Kerenskii and General Kaledin. Anyone refusing to submit to the Military-Revolutionary Committee or who was taking strike action against the Soviet government – a reference to the striking government and bank employees – should be fired. And it continued:

> … We ask all those who stand for the cause of the workers, soldiers and peasants to censure those leaders, who from purely selfish motives abandoned the Congress of Soviets on 25 October, desiring by that action to split and break the united front of workers, soldiers and peasants. Therefore, we have decided that henceforth there should be no party or fractional disagreements in our midst, and that we all, as one person, will defend to the last drop of blood our new Revolutionary Government – the Congress of Soviets of Workers, Soldiers' and Peasants' Deputies and the Military-Revolution Committee that it created, and all other organisations, such as the Committee to Protect Public Safety and party groups, that do not wish to obey and work in close unity with the All-Russian Congress of Soviets, do not enjoy even the smallest degree of our support and will meet in all their actions that are directed against the Congress of Soviets our decisive and unanimous rebuff. Having walked out of the Congress, they went against the workers, soldiers and peasants. Instead of the slogan of unification, they are trying to introduce fragmentation and internal strife …
>
> We demand that the government be responsible solely to the TsIK … Total rejection of representation in the TsIK of organisations that are not represented in the Soviets …

The report to the Bolshevik Petersburg Committee from the Moscow district of the capital similarly stated that workers wanted a coalition with the internationalists, inasmuch as they stood on the platform of the Second Congress of Soviets, but that most were opposed to the inclusion of defencists, although some would accept them if they adopted the platform of the Soviet Congress. In

65 'V Oktyabre v raionnakh Petrograda', *Krasaya letopis*, no. 2 (23), 1927, pp. 173–4.

the Petrograd district, the workers were angered by negotiations that included the defencists. And a resolution adopted by the Petergof district soviet stated: 'We most categorically condemn those who left the Congress, placing themselves in a position of deserters from the revolution and new allies of the hidden and open counterrevolution'.

Especially striking was the strong support for the new government among women workers, since they had generally been the last to embrace the demand for soviet power in 1917. The textile workers' delegates even clashed with their union executive at the end of October over the latter's refusal to give the new government its full support during the negotiations for a coalition. This issue was thrashed out at an angry meeting of union delegates on 26 November. The delegates were particularly angered by the executive's failure at the beginning of November to hand over 4,000 roubles that the workers had collected for the Military-Revolutionary Committee and for the TsIK. As one stated: 'At a time when we decided to give the money of that part of the proletariat that had declared a merciless struggle against capital, the executive shrank from giving these pennies collected from the workers to that proletariat'. Another exclaimed: 'Shame for this conciliationist policy!' The executive, for its part, explained that at that time it had seemed that an agreement was possible and it had wanted to exert pressure on both sides. Now that it was clear that an agreement was impossible, it unconditionally supported the government.

A preparatory meeting of a Conference of Women Workers on 5 November – 500 delegates claiming to represent 80,000 women workers – voted to censure the Left SR and Menshevik-Internationalists, as well as those Bolshevik leaders who had withheld their full support from the new government during the negotiations to form a coalition. (On the latter, see below.) And they reserved particular condemnation for the Bolshevik leaders who had resigned from the government to protest their party's decision to leave the Vikzhel negotiations on 1 November:

> The conference of women workers calls on all socialist internationalists not to sabotage the peasant [!] revolution, to work in a united revolutionary front with all the Soviet organisations, and it declares to the People's Commissars who left and to the internationalists that the proletariat will not forgive desertion from the field of battle when the worker-peasant government needs a total effort for the huge battle with the capitalists.[66]

66 Popov 1918, pp. 306–7.

The workers of the Vyborg district, as one would expect, also adopted the more radical position on the question of a socialist coalition. But here, even the local Left SRs and Menshevik-Internationalists, in apparent defiance of their own party leaders, also supported that position. On 1 November, the district soviet called a meeting of workers that adopted the following appeal, endorsed jointly by the Bolshevik, Left SR and Menshevik-Internationalist fractions of the soviet:

> Steadfastness, courage, unity! Comrade workers!
>
> We, representatives of the three fractions of the District Soviet of Workers and Soldiers' Deputies, consider it our duty to address to you an appeal to end party quarrels and strife – this is not the time for it, when the blood of workers who stand at the same lathes as you is being shed, when discord among us is mockery over their bodies …
>
> Why do we create hostile camps in our workers' family? Who among us does not understand that discord within our ranks is what the counterrevolution needs? Who among us will not understand that the bourgeoisie, having enlisted the support of those who have split away from the revolutionary proletariat, is leading the suppression of the revolutionary movement? Who among us will help it in the criminal matter? Who among us will with his own hands cede his fate to those whose strongest desire is to smother us? No one, of course. Comrades, there are not and cannot be among us enemies of the working class, enemies of themselves. Among us there are not and cannot be traitors, because that would mean to betray oneself …
>
> Comrade-brothers! Think again! Do not attach significance to trivialities, such as are the party disputes at the present moment. It is not a question of parties now but of the fate of the revolution, the fate of the worldwide slaughter; it is a question of our families not swelling up and dying of hunger – that is what the counterrevolutionaries who are marching against us want. Can it be that we will help them destroy us and our children? No, a thousand times no! The worker is not so dull-witted and stupid as the traitors think. He has suffered, suffered too long. But the cup of patience has overflowed – we no longer have strength to remain silent witnesses to our own destruction, no longer strength to waste time on talk when it is action that is called for …
>
> All as one man to the defence of our just workers' cause. And we will be victorious despite the nets of treachery spread before us, we will be victorious despite the teeth-gnashing of our enemies, we will win on

> the condition of the unity and solidarity of all the socialist forces of the proletariat.
>
> Away with the fractional strife!
>
> Long live the united working class![67]

This was an appeal to unity, but from below and in support of the soviets. The reference to 'those who have split away from the revolutionary proletariat' and who support the bourgeoisie was clearly to the defencists.

On the other hand, a large number of factory meetings adopted resolutions of support for the new government that failed even to mention the question of a coalition government. One has to wonder if this was an oversight, given that all the city's main workers' organisations had publicly pronounced themselves in support of a socialist coalition government.[68]

Among the city's Bolsheviks, one could observe the same range of opinion as in the general worker population, although it was even more skewed toward a radical rejection of participation of defencists in the government. The general assembly of the Bolsheviks of the Vyborg district firmly declared: 'No accommodation or agreement with parties and groups that strive to undermine the proletarian-peasant revolution by conciliationism with the bourgeoisie'.[69] When the Petersburg Committee met on 29 October to discuss the Vikzehl negotiations, the Central Committee's decision to participate in them came in for harsh criticism. The meeting adopted a resolution to the effect that any government had to be responsible exclusively to the soviets and that no concessions from the programme of the Soviet Congress were acceptable. And it

---

67 Raisovety, vol. 1, p. 154. For an earlier declaration, see also Dok. Okt., p. 758.

68 Among these factories were the Schlusselburg Power Factory (*Pravda*, Nov. 4, 1917), Admiralty Shipyards, early November (TsGA SPb 9391/1/11/48), Cable (Pravda, 4 Nov. 1917), Petrograd Tram Depot (*Pravda*, Nov. 1, 1917), Petrograd Aircraft Park (*Pravda*, Nov. 4, 1917), Treugol'nik Rubber Factory (*Pravda*, Nov. 2, 1917), Snaryadnyi (*Znamya truda*, Nov. 17, 1917), Sestroretsk Arms Factory (*Znamya truda.*, Nov. 3, 1917), Kozhevnikovskaya textile mill ('*V Oktyabre*', p. 178), Leont'ev Bros textile mill (*Pravda*, Nov. 3, 1917), Novaya Bumagopryadil'nya textile mill (*Izvestiya*, Nov. 2, 1917), Voronin textile mill (*Pravda*, Nov. 5, 1917), Preparatory Meeting of Women Workers (Popov, *Oktyabr'skii perevorot*, pp. 306–7), Executive of the Needleworkers' Union (*Pravda*, Nov. 2, 1917), meeting of the Conference of 2,000 workers and soldiers in the Moscow District (*Pravda*, Nov. 3, 1917), the food plants of Petrograd Food Authority (Popov 1918, p. 309), delegates' meeting of workers and employees of municipal enterprises (Dok. Okt., p. 573).

69 *Pravda* (Nov. 9, 1917).

too passed over the Vikzhel negotiations and the question of a coalition government in silence.[70]

The Petersburg Committee reconvened on 2 November to discuss the latest developments, in particular the defencists' clear rejection of any government responsible to the soviets. It was reported that representatives of the party's Moscow Committee were meeting with the Central Committee and continuing to insist on a coalition with the defencists. Meanwhile, the Left SRs were threatening to walk out of the TsIK unless a coalition government was formed. And those among the Menshevik-Internationalists who had not walked out of the Soviet Congress on 26 October now left the TsIK in protest against its refusal (by a vote of 40 against 31) to include in the TsIK representatives of organisations other than the soviets. Fearing that the Central Committee might yield to this pressure and reverse its decision to end participation in the Vikzhel negotiations, the Petersburg Committee immediately despatched a delegation to warn it against any retreat from the principle of Soviet power. Ya. G. Fenigshtein summed up the sentiment of the majority of the Petersburg Committee:

> The fact that the Menshevik-Internationalists left yesterday and today the Left SRs are threatening to leave does not change the issue. It is not a question of an agreement but of the nature of the Russian Revolution ... If we accept an accord with the defencists, they will introduce changes that will be directed against a worker-peasant revolution. By their entire conduct, they demonstrate [that they believe] that it is necessary to build a bridge between the proletarian-peasant revolution and the bourgeoisie.[71]

The meeting voted to support the TsIK's position and to oppose the inclusion of any groups not supporting the programme of the Soviet Congress.[72]

But the Petersburg Committee was not unanimous on these issues. At a meeting of the party committee of the Second City district on 4 November, it was reported that, under the influence of the Left SRs' ultimatum, Kamenev had succeeded in persuading the TsIK to agree to the inclusion of fifty new members from among the socialist deputies of the Petrograd Duma and to set the Bolsheviks' participation in a coalition government at 'at least 50 percent'. This development, the report continued, split the Petersburg Committee: some

70 *Peterburgskii komitet*, p. 535.

71 *Peterburgskii komitet*, p. 557.

72 *Peterburgskii komitet*, p. 558.

were still unwilling to retreat from the principle of an exclusively soviet government; while others were ready to make concessions, fearing that an exclusively Bolshevik government would be too isolated.[73]

The lower levels of the party, however, suffered much less from these doubts. Of the ten people who spoke at the above meeting of the party committee of the Second City district, all were opposed to any retreat from an exclusively soviet government.[74] Party meetings in other district organisations took the same position. A general assembly of Bolsheviks of the Narva district declared that if the Bolshevik party found itself alone in power, then that was because the other parties had defected, refusing a coalition based on the soviets. Turning to the moderates in the party's Central Committee, the meeting declared:

> No wavering on the part of the leading organs of the revolutionary party. We declare to the commissars who have resigned and to the members of the Central Committee, Kamenev and Zinoviev, that the working class will not forgive them this desertion from responsible posts in so grave a moment.[75]

Other district party organisations also roundly condemned the resignations.[76]

An extraordinary Fourth Petrograd Conference of Bolsheviks on 4 November fully supported the left of the party's Central Committee:

> Our party ... is not in need of the cooperation of the petty-bourgeois political groups but of the whole-hearted support of the toilers. Such support is assured for our party on the condition that its leading institutions, while drawing into the soviet government and its organs all vital elements that are outside the party, at the same time categorically rejects unprincipled accommodation with political and professional élites, whose interests are totally inimical to the proletarian-peasant revolution.[77]

Once again, it was pressure 'from below' (and not Lenin's authority and prestige among the leadership) that decided the question. Lenin's threat to appeal to the party rank and file against the 'deserters' in the leadership was not an empty one.

---

73 *Pervyi legal'nyi PeKa*, p. 345.

74 Ibid., pp. 345–7 .

75 Dok. Nov., p. 167.

76 Ibid., pp. 164–5.

77 Ibid., p. 158. See also 'Chetvertaya Petrogradskaya obshchegorodskaya konferentsiya RSDRP(b) v 1917 g.', *Krasnaya letopis*, no. 3 (24), 1927, pp. 58–64.

The issue of a 'homogeneous socialist government' was finally put to rest for almost all the workers when it became clear to them – some had understood this from the start – that the differences among the socialist parties were based on principle. As Skrypnik told the fifth Petrograd conference of factory committees in mid-November:

> They tell us that it is necessary to reach an agreement, that we need a united front. Yes, we agree. But we need coalitions that are capable of working. But Popular Socialists, SR-defencists and Social-Democratic Mensheviks – have they rejected a coalition with the bourgeoisie? No. We will reach an agreement with the defencists; the defencists with the Popular Socialists; the Popular Socialists with the Kadets, who are enemies of the revolution. One should be magnanimous, but that should not lead to accommodation with the bourgeoisie. A united socialist front means to give up the gains of the revolution.[78]

Sukhanov reached the same conclusion. In an editorial in *Novaya zhizn'* at the end of October, he wrote that the Bolsheviks had made concessions and that all the responsibility for failure of the talks and for the civil war should be borne by the 'right elements of democracy', who rejected a coalition with the strongest socialist party in the name of a coalition with the bourgeoisie.[79] And indeed, Tsereteli, leader of the Menshevik-defencists, declared publicly in November that he was opposed to any government with Bolsheviks, but would welcome one with the Kadets.[80]

The Vikzhel negotiations played an important role in helping workers to understand the real reasons for the failure to achieve a socialist coalition. Once they did, the call for a 'homogeneous socialist government' ceased to be heard. At the same time, the workers' fears of imminent military defeat were allayed by the victories of the Soviet forces in Moscow and outside of Petrograd.

Unity from Below

The Petrograd Soviet met on 6 November to discuss the results of the negotiations. G. Ya. Sokol'nikov, speaking for the Bolshevik fraction, explained that the

78 FZK III, p. 36.
79 *Novaya zhizn'*, Oct. 30, 1917.
80 Ibid. Popov 1918, pp. 351–2.

defencists were in effect demanding a new pre-parliament in which the TsIK would have minority representation and the defencists a majority. Moreover, the soldiers' representatives in this new body would not be elected by the rank and file, as was the case in the TsIK, but by army committees that had been elected back in the spring, when most soldiers still supported the defencists. Furthermore, the latter were demanding an unconditional end to all repressive measures, and, in particular, reopening of all non-socialist papers and the liberation of political prisoners, including the ministers of the Provisional Government, the Junkers who had participated in the uprising of 28 October. Finally, they wanted the militia (municipal police) transferred to the authority of the Duma. Sokol'nikov described this as disgraceful pleading for the bourgeoisie. The Soviet government could only negotiate with the Left SRs. And he urged them to join a coalition government with the Bolsheviks.

He then asked the Soviet if the members of the Soviet government who had resigned reflected the will of the masses. Shouts rang out: 'No!' When he asked for a show of hands of those who could justify these resignations, no hands went up. The Soviet adopted a resolution, with only one person opposing and 20 abstentions, stating that power must remain with the soviets and calling to end negotiations with the 'traitors'–the Mensheviks and SRs. At the same time, it urged the Left SRs 'to adhere decisively to the worker-peasant revolution and join the government'.[81]

In the factories, workers took a similar position. A meeting of 500 workers of the Admiralty shipyard on 7 November, who had a week earlier demanded a homogeneous socialist coalition, heard speakers from the different parties, and then adopted the following unanimous resolution:

> We, the workers of the Admiralty shipbuilding factory ... pronounce ourselves in favour of the full and undivided power of the soviets and against accommodation with the parties of the defencists-conciliators, whose policies have brought the country and the revolution to the edge of ruin. We demand forcefulness from our worker and peasant government, a decisive and merciless policy towards those who sabotage and by other means try to undermine the power of the government of workers and peasants.
>
> We have sacrificed much for the revolution and are prepared, if necessary, for new sacrifices. But we won't give up power to those from whom

81 *Novaya zhizn'* (7 Nov. 1917); *Znamya truda* (7 Nov. 1917).

> we have wrested it without a bloody fight. No wavering, no hesitation, with full faith in our forces and in the success of our just cause – forward![82]

The Left SR party also gave up on the idea of an all-socialist coalition. An editorial of *Znamya truda* on 8 November argued that the slogan had outlived itself. The problem was that some of the people who called themselves socialists turned out, in fact, really to be bourgeois democrats. Even if a 'homogeneous government' had been achieved, it would have turned out in reality to be a coalition with the 'most radical part of the bourgeoisie'. The error became clear 'in the whirlwind of events itself'. 'As soon as both sides understood their error, and the defencists understood it sooner, having adopted an irreconcilable position from the outset, the idea of an accord fell away on its own'.

And so while the Menshevik-Internationalists continued to push for a broad socialist coalition, even while remaining in the TsIK,[83] the Left SRs were now open to a coalition with only the Bolsheviks, as they were the only two parties that supported the principle of government responsible to the soviets. Since the Left SRs' main support was in the countryside, this coalition was enthusiastically welcomed by workers as sealing the worker-peasant alliance. The union was formalised at an Extraordinary All-Russian Congress of Peasant Deputies on 10–25 November in Petrograd. Against the wishes of the Peasant Executive Committee, which had been elected back in May, the delegates to this congress were elected from the country (*uzed*) level, rather than the province (*gubernіya*), as had been the case at the previous congress. They therefore more closely reflected the positions of ordinary peasants, who had been radicalised over the past months. (The congress was called 'extraordinary', since many, but not all, counties sent delegates, as the congress had to be convened over the opposition of the outgoing Executive Committee. However, a Second Peasant Congress in December confirmed the decisions of the one in November.) Among the delegates, there were 110 Left SRs, 50 SRs, 40 Bolsheviks and 15 Bolshevik sympathisers, and 40 unaffiliated. The defencists walked out soon after it opened. The congress endorsed the platform of the Second Congress of

82 TsG SPb 9391/l/11/48. For the earlier resolution of 31 October, see ibid., 9391/l/11/45.

83 The internationalist wing of the party soon after October won a majority in its Central Committee. On 19 November it condemned the party's past policies (I.H. Haimson (ed.) 1975, p. 94). From then on, with the exception of some of the party's right-wing elements, it remained an opposition within the TsIK, rejecting, unlike the SRs, any association with attempts at the violent overthrow of the government. After the German Revolution began in November 1918, the party came around to recognising the 'principle' of a soviet regime, although it remained in opposition to the government.

Soviets of Workers' and Soldiers' Deputies and voted to merge its newly elected Executive Committee with the TsIK of Soviets of Workers' and Soldiers' Deputies.

The strategy of the majority left wing of the Bolshevik Party appeared thus vindicated: the Soviet government's policies on land and peace had won it the support, if not of all the peasantry, then of a very substantial part of it. When the Peasant Congress was told that Russia's troops had concluded a ceasefire agreement with the German army on all fronts, 'something indescribable occurred. In the first moment there was total silence. This was followed by loud, unending applause. The majority of the delegates rose up, and continued to applaud while standing'.[84] When the Bolshevik who read the government's report on the land question told the congress that the government understood that the decree adopted earlier by the Congress of Soviets had come under much justified criticism and that the TsIK had decided to leave the land reform to the decision of the peasants, the alliance was sealed.

Workers met the merger of the two executive committees with enthusiasm. The workers of the third department of the forging, pressing and cutting shop at the Putilov factory adopted the following unanimous resolution:

> Having heard the report of the Soviet of Workers' and Soldiers' Deputies on the unification of the three socialist parties, Bolsheviks, Menshevik Internationalists [!] and Left SRs, we, as one, greet that unification as something long desired and we send our warm greetings to all comrades who act on the platform of the All-Russian Congress of the toiling people – poorest peasant, workers and soldiers.[85]

On 14 November, accompanied by orchestras and an honour guard, the Peasant Congress walked en masse to the Smol'nyi Institute for a joint session with the TsIK of Workers' and Soldiers' Deputies. The mood, according to *Znamya truda*, was 'jubilant. The atmosphere was exalted, joyous. One indeed feels that something great is taking place'. Mariya Spiridonova, one of the most venerable Left SRs, who had spent many years at hard labour for the assassination of the Tsarist official who had repressed the peasants of Tambov province, opened the meeting by declaring that it was the 'first act toward the free union of the toilers of the entire world'.[86]

---

84 *Znamya truda* (Nov. 16, 1917).

85 Ibid., (Nov. 18, 1917).

86 Ibid., (16 Nov. 1917).

The much-desired unity of 'revolutionary democracy' appeared to have been restored, but it was unity 'from below' and not in the form of an all-socialist coalition government. The 'middle strata', the majority of the 'democratic intelligentsia', had for the most part excluded itself from this alliance. Commenting on the congress of the Left SR party at the end of November, *Znamya truda* wrote:

> It is curious to note that all those who gave reports, pointing to the division between right and left [SRs], affirm it was mainly the *intelligenty* who went to the right, forming small groups. But the masses went with either the left SRs or the Bolsheviks.[87]

Similarly, when the All-Russian Congress of Railway Workers and Craftsmen opened on 13 November, it was 'in the almost complete absence of *intelligenty*. Even the presidium consists almost exclusively of rank and file [workers]'. By a vote of 154 against 22, the conference condemned Vikzhel, with its Menshevik-Internationalist majority, as 'the elite of the organisation that in no way reflects the revolutionary will of the proletariat'.[88]

V.M. Levin, a Left SR and a leader of the factory-committee movement, described relations between the workers and the intelligentsia at the end of 1917 in the following terms:

> At the moment when the old bourgeois chains of state are being broken, we see that the intelligentsia is deserting the revolutionary people. People who had the good fortune to receive a scientific education are abandoning the toiling people who carried them on their exhausted and lacerated shoulders. And as if that were not enough, in leaving, they mock the people's impotence, their illiteracy, their inability painlessly to produce great transformations, to realise achievements. And this last thing is especially painful for the people. And inside it instinctively grows a hostility to the 'educated', to the intelligentsia.[89]

October thus marked the culmination of the process of class polarisation in Russian society. This polarisation was not a consequence of the October Revolution – it had very deep roots in Russian society and history. The October

---

87 Ibid., (19 Nov 1917).
88 Ibid., (Nov. 17,1917).
89 Ibid., (Dec. 17, 1917).

Revolution was the expression of that polarisation. As such, it appears as the antithesis of the February Revolution, which for a brief moment papered over class contradictions. The workers' experience over the following eight months had convinced them (some were, in fact, quite convinced from the start) that the propertied classes were implacably hostile to the democratic goals of February and that the defence of those goals required a new revolution, one directed against the propertied classes. This, in its turn, meant that the social content of the revolution would also necessarily change.

CHAPTER 13

The Constituent Assembly and the Emergence of a Worker Opposition

The Elections

The several weeks following the October insurrection were undoubtedly the high point of working-class support for the Bolshevik party and the new regime. Not since February had workers shown the same unanimity as in the elections to the Constituent Assembly, which were held on 12–14 November.

Although the campaign was brief and not especially intense, particularly on the part of the Bolsheviks,[1] 78 percent of the 1,205,737 eligible voters in Petrograd went to the polls.[2] Of these, 45 percent cast votes for the Bolshevik list, a significant increase over the 33.4 percent that the party had received in the city duma elections of 20 August.[3] As before, the Bolsheviks owed most of their support to the industrial workers (see Table 13.1). *Novaya zhizn'* reported:

> In the Vyborg district, inhabited mainly by workers and counting 95,000 voters, the elections took place in a lively yet calm manner ... The largest and exclusively proletarian sector here is the fourteenth ... Here, during the two days, 70% voted. With rare exceptions, it is the Bolshevik list ...
>
> The fifteenth sector of the Kolomenskii district is working class, and list no. 4 is popular ...
>
> The workers and employees of the Moscow Tram Depot vote only for List 4 ...
>
> The fact has to be admitted: the workers of Petrograd again recognised the Bolsheviks as their leaders and those who express their mass opinion in the Constituent Assembly.[4]

---

1 M.S. Uritskii told the Bolshevik Peterburg Committee that 'Even here in Piter, we didn't conduct pre-electoral agitation, since that period happened to coincide with the days of the October insrruection'. *Peterburgskii komitet*, p. 602.

2 *Nasha rech'* (Nov, 17, 1917).

3 See Table 1.1 above.

4 *Novaya zhizn'* (Nov. 14, 1917).

TABLE 13.1 *Constituent Assembly election results in Petrograd by district (as percentage of the total vote in the district)*

District	Bol. %	Int. %	Men. %	SR %	Kadet %	Other [a] %	Total no. votes cast
		Men.					
Admiralteiskii	23.0	0.5	1.4	17.7	43.4	13.8	13,387
Aleksandr-Nevskii	48.5	1.0	1.4	19.4	21.0	8.7	59,713
Kazan'skii	19.9	1.2	2.1	14.0	48.2	14.7	22,475
Kolomenskii	35.8	1.2	2.3	14.5	34.0	12.3	37,951
Lesnoi	47.4	2.2	2.6	12.8	27.6	7.3	21,107
Liteinyi	19.7	1.1	2.4	13.7	47.4	15.7	48,731
Moskosvskii	26.2	1.4	2.5	12.2	44.6	13.0	67,706
Narvskii	48.4	1.0	1.6	18.9	20.5	9.6	91,608
Nevskii	41.3	0.7	1.3	39.0	10.7	6.9	43,736
Novaya derevnya	45.7	1.7	2.3	14.4	25.8	10.1	12,567
Okhtenskii	45.7	0.8	1.4	19.6	23.9	8.6	20,841
Petergofskii	68.2	0.6	0.8	18.7	6.6	5.0	42,144
Petrogradskii	39.1	1.8	3.2	12.4	33.7	9.9	115,623
Polyustrovoskii	57.7	1.2	1.2	24.3	10.0	5.5	23,357
Rozhdestvenskii	28.2	1.4	3.1	14.3	38.4	14.6	54,505
Spasskii	29.5	1.0	1.0	9.7	40.1	18.6	35,202
Vasilevskii ostrov	48.1	1.0	1.5	15.3	24.4	10.3	94,549
Vyborgskii	67.9	1.0	1.3	12.8	11.7	5.3	47,821
Garrison	77.0	0.5	0.6	11.3	5.6	5.0	88,197
Entire city	45.0	1.2	1.8	16.1	26.2	9.6	942,333 [b]

[a] Includes votes for religious parties (4.5% of total), right-wing socialist groups (3.2%) and a few others.
[b] The column adds up to 941,220. The discrepancy with the published figure is explained by the absence of five lists from the district breakdown.
SOURCE: *NASHA RECH'* (NOV. 17, 1917).

Among the 88,000 soldiers of the garrison, too, support for the Bolshevik list was very strong, the SRs' former popularity having shrunk dramatically.

Table 13.2 shows how far the class polarisation had progressed since the spring and the summer. The political extremes, the Bolsheviks and Kadets, both increased their share of the vote in November at the expense of the 'centrists', though the Bolshevik advance since the August elections was much greater, almost double that of the Kadets. In August, the SRs (who can be seen as the 'centre') won majorities or pluralities in ten districts, the Bolsheviks in six, and the Kadets in two. In November, the SRs did not lead in a single district; the Bolsheviks led in twelve – with absolute majorities in three – and the Kadets led in six districts, all in the city's centre and inhabited mainly by well-to-do elements, except for the Moscow district, which had many white-collar employees, shopkeepers, and artisans. The Bolsheviks dominated in all the outlying industrial districts, as well as in the working-class sections of Vasilevskii ostrov and the Petrograd district.[5] The political 'centre' (SRs and Mensheviks), which had been so strong in the spring, had virtually collapsed. Workers and soldiers who had once given it their support now voted mainly for the Bolsheviks. Most of the 'intermediate social strata', on the other hand, had shifted to the right and voted for the Kadets.

TABLE 13.2 *Breakdown by district of returns in elections in Petrograd district Dumas*[a] *(27 May–5 June*[b]*), Central Duma (20 August) to the Constituent Assembly (12–14 November 1917) (percentage of the total district vote)*

District		Bol. %	Men.[c] %	SR %	Socialist bloc %	Kadet %	Others %	Total votes cast
Admiral'teiskii	M	15,8			58,7	23,8	1,8	18,931
(19,761)[e]	A	35,7	2,2	35,8		21,3	5,0	11,865
	N	23,0	1,9	17,7		43,4	13,8	13,387
Aleksandr-Nevskii	M	12,8	10,6	60,5		13,3	2,7	68,318
(96,472)	A	28,0	3,4	52,4		13,8	2,5	43,552
	N	48,5	2,4	19,4		21,0	8,7	59,713
Kazan'skii	M	10,1			41,9	42,5	5,5	22,077
(30,043)	A	17,1	3,5	29,9		41,0	8,6	13,375
	N	19,9	3,3	14,0		48,2	14,7	22,475

5 On the social composition of the districts, see Chapter 3 of the present volume.

TABLE 13.2 *Breakdown by district of returns in elections* (cont.)

District		Bol. %	Men.[c] %	SR %	Socialist bloc %	Kadet %	Others %	Total votes cast
Kolomenskii	M	14,9			55,9	25,2	4,0	40,626
(58,201)	A	29,7	2,3	38,3		26,2	1,5	23,602
	N	35,8	3,5	14,5		34,0	12,3	37,951
Lesnoi	M							
(33,851)	A	36,5	5,3	29,3		24,6	4,3	15,830
	N	47,4	4,8	12,8		27,6	7,3	21,107
Liteinyi	M	8,6			51,5	37,9	2,1	59,423
(64,740)	A	16,9	4,0	35,2		38,5	5,3	31,236
	N	19,7	3,5	13,7		47,4	15,7	48,731
Moskovskii	M[f]	9,7			59,4[g]	31,0		69,942
(100,129)	A	21,3	4,5	34,8		33,0	6,3	39,967
	N	26,2	3,9	12,2		44,6	13,0	67,706
Narvskii	M	17,1			68,9	11,9	2,1	106,392
(128,294)	A	33,3	3,2	50,2		11,3	2,1	69,973
	N	48,4	2,6	18,9		20,5	9,6	91,608
Nevskii	M							
(59,840)	A	20,1	2,8	66,8		8,5	8,5	30,812
	N	41,3	2,0	39,0		10,7	6,9	43,736
Novaya derevnia	M							
(18,921)	A	37,5	4,3	28,1		28,5	1,6	9,805
	N	45,7	4,0	14,4		25,8	10,1	12,567
Okhtenskii	M							
(30,300)	A	31,3	1,8	61,2		4,7	1,0	10,978
	N	45,7	2,2	19,6		23,9	8,6	20,841

District		Bol. %	Men.[c] %	SR %	Socialist bloc %	Kadet %	Others %	Total votes cast
Petergofskii	M							
(59,040)	A	61,7	1,6	31,5		3,4	1,8	27,949
	N	68,2	1,4	18,7		6,6	5,0	42,144
Petrogradskii	M	22,6			54,1	2,8	1,4	134,345
(59,040)	A	38,0	5,4	25,9		26,3	4,4	70,515
	N	39,1	5,0	12,4		33,7	9,9	115,623
Polyustrovoskii	M							
(30,489)	A	39,0	2,3	47,7		9,6	1,3	8,592
	N	57,7	2,4	24,3		10,0	5,5	23,357
Rozhedestvenskii	M	5,0	32,1	28,2		30,5	4,2	59,358
(82,987)	A	15,5	4,9	39,3		33,6	6,6	34,287
	N	28,2	4,5	14,3		38,4	14,6	54,505
Spasskii	M	13,2			44,8	29,0	13,1	37,581
(53,201)	A	16,8	3,6	39,7		33,0	6,8	17,970
	N	29,5	2,0	9,7		40,1	18,6	35,202
Vasilevskii ostrov	M[h]	34,3			45,2	17,7	2,8	108,975
(116,263)	A	38,1	8,2	32,9		17,7	3,1	64,726
	N	48,1	2,5	15,3		24,4	10,3	94,549
Vyborgskii	M	58,2			33,4	6,9	1,5	58,942
(61,134)	A	63,0	3,5	23,9		7,6	2,1	35,711
	N	67,9	2,3	12,8		11,7	5,3	47,821
Entire city	M	20,4			55,0[i]	21,9	2,8	784,910
(1,205,737)	A	33,4	4,3[j]	37,4		20,8	4,0	549,350
	N[k]	45,0	3,0	16,1		26,2	9,6	942,333

[a] Five outlying districts were incorporated into the city after the district duma elections.
[b] Voting took place on May 27–9, except for two districts, where they were postponed a week.

[c] In the November elections, the defencists and internationalists ran two separate lists. The totals have been combined here. See Table 6.1.
[d] The Menshevik-SR bloc ran only in the May elections and not in all districts. In the Kazanskii, Narvskii, Petrogradskii and Vasilevskii ostrov districts, the bloc included the Trudoviki and Popular Socialists.
[e] Total number of eligible voters in the Constituent Assembly elections
[f] Known to be incomplete.
[g] Includes Trudoviki and Popular Socialists, though not running as a bloc here.
[h] This was a Bolshevik-Menshevik-Internationalist bloc.
[i] Includes Socialist bloc, as well as Menshevik and SR votes, where they ran separately.
[j] The Menshevik list in this election was Internationalist.
[k] Includes the soldiers' vote, not included in district totals for the Constituent Assembly elections. See Table 6.1.
SOURCES: ROSENBERG 1974, PP. 162, 220; *DELO NARODA* (AUG. 23–4 1917); *NASHA RECH'* (NOV. 17, 1917).

In Russia as a whole, with its overwhelmingly peasant population, much of which was quite isolated from the centres of national politics, the polarisation was not nearly so pronounced. This partly explains the strength of the 'centrist' vote: the SRs obtained 40.9 percent, and various national and Muslim parties, whose platforms were close to the SRs' – took another 20.1 percent. In the rural areas where peasants were in contact with soldiers or that were located close to urban centres, the Bolsheviks took many votes away from the SRs. But elsewhere, knowledge of recent political developments, in particular of the decrees of the Second Congress of Soviets, was poor, and the peasants remained loyal to their traditional party of 'land and freedom'. Nationally, the Bolsheviks obtained 23.6 percent of the vote; the Mensheviks, also essentially an urban party (except in Georgia, where they had peasant support) – won only 3.0 percent. The Kadets and other right-wing parties obtained 8.4 percent.[6]

The new elections to soviets held in the large and mid-size urban centres in the fall, as well as the party composition of the Soviet Congress, leave no doubt that the Bolsheviks, and to a much lesser extent the Left SRs, had at this time the support of the vast majority of Russia's workers. Petrograd's polarisation along class lines was not exceptional in Russia's urban society. In Moscow's election, the centrist parties won a mere 11 percent (SRs 8.1 and Mensheviks 2.8), while the Bolsheviks won 48 percent and the Kadets 35 percent.[7]

6 O. Radkey 1950, p. 80.
7 Ibid., p. 53. See also *Novaya zhizn'* (Dec. 12, 1917).

But the strong 'centrist' vote in the Constituent Assembly elections did not accurately reflect the political mood of the peasantry. Except for a few provinces, the Left SRs did not present their own list of candidates – they were slow in formally splitting from the rest of the party, which finally expelled them only at the end of October. In constituting the list of candidates, the SR leaders did not respect any principle of proportionality. But at the SR national Council in August, 40 percent of the delegates adhered to the left wing, and at the Congress of Soviets in October, the SR delegation was almost evenly divided between rightists and leftists. A few weeks later at the Extraordinary Peasant Congress, held during the elections to the Constituent Assembly, the Left SRs outnumbered the SRs by a ratio of two to one. The 40 (of the total of 410 seats in the assembly) held by Left SRs did not reflect their real support in the country. In the few regions where they ran their own lists, their supporters strongly outnumbered those of the SRs. Some historians have therefore concluded that if the Left SRs had run independently, the delegations of the two 'soviet parties' (Bolsheviks and Left SRs) would have been in a majority in the Constituent Assembly.[8]

In Petrograd itself, however, most of the 152,230 voters who supported the SR list were, in fact, supporters of the defencists. In new city duma elections held two weeks later, the Left SRs obtained only 26,000 votes, while the Bolsheviks received 358,684 votes, a result close to those obtained in the Constituent Assembly elections.[9] According to *Novaya zhizn'*, 'many who dream of leaving Petrograd to return to the land (cabbies, janitors, doormen, wartime workers, etc.) still believe that only the SRs can give land'.[10] The district where the SRs were clearly still an important political forces (with two-thirds of the votes cast) was Nevskii, itself semi-rural and with a significant group of settled, small property-owning workers.[11] It would become the centre of worker opposition to the Soviet government in 1918.

Among the relatively few votes cast for the Mensheviks, the preference – almost two to one – was for the defencist list rather than the internationalist.[12] The radicalised mass of workers found the Menshevik-Internationalists' position incoherent. V.M. Osokin, an internationalist, told the Menshevik Congress in early December:

---

8 E. Acton, among others, reaches this conclusion in 'The Russian Revolution and its Historians', in E. Acton (ed.) 1997, p. 10.

9 *Pravda* (Nov. 30, 1917); Peka, p. 369.

10 *Novaya zhizn'* (Nov. 16, 1917).

11 See Chapter 3 above.

12 *Nasha rech'* (Nov. 17, 1917). The defencist vote includes those cast for Plekhanov's 'Edinstvo'.

> The coalition enthusiasm of the Mensheviks has lost them any credit in the eyes of the working class – not only among the recently-arrived, temporary masses 'working for defence', but also among the skilled, cadre proletariat ... Only a small old guard – the worker aristocracy, which, to a significant degree, is detached from the masses – has remained in the ranks of Menshevism, and even so – very characteristically – on its extreme right-wing flank.[13]

But even among this so-called 'worker aristocracy', support for the Mensheviks had declined: in December, the printers broke with their longstanding Menshevik tradition and elected a Bolshevik executive to head their union. Simonovich, a delegate from Petrograd to the All-Russian Congress of Printers at the end of December, stated that 'with the election of a new executive, Petrograd's printers have abandoned the purely economic stance of the defencists and have taken the side of the proletariat'.[14]

But the workers' vote of confidence for the Bolsheviks in the elections to the Constituent Assembly does not tell much about how they viewed the latter's role in the political life of the country. One should not conclude that they necessarily saw opposition between the Constituent Assembly and Soviet power. The Bolsheviks, for their part, at least initially, presented the Sovnarkom, the Council of People's Commissars, as a provisional government, one of whose chief tasks was to convene the Constituent Assembly. This had long been a traditional demand of the workers' movement. Some Bolshevik leaders even expressed their concern that the workers would display apathy, or even boycottist attitudes, towards the election. Zinoviev told the Petrograd Soviet on 10 November that 'there is an opinion spreading in some worker and soldier circles that the Constituent Assembly is not needed, since we have already secured all the freedoms and rights and that enough is as good as a feast'. With only four of the delegates dissenting, the Soviet adopted an appeal to the workers and soldiers to participate in the elections.[15] At a meeting of the Bolsheviks' Petersburg Committee on 8 November, a member from the Putilov factory reported that the workers were, in fact, insisting on elections. Another offered that it was rather the soldiers who were asking why they needed a constituent assembly if they already had Soviet power.[16]

13 *Novaya zhizn'* (Dec. 7, 1917).
14 *Znamya truda* (Dec. 30, 1917).
15 *Novaya zhizn'* (Nov. 11, 1917).
16 *Peterburgskii komitet*, p. 565.

Although the election campaign did not generate much passion, the turnout in the working-class districts was equal or even exceeded the average for the city as a whole (although everywhere the turnout was lower than in the May district duma elections). The workers' vote showed two things. On the one hand, they considered the Constituent Assembly an important arena of political struggle. But on the other, by voting massively for the Bolsheviks, they made clear their desire that the Constituent Assembly pursue the policies of the Soviet government. What this really meant was that these workers wanted the Constituent Assembly, which was elected by universal suffrage, to give its national, all-class, endorsement to the policies of the toiling classes. For example, the Conference of Women Workers of Petrograd and Vicinity, attended by 500 delegates representing some 100,000 women, voted overwhelmingly to appeal to workers to vote for the Bolshevik list and at the same time demanded that the Constituent Assembly confirm all decrees of the Soviet government.[17]

From a purely logical viewpoint, this position, of course, was not very coherent. For if a dictatorship of the toiling classes – that was the real significance of Soviet power – was necessary as a temporary measure until the Constituent Assembly could meet, why would it no longer be needed afterwards? Unless, of course, the Constituent Assembly possessed some hidden powers that would be able to heal the deep class polarisation that had led to the October Revolution?

Part of the explanation for this position lies in the workers' emotional attachment to the Constituent Assembly, a demand for which they had fought for many years. But more important perhaps was their hope, however faint by then, that the Constituent Assembly could somehow force the propertied classes to accept their defeat, allowing Russia to avoid civil war. The workers were not prepared to leave any stone unturned to that end. And even those who considered such thinking illusory, understood that the elections had to take place, since the peasantry, as well as part of the army and even the workers, were attached to the idea of a Constituent Assembly. As for Petrograd's Bolsheviks, their organisation called for the strongest possible participation in the elections.

17 *Pravda* (12 Nov. 1917). See also *Novaya zhizn'* (Nov. 17, 1917).

Dissolution of the Constituent Assembly

Once the election returns became known and the failure of the Bolsheviks and Left SRs to win a majority was clear, there could no longer be any hope that the Constituent Assembly would endorse Soviet power or any other equivalent of a government without representation of the propertied classes. The predominance in the Constituent Assembly of 'conciliators' meant that it would, at best, be a repeat of the Democratic Conference, since the SRs and their political allies continued to insist on representation of the propertied classes in government. Accordingly, the Bolshevik and left SR leaders and their press began to declare openly that the Constituent Assembly would be dispersed if it opposed Soviet power.[18] Not long after, the government declared the Kadets to be 'enemies of the people', their leaders subject to arrest.[19] Speaking at the Peasant Congress in December, Lenin stated that the composition of the Constituent Assembly would not reflect the position of the toiling masses, that 'Saturday was created for man, and not man for Saturday', and that the Soviet government in the future would arrest all those who refused to recognise it.[20]

It was against this background that the SRs and some dissident Mensheviks-defencists, the latter in opposition to the policy of their party (now dominated by internationalists), decided to organise a Committee for the Defence of the Constituent Assembly with participation of some workers, district duma deputies, and representatives of political parties. Demonstrations in support of the Assembly were called for 28 November and 5 January.

At this stage, worker support for the Constituent Assembly came mainly from some of the factories that had adopted the Left SR and Menshevik-Internationalist position (neutrality in the civil war and a homogeneous socialist government) in the period right after the October insurrection. A meeting at the San-Galli iron foundry and mechanical factory on 7 December mandated the factory's newly-elected delegate to the Petrograd Soviet to demand that the government consider the views of the minority parties of the TsIK (in reality, only the Menshevik-Internationalists, as the others refused to participate in it) and convoke the Constituent Assembly at once.[21] A meeting at the Reikhel mechanical factory adopted a similar resolution proposed by the Menshevik-Internationalists:

---

18 *Znamya truda* (Nov. 20, 1917); *Novaya zhizn'* (Dec. 3, 1917).

19 *Novaya zhizn'* (Dec. 3, 1917).

20 Ibid. (Dec. 28, 1917).

21 Ibid. (Dec. 15, 1917).

> Only the Constituent Assembly can put an end to the civil war, realise our demands for the conclusion of a democratic peace, the transfer of land to the peasants, and the organisation of state control of production.
>
> At the same time, we recognise that the Soviets of Workers' Deputies must conserve their significance as the institutions that express our interests and that must defend our rights.[22]

The concern to avoid further civil war is evident here. But the insistence on the soviets indicated the doubts even among these workers about the Constituent Assembly.

The above were small factories. But workers in some larger ones that had previously been SR strongholds adopted similar positions. A 'general assembly of workers (peasants) [!]', of the forging shop of the Obukhovskii factory, sent greetings to the Constituent Assembly,

> as the ideal of the Russian Revolution that we have cherished and to which strive all peoples, all the toilers of the whole world ... And, therefore, we, workers of the Obukhovskii factory, despite all the difficulties of the approaching moment in the area of state-building, demand the adoption of the following legislation by the Constituent Assembly, as the spokesman of the will of the people, as the genuine master of the Russian land.

There followed a list of demands, including the immediate proposal of a democratic peace, transfer of all land to the peasants without compensation, the eight-hour day, a minimum wage, workers' control of production, 'as a transitional stage to the socialisation of the mills and factories', social insurance, and free universal education.

> All the above demands of the workers (peasants) of the Obukhovksii factory are demands, are the voice of the toiling people directed to the Constituent Assembly, as the expression of the will of the entire working people ...
>
> And for that goal, we demand of democracy, of the socialists in the Constituent Assembly, to remember that only the class struggle exists, the struggle of labour against capital, and there is no room for dissension in the Constituent Assembly, where the interests of the toiling people stand

22 Ibid. (Dec. 10 1917).

above all individual parties and there is no place for those who would forget the people and follow the bourgeoisie.

And, therefore, we say: No to division among socialists! Down with enmity among the party leaders! Long live the unity of all democracy as the guarantee of the victory of the toiling people! Long live the Constituent Assembly! Long live the socialist revolution!

Unanimous.[23]

Here was a demand for the Constituent Assembly to endorse the programme of the Soviet government, something the Provisional Government had not been willing to do in its eight months of existence, due to the opposition of the bourgeois ministers and the defencists' insistence that the bourgeoisie be represented in the government. The defencists, who were a majority in the Constituent Assembly, had not abandoned that position. Yet these workers, many of whom were recent wartime industrial workers, clung to the belief that the division among the socialists were because of the ambitions of the leaders and not over principle.

On the whole, however, workers' response to the campaign in defence of the Constituent Assembly was very weak. *Novaya zhizn'*, which was not unsympathetic to this campaign, published detailed reports of the demonstrations of 5 January in support of the Constituent Assembly that opened on that day. By then, it was clear that the Soviet government would not tolerate it if it repudiated Soviet power, something it was certain to do. 'All that remains to be seen', commented the paper, 'is the method by which the Bolsheviks will ravish it'.[24]

> [Vasilevskii ostrov] By the start of the demonstration, about a thousand people had gathered, mostly student youth, many from the university, from the Mining Institute, from the colleges and so forth. There are few workers in this demonstration, although there are banners from some factories, such as Trubochnyi, and the like. Small groups of soldiers and sailors also participate in the demonstration from this district ...
>
> [The demonstrators from Vasilevskii ostrov and the Liteinyi district merged on the Palace Square.] The intelligentsia predominated in the large crowd: students, minor officials, and the like. The groups of workers

23 *Znamya truda* (Dec. 2, 1917). See ibid. for a similar resolution adopted by the artillery shop of the Patronnyi factory.

24 *Новаяжизнь* (Jan. 4, 1918).

> from the factories of Vasilevskii ostrov were not large: in each group there were only a few dozen people. There were almost no soldiers ...
>
> The participants of the demonstration in defence of the Constituent Assembly in the Petrograd district ... began to gather at 10 a.m. The crowd consisted mainly of intelligentsia, petty bureaucrats, many women. Rarely did one see small groups of workers. There were almost no soldiers ... [By 11 a.m. about 10,000 people had gathered on the Field of Mars.]
>
> Especially impressive was the demonstration of the Aleksandr-Nevskii district, in which workers of the Obukhovskii Factory, Pal' [textile mill] and other factories of the Nevskii district participated. About 15,000 people participated in this demonstration. The demonstrators walked along Nevskii Prospekt, accompanied by music.
>
> The demonstrators arrive at noon in the square in front of the Tsarsko-sel'skii station. Here is a group of workers from the Westinghouse factory, employees of the Nikolaevskii Railroad, the All-Russian Railway Union, also many students.
>
> Employees of government, public and private institutions also joined this demonstration ...[25]

As these reports indicate, the main participants of the demonstrations belonged to the 'intermediate strata' of society.[26] The same paper later took issue with *Izvestiya*, the government's paper, when it claimed that the demonstrators were mainly 'petty bourgeois and functionaries' and that workers were largely absent. It pointed to the presence of a number of factories that arrived with their banners.[27] But V. Stroev, one of *Novaya zhizn*'s own editors, recognised that 'few workers came out into the street on 5 January for the defence of

25 Ibid. (Jan. 6, 1918).

26 The American historian O.H. Radkey concluded that support in Russian society for the Constituent Assembly was weak: 'Of ... fateful significance was the fact that while the democratic parties heaped opprobrium upon him [Lenin] for this act of despotism [dispersal of the assembly], their following showed little inclination to defend an institution which the Russian people had ceased to regard as necessary to the fulfilment of its cherished desires. For the Constituent Assembly, even before it had come into existence, had been caught in a back-eddy of the swiftly flowing stream of revolutionary developments and no longer commanded the interest and allegiance of the general population, which alone could have secured it against a violent death' (O.H. Radkey 1950, p. 2).

27 *Novaya zhizn'* (Jan. 9, 1918).

a united revolutionary front'.[28] It was the case that the government created obstacles to the demonstrations and that the leaders of the major workers' organisation appealed to stay away. But those measures had not stopped the 'middle strata' from participating in relatively large numbers.

The following resolution adopted by the workers of the Treugol'nik rubber factory provides insight into why the mass of workers refrained from participation:

> We, men and women workers of the Treugol'nik factory, having met on 14 December in the dining hall of the factory and having discussed the current political situation, declare:
>
> 1. The workers, soldiers and peasants, having won power at a terrible price, will not yield to anyone that power that manifests itself organisationally in the Soviets of Workers, Soldiers and Peasants.
>
> 2. To all hypocritical attempts to undermine the power of the Soviets of Workers', Soldiers', and Peasants' Deputies under the slogan 'All power to the Constituent Assembly', we declare: We are also in favour of a Constituent Assembly, but only not the sort of Constituent Assembly that the overthrown government of the bourgeoisie would make for us, but a Constituent Assembly that really expresses the will of the workers, soldiers and peasants, of all the oppressed and disadvantaged. We are only in favour of the kind of Constituent Assembly that will not oppose itself to the power of the Soviets, that will consolidate the policy of peace, the policy of the transfer of lands to the hands of the people without compensation, the policy of establishment of workers' control of production and distribution. But if in the Constituent Assembly, due to abuses allowed during the elections, the will of the toiling masses is so distorted that the Constituent Assembly becomes an obstacle on the path of the development of the worker and peasant revolution, then we will oppose to it all the power and might of the revolutionary working class, of the revolutionary soldiers and peasants, organised in their purely class organisations of Soviets of Workers, Soldiers and Peasants.
>
> 3. We will encircle a genuine Constituent Assembly with a ring of Soviets, and, resting on the power and the authority of the Soviets in the local-

28 Ibid. (Jan. 11, 1918).

ities and in the centre, the Constituent Assembly will be in our hands a formidable battering ram, helping to destroy the old world of violence.

4. But in a genuinely revolutionary Constituent Assembly, there is no room for avowed enemies of the revolution, for members of the party of Constitutional Democrats, who are at one and the same time mobilising their forces under the slogan of 'All Power to the Constituent Assembly', while conducting an open offensive against the revolution with the help of the Kaledins, Dutovs, Kornilovs and Karaulovs.

5. Therefore, we congratulate the Sovnarkom for its energetic struggle against the counterrevolution and we propose to the Sovnarkom to take all measures to verify the elections so that false representatives do not find their way into the Constituent Assembly.

6. The Constituent Assembly, we repeat, must be a Constituent Assembly that reflects the true will of the toiling masses, and the only guarantee of that and of the defence of all the gains of the revolution is the defence and further consolidation of the government of workers, soldiers and peasants, and, therefore, long live the government of Soviets of Workers', Soldiers' and Peasants' Deputies![29]

This was the attitude of most workers: the Constituent Assembly, though elected by universal suffrage, was called upon to endorse Soviet power, which was a government of the toiling classes without representation of the propertied classes – in essence, a dictatorship of the toiling class over the propertied classes. The Kadet party, the hegemonic party of the propertied classes in 1917, therefore, had no place in it. Although the logic of this position was dubious, it was faithfully expressing workers' support for Soviet power along with their reluctance to abandon the traditional, cherished demand for a Constituent Assembly. And it explains why most workers did not support the Constituent Assembly that met on 5 January: if the choice was between the Constituent Assembly and Soviet power – and the election results imposed that choice on the workers – there was no doubt where the vast majority of workers stood.

29 *Znamya truda* (Dec. 16, 1917). For resolutions in a similar vein from the Opticheskii facrory seeibid., and from the new ordnance department of the Obukhovskii factory, see Dok. Nov., vol. 1, p. 189.

But some workers did support the Constituent Assembly. The demonstrations of 5 January were the first occasion in which workers took active part in a protest against the Soviet government. More ominously, it was the first occasion on which forces defending Soviet power directed repressive measures against workers. The first confrontation took place at 11:30 a.m., when some 200 demonstrators were crossing the Liteinyi Bridge. They were confronted by some fifty Red Guards and soldiers, who fired into the air and seized their banners, which they proceeded to burn 'jubilantly' in a bonfire. More serious was the confrontation with the demonstrators from the Nevskii district that left two dead and several wounded. Casualties also occurred in a few other places.[30] Ya. M. Sverdlov, Chairman of the TsIK, informed the Third Congress of Soviets in January 1918 that there had been twenty-one deaths, including those of two workers and a soldier.[31]

These repressive measures served as the catalyst for the emergence of a much more significant worker opposition centred in the Nevskii district. A series of factory meetings that were called to discuss the dissolution of the Constituent Assembly and the events of 5 January attracted large numbers of workers. *Novaya zhizn'* commented that so large an attendance at factory meetings had not been seen for some time. The largest meeting, with up to 8,000 workers, took place at the Obukhovskii factory, some of whose workers had been on the receiving end of the repression. *Pravda*'s distorted portrayal of the events, which placed the blame on the demonstrators, was a source of particular indignation. A large majority supported a resolution of protest against dissolution of the Constituent Assembly and the shooting. It demanded the recall of all the delegates to the Soviet who did not protest against the actions of the Red Guards. Similar resolutions were adopted at the Nevskii shipbuilding factory, the Vargunina paper factory, the Aleksandrovskii locomotive factory, the Pal' and Maxwell textile mills and by the workers of the Nikolaevskii Railroad – all in Nevskii district[32] – as well as by the workers of the ordnance department of Patronnyi, Siemens-Shukkert,[33] Rechkin wagon-building factory,[34] the Otto Kirkhner Printing House and Bindery, and the Markus Printing House.[35]

The workers of almost all the above factories had supported the position of the Left SRs and Menshevik-Internationalists in the October days. An exception

30 *Novaya zhizn'* (Jan. 6, 1918).
31 Ibid. (Jan. 12, 1918).
32 Ibid. (Jan. 11, 1918).
33 Ibid. (Jan. 17, 1918).
34 Ibid. (Jan. 11, 1918).
35 Ibid. (Jan. 9, 1918).

was the Staryi Lessner machine-building factory in the Vyborg district. Its work force was mainly female and it had supported the SRs right up until August.[36] At their general assembly on 10 January, the factory's workers, after hearing a report on the shooting of 5 January, resolved 'to consider Sovnarkom criminal and to hold new elections immediately of our representatives to both the Petrograd and the Vyborg district Soviets of Workers' and Soldiers Deputies'.[37] In an article published some time later, *Pravda* attributed the resolution to the 'accidental composition of the meeting' at this factory that 'never fully supported the Bolsheviks, since the workers are of a petty-bourgeois frame of mind'. After the Kornilov affair, it continued, the Bolsheviks had won the workers' support, but by the time of the meeting in January only some half of the original number of 1,200 workers were still employed there, and the factory's 60 Bolsheviks had left for the civil-war front. This explanation is given some credibility by the results of the new elections in the factory that endorsed the Bolshevik deputy to the Soviet. In the elections to the factory committee, the Bolsheviks won six places, the SRs three and two others were unaffiliated.[38] But even if the resolution reflected only a passing mood, the change in the social composition of the factory's workforce and their political wavering were a foretaste of things to come.

The campaign for new elections to the Petrograd Soviet promoted by the Mensheviks and SRs yielded some positive results for them. In those factories where workers decided to hold new elections in January – many did not see the need – the Mensheviks, SRs and non-affiliated candidates took about half the seats and the Bolsheviks the other half. As a result, an additional 36 SRs, 7 Mensheviks and 6–7 unaffiliated deputies were elected.[39] A serious worker opposition to the government was thus beginning to emerge. But as the results of the campaign indicate, despite the dissolution of the Constituent Assembly and the repressive measures, the Bolsheviks still retained the allegiance of the majority of Petrograd's workers at the end of January 1918.

The demonstration in defence of the Constituent Assembly set a pattern for the opposition in the following months. The main party of opposition among workers was the SRs. And the main centre of workers' opposition was in the Nevskii district. The workers here preferred the SR, seen as the peasants' party, to the Mensheviks, a workers' party. This opposition defended the Constitu-

36 N. Sveshnikov 1923, p. 302.

37 *Novaya zhizn'* (Jan. 11, 1918).

38 *Pravda* (Jan. 31, 1918).

39 *Novaya zhizn'* (Jan. 25, and February 13/26 1918).

ent Assembly against Soviet power. The Constituent Assembly was presented by the defencists as a national (*obshchenatsional'noe*), all-class, government in opposition to the soviets, which were presented as a 'Bolshevik dictatorship'. This was, therefore, not a 'loyal opposition': it did not seek merely to change the Soviet government's policies and its party composition. It sought rather to completely change the regime, with some version of the one that had existed, before the October Revolution. It wanted, in effect, to annul the October Revolution. As will be seen further, despite the rising discontent, most workers could not support that programme.

Although the immediate background of the emergence of a workers' opposition was political, its further growth would owe very much to the deterioration of the economic situation, something that the opposition parties themselves recognised.[40] The bread ration in Petrograd was reduced on 9 January to a half funt (a funt = .45 kg.) and on 9 January, for the first time, it reached the 'truly hungry level' of a quarter funt and even briefly dipped to an eight on 18 January.[41] Typhus, the faithful companion of hunger, made its appearance. Food disorders broke out. In mid-January, for example, a crowd broke into a warehouse of the Food Authority, and the looting continued for three days.[42] Somewhat later, a crowd attacked and looted a food train, until Red Guards arrived to disperse it.[43]

As for industry, the factories producing for the war – the majority – were closed in mid-December for conversion to peacetime production. The conversion was to take place over the following month. But as the date for reopening drew near, it became evident that the shortage of fuel and raw materials did not allow most of them to restart, and certainly not with the same size of workforce.[44]

The *Chernorabochie* and the Upsurge of Anarchist Influence

Another type of worker opposition, which arose before the dissolution of the Constituent Assembly, was linked to the rise of anarchist influence among the *chernorabochie*, the unskilled workers, whose economic situation was partic-

40 Ibid. (Jan. 21, 1918).
41 *Pravda* (Jan. 7, 1918).
42 *Novaya zhizn'* (20 Jan. 1918).
43 Ibid. (Feb. 4/17, 1918).
44 Ibid. (Dec. 22, 1917).

ularly difficult with the accelerating inflation. In the weeks before the October Revolution, the workers' organisations had increasing difficulty restraining these workers, explaining to them that only the political struggle and the transfer of power to the soviets could solve their economic problems. After the insurrection, the unskilled workers naturally looked to the new regime to improve their situation and in particular to bring their wages more in line with those of their more skilled colleagues.

All the workers were suffering. The secretary of the local branch of the Metalworkers' Union in Sestroretsk, most of whose members were employed in the local rifle factory and were relatively skilled, told the union executive that 'there is general dissatisfaction with the [metalworking] branch agreement among the masses, since the rates are low already because of inflation, and it is only the union's authority and the discipline of its members that hold the masses back. But they won't be able to do that for long'.[45]

In other factories, however, discipline was not as strong. At the end of November, the painters at the Metallicheskii factory beat and 'arrested' a representative of the Metalworkers' Union, refusing to release him until he signed a document granting them a fourteen-ruble increase in their daily wage, retroactive to 5 June. According to the worker who chaired the meeting where the incident occurred, antagonism between the skilled and unskilled workers had been simmering since the summer, when the Petrograd Society of Factory and Mills Owners refused the union's wage demands for unskilled workers, while it did accept them for the skilled workers. (The union, in an effort to narrow the gap, had been asking for a large increase for the unskilled workers.) After the October insurrection, the unskilled workers went around the union, and threatening violence, forced the administration to grant their demand. But after this, on 1 December, the administration announced it was closing the factory for lack of new orders from the military. When the workers met in a general assembly to discuss whether they should themselves take over the factory, the unskilled workers burst in, demanding an immediate response to their demands. They would not let anyone speak, pulling those who tried off the platform.

When the Workers' Section of the Petrograd Soviet met with representatives of the union and the factory committees to discuss this conflict, they decided to reject the workers' demands, since they exceeded the branch agreement. And payment of the additional wages to the unskilled workers was stopped.[46]

45 *Metallist*, no. 1 (Jan. 12, 1918).

46 *Novaya zhizn'* (Dec. 2, 1917).

A few days later, another meeting was convened on the topic of 'the struggle against anarchy in the factories'. A representative of the unskilled workers said the following:

> You can't forget the principles put forward by the October Revolution. In this hall ... you welcomed the demand to equalise the material situation of soldiers and officers. And now the unskilled labourers want to be equalised in their material situation with the skilled workers. The social revolution demands that ... If the demands of the unskilled workers are not met, then the government of Lenin will fall, just as the governments of Romanov and Kerenskii fell.[47]

In that period, the press reported a number of similar incidents in which unskilled workers, bypassing the workers' organisations, resorted to violence.[48] A.E. Vasil'ev, chairman of the Putilov factory committee, told a joint meeting of the factory and shop committees:

> Of late, thanks to the agitation of certain elements who consider it their task, not to resolve the common, proletarian class questions, but rather to pursue purely personal, egoistical desires, a movement has arisen that is disorganising the masses. Under the guise of political struggle and of economic demands, a struggle of individual people is being conducted; arguments arise, disagreement on the grounds of purely petty-bourgeois, philistine desires. One sees here the complete absence of a sense of collectivism and the clear emergence of personal interests, dictated by petty-bourgeois, swamp psychology ... Attacks are raining down on both the factory committee as a whole and on its individual members. The committee is accused of conducting political struggle, having forsaken the economic struggle.[49]

The situation became so serious that A. Shlyapnikov, the People's Commissar for Labour, issued a special plea calling for unity in this period when the government's efforts to convert the war industry to peacetime production were being accompanied by a rise in unemployment: 'Chasing after the ruble only

---

47 Ibid. (Dec. 6 1917).

48 See, for example, the *chernorabochie* at Phoenix, ibid., 20 Dec 1917, and further on Metallicheskii, ibid., 22 Dec. 1917. Matters were especially bad in the chemical industry, which had a largely unskilled workforce, ibid., 11 Nov and 21 Dec 1917.

49 *Putilovitsy v trekh revolyutsiyakh*, pp. 419–20.

increases the economic disorganisation ... All demands are now really directed to the workers themselves'.[50]

But the anarchists, who championed the cause of the unskilled workers, portrayed the issue in a very different light, as the struggle of the disadvantaged, unskilled workers against the privileged, skilled workers who occupied the leadership positions in the workers' organisations and whom the Bolsheviks favoured. An unsigned letter from 'a worker of Arsenal', published in the anarchist paper *Burevestnik*, accused the Bolsheviks of abandoning socialist principles:

> When the simple unskilled workers demand an increase in wages, they [the leaders of the workers' organisations] point out to us that we are heavy labourers [*volovye*, from the word *vol* – ox] and we, therefore, must also live like oxen. Is this socialism, comrade Bolsheviks? ... At the Arsenal factory, the Bolsheviks themselves protested against a raise for simple workers, and when they managed anyway to insist on an increase, they gave the larger part to the skilled workers. The bourgeoisie divides the people into higher and lower categories, and the Bolsheviks, the 'party of the people' divides [us] into 'higher workers' and 'lower workers'.[51]

This conflict was not merely over wage differences. It was a clash of different conceptions of the October Revolution. Analysing the economic crisis, the Menshevik-Internationalist Bazarov concluded that the workforce had to be cut and productivity raised:

> This is clear to the genuine proletariat, to the so-called skilled workers. But the *chernorabochie* masses, who consist at present of occasional elements come from afar and transformed into workers only for the period of the war, will recognise neither of these things. And although the worker 'collectives' usually elect skilled workers to the factory committee and other workers' organisations, as they are the most capable [*intelligentnye*], these are in reality powerless to do anything against the dull stubbornness of the demoralised, unskilled crowd. And in many cases they simply do not decide to lay out the real, complete state of affairs before them.[52]

50 *Novaya zhizn'* (Dec. 24, 1917).

51 Cited in *Novaya zhizn'* (Dec. 12, 1917).

52 Ibid. (Dec. 8, 1917).

In the early spring of 1918, *Novaya zhizn'* wrote that 'Experienced observers say that the real instigators of all such [unorganised, violent] actions are the peasants who have only recently entered the factories and who, having obtained several hundred rubles, quit work and depart for the village'.[53] This was also the assessment of the Metalworkers' Union:

> The composition of the working class has been strongly diluted during the war with an element that has come from the village and is unevenly linked to the factory proletariat. Only externally organised and not imbued with the spirit of genuine proletarian discipline and commonality of interest, its backward elements easily succumb to irresponsible anarchist agitation. Its most backward elements still see the entire problem in terms of individuals. They recognize no responsibilities and are still incapable of rising up to a socialist understanding, placing their individual interest above all else and desiring only as big a wage increase as possible, even at the price of the destruction of production.[54]

The deepening economic distress, the start of real hunger, did not favour the growth of 'socialist consciousness', particularly among the wartime workers who did not identify strongly with the working class and its longer-term goals. Most of these workers had embraced the demand for Soviet power only after the July Days and under the impact of the advancing economic crisis. In the weeks before the October Revolution, they were already growing disillusioned with the political struggle and were attracted by anarchist agitation. The October Revolution raised their hopes of a political solution to their economic problems, but the new government was unable quickly or substantially to improve their situation. Hence, the accusation that the factory committees were neglecting the economic struggle and favouring the political one.

Anarchist support grew for a few months after the October Revolution. At one point the anarchists were even able to publish two daily newspapers, *Kommuna* and *Golostruda*. In mid-November, V.P. Polonskii, a Menshevik-Internationalist observed:

> At first insignificant, now the anarchists are a force that will have to be taken into consideration. In one of the factories, I happened to make a critical comment about the anarchists as an element that disorganises the

53 Ibid. (Mar. 22, 1918).

54 *Metallist*, no. 3 (1918) p. 5.

> workers' movement, and I heard back from the crowd: 'That's enough! The anarchists are our friends!'[55]

But the anarchist upsurge proved short-lived. Hunger, which arrived in full force in January, put an end to it. Opposition sentiment among workers looked now increasingly to the Mensheviks and SRs, who were trying to rally workers around the idea of the Constituent Assembly. But even more important in undermining anarchist influence were the factory closures of mid-December, after which many of the wartime workers returned to their villages. By the spring, very little was heard in Petrograd from the anarchists.

The Lines Harden

Despite the rise of oppositional sentiment among workers in the winter of 1917–18, it was still far from presenting a serious challenge to the Soviet government. In particular, those elements of the working class that had been the moving force of the drive for Soviet power from the start did not waver. At the Aivaz machine-construction factory, where support for the Bolsheviks had been consistent from the beginning of the revolution, the workers adopted the following resolution in response to the events of 5 January:

> We grieve for the blood that has been shed on both sides … But to the bourgeoisie and its agents, to the right SRs and the Mensheviks and to all those who are with them, in response to your hypocritical lamentations, we declare:
>
> You yourselves are to blame for the June offensive and the betrayal of Riga that cost the lives of hundreds of thousands of our brothers. You yourselves are to blame for introducing the death penalty for soldiers. You yourselves are to blame for the beatings, both in the jails and outside them, of revolutionary workers, soldiers and peasants. You tore to pieces comrade Voinov [an Aivaz worker] only because he was selling the newspaper *Pravda*. You, who organised the shooting in the October days, and now on the Kaledin front, have absolutely no right to express protest and indignation.

55 *Novaya zhizn'* (15 Nov. 1917).

> The entire blame for the shedding of fraternal blood lies with those enemies of the people's revolution who have set themselves the task of restoring the bourgeoisie to power and do not stop before deception of the proletariat and peasantry. All the blame lies with you.
>
> Peace to the fallen. Disgrace to the living who, through deceit, have pitted brother against brother.
>
> Peace to the fallen. Glory to the living fighters for socialism.[56]

Soon after the events of 5 January, the printers at State Printing House, which printed *Novaya zhizn'*, once again defied the papers' editors and refused to print the 12 January issue. The following day, the editors explained that the paper had failed to appear because the factory committee had taken upon itself the role of censor and had declared that issue to be 'of a pogrom nature' and, therefore, should not appear.[57]

Positions were hardening within the working class. And it is against that background that one should view the events of 5 January and the reactions to them. The Red Guards who fired on the demonstrators do not appear to have been acting on the order of the government, which was badly hurt by those acts. The period following the October insurrection was chaotic, and the soviets sometimes had trouble controlling the Red Guards. In one incident, Red Guards threatened to arrest a district soviet. But the broader background of the shooting of 5 January, which would have been inconceivable in the relatively tolerant atmosphere of the October days, was the deepening resentment among workers over the political strike (the workers saw it as 'sabotage') by government, public and bank employees, the educated 'middle stratum' of society. *Novaya zhizn'* commented on the situation in Moscow, but this paralleled that of Petrograd: 'The strike of the schools and hospitals is seen by the lower strata as a struggle of the bourgeoisie and intelligentsia against the popular masses … This strike creates great difficulties for the Bolsheviks' municipal government, but even more it exacerbates the hatred of the *nizy* [lower levels of society] for the intelligentsia and bourgeoisie'.[58] Meanwhile, news was arriving of the counterrevolutionary army being organised in the South by the generals. Rumours, which turned out to have a real basis, circulated in Petrograd of counterrevolutionary plots. On 1 January, the car carrying Lenin was hit by gunfire. A week

---

56 *Pravda* (Jan. 18, 1918). For similar positions, see the resolutions adopted at Novyi Lessner, *Znamya truda* (20 Jan. 1918); Rozenkrants, ibid.; and Skorokhod, *Pravda* (Jan. 20, 1918).

57 *Novaya zhizn'* (Jan. 13, 1918).

58 Ibid. (Dec. 12, 1917).

later, a large number of officers were arrested for planning a conspiracy that had been scheduled for the opening of the Constituent Assembly.[59]

The Petrograd Soviet discussed the attempt on Lenin's life on 4 January. During the session, a worker deputy declared: 'For each head of our leaders, we will demand a thousand heads of the others. We will know how to reply to black terror with red, more horrible terror. Long live red terror!' This declaration evoked loud applause from the entire hall. Next spoke Sukhanov, who called for cooler heads, reminding the assembly that there had also been attempts on Kerenskii, whom the Bolsheviks opposed. Yet no one blamed the attempts on the Bolsheviks. Terror, he explained, would be the ruin of the revolution. But the speech ended 'amidst noise from the entire hall'.[60] (However, three days later, this same Soviet strongly condemned the lynching of the arrested ministers of the Provisional Government, Kokohskin and Shingarev.)[61]

It was in this increasingly embittered atmosphere that the shooting occurred on 5 January. As the columns of demonstrators in support of the Constituent Assembly proceeded down the street, workers and soldiers on the sidelines hurled the epithets 'saboteurs' and 'bourgeois' at them.[62] When news of the shooting reached the crowd gathered outside the Tauride Palace, shouts of indignation on the part of the defenders of the Constituent Assembly were countered by shouts of 'that's what they deserve!' from the opponents.[63] When the Petrograd Soviet discussed the events, Sukhanov this time narrowly escaped a beating when he insisted on speaking against the resolution that had been proposed, despite the chairman ruling him out of order. He had to be rescued by Volodarskii, who managed to calm the hall.[64]

The same kind of acrimony characterised the Third Congress of Soviets that met in mid-January. When Sukhanov accused the congress of 'declaring civil war against all those who do not agree with Lenin's principles', a shout rang out: 'And we will also go against our own mothers and fathers!' During the discussion of the events of 5 January, the Menshevik-Internationalists Martov and Pobranitskii were shouted down as 'Kornilovists' and 'saboteurs'.[65] The atmosphere was indeed a far cry from the October days, when the Red Guards released General Krasnov on his word of honour.

---

59 Ibid. (Jan. 11, 19, 25, 1918); Dok. Nov., vol. II, p. 36.

60 Ibid. (Jan. 5, 1918).

61 Ibid. (Jan. 9,1918).

62 Ibid. (Jan. 6, 1918).

63 Ibid. (Jan. 9, 1918).

64 Ibid.

65 Ibid. (Jan. 12, 1918).

Workers who supported the Soviet government were particularly angered by the position adopted by the Menshevik-Internationalists. They had been bitter critics of the Provisional Government but were now criticising the Soviet government with equal vigour. Workers took especial offence at the mocking tone of *Novaya zhizn'*, criticising the government for its inability to govern effectively because it did not have the support of the educated elements of society.[66] A group of workers from the Putilov factory sent the following letter to the paper in reaction to its criticism of a demonstration marking the cease-fire at the front and the beginning of peace negotiations at Brest-Litovsk:

> The cannon department of the Putilov factory has resolved to censure you, writers and editors of *Novaya zhizn'*, [such] as Stroev, who was at one time a writer, and also Bazarov, Gimer-Sukhanov, Gorky and all the staff of *Novaya zhizn'*. Your Paper does not correspond to our present common Life, you follow the lead of the defencists. But remember our workers' Life, don't criticise the demonstration that took place on Sunday, it was not organised by you, and it is not for you to criticise it. And in general our party is the Majority and we support our political leaders genuine socialist liberators of the people from the yoke of the Bourgeoisie and capitalists, and in the future if such counterrevolutionary articles will be written then we workers swear – carve this on your foreheads – that we will shut your paper, and if you wish inquire of your socialist so-called neutralist he was at our Putilov factory with his backward speeches ask him if we let him speak or not, and soon you your paper will be forbidden it is approaching the level of a Kadet paper, and if you bitter backward writers also continue your polemics with the government [!] organ 'Pravda', then know that we will end [its] sale in our Narvskii-Petergofskii district.
>
> Putilov Factory, Cannon Department write a resp[onse] or there will be Repressions.

The condescending attitude toward these workers who supported the government was evident in the editors' very decision to print it with all its errors. Gorky's reply was on the same level: 'This sort of ferocity can be observed in the thinking of children who have begun to read the books of Gustave Aimard

66 See, for example, Sukhanov's article in *Novaya zhizn'* 14 January 1918, in which he wrote: 'A whole swarm of paper decrees remain without the slightest practical effect. You cannot even clean the snow off the streets of Petrograd'.

and imagine themselves to be terrible Indians'. He wrote that he had received many such letters.[67]

The Soviet government still enjoyed strong support among Petrograd's workers. A worker opposition had appeared, but it was still weak. It would grow, however, in the following months under the impact of deteriorating economic conditions. And then these worker oppositionists would have to seriously ponder the questions: Was the Constituent Assembly being proposed by the Mensheviks and SRs a real alternative to Soviet power? If not, was there any acceptable alternative?

---

67 Ibid. (22 Dec. 1917). See also Gordienko's account of an encounter between Gorky and three Vyborg workers in Chapter 14 below.

CHAPTER 14

The October Revolution in the Factories

'Active' or 'Passive' Control?

Opposed by the owners, who enjoyed the support of the Provisional Government, workers' control (in the sense of effective monitoring of management, including access to the books and other documents) was not able to make much progress in private factories before the October Revolution, although the committees had done what they could, often expending herculean efforts, to ensure the continued operation of their factories. The transfer of power to the soviets, therefore, quite understandably spurred the action of the committees in establishing control. And now they abandoned their previous refusal to assume responsibility for management, a refusal which, in any case, had been more formal than real if it meant preventing the loss of jobs or closure of the factory. After October, supported by the worker rank and file, the factory committees pressed for the broadest possible freedom of action *vis-à-vis* management, for 'active' control, that is, the power to issue orders that would be binding on management. Opposed to that position were the partisans of 'passive' control, according to which the factory committees would have the right to monitor management, including full access to information, but would not be allowed to directly intervene in managerial activity. This position was defended by many union leaders, by moderate Bolsheviks (often the same people as the first group), and also by the Mensheviks, all of whom accused the factory committees of anarcho-syndicalist tendencies.[1]

On the night of 26–7 October, Lenin wrote the draft of a Law on Workers' Control, according to which the factory committees would have access to all enterprise documents and to stores of raw materials and goods. Their decisions would be binding on management, subject to repeal only by trade-union organisations or conferences of factory committees.[2] In the ensuing discussion, various revisions of the draft law were proposed by different groups. After much deliberation, the TsIK adopted a law on workers' control on 14 November by a unanimous vote (24 voted in favour and 11 abstained). In presenting

1 For a survey of attitudes of various unions and union leaders to workers' control, see FZK III, pp. 115–31.

2 Lenin 1958–67, vol. XXXV, pp. 30–1.

the law to the TsIK, V.P. Milyutin responded to critics who argued that the activity of factory committees should be subordinated to a central economic plan; otherwise, each factory committee would defend the narrow interests of its own workers at the expense of the working class and the economy as a whole. Milyutin recognised that the adoption of a national economic plan should, in principle, have preceded the introduction of workers' control. But 'life demands immediate intervention, and so we had to sacrifice somewhat the planned character of the system'. As to whether control should be organised from above or below, he continued, it was decided to make use of what existed already, that is, the factory committees and their Central Soviet. The latter would be enlarged to include representatives of the trade unions and soviets, and together they would form regional economic councils. The new law accorded management of the factories three days in which to appeal the decision of a factory committee to these new economic councils. In the meantime, the factory committee's decisions would be binding. While the Central Soviet of Factory Committees expressed its satisfaction with the new law, the prominent Bolshevik trade unionist S.A. Lozovskii criticised it as anarcho-syndicalist.[3]

After the law was adopted, the debate revolved around guidelines for the activity of the factory committees. The Draft on Workers' Control, drawn up by the Central Soviet of Factory Committees and published on 7 December, afforded the committees broad powers to intervene directly into the sphere of management:

> Workers' control of industry, as an integral part of control over the entire economic life of the country, should not be understood in the narrow sense of simple inspection [*reviziya*] but, on the contrary, in the broad sense of *intervention* into the disposition by the entrepreneur of capital, inventory, raw materials and finished goods in the enterprise; [it should be understood as] *active monitoring* [*nadzor*] of the correctness and expediency of the fulfilment production orders [*zakazy*], the use of energy and of the work force, and [in the sense of] *participation in the organisation of production itself on a rational basis, etc. etc.* [emphasis in original].[4]

In opposition to this, the draft guidelines adopted by the First All-Russian Council of Trade Unions and by an All-Russian Congress of Trade Unions would

3 *Izvestiya* (Nov. 16, 1917); *Znamya truda* (Nov. 16, 1917).

4 FZK III, p. 146.

have restricted the activity of the factory committees to 'narrow' or 'passive' control, leaving full executive power in the hands of management:

> The control commission does not participate in management of the enterprise and does not bear responsibility for its work and activity, which remains that of the owner ... The control commission itself can petition for sequestration but cannot itself seize and run it [the enterprise].
>
> Management's orders could be countermanded only by government or higher trade-union organisations.[5]

The Petrograd Metalworkers' Union was an important exception to the general support among union leaders for the 'passive' version of control. At a conference of delegates to that union's Petrograd Council, to which representatives of the factory committees had been invited, several speakers, including the secretary of the union's executive, G.D. Vainberg, a metalworker from the Vyborg district, urged rejection of the draft adopted by the trade-union congress. He argued that it 'ties the hand of workers, whereas the draft [drawn up by the Central Soviet of Factory Committees] gives workers broad initiative and makes them in practice the masters of the given enterprise'.[6] The rapporteur on this question, who began by defending the version of the trade-union congress, concluded his speech with a proposal to continue work on both drafts.[7]

The *Sovnarkom* (Soviet of People's Commissars – the national government) did not officially confirm either guideline. Lenin adopted the position that the question could only be decided by practical experience. Both drafts continued to circulate, but the guidelines of the Central Soviet of Factory Committees prevailed in the factories, since the conflicts that arose and the deepening economic crisis were pushing the factory committees to intervene directly in the managerial sphere. The factory committees were unable to subordinate their activity to a national or regional economic plan, as the 'comrades on the right' demanded, for the simple reason that the Soviet government was unable so quickly to establish the necessary regulating and planning institutions, and so no plan yet existed.[8] Responding to criticisms, N. Katyn', a member of the Central Soviet of Factory Committees, wrote in January 1918:

---

5 FZK III., pp, 133, 142, *Izvestiya* (Dec. 13, 1917).

6 *Metallist*, no. 1 (1918) p. 13.

7 *Novaya zhizn'* (Dec. 23, 1917).

8 FZK III, p. 137.

> [… The factory committees] consider themselves to be the basic units of the higher regulating institutions of the economy and are doing everything in their power to follow the path laid out by these organs and institutions. And it is not their fault that all these institutions do not yet exist, or that they are everywhere so closely tied with the tsarist bourgeoisie and the conciliators of our bourgeois revolution, with the result that no one can understand anything and they are themselves incapable of productive activity. It is not their [the factory committees'] fault that, when they find themselves confronted by a complete lack of clarity in this or that matter, circumstances and urgency force them to act at their own risk and peril and on their own responsibility …[9]

In fact, the accusations of anarchism directed at the factory committees by union leaders were to a large extent disingenuous, since every conference of factory committees, before and after October, had insisted that workers' control, in order to be effective had to be exerted within the framework of systematic state regulation of the economy exercised on a national level. The urgent need for the centralisation of economic authority at the regional and national levels was recognised by all factory committee activists, except for the small minority of anarchists. It was clear to everyone that the conversion of military industry to peacetime production, which had begun officially in Petrograd in mid-December but whose realisation met with enormous difficulties, and the allocation of contracts and of increasingly scarce fuel and raw materials, could not be left to individual factory committees.

The need for centralisation was, in fact, a central theme of the Sixth Petrograd Conference of Factory Committees on 22–7 January 1918, at which the Central Soviet of Factory Committees' proposal for the organisation of regional economic councils – *sovnarkhozy* – was discussed and 'met with the warmest sympathy', as reported by the journal of the Central Soviet.[10] According to this plan, the decisions of the *sovnarkhozy* would be binding on local institutions, including factory committees.[11] (The Central Soviet of Factory Committees Council would itself eventually become part of the *Sovnarkhoz* of the Northern Region.)[12] The guidelines on workers' control adopted by the conference

9 N. Katyn', 'Ot rabochego kontrolya k organizatsii i regulirovaniyu proizvodstva', *Novyi put'*, no. 1–2 (5–6) (Jan. 14, 1918).

10 *Novyi put'*, no. 6–8, 1918, pp. 22. The complete protocols of this conference were published in FZK IV (*Oktyabr'skaya revolyutsiya i fabzavkomy*, vol. IV).

11 FZK IV, p. 439.

12 FZK III, pp. 128, 286; FZK IV, pp. 26, 34.

stated that, while the factory committee executes the will of the workers' general assembly, 'at the same time, it executes all the directives and guidelines of the higher economic organs ... The factory committee answers to the government authority for the strictest order in the rational conduct of the activity of the enterprise, in accordance with the needs of the entire working people, and also [answers] for the integrity of the property of the given enterprise'.[13] Other resolutions adopted by the conference called for the centralised distribution of production contracts and fuel.[14]

The guidelines on workers' control, adopted by the conference with only three dissenting votes, also made clear that orders issued by higher authorities that might sacrifice the local interests of workers of a given factory had to be obeyed by the factory committees.[15] To the arguments of anarchist delegates that centralisation 'turns ... into some sort of autocracy', another delegate, expressing the position of the overwhelming majority, replied:

> All the factories have to coordinate their activity. Who will do the coordinating? A higher organisation that will monitor everything, that will know everything, that will distribute orders, that will know what is being done at which factory. We are the control directly in the factory ... We show what we need. But distribution has to be concentrated ... In the conditions of economic collapse that we are experiencing ... we need that like air itself. I emphasise: we need that organisation. We need centralisation ... We need it; otherwise, we will be confused. Otherwise, we will never get out of the present situation and we will never be able to create better conditions for the country.[16]

Another remarked that the anarchists, for all their criticism of centralism, were unable to explain concretely how they would organise the economy. Moreover, if the anarchists were really consistent with themselves, they would oppose even the factory committees, since the latter limit the freedom of individual workers to do as they want.[17]

The delegates, however, were not insensitive to the anarchists' warnings of the dangers of centralism. When one of the latter proposed to amend the

---

13 FZK IV, p. 417.
14 Ibid., pp. 443–4.
15 Ibid., p. 158.
16 Ibid., p. 181.
17 Ibid., p. 197.

guidelines so that the factory committees' obligation to obey orders of higher organs would be conditional on the orders' conformity with the interests of the proletariat, Katyn', speaking for the Central Soviet, replied that the conference's organisers had, in fact, considered such a reservation, but finally decided against its inclusion. He further explained:

> The *sovnarkhoz* that we are organising will not go against us because it is not a bureaucratically created organ, not one appointed from above, but an organ that we ourselves have chosen, that we can recall, and it consists of people that we can remove from their activity ... Don't forget that the sovnarkhoz is a class organ, based on the class of the proletariat and the poorest peasants, and it seems to us that it is hardly necessary, by including such a reservation, to express this sort of lack of confidence in them. If we adopt an attitude of mistrust from the very beginning, then these organs will scarcely be able to function correctly ... Only an anarchist could propose such an amendment, as they reject any kind of leaders and have absolutely no confidence in them. [But] if these organs really do part ways with the masses, then, of course, we will have to introduce such an amendment. And we will have to go further. We will have to overthrow those organs and perhaps make a new revolution. But it seems to us that for now the Soviet of People's Commissars is our soviet, and the institutions that it has established are functioning harmoniously together.[18]

This response reflected the confidence of a working class that had been the leading force in three revolutions.

Although the conference rejected the anarchists' position, the original version of the draft guidelines had, in fact, called for the election of regional *sovnarkhozy* exclusively by conferences of factory committees and trade unions. One might see in this a syndicalist approach to economic organisation. However, the proposal of the Supreme Soviet of the National Economy (*VeSeNKha*) to include also representatives of soviets and cooperatives, as well as of technical and managerial personnel in the *sovnarkhozy*, was accepted by the conference without opposition.[19]

The main issue underlying the opposition from the 'comrades on the right' to the factory committees was not, in fact, any alleged anarchist tendencies of the

---

18 Ibid., pp. 323–4.

19 Ibid, pp. 475–6; *Novyi put'*, no. 6–8, 1918, pp. 22–4.

latter, although the potential for conflict between local and general interests was very real in conditions of deepening economic crisis and shortage. The fundamental issue was really the social nature of the revolution in Russia, since 'active' control meant the workers' radical incursion into owners' property rights and that, in turn, pointed more or less directly to the suppression of capitalism, even if it was not the goal of the factory committees in any immediate sense.

The Bolshevik party itself lacked a clear position on this question. In his 'April Theses', Lenin had written only: 'Not "the introduction" of socialism as our immediate task, but only the transition now to control on the part of the Soviet of Workers' Deputies of the social production and distribution of goods'.[20] Sukhanov, who was a member of the Petrograd Soviet's Economic Department, remarked that, to the extent that the Bolsheviks had an economic programme in 1917,

> it, in essence, did not go beyond the limits of the familiar economic programme of 16 May [1917] that had been adopted by the old Executive Committee [of the Petrograd Soviet] for execution by the coalition government … In essence, it was very far from socialism. But it nevertheless contained an element that has special significance for us. That is the famous workers' control of production. This was the militant point at all proletarian meetings. As a specifically worker's demand, it figures next to land. And here, if you will, the Bolshevik leaders come close to publicly declaring the principle of socialism. But this 'socialism' was, nevertheless, extremely timid and modest: in their theory the Bolsheviks take another path, but they do not go farther than the right-wing Menshevik Groman, with his programme of 'regulation' or 'organisation of the national economy and labour'.[21]

A week before the October Revolution, a Menshevik delegate from Saratov at the All-Russian Conference of Factory Committees argued:

> In order correctly to decide the question of control over production, we have to clarify for ourselves once and for all whether the Russian Revolution is a social one or not. This is the fundamental question that we always pose to the comrade Bolsheviks, but they don't give any reasonable

20 V.I. Lenin 1958–67, vol. XXXI, p. 116.
21 Sukhanov 1919–23, vol. VII, pp. 24–6.

> answer. We say that our revolution is not social, but political with a social leavening, so to speak – in it, questions of vast social significance are posed.[22]

I. Zhuk, an anarchist delegate at the conference from the Schlusselburg Powder Factory, was equally clear: 'We are experiencing a social revolution'.[23] On the other hand, N.A. Skrypnik, a Bolshevik and member of the Central Council of Factory Committees, refused to be pinned down: 'Workers' control is not yet socialism but only one of the transitional measures that bring us closer to socialism'.[24]

As Marxists, the Bolsheviks shared the Mensheviks' analysis of Russian society as one lacking the economic and political conditions necessary for socialism: Russia was a poor country at a relatively early stage of industrialisation, with a small working-class population and a vast peasantry. But the Bolsheviks had a much more realistic understanding of the deeply polarised nature of class relations in Russia. That is the basic reason why, from at least 1912 onward, they enjoyed much stronger support among workers than the Mensheviks. The Bolsheviks, as a party, were prepared to provide leadership for what political circumstances, regardless of Marxist theory, were forcing workers to do. Without that leadership, the workers' struggle would have been dispersed, uncoordinated and inevitably doomed to defeat. The Bolshevik practice followed the maxim that, according to Trotsky, should guide revolutionaries in all great struggles of principle: 'Fais ce que dois, advienne que pourra'.[25] This was the same orientation behind the position Lenin adopted on the question of 'active' or 'passive' control: active control meant the more or less direct overthrow of capitalism, despite the absence of conditions for socialism in Russia. But only concrete practice could resolve the issue. Of course, the Bolsheviks hoped that the October Revolution would precipitate revolutions in the more developed countries of the West, and that these in return would provide support to help the Russian Revolution overcome its contradictions. But that hope in itself did not determine their action.

Mensheviks regarded the Bolsheviks' outlook as irresponsible adventurism. They argued that soviet power and workers' control would inevitably lead the government to adopt socialist measures. But Russia lacked the conditions for

22 FZK II, p. 182.
23 Ibid., p. 183.
24 Ibid., p. 184.
25 Roughly: 'Do what you must – come what may' (Trotsky 1930, p. 418).

these to succeed, and the workers would inevitably be defeated. This was the reasoning by which the Menshevik-defencists explained the necessity of representation in power of the liberal wing of the bourgeoisie, a group that they claimed to exist, despite all evidence to the contrary. The Menshevik-internationalists, who became a majority in the party after the October Revolution, agreed with the Bolsheviks' assessment of the political situation, namely that there was no democratic bourgeoisie in Russia, that the class as a whole was determined to crush the revolution. That ruled out a coalition government with its representatives. But they could not bring themselves to accept a government responsible exclusively to the soviets or workers' control, since they felt that both entailed socialist measures, for which the conditions were lacking. They chose instead to stand by the side and criticise the Soviet government, sometimes in a mocking tone, something Bolshevik workers found especially insulting. Once revolution broke out in Germany in November 1918, the Mensheviks dropped their call for a Constituent Assembly and embraced Soviet power 'in principle', but they refused to support the Soviet government or to participate in it.

Worker activists had difficulty understanding this position. Three Bolshevik workers from the Vyborg district, upset with *Novaya zhizn*'s criticisms of the Soviet government, paid a visit in the early months of Soviet rule to Maksim Gorky, an editor of the paper, who was originally from the town of Nizhnyi Novgorod, like these workers. One of them, I.M. Gordienko, recalled:

> While conversing with us, Aleksei Maksimovich [Gorky], deep in thought, said: 'It's hard, boys, for you, very hard'.
>
> 'But you, Alekei Makimovich, you're not helping us', I threw in.
>
> 'Not only does he not help, but he's undermining our efforts', said Ivan Chugurin ...
>
> 'Ekh, boys, boys, you're great, and I'm sorry for you. You have to understand that you're a grain of sand in this sea, no, in this ocean of petty-bourgeois, elemental peasantry. How many of you are you, such firm Bolsheviks? A handful. In life, you're like a drop of fat in the ocean, the thinnest film that a slight breeze can rip apart'.
>
> 'You're wrong, Aleksei Maksimovich. Come visit us in our Vyborg district and you'll see: where there used to be 600 Bolsheviks, now there are thousands'.

'Thousands, but raw, unshod, and other cities don't have even that'.

'The same thing, Aleksei Maksimovich, is happening in other cities and villages. Everywhere the class struggle is intensifying'.

'That's why I love you – for your strong faith. But that's also why I'm afraid for you ... You'll perish, and then everything will be thrown back hundreds of years. The thought is frightening ...'

A week went by, and we again, the same people, were at Aleksei Maksimovich's place ... But this time, we found Sukhanov and the Sormovo Menshevik who went by the party name Lopata[26] there ... Aleksei Maksimovich again spoke of the petty-bourgeois peasant ocean and he grieved that we, old Bolshevik underground activists, were few, and that the party youth lacked experience. Sukhanov and Lopata tried to back up Aleksei Maksimovich's reasoning with facts. They said that you have to be crazy to talk about a proletarian revolution in so backward a country as Russia. We strongly protested. We said that behind the screen of a classless, all-national [*vsenarodnaya*] democracy they were defending the dictatorship of the bourgeoisie.

'But you have to see that in our peasant country there can be nothing else', excitedly retorted Sukhanov and Lopata. 'That's our tragedy. The peasantry will crush us'. And again – numbers, numbers, numbers ...

In the course of this argument, Aleksei Maksimovich went to the window that looked onto the street, and then he quickly came back to me, grabbed me by the hand, and dragged me over to the window.

'Take a look', he said with anger and resentment in his voice. What I saw was really outrageous. Next to a bed of flowers on a low-cut green lawn, a group of soldiers had sat themselves down. They were eating herring and throwing all the waste onto the flower bed.

'And in the people's house[27] it is the same thing: the floors are waxed, they placed spittoons in the corners and next to the columns, but look

26 V.A. Desnitskii, who also went by the party name of Stroev. After the civil war he was for a time professor at Leningrad University.

27 A cultural and educational institution for the popular classes.

at what they do', sorrowfully said Mariya Fedorovna, who managed the people's house.

'And with that sort of people the Bolsheviks intend to create a socialist revolution', said Lopata sarcastically.

'And who will teach and educate them, do you mean the bourgeoisie?' one of us asked.

'Well, how do you want to do it?' asked Aleksei Maskimovich, smiling already.

'We want to do it differently', I answered. 'First to overthrow the bourgeoisie, and then to educate the people. We will build our schools, clubs, people's houses …'

'But that's not realistic', declared Lopata.

'It isn't realistic for you, but we will do it', I answered.[28]

In a brochure on workers' control, the Bolshevik trade unionist S.A. Lozovsky, one of the authors of the draft guidelines for 'passive' control, made it very clear that underlying union leaders' opposition to 'active' control was, in fact, the question of the social character of the revolution in backward Russia:

> Workers' control … is a transitional revolutionary measure that has been put forward in a transitional revolutionary epoch. Workers' control still does not affect the bases of the capitalist system. It leaves intact private property and the equipment of production and the entire private commercial apparatus – not because it is better that way from the point of view of the interests of the proletariat, but because the proletariat is not capable of doing more in the given historical moment, given its lack of sufficient organisational skills and without a socialist revolution in the advanced countries of Europe. The proletariat can lay its hands on the entire productive apparatus, get close to the entire process of control, limit, with its firm hand, the appetites of the dominant class, but no more.[29]

---

28 I. Gordienko 1957, pp. 98–101.

29 A. Lozovskii 1918, pp. 24–5, cited in FZK III, pp. 133–4.

Lozovsky here envisages a kind of dual power in the economy, by which the capitalists would continue to manage their enterprises but would be regulated by the workers' state in the interests of the workers and be monitored by the factory committees. The advocates of 'active' control were not in principle opposed to this vision, which is also close to what Lenin had initially proposed. The Petrograd Conference of Factory Committees that met on 15–16 November overwhelmingly rejected the calls from anarchist delegates to take over the factories.[30] Skrypnik told the conference:

> We are linked to other countries. But that only shows that the torch, raised by our revolution, can also ignite the proletariat of Western Europe. The working class, step by step, in struggle, is moving toward its ideal. Socialism is not created at once. It is created by the gradual restructuring of the whole of economic and political life. We have entered the first period of that restructuring. We will have to carry out a whole series of measures, such as, for example, control of production and distribution, etc. A whole series of tasks lies before us. We have entered the period of mass struggle. This is not socialism but it is the first step, the path to socialism.[31]

What separated the 'comrades on the right', advocates of 'passive' control, from the factory-committee activists was that the latter, more closely tied to the workers and to the concrete reality in the factories, felt that they needed their hands untied to do whatever might be necessary to save the factories, and so also the revolution. They, too, subscribed to the maxim: 'Fais ce que dois, advienne que pourra'. This orientation, essentially defensive and practical (as opposed to offensive and ideological), had characterised the movement for workers' control from its inception. The factory committees did not begin with the idea of suppressing capitalism. But at the same time, they were prepared to make incursions into private property rights if they judged it necessary. They were not going to remain passive, as in 1905, when a concerted lockout dealt a mortal blow to the revolution.

Even after the October Revolution, workers showed they were willing to limit their control to Lozovsky's conception of dual power, if they considered this to be a realistic option. In a report to the Central Soviet of Factory Committees from 11 January 1918, the committee of the Erikson telephone factory in

30 FZK III, p. 46, 43.

31 Ibid., p. 42.

the Vyborg district stated that management was cooperating with the committee in its efforts to obtain fuel and raw materials, since it did not consider that sort of activity as a challenge to its prerogatives. However, it was resisting the committee's efforts to establish financial and economic control (monitoring), refusing access to documents, even brandishing the threat of collective resignation of the administration if the factory committee decided to force the matter. The factory committee decided not to press its rights at the moment, 'in order to avoid premature complications that could entail the temporary closure of the factory'.[32] *Novaya zhizn'*, which supported the position of the 'comrades on the right', commented:

> One should note that the factory committee at Erikson, acting in full contact with the factory administration, is very intelligently making use of the decree on workers' control and not overestimating its forces. Thus, for example, it froze all the financial assets of the joint-stock company and in that way prevented their disappearance from the enterprise and their transfer abroad. At the same time, the factory committee in no way intrudes upon the economic prerogatives of the factory administration.[33]

In a similar case, the committee of the Tentelevskii chemical factory reached an agreement with the administration, according to which the latter recognised the workers' right to control (monitoring) and the workers recognised the administration's right to manage.[34]

Despite the fears of moderate Bolsheviks and Mensheviks, the factory committees generally showed concern not to alienate management needlessly, but on the condition that they felt management was acting in good faith. In mid-January 1918, the Putilov factory committee reported:

> The committee, defending the interest of the comrade workers, not only adopted the principle of resolving conflicts between capital and labour, it constantly adhered to the tendency of intervention into the economic life of the factory and, as far as was possible, carried that out in practice without assuming executive functions, but only functions of control; and all the gains we made in that area, all the control posts that have been occupied by the committee, were won without open conflict with the

32 Rab. Kon., pp. 325–6.

33 *Novaya zhizn'* (Jan. 23, 1918).

34 Rab. Kon., p. 285.

> representatives of capital, without summoning the masses to defend their positions, but exclusively by means of verbal negotiations and similar means of influence.[35]

When the head of the control commission at the Novaya Bumagopryadil'naya textile mill, a young woman worker, provoked the director's departure by insisting on her right to carefully verify every purchase before she authorised it, the factory committee at once called her out and replaced her. One of its members admonished her: 'How can you not understand that without a specialist we won't be able to manage?'[36]

The situation was more complex at the Keresten knitting mill. In the beginning of December, the workers' control commission discovered that the owner had been shipping out finished goods without its knowledge and was hiding its financial operations from it. It decided to post a guard at the cash desk. But the board of directors announced it would not recognise the decisions of the factory committee, offering as a pretext the fact that the chairman of the factory committee was a worker who had returned from the army after the February Revolution and had been rehired on the sole decision of the factory committee, without management's authorisation. On 4 December, the office employees struck in protest over the brief detention by some workers of the director and the chief bookkeeper. The board of directors announced that the mill would close. The workers' general assembly then decided to keep the mill open under the management of the factory committee and to request the government to sequester it. At this point, the executive of the Textile Workers' Union intervened and convinced the workers to make concessions in order to get the office employees and management to return. An agreement was reached on 8 December, guaranteeing the personal inviolability of the office employees. In return, management agreed to recognise the workers' 'passive' control and to reopen the mill the next week after. But soon after, the owner vanished from Petrograd along with the contents of the factory's safe – 40,000 gold rubles.[37]

---

35 *Putilovtsy v trekh revolyutsiyakh*, p. 432.

36 Perazich 1927, p. 104.

37 Ibid., pp. 105–6, Nats prom, SSSR, pp. 345–6.

Towards Nationalisation

Workers' control in its 'passive' version was premised upon the owners' willingness to continue running their factories, while the factory committees monitored the activity of the administration. On 23 November 1917, the Petrograd Society of Factory and Mill Owners adopted a decision, binding on its members, calling to close any factory in which workers' control was introduced.[38] However, when G.I. Koshurnikov, a representative of the Society, was asked at a meeting of the Petrograd Section of the Russian Leather Manufacturers' Association on 23 January how to interpret that directive, he replied that 'abandoning is conceivable for those enterprises that are already without means, but not at all when the enterprises represent value for the owner'. In the course of the discussion, it emerged that there were two kinds of control – monitoring [*proverochnyi*] control, and executive control. If the first, defended by the trade-union leaders, was considered tolerable by the Society, the second had to be fought.[39]

That position seemed to offer an opening for 'passive' control. But dual power, by its very nature, is always an unstable arrangement. And the reality was that owners were fast losing any interest in the continued operation of their factories. During the war, well over two-thirds of Petrograd's industry was producing for military needs,[40] an activity that was highly lucrative. But the Soviet government had decided to demobilise industry. This meant an end to the high war profits. Moreover, conversion would require new investment. In any case, the very functioning of industry was becoming increasingly problematic as the supply crisis deepened. If to this one adds the owners' heightened insecurity after October about their property and their inclination to use the economic crisis as a political weapon against the workers, one can understand their loss of interest in the continued operation of their factories.

In these conditions, workers were finding that even the 'active' version of control was not adequate. Increasingly, requests came from the factories for nationalisation. In some cases, these were a response to management's rejection of workers' control in any of its forms and to the owner's decision to close. Such was the case, for example, at the Robert Krug machine-building factory. On 12 December, the factory committee informed the workers' general assembly that the administration had rejected the draft guidelines on workers'

38 FZK III, p. 107.

39 Rab. kon. i nats., pp. 339–48.

40 *Peterburgskii komitet RKP(b) v 1918*. SPb, 2013, pp. 212.

control and had announced its intention to cease operations. The meeting decided that the workers should take over the factory, removing the five top administrators. That day, the entire administrative staff vanished along with the factory's operating funds. In its report to its Central Soviet of Factory Committees, the factory committee explained:

> As a result of the criminal sabotage by the board of directors of our factory, we were put before the necessity, in order to avoid the final stoppage of the factory, to convoke a general assembly of workers and office employees, at which the serious situation of the factory was explained and the decision was adopted to take the factory into our hands.[41]

This radical departure from control was still presented as a defensive measure.

As presented earlier, a long chain of conflicts at the Vulkan machine-building factory in the summer and fall of 1917 had led to the establishment of state control with participation of the factory committee and the Metalworkers' Union. On 20 February 1918, the factory committee submitted a request to the *Sovnarkhoz* of the Northern District for nationalisation of the enterprise. It explained that the factory had received a big loan from the Siberian Commercial Bank, which since then had become state property, and that the board of directors was posing insurmountable obstacles to workers' control, continuing to consider itself as the unique authority in the factory. The only way out, argued the committee, was for the state to take over the enterprise.[42] In a letter dated 23 March, it further explained:

> The factory committee, having discussed ... the entire policy of the directors, has reached the following conclusion: since the entire policy of the directors, beginning from July 1917 and until the present time, has been and is being conducted with a definite view to closing the factory (circulars of the board of directors) and [considering] that if the factory is not presently closed, then this support of the life of the factory has to be attributed to the energy of the factory committee, which, encountering every hour in its activity insurmountable difficulties, conducted its entire policy with a view to supporting the life of the factory, [and since] the factory committee considers that the [kind of] control that the administration is willing to accept would be a [mere] palliative, since the

41 Rab. kon. i nats., p. 283.

42 Nats. Prom. SSSR, pp. 350–1.

> administration would continue to be the master of the enterprise, while responsibility for conducting the affairs in the factory will lie fully with the control commission, and consequently, dual power will not be eliminated – the factory committee sees the only way out in the nationalisation of the factory, and this petition once again affirms this.[43]

In this case, the immediate reason given for nationalisation was management's rejection of 'active' control. But this has to be viewed against the background of the factory committees' months-long running battle with the administration to keep the factory operating.

This case was by no means unique. The decision to demobilise in itself led to many demands for nationalisation, since the administration, sometimes with the support of the technical staff, in many cases refused to participate in the conversion, seeing it as an illegitimate initiative of the workers.[44]

The factory committee at Vulkan was one of many that made truly herculean efforts to keep their factory operating. Most did not succeed in the conditions of severe and continually deepening economic breakdown. One of the relatively successful examples was the Opticheskii factory. In a document dated 7 September 1918, the factory committee briefly related its history. Control began on 18 January 1918, when the factory committee held up funds that the administration was attempting to transfer to its parent company in France.

> Gradually taking increasingly greater part in the affairs of management, the factory committee and its ... control commission took over the main functions of management of the enterprise. In the period of demobilisation and the threat of a German offensive [threatening Petrograd], and also in the anxious moments, when dark and malicious elements were baiting the leading organs with the aim of further disorganising the life of the state, the factory committee was forced to assume the entire burden of the struggle to prevent the factory's closing.
>
> During the war, the factory's optical department had been greatly diminished, as operations shifted into the production of grenade detonators. But when the time came to demobilise in January 1918, the municipal power station limited the supply of electricity to two days a week. The factory committee reacted by building its own generating plant, itself purchasing the machinery. This task took three months. Meanwhile, it

43 Ibid.

44 *Novaya zhizn'* (Feb. 4/17 1918). See also *Pravda* (Jan. 31, 1918).

> worked on the development of new models of cinematographic equipment, running the factory legally two days a week, and illegally at night the rest of the time. Those members of the administration who refused to collaborate were gradually dismissed, the factory committee assuming their functions. It also conducted a purge of undisciplined elements among the workers who were having a demoralising influence. As a result, productivity declined here less than at other factories. Eventually, the factory obtained contracts to build projectors for the Commissariat of Education.
>
> The factory committee and its control organ, taking management of production into their hands, knew that they were overstepping by several degrees all the guidelines issued by the higher organs of power to workers' organizations ... Feeling their strength, they confidently took up a great cause, and after a stubborn struggle in all four directions, they were able correctly to approach the task they had set – to keep the plant operating, to create discipline, to organise production on a new basis, and to save the treasury of the People's government many millions in funds that, had the workers' organisation not been up to the task, would have floated away into the pockets of foreign imperialists, as happened in many other cases ... Based on all the foregoing, the factory committee and the control commission ... declare that the time has come to remove the unnecessary obstacles; it is time to take fully into the workers' hands the enterprise that they have put in order, and for that they have people who are prepared to assume the task of managing.[45]

The situation was such that even 'comrades on the right' among the Bolsheviks, like Yu. Larin, until recently a Menshevik and a strong advocate of the 'passive' version of control, were forced to conclude that dual power in the factories, whether in the form of 'passive' or 'active' control, was unworkable. Larin, who was responsible in the Soviet government for economic affairs after the October Revolution, told an All-Russian Congress of the Metalworkers' Union at the end of January 1918:

> We tried in many cases to postpone the moment of full [takeover of management] of the enterprises and to restrict ourselves to control. But all our efforts led to nothing. In the present situation not one of the existing forces can – and sometimes they do not even want to – manage the eco-

45 *Nats prom i org.* vol. 1, pp. 82–6.

> nomy. Example: the Volga merchant navy, whose vessels the industrialists have stopped repairing and which has ceased all activity generally ... Now there is but one way out: either move forward or drown. We have to abandon the idea of workers' control and, whether we want to or not, shift to a system of full management of the enterprises and to management of the country's economy.[46]

Although the conference of factory committees in November 1917 had rejected anarchists' proposals for the workers to take over the factories, insisting that workers' control was not socialism but only a first step toward it, nationalisation of industry was already on the agenda of the conference on January 22–7 1918. M.N. Zhivotov, a Bolshevik electrician at the 1886 Electric Lighting Co., presented the report on that question, explaining: 'A series of requests are being received from factory committees on the need to take the factories into the workers' hands, and so unexpectedly there arises the practical question of nationalisation of enterprises'.[47] He went on to explain that the requests were made in response to the owners' refusal to recognise workers' control or to their refusal to run their factories for other reasons, although there were also some requests for nationalisation that were not responses to these problems.[48] G.P. Maksimov, an anarchist delegate, summed up the situation:

> Each one of us knows that our industrial life is dying and that the moment will soon arrive when all industrial life is dead. We are now living through the final seizures that will lead to the stoppage of our industrial life. And here it is not the question of control that is posed. After all, you can control when you have something to control ... Industrial life is stopping, transport is being destroyed. Everything speaks to the conclusion that it is not control and not regulation that are needed ... No, starting from the farthest right and right up to the most leftist, everyone agrees on one thing: we need to rebuild economic life itself; we need to build economic life on a new basis; we need to organise production and, consequently, we need to discuss here not control but the organisation of production.[49]

The conference unanimously adopted a resolution that called for the nationalisation of industry. But it recognised that this could not be achieved quickly.

46 *Novaya zhizn'* (Jan. 21, 1918).

47 *Novyi put'*, no. 6–8, 1918, p. 24. See also *Novaya zhizn'* (Jan. 28, 1918).

48 FZK IV, p. 290.

49 Ibid., pp. 175–6.

Nationalisation had to proceed in a planned, systematic manner, but the Soviet state still lacked the technical apparatus that was necessary. But it did call for the immediate nationalisation of enterprises whose administration refused to recognise workers' control, openly or secretly sabotaged, or refused to continue operations. If this still could be seen as a predominantly defensive reaction, a new note, one that was clearly offensive in character, appeared in the conference's call to nationalise immediately factories that were in good physical and financial shape and that could be easily and quickly converted to peacetime production. For, it explained, 'the proletarian Republic takes from the predators not only the economy that has been destroyed and lies as a burden on the people's treasury but also those enterprises that are able to operate intensively and give the people goods necessary for the economy that can help to restore to health the people's heritage'.[50]

But this radicalisation was not based on utopian illusions of a socialist paradise waiting just around the corner. The activists of the factory committees had, in fact, an extremely sober, not to say dismal, analysis of the economic situation. One of the delegates summed up the reports on the state of industry in the following words: 'We have heard here of such dislocation, of so terrible a reality, one that we ourselves all experience and know directly, but it nevertheless causes our heart strings to tremble when it is laid out before us by people who are living it'.[51] Nor did the delegates have illusions about the Soviet state being able to turn the situation around quickly. Most of them were Bolsheviks or Bolshevik sympathisers, but they did not spare their criticism of their own class organisations. Running through the conference were complaints about the shortage of qualified people in the economic institutions, and not so much on the local level as in the regional and national economic organisations. One of the delegates told of the shock he received when he went to the *VeSenKha* (Higher Council of the National Economy) and found there a mere ten or twelve people, when, in his opinion, there should have been at least 120 active people. Zhivotov, who answered for the Central Soviet of Factory Committees, admitted that this was unfortunately true, explaining that there were simply not enough competent people to meet all the needs. Even some members of the Central Soviet did not always show up to its meetings, as they were busy elsewhere.[52]

---

50 Ibid.

51 FZK IV, p. 241.

52 Ibid., p. 51; *Novaya zhizn'* (Jan. 26, 1918). Among other things, the panicky, chaotic evacuation, not only of central government institutions but also of some of the factories at the beginning of March in face of the threat of imminent German occupation, was the object

But if the mood was sombre, it was also determined. One of the delegates evoked the concerted lockouts that had dealt a mortal blow to the Revolution of 1905.[53] These workers were determined not to allow a repetition of that defeat.

Nationalisation in practice proceeded slowly over the next months and was carried out mostly on an individual enterprise basis in metallurgy and metalworking, either as a punitive measure or to prevent closure.[54] Following nationalisation of the merchant river fleet, which was repaired by workers without pay over several months, the first complete sector to be nationalised was sugar, in May 1918. It was followed by the oil industry in June, and then the remaining private metalworking enterprises.[55]

As in the case of workers' control itself, nationalisation was not primarily undertaken as a necessary step towards socialism but as a practical measure, one imposed by circumstances, for the survival of the revolution. In a pamphlet entitled 'From Workers Control to Workers' Management in Industry', published in 1918, the prominent Bolshevik I. Stepanov offered this explanation of the shift from workers' control to nationalisation:

> Conditions were such that the factory committees became full masters of the enterprises. This was the result of the entire development of our revolution. It was the inevitable consequence of the unfolding class struggle. The proletariat did not so much move toward this, as circumstances led it to it. It simply had to do what in the given situation it was impossible not to do …

But, he continued, workers were taking too long to organise genuine regulation. The factory committees tended to see things from the vantage point of their own enterprise. That, of course, was only natural, since they saw their primary task as helping the workers of their factory live through the hard times. But measures adopted from the point of view of an individual factory were leading away from the task of conscious, systematic regulation, often complicating the situation in a period of such deep economic crisis. The situation required that measures be adopted on the national level.

---

of very harsh criticism from workers, and not least from Bolsheviks : *Peterburgskii komitet v 1918 g.*, pp. 58–64.

53 FZK IV, p. 174.

54 *Trudy I Vserossiiskogo s'ezda sovetov narodnogo khozyaistva*, Moscow, 1918, pp. 53, 91–2.

55 Carr 1952, vol. II, p. 189.

As terrible as that may seem to many, that means the complete removal of the capitalists from the economy. Yes, 'socialist experiments', as our opponents [reference to the Mensheviks] chuckle. Yes, we have to say it directly: what the working class of Russia has to do now is to remove capitalism and resurrect the entire economy on a new socialist basis. This is not a 'fantastic theory' or 'free will' – we have no choice. And since it is done by the working class and the capitalists are removed in the course of the revolutionary struggle, it has to be socialist regulation.

This has to be understood and said directly. Then, what we did until now by dint of circumstance, with unacceptable waste of effort and time, we will be doing consciously, in a systematic manner, looking further ahead ...

Will this be another Paris Commune or will it lead to world socialism – that depends on international circumstances. But we have absolutely no choice.[56]

56 I. Stepanov 1918, pp. 4, 13–14. Lenin, at the First All-Russian Congress of the National Economy in May 1918, presented a similar analysis of the evolution of economic policy since October: 'We don't close our eyes to the fact that by ourselves, in one country – even if it were much less backward than Russia, even if we were living in much easier conditions than after four years of an unprecedented, horribly painful, difficult and destructive war – we cannot fully realise a socialist revolution by our own efforts. Anyone that turns his back on the socialist revolution that is occurring in Russia, pointing to the clearly insufficient forces available for it, is like the man frozen in his shell, who cannot see past his own nose, forgetting that there has never been a single historical revolution of any major significance without a whole series of cases with a lack of corresponding forces. These forces grow in the process of struggle, with the growth of the revolution. When the country entered the path of great transformations, the merit of that country and of the party of the working class that has been victorious in that country is that we approached on a practical basis tasks that until then had been posed abstractly, theoretically. That experience will not be forgotten. This experience of the workers who are now united in trade unions and local organisations and are tackling on a practical level the task of national organisation of all of production – that experience, whatever happens and no matter how difficult the twists and turns of the Russian and international socialist revolutions – that experience cannot be taken away. It has entered history as a victory for socialism, and on that experience the future international revolution will construct its socialist edifice' (Lenin 1958–67, vol. XXXVI, p. 382).

Management in Nationalised Enterprises

The resolution on nationalisation adopted by the conference of factory committees in January called for nationalised enterprises to be managed by their factory committees:

> But considering that the higher organs of state power do not have special organisations that can manage the enterprises that become property of the Republic, that the government of workers, soldiers and peasants is strong because it is based on the confidence of the toilers and their organisations [and] on its part it should rely on these organisations, therefore [we consider that] in all cases of nationalisation, the workers' committee of these enterprises should be put at the head of these enterprises locally, while working under the leadership of the Councils of the National Economy.[57]

Responding to the idea that factory committees should not assume responsibility for running nationalised factories but should limit themselves to delegating only two or three members to the administration with only a consultative voice, the Bolshevik Zhivotov retorted:

> That is extreme. That is, perhaps, a deformed kind of Bolshevism ... The idea that the factory committees of the enterprises that are being nationalised should not take any part are wrong and incorrect. The main thing, the essence of the question is that when nationalisation of the factory occurs, the factory committee absolutely must be at the head, while, of course, being subordinate to, or under the control of, the state regulating organisation that is now being organised, being formed – the *sovnarkhoz*.[58]

Zhivotov recognised that the factory committees might not always have the required competence. But they could always integrate technical specialists.[59]

However, in March 1918, the *VeSeNKha* issued a decree on management of nationalised enterprises that fell far short of the factory committees' position. While it did not entirely exclude workers' representatives from management, it

---

57 *Novyi put'*, no. 4–5, 1918, p. 14.

58 FZK IV, pp. 294–5.

59 Ibid, pp. 255–6.

called on its *glavky* (branch directorates of *VSNKh*) to appoint a commissar to each of the factories under their supervision, in addition to a technical director and an administrative director. Only the commissar or the *glavk* could overrule the technical director. The administrative director, on the other hand, was to work under supervision of an economic-administrative council, which consisted of representatives of the workers, white-collar and technical personnel, the trade union, and of the local soviet. But workers and white-collar employees could constitute no more than half of the council's members. As for the factory committees, they could not issue orders on their own but had to pass through economic-administrative councils.[60]

In the months that followed, with the outbreak of full-scale civil war in the spring and summer and the deepening economic crisis, the Soviet state was forced into a desperate survival mode. In these conditions, the government's support for centralism at the expense of meaningful worker participation in management was destined to increase. Leaders like Lenin and Trotsky, who had been on the left of their party and had encouraged independent popular initiative, now rallied to the side of the centralisers. (The Mensheviks, who were opposed to 'socialist experiments', limited themselves to demanding trade-union autonomy.) In the Bolshevik party, the cause of the factory committees was taken up in 1918 by the Left Opposition, and later, towards the end of the civil war, by the Workers' Opposition, which defended a syndicalist programme.

The conditions of absolute scarcity and of political-military emergency made it very difficult, probably impossible, to find a suitable compromise between centralism and workers' self-management, both of which are necessary elements of socialism. For self-management to have real meaning, the scope and degree of central control have to be limited to some extent. But a workable solution requires the presence of suitable economic conditions, and first of all the economy's capacity to guarantee the workers' economic security at a decent standard of living. Without that, workers cannot be expected to manifest the kind of consciousness required for voluntary sacrifice of local group interest to the more general good. Those conditions obviously did not exist in Russia in 1918.

The factory committees, elected by the general assembly of workers, were naturally under pressure to give priority to the needs of the workers of the given factory. At the January 1918 conference of factory committees, one of the delegates suggested that the responsibility of factory committees to the

60 Carr 1952, p. 92.

workers' general assembly be limited to issues in which there was no conflict between the overall class interest and that of the given group of workers. On his part, Katyn', a member of the Central Council of Factory Committees, recognised that such conflicts did arise, but he argued that they occurred mainly in factories with a backward composition of workers –

> they are not, strictly speaking, workers, but people who arrived recently from the village, who a month or a year ago were living in a Byelorussian village and by chance, as refugees, find themselves among workers ... As much as I have observed workers in factories, I must say, comrades, we should regard them differently [from what the proposal implies], that is, we should regard them as a conscious element that will always reach the most correct decision, and not as some sort of ugly mass that doesn't understand what it's doing, not as a savage or a child, as comrade Gorky says ... It seems to me, comrades, that it would even be inconvenient for us, who rely on this proletariat, to insert points into our charter that place this proletariat beneath any criticism.[61]

Some of the delegates agreed with Katyn'. But in the course of the discussion, several cases were mentioned that showed otherwise. Replying to the anarchists, a delegate from the Metallicheskii factory stated:

> There are enterprises that absolutely should be shut ... Here we need a state apparatus to see clearly in the situation ... Here is comrade Bleikhman [an anarchist] who says – let's take over the factories and basta! ... I would pose the question to these comrade anarchists – one comrade has already asked it – how do they conduct themselves in the factories with their unconscious masses, how do they talk to them – do they speak openly or not? I don't know how to talk to masses who are demanding money. Yesterday, I wasn't at the conference and today I came late because the situation at my factory is not quite good. We are dismissing one hundred workers. There you have anarchy, and it is not the kind of anarchy about which they [anarchists] speak, not the well-being in the ultimate sense of anarchism about which comrade Bakunin wrote. That would be heaven on earth, but until then we have to live through the kind of misunderstandings from which the heart takes fright and the devil knows what is happening, when people, today's March anarchists, when each worker

61 FZK IV, pp. 319–20.

> tries only to grab [severance pay] not for a month and a half but for two or three months ...[62]

Another speaker cited the example of the Treugol'nik rubber factory, which had reserves of fuel beyond the three-month limit fixed by the Central Council of Factory Committees. Meanwhile, the committee of the Putilov factory was trying to convert the plant to peacetime production and lacked fuel. The committee at Treugol'nik would only agree to part with its surplus at an exorbitant price, saying that it had to cover amortisation of its new fuel tanks that would be left standing empty.

> And the factory committee is so stubborn that it declares outright: Why didn't you Putilovtsy take action in good time? And now you want to take fuel from our workers and leave them without work. You have to worry about yourselves, but we won't give you any. Maybe that's patriotic [in relation to Treugol'nik's workers], but it's not good for the country, nor for the working class, that is struggling so desperately to revive industry.

The conference decided that all fuel beyond a two month's supply should be placed under the control of the regional *sovnarkhoz*.[63]

These sorts of contradictions only grew more acute as the economic and military situations deteriorated. A report dated 11 June 1918 from the Metal Section of the *Sovnakhoz* of the Northern Region stated:

> The Section had, and is having, run-ins with workers' organisations, too, especially with the factory committees. The committees, not taking anything else into account, watch out for the interests of their own parish, trying immediately to obtain one or another subsidy, advances, even though money is given out only after the most careful inspection of the enterprise. The committees try, no matter what, to revive the operation of closed enterprises, even though there is no real possibility of opening them because of the lack of fuel or the lack of a corresponding need for that type of production. The data that we receive from the factory committees, and also from the factory administrations, is all one-sided ...
>
> The factory committees, not taking anything else into account, very often pestered departments and agencies, snatched up orders, obtained

62 FZK IV, p. 284.

63 *Novyi put'*, nos. 4–5 (8–9), 1918, p. 14; *Novaya zhizn'* (28 Jan 1918).

> advances, and without the sanction, without the approval of the *Sovnarkhoz* of the Northern Region, reopened the factories. Unfortunately, the majority of such orders turned out to be unrealisable in practice, not to mention the fact that they severely disorganise the work of the section. The order cannot be realised because many factories are completely unsuited for the given type of production …
>
> The Metal Section will have to intervene in this work, take all orders under its control and, in that way, regroup them in accordance with the interests of the overall state mechanism. This will not happen without the struggle of the workers' government with the workers' organisations.[64]

There were also reports that some factories resisted conversion, the workers demanding first to receive peacetime orders. At Staryi Lessner the workers rescinded their decision to submit to the government's decree to close the factory on 23 December in order to prepare it for conversion after they received unsubstantiated reports that other metalworking factories were refusing to submit. The general assembly decided instead to reduce operations to three days a week, while waiting to obtain orders for peacetime production.[65]

At the First Congress of *Sovnarkhozy* on 26 May–6 June 1918, supporters of the left opposition within the Bolshevik party defended the rights of factory committees against the centralisers. N. Osinskii, who had briefly himself headed the *VeSeNKha*, began by emphasising that the 'absolute decline in material forces of production has reached the limit after which begins the dying of the economy'. The state, therefore, had to shift into a basic survival mode, adopting a 'stingy' (*skarednuyu*) economic policy. The state had to monopolise control of existing productive forces and adopt a policy of the strictest accounting and utilisation of the existing scarce resources. But even though the preceding seemed to argue in favour of centrally appointing commissars to run the factories, Osinskii rejected that, proposing instead that at least two-thirds of the management be elected by the factory's workers. He rejected arguments that this inevitably leads to the defence of local group interests at the expense of the working class as a whole. He cited his recent experience in the Donbass: 'It's all a question of the general conditions in which the enterprise finds itself, whether it has bread and money, whether the directors have been correctly chosen from a practical point of view, whether the enterprise maintains close

64 *Natsionalizatsiya promyshlennosti i organizatsiya sotsialisticherskogo proizvodstva v Petrograde*, vol. 1, 1958, pp. 199–200.

65 *Novaya zhizn'* (Jan. 4, 1918).

contact with the regulating centre'. If there is no bread and no money, he continued, then the enterprise will perform poorly, even if it is run by commissars, because they find that 'they are forced to sell off the monopolised goods or the factory's property [in order to feed the workers]'.[66]

But painting such a bleak, if undoubtedly realistic, picture and calling to shift economic policy into a strictly survival mode, Osinskii was inadvertently providing arguments for the advocates of centrally-appointed commissars. A.I. Rykov, the current chairperson of the *VeSeNKha* and an opponent of worker self-management, cited an article written by Osinskii himself: 'At the present moment, the preservation of the productive forces that are being destroyed by the imperialist war is possible only through their most systematic concentration; the most effective utilisation of the existing technical forces makes nationalised management of these forces from a single centre completely inevitable'.[67] And somewhat later, Osinskii again repeated his error when he opposed the introduction of piece rates as a measure to raise labour discipline and labour intensity. He argued that that sort of measure would further undermine solidarity among workers and foster petty-bourgeois attitudes at a time when 'one observes a great degradation, a great class disintegration [*klassovoe rapadenie*] of the proletariat as a consequence of unemployment'.[68]

A fellow left oppositionist, G.I. Lomov, was caught in the same contradiction. He argued that 'all kinds of commissars not only do not inspire local forces to work to raise production and productive forces in general, but on the contrary, they destroy and decrease the local forces'. Yet again, practically in the same breath, he observed that 'both workers and peasants at the present time, like worms, have retreated into their domestic shells and show any signs of life only insofar as it is necessary for their personal needs ... Everything is broken. We have completely suppressed the vital, creative forces in the country. All of that is retreating into the underground and exists only for itself'.[69] Even though Lomov was, at least partially, blaming government policy for this situation, these were definitely not conditions that favoured the sacrifice of local interests for those of the class as a whole.

Arguments could be made – and were made – in support of both positions. But since everyone agreed that immediate survival of the revolution was at stake, and since the social base of the advocates of worker self-management –

66 *Trudy I Vserossiiskogo s'ezda sovetov narodnogo khozyaistva*, Moscow, 1918, pp. 57–66, *passim*.

67 Ibid., p. 98.

68 Ibid., p. 66.

69 Ibid., pp. 74–5.

the working class – was being dispersed to the civil war fronts and to the countryside or increasingly demoralised by hunger and unemployment, the odds favoured the partisans of increased centralisation and authoritarian management. When Osinksii declared that there was really no solution for the Russian Revolution except for revolutions to break out in the West to end the world war and come to Russia's aid, he was voicing a widely-held view. From that, Osinksii drew the conclusion that socialist principles should not be sacrificed for the sake of the revolution's survival in Russia. But others drew the opposite conclusion: since defeat of the revolution in Russia would be a major blow to the revolutionary movements in the West, it was better temporarily to sacrifice principle. The support later provided to Russia by revolutionary governments in the developed West would help to correct the present distortions. Very few believed that revolution in Russia could survive for long in isolation.[70]

Although the left opposition was defeated on this issue, a recent study of factory management in Petrograd during the civil war, based on the archives

70 Lenin's own position was contradictory. In his speech to the Second All-Russian Congress of Trade Unions in January 1919, he insisted forcefully that socialism means that workers themselves, not bureaucrats, run the economy and the state. The role of the trade unions was to educate workers for that task and to draw them into these managerial functions. He condemned 'that harmful prejudice, according to which the matter of state management is the affair of the privileged, that it is a particular art'. Only if the mass of workers themselves managed, he argued, would the revolution be secure against the restoration of capitalism. And the workers' preparation for those tasks could not be theoretical, not based upon books, lectures or meetings, but upon their actual experience of participation. Yet again, practically in the same breath, Lenin warned the trade unions not to assume managerial functions 'by their own decision'. 'We have moved toward that but we are not yet there'. In other words, not the workers, but the ruling party would control the process of education and decide how and when the masses could assume directly the management of economic and political affairs.

Lenin was undoubtedly aware of this contradiction. But, like most Bolsheviks, he viewed it as a temporary deviation, the product of specific Russian conditions, in which 'because of the mad resistance of the exploiters, because of the offensive of the world-wide union of exploiters against one of the weakest and least prepared countries, when the union of toilers had to make its revolution with furious speed, in conditions when we had to think, not so much of the smooth development of that revolution, but of how to hold on until the West-European proletariat awakens' (Lenin 1958–67, vol. XXXVII, pp. 435–53.) But once the revolutionary upsurge in the West had been conclusively beaten back by the bourgeoisie, making Russia's isolation a long-term prospect and fostering the rise of a bureaucratic ruling caste in Russia, the contradiction, which Lenin had hoped was only temporary, would become permanent. And as Lenin had predicted, without the workers' running their own state, there was no guarantee against a return to a capitalism.

of twelve of the city's largest factories, concluded that not only did workers remain attached to the idea of participation in management, but that such participation itself continued during the civil war. In some cases, even as late as 1920, the factory committees wielded full managerial power, despite official policy. The practice of collegial management also persisted, despite the official policy of one-person management [*edinonachalie*].[71]

71 A.V. Gogolevskii 2005, ch. 6. The author does not make clear, however, to what degree the committees remained responsible to the workers' general assemblies.

CHAPTER 15

Summon Up Every Last Ounce of Strength or Accept Defeat!

Dispersal of Petrograd's Working Class

By the time the Decree on Nationalisation of major industrial enterprises was issued in June 1918, most of Petrograd's factories had in fact ceased operation, victims of the economic crisis and military conflicts. Years would pass before industrial employment in Petrograd would regain its past numbers.

Table 15.1 shows the catastrophic decline in industrial employment over the first eight months of 1918, most of it occurring between the middle of December 1917 and May 1918. By 1 May 1918, little over a third of the industrial workers who had been employed in February 1917 were still working in industry. The chief causes of this decline were the lack of fuel and materials, the result of the transport crisis and the civil war in the south, the demobilisation of Petrograd's swollen war industry, and the panicky evacuation of factories in February 1918, when the German military offensive directly threatened the city.

But workers who kept their industrial jobs were far from privileged. A study of the domestic budgets of Petrograd workers in May 1918 found that the average industrial wage had fallen well behind workers' basic needs. Some of the difference was made up by parcels from relatives in the countryside, where they existed, from the sale of possessions, from renting out rooms and corners of rooms, from borrowing, even begging. Wage increases, such as the 30 percent accorded to unskilled workers in June 1918, did not compensate for inflation: in May–June alone the cost of food rose by 50 percent.[1]

The food shortage became acute. During the first half of 1918, Petrograd received only a little over a third of the grain of the same period in 1917. Rations were below physical requirements, and the price of bread on the free market was seven to eight times above state prices, well beyond the reach of workers.[2] On 18 January, an editorial in *Novaya zhizn'* appeared under the title 'Hunger':

> The bony hand of hunger, with which Ryabushinskii had threatened democracy at the Moscow Conference, has already grasped Petrograd by

1 S. Strumilin 1918, pp. 4–8.

2 A.L. Mil'shtein 1963, p. 129.

TABLE 15.1 *Employed industrial workers in Petrograd and Vicinity, 1 January 1917–1 September 1918*

	1/I-17	1/I-18	1/V-18	1/IX-18
Number of Workers	406,312	339,641	142,915	120,553
As percentage of I/17	100%	83.5%	35.1%	29.7%

SOURCE: *MATERIALY PO STATISTIKE TRUDA SEVERNOI OBLASTI, VYP. V* (PETROGRAD, 1919), P. 23.

> the throat. The population of Petrograd has been put on a quarter-funt [409.5 gm.] ration. A quarter-funt of bread (with straw) a day for an adult person is the bread of unconcealed hunger. It is the harbinger of a hungry death, death from exhaustion, the harbinger of epidemics.[3]

Even during the lean years after the defeat of the Revolution of 1905, low-paid textile workers consumed on the average 1.9 funts of black bread and 0.7 of white daily.[4]

In May 1918, the Petrograd Soviet reported that Petrograd was the worst off of all major cities.[5] Malnutrition was a breeding ground for typhus, which made its first appearance in January of that year and was followed by cholera, once the weather warmed up.[6] On 18 June, there were already approximately 800 reported cases of cholera. That month, the Obukhovskii hospital treated 177 cases of malnutrition, and 30 in just the first three days of July. Two-thirds of these were workers, the rest *intelligenty*.[7]

As a consequence of the deteriorating material conditions and the uncertain military situation, labour discipline and productivity declined in the still operating factories. Drunkenness and pilfering, in particular the use of factory time and materials to make articles for private sale on the market in order to buy food, were on the rise.[8] Factory general assemblies, factory committees,

3 *Novaya zhizn'* (Jan. 18, 1918).

4 Strumilin 1918, p. 5.

5 *Novaya zhizn'* (May 21, 1918).

6 Ibid. (Apr. 30, 1918).

7 Ibid. (July 5, 1918).

8 Ibid. (Dec. 5, 1917, Feb. 1/14, Mar. 22, 1918); Nats. Prom. SSSR, pp. 30, 40; Rab. Kon., pp. 273, 289, 412–13, 422, 424–5, 432, 454.

unions, government – all exhorted workers to greater effort. Piece work was introduced. A merciless struggle against slackers was proclaimed. But none of this did much good. The economist and statistician S.G. Strumilin wrote in the early summer of 1918:

> As before, we come up against the problem: either raise wages [beyond the June increase] or reduce the price of goods, and this has to be decided. For until then, until the worker receives the number of calories needed to work, all complaints about low labour productivity of labour and all talk of raising it by intensifying labour discipline, including the Taylor system and other measures, will remain futile and idle blabbering.[9]

By the summer, the life of employed workers had become so hard that, despite widespread unemployment, factories were unable to hire the skilled, and sometimes even the unskilled, workers that they needed. On 1 September, the managerial collegium of the Izhorskii factory in Kolpino (24 km. from the centre of Petrograd) wrote to the *Sovnarkhoz* of the Northern Region:

> Neither the local labour exchange nor Petrograd's can give, not only needed specialists, but even ordinary unskilled labourers in sufficient quantity. Moreover, there is not the slightest hope that this situation will soon improve at the local labour exchange. The main reason for the absence of workers is the poor state of the food situation and the unwillingness of even the available workers to work in the factory, as they prefer other occupations – trade, private speculation, agricultural work, and the like.[10]

The situation had indeed radically changed from 1917, when an assembly at this same factory condemned workers' engaging in trade on the side as an 'indisputable evil, inasmuch as the striving for profit brings demoralisation to our comradely milieu'.[11]

The decline in employment did not, however, affect equally all branches of industry and all social strata in the working class. Far-reaching changes occurred in the social composition of this class that had important political consequences, which material hardship alone cannot explain. Hardest hit was

9 Strumilin 1918.
10 *Nats. Prom. Petrogradaa*, vol. II, p. 242.
11 *Bastiony revolyutsii* (L., 1967), vol. I, p. 237.

TABLE 15.2 *Changes in sectorial distribution of industrial workers of Petrograd and Vicinity, 1 January 1917–1 September 1918*

Industry	1 Jan 1917		1 Jan 1918		1 May 1918		1 Sept 1918		1 May 1918 as percent of 1 Jan 1917
	Number of workers	%	Number of workers	%	Number of workers	%	Number of workers	%	
Metalworking	249,679	61.5	197,686	58.2	57,995	40.6	45,525	37.8	23.2
Textiles	43,272	10.6	44,416	13.0	30,173	21.1	27,112	22.5	69.7
Chemicals	45,029	11.1	42,126	12.4	10,495	7.3	7,313	6.0	23.3
Print and paper	22,044	5.4	23,531	6.9	19,776	13.8	19,412	16.1	89.7
Food processing	14,291	3.5	11,924	3.5	10,640	7.5	10,278	8.5	74.4
Woodworking	4,715	1.2	3,027	0.9	1,620	1.1	1,206	1.0	25.6
Leather and footwear	11,126	2.7	8,413	2.5	6,045	4.2	5,747	4.8	54.3
Mineral processing	10,237	2.5	2,287	0.7	1,429	1.0	1,301	1.1	14.0
Other	5,919	1.5	6,231	1.8	4,742	3.3	2,659	2.2	80.1
All industries	406,312	100.0	339,641	99.9	142,915	99.9	120,553	100.0	35.1

SOURCE: *MATERIALY PO STATISTIKE TRUDA SEVERNOI OBLASTI*, VYP. 5, P. 23. SEE ALSO *NOVAYA ZHIZN'* (MAY 26, 1918) AND *METALLIST*, NOS. 9–10 (1918) P. 10.

the metalworking sector (see Table 15.2). By May 1918, the number of workers employed in it had decreased by more than three-quarters. The metalworking sector, from which the Bolsheviks drew their strongest support, was still the biggest industrial employer. But metalworkers no longer constituted a majority. Almost half of the workers were employed in the textile, food-processing, paper and printing sectors, sectors whose workers had been among the last to abandon the 'conciliators' in 1917.

Important changes took place within the metalworking sector itself. On the one hand, a large part of the unskilled, wartime, still-semi rural workers left. (In industry as a whole, these had numbered up to 170,000.) But a large part of the skilled, urbanised metalworkers, who were the most radical, active element of the working class, was also gone. The Vyborg district, the vanguard of the workers' movement in Russia since at least 1912, a solid bastion of Bolshevik support, had virtually ceased to exist as an industrial centre by the spring of 1918. In March 1918, only one metalworking factory, Nobel, was still operating there. It was later joined by Arsenal, a state-owned factory, whose workers tended to moderation. What had been the city's largest industrial district in

January 1917 with 69,000 workers (18 percent of the industrial workforce, a quarter of all metalworkers), now employed only 5,000 workers, and some of these were in small workshops.[12]

There were 21 large (500 or more workers) metalworking factories still operating in Petrograd at the end of 1918. Only five of these had been strong supporters of the Bolsheviks in 1917: Aivaz, Lessner, Nobel, the Sestroretsk rifle factory, and the Cable factory, to which one should add the three tram depots. Together these enterprises employed only 5,500 of the city's 45,000 metalworkers. The other sixteen factories (including Obukhovskii, Izhorskii, Patronnyi, Baltiiskii and Nevskii shipbuilding factories, Arsenal, the railway workshops, the Putilov factory), had mostly already been state-owned in 1917, and their workers had been slow to abandon the Mensheviks and SRs. The Nevskii district, the main centre of SR support in 1917, had become the largest industrial district with 25,000 workers, more than 20 percent of the city's industrial work force. It would become the centre of worker opposition to the Soviet government in the spring and summer of 1918.[13]

Moreover, the factories that were still operating were emptied of their most revolutionary and committed workers, the Bolsheviks and young workers. A report on the Putilov factory from April 1918 stated that of the 39,000 workers employed in 1917, only 13,000 remained. The cuts had respected the principle of seniority, so that 'the young, most revolutionary forces have left'.[14] Many of these joined the Red Guard and then the Red Army.[15] (The peasant soldiers in the garrison wanted only to return home as quickly as possible.)[16] Even before the Red Army was formed (the decree was published on 20 January/2 February 1918),[17] 8,000 Red Guards, almost all workers, had left Petrograd for fronts in the Ukraine, on the Don, in Finland and in the West. By 1 April, 1918, 25,000 Petrograders, mostly workers, had enlisted in the Red Army.[18] It was at this time still a voluntary army, and though it provided subsistence for unemployed workers, it also promised risk and hardship. Unemployed workers with any relatives in the village would have been better off there. (In the spring of 1918,

12 I. Shkaratan 1959, p. 21; *Novaya zhizn'* (Mar. 23, 1918). Stepanov 1965, p. 47; K.I. Shelavin 1929, p. 5; Mil'shtein 1963, p. 129.

13 For documentation of the worker opposition here, see E. Tsudsi 2006, pp. 590–648.

14 *Petrogradskaya pravda* (Apr. 7, 1918).

15 V.I. Startsev 1962, p. 280.

16 *Novaya zhizn'* (Jan. 12, 20 and Feb. 1/14, 4/17, 1918).

17 *Gazeta Vremennogo rabochego i kret'yanskogo pravitel'stva*, Jan. 20 (Feb. 2), 1918.

18 V.I. Startsev 1962, pp. 278, 280.

Lenin urged Petrograd's unemployed to go to the countryside, where they could feed their families and organise the peasants).[19]

As a result, the Bolsheviks' Petrograd organisation suffered a steep decline in numbers.[20] At the Sixth Petrograd conference of the party in June 1918, it was reported that only 13,472 members remained in the city's organisation, which had numbered 43,000 in October 1917.[21] By the end of August, only 7,000 were left. A survey of 3,559 of the remaining members found that 40 percent had joined before the October Revolution and 20 percent before the February. Of the total, 81.5 percent were workers. On this basis, one can estimate that by the end of the summer of 1918, there were less than 6,000 Bolshevik workers in the city, whereas there had been 28,500 in October 1917.

But many of those still in the city were no longer working in the factories. At a Bolshevik Conference of the Northern Region in the spring of 1918, a summary of reports concluded:

> In all organisations without exception party-organisational work has been significantly weakened since the October Revolution, and in certain cases – true, they are rare – it has almost completely frozen. Almost all forces of the party have left for government work, the soviets, trade unions, factory committees, food detachments, Red Guards – all this has swallowed almost all the forces of the party.[22]

Thus, what remained of the employed industrial working class had lost its politically most radical and committed elements, those who had been the party's direct source of influence among workers. 'It has disappeared', wrote a Ya. A. Piletskii, a Menshevik-Internationalist in May 1918, 'that vanguard fighter and trend-setter of the working class of Russia, the true pride and glory of the revolution ... Only slowly and gradually will it be resurrected along with the industry of Petrograd. The old social-democratic guard has disappeared'.[23]

---

19 Lenin 1958–67, vol. 36, pp. 357–64.

20 A Russian historian recently attributed the decline in the party's numbers in the factories to disaffection with the government, implying that these Bolshevik workers abandoned the party (D.B. Pavlov 2006, p. 10). If that were the case, one would have to wonder how the Soviet government managed to win the civil war. In fact, party membership in Russia as a whole continued to grow.

21 Mil'shtein 1963, p. 129; *Krasnaya gazeta* (June 18, 1918).

22 K.I. Shelavin 1928–9, p. 113.

23 *Novaya zhizn'* (May 26, 1918).

These workers had not, of course, physically 'disappeared'. They were playing and would play a central role in constructing, administering and defending the new Soviet state. But in the process, they lost their organic ties with the milieu from which they had sprung. The Russian working class, as an independent historical subject, would never regain the strength it expended in defending its revolution. It would not regain the capacity to make a new revolution, the possible necessity for which had been evoked at the conference of factory committees in January 1918.

The 'Obscene Peace'

In the period immediately following the dispersal of the Constituent Assembly, the main political issue confronting the workers was the peace treaty with Germany. In a certain sense, this was the last more or less purely political issue that the workers would face before the start of full-scale war, unleashed in May 1918 by the uprising of Czechoslovak troops in central Russia and Siberia. After Brest-Litovsk, reactions to political issues, at least among workers still employed in industry, would be filtered through the prism of material hardship.

Even so, the choice between an 'obscene' peace (obscene because it ceded large parts of Russia directly or indirectly to Germany and because it was a separate peace that would thus favour one of the imperialist parties), imposed upon Soviet Russia, and a revolutionary war against the German imperialists, already arose at a time of growing disorganisation and demoralisation within the working class. Just before the Germans resumed their offensive, threatening the city, an observer remarked that 'among workers, in connection with unemployment and hunger, interest in political events is being extinguished. At the same time, interest in economic questions becomes more acute. Political meetings and rallies are poorly attended by workers of late'.[24] Reports from mid-March from two Vyborg district factories confirm this assessment. The Phoenix Machine-construction factory, like most in the district, was closed for lack of fuel and orders:

> The mood among the workers is extremely depressed. A general assembly was called three or four times, but only 50–60 people came and it had to be postponed. And only when the committee summoned the workers to clear snow for pay did almost everyone show up. The majority of workers

24 Ibid. (Feb. 3/16, 1918).

> are in an incredibly bad material situation. They come in groups to the factory and, according to the members of the factory committee, 'they ask, beg for work and curse their elected representatives'. They ask to give them 'at least some salted water to alleviate their hunger'.[25]

And at Rozenkrants copper-rolling mill:

> There are about 900 workers working now instead of 4,000. Work proceeds incredibly badly. In the opinion of members of the factory committee, during the eight hours, the workers work barely two. The rest of the time is spent gathered in small groups, discussing the situation. In response to all demands for more intense work, they declare that their energy is sapped by hunger.[26]

Such was the situation when the German Army began to advance toward Petrograd on 18 February (new style),[27] eight days after Trotsky had rejected Germany's terms and unilaterally declared that Russia was leaving the war. The terms, presented in early January, included the separation of Russia from most of her Polish territory, Lithuania, western Latvia, including Riga, the Moonsund Archipelago, and the Ukraine, all of which would come under direct or indirect German control.[28]

Before the start of the German offensive, opinion among the Bolsheviks' national leaders had been divided. (The Left SRs opposed the peace and withdrew from the government when it accepted the German terms.) Lenin, supported by Zinoviev, Kamenev and Stalin, called to accept the German terms, although negotiations should be dragged out as long as possible to allow the revolutionary situation in the West to ripen. Lenin argued that the new Soviet government did not have the means with which to defend itself against a German offensive. Ultimately, survival depended upon revolutions in the West, and there were indeed signs that conditions were ripening. But those revolutions were still some way off. In the meanwhile, the Russian Revolution did not have the right to sacrifice itself without justification. The peace treaty, however onerous, would give the Soviet government a 'breathing space' during which to organise and arm itself, while awaiting and promoting revolutions in the

---

25 Ibid. (Mar. 17 1918).

26 Ibid. (Mar. 20, 1918).

27 The old calendar, abandoned on 1 February 1918, was 13 days behind.

28 Chamberlin 1965, vol. I, p. 396.

West. A compromise with imperialism that is forced upon the revolution by the threat to its existence, Lenin argued, would be understood by Western workers and not be seen as a betrayal.

The Left Communists, led by N.I. Bukharin, opposed a separate peace, arguing that Germany's terms would in any case make the revolution's survival impossible. And they pointed to signs of maturing revolutionary situations in the West: general strikes in Austro-Hungary, Germany, Poland, as well as in Bordeaux and Lyons in France. The peace would be a betrayal of workers in the West, as well as those of Finland, the Baltic countries and Ukraine. They also pointed out how Kornilov had been stopped in August by revolutionary agitation alone.

Trotsky adopted a middle position of 'neither war nor peace', according to which the Soviet government would refuse to sign a treaty and declare unilaterally that it was leaving the war. That would demonstrate in the strongest possible way to the German workers and soldiers that their own government's war was imperialist it would and give a powerful boost to already strong revolutionary anti-war sentiment in Europe.[29]

On 12 January, the Bolshevik Central Committee approved Trotsky's position by a vote of nine against seven. In the Petrograd Bolshevik organisation, sentiment was much more strongly opposed to the treaty. A meeting of the Petersburg Committee on 28 December (by which time German intentions had become clear) called to continue internationalist propaganda among the German troops. If Germany made good its threat, then it would be necessary to wage revolutionary war. The meeting called on rank-and-file members to exert pressure on the party's leadership.[30] A conference of the party *aktiv* on 7 January voted 32 to 15 against the separate peace,[31] and on 18 January the Petersburg Committee formally adhered to the platform of the Left Communists,[32] as did the Fifth Petrograd City Conference that opened on the very eve of the German offensive and had to be suspended.[33]

On 15 February, the Petrograd Soviet endorsed Trotsky's rejection of the German terms and his unilateral departure from the peace talks.[34] The Okhta district soviet declared: 'It is better to die in the struggle for the world revolution

29 Ibid, pp. 398–9.

30 *Peterburgskii komitet RSPD(b) v 1917 g.*, pp. 609–23.

31 *Protokoly TseKa RSDRP(b), avgust 1917–fevral' 1918* (M., 1958), p. 282.

32 M.N. Potekhin 1966, p. 112.

33 Shelavin 1928–9, p. 106.

34 M.N. Potekhin 1966, pp. 112–13.

than to live as the slaves of world imperialism'.[35] The Red Guards, as one might expect, were also strongly opposed to the separate peace.[36]

Attitudes among rank-and-file workers are more difficult to gauge, because meetings became less frequent as the economic conditions deteriorated. Nevertheless, the resolutions of meetings that were published opposed the separate peace. A general assembly held in mid-December at the Opticheskii factory resolved: 'Speaking from the depths of our hearts against a separate peace with the German, we demand energetic steps toward a democratic international peace'.[37] These workers maintained this position even after the German offensive began and the Bolshevik Central Committee had reversed itself on 18 February. They condemned the treaty as a betrayal of the Finnish and Baltic working classes.[38]

Opposition to the treaty was especially strong among traditionally more moderate workers. A joint meeting of the Delegates' Assembly of the Printers Union with representatives of the factory committees pledged full support for Soviet power but declared that the German conditions were unacceptable and called to resist the offensive.[39] Similar positions were adopted at meetings at the Nevskii, Aleksandrovskii, and Baltiiskii shipbuilding factories, and others.[40] After the Sovnarkom telegraphed acceptance of the peace terms, the Menshevik paper *Novyi luch* reported that a series of large factory meetings expressed their strong anger at the government's action.[41] *Novaya zhizn'* reported that information coming from Smol'nyi (seat of the government) indicated that there was strong opposition to the peace treaty among workers, and especially from the district soviets.[42]

Nor was this opposition merely symbolic. Although what still existed of the old army put up negligible resistance – the Germans quickly occupied Revel, Rezhitsa, Minsk and Dvinsk – a significant part of Petrograd's workers were prepared to take up arms. Meetings in numerous factories responded to the offensive with calls to enlist in the Red Guards. Some even called for universal enlistment.[43] Summarising reports from the districts, the Petrograd

35 *Pravda* (Feb. 14/27, 1918).

36 Ibid. (Feb. 10/23, 1918).

37 *Znamya truda* (Dec. 12, 1917).

38 Ibid. (Mar. 1, 1918).

39 Ibid. (Feb. 13/26, 1918).

40 *Novyi luch* (Feb. 8/21, 1918); *Novaya zhizn'* (Mar. 6, 1918).

41 *Novyi luch* (Feb. 8/21, 1918).

42 *Novaya zhizn'* (Feb. 8/21,1918).

43 Such resolutions were adopted at Novyi Arsenal, the Main Workshops of the North-

Soviet concluded on 22 February: 'revolutionary enthusiasm, readiness to fight, the Red Guard is being organised'.[44] The Vyborg district itself sent over 3,000 armed workers to the front before 2 March, and a similar number awaited orders to go.[45] According to the Soviet historian Startsev, in the five days from 25 February to 1 March, 10,000 people, mainly workers, enlisted in the Red Army, bringing its numbers in Petrograd up to 15,300. There was a similar number of Red Guards. Other workers formed special partisan units.[46]

Various observers from different political vantage points contrasted the workers' fighting spirit with its absence among the soldiers of the garrison, who wanted only to return home to their villages. *Novaya zhizn'* complained that the entire burden fell on workers, since the soldiers refused to fight, and there was no sense talking about the peasants in the villages.[47] Speaking before the Petrograd Soviet, Zinoviev, chairman of the Soviet, also drew this contrast, pointing out that the workers of the Sestroretsk arms factory had formed an entire regiment that had left for the front.[48]

But readiness to fight was not the only reaction among workers. On 1 March, A.G. Shlyapnikov, People's Commissar of Labour, informed the Workers' Section of the Petrograd Soviet that, in the face of the Germans' rapid advance, panic was beginning to spread among workers, who wanted to leave the city. Some were quitting their jobs, demanding the legal month-and-a-half of severance pay.[49] In part, he said, these workers had become infected by the mood of the surrounding petty-bourgeois population, thrown into a panic by the approach of German troops. But the Soviet government itself was partly to blame for failing to make the situation clear to workers. In the midst of the mobilisation to defend the city, it issued orders to prepare factories for evacuation or to render them inoperative.[50] These orders were obviously not reassuring. And the most resolute elements of the working class, who might have

---

West Railroad, Russko-Baltiiskii Wagon-construction Factory, a special Conference of the Factory Committees of the Nevskii District (*Znamya truda* (14/27 Feb 1918)); Phoenix, Opticheskii, Treugol'nik and others (ibid. (Mar, 1, 1918)); Dinamo (*Pravda* Feb. 8/21, 1918); Putilov (*Pravda* Feb. 10/23, 1918); Skorokhod, ibid. (Feb. 14/27); Nobel, *Novaya zhizn'* (Mar. 9, 1918).

44 *Pravda* (Feb. 12/25, 1918).

45 Ibid. (Mar. 2, 1918); *Znamya truda* (Mar. 2, 1918).

46 Startsev 1962, pp. 244–5.

47 *Novaya zhizn'* (Mar. 2, 1918).

48 *Pravda* (Mar. 2, 1918).

49 Ibid.

50 Ibid. (Mar. 20, 1918).

calmed spirits, had left for the front, sometimes with the entire factory committee. The government's action later came in for harsh criticism from Petrograd's Bolsheviks, who called it 'not an evacuation but a demoralisation'.[51]

Panic began in earnest on the 'night of alarm', when the factory whistles blew to announce the fall of Pskov, only 250 kilometres from Petrograd. At the Staryi Lessner factory, the remaining 300 workers demanded their severance pay, and no amount of persuasion by the factory committee or by union representatives would deter them.[52] Observing what was taking place at neighbouring factories, the workers at Erikson demanded guarantees that they would not be left without money if the Germans arrived. When they failed to obtain this assurance, they too demanded their severance pay.[53] At the Nobel factory, news of the fall of Pskov prompted a general assembly to call for universal enlistment in the Red Army, and a flying squadron of 700 workers was formed there. But at the end of a tumultuous week, even here the workers decided to close the factory and demand severance pay.[54]

The rapid German advance strengthened Lenin's position and weakened that of the opposition. The Petrograd Soviet reversed itself on 21 February, voting overwhelmingly to approve the Sovnarkom's acceptance of the peace terms.[55] Many factories followed suit, including many of those that had earlier insisted on fighting.[56] Although the Petrograd Trade-Union Council voted 30 to 22 against the treaty, the leadership of the Metalworkers' and Woodworkers' Unions dissented, and a meeting of the Trade Union Council together with 500 representatives of the largest factories voted on 9 March to ratify the treaty, calling at the same time for new elections of the Executive Committee of the Council.[57]

The position changed among Petrograd's Bolsheviks, too. The Fifth Petrograd Conference of the party reconvened after the peace had been signed. Before the German advance, it had overwhelmingly elected a Left-Communist Petersburg Committee. But when the conference resumed after the interruption, it decided to terminate the existence of the Left-Communist fraction in the

---

51 *Peterburgskii komitet RKP(b) v 1918 g.*, p. 61.

52 Ibid.

53 *Pravda* (Mar. 28, 1918).

54 Ibid. *Pravda* (Mar. 28 1918).

55 *Znamya bor'by* (Feb. 13/26 1918).

56 See, for example, Treugol'nik, *Pravda* (Mar. 7, 1918); Okhta meeting, ibid.; Vasilevskii ostrov tram depot, *Petrogradskaya pravda* (Feb. 14/27, 1918).

57 V.I. Nosach 1967, p. 142.

party and to discontinue publication of its journal *Kommunist*.[58] The decision was supported by the Vyborg and other district party organisations, with the exception of Narvskii and a regional party conference of representatives from Sestroretsk, Kolpino, and Finnish Bolsheviks, in all representing 12,582 members.[59]

Workers who had been consistently on the left in 1917 ended up approving the treaty, while many of the more moderate workers continued to oppose it, following the example of the other socialist parties, with the exception of the Bolsheviks. Opposed to the treaty were a majority of the Trade-Union Council (but excluding the leaders of the traditionally radical Metalworkers' and Woodworkers' Unions), workers of the Nevskii and Baltiitskii shipbuilding Factories,[60] some shops in the Putilov factory.[61]

The Left SRs, as mentioned earlier, withdrew from the government over the treaty but continued to participate in the soviets, the armed forces and various other government institutions, until their uprising in June 1918, which was directed against the peace treaty, led to the party's suppression. But M.A. Natanson, one of the party's leaders, told its congress in April 1918 that the decision to leave the government had been nothing more than a 'beau geste' and that it was 'deeply wrong'. 'Whatever our comrades might say, the vast majority of the people were in favour of concluding the peace. The people wanted to save at least a part of what was possible, so that in that part of Russia they could begin to realise the gains of the revolution'.[62]

The Rise and Failure of the Opposition

During the spring of 1918, the Mensheviks and SRs, advocates of replacing Soviet power with a government formed on the basis of the Constituent Assembly, gathered support among Petrograd's factory workers.[63] They called for the 'unity of democracy' and for creation of a '*vsenarodnaia vlast*'' – an 'all-people's' or 'nationwide' government, to be formed by a Constituent Assembly, elected by universal and equal suffrage. They argued that the Soviet regime, because

58 Shelavin 1928–9, p. 106.

59 Ibid.; *Pravda* (Mar. 6, 1918).

60 *Novyi luch* (Feb. 8/21, 1918); *Novaya zhizn'* (Mar. 5, 1918).

61 Ibid. (Feb. 8/21; Mar. 6, 1918).

62 *Partiya levykh sotsialistov eserov, dokumenty i materialy*, Moscow, 2000, part 1, p. 430.

63 Copious documentation of this opposition has been published in Tsudsi (ed.) 2006; and V. Chernyaev et al (ed.) 2000.

of its narrow social base, was incapable of resolving the country's economic difficulties and avoiding civil war.

At the same time, the Mensheviks and SRs denied the existing government any legitimacy. They studiously avoided referring to it as 'the Soviet government', calling it rather the 'Bolshevik dictatorship' – even when it was still a coalition with the Left SRs and far from a dictatorship. Or else they called it a 'Soviet' government with the word 'soviet' in quotation marks. This pointed to a contradiction that was a major weakness of this opposition. Because of workers' attachment to the soviets, the Mensheviks and SRs were rather bashful about saying directly that they opposed the principle itself of government responsible to the soviets. They were reticent about telling workers directly that, in essence, they wanted to restore the kind of government that existed before the October Revolution, a government of 'conciliation with the bourgeoisie', as the Bolsheviks put it. For that was the real meaning of their call for an 'all-people's government'. And the Bolsheviks, on their part, worked hard to make that clear to workers.

That issue arose rather pointedly in June when the Assembly of Authorised Delegates from the Factories and Mills of Petrograd (henceforth: Assembly of Delegates) discussed whether to participate in new elections of the Petrograd Soviet. The assembly was an initiative of the Menshevik-defencists and SRs after the dissolution of the Constituent Assembly, and it became the political centre of worker opposition in the spring of 1918.[64] In discussing whether to participate in new elections, some of the delegates opposed it in principle, and not only because they believed the Bolsheviks would never let them win a majority. One explained:

> We are late in saying our weighty word about the new elections. We have been making a big mistake since we started talking to the workers about the Soviets. Even if the Mensheviks and SRs obtained a majority, the situation would be the same. The isolation of the proletariat from other social classes also existed in the previous [pre-October] Soviets. The proletariat can't shoulder the cause of salvation of the country. That's an impossible task for it alone. We should have gone against the current … If it were not already late, we should be saying: we are opposed to

64 The Menshevik-Internationalists, also opposed to Soviet power, adopted a more neutral, if not unsympathetic, position toward the Assembly. That is why the Menshevik-Internationalist press is a privileged source for this period – and was seen so by workers striving for socialist unity (see Pavlov 2000, p. 14; and Tsudsi (ed.) 2006, p. 528).

> the role of the Soviets that has isolated the proletariat in the course of the revolution, that accelerates the counter-revolution, and pushes non-worker democracy in the direction of reaction ... But until now we have done little in that direction. We would be inserting dissent into the [electoral] campaign that is already beginning.[65]

The growing support for the opposition among the employed workers in the winter and spring months of 1918 was nurtured by economic hardship, hunger and unemployment, and was given an additional boost by the government's occasional repressive measures against protests related to the food crisis. Politicisation of discontent with roots in economic hardship (it will be recalled that worker participation in the protest against dispersal of the Constituent Assembly, when food was still in sufficient supply, had been quite limited) was not without its ambiguities. For if hunger attracted workers to the opposition, it also fostered impatience with 'politics'. And as such, it was a rather shaky foundation upon which to build a political opposition that wanted to change the very basis of political power. In an earlier period, impatience with politics among the less skilled workers had benefitted the anarchists. But the latter's appeal among Petrograd's workers was largely exhausted by the spring of 1918. What workers wanted above all was food and security.

'We are in a period of decline of civic activism in the working class', lamented a Menshevik who was active in cultural affairs:

> At the root of all that, of course, is fatigue ... Lectures by outstanding speakers in the humanitarian sciences attract an average crowd of 20–25 listeners. They attend political meetings only when popular names serve as bait. But alongside that, dance evenings organised by clubs gather crowds of 1,000–1,500.[66]

On 9 May, Zinoviev, Chairman of the Petrograd Soviet, spoke at the Putilov factory, where the opposition had been gaining strength. He explained the precarious political and military situations of the young Soviet republic and warned against the Mensheviks and SRs, who wanted only to lure the workers back under the yoke of capitalism. But the meeting soon grew tired of this analysis. Shouts rang out: 'Enough about politics!' 'About the food ques-

65 Tsudsi (ed.) 2006, p. 251.

66 *Novaya zhizn'* (May 8, 1918).

tion!' When Volodarskii tried to counter the arguments of the Mensheviks and SRs, he too was interrupted with shouts of 'Closer to the question!' 'Speak about bread!'[67]

The early progress of this opposition among workers occurred mainly in factories whose workers had been slow to abandon the 'conciliators' in 1917. In mid-February 1918, local Mensheviks reported from the Kolpino, site of the state-owned Izhorskii ship and machine-building factory and long an SR stronghold, about a certain shift in the workers' mood. As a consequence, they were beginning to think seriously about rebuilding their organisation, which had collapsed after the October Revolution. The workers here had supported the October insurrection and had not participated in the January protests against the dissolution of the Constituent Assembly, but their mood was shifting. Bolshevik-proposed resolutions at factory meetings still won majority support, but those majorities were growing thin.[68] Petrograd's printers, who had elected a Bolshevik majority to the executive of their union after the October Revolution, decided in March 1918 to hold new elections. They took place in April, reducing the Bolsheviks to nine members of the twenty-five-person executive.[69]

March saw the expansion of the activity of the Assembly of Delegates, whose declared goal was to provide workers with an independent alternative to the soviets, and whose political slogan was 'All power to the Constituent Assembly'.[70] But in its early stages, the leaders put the emphasis on the workers' economic problems, and only gradually and rather cautiously moved on to more directly political issues. An appeal to workers at the end of March began:

> The war has ended, but our misfortunes are only beginning. There is little work; the senseless, disorderly evacuation is completely destroying industry. Workers are being thrown into the streets in the tens of thousands. One can't leave, and there is nowhere to go anyway. There is little work everywhere. The last bit of money is being spent. A hungry summer is approaching.

It went on to criticise the soviets and other Bolshevik-led organisations for doing nothing to help workers. But it stopped short of proposing an alternative,

---

67 Ibid. (May 12, 1918).

68 *Novyi luch* (Feb. 7/20, 1918); TsGA SPb f. 171, op. l. d. 10, ll. 10–11.

69 *Novaya zhizn'* (Mar. 26, 1918; Apr. 30, 1918).

70 G. Ya. Aronson 1960, p. 6; *Novaya zhizn'* (Mar. 27, 1918).

stating merely that 'the Assembly discusses all questions of worker life and seeks way to defend workers from the approaching misfortunes'.[71]

This cautious approach took into account the prevailing mood. The workers' dissatisfaction with their economic situation, in most cases, had not yet translated itself into opposition to the Soviet government. But there were signs that this might not be far off. At a meeting of the Vyborg district soviet at the end of March that discussed the plight of the more than 30,000 unemployed workers in the district, a delegate reported that 'among workers a panicky fear is growing in the face of the terrible disaster that is looming'. Another observed: 'A reaction is growing among the workers. For they have received nothing that was promised by soviet power'.[72]

The Assembly of Delegates gradually grew bolder and called openly for the transfer of power to the Constituent Assembly as the only way to overcome the food crisis. The Constituent Assembly, they argued, unlike the soviets, would have broad support and attract competent people to the government and to economic administration. A meeting in May at the Vargunina paper mill in Nevskii district adopted the following resolution:

> After hearing a report on the food question, … [we demand] the annihilation of the civil war in the country, the convocation of the Constituent Assembly and organs of local self-government, city dumas and zemstvos, [elected] on the basis of universal, equal, direct and secret suffrage, the creation of a unified, firm governmental authority to unite the severed country, to put an end to the multiple centres of power [*mnogovlastie*] in the food sector and to organise it on a national scale.

The meeting then elected delegates to the Assembly of Delegates.[73]

A meeting at the Obukhovskii factory in the same district on 12 May heard reports on the food situation from representatives of the Central Food Authority, who tried to show that progress was being made in the face of the very difficult conditions. But other speakers argued that the fact of hunger itself disproved these claims. The meeting then heard a report from a delegation that had been sent by the workers to a meeting of the Bureau of the Assembly of Delegates, after which it adopted a resolution in support of the Assembly.[74]

---

71 *Novaya zhizn'* (Mar. 26, 1918).

72 Ibid. (Mar. 27, 1918).

73 Ibid. (May 14, 1918).

74 Ibid.

A well-attended meeting at the Main Workshops of the Nikolaev Railroad heard a report from a delegation that its workers had sent to Moscow for permission to buy food collectively for the workshops. The permission had been denied, with the explanation that the free purchase and transport of food would undermine the government's efforts to establish a 'food dictatorship', aimed at alleviating the food crisis in the city. After hearing this report, the meeting 'condemned the Soviet government, that has destroyed the food apparatus'. And it demanded convocation of a constituent assembly.[75]

The more penetrating observers recognised that the growing support for the Assembly of Delegates was heavily based on the workers' fatigue:

> The ruling party can, and does, point to the fatigue of the workers of Petrograd, to the temporary decline in their faith in victory near at hand. But is not the proletariat all over Russia tired and is it not being dispersed in a struggle beyond its strength? And can one build a victory against the whole world based on fatigue?[76]

The leaders of the Assembly of Delegates presented the Constituent Assembly as a way to move back from social polarisation and the incipient civil war. The Bolsheviks, on their part, argued that the only real alternative to Soviet power was the victory of the counter-revolution. Their response to the opposition was: 'Not the Constituent Assembly and not the united front, but a decisive struggle!'[77]

It will be recalled that in the days immediately following the October insurrection the workers, including Bolshevik workers, almost unanimously had called for the formation of a united revolutionary-democratic government, a coalition of all the socialist parties. But this demand was premised on the condition that the government give representation exclusively to the toiling classes, breaking decisively with the counter-revolutionary propertied classes, who would have no representation. An end to the nefarious influence of the propertied classes in government had been, after all, the workers' goal in the October insurrection. But the Vikzhel-sponsored negotiations between the socialist parties demonstrated that the much-desired all-socialist coalition was not possible, since the SRs and the Mensheviks insisted on representation in government of the propertied classes, in one form or another. Related to that,

75 Ibid. (May 28, 1918).
76 Ibid. (May 28, 1918).
77 *Znamya bor'by* (May 14, 1918).

they wanted the Bolsheviks, who constituted a majority in the TsIK of Soviets, relegated, at best, to minority status in the government. For the same reason, few workers took part in January in the protests against the dissolution of the Constituent Assembly, since the 'conciliators' were a majority in that assembly. From the workers' point of view, the task of the Constituent Assembly should be to endorse a government representing the toiling classes exclusively, that is, Soviet power or its equivalent.

From that point of view, nothing really changed in the following months to make the 'all-national' government advocated by the opposition any more plausible. But the workers' economic situation had gone from bad to disastrous. And desperation made them more receptive to the opposition's message.

The defenders of Soviet power explained the economic crisis as a consequence of the imperialist war and the policies of the previous governments, of sabotage by officials inherited from the former regime, of the refusal of the intelligentsia to collaborate with the Soviet government, of the German occupation of Ukraine, and the incipient civil war. They pointed to recent events in the Ukraine, where the moderate nationalist Rada (the parliament) had been overthrown and replaced by the counterrevolutionary dictatorship of Hetman Skoropadskii, who was propped up by the German army. 'What the Mensheviks and SRs are proposing', explained the Left SR P.P. Prosh'yan to a meeting at the Putilov factory, 'that is, an all-national [*obshchenarodnaya*] policy at the expense of a class policy, can only lead to Skoropadskii'.[78] Supporters of Soviet power also pointed to what was happening in Finland just to the north of Petrograd, to the mass executions and purposeful starvation of workers and peasants in open-air concentration camps after the defeat of the revolution there. And were not Russia's Kadets, who were also brandishing the banner of the Constituent Assembly, at that very moment, together with Tsarist officers, organising a counterrevolutionary army on the Don? The choice was Soviet power or counterrevolution. Lunacharkii, Commissar of Education, speaking to workers of the Baltiiskii shipbuilding factory, phrased the choice as 'Call forth your last ounce of strength or accept defeat!'[79]

On its part, the opposition continued to hammer away at its central argument: the narrow social base of the Soviet government made it impossible to reverse the economic crisis and avoid civil war. At the end of May, a Menshevik delegate from the Patronnyi factory told the Conference of Worker and Red Army Delegates of Petrograd's the First-City district:

78 Ibid. (May 28, 1918).

79 Mil'shtein 1963, p. 157.

> We warned that if you signed that obscene Peace of Brest-Litovsk, you would by that not end war but expand the civil war. And that fact is now before us. All that must be eliminated, but the government is not capable of doing it ... If the evacuation is carried out without any plan, then one can't count on the factories working. But the government can't do that either. Only a government elected by equal and secret suffrage, that is, the Constituent Assembly, can do that ...
>
> Why do we have raw materials, we have fuel, but the factories are not open? Because our people are not capable of working there. Now in our factory they have made a fitter into a turner, and tailors [are being made] into bailiffs and commissars. In the Third city district, [there is] the honourable comrade Goryachev – a tailor. Now he is a commissar. Of course, he can sew on a good patch. But can he bring any benefit to the state? Hardly.[80]

And another added:

> As often as they might tell you that it is better for a dishwasher, and not General Kornilov, to be a general, that is still open to question ... That all these people are undoubtedly sincere – no one denies. And maybe they work a lot. I know the people about whom comrade Korsakov [Bolshevik chairman of the district soviet] speaks. It is very true that they are most honest people, but they have not collapsed from work, as they have told you here. They have collapsed because they don't know how to work ... It is impossible to demand from a person who is not prepared to carry out all the functions that life has placed upon him. Helplessness is the red thread running through all these reports.[81]

A resolution adopted on 9 May by a meeting at the Putilov factory stated in the same vein: 'Alone, without the help of national, socialist and democratic forces, they [the People's Commissars] cannot handle the task, and we throw before their eyes our will, our worker and revolutionary truth: Unite!'[82]

At the same time, in the context of the economic crisis, workers were feeling that their own organisations – soviets, factory committees, unions – were becoming estranged from them. This, too, aided the opposition. A general

---

80 *Pervaya konferentsiya rabochikh i krasnoarmeiskikh deputatov I-go Gorodskogo raiona*, p. 107.

81 Ibid., pp. 344–5.

82 *Novaya zhizn'* (May 8, 1918).

assembly at the Metallicheskii factory on 18 March discussed the question of severance wages for workers who were being laid off. An agreement had been reached with the Commissar of Labour. But when the government hastily evacuated to Moscow in the face of the advancing German army, the question was transferred to the Soviet of the Northern Commune, which changed the decision, making necessary new negotiations. At the meeting, the laid-off workers demanded to know why they had not received their money. The factory committee explained to them that despite its best efforts – including, at one point, the threatened arrest of the factory's managers – the money could not be had for a few more days, since, on top of everything else, there was a problem finding smaller denominations. This explanation did not satisfy the workers, who chose five people to monitor the activity of their factory committee. One of the workers claimed that the government was exerting pressure on the factory's delegates and hindering their work. Another, referring to the constant appeals for support from the government, asked how they could possibly do more: 'Hold onto the cars' fenders in support, as they drive away?' This was a reference to the government's hasty evacuation to Moscow at the end of February that came in for universal criticism, not least from local Bolsheviks. But another worker suggested that the meeting's nervous mood was best explained by hunger.[83]

Some workers did have a simplistic view of what the relations between workers and a workers' government should be. During the German offensive, workers at the Putilov factory who wanted to leave the city demanded their severance pay at once. At their meeting, one shouted: 'Give us money and [railway] cars too ... Soviet government is our government, and it has to do everything for us. Whatever the rank and file [*nizy*] demand – it must carry out'.[84]

The political opposition, for its part, made much of the conflicts that arose between workers and their organisations, arguing that it had been a mistake for these organisations – soviets, factory committees, unions – to assume governmental and economic management functions. These should be left to institutions elected by universal suffrage and to the capitalists.[85] An appeal in March from the Bureau of the Assembly of Delegates first described the workers' suffering. Then it stated:

---

83 Ibid., (Mar. 22, 1918).

84 *Petrogradskaya pravda* (Apr. 2, 1918).

85 The opposition did not often speak directly of returning the enterprises to capitalists. But it made clear that Russia was not ready for socialist experiments. See, for example, *Pervaya konferentsiya rabochikh i krasnoarmeiskikh deputatov I-go Gorodskovo raiona*, pp. 276, 289.

> One can expect help from no one. Have the trade unions done much for the unemployed? They are not busy with the unemployed nor with the employed. The unions are organising the economy, but not the workers.
>
> The factory committees have become commissions for laying off workers, state institutions that have no need of our confidence and that lost it long ago. They won't help us either ...
>
> And there is nothing to expect from the soviet, since they only judge, punish, collect taxes, organise the Red Guard, and sometimes even shoot ... Workers have to worry about their fate on their own.[86]

In some factories, the workers held repeated elections to their factory committee in the vain hope of obtaining satisfaction for their demands. The general assembly of the Printers' Union explained its decision to hold new elections to the union executive in the following terms: under the Bolshevik leadership 'the activity of a class organisation was replaced by the intervention of state power ... Carried away with affairs of state, it did not wish to, and could not, counteract unemployment'.[87] Similarly, a meeting of workers of the Izhorskii factory resolved:

> Considering that all our workers' organisation – factory committees, unions and soviets – have ceased being independent workers' organisations and have turned into state chancelleries, this assembly protests against such a policy of the Soviet government and demands the return of workers' organisations to their class path.[88]

The change in the activity of workers' organisations from organisations that educated and organised to fight capital into organisations that managed state and economic affairs affected the Bolshevik party itself. R.I. Shelavin, a member of the Bolshevik's Petersburg Committee in 1918, wrote that after the October Revolution

> A series of responsible, highly qualified comrades who had gone through the school of illegality became infected with an exclusively 'soviet' spirit, not to speak of the masses of the younger generation. Even if these comrades did not give full expression to what they thought, they all,

86 *Novaya zhizn'* (Mar, 26, 1918).

87 Ibid.

88 Ibid. (June 1, 1918).

> nevertheless, had a certain difficulty imagining: what, in essence, is left for the party organisations after the victory of the proletariat? Some thought that, in any case, there remained the activity of agitation and propaganda. But they still felt that the real activity now is, for example, to organise the district soviet of the national economy, but certainly not to 'ferment' in the district party committee. Indeed, around them everything was churning; the old was being destroyed and the new was being built; sabotage was being fought; the first new soviet state forces were being recruited; the districts were being organised like independent republics with their own commissars – labour, education, etc.; the best party forces were being thrown into this whirlwind of construction … When the Vasileostrovskii district soviet moved away from the 16th Line to a new building on Srednii Prospekt, they relegated the district party committee to the fifth floor, and their thinking went something like: what kind of particular work can they now have?[89]

This transformation of workers' organisations was, of course, a logical consequence of the October Revolution. The workers had taken power. How else were they to exercise that power but through their own organisations, especially since the old state apparatus was not cooperating? Even under better conditions, some tension was to be expected between the common interests of the class and those of specific groups of workers. But in conditions of economic breakdown, when the new state could not meet even the basic needs of workers, this tension became acute. In such circumstances, it required a strong commitment and class consciousness to continue to identify with this state, rather than seeing it as alien and oppressive.

The Mensheviks and SRs, for their part, actively promoted the latter perception. As noted already, they invariably referred to the government as 'Bolshevik', passing over not only the participation of Left SRs (which continued even after Brest-Litovsk at levels below the national government) and their own refusal to participate in a government responsible to the soviets. But the Bolsheviks, for their part, threw back in the face of the opposition their refusal to work in the government. A Bolshevik delegate to the Conference of workers and Red Army deputies of the First City district at the end of May gave the following response to the oppositionist who criticised the government's inability to solve the problems facing the workers:

89 Shelavin 1928–9, p. 111.

> So it turns out now, that the [district] soviet is doing nothing. From all the reports, they [the opposition] could find nothing [positive]. Then the first question is posed: Please, you are very welcome to come and work [in the soviets and other organisations]. When we proposed to them to take up positions in the TsIK, they said: We will enter the soviet, but only to sit there. And you can work as you like and take power into your hands ...[90]

On the other hand, it is clear that the assumption by governmental and administrative responsibilities and the consequent loss of direct, continuous contact with their fellow workers in the factories, not to mention with the unemployed, tended to foster a certain 'administrative outlook' among those in authority. This could manifest itself in impatience with workers' demands and protests, and, of course, in growing intolerance for the opposition.

Another important factor that facilitated the opposition's growth was the loss to the factories of the most committed, class conscious elements of the working class, the Bolshevik party members, who had assured the party's organic link with the class and had been the principal active force in the October Revolution. Shelavin recalled:

> To the devastation of the ranks of Piter's proletariat in connection with unemployment, plant shutdowns and hunger, one has to add the outflow of party members into the Red Army, food detachments, and the like. At the Seventh Petrograd party conference it was reported: From 35,000 members who belonged to the Petrograd organisation, there are only 15,000 left. In other words, the loss of three months is expressed in the huge figure of 20,000 people ...[91]

And the haemorrhaging did not stop there. By August–September 1918, party numbers in Petrograd were down to 6,000. Of these, 40 percent were 'October Bolsheviks', people who had joined after the October Revolution. The situation became so critical that on 2 August 1918 the Petersburg Committee decided to ignore Lenin's persistent calls to send more party members to the civil-war fronts and to the countryside and categorically forbade members in responsible party positions from leaving the city.[92] In a telegram to the Petersburg Committee, Lenin, Sverdlov and Trotsky wrote: 'Petrograd's complaint that we are

90 *Pervaya konferentsiya rabochikh ikrasnoarmeiskikh deputatov*, p. 334.

91 Shelavin 1929, p. 26.

92 *Peterburgskii komitet RKP(b) v 1918 g.*, pp. 29, 130, 273 and Shelavin 1929, pp. 33–4.

emptying Petrograd of people is unfounded. Where will we take the best agitators and organisers for national tasks, if not in Petrograd?'[93]

The decline in the number of party activists severely affected the party organisation itself in Petrograd, which exerted little influence over the executive of the Soviet. *Pravda*, the party's paper in Petrograd in the first half of 1918, had a total staff of only three, who, 'like all other party workers, are overburdened with work'. The paper was not receiving materials from the districts and factories, and members described it as 'boring, uninteresting and lifeless'.

From a report at a party delegates' conference on 21 May 1918:

> Lately, our party organ is divorced not only from our party masses but from the party institutions. Neither the Petersburg Committee, nor the districts use their organ as a weapon. There is no effort in the districts to help in its distribution. In former times, the party organ was inundated with queries, correspondences, and the like. But now party workers don't use it ... The districts don't support *Pravda* at all. It, therefore, morally hangs by a hair ... Party comrades themselves don't buy it. Members don't distribute, not because they don't share its viewpoint – the right and left both distributed it poorly ... And yet, it is an irreplaceable tool.[94]

In mid-April 1918, the Menshevik-internationalist V. Stroev (Lopata) offered the following analysis of what had befallen the Bolshevik party after October:

> The Party, whose organisational influence had not embraced the entire working class, having driven away the intellectual cadres of the socialist parties with its maximalist intransigence, is all the less able to service even the consciously simplified government apparatus of the Republic of Soviets, which, in the opinion of Lenin, is accessible even to half-educated workers and peasants.
>
> The best workers have been torn away from their class by government work. The still fledgling trade-union organisations of the proletariat have been sacrificed to this same Moloch of allegedly socialist statehood.
>
> The political organisation of the working class – the party of social-democratic Bolsheviks or Communists – has also, in essence, been broken. For, having found itself in power, it has ceased to live as a party that organises the working class and it speaks to it exclusively in the lan-

93 *Izvestiya TsK KPSS*, 1989, no. 5, p. 149, cited in *Peterburgskii komitet RKP(b) v 1918 g.*, p. 258.

94 *Peterburgskii komitet RKP(b) v 1918 g.*, 116–17, 141–2.

> guage of omnipotent benevolence or authoritative prohibition. The natural, healthy growth of the party, the strengthening of consciousness and organisation in the working class, have ceased.[95]

One could take issue with the argument that it was Bolshevik 'maximalist intransigence' that had driven away the left-leaning intelligentsia. After all, Stroev's own paper itself had complained several months before of the intelligentsia's desertion of the working class which, it insisted, had begun well before the 'excesses' of October.[96] But otherwise, Stroev was pointing to an important process, one that certainly made things easier for the opposition, which, for its part, was very present and active in the factories.

Besides the serious deterioration of the food situation in May, two major incidents of repression against workers took place that month that gave a strong boost to the opposition, supporting its portrayal of the Soviet government as dictatorial and hostile to workers. The first occurred in Kolpino, long an SR stronghold in 1917 and where the Bolshevik leaders of the local soviet had been resisting workers' calls to hold new elections. On 9 May, at a time of severe food shortage, women queuing for bread were told that supplies had run out. A large crowd, having failed to find the chairman of the local Food Authority, moved toward the town square. Red Guards arrived and, wielding their rifle butts, stopped a group of women who were trying to reach the fire station to sound the alarm. One youth, however, got through the cordon and was wounded by the assistant commander of the Red-Guard unit. This was followed by a volley fired into the crowd that killed one and wounded three. Upon hearing the shots, workers came running out of the factory but they were turned back by the Red Guards. A general assembly at the factory decided to hold new elections to the local soviet and demanded the arrest of those responsible for the shooting. It also decided to send delegations to Petrograd to discuss a plan of action with other oppositionists. But on leaving the factory gates, the workers were met by Red Guards who again opened fire, killing one and wounding several others. This was followed by searches and arrests, and that evening, the town was placed under martial law.[97]

The other incident took place at Sestroretsk, another small town located outside the capital. But here the workers of the local arms factory had traditionally

---

95 Ibid. (Apr. 20, 1918).

96 See above, pp. 415–16.

97 *Novaya zhizn'* (May 11, 1918). For extensive documentation of this incident, see *Sobranie upolnomochennykh i piterskie rabochie*, pp. 726–812.

supported the Bolsheviks. It, too, began with women enraged by the food shortages. A crowd moved to the factory, where a meeting took place. Some of the speakers called for the overthrow of the soviet regime. From there, a crowd proceeded to the apartments of members of the local soviet and ransacked them. Others went to the soviet, sending the deputies fleeing and beating up the ones that they caught. This was followed by a large number of arrests, including of some factory workers, who were released after a brief investigation. Responding to the arrests, the workers struck and called for new elections.[98]

There were some other, more minor instances of repression. But the period in general was still one of quite broad tolerance of the opposition, especially if one considers that the city was on the verge of starvation and that the civil war was fast heating up in the country. Just how desperate the food situation became can be gauged by Lenin's telegram sent in May to all soviets and food authorities, demanding, pleading for the immediate dispatch of food to save 'red capital on the verge of perishing'.[99] But another element that should be considered in assessing the level of political tolerance[100] in this period and which has already been mentioned, is the fact that this political opposition was not a 'loyal' one but aimed at replacing soviet power with a government in which all classes of society would be represented. In other words, it wanted to annul and reverse the October Revolution.

The Kolpino events, in particular, provoked a series of protest meetings in factories that adopted resolutions calling to transfer power to the Constituent Assembly. At the 11 May session at the Assembly of Delegates, reports from the districts stated that the shooting at Kolpino had overshadowed the workers' preoccupation with hunger.[101] A resolution adopted by a meeting at the Siemens-Shukkert factory declared:

> Having discussed the issues of the current situation and hunger, on the basis of which food disturbances are occurring and the present govern-

98 Ibid. (May 26; June 22, 1918).

99 Ibid. (May 11, 1918).

100 This can be gauged, for example, from the protocols of the Conference of workers and Red Army soldiers of the First City district soviet at the end of May. Although the polemics were heated between the supporters of the government and the opposition, the tone of pro-government speakers was generally respectful. The opposition, for its part, did not complain about its representation or the time that was allotted to it. In only a few cases did pro-government delegates refer to the opposition as 'saboteurs' or 'counter-revolutionary'.

101 *Novaya zhizn'* (May 12, 1918).

> ment uses the force of arms to liquidate them, as the Kolpino events show … we demand the unification of all democratic strata of the population and the establishment of a supreme governmental authority by universal, direct, secret and equal suffrage, that is by the convocation of the All-Russian Constituent Assembly, which alone can ease both the food situation and all public life.[102]

The Bolsheviks and Left SRs were aware of increasing estrangement of the workers from the organs of power and admitted that the attitude of the soviets, which had become engrossed in government administration, was often to blame. They were particularly concerned about the district soviets, the level of government closest to the workers and often the first target of their anger. Partly in recognition of this, and partly in response to the growing support for the Assembly of Delegates, the Petrograd Soviet, on the suggestion of a conference of district soviets, decided in mid-April to convene district conferences of worker delegates 'to elicit the views of the worker masses on issues of the current situation'. The conferences were to be organised by commissions made up of representatives of all the parties present in the soviets. Delegates were elected on the basis of one vote for fifty employed or unemployed workers (the latter's election meetings were organised by the labour exchange), with additional representation given to the district's trade-union organisations and parties.[103] It was later decided to include deputies from Red Army units, which were at that time under jurisdiction of the district soviets.

The decision to hold these conferences was recognition that the soviets, having become organs of government, were neglecting their former functions of organising, representing, and educating workers. The conference in the Narvskii district observed:

> The work of the district soviet can be successful only if our deputies do not look upon their work as bureaucratic and if they conduct a determined struggle against laziness and slovenliness among those who have not yet freed themselves from these vices.[104]

The conference in the First City district, whose proceedings were published in full in 1918, directed the soviet's deputies to maintain closer ties with the work-

102 Ibid. (May 15, 1918).

103 Shelavin 1928–9, pp. 162–4; *Novaya zhizn'* (Apr. 15, 1918).

104 *Petrogradskaya pravda* (June 5, 1918).

ers and to report back to them at least once a month, as well as to the soviet itself. Other decisions adopted by the conference pointed in the same direction. In particular, an agitational commission was to be established with the mandate to keep workers and soldiers informed of the soviet's activities and of the current situation, as well as a department for ties with the unemployed, and a cultural-educational department. One of the pro-Soviet delegates proposed that members of parties that did not recognise Soviet power be excluded from the latter committee. But that was rejected by the majority (made up of Bolsheviks, Left SRs and sympathisers), another sign of the relatively tolerant climate of the period.[105]

The relatively few Bolsheviks who were active in the life of the party itself (as opposed to the soviets, and other governmental and economic institutions) saw an additional cause for worker alienation from the soviets in the latter's detachment from the party. After the October Revolution and for most of 1918, the Petersburg Committee exerted little, if any influence, on the Executive of the Petrograd Soviet. As the editors of the published protocols of the Bolsheviks' Petrograd Committee in 1918 write, 'In the first half of 1918, the party organs did not play a controlling role in the political governance of Petrograd and not even a significant consulting role. Moreover, it is not at all clear that in the post-October months the members of the Petrograd Committee considered that situation in any way abnormal'.[106] The same was true for the relationship between the party's district committees and the district soviets. On 9 April 1918, a member of the Bolsheviks' Petersburg Committee, which numbered only some five people at the time, observed:

> The weakness and incomplete character of party control over the course of soviet work in the districts in the post-October period has led to a series of harmful consequences and has had a deleterious effect on the activity first of all of the district soviets themselves.[107]

The decline of the party's influence resulting from the recruitment of its most committed and gifted members into government, the military and economic administration especially, worried the Left Communists, whose draft resolution, proposed to the party Conference of the Northern Region in April 1918, stated:

---

105 *Pervaya konferentsiya rabochikh i krasnoarmeiksikh deputatov*, pp. 356, 358; Mil'shtein 1963, p. 137. *Petrogradskaya pravda* (June 5, 1918).

106 *Peterburgskii komitet RKP(b) v 1918 g.*, pp. 19–20.

107 *Petrogradskaya pravda* (10 Apr. 1918); *Peterburgskii komitet RKP(b) v 1918.*, p. 86.

> On the basis of reports from the localities, the conference finds that the party's organisational work has declined significantly. The best party forces have left for soviet work. A significant part of the comrades are torn away from party life, which presents a definite danger for the party. Further, the conference finds that the influence of responsible party institutions is extremely weakly felt in the local organs of power.[108]

One of the consequences of this situation, it was argued, was the tendency to adopt an administrative approach to political questions.

Another consequence of the decline of party work, and especially of the weakened party presence in the factories, was the growing influence of the political opposition, whose own members were very active in factories. 'The right forces', complained the Left SR Khmara, 'exploiting the temporary absence of committed revolutionary forces, gain temporary successes among the passive workers'. Another factor in this success was the change in the social composition of the employed workforce – the disappearance of the Vyborg district as an industrial centre and the numerical predominance of the Nevskii district and more generally of workers who had traditionally supported the SRs.

Of course, the most important reason for the opposition's growing strength was the Soviet government's inability to solve the workers' most urgent problems – hunger, unemployment, the civil war. But Khmara's claim finds support in the marked political oscillations among workers during this period: one and the same group could one day vote to support an opposition-proposed resolution and the next, in the presence of capable Bolshevik and Left SR speakers, vote for a pro-government resolution. For example, soon after the Kolpino events, in the absence of the Bolshevik and LSR members of the factory committee, the workers of the Vulkan factory, who had been strong supporters of the Bolsheviks, voted to hold new elections of the factory's Soviet deputies and adopted an opposition-proposed resolution that called for a conference of 'all socialist and democratic forces' – a clearly oppositional formulation – that were prepared to help the toiling masses and collaborate in organising the food-supply system.[109] The opposition press touted this as evidence that even the regime's most stalwart supporters were turning away from it. But three days later, with all the members of the factory committee present, another assembly rejected the resolution proposed by the opposition and adopted a declaration

108 Shelavin 1928–9, p. 115.

109 *Novaya zhizn'* (May 12, 1918).

that asserted that the only way out of the current dead-end situation was for workers and peasants to unite around the slogans of the October Revolution.[110]

Khmara similarly reported that a meeting at the Nobel machine-building factory, whose workers had also traditionally supported the Bolsheviks, would have adopted an opposition resolution to boycott the Mayday demonstration and to demand the convocation of a constituent assembly were it not for the presence of a single Left-SR activist, who was able to explain the real significance of that proposed resolution. He concluded with the appeal: 'We cannot leave the masses in the factories without activists. Comrades in the factories, invite agitators and lecturers. Write about your factory life in the papers. Don't yield to provocation of the conciliationist parties'.[111] This kind of political instability was rare in 1917.

But the classic case of this wavering was the Putilov factory, which employed some 12,000 workers in May 1918. Three consecutive mass meetings took place on 8, 9, and 10 May during work hours, at which the central question was food, and in particular the issue of the government's food monopoly versus free, though in some limited way regulated, trade. The 8 May meeting adopted clearly oppositional resolutions, including the demand to transfer power to the Constituent Assembly.[112] But the next day, a meeting lasting eight hours was addressed by the Bolsheviks' 'heavy artillery' – Zinoviev and Volodarsky – who, however, were continuously interrupted by shouts: 'Enough politics! Talk about bread!' That meeting adopted a pro-government resolution. But towards the end, it also confirmed the previous day's oppositional resolution. *Vechernee slovo*, a paper not sympathetic to the government, concluded: 'Evaluating the meeting yesterday [9 May] of the Putilovtsy, you reach the conclusion that the workers in their mass have not freed themselves from the influence of their former leaders. The crisis of consciousness that the workers are experiencing has still not crystallised into definite, concrete positions'.[113] But yet another mass meeting the next day voted to invalidate the pro-government resolution of the day before, since, it was claimed, the presence of Red Army soldiers had contributed to the pro-government majority.[114] That decision, in turn, was

---

110 *Znamya bor'by* (May 14, 1918).

111 Ibid. (24 May 1918). Shelavin also explained the election in June of opposition deputies in some textile mills, and pro-government deputies in others also by the presence or absence of pro-government activists at the mills (*Krasnaya gazeta* (June 29, 1918)).

112 See *Sobranie upolnomochennykh i piterskie rabochie*, pp. 486–90 for various newspaper reports on the meeting.

113 *Vechernee slovo* (May 10, 1918).

114 *Sobranie upolnomochennykh i piterskie rabochie*, pp. 498–506.

contested by meetings of various Putilov shops in subsequent days.[115] This is how Shelavin explained this wavering:

> The Putilovtsy made the not very great mistake of sending their best to the front. That was an iron necessity, and the ranks of the most active worker-Putilovtsy had to keep flowing into the army, into soviet work, food detachments. At the same time, the proletariat's general situation deteriorated, and the Mensheviks and SRs intensified their activity ... The Putilovtsy remained overall for Soviet power – and that in the most difficult conditions. But it required a great mobilisation of forces to overcome the mood of the masses ... But we did miss the vote in favour of the Constituent Assembly, and that happened because there were no Bolshevik orators on the spot.[116]

On the other hand, workers who were members of the two pro-government parties, and the Bolsheviks first of all, did remain steadfast.[117] *Novaya zhizn'* begrudgingly recognised this, although it curiously explained it by the hold of the 'backward masses' on these conscious Bolsheviks: 'The most conscious workers have long ago understood the hopelessness of soviet intransigence, and only their impotence in the face of the maximalism of the benighted masses and the strong ties to their party keep them captive of the hopeless, makeshift communism'.[118] This was wishful thinking, although it was widespread among Mensheviks. In reality, the opposite was true: in their distress, the less politicised, less 'conscious' workers, that is, those whose identification with the working class and whose commitment to the revolution were weakest, were those attracted more strongly to the opposition's message. Bolshevik workers on the whole did not waver, and the same is true, as one would expect, of workers in the Red Army, who elected 58 Bolsheviks and three Left SR deputies in the June Soviet elections, a result that the opposition parties did not bother to contest.[119]

But despite their support for Soviet power, Bolshevik workers did not hesitate harshly to criticise the government's failures.[120] The latter's handling of the food question, in particular, was the source of much discontent. At an

115 Ibid., pp. 510–11.
116 Shelavin 1928–9, pp. 152, 156.
117 See the *Pervaya gorodskaya konferentsiya* and also Shelavin 1928–9, p. 167.
118 *Novaya zhizn'* (June 1, 1918).
119 *Severnaya kommuna* (July 6, 1918).
120 See, for example, *Pervaya gorodskaya konferentsiya*, and Shelavin 1928–9, p. 167.

enlarged meeting of the Bolshevik Petersburg Committee on 5 June 1918 on the food crisis and the government's decision to centralise the supply organisation, two positions emerged: one supported the government's decision; the other defended the elective principle and continued broad powers for district food authorities. But everyone, as one might expect, rejected the opposition's solution, which was to broaden the basis of government by transferring power to the Constituent Assembly and to municipal governments elected by universal suffrage. If anything, the Bolshevik supporters of decentralisation wanted to restrict even more the social base of the government. They demanded a purge of the 'saboteurs' in the food-supply organisations who had been inherited from the previous regime. They wanted the food-supply administration to be rebuilt 'from below', from supporters of the Soviet regime. Kudeshov, a delegate from the Vasilevskii ostrov district, argued:

> Its [the Central Food Authority's] apparatus is good for nothing. It should have been disbanded long ago. Now they want to change it from above. But that's self-deception. Appointing two or three people won't change anything. The apparatus of the Central Food Authority has thousands who are wall-to-wall saboteurs. Our organisation has always been built from below [*s nizov*]. And so we should do it now. We called long ago to purge the central food authority of our enemies, but up to now that has not been done. As much authority as we might give a commissar, we won't be able to kick out the saboteurs, since you have to prove the reasons, and they won't disband the apparatus.[121]

An article in *Novaya zhizn'* presented the following, no doubt rather slanted, portrait of a rank-and-file worker-Bolshevik. Waiting in line for bread, a group of women is in good spirits because the ration had just been raised to half a funt, a little less than a quarter kilogram. But one of the women remarked:

> 'Don't worry. It will be like the last time. They'll lull us with this for a couple of days and then again start giving out an eighth of a funt, and then nothing at all'.
>
> 'Well, no! This time it will hold. And now there'll be everything – both sugar and butter. During the searches [of food stores], it's amazing how much they confiscated'.

121 Shelavin 1929, p. 74. See also pp. 70–81, *passim*. And *Peterburgskii komitet* RPK(*b*), pp. 160–73, 179.

> This was spoken by Dasha, a tall, pockmarked native of Yaroslavl' province. She never stands at her place in the line but moves from one group to the next, intervening in all the conversations and agitating clearly for the Bolsheviks. There is a terrible muddle in her head, but by temperament she is a genuine revolutionary and demagogue. In her desire to defeat the opponent, she is not choosy about her arguments and expressions. Her voice is low, a bit hoarse; her speech is rapid and energetic.
>
> 'Well, of course, we know you're a Bolshevik!'
>
> 'Naturally, I'm not a *kaledinka* [supporter of white General Kaledin]. I'm a peasant, from the people, and I follow the people. And that's why I like the Bolsheviks, since they bother about the people and show favouritism to no one. Just give them some time, and they'll put them all in their place. Then you'll see what they can do'.[122]

At the First City district conference of worker and Red Army deputies, V. Ivanov, a Bolshevik worker, offered the following response to the opposition's claim that workers had become estranged from the Soviet regime. It deserves to be quoted at length, since it expresses well the thinking of worker-Bolsheviks.

> The comrades ... who pointed out that there is a part of the workers, for example, the Putilovtsy, who criticise this government are perfectly correct. But that still doesn't mean that those workers don't recognise it as their own native [*rodnoi*] Soviet power. In just the same way, we see a mother scold the child she loves, when she fears it is misbehaving. They scold precisely because they love.
>
> But they [the Mensheviks and SRs] will, of course, never understand that, because they have ceased to be a party of the workers; they have left our cause, the cause of the proletarian revolution. Don't be insulted, gentlemen, you who are trying through the Constituent Assembly to slip the bourgeoisie back into power ... I will say, comrades, that only our party, the party of communists, the party of left SRs, only it has remained faithful to our slogan, only it has remained on the revolutionary path ...
>
> We must now say this: we have two paths – the dictatorship of the bourgeoisie or the dictatorship of the proletariat. Each one of us would sooner agree to put a bullet through his forehead than allow the dictatorship of the bourgeoisie, because we know that its answer to our pleas for mercy would be only a bullet in the forehead ...

122 *Novaya zhizn'* (June 10, 1918).

> But you, gentlemen, history will not forget you. It will remember you as would-be socialists, as those who, trembling for their miserable hides, abandoned the common cause, the cause of the proletarian revolution. It will remember you as people, who in such a fearful moment find nothing else to do but speak about your Constituent Assembly, speak about the need to summon the bourgeoisie back to power. History will remember them precisely as would-be socialists, as people who took fright at the hard road that the peasants and workers must tread, and who, therefore, stopped – did not even stop, but went backwards to capitalism.[123]

The results of the general elections of 18–24 June to the Soviet of the Northern Commune (Petrograd Soviet) lend some credence to Ivanov's assessment. A careful analysis of the results indicates that at least a very significant part of the employed workers (the position of workers in the Red Army or in government and economic management positions is not open to doubt) continued to support Soviet power, despite their desperate material situation. Abandoning the usual practice of holding partial elections when workers in a given factory felt the need to recall their deputies, the Executive Committee of the Petrograd Soviet yielded the opposition's demand for general elections. In doing so, it hoped to disprove the latter's claim that the soviets had lost the workers' support as organs of state power.

The general context seemed to favour the opposition, which had begun organising on a national scale and had decided to convoke a national conference in Moscow. Moreover, during the election week, on 24 June, the government announced that the bread ration would be reduced to an eighth of a funt and that on the following two days that would be replaced by an eighth-funt of groats.[124] A Bolshevik who participated in the electoral campaign recalled: 'The meetings in the factories and in the shops were often full of anguish, bitterness and pain. Instead of speeches, the women workers demanded bread. Tears flowed from the eyes of hundreds and hundreds of mothers'.[125] At the same time, Czechoslovak troops on their way to the Pacific Ocean, from there to join Entente armies on the Western Front, had seized Saratov, a major town on the Middle Volga, and towns further east in Western and Central Siberia, cutting off Petrograd from yet another vital source of grain, following the loss of the Ukraine earlier to the Germans.[126] There were also

123 *Pervaya konferentsiya rabochikh i krasnoarmeiskikh* ... pp. 275–6.

124 Mil'shtein 1963, p. 154.

125 *Petrogradskaya pravda* (Dec. 6, 1918).

126 Chamberlin 1965, vol. II, pp. 7–9.

new incidents of government repression against worker protests and against the political opposition. On the eve of the elections, the Menshevik and SR members of the Assembly of Delegates in Sormovo and Moscow were arrested, along with a few delegates from Petrograd who were in Moscow to attend the Assembly's national conference.[127] In incidents in Tula, Sormovo and Moscow, government forces opened fire on protesters. And on 16 June, the TsIK voted to expel the Mensheviks and SRs and recommended that local soviets do the same.[128]

If these things could be expected to boost support for the opposition among workers, the assassination of Volodarskii at the hands of an SR during the elections undoubtedly increased sympathy for Soviet power. Volodarskii, a popular Bolshevik tribune, was shot on his way to an election meeting at the Aleksandrovskii factory in the Nevskii district. Thousands of workers attended his funeral in pouring rain.[129] At the same time, the active involvement of SRs in armed anti-Soviet movements in Siberia and Ukraine no doubt also hurt the opposition among workers.

The election campaign itself took place in conditions of relative calm and freedom, including freedom of the press that included, within limits, the bourgeois (non-socialist) press.[130] The consensus was that the workers had shown a keen interest in the elections and that the Assembly of Delegates conducted an energetic campaign.[131] The opposition did not contest the election results because of any repression but rather because of the mode of representation. Besides workers and soldiers, organisations were also able to elect deputies: the Petrograd Trade-Union Council was allotted one deputy for every 5,000 of its members; individual unions with over 2,000 members could each elect two deputies; smaller unions could elect one – in all, 144 deputies. And district soviets were each allotted three deputies. Finally, factory committees of enterprises that were not at the time operating but which had previously employed a thousand or more workers were each allowed to elect one deputy.

In brief, there were a lot of 'dead souls' participating in the election. This was clearly done with a view to ensure a majority of pro-Soviet deputies. The analysis that follows, therefore, is limited to factories that were operating at

127 *Novaya zhizn'* (June 12, 1918).

128 Ibid. (June 16,1918).

129 Mil'shtein 1963, p. 157.

130 Although Menshevik and SR papers were appearing, the government refused to authorise the Assembly of Delegates its own newspaper.

131 Mil'shtein 1963, p. 146.

TABLE 15.3 *Party affiliation of deputies elected to the Petrograd Soviet from operating factories 18–24 June 1918*

Party [a]	Number of deputies	Percent of all deputies
Bolsheviks	127	48.5
LSRS	32	12.2
Mensheviks [b]	29	11.1
SRS	46	17.6
Unaffiliated	28	10.7
Total	262	100.1

[a] Includes sympathisers.
[b] Includes deputies of United Workers' Party whose platform was close to that of the Mensheviks.

SOURCES: *SEVERNAYA KOMMUNA* (JULY 5 AND 6, 1918); *NOVAYA ZHIZN'* (JUNE 18 AND 26, 1918).

the time of the elections. Their results were not contested by the opposition parties.[132] This leaves aside the vote of the Red Army soldiers, who, as noted earlier, elected 55 Bolshevik deputies and 3 Left SRs. Still, it is worth remembering that these soldiers were mostly former workers.[133]

The most complete results were published by *Severnaya kommuna*, the Petrograd Bolsheviks' newspaper, and they can be supplemented by results published in the Menshevik-Internationalist *Novaya zhizn'* and some other newspapers (see table 15.3). Results from a few operating factories – Vargunina, Pal', Izhorskii, Skorokhod, Sestroretskii arms – were not included in these overall scores. But from other reports, we know that workers in the first three factories tended strongly toward the opposition, while the Skorokhod workers favoured the Bolsheviks.[134] Omission of results from these factories, therefore, probably favours the pro-Soviet parties. On the other hand, smaller factories were allotted a deputy if they employed 300 or more workers, whereas the general norm was one deputy for every 500 workers. This favoured the opposition, since workers in small factories tended to be less radical. Finally, a list of the non-

132 See, for example, *Novaya zhizn'* (June 18 and 21, 1918).
133 See, for example, *Peterburgskii komitet RKP(b) v 1918 g*, p. 137.
134 *Sobranie upolnomochennykh i piterskie rabochie*, p. 714, *Novaya zhizn'*, (May 3, 1918), *Krasnaya gazeta* (June 29, 1918).

operating factories published by the journal of the Metalworkers' Union allows the elimination of deputies elected by 'dead souls'.[135]

According to this data, workers in operating factories elected 262 deputies. At the norm of one deputy for 500 workers, this yields a total number of employed workers that is close to the official statistic for 1 May 1918. Even if one attributes all the unaffiliated delegates to the opposition parties, the two Soviet parties obtained a majority. The Putilov factory, a microcosm of Petrograd's industrial proletariat, elected eleven Bolsheviks, five Left SRs, nine SRs and Mensheviks, one unaffiliated deputy, and four from the United Workers' party, close to the Menshevik-Internationalists.[136] These results are not far from the overall results in working factories. Finally, *Novaya zhizn'*, a moderately oppositional paper, recognised that the results demonstrated the continued attachment among the workers to Soviet power.[137] One of its journalists wrote: 'the working class invariably follows Bolshevism', though he claimed that Soviet power was in the process of decomposition.[138] At the very least, one can conclude that, despite the very difficult situation of workers and other conditions working against the government, the latter managed to hold onto the support of a significant part of the still employed workers in Petrograd.

A more detailed look at the results reveals that the opposition had the best results in factories where the defencists had retained their support the longest in 1917: the Nevskii district, the printing establishments, the railway workshops, state-owned metalworking factories, and municipal enterprises. Workers at the Nevskii, Obukhovskii, Aleksandrovskii, Maxwell, Thornton and Farforovyi factories, all in the Nevskii district, together elected thirteen SRs, one Menshevik, seven Bolsheviks, two left SRs, and five non-affiliated candidates. A majority of the delegates elected by the Vargunina and Pal' textile mills in the same district also belonged to the opposition parties. The vote count at the Nevskii shipbuilding factory was 1,221 for the SRs, 200 for the Mensheviks, and 483 for the Bolsheviks and Left SRs. In the two large railway workshops, workers elected five SRs, three Bolsheviks and one unaffiliated delegate. The state-owned factories Orudiinyi, Arsenal, Patronnyi, Military-Medical Preparations and Baltiiskii elected eight SRs, two Mensheviks, seven Bolsheviks, and five unaffiliated deputies. Thirteen printing plants for which data is available

135 *Metallist*, nos 9–10 (1918), pp. 8–9.

136 *Novaya* gazeta, 29 June, 1918. The results published in the pro-government *Severnaya kommuna* on 4 and 5 July differ slightly.

137 *Novaya zhizn'* (June 18 and 21, 1918).

138 Ibid. (27 June 1918).

elected five SRs, four Mensheviks, four Bolsheviks, one Left SR, while the municipal water and power plants sent three Mensheviks, one Bolshevik and one Left SR.

These results show that the SRs were by far the most popular of the opposition parties. This indicates that the opposition had a stronger attraction for workers whose class consciousness or class identity was weaker, since the SRs were perceived as a peasants' or people's party, while the social-democrats were a workers' movement. On the other hand, the pro-soviet parties, mainly the Bolsheviks, retained majority support in traditionally more radical private metalworking factories, such as Nobel, Vulkan, Podkovnyi, Rozenkrants, Kabel'nyi, Langezipen, as well as in the tram depots. These enterprises together elected fifteen Bolsheviks, two Left SRs, one SR, one Menshevik and a non-affiliated deputy. It is also worth noting that in the textile mills located outside of the Nevskii district, the women workers also tended to support the pro-Soviet parties.

After the elections, the Assembly of Delegates decided to call a one-day, general political strike in Petrograd on 2 July. The decision to call such a strike had initially been adopted in May by the Petrograd Committees of the Menshevik and SR parties in response to the repression at Kolpino, and that decision was endorsed in principle on 12 May by the Bureau of the Assembly of Delegates.[139] However, a new reduction in the bread ration at the end of May provoked a renewed wave of unrest, centred in the Nevskii district. It began with protest meetings, but a strike at the Pal' textile mill eventually spread to almost all the other factories of the district and also evoked a response in the electrical shop of the Putilov factory.[140] But despite urgings from these workers to call a general strike, the Assembly of Delegates on 29 May asked the workers to return to work in order to give it time to mobilise more support for a strike. Although some of the delegates supported the call to an immediate strike, the overall feeling was that the time was not yet ripe, that the workers' mood waivered with the size of the bread ration. The meeting voted 24 against four with 10 abstentions to call the Nevskii district workers to return to work.[141]

The Assembly met again on 1 June to discuss a general strike. Again, some delegates, especially those from the Nevskii District, reported that workers were impatiently awaiting the signal. But others were less sanguine. The overall

139 Ibid. (May 14 and 25 1918). *Sobranie upolnomochennykh i piterskie rabochie*, p. 320.

140 *Novaya zhizn'*, (May 29, 30 1918); *Sobranie upolnomochennykh i piterskie rabochie*, pp. 632–6.

141 *Novaya zinzn'* (May 31, 1918); *Sobranie upolnomochennykh i piterskie rabochie*, pp. 191–200.

feeling was that a call to strike would evoke only a partial response. Izamilov from the Putilov Factory reported:

> The Putilov factory will respond to a call from the Assembly of Delegates. But I wouldn't advise undertaking such a thing right away. We have great wavering at our factory. The general mood is anti-Bolshevik, but the Bolsheviks all the same still have a lot of strength. The people apparently have not yet suffered enough hunger. Besides, a strike now is pregnant with war within the working class. [My comrades] feel that one can't definitely count on the Putilov factory. There is unrest there, but if we act now, then we will win a minimum, and lose a lot.

Grabovskii from the Patronnyi factory said that 'we have to make sure that the strike is not because of an eighth-funt of bread'. The consensus was that the strike would not be general, and the decision was almost unanimous only to issue an appeal to continue mobilising.[142] This was repeated at the next meeting on 12 June.[143]

But on 19 June, members of Moscow's Assembly of Delegates were arrested, along with a few Assembly activists from Petrograd, though they were soon released. Still, the Assembly in Petrograd could not decide to call a strike. At an extraordinary session held that day, N.K. Borisenko, a member of the Assembly's Bureau, a worker at the Trubochnyi factory, told the impatient ones:

> The Petrograd Bureau of Delegates is being criticised for lack of determination in the question of conducting a political protest strike even after such acts of violence as the arrest of the Moscow delegates ... The Bureau of Delegates is not to blame if it does not possess facts that would compel it to decide on a measure such as the declaration of a strike.

A.N. Smirnov from the Patronnyi factory added:

> To call the workers to strike without the firmly expressed will of the delegates would be an adventure. But such a firm will has never yet been expressed at a meeting of the deputies, either because they themselves were absent or because they had no mandate for such a thing.[144]

---

142 *Sobranie upolnomochennykh i piterskie rabochie*, pp. 210–19; *Novaya zhizn'*, (2 June, 1918).

143 *Sobranie upolnomochennykh i piterskie rabochie*, p. 234.

144 *Novaya zhizn'* (June 20, 1918).

A call to strike would finally be precipitated by events involving the Obukhovskii factory, which employed approximately 3,000 people in May 1918. Oppositional sentiment was very strong there, and some of the activists had been fraternising with sailors from the Baltic Fleets' minelayer division, whose small ships were moored nearby in the Neva River. The workers struck on 16 June, declaring that hunger did not allow them to continue work. They demanded an immediate end to the civil war, the immediate resignation of the government, and convocation of the Constituent Assembly. The strike continued the following day, during which an assembly of workers demanded the free purchase and shipment of food by cooperatives and democratic organisations. They appealed for support to the sailors of the minelayer division and called on the Assembly of Delegates to 'declare a struggle against the government'. The next two days were again spent in meetings. Then on 20 June, after the assassination of Volodarskii at the hands of an SR, a popular SR activist at the factory was arrested. This provoked an Italian (slowdown) strike to demand his release, something that was achieved on 22 June following the visit by a delegation to M.S. Uritskii, head of the Petrograd Cheka. That same day a general assembly at the factory called on the Assembly of Delegates to call a general political strike on the 25th. Then on 24 June, sailors from Kronstadt, along with several hundred Red Army soldiers, disarmed the sailors of the mine-layers without using violence. This again stirred up the factory's workers, who spent much of the following day in meetings. That evening, troops conducted searches in the district, arrested four SR workers at the Obukhovskii factory, and closed the two district SR clubs.[145]

On the morning of the 26th, workers arrived at the factory to find a notice on the locked gates informing them that the factory was closed because of the repeated violation of work rules. According to the government's paper, which lamented the wasting of scarce fuel, in May thirteen workdays had been lost in meetings at the factory and seven more in the first three weeks of June.[146] Everyone was fired, and new hiring would be conducted through the labour exchange.[147] (It seems that these same workers were rehired when the plant reopened.)[148] At the same time, the Soviet government definitively shut down the SR party's newspaper *Delo naroda* 'for counterrevolutionary

145 *Severnaya kommuna* (June 26, 1918); *Novaya zhizn'* (June 26, 1918).

146 *Severnaya kommuna* (20 June 1918).

147 For all these events, see *Sobranie upolnomochennykh i piterskie rabochie*, pp. 685–726; *Novaya zhizn'* (June 19, 26, 27, 1918); *Severnaya kommuna* (June 28, 1918); Mil'shtein 1963, p. 154.

148 *Novaya gazeta* (June 28, 1918).

agitation expressing itself in approval of the gang of pogromists calling itself the "Siberian government" and which was keeping back the shipment of grain to Petrograd'.[149]

The Assembly of Delegates could no longer temporise. On 26 June it called a one-day political strike for 2 July. The Petrograd Soviet decided to close down the Assembly on 28 June. By all contemporary accounts, the strike was not a success, even in the Nevskii district.[150] Even the workers of the Vargunina factory, who had been insistently demanding a strike, made their participation conditional on that of a majority of Petrograd's workers. 'In general', observed *Novaya zhizn'*, 'the strike was conducted only at individual factories, and not at the largest ones, at that'. At the Putilov, Baltic and other large factories, workers remained at work.[151] *Vechernee slovo*, hostile to the regime, wrote: 'The general opinion is that the strike did not succeed. The workers have split into two groups, and the opponents of the strike are significantly more numerous than its supporters'.[152]

The bad economic situation, especially the high unemployment, and the government's repressive measures of the previous days no doubt played a role in this. But *Novaya zhizn'*, which by no means claimed that those who did not strike supported the government, wrote:

> It would not be serious to explain the failure of the oppositional parties exclusively by that sort of reasons ... The strike's organisers undoubtedly overestimated the dissatisfaction among rank-and-file workers and paid insufficient attention to the psychology of the working class; they did not consider those threads that, despite everything, still tie the worker masses so strongly to the government so as to make them instinctively reject active measures of struggle.[153]

---

149 Ibid. (June 26, 1918). The Western-Siberian Commissariat was established on 1 June after the first victories of the Czechoslovak troops. It was headed by the SR P. Ya. Derber and based itself on the SR programme: power to the Constituent Assembly with toleration of the soviets and peasant land committee as non-government organisations; gradual denationalisation of industry. But within a few weeks, this regime was replaced by the Kadet-led Siberian Government that suppressed the soviets, permitting only 'non-political' trade unions. Chamberlin 1965, vol. 2, pp. 12–14.

150 *Sobranie upolnomochennykh i piterskie rabochie*, pp. 645–7.

151 *Novaya zhizn'* (July 3, 1918).

152 Cited in *Krasnaya gazeta* (3 July 1918).

153 *Novaya zhizn'* (July 3, 1918).

And even before the strike had begun, Stroev wrote:

> We do not know how broad will be the dimensions it takes: the Communists are too shameless in their use of the police apparatus of state power. Besides that, no matter what attitude one adopts to the dominance of the ruling party or how highly one evaluates the blow dealt to the Bolsheviks by the failure of their candidates to be elected to the Soviet and by the election of representatives of the opposition (Mensheviks and SRs), many workers nevertheless have not yet outlived their Bolshevik 'communism' and continue to consider soviet power – whether good or bad, that's another question – as the representative of their interests. They link their fate and the fate of the labour movement to it.[154]

Another observer, also sympathetic to the opposition, wrote: 'We are convinced that significant strata of workers, despite all their dissatisfaction with the dominant political course, found the strike to be a too strong measure of struggle with the regime that the toilers themselves have established'. He observed that in the course of the debates in the Assembly of Delegates on a possible strike, the delegate from the Putilov factory had expressed doubt about the workers' readiness to move from protest based on hunger to a political strike.[155]

A related cause of this weak response was the workers' doubt about the reality of the alternative to Soviet power that was being proposed by the opposition. Some undoubtedly believed in the Constituent Assembly's capacity to overcome the political polarisation of Russian society and to stop the civil war. But many had been attracted to the opposition out of despair generated by hunger. In arguing their position before workers, the leaders of the political opposition made no attempt to explain the deeply disappointing experience of the eight-month rule of the Provisional Government. It had been, after all, that 'all-national' government for which the opposition was now calling.[156]

A related problem, and one that was evoked by members of the Assembly of Delegates, was fear that the struggle against the Soviets would be exploited by the counter-revolution. This was merely a variant of the first problem – doubts about a reality of the opposition's alternative to Soviet power. At the meeting of 1 June, the Menshevik A.S. Astrov stated:

---

154 Ibid.

155 Ibid. (July 2, 1918).

156 See, for example, the Menshevik and SR speeches at the First City district conference.

> If one were to sum up the reports, one can find arguments for and against a strike. But all the same, these reports say that the more developed workers have left the Bolsheviks. But this ferment is fed by economic causes. One cannot see any political moods. In the worst case, there is a mood that we will not be able to control when they [the masses] begin to manifest themselves. We have vast political work ahead of us. The task is not only to throw off the Bolsheviks, but not to allow forces that are hostile to the proletariat to exploit that overthrow. None among us can say with certainty that that won't happen.[157]

At the same meeting, a printer reported: 'At our plant, the attitude to a political strike is negative. They feel that it can lead to the ruin of all the gains of the revolution'.[158] *Novaya zhizn'* summarised:

> The majority of representatives of the factories, however, and the Bureau which is solidary with them, call for caution. There is an animated debate over the question of the possible appearance of a third force, if a decisive battle occurs between Soviet power and the proletariat in which both sides exhaust themselves.[159]

In the end, most workers agreed with the Bolsheviks' presentation of the alternatives: 'Call forth every last ounce of strength or accept defeat', that is, Soviet power or counterrevolution. But the pro-Soviet activists did not limit themselves to negative arguments, to pointing out the horrors of counterrevolution that the defeated toilers of Ukraine and Finland were already suffering. They spoke also of the prospect of socialism in Russia, while the Mensheviks and SRs were calling the workers back to capitalism. True, Bolsheviks and Left SRs believed that the possibility of socialism in a backward country like Russia depended on the support of victorious revolutions in the developed West, a perspective that the Mensheviks and SRs systematically played down, emphasising how the peace of Brest-Litovsk had allegedly dealt a blow to the Western working class.[160] Nevertheless, the prospect, the hope of socialism was the positive

157 *Sobranie upolnomochennykh i piterskie rabochie*, p. 216.

158 Ibid. p. 209.

159 *Novaya zhizn'* (May 31, 1918).

160 After the German Revolution began in the autumn of 1918, the leadership of the Menshevik party changed its position on the prospects for socialism in Russia and recognised that the October Revolution, despite 'one or another anti-proletarian, anti-democratic or anarchistic tendency, had been a colossal ferment that set in motion a movement in the

dimension of pro-Soviet agitation. The celebrated Left-SR revolutionary Mariya Spiridonova gave eloquent expression to this in her speech to the Conference of worker and Red Army deputies of the First City district in May 1918:

> Everywhere so much stormy electricity has accumulated that it is clear we are living on the eve of an explosion. As we ourselves here, so too it is as if they are waiting for someone to come and save – the gates will open and the liberators will come and give bread. Internationalism in the best sense of the word is developed at present in Western Europe. Europe is on the eve of a tremendous explosion. Never before has the world revolution been so close to realisation as it is now. If we believe that socialism will bring salvation and respite to the world, then we have to join with what is happening and what must happen in Western Europe, and here, locally, we have to be socialists to the last drop of our blood.
>
> We have not yet exhausted all our potential. You have in you so much force for creativity and discipline. You can fight for Soviet Russia and for your liberation with the red banner in your hands. Don't listen to those who call for a cease-fire, for a retreat, to give up all our positions! Go forth, fearing neither the hunger nor the economic ruin. And to those conciliator-gravediggers who come to you with false slogans, say: We, the proletariat and the peasants went hungry for centuries so that a handful of people – factory owners, landowners, oppressors – could live amidst plenty and luxury. The peasantry starved in 1901, 1902, 1906, 1907 and in the 1890s so that a handful of landowners could live idly, gaily, in satisfaction. Now, for the first time in all of world history, the people have to go hungry in the name of their own interests, in the name of their future. Can it be that we will find among the proletariat many who are not prepared to go hungry for themselves but will agree to go hungry for long years for the bourgeoisie and landowners?
>
> It seems to me that when, close to Easter, the homemaker calls forth her last forces, sews, washes, cooks and falls from exhaustion, it is easy for her to bear that suffering, since she knows that Easter will come and she will sit her children down at a full table of food that has been baked and cooked by her own hands. The Russian people is now living through such a

---

entire world'. A party conference in December 1918 recognised the Soviet system 'as a fact of reality, but not as a principle', and declared its solidarity with the government 'insofar as it defends the liberation of the territory of Russia from foreign, in particular, Allied occupation, and opposes all attempts of non-proletarian democracy to expand or maintain that occupation' (A.P. Nenarokov 2001, p. 631).

> Passion Week. The whole insurgent Russian people is suffering passionate torments. But so that Easter comes, complete liberation of your persons, throw off all chains![161]

161 *Pervaya konferentsiya rabochikh i krasnoarmeiskikh deputatov*, pp. 255–7.

Conclusion

This study traced the evolution of workers' attitudes and collective actions in 1917 and the first half of 1918 relating to the basic issues of the revolution. The analysis led to the conclusion that this evolution is most adequately explained by the deepening class polarisation of Russian society that led eventually to military confrontation and civil war. The radicalisation of workers' positions over this period can and should be understood as a fundamentally rational process, rather than a playing out of inherent anarchistic tendencies or of apocalyptic hopes nurtured by Bolshevik propaganda, both variations on an interpretation that has long been favoured by many Western historians. (Since socialism, in the view of these historians, is an evil or impossible project, what could possibly be rational about the suppression of the economic and political dominance of the bourgeoisie?)

When Petrograd's workers, having won over to their side the soldiers of the garrison, overthrew the autocracy in February 1917, they still conceived of the revolution in liberal, 'bourgeois-democratic' terms. This was so even in the case of the most militant group of workers, centred in the Vyborg district. If the latter already in February wanted the Soviet to take power, it was not in order to suppress capitalism. It was rather an expression of their lack of confidence in census society's support for the democratic revolution. And that mistrust was not unfounded. It was based on the experience of the workers' movement since at least the Revolution of 1905. Nor was it only the workers of the Vyborg district who mistrusted the propertied classes. The mistrust was general among workers. Hence, dual-power, that is, the Soviet's support for the Provisional government only 'inasmuch' as it adhered to the Soviet's programme and the latter's mandate to exercise 'control' over it. But the workers did not want to take power themselves. For that threatened civil war. Moreover, they did not believe in their own capacity to run the state and the economy. They opted rather to give a chance to the liberals. For the latter seemed belatedly to have rallied to the revolution.

What happened after that, how workers saw it and reacted to it, is the subject matter of this book. The study showed that even while workers were moving in practice beyond their initial bourgeois-democratic conception of the revolution – in the movement for workers' control and in the attempt in the July Days to force the Soviet to take power on its own – they continued to cling to that conception in their minds. As late as the Kornilov uprising at the end of August, even the most radical workers were summoning the others to 'the defence of freedom', with no mention of socialist goals (although, of course, they were socialists). In the same way, the workers' massive participation in the elections to the Constituent Assembly represented an attempt on their part to reconcile the October insurrection with the February Revolution, that is, a worker-led soviet revolution with a national, bourgeois-democratic revolution: the task of the Constituent Assembly in the workers' view was to endorse Soviet power, a dictatorship of the toiling classes that would exclude the propertied classes from political representation.

What might seem to be a case of consciousness lagging behind practice was, in fact, an expression of the fundamentally defensive character of the process of workers' radicalisation in the course of 1917. In demanding the transfer of power to the soviets and workers' control, workers were reacting to the threat to the democratic revolution from the propertied classes. And the latter, including their representatives in the coalition government, did not hide their hostility to the social and democratic aspirations of the popular classes or 'revolutionary democracy'. In their more candid moments, especially before they decided to join the Provisional Government, the Mensheviks and SRs openly recognised this hostility. But they could not bring themselves to support a break with the bourgeoisie, since, they argued, that would doom the revolution and provoke civil war.

The workers were not insensitive to those arguments. In particular, after the traumatic experience of the July Days, they were acutely aware of the danger of their political isolation from the soldiers and peasantry as well as from the educated 'middle strata', the intelligentsia. The spectre of civil war, along with the looming economic crisis, made them hesitate, despite their overwhelming desire for the soviets to take power and so to exclude the propertied classes from further influence on the government.

This hesitation and the growing insecurity as economic collapse approached were what made the role of the Bolshevik party so critical in the post-July period. Until the defeat suffered in the July Days, the worker rank and file had held the political initiative (in the February Revolution, in the April Days, in the movement for workers' control, in the July Days), and the Bolshevik party followed. Although the October Revolution was anything but the arbitrary, historically illegitimate act that its opponents have claimed, it is true that it would not have occurred without the party's initiative and leadership. Without that, growing despair among workers would have fuelled scattered revolts that could easily have been crushed by right-wing military forces.

But if the party played the leading role in October, it is also the case that the party united in its ranks the most class-conscious, politically aware and committed part of the working class. These workers were able to conceive of their class assuming responsibility for the state and the economy, even without the intelligentsia's collaboration. Therefore, if it is the case that the party's leadership was necessary for the October Revolution, it is also true that its leadership would have been missing, were it not for the pressure exerted on the party's Central Committee 'from below'.

The October Revolution was unable to resolve the problems that had pushed the workers to take power. The economic crisis continued to deepen, bringing mass unemployment and hunger. The treaty of Brest-Litovsk took Russia out of the world war, but at a huge price, and the respite it brought was short-lived, as the civil war, fuelled by foreign intervention, soon heated up. Yet, most workers did not rally to the opposition that was calling for a strategic retreat from October, even though their appeals were tempting to hungry workers whose jobs were gone or were under imminent threat and who were witness to the confusion and incompetence of the early months of Soviet rule.

The arguments of the Bolsheviks and the Left SRs that the opposition was not offering a realistic alternative were certainly not without basis. In his classic study of the Russian Revolution, W. Chamberlin wrote: 'The alternative to Bolshevism, had it failed to survive the ordeal of civil war, would not have been Chernov [leader of the SRs], opening a Constituent Assembly, elected according to the most modern rules of equal suffrage and proportional representation, but a military dictator, a Kolchak or Denikin, riding into Moscow on a white horse to the accompaniment of the clanging of the bells of the old capital's hundreds of churches'.[1] A more recent study of the anti-Soviet uprising in the towns of Votkinsk and Izhevsk by a Russian historian supports that conclusion:

> Everywhere where activists of the 'third force' came to power, events developed in the same manner. They not only cleared the way for the white counterrevolution but they themselves actively participated in the establishment of an all-embracing system of white terror, although they did so under the cover of red banners and revolutionary rhetoric. All the talk of the right-wing socialists about a 'democratic republic' everywhere turned into the establishment of the omnipotence of the military boot and the suppression of all dissent ... In this one should see one of the main reasons for the very short-lived existence of governments that were led by right-wing socialists, wherever they arose – in Izhevsk, Arkhangelsk, Samara and anywhere else. And so one should refrain from speaking about some kind of 'third way' in the years of revolution and civil war.[2]

1 W.H. Chamberlin 1965, vol. 1, p. 371.
2 Dm. Churakov 2004, p. 71.

But rational argument (supplemented, to be sure, by occasional repressive measures) would not have sufficed to convince hungry, desperate workers, had it not found support in the workers' own class consciousness, in their sense of 'class honour' and their historic aspiration to 'class separateness' (more precisely – class independence) from the propertied classes. That was the very essence of Bolshevism, as a workers' movement. It came down, in the last analysis, to a question of dignity. Meanwhile, the Mensheviks and SRs, behind their slogans of Constituent Assembly and 'all-national' government, were in fact calling the workers to a strategic retreat from October, to return under the domination of the propertied classes, who were, in fact, yearning for a military dictatorship to crush the workers' organisations.

Russian workers, like workers everywhere under capitalism, are subordinate people. Most of their lives are spent carrying out the will of others – managers, factory owners, governments, bureaucrats, police, judges. Their sense of self-esteem as workers is not inborn. In Russia, that quality developed over years of struggle with the autocracy and the industrialists. It was already present in the Revolution of 1905–6. The historian N.V. Mikhailov described the Petersburg workers' reaction in the spring of 1906 to the opening of the First State Duma, a miserly concession from the Tsar to the revolutionary movement:[3]

> The convincing victory of the Kadets in the election to the First State Duma evoked a wave of enthusiasm among the liberal strata of society. But among Petersburg's workers it found, on the contrary, no warm echo. They met the day of the opening of the Duma – 27 April – with pointed indifference. In those enterprises where the owners suggested a paid day off, the workers demonstratively refused to accept money they had not earned. Nor did the proposal of Kadet sympathisers among the workers to shift the celebration of 1 May to 27 April find support. 'Let those celebrate who place their hope in the Duma', said the workers. 'We will celebrate instead our proletarian and international holiday – May 1'. They declared that 'it is not their holiday, and so they did not intend to celebrate'.
>
> 'Despite the opening of the Duma', wrote an observer in a letter sent to Geneva, 'the workers worked calmly, so that there was nothing different

3 The Duma was a response to the revolutionary upsurge of 1905. Its powers were very limited, and its electoral law heavily biased in favour of the propertied classes: big landowners elected one deputy for every 2,000 members; capitalists one for every 4,000; peasants one for every 30,000; and workers one for every 90,000. An ironic consequence of this estate-based representation was to strengthen workers' class consciousness and encourage their aspiration to 'class separateness'.

> from any other ordinary weekday. The consciousness of the proletariat is striking. No one conducted any particular agitation in that sense. Yesterday, the proletariat again slapped messieurs the bourgeois in the face with their mighty hand …'
>
> On 1 May, on the contrary, the entire city was excited. According to very incomplete data of the Society of Factory and Mills Owners, a political strike took place in 55 mills and factories …
>
> Two political holidays observed by the Petersburg opposition, the liberals and the workers, and separated by only three days, clearly showed that the abyss dividing people into two hostile camps, that were simultaneously but separately opposing the autocracy, was so deep that they could not come together even at a time of holiday celebrations.[4]

This striking passage should be food for thought for those who would blame the October Revolution, or the dissolution of the Constituent Assembly, or both, for the civil war that subsequently ravaged Russia. To do so is wilfully to ignore the profound class polarisation of Russian society, the irreconcilable abyss separating the toiling and the propertied classes. That polarisation had deep roots in Russian history and society. It was not invented by the Bolsheviks. The opposite is true: it was responsible for a party such as the Bolsheviks. 'They blame us for sowing civil war', stated a Bolshevik delegate to the First City district conference of worker and Red Army deputies in May 1918. 'That is a big mistake, if not a lie … Class interests were not invented by us. That is a question that exists in life, it is a fact before which we all must bow'.[5] To believe that the Constituent Assembly could somehow have overcome that polarisation is to indulge in magical thinking.

Of course, it is tempting to read history backwards, in this case from the murderous, totalitarian regime established under Stalin's leadership back to the October Revolution. In such a reading, the 'seeds' of Stalinism, the 'project' or 'logic' that more or less directly led to Stalin's regime, was already present in the ideology and structure of the Bolshevik party of 1917, waiting only for the party to come to power for it to unfold. It is true, of course, that Stalin's regime did not emerge ex nihilo but out of conditions that preceded it and to which the Bolsheviks contributed. But the present study shows that the Bolsheviks did not start out in October 1917 to establish a party dictatorship, let alone one of its permanent officials (the later Soviet 'nomenklatura'). As we have seen, in

4 N.V. Mikhailov 1998, pp. 68, 71.

5 *Pevaia konferentsia rabochikh I krasnoarmeiskikh …*, p. 248.

the first months, indeed in the first year of Soviet power, the party atrophied, exerting almost no influence on the government in Petrograd. After the October Revolution, the party practically dissolved into the soviets. Party activists felt that its leadership role had come to an end, now that the workers had taken power through their soviets. As Shelavin recalled: 'A series of responsible, highly capable comrades who had gone through the school of the underground became infected with an exclusively "soviet" attitude, not to speak of the mass of the younger generation. Even if these comrades did not give full expression to their thinking, all the same they had some difficulty imagining: after the victory of the proletariat, what is there then really left for the party organisation to do?'[6] Clearly, this was not a party whose ideology contained within itself 'the seeds' of future totalitarianism, as some historians have argued.

If in the course of the civil war the party did eventually supplant the soviets, rather than attributing this to the 'logic of Bolshevism', one should seek the causes first of all in the social, economic and political conditions that favoured such a development. The Menshevik and SR opposition, for its own reasons, almost immediately after October, began calling the Soviet government a 'Bolshevik dictatorship'. They were wilfully silent about the non-elected character of the overthrown Provisional Government and the repressive measures it had adopted, measures that would have been much harsher had the government had at its disposal the necessary repressive apparatus. But more importantly, they wilfully ignored the Left SRs' participation in the government and their own refusal to be a part of any government that was responsible to the soviets. On the other hand, following the October insurrection, the vast majority of Bolsheviks, both leaders and rank and file, favoured an all-socialist coalition government.

Indeed, there is an argument to be made that the Mensheviks' and SRs' refusal to participate in a soviet government was itself a contributing factor to the emergence of a one-party regime. That same refusal also defeated the Menshevik-SR-led Assembly of Delegates, since most workers, despite their discontent, remained attached to the soviets. The incessant criticism on the part of the Mensheviks and SRs of the incompetence and misguided policies of the Soviet regime, in which they themselves refused to participate, was portrayed by the Bolsheviks and Left SRs – not without success – as 'sabotage'. In the popular mind, the Mensheviks and SRs were identified with the intelligentsia, whose members were seen by many workers as having abandoned the people in its moment of greatest need.

6 See above, p. 449.

V.B. Stanekvich, a Popular Socialist and military commissar of the Provisional Government, was one of the few right-wing socialists who argued that participation in the new regime as a loyal opposition was the only rational and honourable option. In an 'Open Letter to Political Friends', written in February or March 1918, he reprimanded his comrades for forgetting that they, the 'ruling parties [from before October], had neither a political programme nor the organisational capacities' for governing the country. And he continued:

> We have to see that by this time the forces of the popular movement are on the side of the new regime ... There are two paths open to them [the former governing socialist parties]: pursue their irreconcilable struggle with the government, or peaceful, creative work as a loyal opposition ...
>
> Can the former ruling parties say that by now they have become so experienced that they can manage the task of running the country, which has become not easier, but harder? For, in essence, they have no programme to oppose to that of the Bolsheviks. And a struggle without a programme is nothing better than the adventures of Mexican generals. And even if there were the possibility of creating a programme, you have to understand that you don't have the forces to carry it out. For to overthrow Bolshevism you need, if not formally, then at least in fact, the united effort of everyone, from SRs to the extreme right. But even in those conditions, the Bolsheviks are stronger ...
>
> There is but one path: the path of a united popular front, united national work, common creativity. That doesn't mean going to Smol'ny with heads bowed ...
>
> And so what tomorrow? To continue the pointless, meaningless and in essence adventurist attempts to seize power? Or to work together with the people in realistic efforts to help it to deal with the problems that face Russia, problems that are linked to the peaceful struggle for eternal political principles, for genuinely democratic bases for governing the country!
>
> Of course, the second path demands significant self-abnegation and self-sacrifice ... But the path of loyal opposition to the present soviet government is the only one possible and the only correct one for all socialist and truly democratic parties.[7]

7 I.B. Orlov 1997, pp. 77–80. This letter was written while Stankevich was under arrest for participating in early attempts to crush the October Revoution militarily and it probably

One can legitimately ask – Western and contemporary Russian historians have generally failed to do so – to what degree the Mensheviks' and SRs' refusal to recognise and participate in the Soviet regime, even as a loyal opposition, itself contributed to the civil war and to the subsequent authoritarian evolution of the state.

The present study shows that certain tendencies that would later become more pronounced under the impact of the civil war could already be observed in the early period of the Soviet regime: a growing estrangement between the still-employed workers and the soviets; the tendency for power to concentrate in the hands of the executives at the expense of the soviet assemblies; and from there to become concentrated in the hands of the central authorities. But these tendencies were not part of a preconceived plan or the expression of any logic inherent in the Bolshevik party. Already in January 1918, the conference of factory committees in Petrograd discussed the conflicts that were arising between workers and their elected factory committees and between local factory committees and their central bodies. These conflicts were generated by the economic crisis, the shortages, the urgency of demobilising industry in order to offer goods to the peasantry in exchange for food. These same conditions were at the root of conflicts that arose between workers and the soviets. And the civil war, which entered its intense phase in the summer of 1918, would only exacerbate these tendencies.

All the delegates to the factory-committee conference in January 1918 were strong partisans of workers' control. And yet they voted overwhelmingly to subordinate their committees to a central economic authority, thus limiting the powers of their own committees and of the workers' assemblies that elected them. This, too, was a response to the economic crisis. The same centralising tendencies, the need for which was recognised by most local activists, were at work in the Food Authority and the Red Army, both of which were initially under control of the district soviets.

Bolshevik workers were not insensitive to the dangers inherent in this centralisation. But they recognised its necessity. One might recall the response of the Bolshevik chairman of the factory-committee conference in January 1918 to the anarchists' proposal to make conditional the committees' subordination to the *sovnarkhozy*:

contributed to his subsequent release. But as the author of the article points out, his later diary entries indicate that these were genuinely held views that did not subsequently change.

> … [But] if these organs really do part ways with the masses, then, of course, we will have to introduce such an amendment. And we will have to go further. We will have to overthrow those organs and perhaps make a new revolution. But it seems to us that for now the Soviet of People's Commissars is our soviet, and the institutions that it has established are functioning harmoniously together.[8]

Victor Serge, a French anarchist who arrived in Petrograd in 1919 and soon expressed his full support for the Soviet regime (in the 1920s he would adhere to the anti-bureaucratic left opposition in the party led by Trotsky), expressed a similar view about the centralism and the coercive powers of the state during the civil war. In an article written in 1920 for his anarchist friends in the West, he explained:

> The suppression of so-called freedoms; dictatorship backed up if necessary by terror; the creation of an army; centralization for war purposes of industry, food supplies and administration (whence state control and bureaucracy); and finally, the dictatorship of a party. In this fearsome chain of necessities, there is not a single link that is not rigorously conditioned by the one that precedes it and which does not in turn condition the one that follows it.[9]

Serge continued that such a state, however justified by the circumstances, generates powerful vested interests that would possibly want to maintain it even after the threat of counterrevolution had passed. His response was to call for vigilance. And, like the worker in the previous passage, he recognised that this might require another revolution. If Serge's views are mentioned here, it is because he did not belong to the Bolshevik or to any other Marxist tradition.

A key factor in the authoritarian evolution of the Soviet state was the dispersal of the working class, which began soon after the October Revolution. The Vyborg district, the radical heart of the workers' movement for all of Russia, vanished within weeks as an industrial centre. And the remnant of the employed working class tended to withdraw from political life in the face of the severe economic hardship. The industrial working class, that had been the main force of Russia's democratic movement, ceased to exist as an independent force, separate from the state. The Bolshevik party claimed to represent it, and

8 See above, p. 403 (Chapter 15).
9 Serge 2011, p. 143.

its ranks included many of the most committed, class-conscious workers. But the party could not be a substitute for the working class as a social force capable of exerting effective control over the state that it had itself brought into existence.

While the much hoped-for revolutionary upsurge in the West did indeed materialise in 1918–21 and played a critical role in the civil war by limiting the scope of direct foreign military intervention, that revolutionary wave was beaten back everywhere, except for Russia. And as the Bolsheviks had foreseen, the isolation of Russia's revolution did condemn it, though its demise played itself out over a long time, and no one could have foreseen the concrete form it would ultimately assume.

Bibliography

I Archives

Tsentral'nyi gosudarstvennyi arkhiv Sankt-Peterburga (TsGA SPb).

fond 171, opis' 1, delo I (Kolpino District Soviet protocols).

1000/73/12 (Petrograd Soviet, Soldiers' Section protocols, 12 Mar. 1917).

1000/73/16 (Petrograd Soviet, Workers' Section protocols, 20 Mar. 1917).

4591/1/1 (general factory assemblies and conferences of the Petrograd Metalworkers' Union, protocols, Mar–Dec 1917).

4601/1/10 (Arsenal Factory committee protocols, 7 Mar.–30 Dec. 1917).

4602/7/7 (Patronnyi Factory general assembly protocols, 3 Mar.–11 Nov. 1917).

7384/7/21 (Mandate Committee of EC of Petrograd Soviet).

7384/9/293 (Petrograd Soviet, factory resolutions on return to work, 6–16 Mar. 1917).

9391/1/11 (Admiralty Shipyard general assembly protocols, 12 Apr 1917–9 Dec 1918).

Gosudarstvennyi istoricheskii arkhiv leningradskoi oblasti (GIALO).

416125/5 (Baltic Shipyard administration – conciliation chamber).

416/5/30 (Baltic Shipyard administration – conciliation chamber protocols, 1917).

Tsentral'nyi gosudarstvennyi istoricheskii arkhiv Sankt-Peterburga (TsGIA SPb).

416/25/5 (Baltiiskii shipyard administration – conciliation chamber).

416/5/30 (protocols – Baltiiskii shipyard administration – conciliation chamber).

II Published Documents and Statistics

Chernyaev, V. Iu (ed.) 2000, *Piterskie rabochie i "diktatura proletariata", oktyabr' 1917–1929*, SPb.

'Chetvertaya Petrogradskaya obshchegorodskaya konferentsiya RSDRP(b) v 1917 gg.', *Krasnaya letopis'*, 3, 24 (1927), 56–64.

Chugaev, D.A. (ed.) 1967, *Rabochii klass Sovetskoi Rossii v pervyi god diktatury proletariata*. M.

Doneseniya komissarov Petrogradskogo Voenno-revolyutsionnogo komiteta, 2 vols. (M., 1957).

Ekonomicheskoe polozhenie Rossii nakanune Velikoi Oktyabr'skoi sotsialisticheskoi revolyutsii, 3 vols. (M.-L., 1957) (Ek. Pol.).

Fabrichno-zavodskie komitety Petrograda: protokoly (M., 1979).

'Fevral'skaya revolyutsiya i Okhrannoe otdelenie', *Byloe*, 7–8 (1918).

Fleer, M.G. (ed.) 1925, *Rabochee dvizhenie v gody voiny* (M.).

Grave, B.B. (ed.) 1927, *Burzhuaziya nakanune Fevral'skoi revolyutsii*, M.

Lenin, V.I. 1958–67, *Polnoe sobranie sochinenii*, 5th edn., M.

Materialy po statistike Petrograda, vyp. I (Petrograd, 1920).

Materialy po statistike truda severnoi oblasti vyp. I (Petrograd, 1918).

Materialy po statistike truda severnoi oblasti, vyp. V (Petrograd, 1919).

Mikhailov, M. 1932, 'Rabochie zavoda Baranovskogo v bor'be za Oktyabr', *Krasnaya letopis'*, 50–1.

Natsionalizatsiya promyshlennosti i organizatsiya sotsialisticheskogo proizvodstva v Petrograde, vol. I (L., 1958) (Nats. Prom. Petrograda).

Oktyabr'skaya revolyutsiya i fabzavkomy, vols. I–III (M., 1927–9) (FZK I–III).

Oktyabr'skaya revolyutsiya i fabzavkomy vol. IV, (St. Petersburg, 2002) (FZK IV).

Orlov, I.B. 1997, 'Dva puti stoyat pered nimi …'*Istoricheskii arkhiv*, 4, 75–81.

Partiya Levykh sotsialistov eserov, dokumenty i materialy, vol. 1, Iul' 1917 g.–mai 1918 g. (M., 2000).

D.B. Pavlov, D.B. (ed.) M. 2006, *Rabochee oppositstionnoe dvizhenie v bol'shevistskoi Rossii. 1918 g. Sobranie upolnomochennykh fabrik i zavodov.*

Perepiska sekretariata TseKa RSDRP(b) s mestnymy organizatsiyami, mart-oktyabr' 1917 (M., 1957).

Pervaya konferentsiya rabochikh i krasnoarmeiskikh deputatov 1-go gorodskogo raiona (Petrograd, 1918).

Pervaya Petrogradskaya obshchegorodskaya konferentsiya RSDRP(b) v aprele 1917 g. (M., 1925).

Pervaya vserossiiskaya tarifnaya konferentsiya soyuza rabochikh metallistov (Petrograd, 1918).

Pervyi legal'nyi Peterburgskii komitet RSDRP(b) v 1917 g. (M.-L., 1927) (Peka).

Peterburgskii komitet RSDRP(b) v 1917 godu (SPb: 2003).

Pervyi s'ezd sovetov narodnogo khozyaistva Severnoi oblasti (Petrograd, 1918).

Peterburgskii komitet RKP(b) d 1918 g. (SPb, 2013).

Piontkovskii, S.A., *Sovety v Oktyabre* (M., 1928).

Popov, A.L. (ed.) *Oktyabr'skii perevorot: fakty i dokumenty* (Petrograd, 1918).

Protokoly TseKa RSDRP(b): avgust 1917-fevral' 1918 (M., 1958).

Putilovtsy v trekh revolyutsiyakh (L., 1933).

Rabochii kontrol' i natsionalizatsiya promyshlennykh predpriyatii Petrograda v 1917–1919, vol. 1 (L. 1949) (Rab. Kon.).

Rabochii kontrol' i natsionalizatsiya promyshlennykh predpriyatii Petrograda v 1917–1919 gg., vol. 1 (L. 1949).

Raionnye sovety Petrograda v 1917 g., 3 vols. (M.-L., 1966–8).

Revolyutsiya 17-go goda: khronika sobytii, vol. IV (M.-L., 1926).

Serge, Victor 2011, *Revolution in Danger, Writings from Russia 1919–1921*, Chicago: Haymarket, 2011.

Shestoi vserossiiskii s'ezd RSDRP(b) (M., 1958).

Startsev, V.I., *Russkie bloknoty Dzhona Rida* (M., 1968).
Statisticheskii spravochnik po Petrogradu (Petrograd, 1921)
Trudy I-go Vserossiiskogo s'ezda sovetov narodnogo khozyaistva, (M., 1918).
Tsudsi, E. (ed.) *Sobranie upolnomochennykh i piterskie rabochie v 1918 g.* (SPb 2006).
'V Oktyabre v raionakh Petrograda', *Krasnaya letopis'*, 2, 23 (1927), pp. 173–8 (V Oktyabre).
Velikaya Oktyabr'skaya sotsialisticheskaya revolyutsiya. Dokumenty i materialy.
Revolyutsionnoe dvizhenie v Rossii posle sverzheniya samoderzhaviya (M., 1957) (Dok. Feb.).
Revolyutsionnoe dvizhenie v Rossii v aprele 1917 g. (M., 1958) (Dok. Apr.).
Revolyutsionnoe dvizhenie v Rossii v mae-iyune 1917 g. (M., 1959 (Dok. May).
Revolyutsionnoe dvizhenie v Rossii v iyule 1917 g. (M., 1959) (Dok. July).
Revolyutsionnoe dvizhenie v Rossii v avguste 1917 g. (M., 1959) (Dok. Aug.)
Revolyutsionnoe dvizhenie v Rossii v sentyabre 1917 g. (M., 1961) (Dok Sept.)
Revolyutsionnoe dvizhenie v Rossii nakanune Oktyabr'skogo vooruzhennogo vosstaniya, 1–24 oktyabrya 1917 g. (M., 1962), (Dok. Nak.)
Oktyabr'skoe vooruzhennoe vosstanie v Petrograde (M., 1957) (Dok. Okt.).
Triumfal'noe shestvie sovetov, vol. I (M., 1963) (Dok. Nov.).
Vserossiiskaya promyshlennaya i professional'naya perepis' 1918 g. (Trudy TsSU) vol. XXVI, vyp. 1 and 2 (M., 1926).
Vtoraya i tret'ya obshchegorodskie konferentsii bol'shevikov v iyule i sentyabre 1917 g. (M.-L., 1927) (Vtoraya).

III Workers' Memoirs

Alliluev, S. 1923, 'V dni Oktyabrya na Elektricheskoi stantsii imeni 1886', *Krasnaya letopis'*, no. 6.
Antonov, A.A. 1957, 'Vospominaniya kommissara Obukhovskogo staleliteinogo zavoda', *Doneseniya kommissarov Petrogradskogo voenno-revolyutsionnogo komiteta*, vol. I (Moscow).
Arbuzova, A. 1923, 'Oktyabr' 1917 na Trubochnom zavode', *Krasnaya letopis'*, no. 6.
Buiko, A., 1934, *Put' rabochego* (Moscow).
Buntilov, A. 1923, *Za pechatnym stolom* (Moscow).
Buzinov, A. 1930, *Za Nevskoi zastavoi* (M.-L.).
Graf, T. 1923, 'Ob Oktyabr'skoi revolyutsii', *Krasnaya letopis'*, no. 6, pp. 164–169.
Ivanov, B. 1919, *Zapiski proshlogo* (Moscow).
Kudelli, P.F. (ed.) 1924, *Leningradskie rabochie v bor'be za vlast' sovetov v 1917 g.* (Leningrad).
Metelev, A. 1922, 'Iul'skoe vosstanie v Petrograde', *Proletarskaya revolyutsiya*, no. 6.

Mikhailov, M. 1922, 'Rabochie zavoda P.V. Baranovskogo v bor'be za Oktyabr'', *Krasnaya letopis'*, nos 50–51, pp. 189–212.

Naumov, I.K. 1933, *Zapiski vyborzhtsa* (Leningrad).

Peskovoi, I. 1923, 'Nakanune Oktyabr'skogo perevorota', *Krasnaya letopis'*, no. 6, pp. 315–318.

'Petrogradskie rabochie ob iyul'skikh dnyakh', *Krasnaya letopis'*, no. 9, pp. 19–41.

Samoilov, F.N. 1924, *Vospominaniya ob Ivanovo-Voznesenskom rabochem dvizhenii*, part II (Moscow).

Shapovalov, A.S. 1934, *V bor'be za sotsialism* (Moscow).

Shlyapnikov, A.S. 1923, *Kanun semnadtsatogo goda* (M.-Petrograd).

Shotman, A. 1935, *Kak iz iskry vozgorelos' plamya* (Leningrad).

Skorinko, I. 1923, 'Vospominaniya rabochego ob Oktyabre 1917 g.', *Krasnaya letopis'*, no. 6.

Sveshnikov, M. 1923, 'Iz epokhi Oktyabrya 1917 goda', *Krasnaya letopis'*, no. 6, pp. 302–307.

Tikhanov, A. 1925, 'Rabochie pechatniki v Petrograde, 1907–1914', in *Materialy po istorii professional'nogo dvizheniya v Rossii*, sb. III (Moscow).

V boyakh za Oktiyabr' (Leningrad, 1932).

V ogne revolyutsionnykh boev, 2 vols. (Moscow, 1967 and 1971).

Vyborgskaya storona (Leningrad, 1957).

Zalezhskii, V.N. 1923, 'Pervyi legal'nyi Peka', *Proletarskaya revolyutsiya*, no. 13.

IV Other Memoirs

Bulkin, F.A. 1924, *Na zare profdvizheniya* (Leningrad).

Dingel'shtedt, F. 1925, 'Vesna proletarskoi revolyutsii', *Krasnaya letopis'*, no. 1(12).

Georgievskii, G. 1919, *Ocherki po istorii Krasnoi gvardii* (Moscow).

Latsis, M.I. 1923, 'Iyul'skie dni v Petrograde', *Proletarskaya revolyutsiya*, no. 5.

Leont'ev. L. 1924, 'V ryadakh "Mezhraionki"', *Krasnaya letopis'*, no. 11.

Maevskii, E. 1918, *Kanun revolyutsii*, Petrograd.

Malakhovskii, V. 1925, *Iz istorii krasnoi gvardii* (Leningrad).

Mstislavskii, S. 1922, *Sem' dnei* (Berlin-Petersburg-M.).

Price, M.P. 1921, *Reminiscences of the Russian Revolution* (London: George Allen & Unwin).

Rafes, M. 1922, 'Moi vospominaniya', *Byloe*, 19.

Reed, J. 1960, *Ten Days That Shook the World* (New York: Vintage).

Shelavin, K.I. 1928–9, 'Iz istorii Peterburgskogo komiteta bol'shevikov v 1918 godu'', ocherki I–III, *Krasnaya letopis'*, no. 2(29) pp. 24–45; no. 3(30), pp. 12–53.

Shelavin, K.I. 1929, 'Peterburgskii komitet bol'shevikov sed'mogo sozyva v 1918 godu', *Krasnaya letopis'*, 2, 29: 24–45; 3, 30: 12–53.

Stankevich, V.B. 1926, *Vospominaniya 1914–1919*, Leningrad.
Sukhanov, N. 1919–23, *Zapiski o revolyutsii*, 7 vols. (Berlin-Petersburg-M.).
Trotsky, L. 1930, *My Life* (New York: Scribner).
Tsvetkov-Prosveshchenskii, A.K. 1933, *Mezhdu dvumya revolyutsyamy* (M.-L.).
Voitinskii, V.S. 1923, *Gody pobed i porazhenii*, 2 vols. (Berlin).

V Press and Periodicals

Byuleten' obshchestva fabrikantov i zavodchikov Moskovskogo promyshlennogo raiona (Moscow region industrialists).
Delo naroda (SR).
Derevoobdelocknik (Petrograd Union of Woodworkers).
Gazeta Vremennogo rabochego i krest'yanskogo pravitel'stva (Soviet government).
Iskra (Menshevik-Internationalist).
Izvestiya (Executive Committee of the Petrograd Soviet and later also of the Central Executive Committee of Soviets (TsIK)).
Izvestiya Moskovskogo Voenno-promyshlennogo komiteta (War-industry committee).
Krasnaya gazeta (Bolshevik).
Metallist (Petrograd Union of Metalworkers).
Nasha rech' (Kadet).
Novaya zhizn' (Menshevik-Internationalist).
Novyi luch, (Menshevik-Internationalist).
Novyi put' (Central Soviet of Factory Committees).
Petrogradskaya pravda (Bolshevik).
Pravda (Bolshevik) (renamed briefly *Proletarii, Rabochii, Rabochii i soldat, Rabochii put'*).
Rabochaya gazeta (Menshevik-Defencist).
Rabotnitsa (Bolshevik, women's bi-monthly).
Rech' (Kadet).
Severnaya kommuna (Commune of the Northern Region).
Torgovo-promyshlennaya gazeta (commerce and industry).
Vechernee slovo (non-socialist daily).
Znamya bor'by (Left SR).
Znamya truda (Left SR).

VI Histories of Factories, Unions, Industries

Bastiony revolyutsii (L., 1960).

Bazilevich, K. 1927, *Professional'noe dvizhenie rabotnikov svyazi* (M.).

Borisov, G. and Vasil'ev, S. 1962, *Stankostroiteli imeni Sverdlova* (L.).

Bortik, M. 1928, 'Na Trubochnom zavode', in *Professional'noe dvizhenie v Petrograde v 1917 g.*, edited by A. Anskii (L.).

Bruk, S. 1928, 'Organizatsiya soyuza metallistov v 1917 g.', in *Professional'noe dvizhenie v Petrograde v 1917 g.*, edited by A. Anskii (L.).

Frantishev, I.M. 1962, *Leningradskie krasnostroiteli* (L.).

Ganichev, L.S. 1967, *Na Aptekarskom ostrove* (L.).

Grebach, V.V., K.A. Kuznetsov et al. 1959, *Rabochie baltiitsy v trekh revolyutsiyakh* (L.).

Istoriya Leningradskogo ordena Lenina i ordena krasnogo znameni obuvnoi fabriki im. Ya. (L., 1968).

Istoriya Leningradskogo soyuza rabochikh poligraficheskogo proizvodstva (L., 1925).

Krasnyi Treugol'nik na putyakh Oktybrya (L., 1927).

Kukushkin, V. 1959, *Sestroretskaya dinastiya* (L.).

Mitel'man, M., B. Glebov, and A. Ul'yanskii 1961, *Istoriya Putilovskogo zavoda*, 3rd ed. (L.).

Moskovskaya zastava v 1917 godu (L., 1957).

Notman, K.V. 1932, 'Trubochnyi zavod na Oktyabr'skikh putyakh', *Krasnaya letopis'*, no.s 50–51.

Ocherk istorii Leningradskogo soyuza rabochikh derevoobdelochnikov za 1917–18 gg. (L., 1927).

Perazich, V. 1927, *Tekstili Leningrada v 1917 g.* (L.).

Rozanov, M. 1938, *Obukhovtsy* (L.).

Rozenfel'd, Ya. S. and K.I. Klimenko 1961, *Istoriya mashinostroeniya SSSR* (Moscow).

Sergeev, N.S. 1967, *Metallisty – Istoriya Leningradskogo metallicheskogo zavoda imeni XXII s'ezda KPSS* (L.).

Shanin, T. (ed.) 1971, *Peasants and Peasant Society* (Harmondsworth: Penguin Books).

Shatilova, T. 1927a, 'Professional'nye soyuzy i Oktyabr'', *Krasnaya letopis'*, no, 2(23), pp. 79–88.

Shatilova, T. 1927b, *Ocherki istorii leningradskogo soyuza khimikov v 1907–1918 gg.* (L.).

Smirnov, A. 1925, *Poslednie dni Utemanov – 1917 na fabrike 'Skorokhod'* (M.-L.).

Suknovalov, A.E. and I.N. Fomenkov 1968, *Fabrika 'Krasnoe znamya'* (L.).

Tanyaev, A. 1925, *Ocherki po istorii zheleznodorozhnikov v revolyutsii 1917-go goda* (M.-L.).

Temkin, Ya. 1958, *U nas na Galernom ostrove* (L.).

Tomkevich, I.G. 1972, *'Znamya Oktyabrya' – ocherki istorii zavoda* (L.).

Tsybul'skii, V.A., 'Rabochie Sestroretskogo zavoda v 1917 g.', *Istoriya SSSR*, no. 7 (1959)

Vasil'eva, M.V. 1968, *Rabochie fabriki Svetoch v trekh revolyutsiyakh* (L.).

VII Secondary Studies

Acton, E., et al 1997, *Critical Companion to the Russian Revolution 1914–21* (Bloomington: Indiana University Press).

A. Anikst 1920, *Organizatsiya raspredeleniya rabochei sily* (Moscow).

Aronson, G. Ya. 1960, *Dvizhenie upolnomochennykh ot rabochikh fabrik i zavodov v 1918 godu* (New York: Inter-University Project on the History of the Menshevik Movement).

Avrich, P. 1973, *The Russian Anarchists* (London: Thames and Hudson).

Avrich, P. 1973b, 'The Bolshevik Revolution and Workers' Control in Russian Industry', *Slavic Review*, vol. XXII, 1.

Balabanov, M.S. 1927a, *Ot 1905 k 1917 g.* (M.-L.).

Balabanov, M.S. 1927b, *Rabochee dvizhenie v Rossii v gody pod'ema 1912–14 gg.* (Leningrad).

Braverman, H. 1974, *Labor and Monopoly Capital* (New York: Monthly Review Press).

Brinton, C. 1958, *The Anatomy of Revolution* (New York: Vintage).

Burdzhalov, E.N. 1967, *Vtoraya russkaya revolyutsiya* (Moscow).

Carr, E.H. 1952, *The Bolshevik Revolution*, vol. II (Baltimore: Penguin).

Chamberlin, W.H. 1965, *History of the Russian Revolution*, 2 vols. (New York: Universal Library).

Churakov, Dm. 2004, 'Pravye sotsialisty i belyi terror: Izhevsik 1918 god', *Al'ternativy*, 2.

Daniels, R.V. 1967, *Red October* (New York: Scribner).

Devlin, R. 1976, 'Petrograd Workers and Workers' Factory Committees in 1917' (PhD dissertation, SUNY Binghamton).

Ferro, M. 1967, *La Révolution de 1917* (Paris: Aubier).

Ferro, M. 1980, *October 1917* (London: Routledge & Kegan Paul).

Gaponenko, L.S. 1963a, *Rabochii klass Rossii v 1917 g.* (Moscow).

Gaponenko, L.S. 1963b, 'Rabochii klass Rossii na kanune velikogo Oktyabrya', *Istoricheskie zapiski*, 73 (Moscow).

Gogolevskii, A.V. 2005, *Revolyutsiya i psikhologiya: politicheskie nastroeniya rabochikh Petrograda v usloviyakh bol'shevistskoi monopolii na vlast', 1918–1920 gg.* (SPb).

Golovanova, L.V. 1974, 'Raionnye komitety RSDRP(b) Petrograda v 1917 g.' (Candidate's dissertation, Leningrad State University).

Grunt, A. Ya. 1961, *Pobeda Oktyabr'skoi revolyutsii v Moskve* (Moscow).

Haison, L.H. (ed.) 1975, *The Mensheviks* (Chicago: University of Chicago Press).

Haimson, L.H., 2005, *Russia's Revolutionary Experience, 1905–17* (New York: Columbia University Press).

Hasegawa, T. 1980, *The February Revolution: Petrograd, 1917* (Seattle: University of Seattle Press).

Istoriya rabochikh Leningrada, vol. I (Leningrad, 1972).

Johnson, C. 1966, *Revolutionary Change* (Boston: Little Brown).

Keep, J. 1976, *The Russian Revolution – A Study in Mass Mobilization* (New York: W.W. Norton).

Kleinbort, L.M. 1923, *Ocherki rabochei intelligentsii* (Petrograd).

Kabo, E.A. 1928, *Ocherki rabochego byta* (Moscow).

Kochan, L. 1966, *Russia in Revolution* (London: Paladin).

Koenker, D. 1981, *Moscow Workers and the 1917 Revolution* (Princeton: Princeton University Press).

Kornhauser, W. 1959, *The Theory of Mass Society* (Glencoe, Ill.: Free Press).

Kruze, E.E. 1961, *Petrogradskie rabochie v 1912–14 gg.* (M.-L.).

Leiberov, I.P. 1964, 'O revolyutsionnykh vystupleniyakh petrogradskikh rabochikh v gody pervoi mirovoi voiny i Fevral'skoi revolyutsii', *Voprosy istorii*, 2.

Levin, I.D. 1925, 'Rabochie kluby v Petrograde (1907–14)', in *Materialy po istorii professional'nogo dvizheniya v Rossi*, sbornik III (Moscow).

Lewin, M. 1975, *Lenin's Last Struggle* (London: Pluto Press).

Lisetskii, A.M. 1959, 'K voprosu o statistike zabastovok v Rossii v period podgotovki Velikoi Oktyabr'skoi sotsialisticheskoi revolutsii', *Uchenye zapiski Khar'kovskogo universiteta*, vol. 103 (Kharkov).

A. Lozovskii, 1918, *Rabochii kontrol'* (Petrograd).

Mandel, P. 1981, 'The Intelligentsia and the Working Class in 1917', *Critique*, 14.

Manning, B. 1978, *The English People and the English Revolution* (Harmondsworth: Penguin).

S.P. Mel'gunov 1953, *Kak bol'sheviki zakhavatili vlast'* (Paris, Éditions La renaissance).

S.P. Melgunov 1972, *The Bolshevik Seizure of Power* (Oxford: ABC Clio).

N.V. Mikhailov 1998, *Soviet bezrabotnykh i rabochie Peterburga v 1906–1907 gg*, SPb.

Mil'shtein, A.L. 1963, 'Rabochie Petrograda v bor'be za ukreplenie sovetov', in *Rabochie Petrograda v bor'be za pobedu sotsializma* (M.-L.).

A.P. Nenarokov, A.P., 2001, 'Politicheskoe porazhenie men'shevikov', in A.I. Zevelev et al., *Rossiiskaya politicheskaya entsiklopedia* (Moscow).

Nikolaev, P.A. 1960, *Rabochie metallisty tsentral'nogo promyshlennogo raiona v bor'be za pobedu Oktyabr'skoi revolyutsii* (Moscow).

Nosach, V.I. 1967, 'Profsoyuzy Petrograda v pervyi god Sovetskoi vlasti', in *Iz istorii Velikoi Oktyabr'skoi sotsialisticheskoi revolyutsii i sotsialisticheskogo, stroitel'stva v SSSR* (Leningrad).

M.N. Potekhin, M.N. 1966, *Pervyi sovet proletarskoi diktatury* (Leningrad).

Pearson, R. 1977, *The Russian Moderates and the Crisis of Tsarism*, London and Basingstoke: Macmillan.

Rabinowitch, A. 1968, *Prelude to Revolution – The Petrograd Bolsheviks and the July 1917 Uprising* (Bloomington: Indiana University Press).

Rabinowitch, A. 2007, *The Bolsheviks in Power* (Bloomington: Indiana University Press).

Radkey, O. 1950, *The Elections to the Russian Constituent Assembly of 1917* (Cambridge, MA: Harvard University Press).
Radkey, O. 1963, *The Sickle under the Hammer* (New York: Columbia University Press).
Rashin, A.G. 1958, *Formirovanie rabochego klassa Rossii* (Moscow).
Rosenburg, W.G. 1974, *The Liberals in the Russian Revolution* (Princeton: Princeton University Press).
Rossiiskii proletariat: Oblik, bor'ba, gegemoniya (Moscow, 1970).
Scott, R.H. 1973, 'The Russian Peasantry in the First and Second Dumas', unpublished paper (Russian Institute, Columbia University).
V.I. Selitskii, V.I. 1963, *Istoriya rabochikh Leningrada*, vyp. II, p. 17 (Leningrad).
V.I. Selitskii, V.I. 1971, *Petrogradskie massy v bor'be za rabochii kontrol'* (Moscow).
Shanin, T. (ed.) 1971, *Peasants and Peasant Society* (Harmondsworth: Penguin).
Shelavin, K. 1923, *Ocherki russkoi revolyutsii 1917 goda, fevral'-iyul'*, part I (Petrograd).
Shkaratan, O.I. 1959, 'Izmeneniya v sotsial'nom sostave rabochikh Leningrada 1917–28', *Istoriya SSSR*, no. 5.
Shkaratan, O.I. and I.P. Leiberov 1961, 'K voprosu o sostave petrogradskikh promyshlennykh rabochikh v 1917 g.', *Voprosy istorii*, no. 1.
Shlyapnikov, A. 1923, *Semnadtsatyi god* (M.-Petrograd).
Soboul, A. 1972, *The Sans Culottes* (Garden City: Doubleday).
Sobolev, O.L. 1973, *Revolyutsionnoe soznanie rabochikh i soldat Petrograda v 1917 g. Period dvoevlastiya* (Leningrad).
S-skii, S. 1923, *Psikhologiya russkogo rabochego voprosa* (St Petersburg).
Startsev, A. 1962, 'K voprosu o sostave petrogradskoi krasnoi gvardii', *Istoriya SSSR*, no. 1.
Stepanov, I. 1918, *Ot rabochego kontrolya do rabochego upravleniya v promyshlennosti i zemledelii* (Moscow).
Stepanov, Z.V. 1965, *Rabochie Petrograda v period podgotovki i provedeniya Oktyabr'skogo vooruzhennogo vosstaniya, avgust–oktyabr' 1917 g.* (Leningrad).
Strumilin, S. 1918, 'Prozhitochnyi minimum i zarabotki chernorabochikh v Petrograde', *Statistika truda*, 2–3.
Suny, R.G. 1983, 'Toward a Social History of the October Revolution', *American Historical Review*, 88, 1.
Tilly, C. 1975, 'Revolutions and Collective Violence', in *Handbook of Political Science*, edited by F. Greenstein and W.W. Polsby, vol. V (Reading, Mass: Addison-Wesley).
Trotsky, L. 1965, *History of the Russian Revolution*, 3 vols. (London: Sphere Books).
Trukan', A.G. 1967, *Oktyabr' v tsentral'noi Rossii* (Moscow).
Ulam, A. 1976, *A History of Soviet Russia* (New York: Praeger).
Volin, S. 1962, *Deyatel'nost' men'shevikov v profsoyuzakh pri Sovetskoi vlasti* (New York: Inter-University Project on the History of the Menshevik Movement), paper no. 13.
Volobuev, P.V. 1962, *Ekonomicheskaya politika Vremennogo pravitel'stva* (Moscow).
Volobuev, P.V. 1964, *Proletariat i burzhuaziya v 1917 g.* (Moscow).
Znamenskii, O.A. 1964, *Iyul'skii krizis v 1917 g.* (M.-L.).

Index of Names and Subjects